MADAME BEY'S:
Home to Boxing Legends

To Pat

[signature]

MADAME BEY'S:
Home to Boxing Legends

GENE PANTALONE

ARCHWAY
PUBLISHING

Archway Publishing books may be ordered through booksellers or by contacting:

Archway Publishing
1663 Liberty Drive
Bloomington, IN 47403
www.archwaypublishing.com
1 (888) 242-5904

Because of the dynamic nature of the Internet, any web addresses or links contained in
this book may have changed since publication and may no longer be valid. The views
expressed in this work are solely those of the author and do not necessarily reflect the views
of the publisher, and the publisher hereby disclaims any responsibility for them.

Any people depicted in stock imagery provided by Thinkstock are models,
and such images are being used for illustrative purposes only.
Certain stock imagery © Thinkstock.

ISBN: 978-1-4808-3644-0 (sc)
ISBN: 978-1-4808-3645-7 (e)

Library of Congress Control Number: 2016914284

Print information available on the last page.

Archway Publishing rev. date: 9/16/2016

Some day some one will write a magazine serial or a movie around the life of Madame Bey, but I question its success. Because the public would consider it too far fetched, too imaginative. I mean things that have happened in the life of Madame Bey challenge credibility. They are not supposed to happen – except in the case of Madame Bey.

—United Press, *Brooklyn Daily Eagle*, Friday, December 10, 1937

CONTENTS

ACKNOWLEDGMENTS

It is the author's goal that Madame Bey's accomplishments have been discovered in this written work. Her accomplishments, which were many, were obscured by the more famous sports figures she aided. Madame Bey was a pioneer of women in business and sport. She entered a field that was the domain of men. Her ability to connect with people, without preconceived notions, was her greatest strength.

Here is an explanation about the style and format used in this work. Most of the book was written to adhere to the style prescriptions of *The Chicago Manual of Style.* That style was used to ensure consistency across spelling, hyphenation, punctuation use, capitalization, and other constructs. The ISO 690 standard was used to format the endnotes to ensure consistency across citations.

Whether supplied through direct contact or exhaustive research, institutions that supplied material to this endeavor were many. The Chatham Township Historical Society, Summit Historical Society, and Library of the Chathams supplied articles producing a local feel. The Library of Congress, whose staff was diligent in their attempts to supply information, or direct me to the appropriate source, helped immensely. Writings from the Chatham Township Historical Society of conversations with one of Madame Bey's granddaughters helped with early history. Caroline Knott, from the Chatham Township Historical Society, gave fact checking and proofreading help that was especially appreciated, as was the Society's Pat Wells for providing photographs and documents. The author's visit to the camp as a young boy in the early 1960s was of little help. Thanks to my brothers Don, Al, and Gary for the camp descriptions. Especially my ten-year-older brother, who worked out at the camp and jogged in the mornings with heavyweight Doug Jones, was of the greatest help. His description of the camp and conversations with the boxers helped with the camp atmosphere.

The Fulton History website, with its newspaper search engine, provided the greatest number of articles. Other websites and organizations that were used for data gathering were the Milburn Free Public Library, Google Newspapers, BoxRec, Cyber Boxing Zone, Museum of Boxing, International Jewish Sports Hall of Fame, *Sports Illustrated* Vault, Corbis Images, Acme Newspictures, US Federal Census, NJ.com, Wikipedia, BBC Sport, the *New York Times*, the *London Times*, Brooklyn Public Library, wn.com, Babylon Wales, Spokeo, East Side Boxing, Christie's, the Statue of Liberty—Ellis Island Foundation, YouTube, Boxing.com, weirdthings.com, Library of Congress, Boxing's Funniest Quotes,

All Time Boxing, census.gov, earlyradiohistory.us, njcu.edu, muhammad-ali-boxing.org. uk, William McKinley Presidential Library & Museum, historynet.com, math.buffalo. edu, American-Israeli Cooperative Enterprise, American Jewish Historical Society, archive. org, International Boxing Research Organization, the Cruelest Sport, Bleacher Report, International Boxing Hall of Fame, Gale US History in Context, independent.co.uk, Journal of Combative Sport, CNN Sports, and ESPN.

The journalists of the era, many of whom came to the camp, wrote articles that were used to develop the narrative for this work and gave a feel for camp life. Journalists were Dave Anderson, Leslie Avery, John Beer, Bob Brumby, Al Buck, Mike Casey, John Coad, Jane Cochrane, Harold Conrad, Jack Cuddy, James P. Dawson, Alfred Dayton, Randy Dixon, Edward P. Duffy, Louis Effrat, Edward Van Every, Jack Farrell, Sid Feder, Frank C. Ferguson, Harry, Ferguson, Tony Galento, Ike Gellis, Alan J. Gould, I. Q. Gross, Jack Guenther, Sam P. Hall, Charles Hecklemann, W. C. Heinz, Thomas Holmes, Sammuel Hubbard, Ed Hughs, Joe Jacobs, James M. Kahn, Jack Kofoed, Martin LaChance, Al Lamb, Jack Lawrence, Perry Lewis, A. J. Liebling, R. G. Lynch, Jack Mahon, Norman Marcus, Charles S. Mathisson, John F. McKenna, Henry McLemore, Ted Meier, Paul Mickleson, Jack Miley, C. F. Moberly, William Morris, Edward J. Neil, Robert Neubert, Joseph Nichols, Frank O'Neil, Dan Parker, Westbrook Pegler, Cy Peterman, Harold Peterman, John Pilgrim, George Plimpton, Anthony J. Pugliese, Willie Ratner, Grantland Rice, Pat Robertson, Stewart Robertson, Gilbert Rogin, Damon Runyon, Max Schmeling, Murray Schumach, Michael Shapiro, Red Smith, Jeff Sorg, Dixon Stewart, Gayle Talbot, Isador Tobias, Raulf Troast, George B. Underwood, Wdward Van Every, Richards Vidmer, Davis J. Walsh, Chster L. Washington, John Webster, Bill Westbrook, Jimmy Wood, Wilbur Wood, and Ted Worner. If someone was omitted, it was unintentional.

Care was given to getting dates and records correct, but there will be discrepancies. BoxRec and Cyber Boxing Zone were heavily relied on to determine dates and boxing records, but other articles from the era were used to determine those, too. People's memories fade from time arising in discrepancies between story accounts. Care was taken to create it accurately. Even Madame Bey's accounts were not always accurate, as when she recalled to Stewart Robertson that Max Schmeling trained for both his Joe Louis fights at her camp, when the truth was he was there for neither. The most glaring problem was the after-fight street brawl between Mickey Walker and Harry Greb. There were three accounts with none in complete agreement. The truth was, as Walker later admitted, the fight never took place.

Additional authors of books, articles, and films were Carlos Acevedo, Cecil Adams, Michael J. Bednar, P. Benson, K. Blady, Kaisa Boddy, Anthony Brockway, Ken Burns, R. Cantwell, Mike Casey, Ruth Churchill, T. Coffman, Monte Cox, Jack Cuddy, John T. Cunningham, Dan Cuoco, Sean Davies, Mohummad Humza Elah, Ross Enamait, Lewis

A. Erenberg, Andrew Fruman, Mark Gado, Paul Gallico, Andrew Gallimore, Robert A. Hageman, A. J. Halford, George J. Hatem, John J. Jarrett, Frances Johnston, Caroline Knott, Margaret Leech,Charles Lesemann, A. J. Liebling, Melarie, Lloyd, Jack Malvern, Norman Marcus, David Margolick, Richard L. McElroy, Roy McHugh, Brian McKenna, John F. McKenna, Joseph Monniger, Jeff Morgan, Wayne H. Morgan, Marty Mulcahey, Robert W. Neubert, Carlos Ortiz, K. Hissner, Andrew O'Toole, Harold Peterson, Neil Prior, Joe Reichler, Mickey Walker, Gilbert Rogin, Jean-Christophe Rose, Jessica Rosero, Rusty Rubin, Tom Donelson, Jeremy Schaap, Murray Schumach, Jeffrey Seibert, James B. Scutt, Bill Stern, M. L. Stoll, Joseph R. Svinth, Raulf Troast, J. R. Tunney, Paul K. Williams, Dominick J. Zimmerer.

When it was determined that enough information could be gathered to give a complete history, work began. It is hoped that the story is justly told.

INTRODUCTION

It was the golden age of boxing. It included the years from the 1920s through the 1940s. It was borne out of the golden age of sports, the decades of the 1920s and 1930s. World War I was over. The booming economy from postwar-related production stagnated in 1918, then more severely in 1920. Those recessions gave way to prosperity that lasted from 1922 to 1929. The annual gross national product increased 40 percent, and the average income per person increased 27 percent.

By 1925, Ford produced a Model T automobile every ten seconds. The price of their automobile, called the Tin Lizzie, dropped from $850 in 1910 to $295 in 1920. In 1927, Ford produced fifteen million automobiles. Ownership swelled from eight million to twenty-three million. Inventions of synthetics, Bakelite, the first plastic, cellophane, nylon, and chemicals were making life easier. Refrigerators, washing machines, dishwashers, vacuum cleaners, and record players were increasing in numbers. The communications revolution caused the number of telephones to double, and the amount of radios increased from sixty thousand to ten million. Cinemas, jazz clubs, flappers, and speakeasies were popular with the public. Wall Street boomed. Businesses increased in number. Skyscrapers, highways, and urban development sprang forth.[1] Americans were confident about themselves, brought on by economic prosperity, and they had money to spend on leisure activities.

One leisure activity increasing in popularity was sports. The top sports were college football, horseracing, baseball, and boxing. College football offered no income. For athletes not of the equine ilk, their only choice for riches and fame were between baseball and boxing. Of those two sports, the one that had worldwide appeal was boxing. Though athletic skills do not always translate between sports, boxing attracted top athletes because of its popularity and lucrativeness if you could get to the top. It also had a color barrier that was easier to overcome.

There was discrimination in boxing, but it was far ahead of other sports for inclusion. African American Joe Gans became the world lightweight champion on May 12, 1902. Jack Johnson followed by winning the world heavyweight championship on December 26, 1908. By August 1938, a total of six of the eight world championships belonged to nonwhites with one weight class vacant. The color barrier in baseball went unbroken until April 15, 1947, with Jackie Robinson.

"I know, but I had a better year than Hoover," Babe Ruth responded in 1930 to his salary of $80,000 being more than President Herbert Hoover's $75,000. The average per capita income for all Americans in 1929, the first year statistics were kept, was $700.[2] Heavyweight boxer Jack Dempsey made over $750,000 in one fight he lost against Gene Tunney in 1926. That was near Babe Ruth's career earnings. In 1921, the sporting world had its first million-dollar gate. It was a boxing match held in Jersey City, New Jersey. The public paid $1,789,238 to watch Jack Dempsey retain the world heavyweight title with a fourth-round knockout over world light heavyweight champion Frenchman Georges Carpentier. Jack Dempsey, heavyweight champion from 1919 to 1926, his manager, Jack "Doc" Kearns, and promoter Tex Rickard, grossed $8,400,000 in five fights between 1921 and 1927 and ushered in a golden age of popularity for professional boxing. Jack Dempsey was, along with Babe Ruth, baseball, Red Grange, football, Bill Tilden, tennis, and Bobby Jones, golf, one of the purported Big Five of sports.

Many boxing matches during this time, about twenty years away from the television era, were social events with many thousands in attendance. It drew mostly men but also many women.[3] They attracted the most popular celebrities and richest people of the era. It also had broad appeal among the less financially fortunate.

They fought in iconic sports venues named Madison Square Garden, the Long Island Bowl, Yankee Stadium, Ebbet's Field, the Polo Grounds, Philadelphia Municipal Stadium, Soldier Field, and many others. These titans of boxing often chose a lesser-known location for their preparation. Located away from the cities, it was an unexpected place to see top athletes of their profession. It was the Madison Square Garden of boxing camps. No fewer than seventy-eight inductees into the International Boxing Hall of Fame and twelve world heavyweight champions would come to the small township. They came to a camp in a pastoral town in the deep woods on a mountainside in New Jersey. An aristocratic woman with roots in government managed the camp in the cruelest sport. It was here that a world-renowned boxing camp called Madame Bey's attracted boxing legends. She stood tall with the giants of the sport.

PART I

CHAPTER 1

A Foundation to Go the Distance

Cigarette and cigar smoke hung heavy in the air, creating a haze in the upper sections of Madison Square Garden. The din of the over-capacity crowd necessitated shouting to communicate with the person beside you. They came to witness an age-old struggle for fistic supremacy. The excitement for the long-awaited bout was palpable. The battle pitted two world champions in the squared ring. The opponents awaited in their dressing rooms with edginess and anticipation. They had trained long and hard, learning how to anticipate their opponent's moves, toughening body and mind. As they exited their dressing rooms, the atmosphere of the Garden intensified. The crowd yelled for and against the adversaries.

In the ring, these men used only the savage, animalistic part of their being. They had put all other thoughts aside, intent on one goal. This state would enable them to punch at an already bruised body, slashing at torn flesh while their body was tired, battered, and depleted. The two men fought at a frenetic pace from the opening bell. They sacrificed their bodies to get close to deliver a solid punch. The closer they came to each other, the harder they fought. Each punch fed the frenzy of the crowd that demanded more and cheered louder with every delivered blow. It was as brutal a fight as one could witness. As the battle progressed, blood covered the fighters, referee, canvas, and press in the front-row seats. Pride does not allow a superior athlete to quit. Only the heart of a fighter can carry battered men to the end.

An aristocratic woman in a coveted seat did not participate in the fervor. Each successive blow weighed heavier upon her. It was one of her boys in the ring. The Garden was unfamiliar territory to her. She could have attended any fight she wanted, but it was her first time at this venue. Though it appeared neither fighter would be able to endure such sustained punishment for the entire battle, they lasted until the end. The woman did not. The ordeal became too much, and she departed before the final bell. She retreated to her home where she had become acquainted with her boys. To her, they were more than fighters.

The woman had been with the world's greatest boxers for the last fifteen years. She gave them a home, attended to their every need, and ensured they were not bothered during their preparation for battle. She shattered the men-only mentality in the institution of boxing. She understood the physical and mental preparations needed to participate in such battles and her boys' sacrifices. Unending labor is the price of preparedness.

"It's dilapidated and somewhat the worse for wear. This is simply a training camp."[1]
—Cus D'Amato, discoverer, manager, and mentor of heavyweight
champions Mike Tyson and Floyd Patterson

Those that chanced by Bey's boxing establishment perceived an ordinary farm indistinguishable from others in the area. Set in Chatham Township, New Jersey, it sat on thirty acres of land. The structures included an unpretentious, yellow clapboard farmhouse with white trim, a garage, a barn, and many shacks.[2] They sat atop a short, steep, brush-covered embankment. The property was bordered by a paved road when most roads were made of gravel or dirt. Near the road, one distinguishable object proclaimed what lay on the property and separated it from other area farms. A square wooden post protruded from the ground with an attached tin sign.

Bey's
Training
Camp

In the pastoral Chatham Township, nestled in the Orange Mountains of New Jersey, thirty miles west of New York City, lived mostly the hardworking farming lot. In front of Bey's modest farmhouse, a road followed the Passaic River contour. It had the apt name of River Road. Across the road, a broad expanse extended to the river. Obscured by trees, the river, about six hundred feet from the farmhouse, split the counties of Morris and Union. Chatham Township resided in Morris County, and across the river was the town of New Providence in Union County. At the juncture of the two counties, the river's water is placid with an observable flow. In summer, rich vegetation encroaches on its dirt banks, sometimes contacting the water. Trees grow close to the water's edge with outstretched limbs that cut the serene water's surface.

In the days of the camp, if you traveled away from the city, it would not be long before farmland and woods surrounded you. The suburbs were not yet in place. The town posed a striking difference to the city, as did the people that lived there. The aristocrats of New York and Washington, DC, which the Beys were part of their entire early adult life, wore dress clothes, had soft, manicured hands, were perfume scented, and had luxurious, sumptuously furnished houses on plots of land in close proximity. The people of the rural land dressed in overalls to attend to their farms, had hands dirtied and leathered from hard work in the fields, and smelled of the land and livestock that provided their subsistence. Their houses on acres of land sparsely spaced and filled with practical furniture were modest.

Less than two miles from the boxing camp resided the town's dairy farm, which was operated by the Noe family and provided milk to surrounding areas. Over 350 cows grazed in the rolling meadows and lazed under the shade of trees to escape a hot sun. The family owned a pond where children and teens swam and cooled off. In winter, the frozen pond was harvested for blocks of ice and stored in icehouses. The Noes used some ice to prepare rose shipments from their greenhouses.[3, 4]

Around the late eighteen hundreds, Chatham Township was known for its rose production. The best-selling American Beauty rose was the town's specialty. The roses grew in large greenhouse complexes. Seen from a distance, they were unmistakable with tall, brick smoke stacks more than one hundred feet high that punctuated the sky and billowed smoke on cold days from coal-fed furnaces. Some were across the Passaic River in New Providence. The largest complexes were in Chatham Township. The neighboring town of Madison, a one-time section of Chatham Township, is still known as the Rose City, though aside from shops and manicured suburban landscapes, the rose is absent.

They were among the largest rose-growing centers in America, some producing carnations and other flowers. Over ninety greenhouses and a million rose plants grew within a five-mile area. Many small greenhouse owners and seven large growers sold mostly to wholesalers in New York City.[5] The most prominent grower, the Noe family, had a specialty, the American Beauty rose, which had a stem five feet in length. Every Christmas, the Noes sent them to European royalty—Queen Victoria of England. They sent fifty on the golden anniversary of her reign.[3]

Miss Margaret Belcher taught at the redbrick two-story schoolhouse, with a one-room classroom, on Southern Boulevard, a little over one mile down the road from the boxing camp. She had an education from the Newark State Normal School, currently Kean University. She taught nineteen to forty students in grades one through four. Some of her students came long distances by bus. Others walked up to four miles. No days off were given because of weather. They arrived in heat, snow, sleet, or rain to the school that sat atop a steep roadway.[6] A high school, located in the Borough of Chatham, taught the older students. The Green Village section of the town had the general store, the foundation of a rural community, called T. Rawsthrone's Groceries. The store had a blacksmith shop for iron products and sold needed commodities.

People knew the town for another famed athlete decades before the boxing camp attracted famous prizefighters. She was a chestnut race mare foaled on April 26, 1837, by William Gibbons, a wealthy owner of a Madison estate that is currently Drew University. Named Fashion, she became queen of the American turf, the greatest American race mare of her time. During Fashion's era, horses ran heats in grueling four-mile races.

Celebrated in her day were North-South sectional matches held in the years prior to the Civil War. The owners of the Southern Boston, a male horse thought unbeatable, challenged the Northern Fashion. On May 10, 1842, at five years old, Fashion met the nine-year-old Boston in a well-publicized four-mile match race at the Union Course on Long Island, New York, with 70,000 people witnessing the event.[7] Carrier pigeons relayed the racing news to New York City newspapers. Boston led for three miles, but as athletes know, it is unimportant how well you perform in part of a competition but how well you do in the entire contest. Fashion took control in the last mile, winning by thirty-five lengths and setting a new world record of seven minutes, thirty-two and a half seconds for a four-mile race. The Northern states adored her.

At eleven years old, the owner retired her after a career spanning eight seasons. She conceded weight and ran in all conditions against younger horses. Of thirty-six races, she won thirty-two and came in second in the four others. She ran in sixty-eight heats and won fifty-five.[8, 9]

A boxing camp rose from the rural hills of New Jersey unlike any other—a place unlikely for prizefighters to train. The camp, built and used by the boxers themselves, attracted many current, former, and future world champions. They used the camp to hone their bodies and skills for upcoming bouts. It became hallowed ground for boxing.

The men that came could absorb tremendous punishment and possessed punches beyond that of normal men. They were born with this punch; no amount of training can bestow upon an individual the powerful punch a boxer has. It is ten times that of an average man. The astonishing differential demonstrates the special talent needed to be a world-class boxer. Genetic constraints separate those men with such power and those without. Their punch could travel at thirty-two miles per hour[10] and strike with a force of 1,300 pounds, which is being hit with over a half ton. A force that is enough to accelerate an opponent's head at a rate of fifty-three times the force of gravity. It takes only 687 pounds of force to break a concrete slab one and a half inches thick.[11]

A boxer enters the ring with knowledge of the risk of severe bodily injury or death. One of the first recorded deaths from injuries sustained in the ring occurred on December 14, 1758, in St. Albans, England, to George Taylor. The first American incident was Billy McCoy in 1841, in Palisades, New Jersey.[12] According to one estimate, boxing has killed 1,865 people from 1725 to 2011.[13]

They came with ferocious names like the Fighting Marine, the Manassas Mauler, the Black Panther, the Black Uhlan, the Brown Bomber, the Ghetto Wizard, the Astoria Assassin, the Tacoma Assassin, the Toy Bulldog, Homicide Hank, and the Herkimer Hurricane. Their real names were Gene Tunney, Jack Dempsey, Harry Wills, Max Schmeling, Joe Louis, Benny Leonard, Paul Berlenbach, Freddie Steele, Mickey Walker, Henry Armstrong, Lou Ambers, Tony Canzoneri, James Braddock, Jack Johnson, and many other world champions. Many trained at the camp, while others came to watch their successors and prospective competition.

Following the top-rated boxers were their managers, trainers, and promoters. They were the best the sport had to offer. Managers Jack "Doc" Kearns, Joe Jacobs, and Al Weill were frequent occupants. Trainers Whitey Bimstein, Charley Goldman, and Ray Arcel had many charges there. Promoters named Uncle Mike Jacobs, Humbert J. Fugazy, Herman Taylor, and Jimmy Johnston came to protect their investments by making sure their boxers were in shape. One of the best promoters the sport ever produced, Tex Richard, did not go to the camp but made sure many of his boxers did to ensure a high-quality performance for his audience. Following them, the leading journalists came to write about upcoming bouts; it was fertile ground for sports columns. These men included Grantland Rice, Damon Runyon, Frank Graham, Al Buck, Jack Miley, James P. Dawson, and Willie Ratner. Celebrities, politicians, and the public followed to watch their favorite fighters. Conveniently, four miles from the camp, the Summit Hotel accommodated many promoters, journalists, trainers, and managers.

Those boxers with the savage names did not intimidate the only woman among these brutes. The camp's proprietor, an improbable person to run a camp for men who made their living by destroying others, was educated, a mother, a mezzo-soprano opera singer, and the wife of a Turkish diplomat and personified sophistication during her years in Washington, DC. President William McKinley and his wife considered her a good friend. Her name was Madame Hranoush Sidky Bey, but everyone called her Madame Bey. She created a home for her boxing clientele in which they could train for their sport. If you intended to stay at her camp, you followed her rules that she expected her boarders to obey. Madame Bey was strict in operating her business. She shunned interviews and photographers until late in her life. She referred to the boxers as her boys. Not wanting for accolades, she preferred to stay in the background while her boys took the tributes.

Madame Bey saw her boys as individuals and not the brutes portrayed in the newspapers. She found that many were intellectual, sensitive men wanting nothing more than the betterment of their lives. Boxing offered that opportunity. It could take them from a life of despair to one that was enviable. She had personal, matriarchal relationships with many of her boys and made a positive impression on them.

"I have succeeded in having all my boys feel responsible toward me," Madame Bey said, "and as a result, I am swamped with remembrances on Mother's Day."[14]

It was a never-ending wonderment to journalists, managers, trainers, and promoters how Madame Bey could exact the finest behavior from these toughest of men. Madame Bey understood people, and the fighters knew that her rigid, structured management was for their benefit. If someone challenged Madame Bey's authority, he would receive the wrath of the other boxers.

Madame Bey was an Armenian Christian, her husband, Sidky Bey, a Muslim. They met in their native Turkey, a country over 95 percent Muslim. Their romance and marriage became as unlikely as their running of a boxing camp. The two, undeterred, married despite cultural and family objections. It was one challenge of many that Madame Bey overcame. If told something was impossible, she figured a way to succeed.

Before her boxing camp, she had danced at the White House and sung in Carnegie Hall. Sidky Bey, her husband, worked as the second secretary of the Turkish Legation in Washington, DC. While in Washington, DC, she became a favorite at the Turkish consulate because of her ability to speak English. She spoke five other languages—Armenian, French, Greek, Italian, and Spanish. She ran a successful oriental rug business with her husband after they left the Diplomatic Corps, but her boxing endeavor she coveted the most.

Madame Bey came to know the meaning of persecution. Her Armenian people were systematically eliminated by executions, deportations, and death marches well after she had departed her native Turkey. The marches consisted of forced treks from Turkey across the vast deserts of Syria with little supplies. Most died from exposure. A report from the *New York Times* stated, "… the roads and the Euphrates are strewn with corpses of exiles, and those who survive are doomed to certain death. It is a plan to exterminate the whole Armenian people."[15] It is known as the first modern genocide where an estimated one to one and half million people perished, and it led to the coining of the word "genocide."

Instead of using these events as a source of bitterness, she chose to understand and embrace differences. Her boys acquired the sentiment of their host. They were there for the sport of boxing. They sought the help of trainers, managers, and sparring partners who would best help them prepare. The person's background did not matter. This contrasted sharply with that which occurred around them. Newspapers printed racist, ethnic, and religious slurs without jeopardy of retribution. Many gifted black athletes were prevented from participating in the sports cultures. Her camp did not discriminate. During a time of deep racism, the camp welcomed anyone who wanted a secluded place to train. Race, national origin, or religious beliefs precluded no one.

Madame Bey proved her camp welcomed anyone, no matter the public opinion of any of her boxing residents. Disagreements were few at her place, and those that arose were more due to egos and higher testosterone levels than racism. Not one racist event at her camp could be uncovered in print.

The former socialite who had been with diplomats, presidents, and queens now ran a prizefighting camp known around the world. There seldom was a time when a champion was absent from the camp when only ten weight classes existed. That was unlike today where the many organizations and weight classes make a title easier to obtain. The camp had a ubiquitous presence in the sports section of newspapers. The newspapers always referred to it as Madame Bey's, and they usually gave the location as Summit, New Jersey, instead of its actual location of Chatham Township; Summit was a larger and a more recognizable town.

Although Madame Bey made the schedules for the use of her facilities by the fighters, she kept away from their training routines. They had only to adhere to her strict rules. The simple formula worked. While three other boxing camps in the town ceased operations in a few years, Madame Bey's endured for decades.

The two-floor wooden clapboard farmhouse was yellow with white trim. A small brick chimney jutted from the back section of the roof. The bottom of the farmhouse had square-shaped lattice. The house front, which faced the road thirty feet away, had a screened porch. The porch had five columns for support with waist-high spindle. A stairway, with spindled support railings, led to the porch from the side near the driveway.

The driveway from the road went past the left side of the farmhouse and curved left. On the other side of the driveway, one hundred feet across from the farmhouse, on a knoll, the combination gymnasium dormitory and a barn stood. Small shacks and many shade trees separated the farmhouse and gymnasium. The gymnasium was a wide, rectangular, low-slung, two-story, wooden barrack structure with windows on three sides. The gymnasium, made of clapboard and set into the knoll, had a door in the front that opened into the first-floor gymnasium.[16]

The low-slung gymnasium housed the indoor ring, training equipment, showers, rub-down rooms, and bedrooms for fighters and sparring partners. It had adequate equipment for training. The front gymnasium door led to the square boxing ring straight ahead. The ring had three strands of rope on each side that were wound with so much tape that the ropes were completely obscured. The taped ropes were covered with years of grime, resin, sweat, and blood, showing the labor of the boxers. Round pipes that provided little to no padding connected the ropes in each corner. For spectators, there were bleachers constructed of dark wood against the right and left gymnasium walls, but they did not extend to the far wall. The walls along the right and left sides were made of exposed cinderblocks, roughly filled with mortar between each. The wall near the entrance had light-colored panels with dark trim. The floor consisted of unfinished, long, wide, knotted, wooden planks. Cast-iron radiators stood on the floor near the walls to provide heat. The ceiling had the same light-colored panels with dark trim at regular intervals. An exercise table, covered in leather, sat against the ring's far side. Aside from using the table for exercise, it doubled as a game table. The boxers, to pass the time when they were not training, would play card games. It became a tradition that persisted through the camp's existence.

A speed bag hung in the back left corner. Opposite the speed bag in the back right corner, the heavy bag hung. Behind the heavy bag was a mirror attached to the right wall where a boxer could observe his form while hitting the heavy bag.[17] Fight posters hung on the cinderblock walls advertising matches from boxers who had trained at the camp, some black and white, and others of bright yellow with large red and black letters, hawking the fighters' names for bouts at Madison Square Garden, Yankee Stadium, and other iconic venues. Black-and-white pictures of past fighters and present boxers, some signed, also hung on the walls. They were a reminder to trainees of what they could become. The wall contained boxing's royalty that had trained there.

Opposite the entrance, tacked on the wall, were more fight posters. Centered on the same wall behind a door were two sets of narrow stairways. One stairway ascended to the floor above the gymnasium where there were evenly spaced small bedrooms, centered by a tight hall, which could accommodate up to twenty-five boxers and their sparring partners. Each cramped bedroom contained a bed, a table, and one or more chairs. The walls were made of compressed wood fiber called beaverboard. They contained markings from the fighters who had trained at the camp and scrawled their names or drawn pictures upon them.[2, 18]

The other stairway descended into the basement where dressing rooms, showers, and massage tables were located. The dressing rooms were made of all wood construction. Inside the dressing rooms, the wall studs, pipes for plumbing, ceiling boards and trusses that supported them, were exposed. Fastened to the studs, a horizontal strip of wood contained hooks where a fighter hung his clothes.

Behind the farmhouse and gymnasium was a field where the Beys grew vegetables and raised chickens, cows, and sheep that supplied fresh vegetables, eggs, and milk for their clientele. Further back on the property, the hillside steepened into a wooded mountainside.

Inside the farmhouse resided Madame Bey's living quarters and bedroom. Five more bedrooms were available to the boxers.[18] An abundance of furniture crowded the rooms. Turkish ornaments decorated them to the extreme.[19] Sidky Bey was an antique collector and expert, and items all had a spot in the farmhouse. In the sunroom, with miniature citrus trees on the windowsills, the boxers would relax in the evenings. The Beys covered the walls with pictures of their earlier life. They included those of Washington society and White House receptions. They gave a spot on the wall of the last posed picture taken of President McKinley alive that included Madame Bey. One room had an upright piano that had ornaments placed on it. There, Madame Bey would entertain those boxers who cared to listen to her operatic voice.

The dining room contained a large Victorian-style dinner table laced with touches of the Near East with high-backed chairs where everyone ate.[20] Madame Bey served meals twice a day. She prepared food consisting of thick steaks or chops at night with vegetables, butter, milk, and fruit pies.[14] Much of the food came from the Beys' farm. She gave second or third helpings to anyone who requested it, as long as they made the request correctly. Sometimes a new boxer, who did not quite comprehend the protocol at the camp, would demand more food. Madame Bey would ignore the request. Until the uninformed new occupant uttered "Please," he received the glare from the more seasoned tenants. Newcomers learned that Madame Bey ruled and had the support of her famous clientele.

The main attraction for spectators was the outdoor ring a few feet in the back of the farmhouse. Many came to watch the public sparring sessions and workouts. It served boxers well on sweltering summer days. When other camps were too hot for training, Madame Bey's was a welcomed alternative. The air was crisp with gentle mountain breezes. The trees filtered the high temperatures created by the sun. The evenings were cool enough to make blankets welcomed.

The early covered outdoor ring was a simple wooden structure that was covered on top with canvas. Later, the covered outdoor ring, constructed of wood, open on all sides, sat upon a platform raised about two feet above the ground. Eight square wooden support posts secured the platform to the ground. Four posts were in each corner, and another four were in the middle of each of the sides. Each of the eight posts had a wooden V-shaped support at the top that secured the hip roof to the platform. Four metal poles were in each corner that held the three layers of the ring ropes. The exposed posts had crude padding for protection but gave little. A canvas tightly laced to the surrounding wooden square frame covered the platform. At the end closest to the farmhouse, a platform on the ring roof supported a speed bag, and a chain wrapped around a rafter supported a heavy bag. The hilly topography that surrounded the ring served as seating. Bleachers were at ringside. This created space for plenty of spectators around the ring.

The outdoor ring would become an important part of the camp. It drew throngs of people to watch boxers train and spar outdoors in preparation for an upcoming battle. Carmine Bilotti, a renowned boxing publicist, recalled River Road lined with limousines and cars to attend Bey's outdoor exhibitions.

"It was a hell of a healthy spot in those days," Bilotti recollected.[21]

If a celebrated fighter was in training, crowds could outstrip the population of Chatham Township. More than two thousand writers, photographers, and fans would descend upon Madame Bey's when the town's population numbered well under one thousand. A sign erected outside informed fans who would be training in the outdoor ring. The sign had the title "TRAINING TO-DAY." Times were listed on the left side in half-hour increments. On the right side, boxers' names slid into slots beside the times.

The boxing exhibitions had the quality that would make a boxing promoter proud. Often they used referees to keep the sparring bouts in control. The boxing exhibitions were an extra source of income for Madame Bey. There was a ticket booth to charge admission. She would stand at the entrance with a large, black pocketbook slung over her shoulder. She would collect one dollar on weekdays and two dollars on weekends from each person who wanted to view the exhibition. She would place the money in her pocketbook. It was customary to give the marquee boxer at camps, the one that drew the biggest crowds, twenty-five to fifty cents per spectator. On nice spring days, boys would drive from Morristown High School or take the Erie-Lackawanna—a train line that served the area—to Summit. From there they would hitch a ride or walk. Most boys had no means to pay to gain entrance. Madame Bey would chase them away and continue to collect from her paying customers. Once the sparring began, Madame Bey would take her seat in the back. She would then give a nod to the boys she had kept away just a short time before. They knew their cue and scrambled to take any unoccupied seats.[21]

All boxers training at Bey's paid the same rate of four dollars and fifty cents a day, giving them room, board, and the use of the gymnasium.[22] An unwritten hierarchical structure existed. The best boxers, champions, former champions, contenders, and Bey's favorites lived and slept in the farmhouse. At meal times, the resident champion garnered the head of the table with the better boxers sitting closest to him.[23] They had conversations at the table with a range that had no limit. World heavyweight champion Jersey Joe Walcott described the relationship that existed.

"It always seemed like a family. Like a bunch of brothers sitting at the table. We were brothers in the same profession."[23]

Besides the singing entertainment Madame Bey supplied, boxers listened to the radio in the evening—no television existed—played cards, and joined Madame Bey at the piano. Sometimes in the early evenings, they would go to the neighboring town of Summit that had a movie theater. Madame Bey often went with them. She had her own seat she expected to occupy.[24] They could do any of these activities, but Bey expected lights out by ten with no exceptions.

One time, heavyweight Charlie Weinert, the Newark Adonis from Hungary, stayed at the camp. He beat Jack Sharkey and fought Gene Tunney twice, losing once by a fifteen-round knockout, and another time in a twelve-round decision. He appeared on the cover of *The Ring* magazine on July 1925. All of this unimpressed Madame Bey. Weinert tried to test Bey's curfew. She stayed awake until he returned.

"When he came sneaking back in the dawn," Madame Bey recalled, "I was waiting for him, but instead of what you would call putting the blast on him, I just said, 'Charlie, I never thought a nice boy like you would be so unkind,' and I walked away leaving him staring at me. Charlie never tried to cheat again once he had made me feel badly. And it affected him when he realized that I had called him a nice boy instead of some of the things he knew he had coming."[14]

Not all of Bey's guests were pleased with the remote camp location. A journalist would follow a boxer for weeks before a marquee fight. He would hand-crank his press release on a mimeograph machine after he had typed it on a stencil, licked the envelopes, and walked two miles into town to the post office.[25] Some sports journalists who had to visit the camp to report on a fighter before a big fight would write about the location and surroundings derisively. One who called Bey's Camp a cross between a chicken farm and a Ninth Avenue, New York, gymnasium wrote:

"There are practical egg laying chickens and a genuine mooing cow, bound in leather and warranted to give milk if properly approached. … there is an open ring, including the bell, under the crab apple tree down behind the cow's apartment …"[26]

In the mid-1920s, Hilario Martinez, a decent welterweight from Barcelona, Spain, dug a hole on the Beys' land for a pet crocodile he had.[27] The crocodile did not stay long, but the pond that the hole had become remained as long as the camp existed. It later became a goldfish pond four feet in diameter with a green-covered bottom. Above, a pipe trickled spring water into the pond. The boxers would grab a glass and hold it under the pipe to receive pure spring water.

Madame Bey succeeded in most endeavors placed in front of her, whether boxing camp proprietor, socialite, diplomatic host, opera singer, or rug merchant. Her respected personality helped her achieve. Her upbringing determined her successfulness in improbable endeavors. Life events shaped her character and accomplishments more than the titles she earned early in her life, and if character creates its own destiny, it created her passion. Her name was imbedded in the consciousness of those at the highest level of boxing. She became an institution in boxing.

PART II

CHAPTER 2

Winners Are Taught Early

Madame Bey was born Hranoush Aglaganian circa 1881 in Constantinople, currently Istanbul, Turkey, to an Armenian father and a French mother. She lived there while it was still under the once powerful Ottoman rule, albeit during the waning years of the 623-year empire that lasted from 1299 to 1923. The Ottoman Empire that at one time controlled most of southeastern Europe, southwestern Asia, and North Africa had only Turkey and some surrounding areas under its rule while Madame Bey lived there.

Madame Bey was a small, slim, elegantly formed woman with a mass of fine, long, dark black hair, thick black eyebrows, fine dark eyes,[1] and a dark complexion. She was a Christian in a country vastly Muslim. Although a minority, the Christians were well educated, owned many businesses, and played a large role in the Turkish economy. It became a source of resentment among the majority, which would cause hatred in later years.

As a young girl, she spent several years in Italy. During her stay, she studied opera and became a mezzo-soprano in the coloratura range. As a young woman, Madame Bey attended the American College for Girls in Turkey,[1] which cost thirty-five Turkish liras, about one hundred fifty American dollars a year;[2] a large sum in the late eighteen hundreds.

The school was established by an Act of the Commonwealth of Massachusetts, United States of America. Christian women of America founded the school in 1871, and it became a college in 1890.[2] The college held a charter from the legislature of Massachusetts and an Imperial Irade, a decree by a Muslim ruler, from the Sultan of Turkey. It was a legally organized body of women in the United States, and the institution's charter included the ability to grant degrees and diplomas in the Commonwealth of Massachusetts. Controls and affairs of the institution were administered by a board of trustees and an advisory board located in Constantinople, which had the authorization to give aid to the college and manage its affairs.

To attend the college, applicants had to pass an entrance examination or have an accredited certificate from a specific list of schools. It was the only college for women in western Asia. Some countries the students came from were Greece, Albania, Egypt, Syria, Russia, Romania, Bulgaria, Turkey, and the region of the Tigris and Euphrates Rivers. Their nationalities included Armenian, Albanian, American, Bulgarian, English, French,

German, Greek, Hungarian, Israelite, Scotch, and Turkish. The college attendance in its early years ranged from 103 to 178 students. The college language was English, but they taught French, German, Latin, Greek, Armenian, Bulgarian, Slavic, and Turkish. Madame Bey would learn many of those languages, becoming fluent in English, Armenian, French, Greek, Italian, and Spanish.[2]

It had a cosmopolitan atmosphere. The women were with others from nationalities and religions they would not otherwise have met outside the college. For many, it was the first time they interacted with people outside their religion. The students had to overcome their prejudices and preconceived notions. Many formed friendships regardless of background.[2] It became an important part of the building of Madame Bey's character. It would serve her well in her future relationships in Washington, DC, and later in her boxing camp with fighters from many different nationalities.

The college curriculum corresponded to that of Wellesley of Massachusetts or Vassar of New York. No single institution had more influence for women in that area. The Ottoman government favored it because of its intellectual and moral training, given by mostly American educators. Most graduates were in demand as teachers in schools for Turkish girls.

While attending the school, Madame Bey met a Muslim man.

"Of course," Madame Bey recalled, "I fell in love—how could I help it—the moment I set eyes on my future husband. He was Sidky Bey, a Turk who was … a blond, blue-eyed, red-cheeked, altogether happy man to whom I gave my heart."[3]

Mehmed Sidky Bey was born circa 1872, ten years Madame Bey's senior. He stood no more than five feet tall. He had a mustache waxed to a point on both sides. His fair skin, blond hair, and blue eyes were atypical for a Turk. Deemed unimportant that Madame Bey was sixteen and Sidky twenty-six, the disparities between the crescent and the cross constituted protestations. Sidky was a Muslim and Hranoush a Christian. They saw no problems, but both families were vehemently opposed to the relationship, and marriage was forbidden. Sidky Bey began to develop a solution to his dilemma.

Sidky Bey began working in Constantinople at the Bureau of Foreign Correspondence at the Foreign Office of the Sublime Porte.[4] The name is a French translation of Turkish meaning "High Gate" or "Gate of the Eminent"—the official name of the gate giving access to the block of buildings in Constantinople that housed the principal state departments. This was the Turkish government's center.

Sidky Bey knew that if he could get to the United States, he could marry Madame Bey despite the objections of their families and the differences in their nationality and religion. Halil Rifat Pasha, the grand vizier of Turkey, was the top minister to the thirty-fourth sultan of the Ottoman Empire, Abdul Hamid II. The sultan wielded absolute control over the empire. As the grand vizier, Halil Rifat Pasha, dismissible only by the sultan, had complete power of attorney. He held the imperial seal and could convene other viziers to attend to empire affairs.

Sidky Bey discovered through a friend connected to the grand vizier that he had a fascination with a new invention—the automobile. They were scarce in Turkey, but Sidky Bey procured one. He presented it to the grand vizier and in return received what he needed. The grand vizier offered him the position of second secretary of the imperial Ottoman embassy in Washington, DC, which Sidky accepted.[5] He could now go to the United States and take Madame Bey with him. Madame Bey's Christianity, which had kept her and Sidky apart, turned into an advantage. Muslim women were forbidden to travel abroad, even if they were married, unless given permission from high officials. As a Christian, Madame Bey had no such restriction. Sidky Bey along with Madame Bey and her mother, Marie Aglaganian, born in 1851, went to Genoa, Italy, where they boarded the steamship *Fulda* and sailed for an Atlantic Ocean journey to New York.

The steamship was built in 1882 by John Elder and Company in Glasgow, Scotland. It was of iron construction and had two smokestacks and four masts. The accommodations were 120 passengers in first class, 130 in second class, and one thousand in third class, called steerage. According to Madame Bey's granddaughter, Madame Bey traveled in steerage.[5] Traveling in steerage on a steamship meant an uncomfortable means of transportation. Each steerage passenger had a fenced-in area, or chalk-marked lines, delineating their space. There was not much privacy, sanitation, nor pleasant sleeping accommodations for the voyage. The automobile favor to the grand vizier granted Sidky Bey a title, not a means of safe passage for others accompanying him.

On July 7, 1897, the ship arrived at Ellis Island, New York, where they were processed. According to the ship's manifest, the Beys were listed as husband and wife and stated both were twenty-six years old.[6] That was the correct age for Sidky Bey but incorrect for Madame Bey. The records were inaccurate; the Beys were not yet married, and Madame Bey was not more than sixteen years old.

"I followed with my mother, and Sidky Bey, and we were married in New York," Madame Bey recalled.[3]

With no family forbiddance in America, the Muslim Sidky Bey married the Christian Hranoush Aglaganian in a union that would last their lives.

CHAPTER 3

Accomplishments Take Work

The same month of their arrival in New York, July 1897, the Beys came to Washington, DC. They went straight to the Turkish legation where Sidky Bey started his position as second secretary of the Imperial Ottoman Empire.

That year, the population of the United States was about seventy million. Republican William McKinley became the twenty-fifth president of the United States after defeating Democrat William Jennings Bryan in the 1896 election. The United States was still in a deep depression that had started with the panic of 1893. The *New York Times* began using the slogan "All the News That's Fit to Print." The first American marathon was run in Boston. The United States signed a treaty annexing the republic of Hawaii. Thomas Edison patented his movie camera. Greece and the Ottoman Empire declared war on each other called the Greco-Turkish War, or the "Thirty Days' War." Although Madame Bey may not have known, or cared, Bob Fitzsimmons became the world heavyweight champion of boxing after defeating James Corbett by a knockout in the fourteenth round on March 17, 1897.[1]

Sidky and Madame Bey became more concerned about settling into life in Washington, DC, at the Turkish legation. Aristarki Bey represented Turkey as the top minister. The legation was a luxurious building, with plush furnishings, located at 1818 Q Street Northwest, less than two miles from the White House. It overlooked the DuPont Circle,[2] which French-born Pierre Charles L'Enfant designed, the same man who planned the street layout of Washington, DC.

The DuPont Circle was a circle within a circle. The outer circle bears no resemblance to the car-infested thoroughfare of today. It was dirt, landscaped with exotic flowers, ornamental trees, and tall gas lanterns. A bronze statue adorned the inner circle's center, which Irish-born American sculptor Launt Thompson created. The statue was of Samuel Francis DuPont for whom the circle was named. He was a rear admiral and one of the most famous Civil War naval figures. It stood tall atop a high pedestal, inscribed "DUPONT" that towered over the area. In 1884, in the presence of the secretary of the navy, naval officers, and DuPont family members, they unveiled the statue. The inner circle, as today, only had pedestrian traffic. The circle's name remains, but the statue was removed and replaced with a fountain.[3, 4]

Madame Bey was an oddity at the Turkish legation. There were women who had come to America from Turkey, but they were Muslim, allowed to leave Turkey only by special permission from the sultan. When they were in America, they were never allowed to attend social gatherings. Preceding Madame Bey, a Muslim wife of a Turkish diplomat along with her sister was not allowed to live in the legation. They lived in Cleveland Park in the northwest quadrant of Washington, DC. They were only allowed to receive women as guests. When they went out, they wore the customary veil and dress required of Muslim women.[2] The Turkish Diplomatic Corps allowed Madame Bey to live in the legation, being an Armenian Christian, even though married to a Muslim. Her husband, Sidky Bey, did not seclude his wife as other Muslims.

"… Of the companionship of a charming wife and family," Madame Bey wrote, "without whom men are not usually at their best; since it requires not less than two heads for a successful household; and a house with but one is not a house."[2]

Regarding politics, Madame Bey did not agree with the tyrannical Turkish rule that her husband worked under. Though she believed in her principles, she could not annunciate or write about them for fear of reprisal. Even after the Turkish regime fell, she wrote about them in anonymity. Despite her misgivings toward the regime and their treatment of women, she settled into the Turkish legation. She was bright and did not lack self-confidence. Later, she wrote of herself and the welcoming of Ali Ferrouh Bey, the incoming first secretary of the legation.

"Having been married just a short time before his departure to America to a beautiful Mohammedan girl of noble family, he could never have become reconciled to the sudden separation and departure during his honeymoon, had it not been that he was welcomed to the luxurious Oriental Legation overlooking Dupont Circle by a fascinating Oriental lady—the wife of Sidky Bey, second-secretary. Sidky Bey had preceded the minister several months, and during the recent and sudden changes of the heads of the legation, upon him devolved the routine duties for several years. His wife proved quite a revelation to American ladies; brilliant in all the arts pertaining to her sex, including that of housekeeping, at a young age she was speaking four languages, as well as her own in addition to English, which she understood thoroughly, having graduated from the American College at Constantinople. Thanks to her mastery of the English language she wielded no little influence on the personnel of the Imperial Ottoman Legation, the members of which were not able to speak English. This fair hostess of the Legation was a great favorite in Washington, especially with President and Mrs. McKinley."[2]

On July 9, 1898, one year and two days after arriving in America, Madame Bey gave birth to a baby boy. He would be the first baby born at the Washington legation under both the American and Turkish flags.[5] They named him Rustem. Sidky Bey and his wife liked the American ways and were determined to raise their son as an American. His playmates were American and introduced him to American customs. Like his parents, he would develop a penchant for languages, able to speak three by the age of twelve.[5]

The pudgy baby Rustem Bey had a dark complexion like his mother and not the fair-skinned appearance of his father. A picture of Rustem appeared in the *New York Herald* under the heading "Babies of Washington Officialdom." Madame Bey would dress her son in bright-colored wool clothes. She was especially fond of red.[6] She frequently took the young Rustem to the DuPont Circle, the social gathering site of the rich and the Diplomatic Corps. It was a playground for children and often strewn with baby carriages along the pathways and beside park benches. Residents strolled along the paths that wound through the trees and flowers.

The McKinleys had no children of their own, having lost two daughters—Ida as a baby and Katherine at three to scarlet fever. It affected Mrs. McKinley's emotional and physical health. Mrs. McKinley would come to the DuPont Circle to interact with the children and their mothers. She enjoyed sitting on the benches and chatting with the children during her forays to the Circle.

On January 1, 1901, Madame Bey became known in the social scene in Washington, DC. The social season began on New Year's and lasted until Ash Wednesday. These were "coming out" events for many new arrivals to the Washington, DC, social scene. The Beys and other guests accepted an invitation to the president's New Year's Day reception.

As was tradition, the White House doors opened at eleven in the morning with guests filing into the reception rooms. They would come in order of official precedence as established in the past. The first person would be the secretary of state, John M. Hay. The president's official household followed Hay. Next, the Diplomatic Corps, which included the Beys, were introduced to the president. At 11:15, the chief justice, Melville Fuller, would enter followed by the associate justices of the Supreme Court and other high judicial figures. At 11:25, the senators and representatives would continue the procession. Officers of the army, navy, Marine Corps, and district militia followed at 11:40. By noon, the heads of bureaus, commissioners, and assistant secretaries joined the gathering. Finally, at 12:25, the White House granted ordinary citizens the opportunity to shake the hand of the president. By one thirty, it ended.

Despite the many people at the reception, Madame Bey was a noticeable addition to the diplomatic list. She was the only feminine representative of the Turkish sultan at the president's reception. She took her place in official society.[6] She and her husband became good friends with the president and Mrs. McKinley. They would receive invitations to many other White House and diplomatic gatherings.

Madame Bey became popular in the capital. The *Chicago Tribune* in 1901 printed after the reception, "Ferrouth Bey's successor, Shekib Bey, is reputed to be a widower. At all events he is unencumbered with womankind. The second secretary, Sidky Bey, has a wife, however, and a charming one, who promises to become extremely popular in the diplomatic set. Mme. Sidky is delighted with the freedom of American society, and takes a naïve delight in each new custom with which she becomes familiar. Her latest fad is the bicycle, and as she is probably the first woman of her nationality who has ever mounted a wheel, her daily appearance in the park is watched for with considerable interest. She is a graceful rider, and wears most distracting bicycling gowns."

Madame Bey would fulfill the prediction. Many other newspapers and society periodicals wrote about Madame Bey in the coming years. She appeared in the May 12, 1901, copy of the *New York Herald*. The newspaper printed a composite picture in the East Room of the White House. She appeared with the president, Mrs. McKinley, and eighty-two other Diplomatic Corps members.[7]

On one occasion, the German ambassador invited the Beys. Sidky Bey did not have the features of a Turk; he looked more like a German. When he entered the embassy, another guest approached him who had thought he was a German embassy attaché. The guest started talking to him in German, of which Sidky Bey understood nothing.

"Sidky Bey," Madame Bey wrote, "not comprehending what had been said to him, in his always ready manner replied: 'Although I look like a German, I do not possess the distinction of being able to speak the language.'"[2]

In the absence of the head of the Turkish legation, more often the case than not, the diplomatic responsibilities fell on the tireless worker Sidky Bey.

"He was always the sole occupant of the desk," Madame Bey wrote, "while other members of Sultan Hamid's Washington cabinet, including the ministers themselves, were enjoying the club and other festivities; for it was Sidky Bey who, owing to his constant devotion to duty, remained throughout the twelve long years while so many changes and abrupt endings of the Washington careers of Turkish diplomats were taking place."[2]

Sidky Bey wanted to stay in America for himself, his wife, and child. The Beys continued their diplomatic conduct with Sidky doing the work of the legation and Madame Bey hosting and attending functions at the various embassies and the White House.

CHAPTER 4

A Knockout

Having a close friendship with the president and Mrs. McKinley, and the president knowing Madame Bey possessed a fine singing voice, the president requested she attend the Pan-American Exposition with them and sing the national anthem.[1] She accepted the honor. The Pan-American Exposition, known as a World's Fair, ran from May 1 through November 2, 1901, in Buffalo, New York. The exposition—embedded in American history because of President McKinley's fateful appearance—was a worldwide attraction. McKinley, in a speech at the exposition, said, "Expositions are the timekeepers of progress. They record the world's advancements. They stimulate the energy, enterprise, and intellect of the people, and quicken human genius. They go into the home. They broaden and brighten the daily life of the people. They open mighty storehouses of information to the student ..."

The event sprawled over three hundred fifty acres. It cost $7 million; Congress pledged $500,000. Eleven million people attended, paying twenty-five cents per ticket. The significant expositions included the X-ray machine by Nikola Tesla, a trip to the moon exhibit, Joshua Slocum's sloop, the *Spray*, on which he had recently sailed alone around the world, and the dazzling nighttime light display of Nikola Tesla's alternate current demonstration of transporting electricity over distances. The alternating current was to the dismay of Thomas Edison, who lost a competing bid. His direct current could not travel the distance. Edison criticized the technology, calling it dangerous. The power that was generated at Niagara Falls, twenty-five miles away, illuminated the exhibits' buildings decked in lights. Taken for granted today, it was a spectacle never before seen in 1901.

President McKinley was to give a speech at the exposition on June 13, but when his wife became ill, he delayed his appearance until September 5.[2, 3] He was at the height, and popularity, of his presidency. The country had recovered from an economic depression and returned to prosperity. The recent victory in the Spanish-American War came just before the 1900 election. McKinley had defeated democratic challenger, William Jennings Bryan, in an 1896 election rematch.

On September 4, 1901, twenty-two Diplomatic Corps members arrived at the Washington, DC, train station. They included members from Turkey, Mexico, Japan,

United States of Colombia, Peru, Costa Rica, China, Venezuela, Korea, and Brazil. Awaiting them were representatives from the Pan-American Exposition, Harry H. Seymour of the Exposition entertainment committee, representing Exposition President John G, Milburn; Colonel William H. Michael, chief clerk of the Department of State of the United States; William C. Fox, director of the Bureau of American Republics; and James S. Murphy, the tourist agent of the Pennsylvania Railroad. A Buffalo-bound special train that consisted of an engine, three Pullman parlor coaches, and a dining car would take them to Buffalo. The Pullman parlor coach was the height of luxury travel. At eight thirty in the morning, the train departed over the Pennsylvania Railroad with Madame Bey, her husband, Pan-American representatives, and the other diplomats.[4, 5]

While the train of the Diplomatic Corps proceeded on to Buffalo without incident, President McKinley's train arrived in Buffalo at six o'clock in the evening from Canton, Ohio. The plans were for a twenty-one-gun salute for the president's arrival. As the train pulled into Buffalo, the cannons started to fire. Someone placed one of the three cannons too close to the tracks. The first of twenty-one shots was fired as the leading train car passed by. All the windows on the one side fragmented, propelling glass shards into the car. The concussion threw the two men in the car across to the other side. Windows in nearby buildings also shattered.[6, 7]

The president's personal secretary, George Cortelyou, rushed to the platform to signal the commanding officer to stop firing. The officer mistook the signal to proceed, and the roaring cannons continued with the twenty-one-gun salute. The crowd was cheering, unaware of what was transpiring. The train's engineer brought the train to a quick stop after seeing what had occurred. The president's personal messenger, Thomas Lightfoot, frantically rushed to the front car shouting, "Where is Doctor Rixey?" referring to the president's physician. Someone told the messenger that he was in the president's car atop the observation deck. Upon reaching the observation deck, he found Doctor Rixey attending to Mrs. McKinley, who had passed out. The cannons' roar caused her distress. A concerned President McKinley, two of Mrs. McKinley's nieces, a nurse, and a maid were there. Doctor Rixey assured the president that his wife would recover in short time. The president moved to the back platform to acknowledge the crowd as the train restarted and proceeded on its journey. No one was seriously hurt.[6]

The Diplomatic Corps train, and its party, arrived at the Exchange Street Station in Buffalo at seven forty-five that same evening without the mishap of the president's train.[8] Abraham Lincoln stopped at this station twice, on his inauguration in 1861 and then during his funeral procession in 1865 after becoming the first president assassinated. Soon the station would achieve the dubious distinction of hosting funeral processions of trains for two assassinated presidents.

After a short wait to change engines, the diplomat's train continued on to the Belt Line station at Porter Avenue. Mr. Seymour introduced the diplomats to the reception committee before boarding their horse-drawn carriages that carried them to the Niagara Hotel where a reception committee greeted them.[5]

After they arrived at the hotel, the group of diplomats gathered in the rotunda. Men were dressed in suits, and women wore gowns. The Turks wore their traditional fez upon their heads, a red cylindrical felt hat with a dark tassel in the middle. The Chinese delegation wore their native dress. The hotel provided the Diplomatic Corps with spacious suites for their stay. Several party members expressed their satisfaction with the trip and accommodations. The Mexican ambassador stated, "We have had a delightful journey. Everything has gone smoothly, and we have not been disappointed in one single detail."[5]

The Exposition designated the next day, September 5, as President's Day in honor of President McKinley. It was to be the highlight of the Pan-American Exposition. Madame Bey and her husband awoke at the Niagara Hotel to a clear, blue, cloudless sky, typical for Buffalo, the sunniest, driest major northeast city. The temperature would climb to an unusually warm eighty-two degrees. The night before, the hotel had arranged for ministers and their secretaries to have a luncheon in the hotel. The Beys attended that luncheon. After completing their meal, the Diplomatic Corps departed the hotel at nine that morning. They took horse-drawn carriages to the Exposition grounds where they had assigned places in the president's stand.[5] The Diplomatic Corps' movements for the rest of the day were the same as the movements of the president.

By the early morning, the Exposition was full of people. The expected appearance of the president, scheduled to give a speech later that day, heightened the festive atmosphere. Over 116,000 people would go through the turnstiles, and more than 50,000 would hear McKinley's speech that afternoon. The exhibitions and sidewalks were full to capacity with at least six different bands playing music to milling crowds. The president was eager to go into the crowd, shaking hands and greeting people in person. Although his staff tried to discourage such close contact, the president refused to be afraid.

"Why should I? No one would wish to hurt me," was his usual response.[9]

With paid and unpaid attendance, the crowds reached 150,000. The official program that cost five cents listed the president's arrival at 10:25 in the morning. The president arrived ten minutes late at 10:35. They received the president upon his entering the Exposition grounds with a twenty-one-gun salute.[10] He then entered a special stand erected at the northwestern part of the Triumphal Bridge positioned over Mirror Lake. The Marine Band located immediately beside the president's stand played "Hail to the Chief." Assembled to the president's right sat the Diplomatic Corps, which included Madame Bey. The Exposition president, Mr. Milburn, rose and looked over the crowd.

"Ladies and gentlemen, the president!"[10]

McKinley wore a tuxedo and held speech notes in his left hand, overlooking the crowd of 50,000. The stage was draped in bunting with stars and stripes in red, white, and blue. The president presented his address. It would be his final.

The Board of Woman Managers scheduled to take Mrs. McKinley by horse-drawn carriage to the Women's Building after the president's speech. They were to have a luncheon in her honor at one o'clock that afternoon. Mrs. McKinley felt too fatigued and left via horse-drawn carriage, accompanied by Director-General Buchanan, back to the Milburn house before the luncheon. She was to rest there before going to the Women's Building in time for the lunch.

Mrs. Horton chaperoned Madame Bey and the other women of the presidential party from the speaking stand after the president's address, to witness the president's review of the troops in the stadium.[11] Driven in horse-drawn carriages and escorted by foot troops, the president, accompanied by the rest of the Diplomatic Corps and invited guests, went to the stadium. There, the president reviewed the troops before an enormous crush of a crowd in attendance. There were over 50,000 attendees in the stadium that was built to accommodate 12,000. Following the review in the stadium, shortly after noon, seven thousand homing pigeons were released from cages at the head of the Court of Fountains in front of the Electric Tower. The presidential party halted to witness the flight.[12]

Madame Bey and the other women of the presidential party went with Mrs. Horton to the Women's Building where they were expecting to honor Mrs. McKinley with the luncheon reception.[11] While Madame Bey and the other women gathered at the Women's Building, the president visited some exhibitions on the grounds after his speech and troop review with the men of the Diplomatic Corps.[13]

The party left the Canadian Building and rode southeast to the Agricultural Building[14] that had been roped off and closed to the public. Diplomats who had no buildings of their own, which included Turkey, received the president in the Agricultural Building. He walked swiftly through the Agricultural Building, passing its exhibits, trying to keep on schedule.[14] Next, diplomats in their own buildings erected by their countries, and containing exhibits reflecting their cultures, received the president.

The presidential party, consisting of the reception committee, diplomats, and newspapermen, continued and entered the Honduras Building flanked by police officers. The procession continued on to exhibits of the Cuba Building that had gained its independence after America's victory in 1898 in the Spanish-American War. There, at the door, the Cuban Pan-American Commission president, Eldelberto Farres, took the president's hand and said, "We are proud to welcome to our doors the great and honored man who promised Cuba her liberty in 1898 and has given it to her. We welcome you with hearts full of love and good will." The president bowed and entered the building.

The Chilean Building came next, followed by the Mexican Building, Dominican Republic Building, and Puerto Rico Building where the president had coffee. The final building visited was the Ecuadorian Building.[14]

Next, the carriages came again, and the president's party went to the New York State Building. The building, closed to the public, had thousands gathered around it. More people clogged the streets leading to it, rendering them impassable. When the president disembarked from his carriage, he walked through the columns of police that were keeping the cheering crowds at bay.[14]

Once inside, the president and his party took a well-deserved one-hour rest before the luncheon. From the 1901 *Buffalo Courier*, "It was as brilliant an assembly of dignity, wealth and talent as has ever been gathered around a banqueting board in the city of Buffalo. Not a man at the tables was without a reputation for his attainments and standing in his community. The names of President McKinley and some of those who sat with him are household names all over the civilized world." There were more than one hundred fifty guests.

The luncheons for the president and Mrs. McKinley were the height of opulence and power. For the president, flags, flowers, and palms decorated the room. Draped across the closed door behind the president's seat stood crossed flags of the United States and New York. Two Pan-American emblems were placed to the outside of the flags. Green and yellow buntings were hung across all four sides of the room. American flags and Pan-American emblems draped the walls. The Exhibition decorated the president's table with flowers grown at the Exhibition, as were all the other tables in the room. The president had a large arrangement of American beauty roses that were placed in front of him, which the other tables did not have.[15]

The president, along with Mr. Lockwood, proceeded down the stairs at two in the afternoon where the dining rooms were. The guests followed in pairs as the orchestra played "Hail to the Chief." The president took his seat at the head of the table. The Turkish minister sat to the far right of the president. The rest of the male Turkish legation sat at a table that included Lieutenant Colonel Aziz Bey, Chigib Bey, Djelal Bey, and Madame Bey's husband, Sidky Bey.[16]

They took one hour for lunch, as the president was due at the Government Building at 3:15. He spent most of the hour eating and talking to one person, Daniel L. Lockwood, seated to his immediate left. They prepared a four-course menu, sherry, and musical entertainment. After the president's luncheon, they distributed cigars. Daniel Lockwood called for attendants to remove the flags behind the president and open the rear doors. The president strode onto the porch that had a grand view of Park Lake and the Exposition grounds. Several members of the public that were in the rear of the building had the surprise of seeing the president. The president took note of one person in particular, a young girl of about ten years old, and bowed to her. The president had been often kind to children.[14]

Madame Bey went to the luncheon given in honor of Mrs. McKinley at one o'clock, along with the other women. The luncheon with sixty-five guests proceeded without Mrs. McKinley. She disappointed the women when she could not attend, even though officials stated that she would after a brief rest at the Milburn House. She still felt the effects of her severe fatigue and missed the lunch in its entirety. Among the women who took luncheon with the ladies of Mrs. McKinley's party, along with Madame Bey, were Mrs. Leonard Wood, wife of General Wood, the governor-general of Cuba; Madame de Wollant, wife of the ambassador from Russia; Senora Don Marcia de Calvo, wife of the minister of Costa Rica; the duchess de Arcos, wife of the Spanish minister; Senora Frederico Alfonso Pezzet, wife of Pan-American Commissioner Pezzet of Peru; and the officers of the Women's Board.[11]

The Women's Building was the only one on the Exposition grounds not erected for the Exposition. The land, leased by the Rumsey family for the Exposition, was the Country Club of Buffalo for golf and polo. That organization constructed its clubhouse in 1889–1890. They turned over the structure to the Board of Women Managers for use during the Exposition. It was a large wood-frame building with broad, shaded verandas on three sides. Located in the southwestern area on the Exposition grounds, the building had gardens of the horticulture exhibit surrounding it. Many found the area to be restful and beautiful compared to the grand scale of the Exposition buildings. The intended building use was for the entertainment of visiting women's clubs, wives of visiting dignitaries, and any other groups that the Board of Women's Managers deemed appropriate. The building was open only to women touring the Exposition. They were free to use the reading room to write, groom, and relax.[17, 18]

Although the luncheon for Mrs. McKinley was not as opulent as the one for her husband, it was not a trite affair. At one thirty in the afternoon, the sixty-five guests sat down to a luncheon served in the reception room, the parlor, and the small rooms adjoining. They decorated the rooms, mantels, tables, and windows with the richest flowers that the Exposition gardens could afford and which the local florists could get. The decoration was a high tribute to the taste, the ability, and the artistic knowledge of the Department of Horticulture. The reception room was a nook of palms, potted plants, and baskets filled with roses. The main dining room was decorated with palms and white asters, and in the magazine room, clusters of beautiful flowers in vases and ornate flower boxes lent pleasing contrast to the general theme of the decoration. They served lobster a la Newburg, sweetbreads and mushroom patties, chicken salad, coffee, ice cream, cake, and bonbons. Miss Effie Greenwood, a soprano, sang several selections for entertainment. The guests in attendance were moved by her rendition of "Ave Maria," by Gounod, which some called "Artistic in the extreme." The women's luncheon had ended just after three o'clock. The women, who were guests at Mrs. McKinley's luncheon, went in horse-drawn carriages to the president's reception at the Government Building.[11]

At three o'clock, after the men's luncheon, the president embarked on his horse-drawn carriage. Along with the Diplomatic Corps and the rest of the party, they went to the Government Building. They gave fifteen hundred tickets to the public to attend the president's inspection of the Government Building. The guests were to enter the building after the president. When the president had not arrived upon his scheduled time, they allowed the guests into the building.[19]

The president advanced through the crowds to the building's south end. General J. H. Brigham, chair of the Government Board, stood in the building's central court to the left of the president in the front of the rotunda. The guests packed the building's south side and filed through a column of soldiers, who allowed one guest at a time toward the president. Although most guests were unknown, General Brigham and his son made the presentations to the president. Mr. Milburn stood behind President McKinley, while R. Rice, a committee member, stood in front of the president and helped introduce the guests he knew. Over one thousand five hundred people shook the president's hand and afterward stood wherever room could be found. The guests included society women in elaborate gowns to people of humbler circumstance who predominated. One guest introduced was Madame Bey. Families of the Government Board and invited guests filled the gallery. Reserved chairs stood at the entrance to the gallery for foreign diplomats where they sat for the reception while the Marine Band played at the building's south end. The entire short reception consisted of the president shaking hands with the guests.[19]

George M. Metcalfe was the last in line to shake the president's hand. The president uttered an audible sigh of relief. The president then shook General Brigham's hand, after which he said, "Well, President, your work is finished here." The soldiers cleared a narrow alley toward the front entrance that the president walked through to embark on his carriage. As he headed toward the Milburn House, the crowd gave him one last cheer.[19]

That evening, Mrs. McKinley was well enough to go with the president to the Exposition grounds to see the lighting of the buildings and the firework display. They went by carriage to the front of the Arts Building. The band began to play the "Star-Spangled Banner" as the lights on all the buildings began to illuminate, which included a searchlight under the Goddess of Light. As the band played on, the light intensity increased until they were at their brightest when the band hit the last few bars.[20]

The McKinleys slept in the Milburn house and awoke on September 6, 1901, to a sunny day without a cloud in the sky as it was the previous day. Before noon, President McKinley along with his wife took a carriage to the station and boarded a train for a trip to Niagara Falls where they took a carriage to observe the sights. Mrs. McKinley, still in fragile health, became ill and returned to the International Hotel. President McKinley continued on to Goat Island.[21] The island, known for its spectacular views, was a common destination for sightseers, but it had no permanent inhabitants.

Scheduled next, the president and his wife were to go to the Temple of Music, a temporary structure costing $85,000 built for the Pan-American Exposition as a concert hall and auditorium. Italian Renaissance influenced the building style. Its façade was constructed of staff, which is a mixture of plaster of Paris and cement molded around a fibrous jute cloth. Molded staff can imitate brick, stone, or other building material. The shaped staff in the Temple of Music resembled a redbrick hall with the exterior in pale yellows with gold and red trim. The panels of the large dome that soared 180 feet from the ground floor were light blue. Both the inside and outside were strung with lights powered by Nikola Tesla's alternate current electricity. Inside, the spacious accommodations seated 2,200 people. It was the ornate centerpiece of the Exhibition and used for national holidays that the Exhibition observed with musical festivals. Many famous bands played there, including the band of John Philip Sousa.[22]

President McKinley reconnected with his wife and took a train back to Buffalo to get ready for his scheduled appearance at the Temple of Music. Mrs. McKinley, still feeling the effects of her earlier illness, returned to the Milburn House.[21] President McKinley proceeded without his wife to the Temple of Music, arriving by carriage. He took his place at the building's center. John Milburn, the exposition's president, stood on the president's left. George Foster, the president's chief bodyguard, was out of position five feet from the president and standing opposite him. The president's personal secretary, George Cortelyou, stood to McKinley's right.[23] Madame Bey stood a few feet from the president.

At four o'clock, the president said to his aides, "Let them come." The doors thrust open to the Temple of Music on the president's orders. It was one of McKinley's greatest pleasures as president to greet the people and go through the handshaking ritual. The president wore a white dress shirt with starched collar and cuffs, pinstriped trousers, a black frock coat, and a black satin necktie.[24] As the outside temperature reached eighty-two degrees, throngs of people crowded outside the Temple of Music waiting for a chance to see the president, though his appearance was only to last ten minutes. As people started to flow in, they played the "Star-Spangled Banner"[25] on one of the largest pipe organs ever built in the United States.

The line moved quickly to greet the president. At seven minutes past four while the organ played a Bach sonata, a little girl approached the president, who greeted her and gave her a pat on the head.[26] The little girl represented two of the president's favorite pleasures—children and greeting the people. She left as the president smiled. Next, the anarchist Leon Czolgosz dressed in a dark suit with a handkerchief wrapped around his right hand approached the president. As the president went to shake Czolgosz's hand, he thrust a .32-caliber short-barreled Iver Johnson revolver pistol, which he concealed under the handkerchief of his right hand, into the president's chest.[27] Two shots echoed as the president slumped forward. He then fell back, and Secretary George Cortelyou and others caught him before he hit the floor.

Madame Bey, a few feet from the president, turned around, leaning back with her arms stretched out, and looked at the president in dismay.[28] Madame Bey later said, "She went through the trying ordeal of standing by the lamented President at the moment he was shot at the Buffalo Exhibition …"

A mulatto man named James Benjamin "Big Jim" Parker, at six feet six inches and weighing two hundred fifty pounds, was standing behind Czolgosz. As Czolgosz prepared to take a third shot, Parker grabbed Czolgosz's right hand with his right hand, and with his left arm he grabbed Czolgosz's neck and yanked it back. His actions prevented another shot.[29] A detective named John Geary and an artilleryman, Francis O'Brien, knocked Czolgosz to the floor as others started punching and hitting him with rifle butts.[30, 31]

"I done my duty," Czolgosz was heard to have said.[32]

"Lynch him!" the crowd yelled.[26]

"Go easy on him, boys," the president said. "Let no one hurt him."[33]

Then the president whispered to Secretary George Cortelyou.

"My wife … be careful, Cortelyou, how you tell her. Oh, be careful."[34]

While the president lay on the floor, Madame Bey went to notify the president's personal physician, Presley M. Rixey.[35] Czolgosz had to be sneaked under heavy protection to prevent the angry mob from seizing him.[36]

"I went to the Temple of Music to hear what speeches might be made," Parker said. "I got in line and saw the President. I turned to go away as soon as I learned that there was to be only a handshaking. The crowd was so thick that I could not leave. I was startled by the shots. My fist shot out and I hit the man on the nose and fell upon him, grasping him about the throat. I believe that if he had not been suffering pain he would have shot again. I know that his revolver was close to my head. I did not think about that then, though. Then came Mr. Foster, Mr. Ireland, and Mr. Gallagher. There was that marine, too. I struck the man, threw up his arm, and then went for his throat. It all happened so quickly I can hardly say what happened, except that the secret service man came right up. Czolgosz is very strong. I am glad that I am a strong man also, or perhaps the result might not have been what it was.

"I am told that I broke his nose. I wish it had been his neck. I am sorry I did not see him four seconds before … I can't tell you what I would have done, and I don't like to have it understood that I want to talk of the matter. I tried to do my duty. That's all any man can do."[37]

Officials gave Parker credit for preventing Czolgosz from taking a third shot. Later, they recanted and could not recall him being there. Parker availed himself for the trial. They never called upon him to testify.

CHAPTER 5

Getting Off the Canvas

At first, the medical staff considered the wounds serious but not mortal.[1] Despite early optimism for the president, he succumbed to his injuries. The secretary of state, John Hay, sent a notification to the foreign representatives. This included the Turkish delegation with Madame Bey's husband, Sidky Bey.

> Department of State,
> Washington. Sept. 14, 1901.
>
> Sir: It is my painful duty to announce to you the death of William McKinley, President of the United States, in the City of Buffalo, at fifteen minutes past 2 in the morning of to-day. Sept. 14.
>
> Laid low by the act of an assassin, the week-long struggle to save his life has been watched with keen solicitude, not alone by the people of this country who raised him from their own ranks to the high office he filled, but by the people of all friendly nations, whose messages of sympathy and hope while hope was possible have been most consolatory in this time of sore trial.
>
> Now that the end has come, I request you to be the medium of communicating the sad tidings to the Government of the honored nation you so worthily represent, and to announce that in obedience to the prescriptions of the Constitution the office of President has devolved upon Theodore Roosevelt, Vice President of the United States.
>
> Accept, Sir, the renewed assurance of my highest consideration.
>
> JOHN HAY[2]

Sidky Bey and Madame Bey would now be serving their nation of Turkey under the administration of the newly sworn-in president, Theodore Roosevelt. As Turkish delegation members, they had duties to perform for the funeral arrangements of the slain president. McKinley would lie in state under the rotunda of the Capitol as done before with Presidents Lincoln and Garfield. They placed him on the same historical bier as those two.

The furnishings were simplistic. There was no sign of mourning except the catafalque draped in black. Above, the gray light came through the long windows of the Capitol dome. Hundreds of spectators found places of observation in window spaces and on the steps winding to the Capitol dome. There were hundreds of flowered gifts filling all the spaces behind the rails. Many floral tributes were elaborate and expensive in character. There were many with clusters of orchids and palms placed in the front rows of chairs for the coffin's arrival.[3]

Toward ten thirty, there were more rapid arrivals. Senators came in from the north side of the rotunda. Headed by Joseph G. Cannon, representatives entered from the House side of the Capitol.[3] The dress of the participants was uncharacteristic of a mourner except for the ex-president's immediate family. Most women were dressed in green and blue, and some bought decorated hats especially for the occasion. Men were in every variety of costume uncommon for those in mourning.[4]

The rotunda usually seated eight hundred, but for this occasion, there were 1,048 seats,[4] some of which were allocated to the Diplomatic Corps. Hundreds were reserved for governors, senators, representatives, cabinet members, and other distinguished guests. The last to enter the rotunda was President Roosevelt and Mrs. Roosevelt, who sat at the end of the row of the cabinet officers. This was to the left of the coffin close to the catafalque. The Diplomatic Corps sat behind President Roosevelt along with many military officers in uniform. The Turkish delegation headed by Shekib Bey wore their native costumes that included the fez. Mrs. McKinley was absent, unable to undergo such an ordeal.[3]

They brought in the coffin bearing the ex-president's remains and placed it upon the historic bier. A prayer echoed through the rotunda given by Reverend Dr. H. R. Naylor, presiding elder of the Methodist Episcopal Church of the Washington District. The words were indistinguishable by most present. A sermon was followed by Bishop Andrew. At the conclusion, those seated exited through the Senate end of the Capitol that allowed citizens to pass the opened coffin, which revealed the ex-president.[3]

Czolgosz's trial started on September 23, 1901. He made a conclusive confession and refused to cooperate with his defense team. The jury convicted him on September 24 after they deliberated for less than one hour. On September 26, the jury recommended the death penalty, and the judge so sentenced him. The judge gave Czolgosz a chance to make a final statement, which he declined. He showed no emotion.[5]

The state executed Leon Czolgosz on October 29, 1901, forty-five days after President McKinley's death, at Auburn Prison in Auburn, New York. Defiant to the end, his last statement was, "I killed the President because he was the enemy of the good people—the good working people. I am not sorry for my crime. I am sorry I could not see my father."[5] The execution was performed by an electric chair with Tesla's same alternating current that had powered the brilliant night lights at the Pan-American Exposition.

In November 1901, the Temple of Music, where the assassination of President McKinley occurred, was demolished along with the rest of the Exposition buildings, as intended prior to the Exposition. Only a stone marker shows the approximate assassination spot. The democracy survived as intended. The smooth transition of power was passed.

Also in November 1901, the Beys moved to their own residence at 2112 Q Street, Washington, DC, described as a cozy home.[6, 7] Sidky Bey still worked as the second secretary of the Turkish Legation, yet most of the operations fell upon him. Despite the traumatic experience of a presidential loss, as with the rest of the country, the Beys were leaving the past to remembrance and continuing their lives.

The year 1901 gave way to 1902, and the new president held the traditional White House New Year's reception. It was the first public appearance by Theodore Roosevelt in his official capacity as the new president. The president disregarded the wishes of his advisors for such an appearance.[8] The assassination of McKinley still weighed on them.

It was a brilliant sunny day of the new year. The White House interior was aglow with electric lights strung throughout. Potted plants and vines hung from the chandeliers. The East Room was spectacular in appearance. Round leaf greenbrier draped over the grand crystal chandeliers with poinsettias, begonias, and tall ferns filling the recesses of the room. In the red and blue parlors were more poinsettias and other flowers to give the same effect as the East Room.[9]

In the outer corridor to the entrance were sixty members of the Engineer Corps Band dressed in brilliant uniforms. Further along in the conservatory was the full Marine Band dressed in bright red uniforms. Leading to the White House, and within its confines, security was added because of McKinley's assassination.[9] Unlike the last appearance of President McKinley at Buffalo, this event went without incident. Dr. Rixey served as President Roosevelt's personal physician, just as he had been for President McKinley. There would be no need for his services for this presidential appearance. Within two months, he would become the surgeon general of the United States Navy, a job promised him by President McKinley. He held the position until his retirement in 1910 with the rank of rear admiral.

The extravaganza started just after eleven in the morning. Horse-drawn carriages bearing guests lined the approaches to the marble portico of the White House well before that time. It began with the Diplomatic Corps, including Sidky and Madame Bey, coming in via the south entrance. The Diplomatic Corps waited in the red parlor for entrance into the Blue Room where the president and Mrs. Roosevelt would receive them.[9]

Mrs. Roosevelt wore a gown of white silk with a ruffle of pleated chiffon. Her waist was of chiffon with lace. She completed her dress with accessories that included rows of pearls around her collar and a diamond pendant that hung from her neck. In her hair, she wore diamond combs and silver leaves. She carried a cluster of purple orchids and shook hands with those that extended theirs first.[8]

The band began to play as the president's party readied to receive their guests. As with McKinley's last public appearance, President Roosevelt enjoyed himself as he greeted all the foreign relations as they passed by him. He smiled as he extended good wishes for the new year over several hours. The New Year's pageant was never complete without the picturesque Turks. This included the newly appointed Turkish minister, Shekib Bey, whose name was alternately spelled Chekib in some newspapers, and his two secretaries, Dejelal Munif Bey and Madame Bey's husband, Sidky Bey. Each wore their customary native uniform and red velvet fez with a dark tassel on top.[8, 9]

Shekib Bey was an enigmatic man. Madame Bey described the new minister as peculiar and superstitious.[10] He had come to Washington two days after McKinley had departed for Canton, Ohio, on route to his ill-fated trip to Buffalo, New York. While Turkey appointed Shekib Bey as the Turkish minister of the United States on August 20, 1900, his arrival from Turkey was delayed for thirteen months. Ferrouh Bey, relieved of the same position, stayed in the United States as Charge d'Affaires until Shekib Bey's long-awaited arrival. Shekib Bey was a widower with two sons, Osman Sureya and Ali Haidas.[11] He had to smuggle in his mother to help care for his two sons because Muslim women were rarely allowed to travel outside their country. As a Turkish diplomatic representative, he was in an unprecedented situation known in the annals of diplomacy. His presence was not recognized by the new Roosevelt administration even after six months in his position since he was unable to present credentials to anyone.[7] Madame Bey's husband, Sidky Bey, was now in the position of being the person having remained at the Turkish embassy longer than any other official representative had. He served in the capacity of acting consul in Washington. Though he did not have the title, he executed the work. This was in addition to his job as vice consul of New York. He divided his time between New York and Washington.[7] Madame Bey, Sidky Bey, and their son, Rustem, would make many trips between the two cities. Having to spend so much time in New York, they lived in a second residence on Long Island.[10] They kept their house in Washington on Q Street.

Madame Bey said of Shekib Bey, "With the waning of the year 1901, came Shekib Bey; but he was not actually Envoy Extraordinary and Minister Plenipotentiary of the Sultan of Turkey. This strange personage was here seven years without having presented his credentials—an unparalleled case in the history of the diplomatic service. He was only an appointed Minister.

"Owing to the peculiar but natural disposition of Shekib Bey, his secretary, Djelal Munif Bey, never resided in the Legation, but instead of this, made his home at the residence of Sidky Bey during the remainder of their time in Washington, accompanying them to New York, when Sidky Bey became acting consul-general in place of Aziz Bey, absent, residing with them at their suburban home on Long Island."[10]

The Beys continued to live as they did under the McKinley administration. They attended many social events at the White House and embassies. Typical of the many White House events they attended was the musical entertainment given at the White House by President and Mrs. Roosevelt on April 14, 1902.[12]

More than three hundred invited guests attended the social gathering with musical entertainment. Besides the Beys, other guests included the secretary of the treasury, secretary of war, attorney general, postmaster general, secretary of agriculture, chief justice, speaker of the House, representatives, senators, high-ranking military officers, and foreign embassy representatives. President and Mrs. Roosevelt received their guests and their wives in the Blue Room of the White House. They decorated the room with potted fragrant primroses and hyacinths. The entertainment took place in the East Room, which was decorated with palms and tropical plants that filled the window recesses. Hyacinths and Japanese lilies in white wicker baskets were placed on the mantels. There was a piano in the center of the room opposite the entrance to the inner corridor.[12]

The music included English ballads and comic songs sung by Mr. Wilford Russell, a versatile baritone from London. Mrs. Wilford Russell and Mrs. J. H. L. Brainard accompanied him on the piano. Ms. Palliser and Ms. Turner sang other classical selections. They printed the selections they sang on plain white cards for the guests. Singers Russell, Palliser, and Turner, referred to as the Southern Trio, had a local following. They also had performed before the king and queen of England.[12]

Typical of the many gatherings given by an embassy was the one attended by Madame Bey on May 6, 1902, at the Mexican embassy hosted by the wife of the Mexican secretary, Madame Godoy. The house was decorated throughout, the dining room being especially attractive in masses of snowballs and green foliage plants. Assisting the host to welcome her guests was Madame Calvo, wife of the minister from Guatemala; Madame Calderon, wife of the minister of Peru; Madame Leger, wife of the minister of Haiti; Madame Torres of the Mexican embassy; Mrs. John W. Foster and her daughter; Mrs. Robert Lansing; and Madame Bey of the Turkish legation. Mrs. Guthridge and Mrs. H. O. Heistand did the honors of the dining room assisted by Miss Calderon and Miss Burke.[13]

For diplomatic gatherings held at the Turkish embassy, Madame Bey acted as the host. It was because of her beauty, charm, and command of languages, particularly that of English, she was the perfect representative of her country. Many society sections of newspapers wrote of her striking beauty, describing her as having a dark complexion, black hair, and fine proportions.[14] She was as beautiful as she was smart and sharp. She was sought after in New York for sittings in the Fifth Avenue drawing rooms where women would pose in the finest gowns. They sketched her for fashion magazines and advertisements. She became referred to in the social circles of Washington as the Armenian Pearl.

Over the years at the Turkish embassy since 1897, ministers, consul generals, secretaries, second secretaries, and Charge d'Affaires came and went. The lone steward was Madame Bey's husband, Sidky Bey, who at one time held many titles as he worked in Washington and New York. He was a tireless worker and kept the daily operations on track despite political changes occurring back in his home country of Turkey along with the personnel changes in America. Corruption was commonplace, but Sidky Bey stayed clear of it.

While Madame Bey and Sidky Bey were at the Turkish embassy from 1897 through 1909, some of those that held titles were Aristarki Bey, Mavroyani Bey, Norigian Ivffendi Bey, Seifed din Bey, Moustapha Bey, Seifeddin Bey, Edhem Bey, Ali Ferrouh Bey, Hussein Bey, Alfred Rustem Bey, Aziz Bey, Shekib Bey, Djelal Munif Bey, Mehmid Ali Bey, Izzet Pacha, Mundji Bey. It confused the American government at times who held what position. No matter who was in charge, unquestionable were the diplomatic skills Sidky Bey possessed. He was the sole diplomat not dismissed, recalled, or reassigned during thirteen years.

"It was in those early days in this country that people spoke of us as Mr. and Mrs. Bey," Madame Bey would write, "… and we found that it was useless to explain that Bey is a Turkish word meaning 'sir' or 'Mister' and that Sidky Bey really translates into Mr. Sidky. Bey came last in our name, as is the Turkish custom, and Bey we were and Bey we are to this day. And as everyone at the Imperial Ottoman Legation carried Bey at the end of their names, it must have seemed as if we were all related."[10]

By 1908, the political climate changed in Turkey. An organization called the Young Turks gained political power. On July 24, 1908, the Young Turks were able to force the sultan Abdul Hamid II to restore the Ottoman constitution. He had suspended it in 1878 to give himself absolute power. The Second Constitutional Era of the Ottoman Empire began.

The changes in Turkey brought about changes at the legation in the United States in the summer of 1908. Turkey recalled Mehmed Ali Bey. They appointed a Young Turks supporter, Mundji Bey, who was consul general in New York, as Charge d'Affaires in Washington. Sidky Bey, second secretary of the Washington legation, kept his position.[15] The Congressional Directory at the end of 1908 had the positions listed as:

(Address of the Legation, 1730 Columbia Road)
Munji Bey, Consul-General in Charge of Legation.
Djelal Munif Bey, First Secretary. (Absent.)
Sidky Bey, Second Secretary, 59 Pearl Street, New York.
Ihsan Bey, Third Secretary.[16]

Mundji Bey said that persons of Jewish extraction would be welcome as readily by the Turkish government and receive the same liberties and protection as the sultan's subjects of the Muslim and Christian faiths. He then set resolutions congratulating Turkey on the adoption of the constitution and pledging the support of the meeting to the establishment of a Jewish state in Palestine, which they wanted to be a part of the Ottoman Empire.[17]

On September 6, 1908, Turks in America celebrated the reinstatement of their constitution. The Young Turks, the Armenian Revolutionary Federation, and the Hunchakist Society assembled a meeting at Carnegie Hall. Ottoman subjects and their sympathizers occupied every seat, with many standing. Congressional representatives and every form of revolutionist from the world, including Turks, Armenians, Macedonians, Syrians, Bulgarians, Albanians, Greeks, and Russians, attended.[18]

They decorated the stage with Turkish flags and small banners with Turkish and Armenian inscriptions, which when translated read:

"Hurrah for the Young Turks!"

"Hurrah for the Armenian Revolutionary Federation!"

"Liberty, Equality, Fraternity!"[18]

The enthusiastic crowd gave a large cheer after Congressman James B. Reynolds, introduced by Mundji Bey, read a letter from the president of the United States:

> Oyster Bay, Sept. 4.
>
> My Dear Mr. Reynolds: Through you may I present my regards to Mundji Bey, the present charge of Turkey in this country, and express my great pleasure on the occasion which gives rise to the meeting next Sunday evening at Carnegie Hall? All men all over the world who believe in liberty and order, who believe in a liberal government, under which Justice shall be done to every man without regard to his creed or race, must feel the keenest Interest in and sympathy with the movement, so full of hope for general progress, which is now taking place in the Turkish Empire. With heartiest good wishes for the success of the meeting, believe me, sincerely yours,
>
> THEODORE ROOSEVELT[19]

Speeches were given in several languages. Sidky Bey gave a speech in Turkish.[20] His wife, Madame Bey, performed a song.[18] The speech given by Mundji Bey expressed the sentiment among the people present with the following passage:

"For thirty-two years," he said, "we have suffered under a despot whom I do not need to name (referring to the Turkish Sultan). You all know his name. If you wish to know how we have suffered you can ask Turks, Armenians, Albanians, and Syrians, who are in the audience, for we have all of them with us. They have all been subjects of the Ottoman Empire.

"But we must be friends and brothers now. We must respect justice. If we use this force which God has given us, we shall be strong and we will fight for liberty with our blood."

Congressman Parsons expressed his congratulations to the "newest torchbearers of Liberty," which he added was the unanimous sentiment among the members of the House of Representatives. Many songs accompanied the speeches and concluded with a national patriotic song of Turkey.[18]

By the beginning of 1909, more changes in Turkey and its embassy in America were occurring. That gave a new life direction to Sidky and Madame Bey. Despite the speech by Mundji Bey and the nationalism exuded at Carnegie Hall the previous year, changes were coming only for the Young Turks.

Mundji Bey wrote letters to Constantinople stating Sidky Bey could not be trusted. Sidky Bey only had a copy of the letter from Mundji Bey that brought about his dismissal.[21] Sidky Bey had an unblemished record, and his devotion for his country had been beyond reproach. The Beys had served under Presidents William McKinley, Theodore Roosevelt, and William Taft. Sidky Bey, for the first time since coming to America in 1897, was without a job.

Mundji Bey was the one who was corrupt and used what means he could to deflect suspicion. He had been living above what his salary of $5,000 could afford.[21]

"His New York residence was the Waldorf-Astoria," Madame Bey stated, "where he enjoyed luxuries that were not permitted by his actual salary. It was not through merit that he succeeded in being appointed Consul-General to New York City, and many were the very handsome presents sent back to the heads of the Turkish foreign office, who had availed themselves of the privilege of appointing him Consul-General to New York City."[10]

As with many of the corrupt, it was a matter of time before one's actions caused their downfall. Such was the case with Mundji Bey. The government of Turkey recalled him when his actions were too much to tolerate.

"Mundji Bey returned to Constantinople almost a fugitive from justice," Madame Bey said. "With Mundji's departure the last vestige of the Hamidian (the Turkish Sultan) regime in America has disappeared. Let us hope that it will never again disgrace the civilized world."[10]

On March 20, 1909, Mundji Bey boarded a ship bound for Turkey in disgrace. With his departure, Riauf Ahmed Bey, first secretary of the Turkish embassy in Washington, levied charges of graft and unauthorized expenditures of the government's money against Mundji Bey.[22] It was a vindication for Sidky Bey, who was without a job due to the hostilities toward him from Mundji Bey. Turkey offered Sidky Bey a post in their Berlin embassy. He declined it, to which Madame Bey concurred.[23] The two had become accustomed to American life, and they wished to stay in the United States. Madame Bey, her husband, Sidky, son, Rustem, and mother, Marie Aglaganian, established residence at Brooklyn Ward 30, Kings, New York.[24]

In 1910, Madame Bey and her husband wrote the book titled *Turkish Diplomatic Life in Washington Under the Old Regime, by the Wife of a Diplomat*. She did not attach her name as the author. It was not until 1913 in *The Cumulative Book Index, Fifteenth Annual Cumulation*, by the H. W. Wilson Company that the Beys were accredited as the book's authors.[25] A copy exists with the inscription and Madame Bey's autograph: "To Mrs. H. Rowe, with compliments of the authoress, H.S. Bey, New Providence (New Jersey), 1914." Even then, she gave her initials and not her full name.[26]

"The old regime in Turkey is wiped out from the face of the earth," Madame Bey wrote after the regime fell, "leaving behind it many a miserable recollection of the days when the young Turks, brave and patriotic, were forced through oppression to take into their hands their own lives, in an effort to propagate their broad-minded views, which have eventually led to the adoption of a new constitution; before which many a day dream and many a night dream did these gallant Turks awake only to find themselves not floating upon the waters of the Bosphorus in golden barge of freedom, but still bound down by the chain of tyranny that for years has been felt by those who have lived under the Turkish rule. But now it is believed that this old form of government is forever gone, and for the first time in its history Turkey can proudly claim a rank among the independent countries of the world, looking forward to freedom and prosperity."[10]

She published those words in anonymity.

The Young Turks in their revolt against the sultan Abdul Hamid II considered the Armenians, like Madame Bey, allies. She could not foresee the events that would unfold. Many of those from the Carnegie Hall meeting became disillusioned with the new Turkish regime they had supported and had so much hope. The new regime succumbed to the devices of power. Their allies were now enemies. The regime used all means to solidify their position, including destruction of perceived opposition. The coalition of representatives at the Carnegie Hall meeting that the Beys had attended was a distant memory.

Returning to Turkey would have been dangerous for Madame Bey. She was Armenian, and stories coming from Turkey of Armenian persecution and genocide were beginning to trickle through. The Young Turks turned on the Armenians.

Madame Bey's fellow Armenians were systematically eliminated by execution, deportation, and death marches. The marches consisted of forced treks across the vast deserts of Syria with little supplies. Most died from exposure. Known as the first modern genocide, an estimated one to one and half million people died. An article in the *New York Times* on April 28, 1909, described a massacre in Adana, Turkey—a harbinger of what was to come in the following years. In that article, the Reverend Herbert Adams Gibbons of Hartford, Connecticut, gave his eyewitness account of the Muslim uprising.

"The entire *vilayet* (the administrative division of Turkey) of Adana has been visited during the last five days with a terrible massacre of Armenians, the worst ever known in the history of the district. The terror has been universal, and the Government is powerless to check the disorders. Adana, the capital of the province, has been the storm centre.

"Conditions have been unsettled for some time past, and there has been animosity between Turks and Armenians, owing to the political activity of the latter and their open purchasing of arms.

"Adana is in a pitiable condition. The town has been pillaged and destroyed, and there are thousands of homeless people here without means of livelihood. It is impossible to estimate the number of killed.

"The corpses lie scattered through the streets. Friday, when I went out, I had to pick my way between the dead to avoid stepping on them. Saturday morning I counted a dozen cartloads of Armenian bodies in one-half hour being carried to the river and thrown into the water. In the Turkish cemeteries graves are being dug wholesale.

"The condition of the refugees is most pitiable and heartrending. Not only are there orphans and widows beyond number, but a great many, even the babies, are suffering from severe wounds.

"The situation in Adana itself is unspeakable. On Friday afternoon 250 so called Turkish, reserves, without officers, seized a train at Adana and compelled the engineer to convey them to Tarsus, where they took part in the complete destruction of the Armenian quarter of that town, which is the best part of Tarsus. Their work of looting was thorough and rapid. It is said that they spread with kerosene and fired the great historic Armenian Church at Tarsus the most important building in the city. They demolished marble statues and shattered important historic tablets. Everything portable was carried away, but the church itself resisted their attempts to burn it. Fortunately few persons were killed here. This was owing to the proximity of the American College, where, 4,000 destitute and homeless persons had sought and found shelter."[27]

Madame Bey and her husband, Sidky Bey, had talents beyond diplomatic life. They would use those talents to enter a new stage in their lives to give them a livelihood to support themselves and their ten-year-old son, Rustem.

CHAPTER 6

A Different Strategy

After leaving the Turkish Diplomatic Corps, Sidky Bey had to find work. Besides having expertise in diplomatic affairs, he was an avid collector of antiques from the Middle East, especially oriental rugs and tapestries. He amassed a large collection during his service in the Diplomatic Corps. His passion for collecting and his expertise in antiques would lead him into his career path after leaving the diplomatic services. He would become a dealer in Eastern antiques and oriental rugs. Madame Bey's talents were in a different area. She had a magnificent singing voice. A voice she had exhibited while her husband was still working in the Turkish diplomatic service.

On May 15, 1908, Madame Bey started using her fine mezzo-soprano voice with a coloratura range that she had trained and cultivated from instructors in Italy as a young girl. One of her first public performances that displayed her exceptional voice came in Bay Ridge, Brooklyn, at the Ridge Club on Seventy-Second Street and Second Avenue when she was twenty-seven years old. She performed the grand aria from the *Il Trovatore* opera by Giuseppe Verdi. After her performance, the *New York Times* printed, "Her voice is a pleasing one, with warm color. It is probable that she will study for the operatic stage."[1, 2]

People noticed, and Madame Bey became a protégé of a famous soprano opera singer, American-born Lillian Nordica.[3] Nordica started singing for the Metropolitan Opera House of New York, the Met, in 1891. Her appeal carried worldwide. By January 1910, the same year Nordica retired from the Met, Madame Bey gave a recital at Carnegie Lyceum, an auditorium of Carnegie Hall. Baritone Eugene McGrail and pianist Georgio M. Sullis assisted Madame Bey in a performance. Madame Bey followed their performance with other selections, including Persian ballads. She performed four songs.[4]

Madame Bey's talents impressed Metropolitan Opera House manager Giulio Gatti-Casazza. So enamored with her performance, he extended her an invitation to join the Metropolitan Opera House.[5] Gatti-Casazza was the picture of sophistication with his three-piece suit, handlebar mustache waxed at the ends and turned upward toward the sky, and beard that came down the sides of his mouth with the rest restricted to just his chin, forming a tuft that hung below. He managed the world-renowned La Scala Opera House in Milan, Italy, from 1898 to 1908 before coming to America to become the manager for the Metropolitan Opera House. He held the job from 1908 to 1935. It earned him two covers on *Time* magazine.

If she accepted, it could have launched Madame Bey into an opera career of international fame. Her husband objected to the idea of his wife working in a career. She had mostly been a woman of society, attending diplomatic events and helping with entertainment at the Turkish embassy. The strong-willed Madame Bey caved and honored her husband's request. Her operatic career ended abruptly. She would use the incident to gain something else she wanted in the future—operation of a boxing camp, something that could not be further from opera.

The Beys concentrated on making a success of their antique business. A month after his dismissal from the Turkish embassy, Sidky Bey started selling antiques in a distinguished art gallery in New York on April 28, 1909. The *New York Times* printed, "A sale of art objects begins today at the Fifth Avenue Art Galleries, and will last four days. They belong to the collection of Sidky Bey, ex-Secretary of the Turkish Embassy in Washington. The collection comprises Persian and Turkish portieres, textiles and embroideries, armor, brasses, and rugs of historical association woven in the sixteenth century."[6] They advertised the sale in newspapers.[7, 8] The four-day sale grossed $52,567. A person paid $1,400 for a royal Persian silk carpet with soft red ground and floral medallion. An agent paid $1,050 for a Persian silk carpet with Koran inscriptions.[9, 10]

His business as a dealer offering his oriental rugs and consignments from others flourished between 1909 through 1911. He used his diplomatic skills to help sell his goods. Before one of his New York sales, he said: "Your women have the most splendid taste in selecting and using Oriental rugs. American women show wonderful versatility in home furnishing; they have learned to place Turkish rugs of large patterns with mission furniture, the lighter and more delicately colored Persian rugs of intricate designs they use with furnishings of lighter types; Kilims and Soumaks they put in bedrooms, and Kivas of rich colorings in libraries and living rooms."[11]

In 1910, Sidky Bey, after a trip to Turkey, secured more rugs. He went to Winnipeg, Canada, to sell them.[12] Starting on May 20, 1911, and lasting three days, the sale exceeded expectations. With the Winnipeg success, he sold more rugs in Montreal, Canada, at the Walter M. Kearns auction.[13] On November 17 and 18 of 1911, Sidky Bey brought his rugs across the country to the Sutter Street Sales Rooms of H. Taylor Curtis in San Francisco for yet another sale.[14] Sidky Bey became known in the rug and antique business, and it afforded him a good living.

By 1915, he went into business with a man from his native city of Constantinople by the name of Ehsan Karadaghli. They named their business the Teheran Rug Company. Adhiel G. Karadaghli became the company's president. Ehsan M. Karadaghli became its vice president. Sidky Bey and the Karadaghlis were directors. The company was located at 244 Fifth Avenue in New York City.[15] It specialized in fine oriental rugs and collectables.

Ehsan Karadaghli was born on November 29, 1889. He was born and raised in Constantinople like the Beys. The small, quiet, dark-hued skinned, steely haired Ehsan immigrated to America in 1914. He was of Persian descent and spoke with a Persian accent. Madame Bey and Sidky Bey would remain best of friends and business associates with Ehsan for the rest of their lives.

Sidky Bey was eighteen years older than the younger twenty-six-year-old Ehsan. Ehsan had connections to Turkey. He would dispatch the profits from the Teheran Rug Company to his father in Constantinople. His father would then send the money to Ehsan's grandfather in Tabriz, Iran. The grandfather helped acquire rugs from the Mideast and ship them to America where the Teheran Rug Company would sell them.[16] It was a perfect business model for Ehsan and the Beys. The rugs in Turkey and Iran were cheap compared to the inflated prices in America. They were making a small fortune on the price difference.

The Teheran Rug Company continued to prosper until 1917. That year the business became challenged when Turkey declared war on the United States as part of World War I.

"We did very well until the World War came along," Madame Bey said, "but after Turkey joined the Central Powers, there was considerable feeling against Turks in the United States."[17]

Despite the challenges of negative feelings toward the Turks, they continued to invest in their business. Their profits over the years had afforded them to live well. They were not privileged to enjoy it much longer.

In 1918, Ehsan and the Beys made a business blunder. They decided to invest their money for larger profits. They had Ehsan's grandfather buy $250,000 worth of rugs and tapestries. The grandfather procured the merchandise and sent them to Trabzon, Turkey, on the Black Sea. He placed the large inventory on a ship destined for America.[16] En route, the Russians, who had declared war on Turkey during World War I, intercepted the ship carrying the rugs. Russia confiscated the cargo, which included the Teheran Rug Company's shipment of rugs and tapestries. Sidky Bey upon hearing the news collapsed.[18] The Teheran Rug Company was insolvent, and the Beys had lost everything.

Before the incident, Sidky Bey had taken some of his money to buy a swath of thirty acres[19] in the small agrarian town of Chatham Township, New Jersey, about thirty miles west of New York City. The land, formerly known as the Smith Baldwin Farm, contained a farmhouse, a barn, a garage, and shacks strewn about. It was a peculiar purchase for Sidky Bey, who along with his wife had lived mostly in cities. The rural area was a departure from their accustomed way of life. The property represented their last major asset.

PART III

CHAPTER 7

Creating Hallowed Ground for Boxing

Madame Bey perpetuated the long run of boxing in Chatham Township, but if it were not for her friend and neighbor Freddie the "Welsh Wizard" Welsh, her boxing camp would never have started. Bey knew nothing about boxing, but Freddie Welsh was the world lightweight champion, a title he held from 1914 to 1917.

He was born Frederick Hall Thomas in Pontypridd, Wales, United Kingdom, on March 5, 1886. It was a working-class town built on coal, iron, and steel. Freddie's father worked as an auctioneer and could afford to send him to a boarding school in Bristol. The schooling helped him become an intellectual, not the usual path of a boxer from Wales, who were mostly impoverished.

He became obsessed with physical fitness at an early age, a result of a breathing ailment he had as a child. He bulldozed through his ailments, countering them by taking long walks. He developed an exercise regimen along with healthy eating habits. He became a vegetarian. The lifestyle made him physically fit.

At fifteen, Freddie went to work in an iron foundry after he completed school. He traveled to America at the age of sixteen in an attempt to find improvement for his health. He found it hard to earn money and returned to Wales. He returned to America a second time, which changed his life direction. He went to Philadelphia where he learned to box. Before coming to America, Welsh had never laced up a pair of boxing gloves. He had his first fight on December 21, 1905, at the Broadway Athletic Club in Philadelphia. It was here he started using the name Freddie Welsh.[1]

He developed a defensive counterpunching style. It was apparent from his early fights that he had the skills and power, winning his first seven bouts. The man Welsh would fight for the world lightweight title, Willie Ritchie, described his boxing style.

"Welsh was a great defensive fighter … Welsh fought typically slugger fashion, all covered up, coming in with his head down, bent over forward … He had his gloves in front of his face, and you couldn't score cleanly with the gloves there."[2]

On July 7, 1914, Freddie Welsh won the world lightweight championship by defeating Willie Ritchie in London, England, in a twenty-round bout by a one-point decision. The referee, Eugene Corri, scored the first nineteen rounds even. He awarded the last round to Welsh.

A newspaper title after the fight stated, "Winning a World's Championship on Carrots, Peas and Spring Water." Another newspaper's title pronounced, "Fred Welsh, Lightweight Champion of England Finds That a Meatless Diet Increases Endurance." Freddie Welsh declared, "Vegetables did it!" The *Los Angeles Times* called him a fruitarian, the vegetarian philosopher phenom.

He was an atypical boxer. He preferred reading to going out to a nightclub. He promoted himself as a brain box with a punch. He dressed well and found his good looks gave him a following with the opposite sex. He did not discourage it,[1] despite having a wife, Fanny, since 1905 and being the father of two children with her. He used it as a ploy to get the largest gates he could entice to his bouts. The way he parlayed his championship into a moneymaking business was brilliant. He boxed in many newspaper fights that were a common practice. This meant that they did not declare a winner. The newspapers would print who they thought had won the fight. Freddie could lose a newspaper decision while retaining his championship title. It brought him riches and fame.

Welsh was to defend his lightweight title against Benny the "Ghetto Wizard" Leonard. In March 1917, Welsh trained for the fight in Douglaston, Long Island. Before the fight, in late March, Welsh searched for a house where he planned to realize his dream of opening a health farm for business clientele. He found one in New Jersey. A wealthy real estate broker, V. F. Pelletreau, built the house as a summer home. He did not save money in providing it with all his tastes dictated for a country home. The estate was listed for sale after Pelletreau died from the result of an accident in Morristown, New Jersey. Thrown from his horse, he was killed instantly. Later, George E. Duncan, a New York merchant who lived there for some time, purchased it. Duncan died in New York the winter before Welsh became interested in the property.[3]

The property Welsh bought was near acquaintances—the Beys. The land was in the same town just one mile down the road from where the Beys lived. Welsh's purchase made more sense than the Beys', who had resided in cities most of their lives. He was a health and fitness fanatic and espoused the virtues of clean country air. He had a brother who owned a car dealership in the larger neighboring town of Summit, New Jersey. The area had its share of affluent inhabitants. Many wealthy people owned country mansions in the area that they used as summer homes. Summit was known as a summer resort town where many of the rich had country homes and vacationed. The Blackburn resort, later the Grand Summit Hotel, was built in 1868. It was a popular summer retreat.

The property Welsh showed interest in had a large house for the era sitting on 162 acres in Chatham Township, New Jersey, at the head of Johnson's Gap.[3] He would call the place the Long Hill Health Farm. Many would refer to it as the house on the hill. Long Hill described the hilly terrain along River Road that extended for miles into neighboring communities.

"For nearly ten years," Welsh said, "I have had this idea in mind. For more than three years, I have been looking for a place to strike my fancy. I wanted one that would both be a good place for my wife and two 'kiddies' to live on and at the same time serve as a training camp. This deal was closed five days ago. Within the next ten days, I intend to take over the title and this spring I expect to have the training farm in first class condition.

"The house there," Welsh continued, "is one of the finest I have ever seen … I intend to have a fine golf course. There will also be tennis, horseback riding, and various other forms of sport to drive away worry from the mind of the tired businessman. I expect to have the training farm in operation by the late spring."[4]

Welsh said that one of the reasons he selected the property was for its convenience to New York. There were eighty trains daily, according to Welsh, between New York and Summit, and the time for the journey was forty-five minutes. On April 3, 1917, Julio J. Julio and Lester S. Duncan, son of George E. Duncan, signed their deeds over to Welsh giving him ownership to the property. That date initiated the introduction of boxing into the small town in the hills of New Jersey.

On May 28, 1917, at the Manhattan Athletic Club, Freddie Welsh fought Benny Leonard for the lightweight title. Leonard was a prizefighter that almost did not make it into the game; he had to overcome his parents' objections.

"I was a Mama's boy. When I was fifteen, I began fighting in the local clubs and I didn't want my folks to know so I changed my name from Benny Leiner to Benny Leonard after the famous minstrel man Eddie Leonard. One night I came home after a fight and my mother was crying. She had found out. My father came in and started yelling at me. 'Viper. Tramp. Fighting, fighting, fighting for what?' I took out the five dollars I had earned and handed it to him. He looked at it, smiled and put his arms around me. 'That's all right, Benny,' he said, 'when are you going to fight again?'"[5]

Welsh lost his world lightweight title that he held for nearly three years to Benny Leonard by a technical knockout in the ninth round. He hit the canvas three times in the final round. Leonard promised him a rematch, but Welsh showed no interest.[6] He had the fulfillment of his dream waiting for him with his newly purchased property.

The house sat on the south side of Myersville Road at the intersection with Fairmount Avenue. Situated atop a long gradual steep incline, the property immediately surrounding the house was mostly free of trees and had little shrubbery, so one could see it from the road. It occupied the entire hilltop overlooking the Passaic Valley and had grand commanding views for miles in every direction.[3] On both sides of the incline were trees, especially an abundance of fruit trees, and shrubbery that went to the top of the property until they were even with the house, at which point they formed a right angle until they met the house. More shrubberies adorned the house front. From the road were a few steps that met a pathway with one shrub to the right. The pathway curved right then left and wound its way up the left side of the property through the trees and shrubbery. Surrounding acreage, owned by Welsh, consisted of many sizeable fields and wooded areas.

The house contained sixteen rooms all furnished with hardwoods of the finest variety, and many of them contained sizeable fireplaces. There were dozens of hunting scenes painted on the walls and many hand carvings imported from Italy. The middle section had three stories, with two two-story wings on either side that angled toward the road. Porches surrounded the house. Most windows had awnings with vertical stripes. The farm cost $70,000 according to the *Lewiston Daily Sun*. Renovations to the house and surrounding property brought the total cost to $150,000, the life savings of Freddie Welsh and an additional $35,000 mortgage.

Welsh renovated the interior with the installation of a gymnasium, a state-of-the-art kitchen, and a grand library. The library had a low oak-beamed ceiling. He equipped the room with rich mahogany furniture, comfortable leather chairs, and bookcases against the walls filled with his books. The furniture was partly in a shadow due to the cathedral light that emanated from the large stained-glass, crown-shaped chandelier. The books included beautifully bound editions of works by Wilde, Brieux, Stevenson, Shakespeare, and other celebrated authors. Some were limited editions and signed by the author.[7] Welsh, an avid reader, filled the shelves with many familiar works. He redid the grounds to include a golf course, tennis courts, and restoration of the pool, which measured seventy-five feet in length and had an ever-flowing spring feeding it.[4]

The palatial home Welsh put to use for the building up of men. One person described it for business and professional men suffering from too much regularity or irregularity, as the case may be, were to come for recuperation and learn the fine art of right living. The high altitude made the air pure, clear, refreshing, and invigorating. Your lungs opened automatically, every cell filled with air, and you felt the thrill of oxygen combining with the iron in the blood. You felt a part of the great force of the universe. Wholesome food, pure air and water, simple exercises—these proportioned made the magic prescription for health. In addition, you had them in an atmosphere of refinement and culture, for Welsh had a library that was worth many thousands of dollars and could discuss the classics with a professor.[8]

In June, the month following the acquisition of the property, Welsh offered sixty acres of the farm to the mayor of the neighboring town of Summit. He wanted the mayor to use it for the construction of an aviation field and general gardening.[9] It was part of his grand scheme to transform the farm into a prime destination for the weary, wealthy businessman.

On August 11, 1917, the Long Hill Health Farm opened with much pomp. Invitees included many celebrities. One guest was Bat Masterson, the famous gunfighter turned lawman, United States marshal, army scout, and gambler. Two years earlier, as a Christmas gift, Welsh gave Masterson a Waltham pocket watch. The watch was constructed with a fourteen-karat gold octagonal case surrounded by silver filigree. Welsh had the inside back cover engraved with the inscription "To Bat Masterson from Freddie Welsh XMAS 1915."[10] Bat Masterson, who now worked as a boxing promoter and sports columnist for the *New York Morning Telegraph*, best described the farm as a "session magnificent house high on a hill, like an acropolis."[11]

The idea of a health club for businessmen seemed appealing. Freddie Welsh had a problem; there were few businessmen interested in staying in shape, though they needed it. The question persisted whether they would frequent Freddie's Farm, or did they not care about exercise. One invitee was world heavyweight champion Jack the "Manassas Mauler" Dempsey.

"Go on and box," Welsh said to one of his guests. "Jack won't hurt you."

After Dempsey gave his promise, the man climbed into the ring. The guest, after one minute, completely exhausted, was unable to continue. Welsh knew the man would not last and already had a second guest laced up with gloves. He lasted a little longer. Though Dempsey did not throw a punch at either of his opponents, the two men could not last the three minutes of the round.

"Don't you fellows ever take any exercise?" Dempsey inquired.

Onlookers were amused. Dempsey was not as he tried to understand. He just shook his head.[12]

CHAPTER 8

The Sports Event of the Century

The Beys settled into their home in Chatham Township, New Jersey. It was all they had left after losing their rug business. Gone was the diplomatic and socialite living in Washington and New York. Madame Bey replaced her gowns with practical clothes. They were entering their third career, their previous vocations as diplomats and antique rug entrepreneurs a memory. With the little they had left, they tried to subsist as farmers. Ehsan, who also lost everything, went with the Beys to their new property. One trait Madame Bey did not lose that remained intact—her fiery spirit. She lost some of life's battles but was not defeated. She would embark on a new endeavor.

Madame Bey, her husband, and Ehsan made their best attempts at farming. They were not good at it. Ehsan, the handyman, kept the place in order. He was a tinkerer and inventor. He applied for and received two patents for his inventions. One was a hose clasp, and the other a grade finder for determining the elevation between two points. Sidky Bey and Ehsan's attorney, F. T. Wentworth, witnessed them both to the United States Patent Office.[1] Neither invention made him money.

While the Beys and Ehsan were struggling with their new vocation, so was their friend down the street, Freddie Welsh. His Long Hill Health Farm was not bringing in the number of people that would fulfill his dream. It struggled so much that he attempted to sell it. At a price well below the $150,000 he spent for the purchase and renovations, he had no buyers.

In October 1918, Freddie Welsh enlisted as a private in the United States Army, leaving his health farm behind. The army attached him to the medical service unit and stationed him in Washington, DC.[2] He worked on the rehabilitation of veterans at Walter Reed Hospital. His duties were to direct physical corrective exercises for wounded soldiers. By January 1919, he was a lieutenant in the sanitary corps.[3] The army discharged Welsh, with the rank of captain, in March 1920 from his reassigned Fox Hills Base Hospital, Staten Island.[4] He returned to his home at the Long Hill Health Farm. Welsh, now thirty-four years old, had little money. He decided a comeback to the ring could bring back his wealth. After three-plus years away from the ring, he started his comeback on December 28, 1920, with a fourth-round technical knockout of a little-known boxer named Willie Green.

The farm continued to languish, but because of Freddie Welsh's fame as a former champion prizefighter, boxers came to his health farm to train. Boxing started to seep into Chatham Township, New Jersey. They came to the Long Hill Health Farm not for its health benefits, as Welsh wanted, but its facilities to train for prizefights. Welsh tried to make the farm into what he had intended it to be, but he did not turn away those boxers who chose to use it as a training facility.

The first notable prizefighter to come to the Long Hill Health Farm to train was the Frenchman Georges Carpentier to challenge for the world light heavyweight championship. It was not his first time in America. On March 13, 1920, Georges Carpentier boarded the French steamship *La Savoie* from Harve, France, along with his bride, Georgette Elsasser.[5] It was part honeymoon and part business. He honeymooned in New York before traveling west to fulfill a movie deal. He was under the auspices of fight promoter Jack Curley, who had him under contract from May 3 to July 17, with an option for five more weeks. During that time, he toured America for exhibition bouts. It was a long and lucrative honeymoon for the Frenchman and endeared him to the American public.

Carpentier was the European heavyweight champion. He was also the last person to hold the world white heavyweight championship. It was a title created once the first black heavyweight champion, Jack Johnson, held the world heavyweight title by defeating Tommy Burns in 1908 and vanquishing all white challengers. It was a title dropped as soon as Jack Johnson lost the championship. Considered a World War I aviator hero, Carpentier was well liked on both sides of the Atlantic. France awarded him two of the highest French military medals, the Croix de Guerre and the Médaille Militaire. With good looks, he had a following with the women. The press called him Gorgeous Georges. He had a ring name unbefitting a boxer—The Orchid Man.

Jack Curley was Carpentier's representative in America but not his manager, which was the French Francois Descamps. Before leaving France for the Levinsky bout, Descamps made a statement.

"Georges will begin immediately to condition himself for the Levinsky bout," Descamps said. "He will work at Freddie Welsh's farm in Summit, New Jersey, and will live a short distance away from the farm. Georges prefers the simple life to the big city hotels. Besides, he will be surrounded by a homelike atmosphere, for Marcel Thomas' sister is the hostess and will provide the cooking to which Georges is accustomed. With us will be Thomas, Charley Ledoux, and Gus Wilson, making our own little family."[6]

On this trip, Carpentier came to America without his wife, who remained home with their first child. His real quest was to get a bout with heavyweight champion Jack Dempsey. On September 13, 1920, he arrived in America aboard the French ship liner *La Lorraine* to fight Battling Levinsky for the world light heavyweight championship. He arrived to cheering crowds and banners displaying "*Vive* Carpentier."[7] Upon disembarking the ship, he addressed the crowd through his manager, Descamps, who acted as an interpreter. After some exchanges, he stated through Descamps:

"They tell me that Levinsky is one of the hardest men in the ring today. But should I care. That makes it all the better for me; that's just why I'm going to fight him. Like you Americans say, 'The harder they come, the harder they fall to the surface.'

"I was really qualified to meet Dempsey right after I knocked out Joe Beckett of England. The people here ridiculed me, though. They said the fight was one-sided; that Beckett wouldn't have had a chance against anyone even slower than I. That's why I'm going to take on Levinsky first."[7]

To show his seriousness, Carpentier forewent going to his American manager and promoter, Jack Curley. He went directly to the camp he had discovered in Chatham Township, New Jersey. It was Freddie Welsh's Long Hill Health Farm. He would do all his training at Welsh's farm for the planned prizefight with Levinsky on October 12 at the Westside Ballpark in Jersey City, New Jersey.

With him, he brought sparring partners French welterweight champion Marcel Thomas, English featherweight Joe Blumfeld, and American heavyweight Joe Jeanette.[7] Freddie Welsh also assisted in his training.[8] The two lighter boxers would help build Carpentier's speed, a method often used in training. Jeanette, his skills diminished, still had abilities that would be an asset in Carpentier's training. Jeanette, born in New Jersey, was regarded highly within the heavyweight division in his younger days. He defeated Carpentier in Paris on March 22, 1914, in a fifteen-round decision. He never received a chance at the heavyweight title. That opportunity went to Jack Johnson. Jeanette held the colored heavyweight title after Jack Johnson had vacated it when he won the world heavyweight title. Jeanette fought Johnson ten times. Jeanette lost twice, won one fight on a foul after two rounds, had two draws, and five no decisions. Johnson called Jeannette "the toughest man I ever fought."

One evening, the Elks Club in the bordering town of Summit invited Carpentier. He brought Joe Jeanette, and they sparred in a ring in front of a small audience. Carpentier, bare-chested, wore shorts. Jeanette wore long pants and a sleeveless shirt.[9]

Shortly after arriving in America, the International Sporting Club (ISC) gave a luncheon for Carpentier in New York City. The ISC introduced him to a burst of applause that lasted for more than a minute. Many prominent people attended to pay homage to their French guest. Those present included William Fox as toastmaster; Senator James J. Walker, father of the law legalizing boxing in New York; Gabriel Delvaux, editor in chief for the *Franco-American Gazette*; Robert Leconte, representative of the French government; Charles H. Ebbets, Brooklyn Baseball Club president; Alfred L. Marilley,

ISC attorney; Tex O'Rourke, ISC matchmaker; promoter Jack Curley; Walter Hooke and Edward Ditmars, Boxing Commission members; M. Ribaute, who greeted Carpentier on the *La Lorraine*; W. A. Gavin, ISC managing director; Benny Leonard, world lightweight champion; Freddie Welsh, former world lightweight champion whose Long Hill Health Farm in Chatham Township, New Jersey, hosted Carpentier's training; and many other prominent people of boxing. Carpentier made a speech at the luncheon.

"I came here a stranger last March and was pleased with the reception which greeted me," Carpentier said. "I returned yesterday and was amazed to experience the same reception, the same crowds again, as if I had never been here. It makes me feel that I am welcome, and I will try to deserve all that has been done for me. I was censured for my activities while here before, but, in explanation, I will remind you I am a professorial man. I must make money, and I had moving picture and circus contracts. The bout I wanted was not available.

"This time it is different." Carpentier added. "I have come here to fight and expect to engage in several bouts and possible arrange for a bout with Dempsey. No matter what the outcome of my fights, whether I win or lose, I hope they are all proper and that the public is pleased. If I lose against Levinsky, I will have no excuse to offer. I am in the best condition and will let the public judge my work as a fighter. Therefore, I say if I do not win, I won't cry.

"When I face Dempsey, it will be the same. I have no fear of him, and, like every other fighter, am confident of myself. What terrors has he to make anyone afraid of him? He is but human; he has two hands and two feet like myself, so that he is only natural. When I meet him, it will be the same as with any other boxer. I will hope and strive for victory."[6]

After the luncheon, Carpentier returned to the Long Hill Health Farm in Chatham Township, New Jersey, to prepare for the Levinsky bout. A seed was planted in the small town that would further its playing host to boxing's best. It would not be until Madame Bey became involved before the seed cultivated Chatham Township into a destination that attracted boxing's elite in large numbers.

The day of the fight, each opponent released a statement.

"I realize that I am under the inspection of a jury of fight fans who know boxing from early childhood. I invite inspection. I am ready. I will win," Carpentier said.

"I am in shape. When I am at my best no man in the world can beat me. We'll see whether this marvelous idol, Carpentier, isn't made of brittle clay. I'm going to knock him over," Levinsky said.[10]

The twenty-six-year-old Carpentier had little trouble with the twenty-eight-year-old Levinsky. He dominated the fight. In the fourth round, Carpentier staggered Levinsky with a left, which he followed with two rights. Levinsky went down for the count.

Carpentier, along with Levinsky's seconds, carried the unconscious fighter to his corner. Carpentier's work for the night was complete. He became the new world light heavyweight champion.[11]

Winning the bout gave Carpentier his long-awaited chance for the world heavyweight championship. On November 5, 1920, in New York City, an agreement was signed by Dempsey and Carpentier; their managers Kearns and Descamps; promoters Tex Rickard, Brady, and Cochran; and stakeholder Edgren. The contract guaranteed Dempsey $300,000 and Carpentier $200,000. Each would receive 25 percent of the movie rights. The promoters posted $50,000 to each fighter for forfeiture. With the deal signed, Carpentier sailed for France the next day, arriving home on November 13.[12]

On January 21, 1921, Tex Rickard took over Cochran and Brady's interest. He gave an extra $66,666 bringing his total forfeiture money to $100,000.[12] It made him the event's sole promoter. He was practicing his lesson he discovered promoting his first bout: you have to provide money to make money. Mike Jacobs, Tex Richard's moneyman, helped Rickard assemble the money. Jacobs raised $100,000 in cash in just eight hours to help Rickard take complete control of the Jack Dempsey-Georges Carpentier world heavyweight championship.[13] Jacobs had met Rickard at the Gans-Nelson fight in 1904, Rickard's first promotion, where he helped him raise money for that fight. He helped Rickard become active throughout the New York area where Jacobs lived.[14] The two would rule boxing from the early 1920s to the late 1940s. They came from different backgrounds—Tex Rickard from the rural Midwest, Mike Jacobs born and raised in New York City.

George Lewis "Tex" Rickard was one of boxing's greatest promoters. In the early years, he ushered in the golden age of prizefighting, the period from the 1920s through 1940s. He was a gambler who would wager on anything.

Rickard was a slender, finely dressed man. His attire included a vested suit with a pocket watch chain above the belt, hat, and cane. He was thin lipped with a half-smoked, chewed cigar protruding from the corner of his mouth. He thrived on exhilaration, saying, "… I've never been far away from excitement …"[15] His stoic expression was unmistakable on his lined, weathered face. It showed the wear as a cowboy from the Midwestern plains of his youth. He had an imperturbable disposition. He neither laughed, except for a fake forced laugh, nor wept.[16] Rickard acquired these traits during his years as a boy and young adult.

He was born January 2, 1870, in Kansas City, Missouri, to a poor family. He had the infamous outlaws Frank and Jesse James, along with their mother, as his next-door neighbors. He was four years old, but Rickard remembered the James brothers and Jesse's thick, rough beard. They would flip coins to Rickard and other kids.[17]

His family moved to Sherman, Texas, when Rickard was still a child. When he was eleven, his father died. He took a job as a cowboy on the plains of Texas with the East Ranch to support his mother and many brothers and sisters.[18] By the age of fifteen, he had ridden through fifteen states on horseback working for the ranch. Not long after, word spread that Rickard was one of the best shots in Texas.[19] An injury from a longhorn ended Rickard's days as a cowboy. At the age of twenty-three, he became the marshal of Henrietta, Texas, and gained the nickname "Tex." In 1894, he married and had a child. Both his wife and child died within a year. Many of his siblings died shortly after.[20] With nothing to keep him in Texas, he went to Alaska. It possessed the potential of fortune that he desired—the gold rush in the Klondike.

In Alaska, Rickard and a partner, George Cormack, claimed an area, which they sold. Rickard received $60,000 in gold dust. "I thought I was fixed for life," Rickard said many years later. Rickard opened a saloon with Tom Turner, and it became the biggest saloon and gambling house in Dawson City.[21] After four months, his gambling took his fortune. In four hours, he lost $150,000, which included the saloon. In St. Michaels, he met Jim White and opened a new saloon in Nome. Here, Rickard promoted his first fight as entertainment for his patrons. After they attracted a packed house, Rickard saw the potential in the sport.[22]

Rickard had recouped almost everything he lost in Dawson City. He left Alaska and went to San Francisco where he accepted a job of promoting the world lightweight title fight between Battling Nelson and the champion Joe Gans. Rickard chose the Casino Amphitheatre in Goldfield, Nevada, to stage the fight. Rickard acted as Gans's manager. He had heated discussions with Nelson's manager, Nolan, about the purse distribution. Rickard never held fight managers in high regard after this.[23] When the townspeople heard what was happening, they gave their support to Gans. Nelson's popularity waned. They guaranteed manager Nolan that if Nelson did not fight, Nolan would be going home horizontally. Nolan withdrew his demands and settled for $22,500. That allowed Rickard to pay Gans $11,000.[23] He would have received nothing if not for Rickard. As much disdain as Rickard had for managers, he sympathized with the prizefighters. In later years, when Gans had no money, Rickard staked him so he could fight. Rickard would repeat the practice with other prizefighters throughout his career.

On September 3, 1909, the fight took place. The large crowd, which included Teddy Roosevelt's son Kermit, paid $69,715 to see the fight. They were decidedly behind the black Gans, not the white Nelson, an unusual occurrence for that time. Joe Gans, the Old Master, lived up to his ring name by out-boxing Nelson despite breaking his hand in the thirty-third round. Nelson reverted to many flagrant fouls that infuriated the crowd to near riot. After forty-two grueling rounds in the searing Nevada heat, Gans took a left hook to the groin that sent him to the canvas. He could not get up. They awarded Gans the fight by disqualification due to the foul.[24]

With this prizefight, Rickard saw the fervor it caused among the people. Rickard did not expect to make money from the fight but had a $13,000 profit. He would be in the fight game for the rest of his life. Two philosophies that were used in the bout Rickard would apply to other fight promotions—you have to provide money to make money, and it attracted attention if you promoted one fighter as the villain and the other a hero. When people would tell him he spent too much, he continued to prove them wrong with increased gates.

Tex Rickard, now a promoter for prizefights, found that he had competition for big fights with other promoters who had realized the financial rewards from successful bouts. Rickard often conceived an angle to outmaneuver his competitors. This became clear when the Jack Johnson and Jim Jefferies fight was announced; everyone wanted to promote it. Rickard befriended Johnson, who told him the highest bid would be $100,000. The principles opened the bids in Hoboken, New Jersey, with Johnson present. A certified check accompanied each bid except one. Rickard's bid contained $101,000 in cash.[25] Rickard had outmaneuvered his competitors. The principles awarded him the fight. He would soon regret the victory.

From the onset, Rickard went through a barrage of protests for allowing a black man to fight a white man,[26] despite Johnson having defended his title in America four times against whites. Given the success and complete opposite sentiment Rickard had experienced when he promoted the black Gans against the white Nelson in a lightweight championship, he did not foresee the fervor with which white America would object to the bout.

Economics overshadowed racism as cities competed to host the event. Rickard had a stadium erected in San Francisco. Governor Gillette cancelled the match due to the ongoing pressure of hosting a mixed-race bout. Rickard lost the money he spent and had to refund the presales. He decided to hold the fight in Reno, Nevada, the same state he had so much success with the Gans-Nelson bout. He built another stadium, costing even more than the one in San Francisco. It became the first time someone erected an arena to hold a bout. When neither fighter could agree on a referee, Jackson suggested that Rickard take the job. To Rickard's surprise, Jeffries agreed, and Rickard with no choice became promoter and referee.[26]

Before a crowd of 15,600 paying $275,000 on July 4, 1910, Jim Jeffries and Jack Johnson entered the ring under the blazing Nevada sun. It was Jeffries's first fight in five idle years away from boxing. At thirty-five, Jeffries lost close to a hundred pounds to get to his fighting weight. Jeffries took the shaded corner. An official reminded him that they had agreed to flip a coin to determine the corner. When Jeffries's manager, Sam Berger, went to Johnson's corner to flip the coin, Johnson told him, "That's all right Sam. You just stay right where you are. This here corner's good enough for us."[27]

Johnson destroyed the undefeated Jeffries. Rickard stopped the scheduled forty-five-round fight in the fifteenth round while simultaneously Berger entered the ring with a towel to end it. Jeffries received $50,000 plus over $66,000 for the movie rights. Johnson received $70,600 plus another $51,000 for the movie rights. They estimated the motion picture money at $270,000.[27]

Among those in attendance was a young fifteen-year-old by the name of William Harrison Dempsey, better known as Jack Dempsey. The youngster came via a Pullman train car for the expressed purpose of watching the championship bout. Days before the bout, he would stalk Rickard in awe of the promoter. He attended the fighters' training camps.[28] Many years later, the two would be formally introduced, producing an epic business association.

Mike Jacobs was born on March 17, 1880, in New York's Greenwich Village. He was one of ten children born to Jewish immigrants Isaac and Rachel Strauss. His family was poor. He dropped out of school in the sixth grade. As a boy in 1890, someone offered him free tickets to a fight. Another person seeing the transaction offered Jacobs two dollars for the tickets, which he accepted. Jacobs was given an understanding of ticket sales. He sold newspapers, candy on Coney Island excursion boats, and began scalping boat tickets. He bought concession rights on all the ferries docked at the Battery and eventually ran his own ferryboats.[29, 30, 31]

Jacobs became the largest ticket scalper in New York. He would buy and sell theater, opera, and sporting event tickets. He began sponsoring events, including charity balls, bike races, and circuses. Jacobs opened a legitimate ticket agency across from the Metropolitan Opera House. He invested his profits in successful enterprises, including real estate development and opera star Enrico Caruso's concert tour. When Tex Rickard staged a fight, he allotted many of the best seats to Jacobs. He sold them at a profit and gave Rickard an agreed-upon share. Both grew rich. Mike Jacobs would not become a boxing promoter until 1934.[32, 33]

Mike Jacobs referred to himself as Uncle Mike. It was a name given to him by Joe Louis. When he was not smoking from his two-pack cigarette habit, he was chewing on a cigar.[31] He had small, round, shiny eyes, an expressionless face, gruff voice, and a set of ill-fitted false teeth. In boxing where profanity was the norm, he used it in excess. He was a realist, accounted as honorable, feared but not disliked, and charitable. He worked long, hard hours.[34, 35] His business found him in New York, but he preferred to live at his estate in Red Bank, New Jersey. It was as a boxing promoter that Mike Jacobs was best known.

His presence in Chatham Township, New Jersey, to look after the fighters he promoted would become commonplace. He would forge a friendship with Madame Bey.

In 1933, Jacobs with sportswriters Damon Runyon, Ed Frayne, and Bill Farnsworth formed the Twentieth Century Sporting Club to promote boxing. Jacobs used the Hippodrome in New York as his primary venue. The Twentieth Century Sporting Club competed with the Madison Square Garden for the biggest boxing promotions but rented the Garden to stage some of its fights.

Through the 1930s and into the postwar period, Jacobs was unmatched as a promoter. In 1935, Jacobs signed the young heavyweight Joe Louis to an exclusive contract. Louis's first bout under Jacobs at Yankee Stadium grossed $328,655 while his fight with Max Baer grossed over $1,000,000.[36] He reached his peak with the second Joe Louis-Billy Conn fight that brought in almost $2,000,000.[37]

Around 1938, Jacobs became the sole owner of the Twentieth Century Sporting Club, compensating Runyon and forcing the other two partners out.[38] Following in the path that Tex Rickard had set for promotions, Mike Jacobs ruled as the dominant boxing promoter from 1935 until 1949. Jacobs was the most powerful man in boxing. He controlled practically every world title bout from featherweights to heavyweights. In his career, he promoted 471 fight cards that attracted 5,071,012 customers paying $25,102,330.[31] In 1942 alone, he promoted two hundred fifty boxing cards and during his career staged sixty-one championship fights. The stretch on Manhattan's Forty-Ninth Street between Broadway and Eighth Avenue became known as Jacobs Beach.[39, 40]

"Nobody else ever exerted such absolute dictatorship as his over any sport," wrote columnist Red Smith.[33]

On April 16, 1921, Jack Dempsey arrived in New York City from the West Coast. He stayed at the Belmont Hotel for a few days. From there he went to Freddie Welsh's Long Hill Health Farm in Chatham Township, New Jersey, where he chose to start preparing for the Carpentier fight, the same facility Carpentier used to successfully train for his bout against Levinsky. Marcel Denis, a French lightweight fighter, was already there. He planned to help Carpentier prepare.[41] Carpentier had planned to use Welsh's place as he did for the Levinsky bout, but Dempsey arrived first.

Jack Dempsey and Freddie Welsh were good friends. For that reason, and the fight was to take place in New Jersey, he chose to start his training there. Dempsey started light training and brought lightweight Joe Benjamin, who was once a sparring mate of the world lightweight champion Benny Leonard, and middleweight Jimmy Darcey, both from the West Coast, to spar with him. Dempsey could earn four hundred to five hundred dollars a day charging admission to have people watch him train. While at Welsh's Farm, he discouraged it; he just wanted to rest. Freddie Welsh was in training, too, as he was in the middle of his comeback attempt, desperate for money. While Dempsey trained with him, Welsh had his second comeback fight on May 3, 1921, in Summit, New Jersey. He won by a knockout in the eighth round. Both comeback fights were with lesser opponents. They were a good tune-up for Welsh, whose boxing skills had diminished.

Dempsey had time for publicity and recreation while at Welsh's farm. If Dempsey had any weakness, it was his affection for kids. He would receive hundreds of letters daily. He cherished and saved the ones written in the typical large letters by children.[42] Freddie Welsh shared Jack Dempsey's fondness for children. Welsh had swings for his own children, daughter Elizabeth, six years old, and son Freddie Jr., five years old. Children would come because Welsh and Dempsey would buy them ice cream. Dempsey and Welsh would roll down the front lawn with them and the Welsh children.[43]

One day, on the hillside of Welsh's Farm, Dempsey and Welsh paused from their training. Dempsey was clad in dress shoes, pants and shirt, tie, and suit vest. Welsh wore dress shoes, pants, tie, and a suit jacket. The children were in their Sunday best. Dempsey and Welsh's son had boxing gloves on. Welsh acted as the referee while the two boxed. Dempsey kneeled on his right knee to come at eye level with Freddie Jr. Dempsey did his typical bobbing and weaving until the little boy connected with Dempsey's head. He pretended Freddie Jr. knocked him down while Freddie Welsh counted Dempsey out. Freddie Jr. joined in on the count.[44]

Dempsey would bail hay with a pitchfork and mow the lawn with a mechanical reel lawnmower for publicity pictures.[44] He was trying to enhance his image to the public that was decisively for the Frenchman, Carpentier, even in America. Dempsey had many detractors who criticized him as being a draft dodger, whereas Carpentier was a perceived war hero. It was a perfect arrangement for promoter Tex Rickard. Adhering to one of his rules, he had his hero in Carpentier and a villain in Dempsey. Rickard knew the hero-villain angle drew people to a fight. He had no idea the magnitude of the event that would unfold.

On April 25, while Dempsey trained at Welsh's facilities, Tex Rickard made the official announcement that Jersey City, New Jersey, would host the bout on July 2. He chose Boyle's Thirty Acres, a plot of land known as Montgomery Oval. There was a problem—no stadium existed there. He had a little over two months to construct one.

The next day, Dempsey announced from Welsh's Farm that he would be moving his training to Atlantic City, New Jersey, before the bout. Journalist Henry Farrell came to the Welsh Farm to spend a day with Jack Dempsey in late April. It gave insight into how Dempsey prepared for a fight and demonstrated how he grew to embrace training in seclusion. Dempsey had no desire to discuss the fight.

"I'm just resting, eating, and having a good time," Dempsey told Farrell.

He woke at six thirty, put on white flannels and a low-necked white shirt, and jogged a couple of miles over the hills. When he returned, he ate ham and eggs and drank three or four quarts of fresh milk. At nine o'clock, he strolled along a small stream with Freddie Welsh, Joe Benjamin, and his trainer, Teddy Hayes. Dempsey grabbed frogs out of the water and used them when he returned to Welsh's house to scare his pet monkey. At noon, he ate a salad, a big piece of tenderloin steak, drank several bottles of milk, and two cups of tea. After that, he played cards and wrestled with friends in the front yard. The rest of the afternoon, he just rested until dinner.

"I'm not going to do any work until we get to our Atlantic City training camp," Dempsey told Farrell. "I'm feeling as good as I ever did and I can get in shape with six week's work. I over trained for Bill Brennan, and I'm not going to make the same mistake this time.

"Yes, I have been dancing a little bit, and I went up to a midnight show last week with Babe Ruth. I know I was criticized for doing it, but a fellow's got to have a little amusement once in a while."

Dempsey liked to golf, but while at Welsh's Farm, he had put his golf clubs away and played tennis and handball.

"I tried pocket billiards, but I was the fish for the whole settlement. Joe Benjamin got rich on me, so I quit."

Farrell asked about the yet to be arranged details of the Carpentier bout.

"I don't care," Dempsey said. "Doc (Kearns) will take care of those things."

When asked if he cared who refereed the fight, Dempsey replied, "As long as he knows how to count."[45]

Dempsey did not wait until he went to Atlantic City and started to intensify his training at Welsh's Farm on May 4 when two more sparring partners arrived. They were middleweight Alex Trambidas and welterweight Steve Latzo. He put them to work immediately.

For training, Dempsey was usually awake early in the morning, and this day was no different. It represented a typical training day that started with roadwork. Trambidas, Latzo, and Joe Benjamin joined Dempsey for his early-morning jaunt. The quartet jogged, raced, and hiked over the roads for approximately four miles. The windy day limited Dempsey's outdoor work, including his infrequent horseback riding.

In the afternoon, Dempsey engaged in a one and a half hour's work. He used the pulleys, punched the bag, shadowboxed, skipped rope, and did floor calisthenics. Next came the sparring. Benjamin went four rounds against Dempsey, working fast throughout.

Trambidas and Latzo each boxed two rounds. In all his sparring, Dempsey took it easy. He encouraged all three of his partners to rush, push, pull, maul, and attempt an attack.

In the evening, Dempsey accompanied Welsh in his car to Morristown, New Jersey.[46] Welsh had another fight scheduled in his comeback attempt against Tommy "Kid" Murphy. Welsh won the fight by a technical knockout in the second of ten scheduled rounds against the less skilled boxer.

The next day on May 5, Dempsey moved from Chatham Township to Atlantic City. On May 7, Carpentier departed from Le Harve, France, with the intention of training at Welsh's Farm where he had successfully prepared for the Levinsky bout. En route, he discovered Dempsey was already there, and not knowing he had switched to Atlantic City, changed his planned training venue. Upon landing on American soil on May 16, Carpentier went to Manhasset, Long Island, where he trained. He had wired Joe Jeanette on April 16 to be his chief sparring partner and advisor, having had so much success with him at Welsh's Farm for the Levinsky bout.[47]

While the two principals continued their training, Tex Rickard completed the stadium on June 28. It was exactly two months from when the first steam shovel started excavating sixty thousand cubic yards of earth. He completed the most extensive boxing arena ever. It took employment of five hundred carpenters and four hundred laborers. Three hundred thousand square feet were built from 2,250,000 feet of pine and spruce lumber fastened with sixty tons of steel nails. The stadium had an octagonal shape. It stood thirty-four feet above the ground and accommodated over ninety thousand spectators. Constructed by J. W. Edwards, brothers of the New Jersey governor, it cost $250,000—twice the original estimate. The last rows of seats were 312 feet from the ring center. They constructed a wooden room under the stands to accommodate the radio broadcast. Telephone lines and a temporary radio transmitter, sponsored by the Radio Corporation of America, were installed at the Delaware, Lackawanna, and Western Railway terminal in Hoboken, New Jersey. The signal would be transmitted from steamship to steamship across the Atlantic until it reached Europe. One of those listening on the other end would be Carpentier's wife with the phone pressed against her ear. Major J. Andrew White would work the radiophone and H. L. Walker the control board. It was the first sports event broadcast on radio, a new mass communication. Promoter Rickard wanted to broadcast the prizefight to advance its popularity throughout the world.[48]

Sale of tickets began on May 13 and ranged from fifty dollars for ringside box seats to $5.50 for the accommodations in the furthest reaches. When the fight sold out, Rickard said he should have doubled the prices.[49] Ticket counterfeiting was a problem, and the police made arrests on June 23. Rickard urged people to buy from authorized dealers.[50]

On July 2, the sky was overcast and the air humid. The media billed the fight as the Battle of the Century. Official attendance was 80,103, including 2,000 women, but the stands seating more than 90,000 were filled. Another 300,000 listened to the fight on the first-ever radio broadcast of such an event. It was sport's first million-dollar gate, with receipts of $1,789,238.[51]

Dempsey was the favorite at two to one. The majority of fans were behind the Frenchman on American soil. Dempsey overwhelmed Carpentier. At 3:27 that afternoon, one minute and sixteen seconds into the fourth round, Dempsey put Carpentier on the canvas. Referee Harry Ertle ended the fight, as Carpentier lay on the canvas unconscious.[52] The event was epic; the fight was not.

CHAPTER 9

Learning the Game

The Freddie Welsh Health Farm was a complete disaster, Welsh's lifelong dream shattered and life savings depleted. On April 15, 1922, his boxing comeback ended when he lost a ten-round decision to an upstart boxer, Archie Walker, with a record of three wins and one loss. Welsh had a comeback record of four wins, one loss, and one draw before retiring for a second time. His career record was seventy-four wins, five losses, and seven draws. He still could not sell his health farm for a fair price.

The formula for success was there for Welsh to see. The biggest financial realization in boxing history had taken place between Georges Carpentier and Jack Dempsey. Both boxers wanted to use the Long Hill Health Farm as their training base. Other boxers trickled in to prepare for their bouts. Welsh continued to promote his establishment for the health of businessmen. He did not pursue making his property primarily a boxing training camp.

On January 30, 1923, a golf and country club was to sign a lease with Welsh. They wanted the Long Hill Health Farm property for its golf course. His home in Bayside, New York, already was under a lease.[1] There are no records that they signed the golf deal. His financial situation continued to deteriorate.

The Beys were not without their own financial problems. They had no source of steady income. On January 24, 1922, in Morristown, New Jersey, a sheriff's sale of part of the Bey's property was executed. A tract of four acres was to be sold to satisfy $18,627.45 of debt.[2]

In the summer of 1923, Welsh told Willie Ratner, a friend and journalist for the *Newark Evening News*, that he would reenlist in the army. He would receive a commission of captain. He needed someone to operate his farm. Freddie Welsh would ask a friend to help run his business while away—Madame Bey. Two signed photographs that Welsh gave Madame Bey documented their friendship. One had Welsh, his wife, son, and daughter. He inscribed it, "To Hranoush With every beautiful wish from the Welsh family." The other had Welsh in his boxing attire inscribed, "To Mrs. S. Bey With every good wish Sincerely, Freddie Welsh."

Welsh asked Madame Bey to operate the everyday management of the farm. The day after Welsh had told Ratner of his intentions, Ratner received a call from Madame Bey. Ratner was also friends with Madame Bey, and she requested him to come over her house. She told Ratner she had something important to discuss with him. Upon his arrival, Madame Bey told Ratner that Welsh had offered her to take over his health farm, and he would allow her to board boxers. Madame Bey said he expected nothing from her, and she would be the boss until he came out of the service.[3]

Madame Bey told Ratner that her husband, Sidky, disapproved of the venture. She consulted with her husband, who did not want his wife running a boxing camp for men. It was the same argument he had given years ago when she aspired to become an opera singer. He opposed that too. Her husband won the opera dispute, but Madame Bey would not surrender this endeavor.

"Now he won't let me do this. What shall I do?" Madame Bey asked Ratner.

"Do it, take it over, you'll be the only woman in the county with a training camp."[4]

Ratner gave her assurances that she would get a million dollars' worth of publicity as the first and only woman to operate a training camp. He would give her all the help he could through his journalism. Unlike the opera incident, Madame Bey won this dispute. She was forty-two years old, and her husband was fifty-two. They had little income; economics dictated the decision.

"We weren't getting any younger," Madame Bey would recall.

Madame Bey went to Welsh to accept the offer. With Willie Ratner present, who advised Madame Bey to agree if Welsh would permit her to board fighters, she accepted.[5]

"Give it to me and I'll make it go," Madame Bey told Welsh.

Due to Welsh's own failure at making the place successful, Madame Bey said, "He told me I couldn't make a go of it but gave me the keys, and I took over bag and baggage."

The next day, Madame Bey and her husband moved a mile down the road to Freddie Welsh's palatial house on the hill. They invited their friend and former business partner, Ehsan Karadag, who had shortened his name from the hard-to-pronounce Karadaghli. Ehsan became a partner and helped with repairs and maintenance. He would stay with the Beys through the duration.

At first, Madame Bey thought Freddie correct in his assessment.

"Nobody came for weeks and weeks," she said.

One day, in late July 1923, a southpaw boxer by the name of Johnny Wilson arrived.[6] He made his way to the house on the top of the hill. Madame Bey had her first boxer, and he was a world middleweight champion.[4] Wilson won the title on May 6, 1920, by a decision in a contested bout over Mike O'Dowd. Though neither Bey nor Wilson knew it, they were about to create a boxing institution.

Bey and Wilson could not have come from backgrounds more different. Madame Bey, the former socialite and Washington insider, Wilson, whose real name was Giovanni Francesco Panica, came from a tough neighborhood in East Harlem. It was nearly all Italian and under the influence of organized crime. Frank Costello lived down the street from Wilson.[7] Johnny Wilson proceeded to become a professional boxer. His friend, Frank Costello, would join ranks with Charlie "Lucky" Luciano and his associates Ben "Bugsy" Siegel and Meyer Lansky. Costello became a powerful and influential organized crime boss. He would lead the Luciano crime family, later called the Genovese crime family.

Johnny Wilson had a record of twelve wins, two losses, and one draw since winning the title. The two losses were not championship fights; he retained the title after those defeats. He chose the Long Hill Health Farm to prepare for a bout against the tough Harry Greb, called the Pittsburgh Windmill or the Human Windmill. Greb trained in Manhasset, Long Island. Wilson used lightweight Sandy Taylor and welterweight George Ward as sparring partners to maintain his speed. Light heavyweight Jack Delaney[8]—who would later become the world light heavyweight champion—also trained with Wilson. He had a bout on the Wilson-Greb undercard.

About a week before the fight, Wilson was sparring with Sandy Taylor, who caught him with a punch to the left eye. A concern came across Wilson's trainer, Harry Kelly, as the eye swelled up. Kelly forbade Wilson from sparring until the eye healed.[9] That did not keep Wilson from continuing his rigorous gymnasium and roadwork.

A week later, on August 28, Wilson's eye had healed. The Greb bout was three days away. Several hundred people came to watch Wilson's workout that day. Most were people who lived in the nearby country mansions. They crowded around the ring and watched as Wilson went through his usual training routine. He shadowboxed and sparred nine rounds with heavyweight Jack Taylor, welterweight Frankie Quill, and middleweight Jimmy Amato.[10] None of the three sparring partners had the ability of Wilson. They were there to help him prepare, but they trained for fights of their own.

"I wish the fight was tonight, so Johnny could step into the ring," Kelly said after Wilson had completed his workout. "Johnny is at weight and ready to go. He is so fine that I had to lay him off roadwork this morning. He took a brisk walk, but that was all. I doubt if any man could be in better shape, and I hope Greb is right, so he will have no excuses."[10]

Greb needed no excuses for the fight and relieved Wilson of the title he had held for over three years. On August 31, 1923, the bout took place at eight in the evening at the Polo Grounds. Greb won a fifteen-round decision to become the new world middleweight champion. Greb never sent Wilson to the canvas but closed his left eye and slashed his mouth open. Many said Greb won beyond argument even though he fought flat-footed.

He was too quick for the plodding Wilson. It was a lackluster fight, and neither was ever close to being knocked down.[11] Many experts ranked Greb as the greatest middleweight of all time, and most had him no lower than third.

Wilson returned to the Long Hill Health Farm after the title loss. He would have success in his next fight in Boston, Massachusetts, on October 19, 1923. He had an easy victory, according to both the *Boston Herald* and *Boston Globe*, defeating George Robinson by a decision.

CHAPTER 10

Remaining Fluid

Johnny Wilson was not alone at the camp. Many top boxers were arriving. They all seemed to come at once. Business picked up. Madame Bey was achieving what Freddie Welsh could not; she was making a success of the Long Hill Health Farm by making it a camp for prizefighters instead of a health club. What looked bleak now appeared promising.

"Then eleven fighters descended at once," Madame Bey said. "Before I knew it, I was right in the midst of a lot of young men who made a living by knocking others for what they called a loop, and I found I enjoyed it."[1]

Of the eleven boxers, many were the best in their weight class.[2] They were among the first boxers of many to occupy what would become a world-renowned camp.

Joe Lynch, a New York City native, came to Chatham Township as the world bantamweight champion. It was a time when the division was stacked with good fighters. He was twenty-four years old. He weighed less than 124 pounds and stood at five feet seven and a half inches. He appeared lanky because of his height and weight. He possessed a stiff jab and a devastating right. In his career, he fought 160 bouts. He was never knocked down and took each of his bouts the distance, except the ones he won by a knockout. Many recognize him as a top-ten bantamweight of all time. While at Chatham Township, he trained with a well-regarded young featherweight, Pee Wee Kaiser,[3] who never fulfilled the hype.

Paul Berlenbach was also a native of New York City. He had made the United States Olympic Wrestling Team in 1920 but could not take part due to injury and turned toward a boxing career. He fought as a light heavyweight. He had just turned professional the same year he came to Chatham Township at the age of twenty-two. Unskilled at boxing, he could hit hard. He would become a world champion in his division and used the ring name the Astoria Assassin. He is considered in the top ten all time as a light heavyweight by many.

Carl Duane was born Carl Duane Yaconetti in New York City. He became the world junior featherweight champion on August 29, 1923, shortly before arriving in Chatham Township.[4] They called him the Bronx Steamroller. He came to train for a successful defense of his title against Frankie Jerome. Duane had fought Jerome to a draw two months earlier. Duane had trained in Red Bank, New Jersey, with Gene Tunney. They had the same manager—Billy Gibson. Tunney was training for a fight against Harry Greb, which would become Tunney's first career loss. Tunney would never lose again. For this fight, Tunney was helping to prepare Duane's opponent, Jerome, in Red Bank, New Jersey.[5]

Bud Gorman born Earl L. Lovejoy in Chicago, Illinois, was a decent heavyweight. His greatest wins were over Jack Sharkey and Tony Galento. Not a prominent fighter, he was in Chatham Township to train for his fight against Homer Smith that resulted in a ten-round no decision.

Sid Terris was a lightweight boxer born in New York City. A journalist dubbed him the Galloping Ghost of the Ghetto after seeing him fight. He relied on his superior speed, using his fast footwork and quick punches to out-box his opponents. *The Ring* magazine called him "the speediest fighter of his generation." Some swore his opponents never hit him in some bouts. His speed was unable to get him the championship belt, but he was a top contender in his weight class. He was a professional fighter for just over a year when he came to Chatham Township at the age of nineteen.

Pancho Villa was born Francisco Guilledo in the Philippines. He was twenty-two years old when he arrived in Chatham Township. He was fast, relentless, and could hit hard with both hands. He always turned away from a fighter he had knocked down before the neutral corner rule. At five feet one inch and weighing between 109 pounds and 115 pounds, he fought in the flyweight division. Arguably, one of the greatest Asian fighters of all time, only his premature death at the age of twenty-three took his championship flyweight belt away from him. His last fight, a loss, did not count as a championship fight. Some experts consider him as the best or second best flyweight of all time.

Harold Smith was a young bantamweight boxer from Chicago. He came to Welsh's Farm to prepare for an October 5 bout at Madison Square Garden against Danny Lee.[6] He won the fight in a twelve-round decision.

Fellow Chicagoan Charley White was at the end of his career when he came to Chatham Township[7] at the age of thirty-two. He was born in Liverpool, England, under the name Charles Anchowitz. Despite never becoming a champion, he was considered one of the best of his era.

Before coming to Chatham Township, Charley White had fought current titleholders four times in three different weight classes, all resulted in losses. He had one of the hardest left hooks. Though he hurt many champions with it, he could never defeat them. He fought featherweight champion Abe Attell twice, featherweight champion Johnny Kilbane, welterweight champion Jack Britton, and lightweight champion Freddie Welsh on Labor Day September 4, 1916, in Colorado Springs, Colorado. It was the fourth time he fought Welsh. Welsh was champion during their first three fights, but they were not for the championship. They were newspaper fights.

During their championship fight, Welsh was winning easily until that left hook caught him in the fifth round and hurt him. He caught Welsh once more in the twelfth, and again, he let him get away. The fight went the full twenty rounds, and Welsh won the decision to the dismay of White and the crowd of 6,000 that had paid $30,000 to see the fight. Upon the rendering of the verdict by the referee, the crowd started throwing bottles and their heavy seat cushions toward Welsh's corner and the referee. The ring was three feet deep in cushions, and many unscheduled fights erupted in the stands. The sheriff, deputies, and police officers rushed into the ring to escort referee Billy Roche to a waiting car.[8]

"I had to fight two men—the referee and Welsh. To win from him, you've got to knock him cold. Referee Roche's decision was the rankest I have ever seen. Freddie Welsh will never lose the lightweight championship, as long as he is allowed to name his own referee," Charley White commented on the fight.

"I think it is time for the press and public of America to demand Freddie Welsh defend his title in a fair and square way. Billy Roche's decision in giving the fight to Welsh was the worst robbery ever perpetrated," White's manager, Nate Lewis, added.

"Welsh hit three blows to White's one. He led the fighting and three-fourths of his leads landed. Roche's decision was right," Welsh's manager, Harry Pollok, responded.

"I fought simply and straight to retain my title. I used every method I knew to pile up points, and I had White topped on that score easily," Welsh responded.

The referee, Billy Roche, defended himself, "I simply decided the fight on points. Welsh landed more blows, which constitute the Marquis of Queensberry rules. White did not fight. He had the chance of a lifetime and didn't take it. Could I give him the championship? No. Could I give him a draw? No."[9]

Now, Charley White was living and training at Freddie Welsh's house, under the management of Madame Bey, for his upcoming fight.[10] White was preparing for a fight at Madison Square Garden against Pat Moran. On October 5, on the same card as Harold Smith, he lost his fight by a technical knockout in the fourteenth round of a scheduled fifteen-round bout. He fought two more times after that bout before retiring with a record of eighty-six wins, sixteen losses, and five draws. He had an additional sixty-three newspaper fights.

Of all the early boxers to come to Chatham Township, one garnered more attention, not as much for his boxing ability but for his lifestyle. Battling the "Singular Senegalese" Siki was one of boxing's most colorful characters. He was one of the five best-known black men in the world. An appearance by Siki could stop traffic in Paris for more than an hour.[11] He was born on September 16, 1897 in Saint Louis, Senegal. Siki moved to France as a child. He was in the French army and wounded in World War I.[12] Siki had gained immediate fame in France when he upset the French hero Georges Carpentier for the world light heavyweight title. Siki became the first Muslim and African to claim a world boxing championship or any sporting title. After winning the title, Siki made an ill-advised decision. For his first title defense, he agreed to fight Mike McTigue on March 17, 1923, Saint Patrick's Day, in the La Scala Theatre, Dublin, Ireland. Mike McTigue, born in Country Claire, Ireland, grew up in a thatched-roof cottage with eleven brothers and sisters. He never laced up a pair of gloves until he arrived in America where he learned to box. Siki lost the twenty-round decision and the title.

His reputation preceded him. He was known for his flashy clothes and wild behavior. Siki was partial to his signature silk hats, swallowtail suits, tan shoes, and bright red neckties. He was asked why he wore evening clothes during the day.

"Ah, everybody wears evening clothes at night," he replied, "but Siki does not wish to be like everybody. So, he wears his in the daytime. Thus, he is different."[13]

Racial epithets were standard in the press. Journalists could espouse their racial and ethnic views without fear of retribution. Siki could not escape ridicule and racism, even from his handlers. He was referred to repeatedly as a "chimpanzee,"[12] a "child of nature," a "natural man," and a "jungle child."[14] Even his manager, Charlie Hellers, said, "Siki has something in him which is not human … There's much of the monkey about him."[15] Siki resented the words, stating, "That talk about the fighting chimpanzee is crazy."[12]

Battling Siki arrived in the United States on September 1, 1923, traveling under the name of Louis Fall on the ship *Berengaria*.[16] He wore a dark gray suit, black hat, dark tie, dull brown shoes, canary-yellow gloves, and a walking stick with an ivory top. He traveled with Louis Defremont and two sparring partners. Siki's fame was clear when he disembarked from the ship to a greeting of throngs of reporters and photographers. It was the largest reception of a European boxer since Carpentier had arrived in America three years before. Mike McTigue had sailed with him on the same ship,[17] but he did not receive the same attention despite still being the world light heavyweight champion.

Before the start of training, Siki went to Canada for exhibition matches. One exhibition bout in Quebec matched him against Jack Johnson, the former world heavyweight champion. Johnson showed all of his past abilities and strategy by beating Siki.[18] Siki found Montreal's alcohol policies and nightlife to his liking.[19] He decided to stay despite a scheduled fight in America one month away. Montreal Chief of Police Belanger received a telegram from Siki's American manager, Bob Levy, asking him to find Siki. Sleuths found the fighter and brought him to headquarters. He informed his questioners that he did not desire to leave the city just yet, as he liked the Canadian metropolis.

"They left me here without any money," Siki said, "if they will send me my money and trunks, I will go back to New York at once, but if they don't do that I will stay right here in Montreal."[20]

Siki's manager, Bob Levy, took Siki back to America.

In early November 1923, Battling Siki climbed to the house on the top of the hill. He was twenty-six years old. Siki had less than three weeks to prepare for his first battle in America. He was scheduled to fight Kid Norfolk at Madison Square Garden on November 20, 1923. Johnny Wilson and Siki would train together. Wilson and Siki were different, but they had the boxing commonality. They had respect for each other.

At Freddie Welsh's Health Farm, Battling Siki also trained with Jack Thompson, who came to Chatham Township for his bout for the world colored heavyweight championship against the titleholder Harry Wills. The twenty-three-year-old Thompson was from Denver, Colorado.[21] In his last fight, he lost to the former world heavyweight champion Jack Johnson in Havana, Cuba. In that fight, the boxers' efforts were so lacking, that the boxing commissioner, sitting at the ringside, fined each fighter $500 for stalling. In the tenth round, the referee left the ring, and promoter Sam Tolan replaced him, while a shower of cushions, soda bottles, and other missiles were hurled at the boxers. A wire service report stated no official decision was rendered.[22] On November 5, Thompson lost to Wills at the First Regiment Armory in Newark, New Jersey, by a fourth-round technical knockout.

With the boxers came their sparring partners, managers, trainers, rubdown men, and seconds. Within a few months of assuming Freddie Welsh's farm, Madame Bey had a camp that stabled some of the best talent in the game. It was buzzing with boxers as well as those who wanted to come see them train.

She kept it simple. She saw that Welsh had no system in place, and Bey liked to do things in a businesslike manner. She gave her boxing clientele two meals a day, a room, made the schedule for facilities use, and then kept out of their way during training. She did impose a few rules she expected her boarders to follow. Those rules instilled discipline. There was to be no alcohol (prohibition was the law at the time), awake by six, breakfast at seven, supper at five, lights out at ten, no swearing, and no women,[1] though it was common for women to come watch the men train and sometimes flirt afterward. She did allow wives and girlfriends to visit at the discretion of the boxers' managers. She broke the alcohol rule on occasion. She expected respect from her fighters. She was not opposed to putting on the gloves, figuratively, with anyone who behaved improperly, the first of whom was, reportedly, Pancho Villa. He was just being a combative youngster that needed some guidance, and she gave it to him. She did not interfere with their boxing routines, which she left to their managers and trainers.

The United Press asked her how a former debutante could run a camp for the most brutal sports figures in the world.

"It makes no difference," she replied, "whether men are kings or tramps, princes or pugilists. I have learned a few rules, and they apply to all men. Feed them well, give them comfortable quarters, and then leave them alone."[23]

The approach served her well. Though she kept away during training, when the training was over, and at meal times, she availed herself to them if they wanted to talk. She built many relations with the boxers that went beyond their business affiliation. Just as she had done in her Washington days, she used her ability to connect with people on a personal basis. She was in the position to judge their character by their discussions instead of the often-erroneous information that journalists penned, which the public used to judge a boxer.

She described the boxers as "complete gentlemen." They saw her as a matriarchal figure and gave her the respect she exacted.

"If you must mother men, and often men expect it, do it unobtrusively. To most of these boys, I was a mother, but I never chased them around with rubbers and mufflers or made them blow their noses," she once told a reporter.[23]

Willie Ratner recalled when Freddie Welsh heard that Battling Siki was at his house—he was furious.

"He was a wild guy," Ratner recalled, "not a bad guy but wild. Used to walk around with wild animals, a lion, or tiger on a leash."[24]

One day, while Johnny Wilson, Battling Siki, and several others were at the Long Hill Health Farm, Welsh telephoned Madame Bey.

"Get that Siki out of my place immediately," Welsh told her, "or you've got to go. I won't have that fellow there. He'll ruin my reputation."[25]

Some believed that Welsh saw how well the business did and wanted it back. Now in a dilemma, Madame Bey conferred with several of her fighters. She discussed the matter with middleweight Johnny Wilson, light heavyweight Paul Berlenbach, and bantamweight champion Joe Lynch. They all said that Siki was not an embarrassment.

"If you put Siki out, I will go," Wilson told her.[25]

Bey saw no problem with Siki either and said that he was always a complete gentleman in her presence. She had the support of all eleven of her fighters.

"Where you go, we'll go," the boxers told her.

She made her decision; she would start her own boxing camp, taking her family of boxers with her.

"But what happened?" Madame Bey said. "The inevitable, for after I had put the camp on a clockwork basis, Freddie thanked me kindly for fixing things up and intimated that he could carry on by himself. That was what he thought, but the joke was that the boys didn't agree with him. They kept telling me that I would have to start a camp of my own, so that they could depend on me."[26]

The rapport she had built in a short time with her boys was unassailable. Not one fighter stayed behind. They all followed Madame Bey to their new home.

In November 1923, the hills had shed their autumn rust. The trees void of most their leaves, clinging on to the last vestige of color, were storing every bit of strength for the onslaught. They prepared all summer, with the long hours of sunlight and a good water supply. They were busy making and storing food—becoming stronger. The days shortened and water harder to get, their goal was to endure what existed ahead. Unencumbered by thought and influence, they readied for the harshness. Without which, inevitable destruction would be their fate.

Winter approached the Northeast when Bey switched the camp location to her farm. The intrepid prizefighters left the comfortable, well-equipped confines of Freddie Welsh's Long Hill Health Farm and marched toward the uncertainty of Madame Bey's farm. They walked past the farmlands and woods. They had a clear line of sight through the trees stripped of leaves as they marched the one-mile distance to Bey's farm. With Madame Bey heading the group, eleven fighters followed her to their new home. It was Johnnie Wilson, former middleweight champion, the first behind Madame Bey. The others following them were Joe Lynch, bantamweight champion, Paul Berlenbach, Charley White, Carl Duane, Bud Gorman, Sid Terris, Pancho Villa, and others.

"They were my first boys," she mused in later years, "and like all the others, they were thorough gentlemen. They marched right over to the thirty acres my husband Sidky, owned, and as they swung along behind me, they marched and shouted hep, hep, hep. That's how Madame Bey's was built."[27]

CHAPTER 11

Change Is Good

Madame Bey and her boxers arrived at her farmhouse a mile down River Road from Freddie's farm. There was a basic problem; it lacked boxing facilities. The thirty acres consisted of a farmhouse, a garage, and a barn. The rest of the property had a few shacks strewn about. Did the prizefighters make a mistake? All they needed was back at Welsh's farm, with one exception—Madame Bey. These were fearless professional prizefighters with relentless perseverance. They attacked the farm as they would a ring opponent.

Some boxers went to the neighboring town of Summit, where they bought bricks, nails, lumber, and other hardware that day.[1] Madame Bey did not have the money, but the boxers had no problem paying for the materials, led by Johnny Wilson.[2] It was a gesture Madame Bey would not forget when boxers came to her establishment without a means to pay.

Johnny Wilson and his manager, Johnnie Buckley, who was a carpenter, did most of the construction work.[3] The others helped, including boxers and trainers. Johnny Wilson later in an interview proudly proclaimed, "Madame Bey's, I built that for her."[4] With hard work and determination, they transformed the shacks into living quarters. They converted the garage into a boxing gymnasium. They did most of the work overnight. If everyone had not yet known it, their fondness for Madame Bey was now unquestionable. It was becoming a family—a family of boxers with a woman giving guidance.

"I will continue operating my training camp as long as I live," Madame Bey once told a reporter. "It is my life work. The boxers are perfect gentlemen—just as gracious to me as the men I knew in the old society days in Washington and New York."[5]

Now they needed to decide where to sleep, which was not problematic at Welsh's large house. The farmhouse could accommodate the Beys, Ehsan, and five boxers for sleeping. Others would have to use the shacks and the gymnasium to get their rest. Battling Siki took a reconstructed shack, preferring to be alone. More construction would follow to accommodate everyone.

The few neighbors in the area would be treated to a new sight that would become a daily routine through five decades. Through the early morning mist, the boxers could be seen for their jogs either in groups or alone. The hilly terrain of Chatham Township and New Providence made for ideal conditions for the boxers' roadwork. The preferred route was to run down the Bey's driveway and a turn right onto River Road. They would jog for a mile and turn right where the road intersected with Fairmount Avenue. As they ran up Fairmount Avenue, they would be able to see Welsh's place on the left. Across from Welsh's were two structures that were boxing gymnasiums owned by Mary Green. Contrary to Willie Ratner, Madame Bey was not the only woman who ran a camp for boxers. The boxers would continue their jog for two miles along Fairmount Avenue that had a spectacular view of the valley to their left. Next, they would turn right on Southern Boulevard as they ran by the small redbrick schoolhouse to their left. Southern Boulevard was a steep road that they ran down until they turned right where it intersected back onto River Road. By the time they returned to Madame Bey's, they had completed a loop of a little over four miles.

Some boxers preferred alternate jogging routes. Some would jog through the woods on pathways. Others would take the same right out of Bey's driveway onto River Road, but when they reached Fairmont Avenue, instead of turning right they would go left onto Central Avenue. On Central Avenue, they would jog across a bridge over the Passaic River that placed them in New Providence. They would continue down Central Avenue until it intersected with Springfield Avenue, where they would turn left. Springfield Avenue would then meet with Passaic Street, where they would again turn left. Passaic Street had a bridge that once more crossed the Passaic River that put them back into Chatham Township. Jogging down Passaic Street, they would go left to return to River Road and make their return to the camp. This loop was shorter at three and a half miles.

Sometimes to make the running more strenuous to build stamina, they would sprint and jog. They would use the telephone poles as reference points. When passing a telephone pole, they would quicken the pace, at times a full sprint. When reaching the next telephone pole, they would revert to their jog. They would continue this process for the entire loop.[6]

If the townspeople were treated to a new sight in viewing boxers in their early morning jaunt, they would be completely unprepared for another sight. It would be the spectacle of Battling Siki jogging. A showman, he was conspicuous among the joggers. He would do his roadwork in a full dress suit, opera cape, and yellow shoes.[7]

The camp's business increased with champion-caliber boxers from all weight divisions descending upon it. As they competed around the country, the first eleven boxers informed others in their profession of a boxing camp operated by a woman in the New Jersey woods.

CHAPTER 12

Competition

Chatham Township, New Jersey, became a center of training for some of the best professional boxers. It had four camps that entertained the presence of professionals. There was Freddie Welsh's Long Hill Health Farm with its state-of-the-art facilities and comfortable living quarters. Across the street from Welsh's Farm were two small gymnasiums operated by "Lovey" Mary Green. Mrs. Green, who hailed from Texas, started her training camp with a man. Her husband stayed in New York City. Green was a stage performer and opera singer. She had been the leading woman in the Moulin Rouge Company in America and Max Spiegel's Winning Windows Company.[1] The camp had a few boxers but no famous ones. She owned a big white polo pony that a Native American working on Welsh's Farm would use to do wild bareback stunts at his camp.[2] One mile down River Road from those two camps was Madame Bey's Training Camp. Another camp, Johnny Collins Camp, was located on River Road along the Passaic River between Passaic Street and Mt. Vernon Road, a little over a mile down the road from Madame Bey's Camp. Of the four, Welsh and Bey's camps would have the greatest impact.

Chatham Township offered what New York City could not. The city had many gymnasiums; Stillman's was the most recognized. They were enclosed, and some were overcrowded, and the stench was at times suffocating. Boxers would get in each other's way. The countryside of New Jersey with its fresh air and cool summer breezes was not for everyone, but enough preferred it as an alternative.

In June 1923, former world featherweight champion Johnny Kilbane was one that did not find the countryside appealing. Kilbane had a fight to regain his title against Eugene Criqui. Kilbane had planned to do his training in Chatham Township but changed his plans upon his arrival there to inspect the facilities. A New Jersey suit—the outcome unknown—against Kilbane alleged that $1,000 was spent on equipping the property as a training camp. Kilbane said he thought he was to train at Freddie Welsh's Long Hill Health Farm but discovered that the training camp selected for him was across the road, which would be Mary Green's Camp. Kilbane would make no statement, but his manager, Brannigan, said he never signed and was waiting until Kilbane looked at the camp.[3] Kilbane lost the bout in the sixth round. At age thirty-four, it became his last fight.

Reporters came to watch Siki train at Madame Bey's Camp, which had been open for less than a week. He continued to prepare for his first American fight against Kid Norfolk. He sparred with the heavyweight Jack the "Nebraska Tornado" Taylor, who hit him at will. Former middleweight champion Johnny Wilson, who was preparing for his next fight against Pal Reed, also trained with Siki. The reporters were unimpressed with Siki's defenseless style of boxing. It signaled trouble with the more skilled American boxers. No one doubted Siki's power, though.

"Don't be too hard on Siki," his manager, Bob Levy, said. "Bear in mind that he has been boxing only three days and has been in the first few days getting all the 'pains' out of his system, running him over the hills around here until his tongue hung out. Some days he did as much as ten miles."[4]

The reporters were more impressed with Bey's new camp than Siki's training. One wrote:

"A gymnasium has been fitted up in the barn. It is a pretty spot and Siki seems to be satisfied with conditions. Judging from the spread provided for the hungry scribes by Levy and the Beys, nobody gets up from the table with that empty feeling."[4]

Wilson defeated Reed on November 16, 1923, in Boston, Massachusetts, in a ten-round decision. Wilson repeatedly scored with straight right hands to the head. Both the *Boston Herald* and *Boston Globe* wrote that Wilson won seven of ten rounds. Wilson received word after the fight that plans were being made for him to fight Harry Greb in a rematch for the middleweight title he lost.

Siki was known for not being serious in his training. The distraction of changing training camps and its unsettled nature made preparing difficult. His fight with Kid Norfolk neared. On the morning of November 15, a day before Johnny Wilson's fight, Siki went to New York City. His new manager, Bob Levy, accompanied him. They met with Tex Rickard in the Madison Square Garden Tower. Siki assured Rickard that he was in shape and that he could beat Kid Norfolk. So confident, he requested that his next match be against Gene Tunney, Harry Greb, Harry Wills, Tom Gibbons, or a rematch with Mike McTigue. Before one thirty in the afternoon, he boarded a train and returned to Madame Bey's Camp to train.[5]

The next three days, Siki put in strenuous workouts before going to New York two days before the fight where he would continue to prepare. When journalists came again to watch Siki train at Madame Bey's Camp, they were still unimpressed, but they did not see the person portrayed in the press. They found their prejudices based on what was written about him unfounded once they talked to him.

"You see a semi-savage when you first look at him," one reporter wrote. "Then come introductions and a surprise. The jungle fades away … You find the black fellow from

Senegal above the ordinary in intelligence. He discourses interestingly … on many subjects … You find him considerable of a linguist, speaking French fluently and having a smattering of English, German, Spanish, Italian, Dutch, Turkish and Arabic."

On his style, the reporter wrote, "… at Summit, N.J. … There is nothing orthodox about his boxing at all. He has a style all his own … He has no defense."[6]

Speaking through an interpreter, Siki stated that he almost destroyed McTigue for sixteen rounds and that he was told to refrain in the last four rounds so as not to get hurt.

"I realized after the fight that I had made a bad match," Siki, quoted as saying via his press agent, "but I insist and will always insist until I am beaten fair and square, that I am the champion in the one hundred seventy-five pound division. If I beat Norfolk—and I am very confident that I will—I stand ready to meet McTigue and guarantee to knock him out. However, my manager tells me that promoter Tex Richard has promised me one of three bigger matches if I triumph over Norfolk, against either Gene Tunney, Harry Greb, or Tom Gibbons. I am in great shape and ready to go. If I don't come through as I think I will with victory, I will have no excuse to offer."[7]

Neither his confidence nor preparation could overcome what he encountered from Kid Norfolk when he met him at one o'clock in the afternoon of November 20, 1923. He lost the fifteen-round decision at Madison Square Garden before a crowd of 12,000. Siki's charging style was thwarted by Norfolk's boxing skills, who beat him decisively. Siki lost thirteen of fifteen rounds. The fights he had proposed to Rickard were no longer obtainable.

For his next bout, Battling Siki once more prepared at Bey's Camp. He would fight heavyweight Jack Taylor, the man who helped him prepare for Kid Norfolk. Siki lost again in a ten-round decision to Taylor on Christmas Day in Philadelphia. Those with better boxing skills in America were neutralizing Siki's powerful punches that had won so many fights in Europe. They were skills that Siki lacked. He would remain at Bey's for seven months.[8] He would have mixed success in his next fights, winning three and losing three. He would never regain the success that gave him so much fame in Europe.

Before 1923 ended, competition between Madame Bey's Camp and Freddie Welsh's Long Hill Health Farm began. Welsh returned home after Madame Bey left with her eleven boxers. Welsh finally saw the value of using his place as a boxing training camp. He needed a means of income, and the health farm was all he had.

If a boxer wanted to train in the New Jersey country hills instead of the city, he now had four choices. Most boxers considered two. Welsh's farm appeared more appealing. It had better facilities, and Welsh, the former world lightweight champion, operated it. Madame Bey's Camp contained makeshift facilities and a woman, Madame Bey, former socialite and a diplomat's wife who knew nothing about boxing, operated it.

Her structured approach to the management of her camp kept everything functioning smoothly. Outweighed and overpowered by her boys, there was no doubt that she was in charge. Given the two choices, the boxers' decisions seemed to be an easy one—Freddie Welsh's Farm. Madame Bey gave the weary brutes away from their loved ones intangibles that Welsh could not provide. Most importantly, she gave them a home.

Though Welsh did lure many boxing greats, Madame Bey attracted them in greater numbers. Needing help for her expanding business, she hired another handyman, Tom Finnegan. He was born in 1882 in Northern Ireland. In 1911, he immigrated to America. He would stay at the camp for the duration of its existence under Madame Bey. He was a single, thin, frail-looking man. He would see boxers progress to championships and others rebuffed. He thought he had predictive powers of which boxer at the camp would win a bout. He came to believe in a white pigeon that would materialize at the camp on occasion. If the white pigeon appeared while a challenger prepared for the title, it meant the camp would have a new champion. No white pigeon meant a challenger would be turned aside.[9] The pigeon worked in the mind of Tom. It became lore of his making. Unfortunately for the boxing challengers, it did not always work for them.

Welsh did have the greatest of all boxers at his camp. In mid-December 1923, Jack Dempsey, a friend of Welsh's, came to his Long Hill Health Club. He had no scheduled bouts.[10] He was there for light training and rest while manager Doc Kearns and promoter Tex Rickard mapped his future.

Dempsey had made two successful title defenses since the last time he was at Welsh's for the Carpentier bout. He had defeated Tommy Gibbons after a two-year layoff by a decision in Shelby, Montana. Promoters canceled most of the undercard due to low attendance. There were just over 7,202 paying customers, and many others watched free after crashing the gate. It almost bankrupted the town of Shelby, which had borrowed money to stage the fight. Four banks in the town failed due to the fight.[11] It was one of boxing's biggest financial disasters. It was the first heavyweight title fight after boxing's greatest success with the Dempsey-Carpentier Battle of the Century.

On September 14, 1923, Dempsey met Luis Firpo of Argentina at the Polo Grounds, New York, with over 80,000 fans producing a gate of $1,250,000—boxing's second million-dollar gate. In a slugging fight, Firpo went down seven times in the first round. At the end of the first, the battered challenger, to everyone's surprise, caught Dempsey with a right that sent him through the ropes. Dempsey barely climbed back through the ropes at the count of nine to survive the round. In the second round, a composed Dempsey put Firpo down four more times. He could not beat the count after hitting the canvas for the eleventh time. It was one of the shortest and fiercest battles ever fought between heavyweights.[12]

While Dempsey was at the Long Hill Health Farm, it hosted sixteen boxers and ten wrestlers from the United States Navy.[13] They were going to battle at Madison Square Garden for the navy titles on December 18. They had all reached the finals through a series of elimination bouts to represent their assigned ship. The eight boxing classes ranged from flyweight to heavyweight. Welsh would supervise their training.

"It is a pleasure to work with these boys after mingling with the professional boxers," Welsh said. "They take such a keen interest in their preparations."

An impressed Dempsey watched the sailors train. He expressed regret that he did not have time to don trunks and go a few rounds with them.[14]

A promising South American fighter, Luis Vincentini from Chile, came to the Long Hill Health Farm while the navy fighters were there. His last fight was his first loss since coming to America. The setback may have sent him home, but he was a protégé of Rickard, who still had faith in him and thought he would be the lightweight champion.[15] Despite having the most famous promoter on his side, he would never become more than average.

In late 1923, Young Stribling, the pride of Georgia, had just turned nineteen one day before coming to Welsh's farm. The brown-haired, blue-eyed, good-looking kid was a promising boxer. Stribling's boxing was a family undertaking. His father managed him, and his mother trained him.[16] He arrived at Welsh's to prepare for a New Year's Day bout against Dave Rosenberg. He hoped to train with his idol, Jack Dempsey. He was a seasoned boxer despite his age. He began boxing professionally at the age of sixteen, compiling a record of sixty-seven wins, three losses, and thirteen draws before arriving at Welsh's, a career for most boxers. Stribling would have a long, prolific career. He would compile a record of 223 wins, thirteen losses, fourteen draws, and another thirty-nine newspaper fights. One year he fought fifty-five times. In total, he fought 291 bouts knocking out 129 opponents, a knockout record only surpassed by Archie Moore.

Earlier in the year on October 4, Stribling fought Mike McTigue in his home state of Georgia for the light heavyweight championship. The fight was a lackluster performance by both fighters. What ensued was not. The pro-Stribling crowd demanded the decision for their fellow Georgian. Referee Harry Ertle, the same referee for the Dempsey-Carpentier bout, called the fight a draw. The angry crowd caused Ertle to award the win to Stribling. He recanted later in safety away from the ring calling it a draw.[17] McTigue remained champion. Stribling held the title for one hour. For that one hour, Stribling was the champion. He would never claim a title again.

Welsh gave the Striblings a wheelbarrow for a publicity photograph. It appeared in newspapers showing Young Stribling pushing Ma and Pa Stribling, which the press dubbed them, and one other person.[18] While there, he fulfilled his wish of training with the heavyweight champion. The youthful Stribling impressed Dempsey with his skills.[19]

On January 1, 1924, despite being the underdog, Stribling defeated Rosenberg. He received a twelve-round decision at the First Regiment Armory in Newark, New Jersey. He won almost every round. Stribling fought six times that January. He won every bout except one he lost on a disqualification. In the loss, he was in the lead, but after repetitive cautions for hitting on the break, referee Phil Pritchard disqualified him. His father then hit the referee.[20] Stribling fought thirty-six times in 1924, losing three bouts.

On December 10, 1923, Harry Greb lost to Gene Tunney by a decision for the American light heavyweight title. In the middle of December 1923, Harry Greb agreed to defend his middleweight title against the man he had taken it from, Johnny Wilson, at Madison Square Garden on January 18, 1924. Wilson signed for the bout, agreeing to the terms Greb and Tex Rickard demanded.[21] Wilson was scheduled to fight Pat McCarthy in Boston before the Greb bout. While Wilson trained for the McCarthy bout at Madame Bey's Camp, his manager, Jim Buckley, divided his time between Wilson's training and finishing the conversion of Madame Bey's garage into a gymnasium.[22] Wilson won the McCarthy fight in three rounds. He returned to Bey's Camp where he trained for the Greb bout. He had worked at Bey's for his three winning bouts since he dropped the middleweight championship to Greb the previous summer. Wilson would lose a close fifteen-round decision to Greb for the middleweight title.

CHAPTER 13

Boxing Recognition

At the end of 1923, it was clear the impact that Chatham Township would have on professional boxing. Of the champions in the eight recognized weight classes, five would train in the town and two would visit often to watch others train. Jack Dempsey, heavyweight; Mike McTigue, light heavyweight; Mickey Walker, welterweight; Joe Lynch, bantamweight; and Pancho Villa, featherweight all trained in the town. Benny Leonard, lightweight, and Johnny Dundee, featherweight, were frequent visitors to watch others train. Only middleweight champion Harry Greb, who had just beaten Johnny Wilson, was not known to have come to the town.

As 1924 started, Bey's Boxing Camp flourished. It was the first full year that Madame Bey operated her camp. Meanwhile, Freddie Welsh's Long Hill Health Farm languished. Bey's Camp hosted the majority of those who wanted to train in the New Jersey countryside. That included camps in the town operated by Johnny Collins and Mary Green. World welterweight champion Mickey Walker used Chatham Township as his base for training in 1924. That year he trained in three camps in Chatham Township—Bey's Camp, Welsh's Camp, and Collins's Camp.

He was born Edward Patrick Walker in the Kereigh Head section of Elizabeth, New Jersey, on July 13, 1901. He initially started to be an architect, but Mickey Walker loved to box. He embarked on a professional career over the objections of his father, who was a friend of the inaugural heavyweight champion John L. Sullivan.[1] Mickey Walker was one of the toughest and most popular boxers of his generation. He had poor boxing skills, and it was rare that he was in proper condition for a fight. He did not like to train, preferring to party. He said he trained in the country instead of the city to avoid giving in to his vices, of which he had many, but Walker had the heart of a warrior. He never shied away from a fight. He stood five feet seven inches, muscled from head to toe, with stocky legs and a pug nose. He had a fierce body punch, one of the hardest left hooks, and a powerful right cross. He could put you down with either hand. Writers marveled at the toughness in his small frame.[2, 3, 4, 5] Against opponents outweighing him by ten or more pounds, Walker had twenty-two wins, two losses, two draws, and thirteen knockouts in his career. He gained the welterweight championship at the age of twenty-one, a title he won by a unanimous fifteen-round decision against Jack Britton on November 1, 1922, at Madison Square Garden.

"He rated close to the top," Nat Fleischer, founder of *The Ring* magazine, wrote about Walker. "A terrific hitter with an abundance of courage, he fought in every division from welterweight through heavyweight. Though far outweighed, he always gave a thrilling performance."[3]

"Walker belongs in that class of fighter called iron men," boxing historian Tracy Callis wrote. "He was tough, rugged, and willing."

Walker said that the bigger fighters hit harder, but they were slower. Walker exploited that slowness. Not any fighter could do that. Walker had the power to fight heavier foes.

A publicity picture of Walker in 1924 while training in Chatham Township showed him fishing by a river. He wore a straw hat and rolled-up pants and had a fishing rod in hand. The caption referred to him as the Huckleberry Finn of boxing.[6] Away from camp, he drank, chased women, and caused a ruckus. Madame Bey harbored no illusions about Walker's exploits away from her camp or that of any of her other boys. When boxers were at her camp, they left their alcohol, women, and indolence behind; they adhered to her rules. There was one purpose for being at Madame Bey's—hard training. Bey lamented that when her boys left her camp, they would train more and listen to their managers.[7]

It was a contrast in personalities between Madame Bey and Mickey Walker. It would appear impossible that Walker could follow Bey's rules, but he did. Walker would be one of Bey's favorites to have at her camp. He spent much time there. Many said he practically lived there.

"The gayest boy I ever had around was Mickey Walker," Madame Bey told a reporter, "middleweight champion of the world, and the wildest, maddest, bravest one I ever saw.

"I call him my lionhearted little Mickey right to his face, and it gets him embarrassed, but we understand each other. There was one boy who loved to fight, and he took a terrible lot of punishment, but never let go, which is why the sportswriters called him the Toy Bulldog. Training was just a lark to Mickey. He would do the work, but he was so sure that he could slap the other fellow silly that he had a good time as well. He was a great dancer, and he liked to sing, and he generally had sparring partners who could keep him company. Some fighters are inclined to be high-hat toward the boys who have to take a hammering every day, but not Mickey. He wouldn't even allow them to eat at a different table, but had them at his own—and, mind you, he was the kind who would knock them senseless every day if he could. Once there were some colored boys—not sparring partners, but rubbers—in his outfit, and they slept in one of the barns. Mickey learned that they were afraid of ghosts, so after filling them up with stories of a New Jersey ghost that walked through the Orange Mountains, he put on a sheet and paraded up and down the camp driveway giving out mournful noises. Believe me, those colored kids nearly went crazy, and never suspected Mickey at all. He had to talk fast to keep them in camp after that, but the ghost did not walk again until the last night, and then the panic was on once more."[7]

In May, Walker trained at Bey's for a defense of his welterweight title against Lew Tendler. He trained with heavyweight Jack Renault, heavyweight Quinten Romero, and South American lightweight champion Luis Vincentini,[8] the Tex Rickard protégé. All were training for their own fights. Walker's defense of his title against Tendler came on June 2 at Shibe Park, Philadelphia, Pennsylvania. It was a unanimous ten-round decision for Walker. Renault and Romero also won their bouts. The Chilean Vincentini lost a decision against tough Johnny Dundee. Vincentini continued to prepare for his next fights at Bey's, but those wins in Chile were turning into losses in America.

On July 5, 1924, Freddie Welsh took a position to be in charge of physical training at the Citizen's Military camp in Plattsburgh, New York, further neglecting his health farm where boxers were preparing without him. Welsh brought his protégé, featherweight Frankie Monroe, who hailed from California, to Plattsburgh. Monroe had won a succession of four round bouts on the West Coast.[9]

While Welsh was in Plattsburgh, his farm still had boxers, but he did not pay attention to them like Madame Bey. He left them there alone. Former junior lightweight champion Jack "Kid Murphy" Bernstein prepared at Welsh's in July for a fight against Jack Zivic on July 23. World lightweight champion Benny Leonard was to fight the winner.[10] Bernstein won the twelve-round decision.

On July 28, 1924, it became clear that Welsh was in jeopardy of losing his Long Hill Health Farm. The Southern Trust and Commerce Bank, a San Diego corporation, sought the sale of Welsh's farm to satisfy the nonpayment of the mortgage. The sheriff listed six tracts of his land for sale. The adjournment of the sale occurred several times until September when Welsh acquired $5,000 to keep his farm. The amount due on the property was $20,257.18.[11]

By the end of July, Welsh made a desperate attempt to rid himself of the farm. He proposed a sale to the National Sport Alliance. The Alliance wanted to use the farm as a training camp for its boxers and as a home for disabled and veteran fighters. They were to use the New York State Athletic Commission's money. Welsh requested that the commission agree to the purchase. They rejected the proposition, citing the commission's funds, attained at a charity bout, were to establish a trust fund for disabled boxers.[12]

In August, Walker left Bey's and went down the street to Welsh's Farm. The fight that was promised to Jack Bernstein against Benny Leonard went to Mickey Walker. Walker would be fighting the king of the lightweights Benny Leonard, vanquisher of Freddie Welsh.

Tex Rickard had planned a long time to arrange a match between Leonard and Walker. He thought the bout could set a gate record outside of the heavyweight division, expecting it to exceed $1,000,000. Benny Leonard had been unbeatable in the lightweight division since 1916. He had had one loss since 1916, and that was against Jack Britton in a welterweight championship fight.

Walker was twenty-four years old while Leonard was twenty-nine. Leonard was a master boxer, Walker a slugger. The setup was perfect. The public wanted the match. Walker needed the match, having put himself in debt spending more than he earned. His manager, Bulger, who had died, would never have allowed Walker to get into debt, but Walker was his own manager now.

The match was scheduled for Boyle's Thirty Acres in Jersey City, New Jersey, the site of the first million-dollar gate between Dempsey and Carpentier. Rickard guaranteed Walker $140,000 and Leonard $100,000.[13] Walker had prepared daily for his fight against Leonard with Jack "Kid Murphy" Bernstein. Bernstein prepared for an upcoming fight against Luis Vincentini. Walker had trained with Vincentini at Bey's in May. At camp, Walker gave what reporters called a prophecy.

"Walker will defeat Leonard; possibly knock him out," he told journalists about himself. "Jack Renault will beat Barley Madden. Harry Wills will stop Luis Angel Firpo. Jack Bernstein will defeat Luis Vincentini."[14]

He was correct on all accounts, except Benny Leonard sustained an injury during training and could not fight. Walker went to Collins's camp to train for a rescheduled Leonard bout.[15] The newly scheduled bout was under a different promoter, Jimmy Johnston, who scheduled the fight for August 20 at Yankee Stadium with Walker to receive 30 percent of the gate and Leonard 20 percent.[13]

Though Walker was almost broke, he bought a $250,000 seventy-five-foot confiscated bootlegger's yacht from the federal government. At auction, Walker bid $50,000 with $5,000 down and the rest to be paid in thirty days. Walker intended to pay for it from his yet-to-be-earned purse from the Leonard fight. The yacht became a daily discussion at Collins's Camp with Walker and his sparring partners, including heavyweight Abie Bain, light heavyweight Jack McVey, Eddie Whalen, and Cy Shindell. They planned their first trip to sail the Atlantic coast to Florida. Walker claimed the captaincy despite not knowing how to operate a boat. The others argued their places on the boat.[1] Walker admitted he did not know how to handle money. Walker had no worry; the Leonard purse would take care of his expenses, buy the yacht, settle debts, and he would still have money left.

Leonard took a warm-up fight with Pal Moran in Cleveland. He won the ten-round decision but broke his thumb. The Walker-Leonard fight was again postponed. A couple of weeks later, Leonard permanently canceled it. Leonard was not in need of money; he had earned over $1,000,000 in the ring and invested in the stock market. Walker would never fight Leonard, who announced his retirement on January 15, 1925.

Walker had accumulated $40,000 in expenses and loans. The $5,000 down payment and the yacht were gone. Walker was broke. He would have to fight his way back to prosperity. Promoter Herman Taylor in Philadelphia offered Walker $25,000 to defend his welterweight title against Bobby Barrett. Walker knocked out Barrett in the sixth round at Shibe Park, Philadelphia, on October 1.

In December 1924, light heavyweight champion Mike McTigue came to Bey's to prepare for Mickey Walker.[16] Walker had won all eight of his fights in 1924. He would move up in class to fight McTigue for his first bout in 1925. He would leave Chatham Township and train in Rumson, New Jersey, where he lived when not in Chatham Township. Some called him the Rumson Bulldog.

On January 3, 1925, just four days away from their scheduled bout, Mickey Walker visited Bey's Camp. He wished his foe Mike McTigue and his sparring partners a happy new year. Walker stayed to watch McTigue train. The meeting was friendly, and McTigue had no objections. When the pleasantries between them finished and Walker had gone, McTigue met with reporters and stated he would win decisively.

Danny Kramer was training at Collins's Camp for his fight against Louis "Kid" Kaplan on January 2, 1925,[17] five days before the Walker-McTigue fight. It would determine the world featherweight championship vacated by Johnny Dundee. Kaplan won every round. By the ninth round, Kramer was so battered, referee Sheridan began to look at Kramer's corner for the towel. They threw it into the ring.[18]

The advice Willie Ratner had given to Madame Bey worked. In addition to Walker and McTigue, the camp saw many fighters in its first full year. In February, one of the most dynamic little fighters ever to lace up gloves, Filipino Pancho Villa, trained to defend his world flyweight championship against George Marks.[19] Villa was a crowd favorite with his relentless punching style. Villa won a unanimous decision. Marks did not make weight, so it was no longer considered a title fight. In April, Mike Burke was training for Young Stribling.[20] Burke lost a six-round decision.

The Hungarian heavyweight Charley the "Newark Adonis" Weinert was training to fight Luis Firpo. Firpo had lost to Dempsey the year before for the heavyweight title. Weinert had daily workouts with heavyweight Joe McCann, heavyweight Sandy Seifert, and heavyweight Sailor Maxted.[21] All were preparing for fights. Weinert lost to Firpo in the second round of a scheduled six-round bout by a technical knockout.

Kid Norfolk, who had beaten Battling Siki and Harry Greb twice, came to Bey's in November. Norfolk trained with Canadian heavyweight Jack Renault for his fight with Tommy Gibbons,[22] who lost a heavyweight title fight to Jack Dempsey the previous year. Gibbons had also defeated Georges Carpentier earlier in the year. Norfolk lost by a technical knockout in the sixth round of a scheduled fifteen-round bout to Gibbons.

Freddie Welsh had many famous friends; they were not the people he needed to help support his farm. Welsh's friend F. Scott Fitzgerald, visited the Long Hill Health Farm in 1924. While there, they had a three-round sparring session. Alun Richards, Fitzgerald's cousin, wrote Fitzgerald was "proud to have boxed three rounds with Welsh." The visit was before Fitzgerald's publication of his novel *The Great Gatsby*. Gatsby and Welsh shared key character traits. Gatsby, whose real name was James Gatz, changed his name at the beginning of his career. Welsh changed his name just before his first fight.[23] Gatsby and Welsh were sportsmen, in the military, rose from being underprivileged to become wealthy, lived on Long Island in extravagant houses, exhibited intellect, and had extensive libraries.[24, 25]

Willie Ratner, the journalist who persuaded Madame Bey to embark on the boxing endeavor, sparred with Welsh, too. Ratner believed in participatory journalism and paid the price for his beliefs. Welsh hit him with a hard punch that made a permanent scar above his left eye. The scar demonstrated daily the effect of the punch.[26] Ratner now knew the power behind a professional prizefighter's blow.

CHAPTER 14

Her Boys Fight Each Other

The two prizefighters who had spent time preparing for fights at Madame Bey's Camp in 1924 would start the New Year in the ring. On January 7, 1925, at the First Regiment Armory, Newark, New Jersey, welterweight champion Mickey Walker fought light heavyweight champion Mike McTigue. Walker weighed ten pounds less than McTigue. The difference in weight classes was twenty-eight pounds.

New Jersey allowed boxing, but it did not allow for a decision rendered. Newspaper columnists had to decide which battler won, coining the name *newspaper fight*. A newspaper decision was not enough to wrest a title away from a champion; it demanded a knockout. They billed the fight as the world light heavyweight championship. Walker would need a decisive knockout to claim that title. Walker won the twelve-round bout according to the newspapers. Unable to knock McTigue out, Walker could not claim the light heavyweight title that day. The smaller Walker showed his toughness against a larger opponent.

In March, Mike McTigue, still world light heavyweight champion despite losing to Walker, returned to Bey's Camp. From there, one day, he went to Madison Square Garden to see Tex Rickard on what he described as "important business." Mike said he had been training at Bey's with Battling Siki, and that the Singular Senegalese was a sure thing to stop Paul Berlenbach when they met in a twelve-round bout at the Garden.

"Siki is going to surprise you," McTigue said. "He is going to turn in just as big a surprise as he did when he knocked out Georges Carpenter in France. … Before the sixth round has been reached, Mr. Paul Berlenbach will wish he was back in Astoria. You will remember that I won the title from Siki in Dublin … He has improved one hundred percent since our bout in Dublin. He is much faster, and he is shooting his punches with deadly accuracy. He is twice as good a boxer now as he was when I met him for the light heavyweight title."[1]

"Me beat Berlenbach," Siki added to McTigue's confidence. "Me beat any German. Him German, *n'est-ce-pas* (French for is he not)? Me fix many German in the war. Me fix this fellow, too."[2]

McTigue's assessment proved optimistic. The crowd for the Siki-Berlenbach bout was close to 12,000 at Madison Square Garden on March 13, 1925. They watched a slaughter.

Referee Eddie Purdy stopped the bout in the tenth round of a scheduled twelve-round bout. The *New York Times* printed that Siki "the former champion had withstood the terrific blows of his rival as long as he could expect to and longer than any ordinary man would have survived."[3]

By May, Mike McTigue was back at Madame Bey's preparing for a fight against one of Bey's first eleven fighters—Paul Berlenbach. Berlenbach had just beaten Battling Siki. The McTigue-Berlenbach fight was for the world light heavyweight championship. It would be held at Yankee Stadium in the Bronx, New York. If McTigue lost by a decision to Berlenbach, unlike the Walker bout, he would lose the title. The New Jersey rules did not apply.

Berlenbach trained for the bout at Madame Bey's neighbor's—Freddie Welsh's Farm. With less than a week and a half before the fight, Berlenbach and his sparring partners readied for their jog. They started down the long winding path from Welsh's Farm to the road. When they passed Madame Bey's Camp, they notice no one was there. Ten minutes later, they noticed something in the distance.

"Here comes McTigue!" someone yelled.

"What will they do?" another queried.

Within minutes, they crossed paths.

"How are you, Paul," McTigue yelled.

"Fine," Berlenbach yelled back, "how do you feel?"

The question went unanswered as neither broke stride.[4]

To help prepare, McTigue engaged two brothers who came from England—Phil and Tommy Walsh. The Walsh brothers became known in the ring of their native country. They had recently come to America seeking fights. Middleweight Joe Skinner and the two brothers would serve as sparring partners for McTigue.[5]

McTigue's daily routine consisted of five to ten miles of roadwork and hill climbing in the morning. Afternoons involved twelve rounds of sparring, shadowboxing, other ring work, and plenty of sleep.[6] As with all her boys, Madame Bey made sure he was well fed. When reporters asked what she thought about McTigue's chances, Madame Bey declared that the champion was never in better shape and that she counted on an easy victory for him when he went against Berlenbach.[6] When asked who would win an upcoming bout, Madame Bey's response would always be the one in her camp. She would exhibit that confidence about any of her boys. She had the attitude that an athlete must have. She expressed more confidence in her fighters than they expressed in themselves.

While at Madame Bey's Camp, McTigue admitted he did not learn how to box in Ireland. He started boxing after he came to America.

"I had never seen a boxing glove before I came to this country," he said.

Reporters asked McTigue what he thought his chances were. He exuded confidence.

"I have forgotten about the past for the time being because I know my hand is not going to be a drawback to me as it has been in my last few bouts. I am going in to whip Berlenbach and don't be surprised if I drop him for the count."[6]

Two years before, prior to the Young Stribling bout, McTigue broke his hand but fought because of fan pressure in Stribling's home state of Georgia.

On May 30, 1925, the two men fought at Yankee Stadium as part of the annual Hearst Milk Fund Charity. Mrs. Hearst ran the charity where some of the proceeds went toward milk for America's poor children. McTigue tried to out-box Berlenbach and tire him out. Berlenbach lasted the fifteen rounds and overpowered his opponent before the crowd of 45,000. Berlenbach won the decision and became the new world light heavyweight champion. The crowd, which favored McTigue, booed the decision. The more objective newspapers wrote that Berlenbach had won by a comfortable margin.[7]

On June 24, 1925, a boxing first occurred at Bey's Camp. Heavyweight Charlie Weinert was training for a bout against Harry Wills at the Polo Grounds, New York. A radio was installed at the Bey's farmhouse where Weinert sat, headset clamped to his ears. His manager, Billy McCarney, at a remote location spoke over the radio giving Weinert instructions and telling the world how he would upset Harry Wills. It was the first time a manager talked to his boxer over the radio.[8] The bout was to be fought on the undercard of the championship title fight between Mickey Walker and Harry Greb. Greb still held the middleweight title he had taken from Johnny Wilson in August 1923. Since winning the title, Greb fought thirty-nine times. He lost only to Gene Tunney and Tommy Loughran in close decisions and Kid Norfolk on a foul in what was called a disgraceful and dirty fight. The three losses were all above his weight class in the light heavyweight division, so he still held onto his middleweight title. Mickey Walker was the welterweight titleholder. Harry Greb was to train at Madame Bey's Camp but changed his mind and trained in Manhasset, Long Island.

Walker was in California before the fight with Greb where he met with Jack Dempsey's manager, Jack "Doc" Kearns.

"It had been at Dempsey's urging that I took on Mickey Walker," Kearns wrote," whose manager had died. Dempsey had warned Walker that I was an 'expensive manager,' but he also realized that I could help Mickey as no one else could. … I offered him a 50-50 deal, we shook hands on it and that was the only contract we ever had. He had two girls with him at the time and we even split them."[9]

Walker explained to Kearns that he would get $20,000 for the Greb bout. Kearns thought he should have received much more. Kearns would be instrumental in getting

Walker more money in future bouts. Kearns and Dempsey ended their boxer-manager relationship shortly after Kearns became Walker's manager. The split caused a long rift between Dempsey and Kearns.

Walker returned east to New York to ready for the Greb fight. Joe Degnon and trainer Teddy Hayes accompanied him. Kearns was to arrive later. When he disembarked from the Broadway Limited train, a band played, and the crowd was greater than when the heavyweight champion Jack Dempsey recently arrived. Walker, usually conservative in dress, wore a black coat with a broad white stripe, brown silk shirt with a white stripe, gray trousers with a blue stripe, a gray and red necktie, and a kerchief of the brightest cerise hue with a border of white poking out of his coat pocket. Mickey's outward appearance had changed. He went to the Biltmore where the champion promised that "win or lose, Mr. Greb will know that he's been in a fight after our meeting at the Polo Grounds."[10]

When serious boxing preparation started, Walker chose to train down the road from Bey's Camp. He would do his preparation at Johnny Collins's Camp. Walker put away his new clothes. Donning the clothes of a boxer, he trained for the most important fight of his career. Walker dreaded training but understood he had to put in the work.

On July 2, 1925, Humbert J. Fugazy promoted what boxing buffs recalled as the greatest fight card in boxing history. Many who remembered it would still discuss the card forty years later. The spectacle at the Polo Grounds attracted about 50,000 fans and a record gate of $480,000 for the welterweight class.[11] This was $260,000 more than Tex Rickard, Fugazy's rival promoter in New York, had been able to draw three weeks earlier with Berlenbach and Young Stribling. The principal bout matched the middleweight champion Harry Greb against Mickey Walker, the welterweight titleholder. The supporting bouts brought together Dave Shade and Jimmy Slattery, welterweights; Harry Wills and Charlie Weinert, heavyweight contenders; and Joe Lynch and Jackie Sharkey, featherweights.

The fight before Greb-Walker was Weinert-Wills. Billy McCarney's talk to Weinert on June 24, 1925, on the first such radio broadcast at the Bey's farmhouse did him no good; Wills knocked Weinert out in the second round.

The Greb-Walker bout was hard fought. Kearns proved right; Walker should have received more than the $20,000. It was the peril of being your own manager. When it was over, Greb had retained his middleweight title by a unanimous decision.

Grantland Rice wrote in the *New York Herald Tribune*, "The second round was sensational, one of the greatest of all time. In the 14th round, Walker was hammered all over the ring after being staggered by a right to the jaw."

Damon Runyon, in the *Universal Service*, reported this fight as being close, with Walker outfighting Greb in the fifteenth.

A story was rumored about a street fight after the bout between Greb and Walker outside the Silver Slipper nightclub. The story has been passed down by accounts from Kearns, Walker, and others. No one ever knew the validity of the story until decades had passed. A journalist visited Walker in his later years and asked about the incident.

"Nah, never happened," Walker said.[12]

Walker and Greb formed a friendship that did not last long. Less than sixteen months later, Greb was dead. On the night of August 20, 1926, Greb rolled his car twice. Greb was admitted to the hospital with a broken nose. Later, he went to Atlantic City for an operation on a bone near the base of his skull. He failed to recover from the anesthetic.

"One of the few times I ever cried in my life was when he died," Walker admitted.[13]

Walker fought Sailor Friedman after the Greb bout, in Chicago, winning the decision. After the fight, Kearns negotiated with promoter Tex Rickard. He got Walker a $100,000 guarantee to defend his welterweight title against Dave Shade. When he secured the deal, Kearns hastened to Chatham Township, where Walker was training, to hold a press conference. They had to provide a $10,000 bond to bind the match.[14] Walker now knew the advantage of having a good manager, even if he took a hefty percentage.

On September 21, 1925, before a crowd of 40,000 at Yankee Stadium, the Walker-Shade bout took place. The gate receipts reached $200,000. It exceeded expectation. Walker won a controversial split decision to retain his title. James P. Dawson reported in the *New York Times*, "… one of the most exciting, bitterly contested ring battles of the year."[15]

At the Long Hill Health Farm, it was becoming clear that Freddie Welsh was not attracting many boxers. He was in need of cash. By his actions, he was conceding the boxing camp business to Madame Bey. He decided he would turn his farm into a fox ranch. The plan was to breed them as a producing unit with the Pontiac Strain organization, the largest fur producer in the world.[16] It was a desperate attempt to bring in money. It did not work.

He tried health farm, boxing camp, boxing manager, golf course, and fox breeding. All failed. It was rumored that the financial difficulties were putting a strain on Freddie Welsh's marriage and health. They were saying he started to abuse alcohol, a vice one would have thought unthinkable of the man who espoused the virtues of healthy living and exercise. By November, Welsh's health worsened. He was admitted to a nearby hospital in Summit, New Jersey. He suffered from recurrent heart attacks.[17]

Tragedy struck former Bey Camp residents in 1925. Pancho Villa died at the age of twenty-three in San Francisco. He was the current world flyweight champion. Villa had developed an infection in the mouth. He disregarded a dentist's advice to rest. The infection worsened, and his trainer, Whitey Ekwert, rushed him to the hospital. He suffocated under the anesthetic while doctors readied to operate.[18] Pancho Villa was thought by many to be one of the best flyweight and Asian boxers ever to step into the ring.

"Pancho Villa is the best fighter of his weight in the world," journalist Damon Runyon said. "He is even greater as a flyweight than Dempsey is as a heavyweight."[19]

Another of the Bey's first boys, Battling Siki, who was the reason for Bey starting her camp, was murdered. It occurred on December 15, 1925, in the Hell's Kitchen section of New York along West Forty-First Street near Ninth Avenue. It was close to where someone stabbed him a few months before. The twenty-eight-year-old Siki, wearing one of his signature silk hats, was shot twice in the back at close range. Patrol Officer Meehan discovered the body. The two knew each other from Siki's frequent encounters with the law. Meehan had seen Siki four hours before. He reported he was drunk and unsteady. Police searched speakeasies, but they never found the killer.[20]

"When they brought me the news that he had been murdered in a New York Street," Madame Bey said, "I could think of him only as one of the most courteous men I have ever known."[21]

Siki at times displayed unsavory behavior but always presented his best conduct in the presence of Madame Bey. People acted differently when they were at the camp in the presence of Madame Bey. She understood the locker room protocol. Whenever asked about one of her boys, she replied with kind words. If she had a problem with a fighter, she resolved it in private.

CHAPTER 15

An Assassin Appears at Camp

Paul the "Astoria Assassin" Berlenbach was one of Madame Bey's first boys. Early in 1925, he defeated many of whom trained at Bey's Camp. This included gaining the world light heavyweight title by defeating Mike McTigue. Berlenbach fought three times—two wins and one no contest—since winning the title in May 1925. He came to train at Bey's, again, in November 1925.[1] He was to defend his title against Jack Delaney on December 11, 1925, who knocked him out in their previous meeting in March 1924. Berlenbach did not have brilliant boxing skills but could punch hard. Not conflicted about using boxing or defensive skills, he just delivered a hard hit.[2]

He started as an amateur wrestler before becoming a boxer. He had a second ring name, Paralyzing Paul, because of his debilitating body punches that would crumple an opponent. They called him Paulie or Berly at camp. At first, not a fan favorite, he became one as demonstrated by the crowds that came to see him at Bey's Camp. It was not only because of his boxing ability but also because of what he had overcome to obtain his achievements.

Paul Berlenbach was born a deaf mute on February 18, 1901, in New York City to French and German parents. At the age of eighteen, he worked as an instructor at the Westchester County institution for deaf mutes. One day, a youth flew a kite that became caught in electrical wires twelve feet above the ground. Berlenbach climbed the pole to disentangle the kite. In doing so, he encountered a wire. The electricity coursed through his body as he fell unconscious to the ground. At first, he was thought dead, but people performing first aid revived him. To his astonishment, he found he could hear. The event caused much interest among the medical community. Over time, he was able to develop his speech.[3, 4]

Berlenbach's manager, Dan Hickey, was at Bey's to help his charge. Hickey, a former fighter, was born in Australia. He came to America at the age of sixteen. He was lanky in a six-foot, 155-pound frame. Hickey was knowledgeable about boxing skills and tactics. He had trained world heavyweight, light heavyweight, and middleweight champion Bob Fitzsimmons, sparring with him regularly. He seconded him in many bouts. Many had credited Hickey with the development of the solar plexus punch that enabled Fitzsimmons to defeat James Corbett for the world heavyweight championship.[5, 6]

As most champion boxers did, Berlenbach would take along his sparring partners. His spar mates were professional fighters, not the caliber of Berlenbach, training for their own bouts. Some would be on the Berlenbach-Delaney undercard.

Berlenbach's favorite dog breed was the Great Dane. He owned three of them. One was a prize-winning dog, Shorty, that garnered most of his affection. Shorty had the honor of accompanying Berlenbach to Bey's Camp. Madame Bey had no problem with faithful companions. Many boxers would bring their welcomed dogs.

Berlenbach loaded his convertible Packard Model 326 Phaeton automobile with six or seven new punching bags because he would slam them to pieces during his training.[7] He also brought gym equipment, a saxophone, and Shorty. The Great Dane sat in the back on the retracted roof. Berlenbach drove into Bey's Camp with his driving flat cap and Shorty towering over him by two feet.[8]

For leisure time, he played his saxophone, which he said helped build up his lungs. At Bey's, he could play with no one to complain. He would sit under a tree with Shorty. The dog appeared content listening to his master's somber style.[9]

Berlenbach had time for some songwriting to parody what a great champion he was. One of his songs had a refrain:

"If you know Paulie, like I know Paulie, you wouldn't bet on Delaney."

Another started:

"Oh, what a champ is Paulie."

While he trained at Bey's for the Delaney bout, Berlenbach worked hard. Promoter Humbert J. Fugazy conducted trips for the press to Berlenbach's camp at Madame Bey's and Delaney's Camp in Bridgeport.[10] Journalists who came to see Berlenbach remarked how much bigger, stronger, and more confident he looked.[11]

Berlenbach would do his roadwork in the morning with Shorty setting the pace.[12] In the afternoon, he would box with various sparring partners, skip rope, and do calisthenics. His wind was excellent, as he was not breathing hard. He felt confident and told journalists he would score decisively over Delaney.[13]

A few days before the fight, two members from the New York State Athletic Commission came to the camp to see if Berlenbach was in shape. They had done the same at Delaney's Camp the day before.[14] This was a common practice. The promoters did not want out-of-shape boxers making a mockery of their boxing cards.

They fought, as planned, at the new Madison Square Garden on December 11, 1925. An over-capacity crowd of 23,000 people paying $60,000 attended. It was the second boxing card held at the new Madison Square Garden, which did not officially open until December 15. It was the third building to hold the Garden name. The current Madison Square Garden that opened in 1968 was the fourth. The Garden of 1925 was the creation of Tex Richard. He financed it with a group he called his "six hundred millionaires," a number of wealthy friends.[15] He built it at a cost of $4,750,000 in 249 days. The media called it the House That Tex Built.[16]

The new 1925 Garden held many historical events through its existence, but its main purpose was to host boxing events,[17] for which it could accommodate 18,500 fans, with seating on three levels. It measured two hundred feet by three hundred seventy-five feet. Though designed by noted architect Thomas W. Lamb, it had poor viewing for some seating. Deficient ventilation would give a hazy appearance inside, especially in the upper seats, due to permitted smoking.[16]

The fight was an epic one for the new Garden. Delaney knocked down Berlenbach for a count of three in the fourth round and hurt him in the sixth and seventh. Berlenbach came back in the last six rounds with a rally, which showed his courage and determination when he appeared defeated. The scoring was close, but Berlenbach retained his title. Newspapermen at ringside gave him seven rounds to six for the challenger, with two even.[18]

Late February 1926, Berlenbach and Shorty were back at Bey's Camp. Berlenbach would be training at Bey's while Mike McTigue was there training for a fight with Jack Delaney. Berlenbach was to fight the McTigue-Delaney victor.[19] While Berlenbach waited for the winner, he received permission from the Boxing Commission to rise in weight class. He would fight the Canadian heavyweight champion, Jack Renault. Berlenbach wanted heavyweight contender recognition. The commission gave him the stipulation that he must weigh in at 175 pounds or less, the light heavyweight limit. Renault was unenthusiastic about the fight, feeling he had nothing to gain from it and could make more money with a different opponent.[20] Renault withdrew, and the commission replaced him with Johnny Risko. They called Johnny Risko the Cleveland Rubber Man because he could absorb so much punishment and still not go down. Gene Tunney fought Risko on November 18, 1925. Shortly after the beginning of the fight, Tunney injured his right hand with a blow to Risko's iron jaw. When the bout ended, Tunney had won, but both of his hands were swollen.

While Berlenbach and McTigue trained for their upcoming fights at Madame Bey's Camp, Freddie Welsh's troubles mounted. Myrtle Wilson—the same name F. Scott Fitzgerald used in *The Great Gatsby* where an automobile crash kills a Myrtle Wilson—sued for an automobile accident involving Welsh in Summit, New Jersey. The plaintiffs, Myrtle Wilson and her father, William Wilson, of West Orange, New Jersey, charged that on October 11 an automobile driven by Welsh crashed into a car, which Myrtle Wilson was riding. Myrtle Wilson claimed she was injured and permanently disfigured. She sued for $20,000, and her father sued for $1000. On February 26, 1926, Judge W. F. Mountain adjourned the case for March 1, 1926, when Welsh was to appear in the circuit court, Newark, as a defendant in the two suits for damage.[21] The outcome of the lawsuit is unknown.

McTigue lost to Delaney on March 15, 1926, in the fourth round by a technical knockout. On March 19, at Madison Square Garden before a crowd of 18,000, Berlenbach fought in the heavyweight division. Risko outweighed him by fifteen pounds. Risko caught Berlenbach with a left hook to the jaw in the first round. Everyone wondered how he would be able to continue. The bell saved him. For the next nine rounds, Berlenbach was hit hard many times. He held on to complete the ten-round fight. To many, Risko's win was less impressive than the courage of Berlenbach, who took such a beating.[22] Berlenbach lost the decision but retained his light heavyweight title because the fight was in the heavyweight division. This fight stamped twenty-two-year-old Risko as a heavyweight contender. Berlenbach retreated to the light heavyweight division.

Berlenbach chose an easier rival the next time. He defeated opponent Ray Neuman on April 5 by a decision. His next bout would be against Young Stribling, the youngster who had trained with Dempsey at Welsh's in 1923. Stribling was twenty-one years old and had compiled a record of 121 wins, five losses, and fourteen draws. While preparing at Madame Bey's for Stribling, one of the greatest crowds gathered at the camp to witness a champion in training.[23] Berlenbach would risk his light heavyweight title at Yankee Stadium on June 10 in front of a crowd of 56,000. Berlenbach received $78,000. His opponent collected $26,000. The fight would be their second; the first resulted in a draw in 1924.

Stribling was impressive in the first three rounds. Berlenbach looked slow at the start. In the fourth round, Berlenbach landed a hard left hook just over the heart of Stribling that hurt him. From that point, the champion gave Stribling a severe beating. Stribling went to the canvas in the seventh round. Berlenbach retained his title with a unanimous fifteen-round decision.[24]

Berlenbach's popularity increased daily. He attended the Mickey Walker versus Joe "Baltimore" Dundee fight at Madison Square Garden on June 24, 1926. Somebody recognized Berlenbach as he approached his ringside seat. He started chanting, "We want Berlenbach!" Soon, the crowd of 15,000 joined the repetitive chant. It became so loud they drowned out ring announcer Joe Humphries, preventing him from introducing Walker and Dundee. Berlenbach smiled as he took his seat.[25] Dundee defeated Walker by a technical knockout in the eighth round. Walker's eyes were cut from repeated head butts from Dundee, which impeded his vision.

Berlenbach would leave after the bout and went directly to Bey's Camp. A second fight against Jack Delaney had been arranged. Once again, he prepared for him at Madame Bey's Camp. He brought the greatest sparring partners any champion ever had.[26] They were Martin O'Grady, a Canadian lightweight, who went seven rounds with Delaney in a bout a few weeks before, Monte Munn, a large six-foot-four two-hundred-plus-pound heavyweight; welterweight Johnny "Kid" Alberts; and middleweight Charlie Nashert to help build speed. A theme of his training for this fight was to get used to facing speed.[25] Phil McGraw was also training daily at Bey's with Paul Berlenbach for his fight with Georgie Balduc.[27] McGraw won the ten-round decision on June 26.

Tex Rickard planned to promote the Berlenbach-Delaney fight. While he was busy trying to create another match, he lost the rights. His competitor Humbert J. Fugazy saw an opening and took it. Promoting the fight would be lucrative for Fugazy. The work that had distracted Rickard was a Dempsey-Tunney match. Rickard lost the short-term gain but had prepared a more lucrative venture for the long term.

Berlenbach's manager, Dan Hickey, was convinced that his boxer was in the best condition he had ever known. He accredited it to the exceptional training facilities at Madame Bey's Camp. He believed the out-of-the-way location was ideal to get into the best possible form. He brought Berlenbach's training along slowly, saving the heavy work for the conclusion.[26]

Berlenbach's sparring partner, Monte Munn, was a heavyweight who shared Dan Hickey as a manager. Hickey had lofty hopes for Munn, called the Nebraska Giant. He was undefeated since becoming a professional on April 24, 1926. The twenty-five-year-old was a former University of Nebraska football player. He came from a family of large men. His brother, Wayne, was a renowned wrestler. At Bey's, Munn recalled that former heavyweight champion Jim the "Boilermaker" Jeffries was the sparring partner of former heavyweight champion James Corbett. His hope was to follow that path. Dan Hickey knew the path well. He was training with former heavyweight champion Bob Fitzsimmons in those days. Munn would defeat Jack Shaw on the McTigue-Risko Madison Square Garden undercard on July 1.

Crowds at Madame Bey's Camp became commonplace. There were so many champions and skilled fighters that reporters, photographers, and fans swamped the camp to watch them train. For Berlenbach, the crowds were heavy every day, but no one expected the crowd that appeared on July 4, Independence Day. Over two thousand people came to watch Berlenbach train for Delaney, more than double the town's population. Automobiles and limousines filled Bey's driveway and lined the street as far as one could see. Other people arrived by train at the stations in neighboring Madison and Summit and then walked or hitched a ride to the camp.[28]

The spectators were given a fine show for their money. Madame Bey was rivaling cards at Madison Square Garden with her exhibitions. They watched Berlenbach work four rounds against Johnny "Kid" Alberts. The reporters were impressed. Other boxers were on display for the crowd. European featherweight champion Andre Routis of

France, who had just come to America, fought an exhibition against the former world bantamweight champion Eddie "Cannonball" Martin. In what reporters called an excellent encounter, the boxers showed their tremendous speed. European lightweight and welterweight champion Fred Bretonnel of France then went some easy rounds with Johnny "Kid" Alberts.[28]

The Berlenbach-Delaney light heavyweight championship bout was highly anticipated. Advanced ticket sales were strong. Seat prices ranged from $3.30 to $27.50. On July 16, 1926, the bout took place at Ebbet's Field, Brooklyn, New York. Attendance was over 45,000. The gate was an estimated $520,000.[18] Madame Bey had a coveted ringside seat.[29] It was the first time she had attended a match despite the many opportunities she had been given. Fighters at her camp were always offering her ringside seats that she repeatedly rejected.[30] In a preliminary bout, Monte Munn, who trained at her camp and was Berlenbach's sparring partner, won his fight on the undercard.

In the main event, Berlenbach beat Delaney in the early rounds with persistent rushes. In the eleventh round, Delaney opened with a hard punch to the champion's stomach. From that round on, the challenger took control. Where Delaney had seemed tired, he was now aggressive. Berlenbach rushed in, occasionally connecting with his left to the body or hitting Delaney's head, but the challenger thwarted his attempts with his defense. Berlenbach absorbed terrific punishment in the closing rounds.[18, 31, 32] The fifteen-round unanimous decision went to Delaney. There was a new world light heavyweight champion.

It would be the last fight Madame Bey would attend for years, preferring to listen to the radio at her home where she did not have to endure the visual brutality. She preferred to see her boys as gentlemen, as she would call them.

After the fight, Delaney spoke to the press.

"I am mighty glad to be the champion of the light heavyweight division. It was a hard fight, but I felt that by the twelfth round, I had long lead and would surely win. I want to give credit to Berlenbach though for being one of the gamest men in the ring, and also the possessor of the hardest left hand punch I ever took. I tried hard to land a right that would end the fight, but Berlenbach took all of them and stood up. I am going to take a rest for a month or so and then I shall make plans for the defense of my title."

At Berlenbach's press conference, he spoke.

"I fought the best fight I was capable of, and I have no criticism to make of the decision; I felt strong all through the fight, and I was never in serious trouble, but I could not land my lefts effectively. Delaney is one of the cleverest men in the ring today, and I could see early in the fight that he was fighting for a decision when he found he could not drop me with his right. I only hope that he will give me a return fight, just as I gave him another chance after I defeated him last December."[33]

Berlenbach wasted no time scheduling his next bout for August 20. He would not be back at Bey's Camp. He chose to train in Pompton Lakes, New Jersey. His opponent, European light heavyweight champion Francis Charles, was already at Bey's with two other French citizens—European featherweight champion Andre Routis and European lightweight champion Fred Bretonnel. The three Frenchmen arrived in America on June 30 with Gus Wilson undertaking their management.[34] Barney Cantor, the mayor of Bensonhurst, had arranged for the three to come to America.[35] The media called them France's Three Musketeers of *Ringland*.[29] The camp was perfect for them. The three would fight ten-round bouts on the same August 20 card at Ebbet's Field promoted by Humbert Fugazy. Charles's training impressed the media. He said of his fight, "I saw Berlenbach train for Delaney at Summit and I know I can beat him."[36]

One day, some of the French fighters may have thought their presence gave them preference. They tried to show their superiority when they demanded lobster salad for breakfast.[37] Bey's tolerance tested, she chose to ignore their cries. The request went unfulfilled. Not much intimidated Madame Bey. If the French fighters questioned who was in control, there was no doubt that it was Madame Bey after the incident.

On August 20, all three Frenchmen fought on the card at Ebbet's Field. It took Berlenbach one minute, nine seconds in the first round to secure victory. Berlenbach knocked Charles down three times before the referee stopped the fight.[38] It was Charles's lone fight in America.[37] Bretonnel went the distance with Johnny Dundee, who broke a bone in his right arm just below the elbow during the third round. He used one hand for the rest of the fight. He beat Bretonnel in a decision despite the handicap. Routis, in his American debut, the best of the three Frenchmen, beat Cowboy Eddie Anderson in a decision. Routis, knocked down in the third by a left hook, rallied to win the decision with his two-fisted attack. He would have a better boxing career and a more fortunate life than his French compatriots would.[38]

France's Three Musketeers of *Ringland* represented a small-scale version of the best and worst in the sport of boxing. There was the sheer brutality, psychological impact, vulnerability of superior, powerful athletes, and the ecstasy, money, and celebrity status that came with achieving a championship.

After the loss, a dejected Francis Charles returned to Europe. He would fight three more times with no wins. This included his second-to-last fight against twenty-one-year-old Max Schmeling. His last fight was on December 13, 1927, in Paris, France, against Moise Bouquillon for the French light heavyweight title. The bout ended in tragedy. The brutal hits that Charles took caused a stoppage of the fight in the second round. The injuries left him blind.

Tragedy struck Fred Bretonnel, like Charles. Bretonnel fought four times in America with one win, two losses, and a draw before returning to France after his last American bout on Christmas Day 1926. On October 4, 1928, he committed suicide by hanging at the age of twenty-three.

Andre Routis, a resilient fighter, installed Joe Jacobs as his manager early in his American career. He lost but one fight that did not go the distance or involved a disqualification. That one fight was in 1922. He was the toughest of the French Musketeers. His two future championship title bouts against Tony Canzoneri were brutal, epic bouts that left both battered. When he first came to America, he had become homesick. He found relief in the kindness of Madame Bey. She spoke fluent French and could prepare French cuisine. She made him feel at home so far away from France. He proceeded to win the world featherweight championship in 1928. Along with the title, he would know what success in the ring could bring to one's life.

Routis's new manager, Joe Jacobs, had guided Mike McTigue to the world light heavyweight title against Battling Siki. Jacobs and McTigue had parted ways in 1923 after much bitterness. There were lawsuits between them involving slander, contractual obligations, and money.[39]

Joe Jacobs was born circa 1898 to Jewish parents who had emigrated from Hungary. His parents raised him in the tough Irish West Side of New York in the Hell's Kitchen section. He became one of boxing's most charismatic and influential managers during its golden age. He managed his first fighter, a bantamweight named Willie Astey, while still in Commerce High School. He had fast hands, not for boxing but for typing, being the fastest typist in his class.[40] He would say, "Good managers are few and far between as good fighters. I think that good managers are born, just as good fighters are."[41]

A boxing manager called Dumb Dan Morgan hired Jacobs. Morgan employed him as a secretary for his typing skills. Morgan, from New York City, boxed as an amateur before turning professional in 1894. Dorgan, the sports editor from the *New York Journal*, dubbed him Dumb Dan because of his nonstop talking. An astute Irishman, he was anything but dumb. Morgan managed many fighters, including world welterweight champion Jack Britton, world middleweight champion Al McCoy, and world light heavyweight champion Battling Levinsky. When Dumb Dan Morgan took over one of his charges, Barney Williams, he had him change his name for economic reasons.

"You'll never win a world title with a name like Williams. For one thing, the fans won't know you're Jewish, and that's bad publicity, as they all know that Hebrew fighters are some of the best you can get. We'll change your name to Battling Levinsky, and that will cover up the fact that you're a counterpuncher."

As rapid as Morgan talked, Jacobs typed faster. He corrected his grammar as he dictated. This impressed Morgan with the young Jacobs, who soaked in all that he could learn so he could make a career in boxing as a manager.[40]

Jacobs was a short, energetic man. The ever-present black cigar that protruded from his false teeth was as much a part of his facial features as were his ears, eyes, nose, and mouth. He spoke in a hurried fashion in a language that sounded like a cross between English and Hungarian. He would hardly finish a sentence before he proceeded to the next.

If you had the opportunity to go on one of his many late-night adventures, you needed not worry about who was going to pay the tab. Jacobs was always there with the cash. He spent his money as fast as he made it.

There were many notable boxers at Bey's in 1926. Mike McTigue returned to Bey's in March.[42] He would lose to Jack Delaney in the fourth round by a technical knockout. Tod Morgan trained at Bey's for three defenses of his world junior lightweight title in 1926.[43] He once sold newspapers on the streets of his hometown, Seattle. Paul Berlenbach and Willie Harmon, who were campmates, expressed admiration toward Morgan while he was training for Kid Sullivan.[44] On June 3, he won by a technical knockout over Steve Kid Sullivan in the fifth round at Ebbet's Field. On September 30, he won a decision over Joe Glick at Madison Square Garden. The ninth of November brought a unanimous decision over former Bey resident Carl Duane, also at the Garden. Tod Morgan's manager, Frank Churchill, realized that he needed arduous training to go against these hard-hitters. Churchill's choice of Bey's proved the perfect spot, giving his charge wins in all three title defenses.

Willie Harmon trained at Bey's Camp for his welterweight championship title challenge. He was training to fight Pete Latzo, who had just claimed the crown by defeating Mickey Walker on May 20. Latzo was training down the street at Freddie Welsh's place.[45] Harmon came from New York's Lower East Side, like so many other Jewish fighters of his era. He was a top welterweight contender in the mid-1920s. *The Ring* magazine ranked him the number-six welterweight in the world for 1925. They met on June 29 at Dreamland Park, Newark, New Jersey. Though Latzo came in overweight, the fight occurred anyway. Latzo knocked Harmon out in the fifth round of a scheduled twelve rounds.

Ruby "Jewel of the Ghetto" Goldstein trained at Bey's for a bout with Ace the "Nebraska Wildcat" Hudkins, who trained at Pompton Lakes, New Jersey.[46] Goldstein carried an undefeated twenty-three-win record into the ring. Well regarded, he was featured on the cover of the October 1925 issue of *The Ring* magazine. He hoped for a chance at the lightweight title with a win. Hudkins dashed those hopes when he knocked him down in the fourth round at the Coney Island Stadium, referred to as the Fugazy Bowl after the promoter. In August, Hudkins would be at the same venue to defeat Phil McGraw, who had trained at Bey's Camp.[47]

Ruby Goldstein would become one of the best boxing referees, despite criticism for his refereeing of the Benny "Kid" Paret-Emile Griffith bout where Paret died.[48] Paret trained at Bey's for that fight. Goldstein refereed for twenty-one years, including thirty-nine world championship fights.

Of all the fighters that came to Madame Bey's in 1926, one would rule boxing for the next two years. He had come that year with no planned fight. He was there to keep in shape until his chance emerged. The Fighting Marine would be the biggest name to come to the camp that year. Gene Tunney had arrived.

CHAPTER 16

A Fighting Marine

Gene Tunney had already been the American light heavyweight champion when he came to Madame Bey's on July 18, 1926,[1] at the age of twenty-nine. He fought on the undercard of the world heavyweight championship between Jack Dempsey and Georges Carpentier on July 2, 1921, in sports first million-dollar gate. He wanted to achieve the most ambitious goal in boxing—the world heavyweight championship. Jack Dempsey was the current champion. Tunney spoke in a deep, cultivated voice. He was handsome and vigorous, with dark brown hair.[2] He looked more like a studious youth than a rugged prizefighter. Studious he was, not just in his love of reading classical literature but the study of boxing. He had what the best of athletes possess—drive, goal setting, perseverance, and the willingness to make tremendous life sacrifices to achieve their goal. He was strict in his technique, resolute in his fighting.

Tunney was at Bey's to do light training; he had no fights scheduled. He would spar with featherweight contender Babe Herman[3] to keep his speed sharp. He waited for his chance with Dempsey, who had held the title for seven years. Dempsey won the title when he defeated Jess Willard, who had claimed it by beating Jack Johnson in the twenty-sixth round of a scheduled forty-five-round fight. Dempsey had defended his title six times after taking the crown. It was three years since his last fight. Tunney had knocked out Georges Carpentier and Tommy Gibbons, who had withstood Dempsey for fifteen rounds in Shelby, Montana, in 1923. He deserved a chance for the title.

He was born James Joseph Tunney in New York's Greenwich Village on May 25, 1897, the same year Madame Bey arrived in America. His parents were Irish immigrants, and his father worked as a dockworker. His family started calling him Gene because his little sister had trouble pronouncing his name. He learned to fight on the tough streets of New York before finding an organized venue at the Greenwich Village Athletic Club. At the age of eighteen, he embarked on a professional career. It continued through his enlistment in the marines during World War I on May 2, 1918. He never saw combat and continued to fight while stationed in France with the Marine Corps' approval. It earned him his ring name, the Fighting Marine. After his discharge, he continued his boxing career with intensity.[4]

He was meticulous and one of the first boxers to use films of his opponents to discover their weaknesses. He planned for every contingency he could think of that would occur in the ring. He ran backward during training, a practice commonplace today, to simulate backpedaling in a bout. Tunney was a thinking boxer, an unpopular style when sluggers and brawlers were favored. Boxers such as James J. Corbett and Benny Leonard influenced his style. Tunney's boxing style was to hold his hands low for greater power. He had fast footwork that adjusted to his opponents' moves. His counterpunches were quick and accurate. He was knocked down only once in his career and never knocked out.[5] Tunney used rapid-fire combinations and threw lead right hands that baffled his opponents. He was always moving and boxing behind a left jab, and pivoted to create angles for hooks and uppercuts.[6] He had vicious body punches. Tunney would study his opponents from the opening bell, exploiting their styles.[7] He rarely fought toe-to-toe.[8]

With only one career loss, he was never given credit that he had due. One of the best ever cornermen, Whitey Bimstein, said of Tunney, he "was the finest fighter I've ever seen. He was cool, calm, and collected. Nothing ever bothered him. He was always underrated. In my book he could have licked them all, from John L. Sullivan to Rocky Marciano."[9]

In 1926, he had compiled a record of sixty-two wins, one loss, one draw, and no one had knocked him down. The one loss came against light heavyweight boxer Harry the "Human Windmill" Greb by a unanimous decision. In that fight, Tunney stayed on his feet for fifteen rounds despite receiving a beating. Tunney out-pointed Greb in a return bout and then beat him two more times and drew him in a newspaper fight. All fights went the scheduled number of rounds. The five bouts against Harry Greb demonstrated Tunney's vicious body punching. During the closing rounds of their last fight, he had the satisfaction of hearing Greb whisper, "Don't knock me out, Gene. Let me stay."[2] Tunney obliged his request.

Tunney preferred reading classics to the card playing that many boxers at Bey's would do to pass the time. When others would play cards after dinner, Tunney did not.

"How can they waste their time like that?" Tunney would say.[10]

He would go to another room to read classical literature. He had a reputation of being a snob. Some would refer to him derogatorily as Shakespeare Gene. He later developed friendships with writers George Bernard Shaw and Ernest Hemingway.

Tunney did not hide his disdain for the press, which they reciprocated. Will Rogers, a humorist, social commentator, cowboy, actor, and a popular celebrity in the 1920s and 1930s, wrote in his newspaper column, "Let's have prizefighters with harder wallops and less Shakespeare." Sportswriter Paul Gallico, from the *New York Daily News*, wrote, "I think Tunney has hurt his own game with his cultural nonsense."

Dempsey was not well liked either, but Tunney was the least liked. People appreciated Gene Tunney more for his boxing skills after he had retired. We treat prizefighters like other athletes, celebrities, and politicians. We only appreciate their accomplishments after someone else comes along we hate more, they retire, or have been sprawled on the canvas. Once they took the time to get to know him, they would discover their assessment derived from first impressions, or journalists, which was not always accurate.

Madame Bey did not judge someone based on what was written in a periodical or what others had to say about them. She had the man in front of her and could make her own determination about character. Gene Tunney would become one of her favorites, and she would talk about him enthusiastically whenever asked about him. She had her own name for him—my polished emerald.

"That dear Gene!" Madame Bey described Tunney. "That marvelous, handsome, intelligent Gene Tunney – ah, there is a man for you! He is fine inside and outside, and he deserves everything good that life can give him. Night after night, he has sat in this very chair, talking about music and books, and about his future, for Gene has always believed that he is a man of destiny. He would tell me of how he would win the championship, and how he would keep it, and of his plan to retire and make good in business."[11]

Tunney bided his time at Bey's Camp, relaxing and continuing his light workouts. He would take lengthy, solitary, reflective walks during the day and read books at night.[12] He would later say that he did six years of planning to win the championship from Jack Dempsey. He knew from his manager, Billy Gibson, a match with Dempsey was being discussed with promoter Tex Rickard, but an obstacle stood in the way.

Dempsey contracted to defend his title against Harry the "Black Panther" Wills. Harry Wills, like Jack Johnson before him, had to break the color barrier. A Dempsey versus Wills fight was controversial. Tex Rickard promoted and refereed the Jack Johnson versus James Jeffries fight on July 4, 1910, in Reno, Nevada. The match resulted in deadly riots following Johnson's victory. A black man had not fought for the heavyweight championship since Jack Johnson lost to Jess Willard on April 5, 1915. There was no difficulty arranging fights with whites for championships in other weight classes or nontitle bouts in the heavyweight division, but a heavyweight title remained unacceptable.

With Tex Rickard as the promoter, Jack Dempsey and Harry Wills signed their first contract to fight for the championship within sixty days on July 11, 1922. Wills's manager, Paddy Mullins, provided $2,500 the month before to the commission as a forfeit fee.[13] If they withdrew from the fight, they would lose that money. Contracts in boxing did not mean much in those days; they were often broken. Fighters and managers would sign a contract with one fighter just to help get a fight with someone else. It can be called racism, but for Rickard, it was always about the money. Though he had promoted mixed-race fights before, he now thought a black champion would not be worth as much at the gate as a white champion would.

With much wrangling with the commission, the fight never took place. Dempsey successfully defended his title against Luis Angel Firpo instead, in boxing's second million-dollar gate, despite the objections of Wills and his manager. The attempt by Wills's team to stop the Firpo-Dempsey fight angered Dempsey. He said Wills would never get a chance to fight him.

"I would have fought Wills," Dempsey told the *New York Post* in 1953, "but nobody would promote it. When Wills challenged, Tex Rickard would have nothing to do with the fight. He said he had instructions from Washington not to promote a mixed[-race] bout for the heavyweight title."

On September 9, 1925, Dempsey, and heavyweight contender Harry Wills signed a second contract with promoter Floyd Fitzsimmons in Niles, Michigan, to fight for the championship in 1926. They gave Wills $50,000 and promised Dempsey $125,000.

"The facts clearly show that in 1926, I tried desperately to arrange a fight with Harry Wills, but the deal collapsed when my guarantee was not forthcoming," Dempsey said in a 1950 *Ebony* article.

Dempsey said he met Fitzsimmons in Dayton, Ohio. The promoter handed him a certified check for $25,000 and a promise to let him have the balance. Dempsey balked and demanded the full amount. Fitzsimmons called the bank where he said he had deposited the money. The bank informed Fitzsimmons he did not even have enough to cover the $25,000 check he had given Dempsey. Furious, Dempsey returned the check to Fitzsimmons and told him he would not fight. Later, the Fitzsimmons syndicate financing the fight sued Dempsey for failure to honor the contract. Dempsey won the case.[14]

The ordeal persisted. Tex Rickard and Tunney's manager, Billy Gibson's, main impediment was now with B. C. Clements, who was president of the Coliseum Athletic Club. On July 19, 1926, Clements claimed that he held the Dempsey and Wills contracts. He said if Dempsey were to fight in Chicago, it would have to be against Wills. Billy Gibson wired Rickard requesting him to delay a Dempsey-Tunney announcement. Gibson wanted to wait for the Illinois State Athletic Commission scheduled meetings to fix any issues.[1]

On July 21, 1926, after three days of conferences, Tex Rickard announced what Tunney had long been awaiting. Dempsey would defend his title against Tunney in September with Chicago's Soldier Field as the probable site. Both New York and New Jersey, that were hoping to host the fight after discussions with Rickard, expressed disappointment in the choice of Chicago. Rickard expected a gate of more than $2,000,000. He would divide 55 percent between the principles. He declined to announce how he would split the 55 percent but would give them an option of cash compensation instead. He further pledged that he would donate $150,000 of the proceeds to the Widows and Orphans' Fund of the Chicago firefighters and police.[15]

Clements protested the decision, insisting that Dempsey must fight Wills. The Illinois State Boxing Commission declined comment, which cast doubt on the fight. It was later reported that Clements had acquired the contracts from Fitzsimmons for payment of ten dollars. This prompted Dempsey to go public on July 23, 1926, stating he had no contract with Clements.

"I don't see how Dempsey can get out of fighting Wills," Paddy Mullins, Wills's manager, said.[16]

Another heavyweight title fight with a black man would not occur until Joe Louis fought James Braddock in June 1937.

Tunney, still at Bey's, did not hear about the dealing. Willie Ratner, the journalist who advised Madame Bey to start the camp, received the news when a bulletin came over the Associated Press wire stating that Jack Dempsey and Gene Tunney had been matched. Ratner tried to contact Tunney at Bey's Camp, but the telephone was not working. He took a cab to the training camp. Upon his arrival, he discovered Tunney sitting in a rocking chair on the Beys' farmhouse porch, oblivious to all that had occurred. Ratner handed him the message just as it had come over the wire. Tunney jumped from his chair, changed his clothes, and went to New York to learn more about the good news.[17]

Tunney heard from his manager, Billy Gibson, about the fight details after he returned to Bey's Camp, where he expressed regret that New York was not granted the fight.

"The news that I finally am to get a crack at the title is great," Tunney said, "but at the same time, I am disappointed that I can't fight for the championship in my hometown. However, I am satisfied with Chicago, for at least I know I will be fighting where there won't be any political interference."[18]

Tunney stated he cared nothing about earning twenty-five and fifty-cent training gate receipts, customary for famous fighters training for marquee fights.

"I am out to win the title," Tunney said, "and nothing else counts. I want to train where I can whip myself into the best possible shape."[18]

On July 22, 1926, Tunney left Bey's to train in Saratoga Springs, New York. From there he went to Wisconsin to train for the Chicago fight. It would have been a boon for Bey's Camp if Tunney continued his training there. Madame Bey may not have known much about the boxing technical craft, but she understood the business aspect of boxing. Boxers, especially for high-profile fights, were at the disposal of promoters, managers, and trainers. They could not always train where they wanted. Promoters, who provided the purse money, had influence on where training would occur. You did as told. Despite Tunney leaving, he would remain one of Bey's favorites. She often heard from Tunney and kept his letters among her many mementos gathered during her operation of the camp.

There were still many obstacles to holding the fight in Chicago, which eventually prevented the fight from occurring there. Rickard agreed to change the venue to Yankee Stadium, New York, where Tunney wanted it anyway, with a new date of September 16.

If Tunney had been elated with the venue change, it would not be for long. The New York State Athletic Commission denied issuing a license to Dempsey despite the fact that the attorney general, Albert Ottinger, had rendered an opinion that he was entitled to one. The New York option was gone unless Rickard wanted to wage a court battle, which he did not. On August 19, Rickard released a long statement, with the opening paragraph:

"After much and careful consideration, I have decided to take the Dempsey-Tunney bout to Philadelphia. I have made every effort to hold this match in New York, because I felt that New York was entitled to the match and that I had no right to take it from the State in which I have so many interests, the money which will accrue, directly or indirectly, from this bout. I received strong and generous efforts from Commissioners George E. Brower and William Muldoon, but the time came when they could do no more. The only recourse left to me was the courts. After considering the matter, I am unwilling to proceed to this extremity."[19]

The final site and date was determined when Rickard decided to hold the fight at Sesquicentennial Stadium, Philadelphia, on September 23. Pennsylvania assured he would receive no opposition. He would get cooperation from the Pennsylvania State Athletic Commission and the Pennsylvania governor, Pinchot.

Tunney was in Lake Pleasant, New York, at his training camp working hard while Rickard resolved the fight logistics. He was awaiting Bud Gorman, who was still training at Bey's Camp, to come to Lake Pleasant to be his sparring partner along with Johnny Grosso.[20] Both Gorman and Grosso were already decent professional fighters in the heavyweight division. Gorman was in training for his fight on September 10, as was Grosso for his fight on August 31.

On September 2, Tunney shifted his training camp to the Glen Brook Country Club in Stroudsburg, Pennsylvania. The day before, while traveling through Philadelphia, he was surprised by the number of people that came to see him. Marine Corps members especially stunned him when they rushed him and hoisted him up. Reporters asked if he worried about the fight, to which he said he was not.

"As soon as I worry, I stop training."[21]

There were no boxing facilities at the country club, but they erected a ring and assembled other equipment just to get Tunney to come. His manager, Billy Gibson, came before Tunney and gave his approval to the facilities.[22]

The fight occurred as planned on September 23. The mayors of Philadelphia and New York City attended. The Pennsylvania governor, Pinchot, and other governors from across the country attended. Dignitaries included the secretary of the navy, Curtis Wilbur, and many millionaires and notable people.[23] Extra train service was scheduled to transport fans from New York, New Jersey, Illinois, and other locations. Those that could not attend listened to the fight on the radio. Others followed telegraph reports dispatched around the world.[24]

The crowd was 144,468,[25] the largest paid attendance ever for a boxing match and remains an American record. According to Rickard, based on tickets and badges used to gain admittance, the fight produced a record of $1,895,733.[26] It was boxing's third million-dollar gate, Dempsey-Carpentier and Dempsey-Firpo the other two. Dempsey earned $770,000. Tunney received $200,000. The Philadelphia Chamber of Commerce estimated city businesses made an extra $3,000,000 in revenue through purchases of meals, hotel rooms, train and taxi rides, and other items from those attending the fight.[24]

The majority favored Dempsey to win. They fought in a driving rain that increased in fury, as did Tunney's punches, as the fight progressed. The ring flooded, and the rain drenched spectators and the fighters.[27] Dempsey's estranged manager, Doc Kearns, had a seat at the fight beside Bernard Gimbel, the department store tycoon.

Tunney out-boxed the champion to take the title by a unanimous decision. Madame Bey's polished emerald, Gene Tunney, won the world heavyweight championship just as he told her he would. There were no knockdowns by either fighter. *The Ring* magazine declared it the Upset of the Decade. Tunney's six years of planning to beat Dempsey paid off. Madame Bey had her first world heavyweight champion in a little less than three years after she opened her camp. It would not be her last.

Tunney would again fight Dempsey on September 22, 1927, at Soldier Field, Chicago. Dempsey had knocked out Jack Sharkey on July 21, 1927, in the seventh round of a scheduled fifteen-round fight. For Tunney, it would be his first fight since the last time he fought Dempsey. A Dempsey team member, Gus Wilson, inquired about training at Madame Bey's for the fight.[28] They decided on other accommodations. The numbers for the next fight were staggering, surpassing most numbers from their encounter in Philadelphia.

Attendance at Soldier Field was 104,943. Another 50,000,000 listened to the fight on the radio[29] when the population of the United States was just over 119,000,000. It produced a gate of $2,658,660.[26] Dempsey's purse was $447,500, and Tunney's $990,445. Tunney received a check for $1,000,000 after he paid the promoter, Tex Rickard, the difference. Tunney, with his payment, became the first athlete with a $1,000,000 payday. From the receipts, $250,000 went to federal taxes, and $225,000 went to state taxes. Preliminary fighters received $180,000. The stadium rental cost $100,000, and other incidental expenses were $156,500. That gave promoter Rickard a profit of around $250,000. To put those numbers in perspective, Babe Ruth, who hit his record sixty home runs that year, made an annual salary of $70,000 as the highest paid baseball player.

The fight would forever be known as the Long Count Fight. It has been argued for ages if Dempsey had won the fight by a knockout. Tunney was winning with a skilled display of boxing when Dempsey caught him with a combination in the seventh round. Seven consecutive punches from Dempsey sent the champion to the canvas. Dempsey did not go to a neutral corner as a new rule dictated. He was used to waiting by an opponent, so he could hit him when he got up. The referee told Dempsey to get to a neutral corner.

"I'll stay here," Dempsey said.

The referee waved Dempsey to a neutral corner before he began his count. By the time the referee, Dave Barry, had gotten him to go to the correct corner, five seconds had passed. Tunney, down for the first time in his career, sat hanging on the middle ring rope with his left hand and listening to the count, getting up on the nine count. Fourteen seconds passed. No one will ever know if Dempsey sufficiently hurt Tunney, or he took advantage of the situation and waited to hear nine from the referee. By the eighth round, Tunney recovered and took control, knocking Dempsey down with a right. Tunney won by a ten-round unanimous decision. The seventh round was the only round he lost.[30]

After the fight, someone asked Dempsey why he did not go to the neutral corner.

"I couldn't move. I just couldn't. I wanted Tunney to get up. I wanted to kill the S.O.B.!

"I won the championship but didn't get it because they gave Tunney fifteen seconds to recover from the knockdown in the seventh."[30]

Tunney said after the fight about the knockdown, "My first thoughts were: 'What is this? How did I get here? I ought to be ashamed of myself.'

"That smash stunned me, but I could have gotten up all right at the count of five."[31]

Tunney's last bout would come against the New Zealand-born Irishman Tom Heeney. Tunney trained in Speculator, New York. Heeney trained at a camp in Fairhaven, New Jersey. Jack Dempsey would be in Heeney's corner. Heeney had earned a chance at the title by fighting his way through the best heavyweights America had. He drew Jack Sharkey then won a decision over Jack Delaney in his last fight.

The fight occurred at Yankee Stadium, New York, on July 26, 1928, before a crowd of 50,000. Attendance and revenue were lower than expected. It was a disappointing showing compared to the Dempsey fights, and Rickard admitted it was a financial failure. It enabled Tunney to fight a championship bout in his hometown. He heard cheers instead of the jeers of his previous championship battles. It was clear that Tunney was a far superior fighter. He knocked Heeney down in the tenth round. Only the bell saved him. Heeney's seconds carried him back to his corner. No one would have blamed him for not answering the bell for the eleventh round, but he fought on. Tunney continued his beating while Heeney was bleeding from several areas of his face. At two minutes, fifty seconds into the eleventh round, the referee, Eddie Forbes, stopped the fight.[32, 33]

A few days later, Tunney announced his retirement in a written statement to the press. He retired as the second richest man in sport, only Jack Dempsey had more. Money made in other sports could not approach that made in the ring by the best fighters. Tunney had made over $2,000,000 in his fights, most of that coming from the last three. The two Dempsey fights made him $1,200,000. He received $525,000 for the Heeney fight, which was the first financial loss for promoter Rickard, who said his loss was $155,719,[33] since 1906. Tunney's lengthy retirement statement read in part:

"I have fought my last bout as a professional boxer.

"It naturally is with a certain regret that I announce my permanent retirement from the ring. No man realizes more than I do my debt to the game. It has treated me well. To it I owe such fame and fortune as I possess and it has given me something less ephemeral than fame – many real and warm friendships, which I hope and expect to keep through all the years to come.

"I shall always take a live and active interest in boxing. There is no finer physical exercise or more engrossing science. It is a game which, properly conducted, teaches and develops such qualities as stamina, confidence, patience, self-denial, bodily fitness, mental alertness and courage."[34]

One of those friendships mentioned in his statement was Madame Bey. He would send her letters and return to the camp where he first heard about his chance to fight for the championship against Dempsey. He would go there to watch the boxers train and have talks with his friend Madame Bey.

Years after his retirement, Madame Bey still praised Tunney when asked about him.

"And that dear Gene, whom I will always call my polished emerald, has married into society and is a great man now apart from the ring, yet he is always the same to me whenever he calls to see someone in training."[11]

Bey was referring to Tunney's marriage to Miss Mary Josephine Lauder, better known as Polly Lauder, on October 3, 1928, in Rome, Italy. She was a Connecticut socialite and an heir to the Andrew Carnegie fortune via her grandfather George Lauder, a first cousin and business partner of Andrew Carnegie. Andrew Carnegie was a philanthropist and one of the richest men in the world. He had made most of his money from the steel industry that included his being a principal owner in United States Steel, the first company in the world with a market capitalization of over $1 billion.

All of Tunney's predictions told to Madame Bey from a chair in her farmhouse had come true. As Bey called him, he had become a man of destiny. He created a plan and executed it. He won the championship, kept it, retired, and made good in business, becoming the chairperson and director of many companies.

CHAPTER 17

Last One Standing

While Gene Tunney was conquering the heavyweight division, a steady stream of fighters continued to flow into Madame Bey's Camp. In 1927, her camp was the only one remaining in Chatham Township. A fire partially destroyed Mary Green's Camp, and it discontinued operations. Newspapers no longer mentioned Johnny Collins's Camp as no one trained there anymore.

Where it all started, Freddie Welsh's Long Hill Health Farm went into foreclosure. It was the attainment of his dreams and the cause of his anguish. Welsh's farm was to be sold in November 1926 to settle the mortgage. Welsh did not let the farm go without a fight. After the foreclosure had been signed, Welsh obtained a thirty-day extension. After the thirty days expired, Welsh received an additional thirty days after he told the court through counsel he had received a loan of $45,000, but the lender withdrew because of litigation, delaying the transaction. Then Welsh induced William C. Armstrong of Chatham Township to advance him the money. Before the loan occurred, Armstrong came to his tragic death in an automobile accident. In April 1927, Albert Berkenmeier and a syndicate of eight other Newark businessmen offered to fend the final blow. Mr. Greene, representing Welsh, told the court about the syndicate and that Welsh had declined offers of $35,000 and $50,000, declaring them inadequate, and the persons making the bids were trying to take advantage of Welsh's financial predicament. The court gave Welsh another thirty days to complete the financing.[1] The money never materialized. Then Welsh filed suit for $150,000 in the Supreme Court of Newark, New Jersey, charging the nine Newark businessmen with failing to fulfill a promise to help him buy back the farm. The court set the sale aside and gave Welsh until April 29, 1927 to repurchase the farm.[2, 3] He never secured the money.

In May 1927, the final blow was struck, and they foreclosed on the farm to meet the $30,000 mortgage. George T. Brown, a onetime friend in better times, held the mortgage.[4, 5] The contents of the house included signed first-edition books, original manuscripts of Welsh's late friend Elbert Hubbard, bronzes, and prizefighting trophies.[6] Welsh considered the items priceless. The court considered them payment on the mortgage.

Life for Welsh spun out of control. He drank and worried about his finances. Welsh's health was failing, and he was getting into fights outside of the ring. On July 17, 1927,

Welsh appeared in a New York court with a black eye and bruises. Welsh received the worst from a fight that had escalated from a quarrel with a person named Edward Delaney of New York. A police officer saved Welsh from a more severe beating. This resulted in a police charge of disorderly conduct. The judge said it was a friendly fight and dropped the charges against both men.

Welsh stayed in the Hotel Sydney in New York to recover from the beating. He received visits from some friends who said Welsh looked terrible. On July 29, 1927, at the age of forty-one, Freddie Welsh fought his last bout. It was not against a ring opponent but his own demons. A maid discovered Welsh dead in his room at the Sydney Hotel. Dressed in pajamas and a bathrobe, it appeared he was sitting behind a desk when he fell over from an apparent heart attack. A copy of *Elbert Hubbard of East Aurora* by Felix Shay lay on his bed. The book was open.

"Get your happiness out of your work, or you will never know what happiness is," the open page started with.

Welsh's estranged wife of the last few years was bitter and tearful upon hearing of Welsh's death. She assailed Welsh's boxing friends.

"When you're up you're way up," she said, "but when you're down you are sure down. Freddie knew them all when he was on top, but none of them knew him when he was down and out."[2, 3]

Even in death, the farm continued to haunt Freddie Welsh. On October 13, 1927, the Long Hill Health Farm ceased to exist. A fire swept through the grand house on the top of the hill. It was determined to have started from one of the fireplaces.

"I remember when it caught fire," a neighbor Mrs. Clingen said, "my father went to help pull out the furniture and give the firemen a hand with the water buckets."

Her father said that people were taking the furniture off the lawn as fast as it came out of the burning house and carrying it back to their houses.

"In those days when people saw smoke," Mrs. Clingen continued, "for some reason, they took advantage of the situation."[7]

Left behind and destroyed were all Welsh's physical possessions. There were two occupants at the time of the fire, George T. Brown, the man who had foreclosed on the house, and his wife. They both escaped unharmed.

While Freddie Welsh's life ended in 1927, Paul Berlenbach was welcomed to Bey's Camp in January of that year. He came to the camp where he had so much success. He prepared to fight Mike McTigue, the man from whom he had won the light heavyweight title. The press called it the Battle Between Ex-Champions.

Berlenbach had not fought since defeating the Frenchman Francis Charles, who had trained at Bey's Camp. The journalists at Bey's had mixed opinions about how Berlenbach trained. Some thought he appeared sluggish after a six-month layoff. Others thought he punched harder than ever. Photographs in the newspapers showed that Berlenbach's Great Dane Shorty, who seemed to get as much attention as his master, was in fine shape. McTigue went through the last six months performing well in his bouts. He had added incentive in that Berlenbach had taken his light heavyweight title from him.

Berlenbach brought with him heavyweight Bud Gorman, who had just loss to Jack Delaney, and heavyweight Harold Mays as sparring partners. Berlenbach stated that he would never try to box again but fight in his natural style. He felt he lost to Delaney by trying to box instead of relying on his powerful punch.[8]

Berlenbach was the favorite. McTigue was ten years older than the twenty-five-year-old Berlenbach. A crowd of 18,000 on January 28, 1927, at Madison Square Garden roared encouragement as McTigue overwhelmed his youthful rival with a savage attack. In the fourth round of a ten-round bout, Berlenbach hit the canvas three times. Berlenbach was out on his feet, and his instincts and courage allowed him to continue. The referee, Kid McPartland, stopped the fight to save him from further punishment.[9] McTigue won by a technical knockout. It was Berlenbach's fourth career loss in thirty-seven fights.

The Associated Press reported, "Drawing power from some fistic fountain of youth, 35-year-old Mike McTigue, battle-scarred veteran of many years campaigning, knocked out Paul Berlenbach tonight in one of the most dramatic upsets the ring has seen in many years."

"Youth must be served with rights and lefts to the jaw,"[10] Mike McTigue said after turning "Paralyzing Paul into Pulverized Paul," according to one writer. McTigue now wanted a title chance against Jack Delaney. The light heavyweight division consisted of many good men that he would have to fight to get another championship bout.

Andre Routis, using Bey's as his base, started his American campaign with much success. He won five times and lost once in 1926. He trained at Bey's for all fights except one—a close loss to Tony Canzoneri, who would become a five-time world champion in three different weight classes. The featherweight Routis had mixed results in 1927. He compiled a record of five wins, four losses, and a draw. The last fight took place in France during December when he returned home for a short time. After one more fight in France, he returned to America and his second home at Madame Bey's Camp.

The camp welcomed the arrival of another promising boxer from Europe in 1927. He was the European heavyweight champion Paulino Uzcudun. They called him the Basque Woodchopper or the Basque Bull. The press used Paolino as an alternate spelling of his name. Newspapers called him by his first name, Paulino, or simply the Spaniard. Madame Bey called him her rough diamond. He remains the best heavyweight Spain has ever produced.

Paulino fought from a crouch and had a terrific left hook. He was short and stocky with tremendous shoulders that would bulge from his tattered brown shirt he wore often at Madame Bey's Camp. His fighting height was stated as five feet ten inches, though some said he stood no more than five feet seven inches. He weighed a little over two hundred pounds. His ruffled, black hair gave him a rough appearance, but when he bared his teeth, gold filings shined. He was as rugged as the Pyrenees Mountains from which he came. His family hailed from the Basque region of Spain. The youngest and smallest of ten children, his seven brothers and two sisters were all over six feet tall and powerful. He was a butcher by trade and had aspirations of becoming a bullfighter. He thought he was good at fighting the bulls. When someone saw his agility in the bullfighting ring, he suggested Paulino try the boxing ring instead.[11] Paulino took his advice and put away his bullfighting swords. He had dispatched his last bull.

At twenty-six years old, he came to America. In Europe, he had compiled a record of twenty-five wins with twenty-one knockouts, two losses, and a draw. The Spaniard had his first American bout during January in Tampa, Florida, which resulted in a win. In February, he came to Madame Bey's Camp. Like many foreign fighters, he would make it his home. The secluded location suited his introverted personality. Paulino's English was not good. Conversing would be no problem with Madame Bey's Spanish language mastery.

Paulino would be at Madison Square Garden on February 25, 1927 for his next fight. He fought in the main event. On the undercard, New Zealand heavyweight champion Tom Heeney fought Charley Anderson. The winners of each bout were to fight each other. Heeney won his bout by a technical knockout. Paulino won his bout with a decision over Knute Hansen.

Paulino returned to Bey's to prepare for Heeney. At his weighing in, the press asked his opinion about the fight outcome. In broken English, he told reporters that he would hit Tom on the chin, and Tom would hit the canvas.[12] Tex Rickard was hoping Paulino was correct in his assessment. Rickard was trying to build the Spaniard into a box office draw with an international appeal. On April 1, 1927, Paulino did not disappoint. He defeated Heeney in a ten-round decision at Rickard's new Madison Square Garden. Paulino would say Heeney was his toughest opponent that year. Paulino exited the fight with a broken rib and an injured arm.

His next bout was to be against Harry the "Black Panther" Wills. Uzcudun had ignored his contract with Tex Rickard to fight Wills, after he had been abandoned from Rickard's heavyweight elimination tournament when Jack Dempsey refused to fight in more than one preliminary bout preceding a fight with Gene Tunney. Rickard's original plan was to match Uzcudun with Dempsey and have the winner meet the survivor of the Jack Sharkey-Jimmy Maloney bout. Once again, Paulino returned to Bey's Camp.

On July 13, 1927, at Ebbet's Field, the scheduled fifteen-round fight took place. Paulino sent Wills to the canvas in the fourth round while the referee counted to nine. Wills rose only to be hit with a barrage of punches that put him under the lower rope. He remained there supported on his elbows while referee Lou Magnolia counted him out.[13] The thirty-eight-year-old Wills, no longer in his prime, was no match for the younger Spaniard.

Paulino was attracting attention in the heavyweight division. He had four consecutive wins since arriving in America. People became aware that he was making his headquarters at Bey's Camp. Crowds were coming to see the Basque Woodchopper train, and reporters were there to report on his progress for fans.

His next fight would be in less than a month against the light heavyweight champion Jack Delaney, who was moving up into the heavyweight division. While preparing for Delaney, Paulino thrilled the crowds at Bey's in early August. In what was representative of Bey's international appeal, the Spaniard sparred with French middleweight Felix Sportiello, who would fight on the Delaney-Paulino undercard. Other spar mates were Chilean heavyweight Romero Rojas and Australian heavyweight Blackie Miller.[14] Light heavyweight Maxie Rosenbloom joined the sparring partners after winning a bout on August 4 in Detroit.[15] He was a promising light heavyweight given the colorful ring name of Slapsie Maxie.

"Delaney may box rings around my man in the first four or five rounds," Al Mayer, a spokesman for Paulino at Bey's, said, "but he'll be made to run to cover beginning the sixth. Paulino will punch him full of holes. A left hook to the body will lay low Delaney. That's as sure as the sun shines."[15]

On August 11, 1927, before a crowd of 25,000 at Yankee Stadium, the sun did not shine; the bout was held at night. Delaney was the quicker man and proceeded to out-box Paulino. The Spaniard did land his powerful left to the body that doubled up Delaney and hurt him, but he held on. In the seventh round of the scheduled ten, the referee disqualified Paulino for a low blow after having been repeatedly warned about the infractions. Writer Roscoe McGowan called it an invisible foul. A win would have matched him against the highly regarded Jack Sharkey and a possible title chance.

Paulino's next opponent would be a rematch against Tom Heeney. Despite his loss to Delaney, the crowds that came to watch him prepare at Bey's did not abate. At the camp, two days before the bout, he spoke through an interpreter, Charlie H. Harvey.

"I do not choose to win on points. I am sure I will knock out Heeney inside of the fifteen scheduled rounds," declared Paulino. "After I beat Mr. *Upsidedown*, I am going to challenge the winner of the Dempsey-Tunney fight."

Mayer, at the camp, said, "Right after the fight, we'll take the first train to Chicago and see the big fight (referring to Dempsey-Tunney). Paulino will visit the camps of both fighters, and perhaps he will have a little bet down. Right now, he's picking nobody. He wants to get an eyeful before making a prediction."[16]

On September 8 at Madison Square Garden, Uzcudun and Heeney met. It was a lackluster fight that resulted in a draw. It had none of the excitement or viciousness of their first encounter. A win would have made either a contender for the heavyweight title.

Paulino was scheduled to fight English heavyweight Phil Scott in his next bout on November 4 at Madison Square Garden. Jess McMahon, cofounder of the World Boxing Association (WBA), and whose family runs the Worldwide Wrestling Entertainment (WWE) business, arranged the match for the Garden. Paulino complained about back problems and canceled the match. He claimed he injured it reaching across Madame Bey's dining room table for the last pork chop.[17] The Garden sent a doctor to Madame Bey's to ensure the injury was legitimate. Dr. Joseph Bier examined Paulino, diagnosed him with low back pain, and said he would be unable to train for a week. When Jess McMahon received the report, it sent him scrambling to put together another boxing card.[18]

Dr. Bier made the trip to Madame Bey's because the commission and promoters wanted to protect their financial interests. They wanted to make sure boxers they signed were in shape and ready to perform for their paying patrons. With Paulino, they wanted to make sure any purported injuries were not just a ruse for the boxer to withdraw from the signed match. Dr. Bier owned his own camp in Pompton Lakes, New Jersey. It became one of Madame Bey's biggest competitors. Like Bey's Camp, it was away from the city in a secluded area.

The fight with Phil Scott never occurred. Instead, Paulino fought Johnny Risko. In November, a few days before Paulino's bout against Johnny Risko, reporter Thomas Holmes went to Madame Bey's Camp for an interview with Paulino. Upon reaching his destination, Sidky Bey greeted him. Holmes inquired where he could find Paulino. Finding him and getting through the language barrier would be a task.

Sidky Bey asked Murray Gitlitz, a light heavyweight and sparring partner, where they could find Paulino. Gitlitz asked Paul Arthus, Paulino's manager. Arthus relayed Paulino's interview acceptance to Gitlitz, who told Sidky Bey, who then told reporter Holmes. Then Sidky Bey escorted Holmes to Paulino, who was relaxing after a hard day's work. He had done his early morning roadwork followed by an afternoon of six rounds of sparring, which had just completed one hour before. He was playing beret—a card game like rummy—with a fellow Spanish citizen. He wore a tattered brown shirt that defined his broad muscular shoulders.

The reporter, Holmes, needed an interpreter to question Paulino. The interpretation process became complicated. Holmes spoke English to sparring partner Gitlitz to tell him what he wanted. In a mixture of French, English, and sign language, Gitlitz talked to Arthus, Paulino's manager. Arthus questioned Paulino, who then answered. In cases of extreme difficulty, Pierre Gandon, a French middleweight, intervened and tried to resolve misunderstandings. Paulino's answer took the reverse path. Sidky Bey, placed at the door as if standing guard, offered no help. He could speak French and English but abstained from helping and said nothing while watching the situation transpire.

"He can keep on going at top speed all day long," Murray Gitlitz said in awe. "He tires us all out, but he never gets tired himself."

The reporter, Holmes, got his interview, and they told him about Paulino's upbringing in the Basque Pyrenees Mountains with his family. Paulino told the reporter of his aspirations to bring the heavyweight title back to his Basque homeland. He told him he worked as a butcher. He chopped wood as a diversion, and it served to build strength. He was a good bullfighter, he told the reporter, but chose the boxing ring over the bullring. He shook hands with his seven brothers, kissed his two sisters, packed his bag, and said good-bye. He then met Arthus and agreed to a business deal. Within a year, he was a Basque boxing hero. The next year, most of Europe knew his name. He only lost one bout and that was to Australian George Cook in London, inferring the decision was biased. He and Arthus decided to come to America in the quest of the heavyweight title. Paulino smiled and said through the series of interpreters that none of his bouts in America was tough. As Gitlitz told everyone in English, laughter erupted.

"And don't think he doesn't mean it," Gitlitz said. "You couldn't hurt him if you hit him over the head with a church. I've thrown my hardest right hand swings at him, and he doesn't even blink. Just smiles a bit and keeps on plugging right along."

Gandon and Mickey Davis, Paulino's other sparring partners, agreed. The interview ended, and Thomas Holmes said Paulino was a hero at Bey's Training Camp and the entire Spanish colony of New York.[19]

The fight with Johnny Risko, in front of 15,000 at Madison Square Garden on November 25, 1927, needed no interpretation. Risko won the first three rounds against a lethargic opponent. Paulino started an attack to the body in the fourth that had Risko holding for the first time. Risko then won the fifth with Paulino winning the sixth and seventh, while the eighth was even. Risko won the final two rounds beating Paulino and spoiling his ambition of a title.[20]

In 1927, many other boxing's greats came to Madame Bey's Camp. The highly regarded trainer Ray Arcel brought his charges Phil "KO" Kaplan and Ace the "Nebraska Wildcat" Hudkins to Madame Bey's Camp in May 1927. Arcel trained Kaplan for his ten-round battle with George Courtney at Ebbet's Field on June 8. He readied Hudkins for his welterweight fight against Al Mello at Queensboro Stadium on June 1.[21]

Arcel was born in Terre Haute, Indiana, on August 30, 1899. He would train twenty-two world champions in his career. He wanted fighters who were smart. He taught his charges values in addition to boxing. As a child, his family moved from Indiana, and he was raised in New York's East Harlem. He said they were the only Jewish family.

"Because of that, as a kid, I was in a fight every day," Arcel said.[22]

Under Arcel, Hudkins defeated Al Mello. He returned to Bey's to train for his next fight at the Polo Grounds against Sergeant Sammy Baker. Hudkins trained at Bey's with lightweight Billy the "Fargo Express" Petrolle,[23] who appeared on the cover of the May issue of *The Ring* magazine that year. Petrolle would appear on the cover three times in his career—May 1927, March 1931, and May 1932. In attendance for the Hudkins-Baker fight was Charles Lindberg,[24] who had just become the first to cross the Atlantic by airplane the previous month. Hudkins lost due to a bad cut received during the fight above his eye. He beat Baker the following month in a rematch.

Joe Dundee trained at Bey's in May for his welterweight championship fight against Pete Latzo.[25] On June 3 at the Polo Grounds, Joe Dundee won the title in a fifteen-round decision. At the end, Latzo was battered and bruised—a beaten champion—while Dundee bore hardly a mark. Phil Kaplan lost on the undercard.

Other fighters in 1927 at Bey's included Jackie Fields, Johnny Green, Henny Goldberg, Charlie Rosen, and Walter Hogan. They all arrived in May.[26] In September, lightweight Hilario Martinez prepared for one of Bey's early boys, Sid Terris.[27] Martinez said to his manager at Bey's Camp, "… you can go and bet that if I get him down there, he will stay put. He'll never get back up, if I drop him."[28] Martinez won by a decision. Many of the sparring partners were professional boxers who fought that year from Bey's Camp.

Madame Bey's son, Rustem, turned twenty-nine years old in 1927. He showed no interest in the prizefighting business though he had physical traits of a boxer. Technically born on Turkish soil in the embassy in Washington, DC, he became a naturalized American citizen. Rustem was a strong, powerful man. Embarking upon a professional career, Rustem went to the Dental College in New York for half a year but later decided that he did not want to be a dentist. In March 1920, he started in the billing department of the H. & D. Folsom Arms Company in New York City. Then he sold equipment for the company to police departments in New Jersey, and Westchester and Nassau Counties in New York. In 1927, Rustem was appointed as a special police officer under Township Police Chief Herbert L. Rowe. He would serve the Chatham Township for the rest of his life. People would start calling him Russ instead of Rustem.[29] Rustem married Mildred High, who came from New Providence across the Passaic River from Chatham Township. They would have two children—Muriel, born in 1925, and Bette Ann, born later in 1929.

CHAPTER 18

A Winning Streak

In February 1928, the camp was full of top professional fighters and the grounds blanketed in white. It was Madame Bey's friend and business partner, Ehsan Karadag, who had the job of removing the snow. There were always willing fighters to help. Ehsan said when the world light heavyweight champion Mike McTigue was at camp, he would ever be there with a shovel.[1] For the fighters' early morning roadwork, they would wear overshoes, sometimes having to traverse through snowdrifts. They did their work no matter the conditions. There were fights for which to prepare.

The camp prospered so much that before the decade ended, Madame Bey hired additional help. She employed the help of Luther Coleman, a young man in his early twenties from Virginia,[2] and she still had handymen Ehsan and Tom Finnegan.

Madame Bey started 1928 with her two European boys, Andre Routis and Paulino Uzcudun, still making their home at her camp. They were still on their quest for a championship. Spanish welterweight Hilario Martinez and Chilean lightweight Luis Vincentini joined them in February.[3] They were good boxers but lacked the talent of Paulino and Routis. Paulino was enough of a draw that he was making money but lost key bouts that kept him from a championship. Routis had a disappointing 1927 where he lost four of his ten fights with one draw but was gaining form by the year's end.

Gene Tunney would never train at Bey's again. He held the world heavyweight title after defeating Jack Dempsey twice and Tom Heeney in July, but when he announced his retirement after the Heeney fight, the heavyweight title was vacant. That left Tex Rickard in the position to determine a method to award the vacated world heavyweight championship.

Tex Rickard, who ruled boxing by his undeniable success at promoting fights, devised a plan in 1928 to crown the new heavyweight champion. He intended to arrange a series of elimination matches with the winner to fight Jack Dempsey. Although Dempsey had announced his retirement, he hinted at a comeback.

Rickard wrote an article for *The Ring* magazine that year.

"Jack Dempsey has decided to make a determined effort to the championship. … there are thousands of fight fans throughout the world who feel that Jack Dempsey is the uncrowned world's heavyweight champion."[4]

Rickard planned to match Jack Dempsey against the winner of his heavyweight elimination bouts.

Rickard ranked fighters in each boxing weight division by whom he thought was the best, not always being the titleholder. In each weight division, he further divided the fighters into classes. Class one contained the top contenders. Classes two and three contained the next tier of contenders. In the heavyweight division, Rickard considered Gene Tunney and Jack Dempsey the only two deserving to be in class one, although both were retired. In class two, he placed Jack Sharkey, Boston; Young Stribling, Atlanta; Paulino Uzcudun, Spain. In class three, he placed Tom Heeney, New Zealand; Jimmy Maloney, Boston; Johnny Risko, Cleveland; George Godfrey, Philadelphia; Paul Scott, England.[5]

Of those heavyweights he ranked, Chatham Township had hosted, at some time, Jack Dempsey, Gene Tunney, Young Stribling, Paulino Uzcudun, Jack Sharkey, and George Godfrey. For each of the other weight divisions where Rickard ranked his top contenders, many would use Bey's as their camp at some point.

To show the impact of Chatham Township and Madame Bey's Camp—just over five years after it had opened for business—at the end of 1928, you needed to look no further than *The Ring* magazine's ranking of each of boxing's weight classes. Many champions listed, and many of their opponents, trained at Bey's at some point in their careers.

Like Rickard's heavyweight rankings, for 1928, *The Ring* magazine had the title vacant with the retirement of Gene Tunney. Four contenders in the division had all trained in Chatham Township. They were Jack Sharkey, Young Stribling, George Godfrey, and Paulino Uzcudun. In the other weight divisions' rankings, many trained at Bey's during their careers. They were light heavyweight champion Tommy Loughran, middleweight champion Mickey Walker, welterweight champion Joe Dundee, junior welterweight champion Mushy Callahan, junior lightweight champion Tod Morgan, and featherweight champion Andre Routis. Seven champions from the ten weight class divisions trained at Bey's at some time. This would not be an unusual occurrence for the camp. The five years before 1928, and the many years that followed, saw the same caliber of boxers. The champions and their foes would be a constant in the deep woods of New Jersey preparing, in earnest, for battle.

Many of her boys left behind signed pictures that would hang on the gymnasium's rough walls. In 1928, she had signed pictures from many famous boxers.[6] They included Gene the "Fighting Marine" Tunney, world heavyweight champion; Paulino the "Basque Woodchopper" Uzcudun, the best heavyweight ever from Spain; Martinez Gibbons; Mickey "Toy Bulldog" Walker, world middleweight champion, world welterweight champion, and heavyweight contender; Eddie "Cannonball" Martin, world bantamweight champion; Charles Rosen; Phil "KO" Kaplan, contender in the middleweight division; Sid Terris, lightweight division contender; Ace the "Nebraska Wildcat" Hudkins, fought in the lightweight through heavyweight divisions losing twice in championship middleweight titles and becoming California's heavyweight champion and that state's most popular boxer in the 1920s; Romero Rojas, an insignificant Chilean heavyweight but did beat world heavyweight champion Jack Sharkey early in his career; Felix Sportiello, not a celebrated fighter but fought two losing efforts for the French light heavyweight title; Mike McTigue, Irish-born world light heavyweight champion; Andre Routis, world featherweight champion; Tod Morgan, world junior lightweight champion, California lightweight champion, and Australian lightweight champion; Battling the "Singular Senegalese" Siki, the colorful Senegalese who held the world light heavyweight championship; Pancho Villa, first Asian/Filipino world champion and named flyweight fighter of the century by the Associated Press; Benny the "Ghetto Wizard" Leonard, world lightweight and welterweight champion making over $1,000,000 in his career before his first retirement in 1925; Paul the "Astoria Assassin" Berlenbach, world light heavyweight champion, and dozens of others. Throughout the upcoming decades, dozens more would join others on the walls. Such names as James "Cinderella Man" Braddock, world heavyweight champion; Red Burman, who fought a losing effort to Joe Louis for the heavyweight championship; Tony Canzoneri, five-time world champion and the second boxer to win world titles in three weight divisions—world junior welterweight champion, world lightweight champion, and world featherweight champion.

Not appearing on *The Ring* magazine's list, or Tex Rickard's list, was a little-known twenty-two-year-old German heavyweight. He had achieved recognition in his country by winning the European light heavyweight title in 1927 at the age of twenty-one. In 1928, he won the German heavyweight title. He went unnoticed in the America, except by the most ardent of boxing followers. Paul Gallico, *New York Daily News* columnist, could read German newspapers.[7] He saw the potential in the young German fighter. Tex Rickard made the German an offer to fight on the Tunney-Heeney undercard, which he declined.[8] Under the advice of others and his own ambitions, the German went to America at the age of twenty-two. He sought bigger fights and larger purses. He would be smart, hit hard, become controversial, and expose the kindness in Madame Bey, who would pay for his early American stay. Max Schmeling would arrive in America.

CHAPTER 19

My Max

Maximillian Adolf Otto Siegfried Schmeling was born on September 28, 1905, in Klein Luckow, Germany. At the height of his career, he stood six foot one and weighed a little over 190 pounds. He looked rugged with raven-black hair and eyebrows. It earned him the nickname the Black Uhlan of the Rhine. Manager Joe Jacobs gave him the colorful ring name.

He would become close to Madame Bey when he came to America. Though Bey knew many languages, German was not one of them. She soon learned it from Schmeling and added it to her repertories of spoken languages. She would teach him English. In addition to Schmeling's native language of German, he knew enough French to converse. French was a language Madame Bey knew. Like Madame Bey's polished emerald, Gene Tunney, Schmeling was an avid reader.

"I wonder what they will think when I say that I not only like to read good books, but paint pictures, too," Schmeling said. "It is fine recreation, putting people and scenes down on canvas in colors. However, I am not so very good at it and will stick to fighting."[1]

His penchant to read and paint was something fans and journalists never understood in a prizefighter. He was not criticized for it, as was Gene Tunney.

His interest in boxing became clear on July 2, 1921, when at fifteen years old standing outside a newspaper office in Cologne, he followed the Jack Dempsey versus Georges Carpentier fight as it crossed the wire from the United States. Schmeling idolized Dempsey and rooted for him. He went many times to watch the fight in theaters. He begged his father to pay for boxing lessons. His father relented and bought a used pair of gloves that Schmeling hung over his bed.[2]

In 1924, when Schmeling was nineteen years old, he talked to a coworker.

"Max, what are you doing tonight?"

"Nothing," Schmeling answered. "I have no money to spend foolishly on theaters."

"Come with me. We will go to the athletic club and see the fights."

It was the first time Schmeling saw a live boxing match inside a ring. His interest in boxing grew that night. He was offered to fight as an amateur a short time later at the Sports Club Colonia in Muelheim, Germany. His opponent was an experienced city amateur champion. For the first few rounds, Schmeling was hit all over his body.

"Then he hit me a hard blow," Schmeling said. "It hurt, and I became angry. I hit back as hard as I could. The blow I struck, friends later told me, was a right cross. The other fellow fell to the floor and did not rise again. He was knocked out."[3]

Schmeling discovered his boxing punch, more powerful than an ordinary man, was a right cross. It would be his most potent weapon throughout his career. Schmeling had his first taste of victory. He now understood the exhilaration of winning. Once experienced, and adrenaline is pumping, you want more and the euphoria that it creates. It is a feeling like no other. It is only satisfied by another win at greater stakes.

On August 2, 1924, Schmeling became a professional boxer when he fought Hans Czapp. He won that fight and thirteen of his first fourteen bouts. Something more inspiring to Schmeling than becoming a professional was about to happen—a meeting with Jack Dempsey.

Jack Dempsey came to Cologne, Germany, in 1925. Promoters gave him $7,500 for a three-day appearance in the city. The reason for Dempsey's visit was three one-round exhibitions with three German boxers. Schmeling was one chosen. He would get into the ring with his idol and the world heavyweight champion.

"My greatest thrill—climbing through the ropes to meet the greatest fighter of all time—Jack Dempsey," Schmeling said. "I shall never forget that afternoon."

Schmeling saw Dempsey mobbed by admiring fans. They brought him over to see Schmeling and told him he was one of the men he was to box. In German, Schmeling told Dempsey he was pleased to meet him. Dempsey climbed into the ring, and Schmeling watched as Dempsey fought other boxers. Then Schmeling's turn came. Though just an exhibition, Schmeling threw a hard right into Dempsey's elbow. At this point, Dempsey's competitive spirit awoke. No longer was it a simple exhibition match. Dempsey transformed into a devastating fighting machine. The young and inexperienced Schmeling was unprepared for what Dempsey was to unleash upon him.

"Dempsey's smile vanished," Schmeling said. "His lips curled back. His eyes dilated. I heard a snarl as he tore at me with a fury I have never seen in a man before. The next instant a left hook smashed against my ribs. I thought that rocky fist had crashed through and snapped my spine. My side was ablaze with pain. The bell rang. Oh, how wonderful it sounded! I was certainly happy the short bout was over. Dempsey was smiling again when we shook hands."

That night, at Dempsey's invitation, Schmeling went to the hotel where Dempsey was staying. He told him to "train hard, live cleanly, and keep fit even when you're not training for a fight, and you will be a great boxer someday."[4]

The impact should not be underestimated when an athlete with the stature of Jack Dempsey bestows on a younger athlete advice and accolades. Schmeling had talent. Now he had the incentive to develop that talent. Schmeling wanted what he saw in Dempsey.

"His fine clothes, his wealth, the great reception given this foreign fighter by my own people fired my ambition. I must go to America!" Schmeling recalled.[5]

The young Schmeling took his advice. He lived a clean life and did not indulge in alcohol. When Schmeling met Dempsey in the United States years later, he reminded him what he had told him as a youngster. Dempsey laughed and told him that is what he told all the young fighters.[6] Whether sincere or not, it inspired the youthful Schmeling.

Schmeling met another American heavyweight while Dempsey was in Germany. Bud Gorman was touring Europe. Gorman told Schmeling about a camp in American run by a woman in the countryside. He recommended Madame Bey's to him if he should come to America.[7]

Three years after Schmeling turned professional, he won the European light heavyweight championship in 1927. He became the first German to attain the achievement. He found himself a celebrity among the German elite. Just eleven days after winning that title, he made his first trip outside of Germany. He attended a middleweight world championship bout in London. It was Madame Bey's lionhearted little Mickey Walker against Tommy Milligan. Walker Destroyed Milligan. The fierce, relentless style of Walker made an impression on Schmeling, as did the high-society audience that attended.

Schmeling was soon a celebrity in the Weimar Republic of Germany in Berlin. It was a time where race, color, sexual preference, and religion had no bearing on affiliations. This was in sharp contrast with what was on the horizon under the Third Reich of Adolf Hitler. Schmeling was a star in the cosmopolitan atmosphere where actors, artists, and writers gathered nightly. They were fascinated to have a prizefighter of his stature among them. He made many friends with this exclusive society. Artists and sculptors used him as a model for their works.[8]

Though he was famous in Europe by 1928, he went unnoticed in America with a few exceptions. American promoter Tex Rickard took note of his boxing skills with interest and invited him to America to fight. Rickard sent Schmeling a telegram offering him a fight on the undercard of the Tunney versus Heeney heavyweight championship bout for $6,000 with travel costs paid. Schmeling declined the offer.[9] He had just won the German heavyweight championship with a victory over Franz Denier on April 4, 1928. By winning the fight, he held three titles—the European light heavyweight championship, German light heavyweight championship, and German heavyweight championship. During the Denier fight, Schmeling broke his left thumb, for which German doctors prescribed rest. His manager, Arthur Bulow, told him they should go to America.

With no boxing prospects, on May 28, 1928, at the age of twenty-two, Max Schmeling disembarked from the ocean liner *New York* onto American soil with his manager, Arthur Bulow. Their goal was to participate in American boxing for fame and fortune. If he thought he would be as famous as in Germany, he was mistaken. America was dismissive or uninterested in his European accomplishments. He would have to build a new reputation in America.

"1928 saw the realization of one of my greatest dreams," Schmeling said after coming to the United States. "My broken hand, smashed in the Franz Denier fight, was still in such bad condition that I would not be able to fight for some time to come. So, it was not with the intention of immediately meeting American boxers that Bulow and I came here so early. I wanted to become acclimated."[10]

Schmeling and Bulow stayed in New York. Schmeling found that living in New York was expensive, and his money was becoming depleted. Being a German and European champion did not help him obtain fights in the United Sates. Americans did not have high esteem for European fighters. They saw many hyped foreign fighters with good records fail in America. They thought Schmeling was no different. The best the newspapers would write about him was that he looked like Jack Dempsey. The facial similarities were stunning. Later, because of the likeness, they referred to him as the German Jack Dempsey.

Schmeling was broke financially and physically and had no place to stay. He could not fight for a living while his hand was broken and had no means to repair it properly. The American dream he had heard about was looking bleak. There was that camp that Bud Gorman had recommended to him in Europe. It would change his fortunes.

Schmeling became frustrated, and his relationship with his manager, Bulow, became strained. If it had not been for the charity of one person, he might have remained a broken man and returned home without showing America his abilities. That one person was Madame Bey. One day Max Schmeling appeared on her doorstep with no means of payment to stay. When Madame Bey had no money, her boys paid for the building of her boxing camp. Max Schmeling was welcomed.

"He was unknown," Madame Bey said, "and all the papers would say about him was that he looked like Dempsey. Besides that, he had quarreled with his manager, who was a countryman of his but couldn't get any fights for him, and so he came to ask my advice."

Madame Bey gave Schmeling and Bulow each a single room for no charge.

"Machon introduced me to Madame Bey—the exalted wife of the retired Turkish ambassador—who had a training camp in Summit, New Jersey," Schmeling recalled in his autobiography.[9]

"That was not an easy time for me," Schmeling said. "I was lonesome. I didn't have any money, and I didn't feel very good. I couldn't speak English, and I couldn't understand what the people around me were saying. It was all strange to me, this country, and many nights I wished I had not come here."[11]

Uzcudun and Routis were at Madame Bey's when Schmeling arrived. Schmeling and Uzcudun knew each other in Europe before either came to America. It was not one of admiration. Schmeling's European popularity was on the rise to which Uzcudun scoffed. Their feud continued while both trained at Bey's Camp. It was different with Andre Routis. The two became good friends. Schmeling knew enough French to converse, and the two grew close. Routis, along with Madame Bey, were indispensable to Schmeling in learning the ways of American boxing.

Andre Routis's manager, Joe Jacobs, came to Madame Bey's to see Routis. Through Andre Routis, Jacobs met Max Schmeling.

"After the work was over," Jacobs recalled about Routis's introduction of Schmeling, "he called to a large, dark, solemn-featured man, and said, 'This is Max Schmeling, Joe, the German heavyweight.'

"I nodded briefly—I had met fighters before," Jacobs continued. "I little realized the drama of those few moments then. I had heard of Schmeling and his extraordinary physical likeness to Jack Dempsey, but he hadn't fought in America."[12]

Schmeling began his training regimen. After using his left hand, it was apparent the thumb had not healed despite the rest. Madame Bey recommended a specialist, the New York sports surgeon Dr. W. G. Fralick. He was the doctor that most high-profile boxers would use when confronting an injury. Not only did Madame Bey allow Schmeling to stay without paying, but also she gave him the money to get his busted hand fixed.

Schmeling went to Dr. W. G. Fralick and had the hand X-rayed and corrected. Fralick operated on the hand and removed a small bone splinter that had caused the hand to become inflamed.[13] The rest that Schmeling's previous doctors had prescribed would never have fixed the problem. A few days later, Schmeling returned for a follow-up visit. While he was there, he met another boxer—Jack Sharkey.[9] It was a chance meeting of future foes.

After a while, Schmeling was back to full training for a fight that did not exist but felt strong and returned to his training routine. On July 26, Schmeling paused from training at Bey's Camp. He went to New York with Bulow and Machon to watch the Tunney-Heeney fight at Yankee Stadium[14]—the fight card that Schmeling was invited to fight in by Rickard.

Schmeling's manager, Arthur Bulow, was still ineffective at getting a fight in America. Bulow, who arranged fights in Europe, could not duplicate the effort in their new country. It did not help that the last heavyweight championship fight between Tunney and Heeney was a financial disaster. It made promoters cautious. The press called the fight the Headache of the Century.[13]

"Max was moody and very quiet," Madame Bey recalled, "and he was worried about the money he owed for his keep. But I told him to forget it until he was on top. He used to smile rather sadly when I said that …"

"Stay," she said, "stay as long as you wish. Some day you will be a champion, and you will remember me then."[15]

The kindness she showed Schmeling was a practice Madame Bey would continue. If a young fighter approached her, or an old, broken-down fighter making a comeback, she would make accommodations if they had no means of support. She did expect something in return. There were plenty of chores needed done on the premises for them to earn their keep. If a boxer could pay or did not make alternate arrangements ahead of time, Madame Bey did not exempt him from the bill. She would not be taken advantage of by her boxers. She demonstrated this in 1930 when she instituted legal action against heavyweight Frank the "Madison Butcher Boy" Montagna, who was in her camp when Schmeling was there. District Court Judge Edward A. Quayle awarded her a judgment of $432.10 for training expenses, room, and board, for the time Montagna trained at Madame Bey's Camp.[16]

Madame Bey had faith in the German.

"He was a dispirited boy about ready to give up and go home," Madame Bey said, "but I suggested that Joe Jacobs was a pretty smart fellow and maybe could do something for him."[15]

Schmeling asked his friend and fellow boxer Andre Routis for advice. Routis gave Schmeling the same advice that Madame Bey had given him.

While the Schmeling team toiled trying to get a fight, Routis and his manager, Joe Jacobs, were fighting their way to the featherweight division title. In his last six fights, he had five wins and one draw. That gave him a chance at the featherweight title. It would be against Tony Canzoneri, the man he had lost to in a close decision two years before.

Routis was training hard for the bout at Bey's Camp. Writer Roscoe McGowen when at Bey's said Routis would not look natural if he was not sporting a black eye.[17] Bey's boys trained hard, and sparring took its toll on their faces and bodies. For the last two weeks leading to the fight, Routis went four rounds every day with a lightweight countryman Benny the "French Flash" Valgar.[18] A Ray Arcel trainee, Valgar, was a featherweight in 1920. He had a title fight against champion Johnny Kilbane. The fight was a newspaper fight. Valgar won the newspaper decision decisively but did not knock Kilbane out. That was not enough to claim the title.

After spending a little over two years at Bey's preparing for a championship match, on September 28, 1928, Routis received his opportunity. He met Tony Canzoneri for the second time at Madison Square Garden before 10,000 fight fans. Throughout the first half of the fight, Routis, hopelessly outclassed, was knocked down once in the opening round and badly battered. He started outfighting Canzoneri in the eighth round. Canzoneri fatigued under Routis's persistent onslaught and lost the commanding lead he once held. The enthusiastic crowd, the largest in a while, watched one of the most remarkable ends to a fight. It was a close decision, but Routis won the verdict. It was one of the most savage fights ever waged for the featherweight title.[19] Routis achieved his goal—he was the world featherweight champion.

The win gave his manager, Joe Jacobs, two current world titleholders. Jacobs managed world flyweight champion Frankie Genaro, whom Jacobs also had training at Bey's Camp.

"Genaro was a wonderful little boxer who could give and take a punch," Jacobs said. "With his swarming style, he was the nearest thing to Harry Greb that I've ever seen. He had a heart bigger than himself, and he would go on fighting till he dropped dead."[12]

If Schmeling had not yet been convinced a manager switch to Jacobs would be advantages, his adept handling of Routis and managing two current world champions would leave him no doubt.

Bulow heard about Schmeling's disenchantment and his consideration of making Jacobs his manager. He started looking for fights with more urgency. He went to see promoter Tex Rickard, still considered the best promoter in the business. After all, Rickard had offered them a fight, which they declined, on the Tunney-Heeney undercard. Rickard must still want him? Bulow was seeking a fight at Madison Square Garden, considered the fountain of gold by prizefighters. Rickard had no problem with foreign European fighters, as long as they had a following. He had been successful when promoting them in the past. Fights with an international flare meant large gates and followings from other continents. The fights had meant million-dollar gates in the past. Rickard listened to Bulow's pitch.

"Yeah?" Rickard told him in his drawl, "I expect I kin use him somewhere. But, right now I don't see a spot. Come Back."[13]

Bulow was getting deeper in debt and considered selling Schmeling's contract. If he thought trying to get a fight was hard, he found trying to unload the contract more difficult. Marty Forkins, an above-average manager, who had had a middleweight contender, offered $17,500 for the contract. The deal faltered when Forkins declined to provide an extra $7,500 for a $25,000 total.[13] Doc Kearns, Dempsey's former manager and Mickey Walker's current manager, also balked at a deal.

"If Gaines and Daniels licked him, he can't be much," Kearns reasoned.[13]

Gains and Daniels were fighters of lesser merit.

Bulow did not speak much English, which compounded the difficulty in getting Schmeling a fight. Schmeling knew he was trying but also knew he was not succeeding.

"Bulow began to haunt the office of Tex Rickard at Madison Square Garden," Schmeling said. "He asked again and again a place for me in one of the Madison Square Garden's boxing shows, but always was turned down."[10]

"Can't you get him a fight, Joe?" Routis asked Jacobs. "Things aren't going too well with him, and I know he'll make good."

"Eventually, I agreed to see about it," Jacobs recalled, "and I pulled a few strings to get Schmeling matched with Joe Monte, a fair to middle heavyweight.

"At this period, I hadn't the slightest idea of managing him, and it was only to please Andre that I bothered at all."[12]

That was the break Schmeling needed. Bulow negotiated the match. Madison Square Garden boxing matchmaker, Thomas McArdle, arranged the bout for Schmeling. McArdle matched him against Joseph Monte, a heavyweight considered hard to knock out. McArdle figured Monte would knock out Schmeling, ridding him of the German. Schmeling knew this, and it gave him added incentive.

"Finally, Thomas McArdle, the Garden matchmaker," Schmeling said, "consented, and arranged a fight between Joseph Monte, a Boston fighter, and me. Monte was considered a hard man to defeat, and McArdle probably thought he would knock me out and thus dispense with me, a troublesome German fellow once and for all."[10]

If Bulow had thought he had fallen back into good favors with Schmeling, he was mistaken. Schmeling was angry about the deal signed for $1,000. It was much less than the $6,000 offered from Rickard previously.

"They could not seem to hit it off and Max was getting nowhere," Jacobs recalled. "Madame Bey told me it was one continuous scrap between the pair."[20]

When asked about the night he climbed into the ring with Monte in the Garden and was he nervous?

"Nervous?" he repeated.

"No, not exactly nervous. But I—well, there was the language again. I did not know what they were saying around me, and what was going to happen. But when I got in the ring, and the fight was ready to start, I was all right; I knew what to do then, all right"[11]

On November 23, 1928, Schmeling made his American debut at Madison Square Garden. Tex Rickard watched from a front-row seat. Schmeling knocked Monte out in the eighth round with a right cross. Behind him at ringside, he could hear the usually reserved Tex Rickard jump up thumping his cane on the floor, amazed at the power in his right hand.

"That feller is great!" Rickard yelled while chewing on his cigar. "I ain't seen nothing like him since Dempsey!"[21]

The German was not going away. Rickard had another foreign menace for the American boxing scene.

Schmeling returned to Bey's Camp. Other managers may not have wanted Schmeling, but it was clear that Jacobs now did. After several weeks and the advice of Madame Bey and Andre Routis, Schmeling made Joe Jacobs his manager and signed a contract with him. It earned Joe Jacobs the nickname of Yussel the Muscle, Yussel being a Yiddish word for Joseph. Muscle, because he muscled in to take Schmeling away from his current manager, Bulow. Jacobs saw something special in Schmeling and worked for no fee until Schmeling's contract with Bulow expired.[22] Schmeling's next fight was not hard to get with his stunning defeat of Monte. It would be against the blond-haired Joseph Sekyra of Dayton, Ohio, on January 4, 1929, at Madison Square Garden.

While Schmeling trained at Bey's for his second fight in America, Tex Rickard arrived in Miami Beach on December 28. He was there to arrange one of his heavyweight elimination bouts between Jack Sharkey and Young Stribling and discuss with Jack Dempsey his proposed comeback. Early on New Year's Day, he complained of pains, and the doctors rushed him to Allison Hospital for an emergency operation. On New Year's night of 1929, Tex Rickard was operated on and his appendix removed. The next day, he showed signs of a quick recovery. Despite the early optimism of the doctors, Rickard's health deteriorated.[23]

While Rickard lay on his hospital bed, his condition worsening, the Schmeling-Sekyra bout was held as planned in Rickard's Madison Square Garden. Schmeling won a unanimous decision. The crowd of 14,000 at the Garden cheered the verdict. The unknown German was gaining popularity. The Garden saw demand for the German. The *New York Time's* journalist James P. Dawson wrote, "Schmeling left the ring after giving the throng a reminder of what Jack Dempsey was in his earlier days as a fighter."[24]

The day after Schmeling's second win in America, the hospital where Rickard still lay ill released a bulletin at midnight.

"Practically the same condition existed tonight as this afternoon. Mr. Rickard's resistance was possibly slightly lower. His temperature remained at 103, and his pulse had increased from 132 at 4 p.m. to 140 at this time." Signed Dr. E. H. Adkins.

The hospital allowed Dempsey, who had arrived in Palm Beach, to see Rickard for a moment. When he left the hospital, he said the promoter told him, "'Jack, I've got this fight licked.'"

Before lapsing into a coma from which he never rallied, he turned to his wife and friends who gathered at his bedside with the assertion that he was "getting a tough break, but I'll fight." Then he grasped the hand of his wife and in a concerned, feeble voice inquired about his eight-year-old daughter, Maxine. When told that Maxine was all right and wanted her father to get well, Rickard said, "Help me over this, sweetheart, I'm fighting my …" He did not finish the sentence, and in two hours[25] the man who was not just associated with boxing, he was boxing, was dead at fifty-nine.

The body of Tex Rickard came to New York in a great $15,000 bronze casket.[26] Jack Dempsey and Walter Fields, brother of comedic actor W. C. Fields, were among the pallbearers.[27] The casket lay in state at Madison Square Garden, "Rickard's own Temple to *Fistiana*,"[28] where Schmeling had fought just days before. Huge crowds came to pay their last respects.

"My sympathy goes out to Mr. Rickard's family," Gene Tunney said from a vacation spot. "I feel his death keenly as one of his myriad of friends. The world of sport has undoubtedly lost a genius. There probably never will be another promoter so capable of stirring the public interest. It might truly be said that whatever his hands touched turned to gold."[29]

"My best pal is gone!" Jack Dempsey said. "Quietly and nobly he slipped away. His greatest fight was lost … Ten minutes before the end Tex opened his eyes. His hand lay in mine. … His eyes carried the message that meant only one thing. He knew then that the battle was over … For twelve years Tex was my loyal friend."[30]

With the death of Rickard died any thought that Jack Dempsey would make a comeback.

"The secret pact that we had made ended with his tragic passing," Dempsey said. "My conditional promise to fight again so that he might perhaps realize his final ambition of 'Just one more million dollar gate' is automatically shattered."[31]

Rickard's planned match between Sharkey and Stribling occurred on February 27, 1929, at Flamingo Park, Miami Beach, Florida. Sharkey won the ten round decision.

Rickard died one of the wealthiest men in sports. His estate was estimated at $2,000,000.[27] For a man who started with nothing from the Missouri plains, it was a sizable sum. The New York Trust Company, executer, refused to divulge the exact amount. The will provided for his widow, daughter, mother-in-law, sisters, nieces, nephews, and a cousin of his first wife. His estate included properties in Boston, Miami Beach, South America, securities in South American corporations, the Cattle Company of Paraguay, and brokerage accounts and bank accounts in New York and Florida.[32]

Promoters thought to take Rickard's place were Humbert Fugazy, Jim Mullen, Jimmy Johnston, and Paddy Harmen.[33] None would obtain the stature of Rickard, but one man who had worked closely with Rickard in his biggest promotions would wield the power in boxing that Rickard had. He would not get involved in boxing promotion for another five years. When he did, it would be with absolute power. Mike Jacobs would be a man who would rival Rickard's accomplishments.

Once again, Schmeling returned to Bey's after the Sekyra fight. The feud between Schmeling and Uzcudun reached a climax when a group of photographers from New

York newspapers arrived at Bey's after Schmeling defeated Sekyra. Uzcudun thought the photographers were coming for him. He spent time that day making himself presentable. He came outside ready to pose for the photographers when one approached him to inform him that they were there for Max Schmeling.

"That broke Paulino's heart," Joe Jacobs recalled. "He had to stand aside and watch a couple of hundred of pictures taken of Maxie. Paulino never got over that. The next day he refused to even recognize Schmeling, and since that time the two have never spoken."[34]

Schmeling's next fight came on January 21, 1929, seventeen days after defeating Sekyra. It was against Pietro Corri at Laurel Garden in Newark, New Jersey. Corri had a losing record, and it showed. Prior to the crowd getting a chance to realize what was happening, Corri charged out of his corner and was stopped by a left. They sparred for half a minute before Corri charged again. Another left straightened him, and then Schmeling threw his powerful right into Corri's jaw. Corri went down, and the referee counted him out at one minute, two seconds of the first round of a scheduled ten-round fight.[35] It was Schmeling's third American victory in as many starts.

In late January 1929, Max Schmeling returned to Bey's to train for his next fight. He would fight Cleveland's Rubber Man Johnny Risko. He was the man who had the ability to absorb much punishment in the ring. The last few years, he defeated prominent heavyweights Jack Delaney, Paulino Uzcudun, Jack Sharkey, and George Godfrey. He would be Schmeling's toughest opponent to date. It did not instill confidence in Schmeling when his friends told him Risko could not be knocked out.

"'He was tireless,'" Schmeling said they told him. "'He had a hard punch. He was very smart. He was one of the strongest men in the ring. In fact, it was sad that so early in my career I must meet and be defeated by this fellow.'"[36]

Schmeling trained with rigor. He knew this fight would determine his position in the heavyweight division. "Max," Schmeling said to himself, "this is the Franz Denier fight all over again. If Risko beats me, I may as well take the next boat home to Hamburg. If I beat him, I will become as famous and as popular over here as I became in Europe."[10]

The crowds were increasing in size at Madame Bey's to watch the German prepare for the Johnny Risko match. The once unknown Schmeling had a growing following, and now they knew he had potential. The deluge of people was making training difficult. Madame Bey developed a solution at Schmeling's suggestion—she prohibited fans from coming to her camp, only allowing reporters, photographers, and friends. Her reason for the drastic step was "too much hero worshipping." Joe Jacobs and Doc Casey, Schmeling's American trainer, concurred with the decision.[37]

On February 1, 1929, Schmeling met Risko in front of a crowd of 20,000 at Madison Square Garden. Schmeling climbed into the ring amidst the cheering crowd. He forgot his managerial problems, eager to fight.

"After they had pulled the stool from beneath me," Schmeling recalled, "I stood in my corner, my back to Risko, pulling the ropes and shuffling my feet as I had seen American fighters do. I tried to appear unconcerned. The bell rang, and I rushed at Risko. His first blow told me: 'Max, here is a fight.' And it was. For the first five rounds, Risko gave me the hardest fight of my career."[36]

In the first round, Schmeling put Risko on the canvas with that hard right of his, something only one opponent had done before. Risko got up without a count from the referee. In the seventh round, Schmeling hit the Rubber Man so hard he went down a second time. He did it again in the eighth. In the ninth, he sent him down for the count.

"I was getting set for the knockout," Schmeling said, "when referee Arthur Donovan stopped the fight to save Risko from the disgrace of being knocked insensible. Donovan raised my hand and in all my life, I do not believe I heard such cheering. I was a hero! The crowd applauded me as though I was one of their own. It was a wonderful feeling."[36]

The Ring magazine called it the fight of the year. Schmeling was now a heavyweight contender with this victory and one of the best foreign heavyweights the American ring had seen during recent years. Now, everyone wanted Schmeling.

The next day, his friends who had told him he did not have a chance started calling him a champion, telling him he would soon win the crown.[36] Writers and photographers flocked around Schmeling as he went to manager Joe Jacobs's office. The German ambassador, Baron von Prittwitz, gave a reception for Schmeling. For a man no one noticed when he arrived in America, everyone now wanted his life story and as many pictures as they could take. On this day, he arrived in America.

With Schmeling's stunning victory over Risko, his managerial problems exacerbated. Bulow signed for fights and had no problem getting them for the in-demand Schmeling. He agreed with promoter Humberto Fugazy to have Schmeling meet Phil Scott. Bulow sold contract percentages to some men in New York who liked investing in fighters. Schmeling refused to accept any more bouts under Bulow's direction.[38] Schmeling; Joe Jacobs, his manager; Max Machon, his trainer; John S. Hammond, director of Madison Square Garden affairs; and Tom McArdle, Madison Square Garden boxing matchmaker came to an understanding that Madison Square Garden, which shunned Schmeling earlier, would get exclusive rights to his fights.[39] Schmeling considered Jacobs his manager, but the Bulow obstacle remained with fourteen months left on the contract.

"If I wasn't satisfied with Jacobs, I wouldn't be here now. He has guided me satisfactorily since we became associated, and I see no reason for ending our association, regardless of whether I am successful in breaking my contract with Bulow while at home. I know others will be after me and are after me now. But I'm satisfied to go along the way I have been going with Jacobs."[40]

From four fights in America, Schmeling received $23,000. That did not include the money withheld because of the ongoing dispute over his managerial predicament. Schmeling could have trained anywhere after his last fight with Risko. He chose to return to the person who gave him a home when he had nothing. He returned to his good friend Madame Bey, from whom he no longer needed charity. During his stay, he made plans to return to Germany for a while. When asked if he had a girlfriend in Germany, he replied:

"Yes, my mother will be glad to see me. She's my girl."[40]

Schmeling sailed for home just over two weeks after the Risko victory. Jacobs, Machon, Herman Herse, his middleweight sparring partner, and a cousin Albert Fuchs boarded the *Deutschland* of the Hamburg-American Line with him. In sharp contrast to his arrival in America, a great many of his recently uncovered followers arrived to watch his departure. Among them was Schmeling's close friend, to whom he had owed much of his success— Madame Bey. Her astute language teaching was clear when Schmeling spoke with the press. He asked the American public, in respectable English with a German accent, not to forget him as he waved good-bye. In testament to how far he had come in American boxing, Walter St. Denis, representing Madison Square Garden, Doc Casey, his trainer in America with Machon, and Doctor Alex Schiff, representing the Boxing Commission, came for his departure.[41]

Upon his arrival in Germany, people greeted him by the thousands. He now knew how Jack Dempsey felt in Germany when he received the same admiration. He told his manager, Joe Jacobs, he planned to stay in Germany until October of the following year. That was when his contract with manager Arthur Bulow would expire. After spending only a few weeks in Germany, on April 30, 1929, he boarded the SS *Reliance* to the surprise of many to journey back to America via Montreal, Canada.[42] The American boxing scene beckoned.

Upon his arrival in Montreal, he met with Madison Square Garden President William F. Carey, Joe Jacobs, and representatives of the Hearst Milk Fund. The meeting was held on May 10 to discuss a proposed fight with the Spaniard Paulino Uzcudun. The proposal was for them to fight in New York on June 27. The match was set as proposed.

Schmeling returned to Bey's after his business in Montreal. There was one problem— Paulino was still there training. The animosity between the two fighters grew as both trained at Madame Bey's for their bout. Uzcudun treated Schmeling with disdain. He would not eat at the same table with him. When their paths crossed on the grounds, Uzcudun would look the other way. Although Uzcudun ignored Schmeling, he did not do the same. Schmeling took every opportunity at Bey's to study Uzcudun's boxing style to find weaknesses.[34]

"Paulino is a fighter with a set and fixed style," Joe Jacobs said. "What he does in one round you may be sure he will do in the next. You can take it from me that Schmeling has got his number and will make a monkey of him when they meet at Yankee Stadium on June 27."[34]

As late as May 26, the two were still at Bey's training for their Yankee Stadium bout a month away. That was about to change. Though both started their training at Bey's, neither would stay. Schmeling went to train at a camp in Lakewood, New Jersey. About the same time, Paulino went to a camp in Hoosic Falls, New York. Both fighters made their final preparations at those camps. As with Tunney, others dictated where the two trained. Again, Madame Bey understood it as the business of boxing.

Much of Schmeling's money from previous fights had gone to paying debts. More was held by the New York Athletic Commission because of Schmeling's managerial entanglements, but still he had enough to buy a new car. While training at the Lakewood camp, he brought an Italian made Lancia automobile.

The feud between the two European heavyweight prizefighters came to public view on American soil at Yankee Stadium on June 27, 1929. In attendance were Jack Sharkey, top heavyweight contender after defeating Young Stribling earlier in the year; Tommy Loughran, world light heavyweight champion; and James Braddock, who would fight, and lose, to Loughran for the world light heavyweight title on July 18.

Ringside seats cost fifty dollars, and the total receipts that night amounted to $378,000. From the proceeds, 40 percent went to the fighters. The Hearst Milk Fund also took a share. A crowd of 45,000[43] came to watch Madame Bey's Max fight her rough diamond. Many more listened to the fight over the radio. The Europeans, especially those in Germany and Spain, listened to the round-by-round descriptions. Cuba, with its heavy Spanish population, assembled the greatest bulletin-board crowd in Cuba's history. They wagered $100,000 on their fellow Spaniard. More than 250,000 received the Associated Press description broadcast by radio from the Havana newspaper *Diario de la Marina*.[44]

The thirty-one-year-old Paulino was no match for the younger Schmeling. He was so bloodied, swollen, and bruised by the fifteenth and final round that referee Arthur Donovan asked, "Are you all right? Can you go?"[43] Paulino gave a nod as any warrior would, and the fight went the distance. The decision was a unanimous one for Schmeling. It established him as the top contender to challenge for the world heavyweight championship vacated by Gene Tunney.

The Germans hailed Schmeling as a hero. There was no shortage of admiration in German newspapers for their fellow citizen. His mother's phone never ceased ringing, prompting her to say, "Now I know what it means to be the mother of a famous son." One of the calls was from Max asking her if she was "glad" and if the German people greeted the decision with enthusiasm. For Paulino, Spain accepted the results with surprise, rationalizing the loss by saying, "Anyhow, our Paulino made a good fight and was not knocked out."[44]

Schmeling, undefeated in America, had arrived at this point with his hard right and tactical boxing skills, knowing that Madame Bey had afforded him the opportunity. Through her generosity and guidance toward the correct medical treatment of his broken hand, and advising him of a managerial change, he had achieved this height. It would be another year before Schmeling would fight again. That would be against the man he had first encountered in Dr. Fralick's office when he had his hand repaired—Jack Sharkey. The bout would determine the world heavyweight champion.

With Max Schmeling gone from the camp, the headline boxer would be Madame Bey's lionhearted little Mickey. In July 1929, Mickey Walker returned. Having lost the welterweight title, he returned with a new title. He had moved up in weight class and was now the world middleweight champion, having defeated Jock Malone in June 1928. In his last fight, he had risen in weight class again to fight for the light heavyweight championship against Tommy Loughran.

The Walker-Loughran bout took place on March 28, 1928, in the new $7,000,000 Chicago Stadium in front of a crowd of over 20,000. Loughran fought well. Walker had a chance in the fifth round when he hit Loughran with a right cross to the jaw. Loughran survived the round and then took control of the fight. Walker lost the split decision with Loughran retaining his light heavyweight title. Loughran obtained the verdict of the two judges, Eddie Klein and Phil Collins. The referee, Davey Miller, chose Walker.[45]

Under the terms of the contract signed by Loughran, he received 55 percent or approximately $67,000. Out of that amount, Loughran was required to pay Walker $50,000 and $13,000 to Leo Lomski and Tuffy Griffith, two men who fought on the undercard. That left Loughran and his manager with $4,000, which also went to pay their expenses.[46] Walker's hiring of Doc Kearns made him look smarter every fight.

Walker returned to Bey's to prepare for his next fight with Leo Lonski. He had his obligatory publicity photograph while at Bey's Camp. Huck Finn was gone; now he was seen in casual clothes feeding the Bey chickens that gave the fighters their early morning fresh eggs. The heading read, "It's Back to the Simple Life for Mickey Walker."[47]

On August 19 at Municipal Stadium, Philadelphia, Walker met Lomski. Until the fifth round, Lomski was superior, and in that round, he almost knocked Walker out. Then Walker performed a dramatic, courageous comeback and won the decision.

CHAPTER 20

A Heavyweight Title for Her Boy

As with his last fight with Paulino, Max Schmeling would not be training for his heavyweight title bout at Madame Bey's Camp. His manager, Joe Jacobs, sent him to Endicott, New York, to train. He would fight Jack Sharkey for the heavyweight championship.

Jack Sharkey was born Joseph Paul Zukauskas on October 6, 1902, in Binghamton, New York, but moved to Boston. It earned him the ring name the Boston Gob. He created his name based on his two idols—Jack Dempsey and Tom Sharkey. He was the son of Lithuanian immigrants. He had the distinction of being the only person to fight heavyweight champions Jack Dempsey and Joe Louis. He was ahead in the Dempsey fight but became careless in the sixth round, and Dempsey knocked him out. He had good boxing skills with decent power. He had an ego and was not shy about telling the press about his confidence in an upcoming fight. This was in contrast to the reserved and modest Schmeling. He was inconsistent, never able to put together a series of good bouts.[1]

Max Schmeling, the man few people knew when Madame Bey took him in with no money, was now at the top of the boxing world. The man she had consoled, financed, and paid to have injuries fixed was going to fight for the world heavyweight title. America knew him now. A New York State trooper stood guard at his Endicott camp entrance. Most fighters before a big fight just wanted to be alone. Schmeling was different. The trooper made sure uninvited guests did not wander onto the training facility. Reporter Ed Hughes interviewed him on the eve of the fight. Hughes did the best he could to capture Schmeling's words that he gave in English through his thick German accent. Hughes could not get Schmeling to talk derisively about his opponent. Schmeling, as any good athlete, exuded confidence.

"Yes, I will win," Schmeling stated.[2]

On June 12, 1930, in front of over 79,222 fight fans, the twenty-five-year-old Max Schmeling met Jack Sharkey at ten in the evening. Expected gate receipts were to be more than $750,000. The bout held at Yankee Stadium was the first heavyweight title match since Gene Tunney's victory over Tom Heeney on July 26, 1928, at the same venue.

Special trains arrived from Chicago, Cincinnati, Detroit, Scranton, Washington, DC, Boston, and other cities. Millions more listened to the radio. Twenty-five percent of the crowd were expected to be German or of German descent. Attendees included the last two heavyweight champions, Gene Tunney and Jack Dempsey; Paulino Uzcudun, the last person Schmeling fought; heavyweight Johnny Risko; twenty-eight-year-old actor Marlene Dietrich; and automobile businessman Walter Chrysler. Miss Carmen Ogden gave a ringside discussion of the fashions worn by high society attendees, a commonplace practice on red carpets today. About one thousand newspaper reporters were set with pencil and paper as others sent the news over the telegraph.[3, 4]

Sharkey, the better boxer, was superior to Schmeling through the first three rounds. Schmeling was a notoriously slow starter. In the fourth round's waning seconds, Sharkey bounced off the ropes and threw an unblocked left hook. It landed into the groin of Schmeling. He went down in a heap.

"Count him out! Count him out!" Sharkey's manager, Buckley, yelled toward the referee, Crowley.

Referee Jim Crowley looked confused. He started counting the withering Schmeling out. When he reached the count of six, the bell ending the round rang. Schmeling's handlers came to gather their fighter. One grabbed his arms, the other his legs. They carried him to his corner. Pandemonium ensued. Sharkey's manager, Buckley, implored Crowley to count Schmeling out as he sat on his stool in the corner.

"Don't let him bluff you!" Joe Jacobs snapped. "The blow was low!"[5]

Sharkey came over to Schmeling's corner. After a few seconds, Sharkey jumped off the canvas as he pounded his gloves together. He looked like a man in trouble as he walked away.[6] Crowley did not know what to do. One judge, Barnes, at ringside was adamant that the punch was below the belt. Crowley had no choice but to disqualify Sharkey. He told him in the middle of the ring. Schmeling was the world heavyweight champion on a foul. It was the first championship due to an infraction. He became the first non-American to win the heavyweight title since John Sullivan.

"I knew Schmeling was hit low," referee Crowley said, "but I hoped that he would get up and fight anyway. People paid almost three-quarters of a million dollars to see this fight. It was a shame to have it end in a foul. I knew Schmeling was hurt, but I thought he might want to continue."

"Do you blame him for not getting up?" someone asked the referee.

"I guess he was smart," he replied.

Joe Jacobs, his trademark black cigar stuck in one corner of his mouth, had a different view.

"Max was just beginning to fight. You can shake off a sock on the jaw, you know, but a low punch is something else again," he said.[7]

"It is up to the manager to see that his man gets a better than even break in such matters," Jacobs said of his boxing philosophy in later years, "because hundreds of thousands of dollars can hang on a single decision, and a fighter can be made or marred by a single verdict."[8]

"It is unfortunate for Schmeling, the victor, and Sharkey the loser, that it ended in a foul," Dempsey declared.[9]

"I guess it's just not in the cards for me to win the championship," Sharkey said after the fight.[10]

Each fighter received over $177,000. Sharkey's lifetime earnings surpassed $1 million. Schmeling's crossed over the one-quarter of a million mark.[3]

As soon as Schmeling won the fight, the press referred to him as the Low Blow Champion. When Schmeling recovered in the dressing room, he was despondent over the way he had won the bout. Joe Jacobs was not. He told him that he would have to beat the next opponent.[5] The New York State Boxing Commission did not have his name engraved on the Tunney-Muldoon Trophy for heavyweight champions. William Muldoon was the trainer of many champion boxers. He also served as the first New York State Boxing commissioner. Muldoon declared the blow by Sharkey was fair, while Tunney said it was a foul. The examining doctor found a distinctive spasm of the left side of Schmeling's scrotum. The doctor said, "Schmeling could not produce this condition unless he was hit low."[11]

Joe Jacobs and Max Schmeling were in no hurry to defend the title. The candidates were Stribling, Carnera, and a Sharkey rematch. Instead, they arranged a forty-city tour of America to stage exhibition bouts.[12] Not an original idea, Jack Dempsey, Freddie Welsh, and others did it in the past. It was a lucrative endeavor with no chance of losing the title. Joe Jacobs was trying to get everything organized with his other fighters, so he could join Schmeling on the tour.

In the middle of January 1931, while Schmeling was in Germany, the next world heavyweight championship bout was announced. Young Stribling would challenge. Under terms of the contract signed, Schmeling and Stribling would meet in a city selected ninety or more days before the match. The winner would defend the title against Primo Carnera in 1932. Representatives from the three heavyweights signed the contract with the Madison Square Corporation of Illinois, a New York Garden subsidiary.[13]

In the last week of January 1931, Schmeling returned to America. He had spent time in Germany after his win over Sharkey. He disembarked the ship with his trainer, Max Machon, fourteen pieces of luggage, and Cilly, a ten-month-old brown dachshund. The prior year, he brought a chest of cuckoo clocks as gifts. On this trip, they were absent. American customs gave him a hassle over the clocks the last time.[14]

"I am going to loaf around for a couple of days and then I will go to Madame Bey's and resume training so that I will be ready to start my exhibition tour on February 9," Schmeling stated after arriving.[15]

He stayed in a suite at the Commodore Hotel, New York. It was after midnight when he took questions from the press in his room. Everyone wanted to know his thoughts on Stribling.

"Stribling is a man who got plenty of lickings in his life. How old is he? He was about twenty-two when he met Berlenbach, and he'll never lose that beating," Schmeling said.

"And don't forget that Tuffy Griffiths just gave him a hard fight," cut in manager Joe Jacobs.[14]

With his title bout set and the tour near, Schmeling returned to his American roots. By February 1931, he was back at Madame Bey's Camp to get into condition. Madame Bey had her Max back. With the fame and money that came to an athlete like Schmeling befell unwanted accompaniments. Now a celebrity, he was a target, whether just or unjust, for lawsuits. On February 5, Max, his manager, Joe Jacobs, and some friends had just completed nine holes of golf at the Summit Golf Club. They were having lunch when deputy sheriffs disrupted the golf outing to serve a court order demanding Max to be taken into custody to post a bond of $10,000 for his attendance in a trial for a lawsuit. Joseph Rahl, twenty years old, a process server of New York, was suing Schmeling for $25,000, claiming he flung him down the stairs of a New York hotel when he attempted to serve papers in a different lawsuit. Rahl filed the suit in the Union County, New Jersey, Circuit Court. Max changed his clothes, and everyone preceded to Elizabeth, the county seat, for a bout in the New Jersey courts where before a Supreme Court commissioner, he posted the required bond.[16]

Lawsuits aside, at Bey's Camp, Schmeling trained with middleweight contender and future world middleweight titleholder Vince Dundee. Schmeling and Dundee were together most of the time and became friends.[17] Dundee was training for a bout against Englishman Len Harvey, the European middleweight champion.[18]

"Dundee was always a gentleman," Madame Bey recalled, "and one of the best *ringmen* I ever saw."

On February 13, Dundee won a twelve-round split decision at Madison Square Garden.

Schmeling's stay at Bey's was not a long one. His tour was a few days away.

"That is going to be a long tour," Schmeling said, "but after it is finished, I will go someplace and rest myself for maybe three weeks before I start training for the Stribling fight."[15]

After the tour, Schmeling trained in Conneaut Lake Park, Pennsylvania, for the Stribling heavyweight title bout. The fight was first scheduled in Chicago but changed to Cleveland. Stribling's camp in Geauga Lake, Ohio, was ninety-three miles away from Schmeling's camp.

Stribling, accompanied by a New York newspaperman, borrowed a friend's plane in Akron, Ohio. Stribling flew over his training camp and then proceeded to the Pennsylvania border and Schmeling's camp. Schmeling was in the ring sparring in the second round with George Panka of Pittsburgh when Stribling flew his plane overhead. The plane was not more than two hundred feet above the spectators as they gasped. He returned twice to repeat the bold feat and then hurried back to the Cleveland airport to receive a reprimand from his father.

"It seems that Stribling broke away from the apron strings," Nate Lewis said, a Stribling camp member. "He probably will do the same thing when he gets into the ring with Schmeling Friday."[19]

On July 3, 1931, the two met for the world heavyweight championship. Stribling was no longer the teenager that had come to Freddie Welsh's Long Hill Health Farm to train. He was twenty-six years old. Schmeling was less than a year younger. They fought at Cleveland's new Municipal Stadium on the shore of Lake Erie before an estimated 35,000 spectators. The disappointing crowd occupied a third of the big double-decked structure. The gate approximated at $323,000 was one of the smallest in heavyweight title history since the post-World War I boom days began. The depression that started in 1929 was affecting boxing.

Schmeling had Stribling bruised and bleeding in the last half of the fight. In the fifteenth and final round, Schmeling connected with his lethal right to Stribling's chin. Stribling went down and looked unable to rise but beat the count at nine while clutching onto the ropes. He appeared out on his feet. Schmeling dashed toward him while the crowd yelled, "Stop it!" With fifteen seconds left in the round, Stribling's father tossed in the towel. Referee George Blake stopped the fight, lifting Schmeling's arm in victory. It was a technical knockout in the fifteenth round for Schmeling. A boxer for the first time stopped Young Stribling. Schmeling was euphoric but brought the stunned Stribling to his corner.[20]

After the fight, Stribling said it was an injustice to stop the fight with fourteen seconds left. Stribling argued that Schmeling knocked him down only once, and he might have continued to the end. The Garden crowd, including his father, saw Stribling was in no state to continue, and another vicious hit could have caused a severe injury.[21] Boxing finally recognized Schmeling as the legitimate titleholder. *The Ring* magazine declared their bout the 1931 Fight of the Year. The New York State Boxing Commission finally had Schmeling's name engraved on the Tunney-Muldoon Trophy for heavyweight champions.

In August 1931, the man that Andre Routis had defeated to gain the featherweight title was looking for a place to train. The Brooklyn-born Italian, Tony Canzoneri, had risen in weight class to the lightweight division after the Routis fight. After losing to Kid Berg and Billy Petrolle a year before, boxing considered Canzoneri finished. He showed that his slump was temporary. On November 19, 1930, Canzoneri won the world lightweight title over Al Singer with a first-round knockout. Then he won the world junior welterweight championship by a third-round knockout of Jack "Kid" Berg on April 24, 1931. He held the two titles simultaneously. In an era of excellent fighters with only ten weight classes and one champion in each, Canzoneri became the second person to win titles in three divisions and the first person since Bob Fitzsimmons in the nineteenth century. Canzoneri was just twenty-two years old. Before his career ended, he would win five titles. He was the featherweight, twice lightweight, and twice junior welterweight world champion. Many called him the best pound-for-pound fighter of his era.

Canzoneri would train for a return title fight against Jack "Kid" Berg, where he would risk both his lightweight and junior welterweight titles. First, he planned on training in Massapequa Park, New York, where Jimmy McLarnin had just left. Canzoneri changed his mind. Next, he checked Poughkeepsie, New York. When he heard they were moving cattle to start a large dairy near the camp, he crossed that out. His old camp was in Orangeburg, New York, but the big heavyweight contender Primo Carnera was there, and they humorously said he took too much space. Jack Sharkey occupied Dr. Bier's in Pompton Lakes, New Jersey, so he did not want to go there either.[22] On August 30,[23] he chose to go where the man who had taken away his featherweight title, Andre Routis, had trained—Madame Bey's Camp.

His manager, Sammy Goldman, retained trainer Lou Fink. Gene Tunney used Fink for some of his greatest battles. His manager brought other fighters to help Canzoneri. He would have no trouble making weight; he was already below the limit. He did vigorous training to build more power.[24, 25]

Canzoneri's confidence was building as the Berg fight approached. Even before the Berg fight had commenced, he was planning his next succession of fights. With confidence, he told of his ambition for the first time on September 4 in an interview with the United Press at Bey's Camp. He gave them his plan for his upcoming fights.

"After I prove my right to the lightweight and junior welterweight titles which I now hold by beating Jack 'Kid' Berg at the Polo Grounds. Next Thursday, I'll be ready to meet Billy Petrolle, the only other serious contender for these titles," Canzoneri said. "Then I'd like to go back into the featherweight class and fight Kid Chocolate for the championship and take on Benny Bass for the junior lightweight crown. If I regain those titles, and I'm sure I can, I'll ask manager Goldman to get me a shot at welterweight champion Jack Thompson.

"I still can make the featherweight limit although I've been fighting among the lightweights ever since I lost the one hundred twenty-six pound title to Andre Routis in 1928. I weighed only one hundred twenty-nine pounds when I knocked out Berg at Chicago in April and I wasn't even trying to get down then. When I win the five titles, I'll be satisfied. I can't make the bantamweight limit and never will hold that title, although I got a draw in a championship fight with Bud Taylor when he held the title. And I guess the middleweights are a little too big for me unless I pick up a lot of pounds before I get too old to fight any more."[26, 27]

After one time at the camp, Canzoneri left Madame Bey a signed picture that summed up most boxers' feelings toward her. He inscribed it:

"To Madame Bey, a mother to boys from one of her boys. Tony Canzoneri."

On September 10, 1931, at the Polo Grounds before 18,000 thousand people, Canzoneri fought Berg. It was one of the year's largest crowds. The original venue changed from London, England, Berg's home country. Canzoneri sent Berg to the canvas in the first round for an eight count. A body punch sent him down again in the eighth. The obvious low blow had the 18,000 fans shouting protests.[28] With Schmeling winning the heavyweight title on a foul, the New York State Athletic Commission had instituted a new rule that a fighter could not win or lose on a foul. The rule did not matter as referee Haley counted over Berg as though Canzoneri sent him to the canvas by a legitimate blow. He beat the count. Berg staggered through the last five rounds as Canzoneri attacked his head and body. Berg never quit trying.[28] Canzoneri won a fifteen-round unanimous decision. The Associated Press scorecard gave Canzoneri an edge in ten rounds, with four for Berg, and one even.

A new Bey resident was about to arrive during the summer of 1931, the brilliant Cuban fighter Kid Chocolate. Others called him the Cuban Bon Bon. His real name was Eligio Sardiñas Montalvo. He was sleek in appearance. He had speed and could box and throw a hard punch. His manager, Luis Gutierrez, pronounced his name *Keed*. It reverberated through the press; columns would print the *Keed* when referring to him. Chocolate developed his hard left jab by studying films of Joe Gans in his Goldfield fight against Battling Nelson—Tex Rickard's first big promotion.

"We studied how Gans used his left hand. Then the *Keed* would go to the gym and practice throwing his left hand exactly as Gans did. Study pictures of Gans and the *Keed* and you'll see that Chocolate's left hand was just like Gans," Gutierrez said.[29]

Later, Sugar Ray Robinson studied Kid Chocolate's style. "Sugar Ray Robinson was an admirer of Kid Chocolate," Fausto Miranda said, a former Cuban journalist who covered many of Chocolate's fights. Sugar Ray Robinson, stated he never saw anyone box like Kid Chocolate.[30]

Kid Chocolate not only learned how to box by studying the films of the legends, he was "a living, breathing boxing instruction book," boxing film historian Mike Hunnicutt noted. "He had as many or more moves, feints, head, and body positions as any boxer who ever lived. He had more moves than any boxer I've ever seen on film. He is perhaps the one man aspiring boxers should study for all around boxing technique."

The *Keed* started his training for a title bout at the Dougherty's Camp in Leiperville, Pennsylvania. It was a scorching, oppressive July in 1931. Kid Chocolate went through a hard workout. He was hot and tired due to the unrelenting heat.

"Too hot," Kid Chocolate muttered.

Trainer and boxer decided the cool breezes at Madame Bey's would be less stifling.

"I don't care a hang about anything but having that boy in the best shape of his life," Gutierrez said. "There isn't any nourishment for the *Keed* in burning himself out under that blazing sun, and so we are going to Summit. That's all there is to it."

In July, he was at Bey's preparing for his world junior lightweight title bout against Benny Bass. He was attempting to become the first native Cuban to hold a world boxing title.

On July 10, four hundred fans came to Madame Bey's to watch Kid Chocolate train. He sparred with "Knockout" Johnny Alva, a rugged New York junior welterweight. Chocolate knocked Alva down with a right to the heart at the end of the second round. Alva was unable to continue. Chocolate also sparred with Eddie Reed of Philadelphia, Dave Adler of New York, Al Tedesco of New York, and Young Zazzarino while at the camp.[31]

On July 15, 1931, in Philadelphia at Baker Field, Kid Chocolate had little trouble defending against Bass's punches. Bass tried to pond the *Keed* in close, but Chocolate known for his boxing ability surprised all by outslugging Bass. Bass never went down but looked out on his feet. The referee, Leo Houck, saw enough and halted the bout at two minutes, fifty-eight seconds of the seventh round. Kid Chocolate was at pinnacle of boxing's 130-pound weight class with a title and sixty-two wins, three losses, and one draw. He became the first Cuban fighter to win a world boxing championship. The United Press printed, "Cuban Kid Chocolate, one of the finest boxers seen in the American ring during the past decade, today held the world's junior lightweight championship."[32]

Mickey Walker and his manager, Doc Kearns, planned to make an assault on the heavyweight division. They had set their goal for the world heavyweight championship in 1929. Walker surrendered his middleweight crown—he was undefeated while holding the middleweight title—to pursue the largest prize in boxing. Walker's diminutive size and weight compared to those he would fight showed the fearless nature of his character. Walker's goal was to fight the current heavyweight champion, Max Schmeling. The lower weight classes could not compare with the fame and money that could be earned with the heavyweight title. It was the ultimate prize in boxing. The press called it the million-dollar title because that was what the holder could expect to earn.

Walker trained at Bey's in January 1931 for a light heavyweight bout against Matt Adgie. Walker, despite being outweighed by ten pounds, knocked him out in the first round. He then won his next four fights, including his last two against Johnny Risko and Bearcat Wright. Both were heavyweights. Risko, at 194 pounds, outweighed Walker by over twenty-eight pounds. Wright, at 210 pounds, outweighed him by forty-two pounds. Walker lived up to his name, The Toy Bulldog, in those fights, winning both by a decision. He had won his last twenty-two fights. His next bout was against Jack Sharkey.

The press started using Madame Bey's name for Walker when articles for the upcoming fight with Sharkey referred to him as lionhearted little Mickey.[33] At first, Walker was to train at Madame Bey's,[34] but he went to Orangeburg, New York, instead. Sharkey trained at Dr. Bier's in Pompton Lakes, New Jersey. Dr. Joseph Bier, who had come to Madame Bey's to examine boxers' health for the New York Commission, was running a camp that was Bey's biggest competitor in New Jersey.

Sharkey outweighed the fearless Walker by twenty-nine pounds when they met at Ebbet's Field on July 22, 1931. The crowd was a larger than expected 32,000 paying $210,000. Walker took the fight to Sharkey early. Sharkey, toward the later rounds, was using fouls. Referee Donovan gave him repeated warnings. The crowd displayed its disapproval with jeers. If they had not been already, the crowd was now behind the smaller Walker, who no one thought had a chance against the larger Sharkey. At the end of the fight, Walker looked the more battered as blood coursed down from a gash above his right eyelid. The fight ended in a draw. The crowd believed Walker had won and expressed their anger.[35] Judge Kelley gave the decision to Sharkey, but referee Donovan gave the decision to Walker. Judge Charles F. Mathison called the contest a draw.

"Jimmy, who won?" a fan shouted as New York City Mayor James J. Walker was leaving the park.

"Jimmy Johnston, the promoter," the mayor replied without missing a beat.[33]

Kid Chocolate was scheduled to rise in class and attempt to take away Tony Canzoneri's two titles. Kid Chocolate would train at Bey's for two tune-up bouts before meeting Canzoneri.[36] He would knock out Buck Oliva in the second round on October 26 and win a unanimous decision over Lew Feldman on November 2. He won his previous eleven fights in 1931 before meeting Canzoneri. Neither Canzoneri nor Kid Chocolate would train at Bey's for their big bout.

The widow of Freddie Welsh gave his championship Lonsdale Belt to promoter Jimmy Johnston days before the bout. It was to be awarded to the winner. The boxers met on November 20 at Madison Square Garden. Kid Chocolate built an early lead over Canzoneri with a relentless onslaught. Toward the finish, Canzoneri mounted a comeback and won the tenth, eleventh, and twelfth rounds. Chocolate took two of the last three rounds but lost the decision. The crowd booed for ten minutes. It was one of the greatest lightweight championship fights.[37] If Canzoneri made the 130-pound limit for the bout, he would have been given Kid Chocolate's junior lightweight title and would have become the first four-division titleholder ever.

Also in 1931, Victorio Campolo, the heavyweight champion of Argentina, came to Madame Bey's with his brother Valentin to prepare for his Primo Carnera fight. The New York Sports Athletic Commission was attempting to create a new weight class. The fight would determine the first champion in the class the commission called the dreadnought division. It was for men above two hundred pounds.

Victorio Campolo was born in Reggio Calabria, Calabria, Italy. His hometown away from America was Quilmes, Buenos Aires, Argentina. He was a butcher in his father's meat shop in Argentina before becoming a professional boxer. Gustavo Leneve, Luis Guiterrez, and Jess McMahon managed him during his career.[38] He had an extraordinary reach, reported to be eighty-six inches.[39] The October 1931 issue of *The Ring* magazine featured him on the cover.

On a balmy, sunny, late November day, journalists and photographers came to Bey's to interview Campolo. He wore an orange sweater, grayish brown pants, and a dark blue beret. They discovered the 220-plus-pound Campolo with his legs wrapped around a branch of an oak tree. Smiling, he glanced and waved to the journalists and photographers. He described to them in broken English how he spent time, when not training, playing with the cows, chickens, and dogs dispersed around Bey's Camp. He also liked to read Spanish novels and listen to Latin music on a tin-horned phonograph. He told the reporters if he did not beat Carnera, he would devote himself to helping his brother Valentin in his boxing career. He sparred with several boxers, including his brother. The weather was sufficiently pleasant to train in the outdoor ring, but Campolo wanted to train in the indoor gymnasium. The reporters said he was using a left hook and no longer appeared "right hand crazy" as the press had referred to him.

Reporters asked Campolo about the fight. He explained how he would win, and it was the biggest fight of his career. Later, when the reporters were departing, one called to Campolo. He said that odds makers would most likely favor him over Carnera.

"I don't care," Campolo said with a shrug of his shoulders and a Spanish accent, "because I will win anyway."[40]

On November 16, Vittorio Campolo's younger brother, Valentin, won his second fight in as many attempts. Valentin would later fight for the South American heavyweight title three times, winning it once in the biggest fight of his career against Arturo Godoy. Godoy would take the title in their rematch, which was Valentin's next bout. Valentin would lose the last fight of his career against Buddy Baer in 1940.

On November 27, 1931, attendance was 12,000 at Madison Square Garden to determine the inaugural world dreadnaught champion. Carnera weighed 226.5 pounds, forty-two pounds more than Campolo. Carnera hurt Campolo in the second round and sent him to the canvas for the second time in the round. He did not get up until after referee Gunboat Smith, former white heavyweight boxing champion when Jack Johnson held the world title, counted ten. After rising, he went to his corner. Carnera had knocked Campolo out in the second round, becoming the first world dreadnought champion. The commission did not carry the weight class forward. Campolo would continue his boxing career with mixed success.

CHAPTER 21

Lionhearted Little Mickey Returns

On March 19, 1932, Mickey Walker's wife gave birth to a seven and a half pound boy. The proud dad said, "I hope we have another champion."[1] Mother and son would visit Mickey at Madame Bey's later in the year, but Walker's boxing schedule would prevent him from spending much time with his new family addition. Away from the ring, his social life and late-night exploits took much of his other time.

Madame Bey's lionhearted little Mickey returned to her Camp on April 4, 1932. Walker was there to train for his heavyweight fight with King Levinsky on April 29. Eleven days after the Levinsky bout, he was to fight Johnny Risko. The heavyweight contenders, in order, for Max Schmeling's title at the start of 1932 were Jack Sharkey, Ernie Schaaf, Primo Carnera, Mickey Walker, Max Baer, King Levinsky, Young Stribling, Steve Hamas, Tuffy Griffiths, and Paulino Uzcudun.[2] Walker at number four put him within reach of his goal of challenging for the heavyweight title.

Mickey Walker's last six fights were all in the heavyweight and light heavyweight divisions. Opponents outweighed him by as much as forty-two pounds. He won five and drew the one against Jack Sharkey. In his last fight on March 11, 1932, Walker defeated heavyweight Jimmy Mahoney by a second-round technical knockout in Salt Lake City, Utah. Walker knocked Mahoney down three times in the opening round. In the first minute of the second round, Mahoney hit the canvas two more times. Walker helped an unsteady Mahoney back to his corner. Referee Ira Dern stopped the contest.[3] That fight occurred three days after his fight against Jackie Williams in Denver, Colorado, which Walker won by a second-round knockout.

Promoter Jimmy Johnston visited Walker at Bey's to talk about a fight with Paulino Uzcudun, but no deal was made. Eight days before the Levinsky fight, Johnston sent his assistant, Sam McQuade, to Madame Bey's Camp. McQuade came to have Walker sign a contract to fight Paulino Uzcudun for a May 26 bout. After going three rounds each with three sparring partners, Walker signed.[4] Under the direction of his manager, Doc Kearns, he had three heavyweight bouts scheduled between April 29 and May 26. He was going to be busy for the next month trying to fulfill his goal to get a bout with Max Schmeling for the heavyweight title.

Walker's West Coast trainer, Teddy Hayes, was in California when Walker was preparing for Levinsky. Bloxham, his usual trainer, was engaged elsewhere. Chippy Grill was asked to train Walker for a short while at Bey's Camp. Chippy was a part-time trainer of boxers. His full-time job was training pedigree dogs. Pending permission from his canine clients, Chippy would accept the offer.[5] It was the first time he trained a human toy bulldog.

Walker met King Levinsky at Chicago Stadium on April 29, 1932. Levinsky had beaten some top heavyweights and had a record of forty-one wins, fifteen losses, and four draws. Walker was outweighed again, this time by twenty-three pounds. A few seconds before the first round ended, Levinsky dropped Walker with a left hook followed by a hard right to the head. He bounced off the canvas without taking a count. Still dazed after the bell, he walked to Levinsky's corner instead of his own. His courageousness carried him forward. He was more cautious the next few rounds. After the fourth, Walker used a succession of punishing body punches. He knocked Levinsky down in the seventh and proceeded to win a ten-round split decision. The crowd of 19,995 that paid $78,892 approved the verdict.[6, 7]

"… I almost fainted when Mickey walked out in the first round, and the Kingfish dropped him to the deck. But thereafter, Mickey wrapped it up," Kearns recalled.[8]

There was a postponement of Walker's next bout against Risko on the day of the fight. Walker said he had boils that made it impossible to fight.[9] Walker had beaten Risko two times before. The Levinsky fight was brutal, and Walker's team had spaced his fights aggressively. That meant his next fight would be against Paulino Uzcudun. Once again, he came to Madame Bey's for this fight. Paulino trained in Orangeburg, New York.[10]

While Walker was training for Paulino at Bey's, world junior lightweight champion Kid Chocolate was there training for Mike Sarko. A fight he won. The *Keed* had won his last six fights since losing to Canzoneri.

Walker was still having problems with his boils while training for Uzcudun. He had one removed from the back of his neck that left a hole over an inch in width. Walker refused to postpone the fight.

The Walker-Uzcudun fight took place at Madison Square Garden on May 26, 1932. The crowd was a disappointing 8,000. Walker, outweighed by thirty-seven pounds, fought with confidence and a hole in the back of his neck. Hits after the bell blemished the bout. Paulino had landed a left hook to the body just after the eighth-round bell. He dropped his hands and stepped back, when Walker threw a right, ripping Paulino's left eyebrow open. Walker hit the cut with his first punch in the ninth round. Blinded by blood that seeped into his eyes, Paulino could do little from then on. The punch after the bell in the eighth changed the sentiment of the crowd against Walker, who won the ten-round decision. The Garden crowd booed Walker as he left and cheered for Paulino. The victory did not enhance Walker's chances at the heavyweight title. The late hits played a major role in that.[11]

While Walker was training for Risko, a rematch took place between Max Schmeling and Jack Sharkey for the world heavyweight championship. Neither fighter prepared at Madame Bey's Camp. They fought on June 21, 1932, at the Madison Square Garden Bowl, Long Island City, New York, before 70,000 paying over $400,000. The fight was dull.[12] Neither put in an effort of a championship caliber. The judges were far apart on their scorecards. One judge voted for Schmeling ten to five, the other Sharkey eight to seven. The deciding vote by the referee, Ed Gunboat Smith, gave the split verdict to Sharkey, scoring it seven to three. Much of the crowd disapproved. People argued the result for a long time. The controversial decision caused the New York State Athletic Commission to bar all but boxing experts—sportswriters, referees, judges—from broadcasting descriptions of future matches.[13] After the fight, Joe Jacobs uttered his enduring quote.

"We was robbed!

"They stole the title from us!" he added.

Sharkey said that he would not fight again for a year. His next fight would occur in June 1933.

A championship fight with Schmeling was no longer a possibility for Walker. A Schmeling-Walker fight almost happened earlier in the year, but promoters said there was not enough interest. Walker's next bout was a rescheduled bout with Johnny Risko, the man Walker had beaten the last two times. The highly regarded Risko was the man that Schmeling beat, which made him known to Americans. Max Schmeling owned the only knockout against him that occurred in 1929.

On June 24, 1932, at Cleveland Stadium in front of a home crowd of 15,000, the Cleveland Rubber Man, Risko, won a unanimous twelve-round decision over Walker. Walker could not overcome the twenty-seven-pound advantage that Risko had. Walker went to the canvas and arose without a count, just as in the King Levinsky fight, but unlike that fight, he did not recover. Levinsky repeatedly forced Walker to the ropes. Both of Walker's eyes were bleeding after a ferocious finish by Risko.[14]

Despite the beating Walker took, he was back the following month to fight Italian heavyweight Salvatore Ruggirello. The Italian had a losing record. Ruggirello fought some of the best heavyweights in the last year. He fought Joe Sekyra, Young Stribling, and twice Ernie Schaff. They all resulted in losses. The fight appeared to be a confidence builder for Walker. He showed superiority despite a large height and weight disadvantage. Walker was seven inches shorter and was outweighed by thirty-six pounds. The fight took place on July 25, 1932, at Dreamland Park, Newark, New Jersey, scheduled for ten rounds. The crowd had not all settled into their seats before it was over. Walker needed one minute, ten seconds to dispatch Ruggirello. He used three punches. Two lefts to the body and one short right knocked Ruggirello down.[15] It was so quick that the New Jersey State Boxing Commission withheld both fighters' purses pending an investigation.[16] The purses were released the next day when the commission found no grounds for foul play. The commission gave Ruggirello a thirty-day suspension for "unsatisfactory performance."[17]

After the easy win over Ruggirello, Walker signed for the fight he wanted, but it no longer included the title he sought. He signed to fight Max Schmeling. The fight would take place on September 19. Jimmy Johnston, promoter and boxing director for Madison Square Garden, was responsible for the signing. It was in association with the interests of the Free Milk Fund for Babies, which would take a percentage of the gate for the charity. Mrs. William Randolph Hearst was chairperson. They would fight at the Garden's Long Island City Bowl.[18]

"Things began to look even better for us when he knocked off Paolino Uzcudun, the wood-chopping Basque, in New York," Kearns recalled. "But then, three days after Sharkey's decision over Schmeling to take the heavyweight title, we lost a decision to Johnny Risko in Cleveland. So I settled for a shot at the beaten Schmeling, figuring that if we whipped him, we'd get the Sharkey match."[8]

It would be Schmeling's first fight since losing the controversial decision, and the world title, to Jack Sharkey. Now both men who thought they had beaten Sharkey would face each other. Schmeling was to receive 40 percent of the gate. Walker would receive 15 percent despite Kearns requesting 22.5 percent. The official signing took place at the Hotel Forrest in New York City. Speculation was that the winner would face Sharkey for the heavyweight championship sometime in 1933. If Walker were to win, it would give him a chance to equal the record held by former heavyweight champion Bob Fitzsimmons of capturing three boxing titles. Fitzsimmons held titles for the middleweight, light heavyweight, and heavyweight. Walker had held the welterweight and middleweight titles.[19]

The fighters were two of Madame Bey's favorites. She did not disclose whether she preferred her lionhearted little Mickey or her Max. Mickey Walker got the advantage over Schmeling, who was still in Germany, and returned to Madame Bey's Camp. This would be his most important heavyweight fight. Walker had been training in Chatham Township with his trainer, Bill Bloxham, intermittently for nine years.[20] It was Walker's home when not in Rumson, New Jersey. At Madame Bey's for the Schmeling fight, he used rooms for his sparring partners, rubdown men, manager Doc Kearns, brother Joe Walker, and one just for his equipment.[21]

Schmeling decided to use Speculator, New York, to train. Speculator was where Gene Tunney had trained for many of his matches. After arriving in New York City from

Germany, he traveled to Speculator on August 29. Bill Osborne, who was in Speculator, sent an amphibious airplane to pick up Schmeling and his party.

The departure was to start from the end of West Ninety-Sixth Street. The aircraft taxied to the river for the takeoff when a wing hit a small boat. An examination showed that the damage was inconsequential. Shortly afterward, a fire started near the engine that was doused with fire extinguishers. The airplane was returned to the shore. They deserted the airplane for the railroad. After communicating with Osborne at Speculator, Schmeling boarded a train at three o'clock.[22] The man who put his life in jeopardy many times in the ring nearly became an early aviation statistic.

Walker started camp in the middle of August. He was going to put more work in for this fight than ever before. His manager, Doc Kearns, could not have been happier with the camp selection. He would boast about the advantages of the camp and that there was a terrific golf course two miles away. Walker and Kearns were avid golfers. They would play while training for a bout. Reporters liked the fact that Bey's Camp now had a wire room where they could dispatch their stories as fast as their fingers could type them.[20] No longer did they have to go to another town to wire their columns or send mimeographed copies by mail.

Walker followed his training program with rigor. He would awake early in the morning to do his roadwork. He followed that with ten rounds of work in the gymnasium. The work included calisthenics, shadowboxing, bag punching, and sparring.

For sparring partners, Walker used Johnny Indrisano of Boston, a welterweight who had fought four world champions; heavyweight Al Fay of Pittsburg, Pennsylvania, who fought on the Stribling-Schmeling card; and an unnamed burly-looking person Kearns picked up in Cleveland during the Risko fight. Walker would finish his days' workouts by working on his speed with Jimmy Donato, a bantamweight from Red Bank, New Jersey. Donato had a few professional fights, but they were meaningless bouts at local athletic clubs at the New Jersey Shore. He was mostly a sparring partner. Donato would gush over the wonderful treatment he said he received from Madame Bey. He claimed her food was the best tasting he ever had.[21]

Mickey Walker had never-ending energy. With taxing workouts, he still made time to work on his golf game. There was a golf course in nearby Short Hills. He played eighteen to forty-five holes every day. He would play with his brother Joe and manager, Doc Kearns.[21] Often he would work his golf game in between his morning roadwork and his late-afternoon sparring and gymnasium work.

Mickey Walker, hailing from New Jersey, was always a popular attraction at Madame Bey's Camp. For a matchup with Schmeling, admirers and the inquisitive streamed in greater numbers to watch Walker train and spar in the afternoons. They would sit on the terrace and hillside overlooking the outdoor ring as Walker went through his workouts. With five weeks of training planned and the crowds that were attending daily, sports journalists were certain that Walker would break all attendance records for the camp. One interested observer was Tony Polazzolo, the trainer of the current world heavyweight champion Jack Sharkey.

"Walker's style is very likely to lick Schmeling," Polazzolo declared. "It should be much easier for Mickey than it was for Sharkey. Mickey is shorter, is a pretty good weaver and a sweet left or right hooker. This is the type of fighter that should give Schmeling a heap of trouble.

"I thought at first that Walker started the grind a little too early, but after watching him sparring with such speedy fellows like Al Fay, heavyweight, and Johnny Indrisano Boston, middleweight, I changed my mind. He knows how to gait himself and no fighter who does that will leave his fight in the gymnasium."[23]

"Max Schmeling has never met a man possessed of such powerful body punching ability and relentlessness in attack as Mickey Walker," Doc Kearns said. "Mickey's style is ideal for Schmeling, and it won't surprise me in the least if the German yells 'quit' before the tenth round."[24]

Doc Kearns made an announcement in the first week of September. Walker was searching for forty men of differing styles and dimensions to help in preparation. When the word was released, aspiring fighters and other jobless men wanting to work inundated Madame Bey's Camp. Kearns assembled a group of sparring partners from the arrivals. Walker said after eight days of working on speed with lighter fighters, he was ready for as many big men they could lure to the camp. Walker would do everything he could to prepare for this bout. His concerns were speed and punching power. He wanted to hone his skills to perfection before the bout.[24]

In Walker's autobiography, he wrote that after having a case of champagne delivered to Madame Bey's Camp, golfing with Kearns, the two inebriated men jumped a picket fence, and Walker cut his forehead, opening a huge gash over his left eye.[25] The commission and the press reported the problem was that Walker was having boils again. Doc Kearns requested the fight be postponed after he said Walker had again developed a boil on his left arm that brought his training to a virtual halt. A doctor lanced the boil, and it needed time to heal. On September 11, Deputy Daniel H. Skilling of the State Athletic Commission visited Walker at Madame Bey's Camp. Promoter Jimmy Johnston, Dr. Vincent Nardiello of the commission's medical staff, and Edward C. Hoofnocker accompanied him. Johnston enlisted the services of Hoofnocker, who was a specialist.[26]

Jimmy Johnston agreed to reschedule the fight. Johnston announced a four-day postponement with the consent of Commissioner William Muldoon and Brigadier General John J. Phelen of the State Athletic Commission. The fight would be on September 23.[26, 27]

Walker became discouraged at the wasted hard training he had done to get into top shape and the prospect of more time of tough conditioning. He reached a peak and knew that it would be difficult to retain his form. When word arrived at Schmeling's camp, Joe Jacobs cried foul when told the boil story. He went to New York City to meet with Johnston to file a protest. He had designed Schmeling's schedule for him to be in peak condition for September 19, explained Jacobs. Johnston was sympathetic, but the new date stood.[27]

"I am astounded at the sale," Johnston said a few days after the bout was delayed. "The postponements haven't hurt the advance sale one bit. In fact, to be truthful, they have helped considerably. Only today, I received an order for fifty tickets from Chicago. Dr. J. P. O'Connell wired for twenty ringside tickets. There is also a good crowd coming from Speculator where Schmeling is training, too."[28]

As his wounds healed, Walker went back into the ring. He had what was left of the cut from the boil bandaged to prevent infection. The cut on the bridge of his nose and a gash on his left eye were hardly evident. He wore two patches on his face so as not to aggravate the face wounds. When he sat on his corner stool between rounds, Teddy Hayes smeared Vaseline on his face in excess. Walker did not accept the treatment willingly, squirming when the Vaseline was applied.[29]

Dr. Vincent Nardiella of the New York State Athletic Commission was staying at Madame Bey's Camp to examine Walker. He would tend to change the dressing for the boil every day.[30] For a fight of this caliber, the promoters, Garden, and commission wanted their investment protected. They did not want to stage a fight with an injured fighter. It was just as important to their investment in this fight as it was to stage a good exhibition for later fights. A one-sided fight would be disastrous for future marquee fights. They again postponed the fight because the doctor decided Walker needed more time. The new date was September 26. This time Walker objected.

"I'll be all right," Walker declared. "Let's get it over with."[30]

As the fight drew near, rumors were spreading that Walker had developed more boils and a further postponement persisted as a possibility. Dr. Vincent Nardiella dispelled the rumors by pronouncing Walker fit to fight. Both camps were getting an influx of journalists to get the fighters' perspective on the bout. Sports columnist Jack Kofoed, who had a column called "Thrills in Sports," spent the last few days at Madame Bey's Camp for Walker's training before the bout. Kofoed talked to Walker two days before the fight.

"I've got to lick this Schmeling. I've just got to," Walker said with conviction.

"Why?" Kofoed inquired.

"Well, it's on account of Doc Kearns. He thinks I'm going to win. He's told everybody I'm to win, and I don't want him to be embarrassed."

That exchange prompted Kofoed to write in his column, "There's an angle for you. The old fox Kearns used to drill the same idea into Jack Dempsey and the Man Mauler was fighting for his manager as well as himself. The old college spirit was evident all the way."[31]

As with Schmeling, it was unlike Walker to deride an opponent. Walker always had confidence in his ability to win. The only shred of doubt Walker exhibited was in an exchange with another reporter.

"Because Schmeling is strong and can take a punch a bit better than the majority of heavyweights, I look for a hard fight," Walker stated. "But I don't doubt my ability to whip the German. My only worry, if any, is that he may nail me."[32]

It was a concern well founded. Schmeling had the power of a heavyweight but the speed of one attributed to someone of a lower weight class.

Kearns was going to wager a sizable sum of money on Walker. It was as much psychological as it was on his conviction that Walker would win. Negativity in sports is an enemy. You still may not win, the opposing side has just as much positivity, but as soon as you doubt yourself and the team around you, all is lost. The best athletes understand this concept. Even in defeat, you must remain positive. Walker understood it. Kearns understood it. Their problem was not their own hesitation but on the other side. Max Schmeling and Joe Jacobs knew it just as well.

Walker had spent more than forty days of training—twenty-two days devoted to boxing. He had sparred 112 rounds and logged many miles of roadwork. Those that saw him before the postponement said he looked in the best shape of his life.[33] He had the confidence, and of those around him, that he could win. His training in the last three weeks lacked intensity. Some days he had foregone training altogether. Teddy Hayes, his trainer, had to try to keep him sharp the final few days.[34]

Walker recalled that he was unrecognizable as the same man. Flabby and not in shape, he neglected to train.[25] He would come into the ring against Max Schmeling weighing his heaviest ever. He had gained sixteen pounds since the postponement.

"Mickey or Max," that is what the newspapers professed. Kofoed, who had spent time with Walker, gave the advantage to the bigger Schmeling. He thought his size, power, and quickness would be too much to overcome, as did many others. He said he had seen too many others that appeared in outstanding form and "were certain of a win end up with smelling salts under their noses."[35] Columnist Willie Ratner thought the tenacious Walker would once again overcome the height and weight disadvantage. World heavyweight champion Jack Sharkey—who had accepted his invitation to the fight—had boxed both and gave the nod to Schmeling. Jack Dempsey, too, sided with Schmeling. He reasoned, "A good little man could not beat a good big man."

Bookmakers favored the twenty-six-year-old Schmeling over the thirty-one-year-old Walker. The bout would be the last to take place during the outdoor season. Schmeling was six and a half inches taller. He weighed twenty pounds more. He had a six-inch reach advantage. In every statistical category, Schmeling was bigger except for Walker's stocky thighs and thick wrists.[36] Walker could beat heavyweights with his superior speed and equal punching power. Schmeling was different. He had the speed and agility of a lighter class fighter wrapped in a heavyweight's body. He was a patient fighter waiting for the right opportunity. He viewed fights as marathons, not sprints. He would be in condition to go the distance if needed.

Before the fight began on September 26, 1932, in front of an estimated 60,000 fans, the announcer made introductions for heavyweights Jack Dempsey, Johnny Risko, Primo Carnera, other heavyweights, and welterweight Jimmy McLarnin. Walker stormed Schmeling from the start, hitting hard and often. It was clear early that Walker's blows, though many scored, were ineffective. At the end of the first round, Schmeling caught Walker with his lethal right that sent him to the canvas. Walker got up and charged Schmeling just as the bell sounded.[37, 38]

Schmeling let Walker exert his energy. His plan appeared to be to let Walker tire himself, evidenced by the fact that Schmeling did not throw punches even when an opening became available. As long as Walker ran around, Schmeling waited contently. Schmeling's plan worked to perfection. Walker won some early rounds, but by the seventh, he was spent. In the eighth round, Schmeling went to work with punishing blows. The openings foregone in the earlier rounds, he exploited with speed, precision, and power. He knocked Walker down twice with the right for counts of six and nine seconds. Walker's left eye swelled shut, and his right eye was cut. Blood gushed from wounds on his nose and mouth. A hard fight to watch, the crowd pleaded with the referee to stop it. They sensed the lionhearted little Mickey would fight until nothing was left of him. The onslaught of Schmeling's punches continued, but they were unable to knock Walker down for a ten count. At the bell, Walker staggered to his corner.[37, 38]

By the eighth round, while Walker might have been able to take it a little longer, Kearns could not. Doc Kearns notified referee Jack Denning to end the fight. For the first time since 1926, Walker did not finish a fight. Schmeling scored an eighth-round technical knockout.

"I guess this was one we couldn't win, Mick," Kearns said.

"Speak for yourself, Kearns," he said, spitting blood on the floor, "you threw in the sponge, not me."[39]

The fight was not broadcast.[36] Fortunately for Madame Bey, she would not hear the tremendous punishment her Max had inflicted on her lionhearted little Mickey. She would have to read about it in the paper.

Some writers blamed the loss on the structured system Kearns made Walker endure at Madame Bey's Camp. They said he looked chunky in the fight. He was at his heaviest weight of 174 pounds. No one mentioned his many successes at Bey's Camp in the previous nine years.

Walker decided to retire after the Schmeling fight. Walker had taken a bad beating. After a month, the restless Walker, wounds healed, decided to fight again. He would fight heavyweight Arthur De Kuh whom Walker had trained with at Bey's in July 1930.[40]

The press no longer considered Mickey Walker a contender in the heavyweight division after his dismantling by Max Schmeling. Walker took his frustration out on Arthur De Kuh at the end of 1932 on December 6. De Kuh had a record of forty-four wins, thirteen losses, and one draw. De Kuh weighed 223 pounds when he fought Walker at the Olympic Auditorium in Los Angeles, outweighing him by forty-eight pounds and standing eight inches taller. Walker knocked out the twenty-seven-year-old De Kuh in the first round. It would be De Kuh's next to last fight.

Walker still had the power to knock around the big men, just not the contenders. Walker would fight in the light heavyweight and middleweight classes for the rest of his career with mixed success. He fought a light heavyweight title fight against Maxie Rosenbloom in 1933 and lost by a decision. Kearns would part with Walker in 1934. Walker would continue to fight for another year before realizing his boxing career was over.

CHAPTER 22

Boxing Hits a Depression

The Great Depression in America affected boxing like any other business. America's unemployment rate reached 25 percent in 1933 from 3.2 percent in 1929. It meant people had less to spend on leisure. Promoters offered less money to fighters. Boxing offered people a diversion from their plight, but they came in lesser numbers to watch live matches. The million-dollar gates for the 1921 Dempsey-Carpentier, 1923 Dempsey-Firpo, 1926 Dempsey-Tunney, and the 1927 Dempsey-Tunney fights were in the past. There would be only five more through 1971.

Madame Bey's did not escape the Depression. Articles in newspapers did not mention her camp as often. In 1933, her clientele included champions but to a lesser degree than in the past. She had some top names in the lower weight classes, but the heavyweight contenders were training elsewhere.

Vince Dundee arrived at Madame Bey's in March 1933. He would fight Ben Jeby for the world middleweight title. He trained hard and did everything conceivable to realize a triumph.[1] If he won, he would be the second family member to claim a championship. Joe, his older brother, held the welterweight crown when he beat Pete Latzo—who won it from Mickey Walker in 1926—on June 3, 1927.

On March 17, 1933, they met at the Garden. The fight lacked championship quality. At the end, Jeby appeared to have received a beating. Dundee had outclassed him. In the opinion of boxing critics at ringside, Dundee deserved a unanimous decision and the title. Those that counted called it a draw. One judge voted for Jeby, the other for Dundee, while the referee declared the bout a draw. Jeby retained his title. The decision shocked the 12,000 fans in attendance.[2] Many columnists thought Dundee had won. Wilbur Wood, a week after the fight, expressed with sarcasm the unpopular decision.

"… Ben Jeby, middleweight champion, was married yesterday to Miss Evelyn Seidman … Maybe the officials who enabled Ben to get a draw in his recent bout with Vince Dundee knew about his coming marriage and adopted that means of making him a substantial wedding present."[3]

Dundee would win the title later in the year. Lou Brouillard defeated Jeby for the title in August. Vince Dundee took it from Brouillard in October.

The only heavyweight of note to appear at Bey's in 1933 was Don McCorkindale[4] of South Africa with a record of twenty-three wins, nine losses, and four draws. Many of his recent fights were in the United Kingdom. He would launch his American debut from Madame Bey's Camp. He lost his last fight in Spain on July 1, 1933, to Madame Bey's rough diamond—Paulino Uzcudun. McCorkindale, before that, had beaten the tough German Walter Neusel, albeit via a foul.

McCorkindale's debut at Madison Square Garden against Patsy Perroni on October 9, 1933 resulted in a win. One judge gave it to McCorkindale; the other made it a draw. The referee gave the deciding vote to McCorkindale. In his next fight, McCorkindale fought against heavyweight contender King Levinsky. Held in December at Chicago Stadium, Chicago, he was no match for Levinsky. McCorkindale hit the canvas four times in the first round, and once in the fourth, eighth, and tenth. McCorkindale retreated to the United Kingdom and never again fought in America.

Most of Tony Canzoneri's fights early in 1933 were out of the area. He won the world junior welterweight championship when he defeated Battling Shaw earlier in the year by a unanimous decision in May at Heinemann Park, New Orleans. He now held the junior welterweight and lightweight titles.

In June, for his next bout, just one month after winning the title from Shaw, Canzoneri fought Barney Ross at Chicago Stadium. Ross landed more punches with his sharp left jab and demonstrated a superb defense. Canzoneri hit harder and took the fight to Ross. The two judges' scores favored Ross, while the referee had it even. The fight was close. The *Chicago Tribune* reported, "The fight was razor-sharp close and was replete with action. No title fight in Chicago was better fought." Canzoneri lost both of his titles. The two men fought again in September at the Polo Grounds, New York. Ross won once more in a split decision. Canzoneri lost three rounds due to low blows.

Canzoneri beat Frankie Klick in his next fight. After that, he prepared at Madame Bey's Camp for another match against Kid Chocolate, who he had beaten by a decision. For his last fight against Barney Ross, Canzoneri spent over four weeks training. He had to stop and start during that time because he felt he was getting stale. Canzoneri would spend two weeks training at Bey's Camp. He said that amount of time would be right for him to be at his peak.[5]

Canzoneri employed a young, promising lightweight named Lou Ambers as a sparring partner at Bey's Camp.[6] Ambers had a record of twenty-five wins, no losses, and three draws. He would win his next fight three days after Canzoneri's battle with Kid Chocolate. The young Ambers would soon be known in boxing.

There were 12,000 attendees at Madison Square Garden on November 24, 1933. Despite the brevity of the fight, the press described it as the most spectacular lightweight battle since the night Benny Leonard stopped Richie Mitchell.[7] In the second round, Canzoneri strode back, measured his distance, and unleashed a devastating right that found Chocolate's chin. The blow left Chocolate senseless. He stiffened and collapsed headfirst. His body so rigid, he fell with his forehead hitting the canvas first. At a count of seven, he rolled over onto his back trying to get his legs under him. Still dazed at the count of nine, he tumbled onto his back. Referee Arthur Donovan completed the count at two minutes and thirty seconds of the second round. Canzoneri scored a second-round knockout. It was the first time the *Keed* had been knocked out, with a record of ninety-two wins, five losses, and one draw.

"I was in better shape this time than I was for the last fight with Ross," Canzoneri told reporters. "… Yes, I still think I can beat Ross and get the title back, and I hope I have earned another chance."[5]

After defeating Kid Chocolate, Canzoneri won a fight in Cleveland. Then he returned to Bey's to prepare for a bout with European lightweight champion Cleto Locatelli in December 1933. Locatelli was a man of Canzoneri's ancestry. He came from Italy with a record of sixty wins, eight losses, and six draws. This would be his American debut. It would be Canzoneri's fourth fight in a month.

Canzoneri fought an awkward, resilient Locatelli when they fought at Madison Square Garden on December 15. It began as an unexciting fight that turned into a scrap. Many thought Canzoneri should have kept his distance. Instead, he fought Locatelli in close and became reckless. In the ninth, Locatelli won the round. In the tenth and final round, Canzoneri out-boxed his opponent and won the fight by a unanimous decision. The decision did not appeal to the crowd of over 8,000. Locatelli admitted after the battle that Canzoneri deserved the decision. He blamed his defeat on Canzoneri's spectacular rally in the tenth.[8]

"I didn't think Canzoneri was as good as he is," Locatelli said in Italian to his manager and interpreter, Al Francis.[9]

After his fourth fight in a month, Canzoneri went to his farm in Marlboro, New York. He enjoyed a well-deserved rest until after the Christmas and New Year holidays. Negotiations occurred for a bout in Chicago with Sammy Fuller late in January.[9] Negotiators canceled those plans because Locatelli's valiant effort earned him a rematch at Madison Square Garden on February 2, 1934. On January 13, 1934, Canzoneri left his home in Marlboro and returned to Madame Bey's Camp.

Canzoneri started with ten days of light training, followed by training that was more strenuous. Canzoneri trained hard, determined to show a better effort against Locatelli, who trained at Saint Nicholas Gymnasium, New York. At Bey's Camp, Canzoneri voiced immense confidence to win by a convincing decision or a knockout.[10]

The Canzoneri-Locatelli rematch took place at the Garden, as planned, on February 2, 1934. Locatelli went down in the second and third rounds. Canzoneri would not make the same mistake he did in the first fight. Once he had the advantage, he coasted until the later rounds when he started to fight harder. Once again, Locatelli showed his toughness by enduring the twelve rounds. The announced decision of a draw brought jeers from the crowd of 5,000. It turned to laughter, as it was obvious that Canzoneri had defeated Locatelli. Pandemonium in the ring ensued as the judges showed bewilderment about the verdict. Then they withdrew the verdict—the first time in Garden history a boxing decision had changed—and awarded the victory to Canzoneri.[11]

After two more wins, Canzoneri was still unable to get the title chance against Ross he desired. Instead of Ross, he would fight against Frankie Klick, who had boxed Ross to a draw in his last fight for the junior lightweight title. Two fights before the Ross fight, Klick became the second person to knock out Kid Chocolate. Canzoneri started training, again, at Bey's Camp. Klick did his preparation at Dr. Bier's in Pompton Lakes, New Jersey.[12]

On June 28, 1934, the two met at Ebbet's Field in front of a crowd 12,000. Both went to the ring center and slugged each other from the beginning. Klick won the first two rounds, but Canzoneri took over in the third. In the fifth round, Klick's right eye swelled, blinding him in that eye. Canzoneri exploited his foe's handicap. In the sixth round, he hit Klick with a barrage of punches. Klick wobbled but never hit the canvas. By the ninth round, the referee stopped the fight. Klick was near defenseless because of his right eye.[13] Canzoneri scored a ninth-round technical knockout. Ross was to fight the winner but did not.

CHAPTER 23

Down in a Blaze

Chatham Township established the Long Hill Volunteer Fire Company on September 8, 1925, at Collins's Camp—the same camp used for training by boxers like Mickey Walker—with twenty-nine residents in attendance. In 1926, the town built a new firehouse at 495 River Road. This was across the street and down the road from Madame Bey's Camp. It was less than one-tenth of a mile away—a two-minute walking distance. In 1927, the fire department acquired their first truck, a 1927 Reo chemical truck. For the first few years, firefighters responded mostly to brush fires. The department issued all firefighters their own brush brooms. They carried them to all fires, using them to sweep out the flames.

The fire department used large metal rings to announce fires. The rings were made from decommissioned steam locomotive engines. They cut them to give a ringing sound when hit. Each had a sledgehammer hanging by them to hit the ring to summon the firefighters. There were two rings—one located at the River Road Fire House and the other at the intersection of River Road and Passaic Street.[1]

On November 12, 1934, in the dark early hours of the morning, a mass of flames cut through the night. Motorists discovered the fire about one thirty. Flames engulfed the two-story gymnasium, and the fire had spread to other buildings and set them ablaze. When firefighters arrived, the Beys were asleep. After waking them, the firefighters attempted to save the farmhouse, which was the only structure not on fire. The New Providence and Long Hill fire departments fought the blaze, the cause of which was undetermined.[2]

The gymnasium and other buildings of the training camp were completely lost. The loss was estimated at several thousand dollars. Madame Bey's home, and that of some of her boys, was the lone building saved. With no gymnasium, Madame Bey could not operate the camp. That would prove to be temporary.

A plaintive, distraught Madame Bey, through tears, attempted to talk.

"What I hated most was losing all those autographed pictures. I'll build a new gym," she stated.[3]

"The pictures of all my fighters were in there. I wouldn't have taken a million dollars for that collection. Some of the autographs were so sweet."[4]

The pictures represented her extended family of the past eleven years. Some left simple autographed photographs, while others left autographs with heartfelt wordings of appreciation toward Madame Bey. They plastered the gymnasium walls and told the story of her improbable success. They were from some of the best and toughest fighters. There were photographs autographed by Gene Tunney, Paul Berlenbach, Mickey Walker, Vince Dundee, and many others. Men who could knock you out with one punch always exposed their soft, human side to their beloved Madame Bey. The fighters expressed those sentiments in the photographs.

In April 1935, Madame Bey's Camp reopened with a new gymnasium. It was six months since the fire. Present was Stan Thomas, the brother of Freddie Welsh, without whom Madame Bey would not have gotten into the boxing game. Stan Thomas worked as a businessperson in neighboring Summit and owned a car dealership. Robert J. Murphy, the local Lackawanna Baseball League president and mentioned as the next state boxing commissioner, also attended. Murphy declared the camp one of the finest gymnasiums in the country. He said Madame Bey would need only to get one nationally known fighter at her establishment, and once the place was discovered, the fighters would keep coming.[5] Madame Bey could not rely on her past success. She needed to attract top-name boxers as she had done before the fire. It was clear by the last four months of 1935 that the camp had regained its favor with the top-ranked boxers. Once again, boxers swamped the new facilities wanting to train there. Reporters, photographers, and fans followed.

Heavyweight Two-Ton Tony Galento became one of the first men to come to the new camp. In early May, a few weeks after the facility reopened, Galento along with his new manager, Joe Jacobs, arrived.[6] It was a start. Not considered among the best heavyweights, he proved to be one of the hardest hitters. He had a devastating left hook.

Jacobs pointed out that Galento had knocked out Natie Brown and Red Barry in one round. Brown had gone the distance with the well-regarded young Joe Louis, and Barry had gone three rounds with Louis.[6] Galento was going to fight on the Max Baer-James Braddock world heavyweight championship undercard held on June 6 at the Madison Square Garden Bowl, Long Island.

Galento, one of the most colorful heavyweights ever to don trunks, was paired with one of the most colorful managers—Joe Jacobs. The two would make quite a pair in the years to come. Their antics were legendary, sometimes to the annoyance of promoters and commissioners. The outspoken, free-spirited Galento gave the appearance of disdain for the strict Madame Bey and her rules that governed the camp. Galento followed one set of rules that presided over his boxing and life—his own. Joe Jacobs brought most of his charges to Bey's with outstanding results. McTigue, Routis, Genaro, and Schmeling had all trained there for Jacobs and had won championships.

On June 13, 1935, at the Madison Square Garden Bowl, Long Island, all six bouts were contested in the heavyweight division. Galento garnered the second billing under the Baer-Braddock main event. Galento wasted no time dispensing with Anthony Ashrut with a first-round knockout. Following Galento, James "Cinderella Man" Braddock defeated Max Baer by a fifteen-round decision in Baer's first title defense since winning the title from Primo Carnera. Braddock's win was a large upset.

In August 1935, twenty-two-year-old Lou Salica came to Madame Bey's Camp. He used the camp to train for his bout against Sixto Escobar, the first Puerto Rico native to hold a world boxing title. It would be for the world bantamweight championship. Aside from Canzoneri and Al Roth in the heavier lightweight division, many considered Salica to have one of the hardest punches in the lighter weight classes.[7] His most powerful punch was a right hook, and he was difficult to hit. He was a fast, light, strategic boxer with a swift attack followed by immediate withdrawal. In his career, he won ninety-five of his one hundred amateur and professional victories by outpointing his opponents.

"Salica was a fine fighter," boxing historian Jerome Shochet said. "He beat top-notch people … he was fighting in a division that not many people pay attention to. There were, on the other hand, those times when he didn't duck. Once … he was caught with a punch that hit him so hard he doesn't actually remember it to this day."[8]

Salica was born Luigi Salica and raised in Bath Beach, Brooklyn. They called him the Bath Beach Slugger. He stood five feet four inches and weighed no more than 122 pounds. He parted his dark hair just to the left of the middle. He was twelfth in a family of twenty-one Salicas.[7] He quit school in the seventh grade. At fifteen, Salica met fourteen-year-old Grace Prince, his future wife. He won the 1932 Golden Gloves championship in the 112-pound class and a bronze medal in the 1932 Olympics. Salica and the other boxing medalists received a ticker tape parade in New York.

Because of his Olympic medal and professional boxing career, Salica was known in Los Angeles boxing circles and spent many hours at a boxing venue there. The movie people used Hollywood Post No. 43, American Legion, which conducted weekly shows in a stadium accommodating 8,000 persons. They called it the Hollywood Legion Auditorium.[9] It was a favorite site not so much for the night boxing matches but for the celebrities that frequented it. People were more concerned with whom they could sit beside than what boxing event took place. Many of them paid little attention to what was occurring in the ring.

On September 7, 1934, Lou Salica was to fight Young Tommy, a Filipino, in the headliner at the Hollywood Legion but was out-staged. That night, the comedian and actor

Joe E. Brown staged an impromptu wrestling bout with actor and singer Eddie Cantor until both were stripped nearly to their shorts. After that act, the crowd had its money's worth.[9] If anyone cared, Salica beat Tommy by a decision. Salica was seen frequently with Hollywood personalities. Mae West invited Salica to her house on occasion. George Raft was a frequent dinner companion, and Grace Prince gushed over meeting with John Barrymore.[8]

He brought some of his younger brothers to Bey's Camp. He would get unintended roadwork from his playful younger brothers. One day, in the early morning hours, Lou Salica ran after his young brothers because they stole all his polo shirts. That left Lou with only a sleeveless sweater. Newspapermen came to the camp to watch a typical workout. Salica boxed two rounds apiece with Artie Wineberg, Freddie Latanzio, and Billie Skidmore. He followed that with two rounds of shadowboxing, one on the bag and one with the jump ropes. He finished as strong as when he started.[7]

Salica trained well enough to win the title from Escobar on August 26, 1935, in a fifteen-round decision. The crowd jeered the decision as Phelan and his commission left. The Associated Press scored the victory for Escobar, winning eight, losing five, and two even. The judges rendered a split decision. Referee Arthur Donovan scored the fight seven to seven, with one even, but voted for Salica on the grounds of "more effective punching and in better physical condition at the end of the bout." The decision that counted made Lou Salica the new world bantamweight champion. Phelan said they would investigate.[10] The commission upheld the decision. The bout was described by one sportswriter from the *Pittsburgh Post-Gazette* as one "of the most savagely fought battles ever staged by little men in the New York area."

Tony Canzoneri, still seeking a fight with Barney Ross, who took his titles away, had found another place to train while Madame Bey was rebuilding her camp from the fire. Canzoneri would never fight Barney Ross again. Ross had not defended his lightweight title since 1933. He only defended his junior welterweight title. In 1935, Ross vacated his lightweight title. Boxing officials arranged a series of elimination bouts to determine the lightweight champion. Canzoneri and Ambers won their elimination bouts. The two fought at Madison Square Garden on May 10, 1935, to determine the lightweight title. Ambers was the youngster who had earlier served as a sparring partner for Canzoneri at Bey's Camp. He had lost only once in his fifty-one fights before meeting Canzoneri for the title. Canzoneri put Ambers on the canvas twice in the third round and once in the fifteenth. Canzoneri won by a unanimous decision, becoming the first man to win a fifth title. An amazing feat at a time when there were only ten weight classes and one title holder in each class, compared to the many governing bodies today, with each having their own title holders.

Canzoneri won his next four fights in as many months after the Ambers bout. His next bout would be against Al Roth. Canzoneri was not training at Bey's Camp; he trained at his home in Marlboro, New York. His challenger came to Bey's Camp in September.[11] Roth was to meet Canzoneri for the world lightweight title on October 4 at Madison Square Garden. A decent fighter, Al Roth had a record of twenty-eight wins, eleven losses, and nine draws. His most powerful weapon was the overhand right, a punch that two years before nearly killed the undefeated Jerry Mazza who had eighteen fights. Mazza was near death and in the hospital for days. He had a severe concussion but made a complete recovery.

With Roth at the camp were his trainer, Yussel Levy; his roommate, heavyweight Eddie Mader; and two other sparring partners. Mader was scheduled to fight Hank Hankinson on the Joe Louis-Max Baer undercard. Max Baer had just lost the heavyweight title to James "Cinderella Man" Braddock in his previous fight.

Roth was becoming known at Bey's for activities not related to boxing. Roth excelled at pinochle. He stayed in a room above the gymnasium. He preferred the room to one at the farmhouse. It kept him closer to his prey. He had people in camp owing him money from his card playing.

"I like to play cards, and the boys are willing to oblige," he explained.[12]

Card playing was a way of life at Bey's Camp. It was a way of relaxing when not training. Friendly wagers were often involved.

Al Roth knew why he was training at the camp. He trained hard. Roth would awake every morning at seven. The first thing he would do after dressing was to milk Madame Bey's cows. He claimed it helped strengthen his hands. He remembered that heavyweight Tommy Gibbons used to jog while squeezing a rubber ball to strengthen his hands. Roth's method was less conventional, but Madame Bey had a free laborer. After he gave the milk to Madame Bey, Roth would jog for three to four miles. Next, he would eat breakfast and then go to the hills to chop wood. Mader would remind Roth that he did his wood chopping at night when Roth was trying to sleep; Mader owed Roth money from losing at cards. Featherweight Al Dubar, training for his own bout, and Freddy Landry would spar with Roth in the afternoons.[13]

He started using other fighters that were training for fights at the camp for sparring as his training progressed. They were fellow lightweight Custer Perry and Freddy Buster. Four days before Al Roth was to meet Tony Canzoneri for the lightweight title, another fighter joined him at the camp.[14]

Primo Carnera the native Italian and former world heavyweight champion lumbered into Madame Bey's on September 30 at five-thirty in the afternoon. Carnera, age twenty-eight, in his last fight lost in the sixth round by a technical knockout on June 5 to young Joe Louis who had nineteen wins with no losses.

Carnera was a giant of a man. They gave him the ring names of the Ambling Alp, the Man Mountain, and Da Preem. The first two names embodied his huge physical presence. He was six feet seven inches and weighed 270 pounds with an extraordinary physique. Not impressive by the size of today's athletes, but in Carnera's day it constituted a tremendous size advantage. He was the heaviest heavyweight champion of his time. He was slow in movement and awkward. He had custom boxing gloves made to fit his large hands. His image appeared on the cover of the October 5, 1931, issue of *Time* magazine. The magazine referred to him as the Monster.

"For Breakfast," his publicist commented, "Primo has a quart of orange juice, two quarts of milk, nineteen pieces of toast, fourteen eggs, a loaf of bread, and a half a pound of Virginia ham."[15]

"Carnera was the only giant I have ever seen who was well proportioned throughout his body for his height," writer Paul Gallico described him. "His hands were like Virginia hams, and his fingers were ten red sausages. His head was large, and he had a good nose and fine, kind eyes. His skin was brown and glistening and he invariably smelled of garlic."[16]

Upon Primo Carnera's arrival, Madame Bey gave him Gene Tunney's old room.[12] Everybody wanted Gene Tunney's old room. Al Roth took Carnera's size-18 shoes just after he had arrived. He filled the bathtub and placed Carnera's shoes into the water. Roth thought if he could get a miniature outboard motor, he could make a motorboat out of them. Carnera refused to allow Roth to use his twenty-two-ounce boxing gloves for wading boots.[14] The launch of Carnera's shoe boat would have to wait. The fun over, the more serious matter of training remained.

Carnera expressed his pleasure with the facilities. People flocked to Bey's when word spread that the anomaly of a man, Carnera, trained there. He had always been an attraction because of his size and physical appearance more than his boxing skills. Madame Bey recalled her first impression of Carnera.

"I remember the first time Primo squeezed himself in that door, and I wondered how in the world I would keep him fed. What a giant of a man, I thought, and when I looked at his huge feet, hands, and shoulders, I felt a little repulsion. But then, I noticed his eyes. Such large, brown, and kind eyes!"[17]

As with her other fighters, Madame Bey became to know Carnera on a personal basis. She found that he was not the person the media had tried to portray him. That was only good for newspaper readership and promoters' need for large gates at their fights. She found him to be a kind and intelligent person and not the naïve boxer that journalists depicted.

"No wonder poor Primo could write poetry—he had soul if you understand me— but the sportswriters never noticed it. And to my surprise, the enormous Primo ate very little—certainly no more than a normal size man," Madame Bey noted.[17]

The media questioned many of his fights as being "fixed" due to the relationship of his handlers to organized crime. Many believed the accusation. The three years before coming to Bey's, Carnera had fought his way to the top, then tumbled to disgrace.

In 1933, Carnera and the other top heavyweight contenders trained elsewhere for important fights away from Madame Bey's Camp. A fight between Carnera and top heavyweight contender Ernie Schaaf was originally planned with the intention of having the winner meet Jack Sharkey later in the year for the heavyweight championship. There was public protest because Sharkey had part ownership of Schaaf's contract and was in his corner for many of his fights. It forced the Garden management to announce that only if Carnera won would a championship bout be arranged. As a result, Schaaf entered the fight with nothing to gain and everything to lose.

On February 10, 1933, at Madison Square Garden, Primo Carnera fought Ernie Schaaf. The enormous Carnera outweighed Schaaf by forty-three pounds. Looking clumsy, Carnera was winning most of the rounds according to experts at the ringside. The crowd thought the bout fixed,[18] as was the case with many of Carnera's fights. The crowd knew champion Jack Sharkey owned half of Schaaf's contract. The fight lasted thirteen rounds as the suspicious 20,000 Garden crowd voiced their disapproval. Many thought Schaaf did not try to defend himself. Schaaf went down after a solid jab landed into his face. He did not get up. Seconds rushed into the ring, which included Jack Sharkey, and carried Schaaf to his stool. Later, they brought Schaaf across the street to the Polyclinic Hospital.[19]

Schaaf tried too hard to lose if there was a fix. He suffered a brain hemorrhage, and his left side became paralyzed. He underwent an operation to remove a blood clot from his brain to relieve pressure. He died on February 14, 1933, at the Polyclinic Hospital at the age of twenty-four.

Governor Lehman ordered an immediate investigation. The legislature threatened to repeal prizefighting in New York State. Others wanted to banish Carnera from boxing due to his immense size. Authorities lodged homicide charges against Carnera.[20] General John J. Phelan and William Muldoon of the commission threatened to reintroduce the dreadnaught weight class for oversized heavyweights. The same one Carnera had held until the commission abandoned it. Carnera would have to fight opponents only from that class. They would be taller than six feet two inches and weigh more than 220 pounds.[21, 22]

There remained some discrepancy over the exact cause of Schaaf's death. Some medical experts said the injuries received during the bout caused his death. Others said that Schaaf already had some tumor, cyst, lesion, or old brain injury that contributed to his death. Schaaf had suffered a bout of influenza before the fight that left him in a weakened state.[23]

Carnera had won the fight, which should have given him a title bout with Sharkey. With the death of Schaaf, he was under investigation for manslaughter. Further, a dreadnaught weight class would have barred Carnera from fighting in the heavyweight division. In time, the outcries ceased. The new weight class was dismissed along with criminal allegations against Carnera.

Tragedy or not, fix or not, Carnera had beaten Ernie Schaaf and was awarded a bout against the heavyweight champion, Sharkey. A Sharkey-Carnera heavyweight championship bout was set for June 1933. The Garden promoter, Johnston, had ruled out a Sharkey-Schmeling rematch. Many thought Schmeling lost a chance for the title because of his strained relationship with Johnston. This left an opening for a new promoter to the game—ex-heavyweight champion Jack Dempsey. He would pit Schmeling against a hard-hitting heavyweight from California—Max Baer. The planning for the two matches started to solidify in March. Published reports stated that the Schmeling-Sharkey match would have been held at the Garden, but Johnston's disdain for Schmeling jeopardized it.

"There is absolutely nothing to that yarn," Dempsey said. "I have the best match of the two, and it will go on in either the Yankee Stadium or the Polo Grounds the night of June 1. After Schmeling and Baer have fought, Sharkey can meet the winner for the champion's percentage in the fall if he likes, but it must be under my promotion."

Johnston, at the Garden, was strong in his denials.

"The Garden is going ahead with its plans to promote a Sharkey-Carnera match for the heavyweight championship," he said. "We have not yet decided upon a date, but we have no intention of joining hands with Dempsey. Articles have been signed for weeks by Sharkey and Carnera. We are perfectly satisfied with this match."[24]

On June 8, 1933, at Yankee Stadium, the bout between Schmeling and Baer took place. The original date of June 1 was changed. It was Schmeling's first fight in over eight months when he beat Mickey Walker. A crowd of over 60,000—including Jack Sharkey and Primo Carnera—paid $239,676. It gave Jack Dempsey a profit from his first big promotional venture.[25]

The fight started uneventfully in the early rounds and met with some jeers from the crowd. They sparred in the ring center for most of the fight. Baer showed Schmeling his mocking smile throughout the bout. Then came the tenth round. The Baer smile dissipated. His punches were finding their target. Everything Baer threw connected. Schmeling did not land one punch in the round. Baer sent Schmeling to the canvas. He managed to get to his feet at the count of nine, still hurt and stunned. Referee Donovan halted the bout, saving Schmeling from a knockout.[26]

Schmeling's chance at another title fight was set back with the defeat. He sat in his locker room wondering what happened. He was the one-to-two favorite going into the bout. Schmeling rationalized, shaking his head.

"It was the heat," he said. "It was terrible. It was too hot for a European not used to it. Perhaps Baer, being from California, was more used to it, but it robbed me of my strength.

"He did not hurt me before that last round. I caught most of his blows here," Schmeling said while patting his elbows, "but I had no strength to hit him. I could hardly raise my arms toward the last. I saw the punches coming, but I could not block them."[27]

In contrast to the dejected Schmeling, Baer exhibited jubilation. Police had to block his dressing room to stop the mob trying to gain access. As he stood under his shower, Baer thrust his huge fist from the shower and yelled to them.

"Boys, I'm going to win that championship! I told you so. I'm going to win that championship!"[27]

On June 29, 1933, before a crowd of 40,000 in the Madison Square Garden Bowl, Long Island City, Carnera got his chance to fight Sharkey a second time. He lost to him in 1931. It was clear in the previous fight that Sharkey had out-boxed Carnera in a fifteen-round unanimous decision, a year before Sharkey defeated Schmeling for the title.

For this fight, Sharkey seemed intimidated by Carnera. In the sixth round, a right uppercut hit Sharkey that ended the fight. The knockout occurred at two minutes and twenty-seven seconds of the sixth round. Carnera became the world heavyweight champion to a skeptical public that thought, again, the fight was fixed. It was an enormous upset, one of the biggest in the decade. Many speculated that Sharkey threw the fight. Though questioned the rest of his life, Sharkey always denied the allegation.[28]

Carnera's first heavyweight title defense came against Paulino the "Basque Woodchopper" Uzcudun. They fought on October 22, 1933, in the Piazza di Siena, Rome, Lazio, Italy. He fought in front of a home crowd of more than 70,000 that included the premier, Benito Mussolini. Also present was James Roosevelt, the oldest son of President Franklin D. Roosevelt. Carnera had no problem with the older thirty-four-year-old, and lighter by sixty-five-pounds, Uzcudun. Despite the win, his fellow citizens booed him—they wanted a knockout.

Carnera's second heavyweight defense came against Tommy the "Phantom of Philly" Loughran. He was the former light heavyweight champion and *The Ring* magazine's fighter of the year in 1929 and 1931. The fight took place in Miami on March 1, 1934, at the Madison Square Garden Stadium. Carnera had advantages in almost all statistical categories. He stood seven inches taller. He weighed seventy-four pounds more. He was five years younger. He had a ten-inch reach advantage. He was a three-to-one favorite to maintain his title. Carnera, unable to knock down Loughran, won the decision. The fight was a financial disaster. It drew just 15,000 spectators and had receipts of $40,000 to $50,000.

With Baer defeating Schmeling in his last fight, he was given a title fight against Carnera. The two met on June 14, 1934 at Madison Square Garden. Nat Fleischer stated in the August 1934 issue of *The Ring* magazine that Carnera was down twelve times, and one was a slip. He gave Baer three knockdowns in the first, three in the second, one in the third, three in the tenth, and two in the eleventh. He said that Carnera slipped in the eighth after missing a punch. The referee stopped the fight at two minutes, sixteen seconds of the eleventh round as Carnera was wobbly and receiving too much punishment.

"I no lay down," Carnera said after the fight. "I fight good and he fight good, too."[29]

Fixes are subjective. Carnera may not have been the most elegant of fighters, but he did have size and power winning eighty-eight fights, seventy-one by knockout, of his 103 career bouts. His fame went beyond boxing. In 1933, Italy put him on a postage stamp. He was a favorite of Italy's Premier Benito Mussolini until his embarrassing loss to Baer. He appeared in the movie *The Prizefighter and the Lady* with actor Jean Harlow in which he played himself. In one scene, he fought Max Baer's character before they met for the heavyweight championship in reality.

Carnera had come to Bey's to train for his next fight against Walter "Der Blonde Tiger" Neusel, the German-born heavyweight. Neusel had won all six of his bouts in America. He had just returned from Europe, where he had fought in the last year. In four bouts there, he lost only to Max Schmeling, who knocked him out before a record European crowd of 102,000 on August 26, 1934. Carnera was unimpressive in his last two fights. They resulted in a loss to Joe Louis and a win against an amateurish Ray Impelletiere. The Ray Impelletiere fight had Jack Dempsey, with yet another vocation, as referee.

On March 15 at Madison Square Garden, Carnera looked sluggish in the beginning of the bout, and Impelletiere out-boxed him. In the sixth round, he forced through Impellitiere's defense with a decisive left hook, causing Impelletiere to tremble. From that point, Carnera was in control and won in the ninth round by a technical knockout.[30]

The fight against Neusel was scheduled to be at Madison Square Garden on November 1. It was an important fight in that promoters wanted to determine if someone other than Joe Louis could draw big crowds. Carnera's training went well at Bey's Camp. He jogged an unusual eight miles a day.[31] He worked hard at camp. He sparred with heavyweight James Merriott,[32] who would fight on the Carnera-Neusel undercard. For the Bey Camp, an unusual occurrence happened with Carnera and another fighter. Boxers were usually too busy preparing for their ring opponents to involve themselves in extracurricular bouts. Carnera subjected himself to a scuffle with a fellow heavyweight that escalated into a fistfight. It occurred just two weeks before his bout with Neusel. It happened with one of his sparring partners, Willie McGee, a lesser-known boxer with a losing record, after a workout. The fight caused McGee to leave the camp.

A crowd of 12,768 paying $31,621 at Madison Square Garden watched as Carnera pounded Neusel. Carnera came close to knocking Neusel out in the first and second rounds. Then, two minutes and twenty-three seconds into the fourth round, Carnera tried to hit him with his right but caught Neusel with his elbow, opening a gash that caused blood to flow. The blooded Neusel threw his hands in the air and walked to his corner. The referee stopped the fight. Carnera won and led in every round.[33]

The fight between Roth, training at Bey's, and Canzoneri was held at Madison Square Garden on October 4, 1935. The crowd of 14,210 saw one of the best lightweight fights in years. Canzoneri dropped Roth in the third round with a left hook followed by a right. Roth got up at the count of nine. Canzoneri won most, if not all, early rounds. Roth looked beaten until the twelfth round of the fifteen-round bout. To the amazed Garden crowd, Roth made a comeback and rocked Canzoneri the rest of the fight. He hurt Canzoneri, but he did not go down. The crowd cheered throughout. Canzoneri retained his title by a unanimous decision. The Garden crowd cheered more as Canzoneri left and gave a huge ovation to Roth, usually reserved for the victor.[34]

In November, Lou Salica, world bantamweight champion, returned to Madame Bey's to defend his title in a rematch against Sixto Escobar. He declared Madame Bey's Camp a lucky spot just before going to the gymnasium to train.

"Look what happened last week," the champion explained. "Primo Carnera, Eddie Mader, and Jorge Brescia all trained here. They all won in the Garden."

A reporter queried Salica about James Merriott, who also trained at Bey's Camp and lost on the same card with Carnera.

"Merriott was Primo's sparring partner," Salica answered. "Besides, he lost to George Turner."[32]

Hymie Caplin managed Salica and Turner. Salica accounted for Merriott's defeat to the better manager.

Primo Carnera also returned to the camp for a November 25 bout against Ford Smith in Philadelphia, twenty-four days after his last fight. The man he just vanquished, Walter Neusel, followed him to the camp. It was a recurring theme that a beaten fighter would go to Madame Bey's where his vanquisher had trained. Like Salica, many considered it a lucky spot. Al Roth and Eric the "Jewish Wildcat" Seelig joined Salica, Carnera, and Neusel at the camp. Al Roth was to fight Frankie Klick, with the winner having an opportunity to fight Tony Canzoneri for his title. Eric Seelig was going to fight Charlie Belanger.

In March 1933, Adolph Hitler, with a stroke of a pen, relieved Seelig of the German middleweight and light heavyweight championships. The Nazi government stripped all

Jewish champions of their titles. Then the Nazis expelled Seelig and his family from Germany.[35] If Seelig had not been a distinguished boxer, his fate may have been far worse than expulsion. He fought in Belgium, France, and then England the next two years before going to Cuba and America in 1935.

Madame Bey and her boys welcomed Seelig when he came to the camp, as with any boxer trying to find a home. The Seelig for Champion organization, which counted among its members Lou Salica and Al Roth, was formed at the camp.[36]

Madame Bey told the press the German titles would soon be forgotten. She declared that Seelig would be the next middleweight champion. She had predicted that her Max Schmeling would become the world heavyweight champion before anyone knew him, which came to fruition.[37]

"I predict a wonderful future for the boy," Madame Bey said. "He reminds me of Max Schmeling when he first came here. Seelig, like Schmeling, is very serious."

"Seelig is very strong and very tough," Lou Salica added.

Someone scrolled a freehand sketch of Hitler on the punching bag. Eric Seelig appreciated the gesture by his fellow boxers, but it could not change the indignities subjected to his people.

"I would fight him for nothing," Seelig declared, referring to Hitler, not his opponent Belanger a few days away.

He would concede to the press that the current victory was with Hitler.[36]

On November 11, the day of his Belanger bout, publicity pictures were printed in newspapers describing Seelig as a Jewish-German refugee. Photographers took the pictures at Madame Bey's Camp. They showed him shoveling dirt with a caption that stated he was limbering up his shoulders for the Charley Belanger fight. Another two showed him feeding Bey's chickens. Finally, another showed him in his boxing stance inside Bey's gymnasium.[38] Seelig would show his power and skills by dispensing with Belanger in the fourth round with a knockout. It was his second bout in America. After the win, Seelig was offered a bout on the prestigious Joe Louis-Paulino Uzcudun undercard. He declined because of his religious beliefs;[39] it was on a Friday night. Seelig would win all his American fights in 1935, a total of four, including a technical knockout of Mickey Walker to finish the year.

The bantamweight Salica and the heavyweight Carnera became good friends. They could be seen jogging together along the wooded paths around Bey's Camp. Salica would hop on Carnera's broad shoulders part of the way. Carnera wanted to get on Salica's shoulders, but he could not support the weight of the Italian giant. Carnera had to play leapfrog instead. That did not last long because Salica tired of picking himself out of the leaves when Carnera thrust his enormous body over him.[40]

In a friendly bet of ten dollars, Carnera challenged Salica that he could keep his mouth shut all day and not speak before him. The wager was accepted. Salica taped his mouth shut to keep silent. Carnera found out, and Salica removed the tape, and some skin came off his lips. With the cold November air, Salica's lips became severely chapped. Salica said he would never again use tape as a speech suppressor.[41] The wagering outcome went unrevealed.

On a rainy November day, reporters inundated the camp to report on Salica. They watched him, and his chapped lips, do serious preparation for his title bout with Sixto Escobar at Madison Square Garden a week away. He sparred with featherweights Dick Welsh and Johnny Mauro. Salica demonstrated his powerful punching combinations.

From the ring, the reporters, photographers, and Salica dashed through the rain to Madame Bey's living room. There, Al Roth, Walter Neusel, Eric Seelig, and a bunch of sparring partners welcomed him. They would play a game to see who could gain control of a piece of furniture. It was roughhousing and childish, but they were just trying to unwind after a long day's work. A struggle ensued to see who would win sitting honors on Madame Bey's famous green piece of furniture from France. It was a *tete-a-tete pour trois*, known in English as a love nook for three. It had a peculiar seating arrangement with three distinct parts. Each part faced in a different direction, and a lamp sat between, which was part of the chair. No matter where you sat, you had your back to the other two in the chair. The boys tussled as Madame Bey watched.

"Hey, take it easy. Watch those punches," Madame Bey said.

"That's all right. Come on and punch," Salica said with a grin.[41]

Salica would lose the title in his rematch to Escobar on November 15, 1935, by a unanimous decision. He would fight many more times at the Hollywood Legion Auditorium and regain the bantamweight title in 1939 and hold it until 1943.

Frankie Klick came to Bey's in December.[42] It was after beating Al Roth, who had trained for their fight at Bey's Camp. He was to fight Lou Ambers in January. Ambers, with a record of forty-nine wins, two losses, and five draws, was still a promising young lightweight even after losing his title bout to Canzoneri. Ambers would defeat Klick in a ten-round decision. Ambers had not lost since his defeat to Canzoneri.

CHAPTER 24

The Herkimer Hurricane Hits

As the cold December air turned 1935 into 1936, Madame Bey's Camp was once again the center of training for top quality prizefighters. Just over one year after the fire had occurred, and six months since the camp reopened, the press was referring to her camp as Madame Bey's Training Emporium in their columns. Primo Carnera was still the headliner. Since his loss to Joe Louis, the Ambling Alp won his last three fights while training at Bey's Camp. He was now trying to make it four with a scheduled bout against Isidoro Gastanaga on March 6 at Madison Square Garden. The press billed Gastanaga as the "man Joe Louis refused to fight."[1] Joe Louis's team avoided him for business reasons, not fear.

Days before the fight, newspapers were printed with Carnera and a German shepherd at Bey's Camp. The caption with the picture read in part, Da Preem frolics with a canine friend at Madame Bey's Camp in Summit, busily preparing for Friday night's bout with Izzy Gastanaga at the Garden.[2] The fight had been problematic days before it occurred when newspapers printed columns about the questionable relationship between the two foes. The accusation was that the rival managers were business partners, and the fight was nothing more than a proposition among business associates.[1] Before the fight started, people thought it was fixed.

The public showed their disapproval with an attendance of 8,834 paying $18,380. Carnera won the bout early in the fifth round when referee Arthur Donovan stopped the fight because of a ragged cut above the left eye of Gastanaga. It was Carnera's fourth consecutive victory but the start of more accusations levied against him. Commissioner John J. Phelan said after the bout that he was satisfied with the honesty of the fight. The commission held the purses until an investigation into the matter was completed. Phelan added that the investigation was precautionary.[1] Carnera was cleared, but it did not matter; public opinion on the legitimacy of his fights, which had always been in doubt, had already been determined.

Carnera fought ten days later against Leroy Haynes at the Arena Philadelphia before 10,000 fans. The fight was advertised with posters printed with the words "Can Joe Louis fight? Wait till you see LeRoy Haynes."[3] Young Jersey Joe Walcott, future heavyweight champion and Madame Bey Camp trainee, fought a winning fight on the undercard. Haynes rocked Carnera in the first round. Carnera had Haynes cut in the second, but it did not stop him. Haynes sent Carnera halfway through the ropes with his relentless attack. In the third, Carnera was dazed and defenseless against Haynes, who put him on the canvas near his corner. Carnera got up without a count. Hurt, he hung on the ropes with his back toward Haynes. It appeared Carnera was appealing to his manager, Bill Duffy, to stop the fight. The pleas would not matter. Referee Matt Adgie stepped in between the two fighters and put his arms around Carnera.[4] The fight was over.

Undeterred, Carnera returned to Madame Bey's Camp for a rematch against Leroy Haynes. Two former world champions accompanied him at camp—ex-light heavyweight champion Bob Olin and ex-middleweight champion Teddy Yarosz. Ray Arcel trained all three.

Teddy Yarosz did not have a hard punch but compensated for it with his tenacious infighting and endurance. He defeated Vince Dundee—who had trained at Bey's for the fight[5]—for the middleweight title on September 11, 1934. On New Year's afternoon, 1935, Yarosz fought Babe Risko in Scranton, Pennsylvania. His title was not at stake. Yarosz injured his right knee during the fight. The knee damaged, Yarosz fought with one good leg. Yarosz lost by a technical knockout in the seventh round. For the first time, he was stopped.[6]

Yarosz went to the Mayo Brothers in Rochester, Minnesota, where they fixed a torn ligament. Yarosz started training again for a rematch with Risko in Pittsburgh. This time it was a fight for the championship. During the fight on September 19, 1935, his right knee became injured again. Showing his tenacity, Yarosz continued to fight in pain. He lost his title to Babe Risko by a decision.

Dr. John Moore of Temple University in Philadelphia repaired the knee a second time. In January 1936, against the doctor's advice, Teddy Yarosz decided to try a comeback. He took a train to New York and went to Stillman's Gymnasium.

"Ray," he said to Arcel, "I gotta fight."

He began to use two large bags filled with salt to strengthen his knee over four months. To the astonishment of many, the leg improved. Yarosz started training again. Then he accompanied Arcel to Madame Bey's where Arcel's Primo Carnera and Bob Olin were training.[6]

Arcel traveled from Madame Bey's Camp to Hickey Park, Millvale, Pennsylvania, when Yarosz fought Bob Turner. The leg was noticeably impaired, but Yarosz defeated Bob Turner in a ten-round unanimous decision. Arcel went back to Madame Bey's that night to train Carnera. Carnera and Olin sent to Yarosz a telegram, wishing him "loads of luck" in his comeback. The twenty-five-year-old Yarosz placed it into his scrapbook.[7]

While at Bey's, Arcel liked to tell a story about Carnera and Max Baer for anyone who wished to hear it. Like card playing, storytelling was a popular past time at Bey's Camp. He would tell them about the time they were in Hollywood making the picture *The Prize Fighter and the Lady*. Jean Harlow accepted Carnera's dinner invitation, but she slighted Baer's invite. In the movie fight scenes, neither was to hit, just act, but it transpired into a real fight.[7]

In 1936, Carnera, still training for his rematch against Leroy Haynes, did some charity on an April evening. As a guest of the Cub Scouts, he attended a boxing match in the nearby town of Short Hills. While he was there, he refereed six boxing matches in front of one hundred boys and signed autographs at the end of the meeting. He reciprocated the invite by asking the Cub Scouts to come to Bey's to watch him train.[8]

On May 27, 1936, at Ebbet's Field, Brooklyn, New York, Carnera fought Leroy Haynes in a scheduled ten-round bout before a crowd of 20,000. Apparent from the start, Carnera would be no match for Haynes despite his sixty-four-pound advantage. Haynes struck him unrelentingly in the seventh and eight rounds. At the end of the eighth, Carnera staggered to his corner and dragged his left leg. Carnera showed courage by continuing into the ninth. Forty seconds into the round, Carnera, without being hit, fell sideways into a half spin, saying something inaudible to the referee. The referee gathered him and helped him to his corner; the fight was over.[9] It would be his last professional fight in America.

Carnera suffered kidney damage and paralysis of his left leg. He spent time in the hospital but did recover. He was relegated to a second-rate heavyweight. No one cared about those sensitive eyes or his poetry writing like Madame Bey did. He was no longer a top contender, and that was all anyone cared about. There was no humanizing a fighter, except by a few, as Madame Bey did.

Carnera had won over $1 million in prize money but had nothing remaining. He involved himself with too many unscrupulous people. Carnera was left without money, friends, and alone in a New York hospital with one leg paralyzed.

"I lay in the hospital bed for five months," Carnera said. "My whole left side was paralyzed. I was in much pain. During all this time, not one of them came to see me. Nobody came to see me. I had no friend in all the world."[10]

He returned to Europe and fought there seven more times professionally. He never recaptured his glory. He was thirty-nine years old at the time of his last fight in 1946.

In October, Argentina's heavyweight Jorge Brescia came to Bey's Camp. He had trained three weeks in Speculator, New York,[11] before he came to the New Jersey countryside. He prepared to fight Joe Louis, who had compiled a record of twenty-six wins and one loss. Louis's one loss came two fights before on June 19, 1936. It was against Madame Bey's

Max. The odds were ten to one Louis would win, four to one he would win by a knockout, and two to one Schmeling would not last seven rounds.

"When Max was training for the first Louis fight no one thought he had a chance, and he knew their feelings, so he was worrying about it," Madame Bey recalled.[12]

Since Schmeling did not train at Madame Bey's for the fight, she came to him. Max suddenly stopped his training and came out of the ring to embrace Madame Bey.

Choked with emotion, Madame Bey said, "Max, you're still the champion."[13]

Schmeling exploited a weakness he saw in Louis. Every time Louis threw a left jab, he would drop his shoulder and hand, making him a target for a right cross, Schmeling's best punch. Schmeling studied film of Louis's fights against Primo Carnera and Max Baer. He attended the Joe Louis-Paulino Uzcudun fight on December 13, 1935, at Madison Square Garden.

"I saw something," Schmeling stated.

"Everybody laughs when Jack Johnson says Louis has a weakness, and says that he is jealous," he told the *Saturday Evening Post*.

Joe Louis knocked out Paulino Uzcudun in the fourth round. It was the Basque Woodchopper's last fight.

Louis was undefeated with twenty-four wins, twenty by knockout. Schmeling, former world heavyweight champion, had forty-eight wins with thirty-four knockouts, seven losses, and four draws. Mike Jacobs promoted the fight. The bout was delayed a day because of rain. The next day, an estimated crowd of 60,000 arrived on June 19, 1936, at Yankee Stadium. The gross gate was $547,531, and the net $464,945. Louis's gate share was $139,483.50, and Schmeling was guaranteed $150,000, tax-free. Veteran manager and promoter Tom O'Rourke died of a heart attack in Schmeling's dressing room shortly before the start of the bout. Schmeling knocked Louis down in rounds four and twelve as Schmeling exploited Louis's flaw with a right over the dropped hand. By the thirteenth round, the referee stopped the fight. Schmeling had accomplished one of boxing's biggest upsets.[14]

In later years, Louis said when he was knocked down in the second round, he could not remember the rest of the fight.[15]

Retired and former world light heavyweight champion "Philadelphia" Jack O'Brien had spent several weeks at Madame Bey's helping Brescia prepare for his Louis fight. O'Brien retired from the ring in 1912 with a record of ninety-two wins, eight losses, and fourteen draws. He acted as the chief second to Jack Dempsey in the first Jack Dempsey-Gene Tunney bout in 1926 in Philadelphia.

Jack O'Brien fought many of the best fighters. He did battle with four future, current, and past world heavyweight champions on seven occasions. In 1909, O'Brien fought Jack Johnson when Johnson held the world heavyweight championship, in a six-round bout. Deemed a draw, it was a nontitle newspaper fight; some newspapers favored Johnson, while others O'Brien. Less than two months before the Johnson fight, O'Brien fought Stanley Ketchel. He fought Ketchel again less than three weeks after the Johnson bout. He lost the fights, one by a decision and the other by a knockout. Nat Fleisher, the founder of *The Ring* magazine, considered Ketchel the greatest middleweight ever. Ketchel was murdered at age twenty-four, a year and a half after their second fight.

In 1904, Jack O'Brien defeated Tommy Burns two years before Burns became the world heavyweight champion. In 1906, Jack O'Brien fought Tommy Burns for the world heavyweight championship. Before the fight, former heavyweight champion James Jeffries stated that he thought O'Brien was the better man. The twenty-round bout ended in a draw. In 1907, O'Brien fought Burns again for the world heavyweight title. O'Brien lost a twenty-round decision.

In 1905, O'Brien defeated former world heavyweight champion Bob Fitzsimmons in round thirteen of a scheduled twenty-round bout. He lost to Fitzsimmons the previous year. In 1903, O'Brien lost a six-round newspaper decision to Marvin Hart, who won the heavyweight title two years later.

Jack O'Brien was fifty-eight years old when at Madame Bey's Camp. He thought that Brescia had a chance against Joe Louis.

"This Brescia is a big, strong, fast fellow," O'Brien said. "He can box and he can punch, and I think he is dead game. He has picked up fast in his schooling, and I believe he will give a mighty good account of himself against Louis.

"You remember what I say," Philadelphia Jack O'Brien warned. "Brescia is going to do better than you think."[16]

"He will surprise you," predicted Brescia's manager, Louis Soresi. "He will beat Louis like Max Schmeling beat him; only he will beat him much quicker. Jorge has a faster right hand than Schmeling."

The press pointed out that Brescia had not displayed his right as a destructive weapon in his six-round bout with Frankie Connelly and his four rounder with Abe Feldman.

"Wait and see," his manager assured.[17]

Brescia's trainer, Billy Defoe, did not bestow as much confidence, taking a practical approach.

"I am not saying Brescia is going to win, but just the same, I know he has a great chance.

"It was not so long after Louis Soresi picked up Brescia that I became impressed with Brescia's possibilities; so much so that Primo became a bit jealous of my attention to Jorge.

When it came to a showdown, where I had to confine my job as trainer to one or the other, I gave the preference to Brescia," DeFoe explained.[11]

Brescia, physically, had the advantages. They do not award wins on appearance. Brescia stood three-quarters of an inch taller, at least five pounds heavier, a six-inch edge on reach, and a chest expansion four inches bigger. Eddie Blunt, Jack Rose, Jack Moran, George Nicholson, and Paul Pross were the sparring partners for Brescia. He trained six and seven rounds a day.

Louis completed his training at Bier's in Pompton Lakes, New Jersey. Having just beaten Al Ettore, he required only five days of training.

"Ah think Chappie'll win this one quick," trainer Jack Blackburn declared as Louis scaled 206 pounds following his last workout. "He's heavier than ever before."[17]

Days before the fight, Brescia and Louis went to the New York Boxing Commission for their physical checkups. The doctor gave his approval to both. A confident Louis went to a ball game. Brescia returned to Madame Bey's Camp.[11]

Journalist Damon Runyon had seen this scenario before—the young fighter with all the promise challenging an established foe. Runyon wrote, "It is quite likely that Brescia has been well grounded in his fistic education. The trouble with these youngsters is that while they can do everything they have been told and taught in a gymnasium, the minute they are tagged in the ring they start to forget."

On October 9, 1936, the Mike Jacobs's promoted fight drew few to the Hippodrome in New York. A cautious Brescia was no match. He rolled over on his blood-spattered face after two minutes and twelve seconds of the third round. He lay unconscious for one minute. Joe Louis won by a knockout.[18]

Since losing to Schmeling, Louis defeated Jack Sharkey in three rounds, Al Ettore in five, and Brescia in three. Brescia would be the start of a long list of fighters to train at Madame Bey's for a chance to defeat Joe Louis. Her Max remained the sole blemish on Louis's record.

In November and December 1936, contenders and champions filled Madame Bey's Camp. A twenty-four-year-old Chilean named Arturo Godoy was becoming known in the heavyweight ranks. In his New York debut, he fought Leroy Haynes to a draw in October. Now at Bey's Camp, he readied for his second fight since returning to America—he had fought in Miami earlier.

Godoy weighed around 190 pounds. His hair was black and eyes dark, with high cheekbones that were scarred from punches. He liked to fight ruthlessly with his sparring partners. He drove five sparring partners out of Bey's Camp. Lou Brix, his manager, told him to pull his punches next sparring session. Godoy could not heed his manager's advice.

In the second round of his opening sparring session, his competitive spirit taking charge, he knocked out his opponent unconscious. People hurried to the fallen victim with concern. No one could remember if he had a mouthpiece and feared he had swallowed it. They unbuckled his headgear to check his mouth. They were relieved when they discovered the mouthpiece had not been worn.[19] Some first-time reporters at the camp had heard that they worked at full speed in sparring but had never seen it and were unprepared. Some said that more people had been hurt at Madame Bey's than at Madison Square Garden.

Columnist Frank Graham rode to Bey's on a sunny afternoon in early November to watch the foreign invader Godoy and the Puerto Rican Sixto Escobar. Ray Arcel trained Escobar, and his former partner, Whitey Bimstein, trained Godoy. Graham knew the current world bantamweight champion, Escobar, was a good fighter, and he had heard Godoy was. He knew the Beys' history, too. He called the Beys world travelers, sophisticates, persons of charm and culture. Then, added the Beys were the most extraordinary pair that ever conducted a training camp for prizefighters. When Graham asked Madame Bey regarding her boys who had trained there, she talked about some of her greats—Max Schmeling, Paulino Uzcudun, Paul Berlenbach, and the big, good-natured Carnera. She reserved her highest praise for Mickey Walker.

"Such a nice boy," Madame Bey said. "Always the same. We had him here when he was just a little boy. We watched him become a great fighter. And he was always just the same."

During the fighter's workouts, Graham asked Sidky Bey, a man he described as gray-haired, quiet, and gentle, if he liked boxing.

"Oh, yes," Sidky Bey replied. "I am very much interested."

"And Madame?" Graham queried.

Sidky Bey shook his head and smiled.

"Not when one of the boys who has trained here is fighting. She cannot go. She is afraid for them. She is too nervous."

Godoy told columnist Frank Graham he did not intend to be a fighter. He was in the Chilean army when ordered by his captain to box a man from another regiment. Godoy knocked him out. He proceeded to knock out other soldiers during his enlistment. Godoy, like so many other fighters, discovered he was born with a punch beyond that of ordinary men. After the army, he turned professional. He fought in South America, Miami, Cuba, Europe, and then New York.

Graham asked Godoy if he had much money from his fights.

"In Argentina, I make a little," Godoy replied. "I need to make a lot. I have a big family. My mother and eight brothers."[19]

Escobar sparred with former Puerto Rican flyweight champion Christobal Jarmilla and blond-haired featherweight Joey Wach. Escobar deemed the two boxers his closest friends in America. Escobar had imparted Wach with all he knew about boxing after he discovered his trainer, Ray Arcel, befriended Wach after his mother died. Escobar and Wach ate at the same table, slept in adjacent rooms, and played pinochle. They spent the entire day at Bey's Camp together yet never spoke much to each other during a day.[20, 21]

"Why all the heavy silence?" the press demanded.

"Well, Joey and I are both in training, and we haven't any time for talk," Escobar replied.[20]

Along with Arturo Godoy, Escobar and Wach found time to put rocks, gravel, and cereal in each other's bed every night. Escobar would give Joey Wach a "hot foot" or a "hot seat," and one night Wach, Escobar, and Godoy nearly set welterweight Canada Lee's room afire when an attempted "hot foot" set the bed sheets aflame. Their friendship was undetectable when sparring. Gloves laced, friendships put aside, Escobar displayed his boxing proficiency.[20, 21] Escobar's title fight with Indian Quintana was a few days away.[22]

On November 11, 1936, Godoy's bout at the Hippodrome in New York ended in a draw against the ninth-ranked heavyweight by *The Ring* magazine, Al Ettore, who had lost to Joe Louis in his last bout. On November 13, Sixto Escobar retained his world bantamweight title with a first-round knockout against Indian Quintana at Madison Square Garden in the feature bout. Not as skilled a boxer, Joey Wach lost to Al Reed on November 12 and in a rematch on December 9.

In November 1936, the next big-name boxer to come to Madame Bey's was the world lightweight champion Lou Ambers. He had come to train for a nontitle bout with Jimmy McLarnin. Ambers's record in sixty-seven bouts contained two losses, both by a decision. One of those losses came in a lightweight title bout, which Barney Ross had vacated, against Canzoneri. In September 1936, Ambers reached the pinnacle of a boxer's journey—he became a world champion. Ambers earned the lightweight title on September 3 at Madison Square Garden with a fifteen-round unanimous decision in a rematch over Tony Canzoneri.

He was born Luigi Guiseppe D'Ambrosio, into a large family, including five brothers, in Herkimer, New York, on November 8, 1913. He hid from his mother that he was a boxer, as many professional fighters were prone to do, by changing his name. They gave him the ring name the Herkimer Hurricane for his aggressive fighting style and the town from where he came. The Italian-heritage Ambers had hunched shoulders and brown hair. His head was large with a long, hollow jaw that gave his face a drawn appearance. A huge scar adorned his back.[23] He looked like a teenager rather than his twenty-three years. The looks were deceiving, as he showed a ferociousness and toughness in the ring. In 1935, in a fight against Fritzie Zivic, Ambers's jaw was broken. Ambers continued to fight and won the decision over Zivic.[24] Ambers had unbounded energy in and out of the ring. He packed it into his five feet four inches and 135-pound frame. Not known to have a hard punch, he compensated for it with quick hands, feet, and hitting often. He could get in close to an opponent for a strike and then quickly withdraw. He was expert at measuring the range for a punch. One of his opponents, Henry Armstrong, called him "a jumping jack, always in motion, constantly going away from punches."[25]

Ambers was taught boxing in the basement of his Catholic church, St. Anthony's, by a priest, Father Gustave Purificato. Ambers developed a friendship with Father Gustave Purificato, who went to all of Ambers's fights. Known to be close to his mother, he would call to reassure her he was unharmed after a fight. He would sing the song "I Want a Girl Just Like the Girl Who Married Dear Old Dad" in his dressing room.[26]

He could play piano and clarinet but did not have much of a voice. That did not stop him from singing. Ambers had another trait—he appeared to be in a state of perpetual happiness. He would spontaneously begin performing song and dance for no reason. If bloodied and battered after a fight, he still joked, laughed, and sang.

As fight time neared, he was unapproachable. He admitted he would snap back at his trainer, manager, and anyone else nearby. It was the body's natural reaction to the adrenaline, testosterone, and anxiety of an upcoming fight. A condition not unique to Ambers, he was a fighter on edge. Madame Bey took note of this with her other boys when they were in the throes of training, close to a fight.

"That is what makes most of them … so hard to get on with as fight time approaches …" Madame Bey said. "It is no wonder the boys feel a little savage towards their opponents."[12]

Ambers had one of the best teams, consisting of trusted second Frank "Skid" Enright, manager Al Weill, and trainer Morris "Whitey" Bimstein.

Skid, like Ambers, hailed from Herkimer. He was there as a friend for Ambers throughout his career. The two were together when Ambers started as an amateur fighter. It was rare for them to be apart. To Skid, Ambers would always be the best 135-pounder who ever lived. Nobody could tell him anything different.[27]

Al Weill was born Armand Weill in France. He came to New York at thirteen. Boxing regarded him as one of the most astute boxing managers in history. Weill was short, rotund, with a round face that held glasses. Despite his physique, he had agility, which he demonstrated slipping through the ropes to get to his fighter's corner between rounds. He was smart, energetic, aggressive, and demanding of his fighters. Al Weill was a champion—a champion waltz dancer.[28] He had an ashen complexion matched by the suits he wore with cigar ashes spilt on them.[29] Invariably, he wore a vest, and the journalist Dan Parker jokingly called him the Vest, a name that he carried. He had the ability to recognize and evaluate a boxer's technique. Aside from Ambers, Weill managed other champions.

They included featherweight champion Joey Archibald, welterweight champion Marty Servo, heavyweight challenger Arturo Godoy, and undefeated heavyweight champion Rocky Marciano. He worked as the matchmaker at Madison Square Garden for Mike Jacobs from 1949 to 1952. Weill also promoted bouts at many East Coast venues that included such renowned boxers as Kid Chocolate, Barney Ross, Tony Canzoneri, and Max Baer.[28]

Unlike other leading managers of the era, like Doc Kearns and Joe Jacobs who spent money freely, he was frugal. He expected no less from his fighters. Weill had no tolerance for a fighter that gambled. He told author A. J. Liebling in later years his thoughts.

"Every kind of serious trouble a fighter can get into has its origin in the disbursement of currency, rich food, liquor, women, horserace betting, and fast automobiles."[29]

Weill found Ambers when Lou boxed in the small clubs. He sometimes managed Ambers in person and other times remotely. They had a close relationship. The press thought them inseparable. It appeared to them that Ambers never would have another manager and that when the time came for him to hang up his gloves, he and Weill would still be friends.

Morris "Whitey" Bimstein was raised on Manhattan's Lower East Side. They called him Whitey because of his white, thinning hair and pale skin. Whitey was a former boxer of little talent who started as a bantamweight, or what he termed a "bantyweight." Father Ryan at the St. Jerome Catholic Church taught the Jewish Bimstein how to box. He fought under the name Johnny White and had seventy bouts before becoming a trainer. With the onset of World War I, the nineteen-year-old Bimstein joined the navy and served as a boxing instructor.[30] He was small in stature, attested to by the 118-pound bantamweight limit. He had an uncanny knack to recognize gifted young boxers by their movement while fighting. He saw latent talent before the boxer knew he had it. He was expert in extracting that talent.

Whitey was a legendary trainer and cut man. They called him King of the Minute Men, the time he had to repair a fighter's damage between rounds. He was considered a master of repairing the cuts his fighter sustained.[31] He came to the corner with swabs, antiseptics, ice bags, mild stimulants, and astringents. Some were homemade secret concoctions.[32] It was not only the quantity of the items he brought into the ring, but also he knew when and how to use each one. Having Whitey in the corner was as important to a fighter as his purse cut.[33] He motivated using psychological and physical means. He was not adverse to a slap in the face or a needle to the backside to get results.[34]

Starting in 1925, he collaborated with another legendary trainer—Ray Arcel. The press called them the Siamese training twins. They both learned their trade from Frank "Doc" Bagley, who trained world champions Gene Tunney and Jimmy McLarnin. They trained boxing's elite. The two split in 1934. Whitey, in high demand, handled the best talent boxing had. Whitey trained over fifty elite fighters in his career, half of whom were champions. Whitey worked in James "Cinderella Man" Braddock's corner when he upset Max Baer for the heavyweight championship the year before arriving at Madame Bey's with Ambers.

The list of greats he trained, or acted as a second to, was never equaled. It included Fred Apostoli, Max Baer, Jack Berg, Maxie Berger, James Braddock, Lou Brouillard, Primo Carnera, Georges Carpentier, Jack Dempsey, Sixto Escobar, Tony Galento, Arturo Godoy, Rocky Graziano, Harry Greb, Ingemar Johansson, Louis Kaplan, Benny Leonard, Rocky Marciano, Maxie Rosenbloom, Barney Ross, Lou Salica, Gene Tunney, Paulino Uzcudun, Mickey Walker, and Fritzie Zivic.

Of all the champion fighters he worked for, he would later recall, "I guess my favorite was Lou Ambers. He was the easiest to handle, like Sixto Escobar and Paolino Uzcudun. I had a lot of champs, Escobar and Ambers and Braddock and Graziano. There were others, but I remember Ambers best. It was always fun working with Ambers. You didn't have to drive him. My job with him was to keep him from working too much."[35]

It is the dichotomy in sports. Outside the arena, the affable, smiling, boyish-looking Lou Ambers was unthinkable of possessing such cruelty toward another person. Inside the arena, he was ruthless, unforgiving, with a focus of destruction of his opponent. Ambers was at the lowest point of his career in March 1936, six months removed from winning the world lightweight title. He fought Tony Scarpati in the Broadway Arena, New York. In the seventh round, Ambers connected flush on Scarpati's jaw. The hit so hard it knocked him off his feet. Scarpati's head hit the canvas when he went down.[36]

Ambers left the ring and went home without taking a shower. The next day, Ambers discovered that Scarpati had a concussion. It was far worse. Three days later, Scarpati died of a cerebral hemorrhage. Ambers, devastated, called it his worst fight. He told Al Weill he would quit fighting, but Weill convinced him not to abandon the sport.

Three weeks later, Weill arranged a bout for Ambers with Pete Mascia in the same ring at the Broadway Arena where he killed Scarpati. Unimportant was the result of the match, which Ambers won. The proceeds went to benefit the Scarpati family. It enabled everyone to reconcile the tragedy. Ambers said he would sometimes see Scarpati in his opponents when he fought.

Lou Ambers first came to Madame Bey's in 1933 in his second year as a professional fighter. He was the little-known boxer who had come to the camp as a sparring partner for Tony Canzoneri. He helped Canzoneri in his preparation for Kid Chocolate. No one gave Ambers much attention. Madame Bey assigned a small room to him upon his arrival. It was the same kind of room that all the sparring partners received. It was cozy and comfortable but modest compared to Canzoneri's room. Canzoneri, being a champion, had his choice of rooms.

In November 1936, Ambers returned to Madame Bey's Camp as the world lightweight champion. With him were Al, Whitey, and Skid. Madame Bey showed Ambers to his room to see if it met his approval. In front of the humble Ambers was Canzoneri's old room.

"All this for me?" Ambers queried as he looked over the well-fitted room.

"Most certainly," Madame Bey assured Ambers, "for now you are the champion."

"Thanks a lot, Madame Bey," Ambers said, "but if I can have my own choice of a room, won't you please see that I get the same one that was mine when I was here last?"

As champion, Madame Bey granted his wish. A writer wanted to know why Ambers declined Madame Bey's star guestroom in preference for the more modest one.

"Aw, I don't know," Ambers answered. "I guess it is because it is more fun just being one of the bunch. I'd rather hang around with the boys who I knew in the days when being champion seemed a long way off. I'll tell you, I don't want to get swell-headed. Canzoneri never did, and I want to be like him as much as possible."[37]

Kid Chocolate, the man Ambers helped Canzoneri prepare for in 1933, was already at Madame Bey's Camp training for a December meeting with Phil Baker.[38] Chocolate had just returned from his native Cuba, where he had been for almost two years, having won his last eight fights.

Ambers settled into camp life. He would use Madame Bey's as a staging ground for many of his future fights. His daily routine consisted of waking at seven o'clock and running three or four miles, followed by a shower. At nine o'clock, he ate breakfast made by Madame Bey. He then walked and then just stayed in the house reading or lazing around. At ten o'clock, he hiked the hills to clear his head. Next, he would try to sleep a while. He went to the gymnasium in the afternoon and trained an hour to an hour and a half. His training entailed of two or three rounds of sparring, one or two rounds of heavy bag punching, punching the small bag, and one or two rounds of skipping rope. He would complete ten to twelve rounds of work followed by another shower and a rubdown. He lay on his bed by nine o'clock every night.[15]

Again, the reporter Frank Graham came to Bey's Camp. He arrived to see Lou Ambers train for a nontitle bout against Jimmy McLarnin. Whitey Bimstein, Amber's trainer, answered Graham's knock at the door.

"Come on in," Whitey said. "He's upstairs. He won't work until two o'clock, and you can put on the feed bag first."

Everybody went into the dining room and sat. Whitey Bimstein stood at the bottom of the stairs.

"Come downstairs. Lou," he called. "There's somebody here to see you."

Ambers wore baggy pants, a wool shirt, and a pullover sweater. He bounded down the stairs singing.

"Sometimes I'm happy ... Sometimes I'm sad ..."

"I should think you would be sad with that voice," Pete Smith, who drove Graham to the camp, said to Ambers.

Ambers gave a friendly dig back at him.

"Going to eat first?" Ambers asked.

"Yes," Whitey replied. "They got time to eat before you work."

"Sure," Ambers concurred.

"I want to make some pictures of you," a photographer said.

"All right," Ambers said.

Ambers put on a lumber jacket and a faded blue beret while singing and doing a jig at the same time.

"I want a girl just like a girl that married dear old dad."

"That makes you look like a sissy," a reporter told him.

"He is a sissy," Whitey joked.

Ambers laughed and then went with the photographer outside. Everyone else sat at the table to eat.

Madame Bey prepared a typical training camp meal. She was used to preparing meals for many men. She had as many as thirty guests and sometimes more when the media came. She gave them broiled steak, mashed potatoes, milk, bread, and lettuce with oil and vinegar. For dessert, she made stewed pears with coffee.

"Anybody want a drink?" Whitey asked; the Madame Bey rule of no liquor was not always followed.

Nobody replied.

"Go upstairs, Skid, and get that bottle out of my bag," Whitey said.

Skid climbed upstairs and retrieved the bottle.

"This is some Summit rye," Whitey said. "I don't know how good it is."

"It looks like hop, skip, and jump liquor," Harry Newman said.

"Or block and fall," another reporter said. "You drink it, walk a block, and fall."

Whitey put glasses on the table, but everybody was eating, and nobody took a drink. Whitey put the bottle down on the sideboard.

Ambers's manager, Al Weill, walked in. He spotted the bottle.

"Where did that come from?" Weill asked.

"We just took it from Ambers," a reporter said.

"He said he was tired of rye and wanted scotch," another said.

Weill laughed.

"That's one thing I don't have to worry about."

He looked around the table and added, "What's the matter? Isn't anyone drinking?"

"No," somebody said.

"Well," Weill said, "I guess I'll take one for my cold."

When dinner finished, everyone went outside. They all took the short walk from the farmhouse up the slope that led to the gymnasium.

"He's in the dressing room," Whitey said. "You want to talk to him, don't you?"

The reporters filed into the dressing room. Ambers was still half-dressed and lacing his shoes.

"How do you feel?" they asked him.

"I feel swell. I'm punching good," Ambers replied.

A reporter asked him how many times he had seen McLarnin fight.

"I saw him twice. I saw him fight Barney Ross and saw him with somebody else," Ambers said.

"You saw him with Canzoneri," Skid said.

"That's right," Ambers said. "Canzoneri."

"Which fight?" a reporter asked.

"The first one," Ambers said. "No, the second one. Lemme me see, now …"

"Who won it?" a reporter asked.

"Canzoneri," Ambers replied.

"It was the first fight," a reporter said.

"That's right," Ambers said. "He nearly knocked McLarnin out in the first round, and then McLarnin nearly knocked him out in the second round."

"No," the reporter said. "It was just the other way around."

"That's right," Ambers said.

"How long have you wanted to fight McLarnin?" another reporter asked.

"I don't know," Ambers said.

"Well, who's idea was it, yours or Weill's?" the reporter asked.

"I'll fight anyone Al wants me to," Ambers said. "If he says I fight McLarnin, all right, I fight McLarnin. He makes the matches, and I do the fighting."

"Do you remember," a reporter asked, "when you were named the number-one lightweight contender in this state, and Barney Ross resigned the lightweight title because he didn't want to fight you?"

"Yes," Ambers said.

"Well," the reporter said, "if you beat McLarnin, you may get a crack at Ross for the welterweight title. Do you know that?"

"Gee," Ambers said, grinning. "That would be great, wouldn't it?"

"What happened to you in that Cool fight in Philadelphia?" a reporter asked. Eddie Cool was a boxer.

"I don't know what was the matter with me," Ambers said.

"Ed Van Every said you won the fight all right, but you didn't look good," the reporter said. "A fight like that shouldn't have been close. Didn't you feel all right?"

"Yes, I felt all right," Ambers said.

"Well, what was the matter?" the reporter asked.

"Maybe I was a little nervous," Ambers said. "It was my first fight since the champion. I guess I was a little nervous."

"You told me once that you were always nervous before a fight," the reporter said.

"That's right," he said. "Sometimes I get on edge, and I speak back to Whitey and Skid. I don't mean to. But I'm just on edge."

"Benny Leonard says when a fighter is on edge it is because he knows he's due to get licked," another reporter said.

"Is that right?" Ambers said.

Ambers laughed.

"Did he say that?" he asked.

"Yes," the reporter said. "You weren't afraid of getting licked by Cool, were you?"

Ambers laughed again.

"No," he said.

"Are you on edge now?" another reporter asked. "After all, this McLarnin looked pretty tough in the last fight with Canzoneri, and you wouldn't want all the boys back in Herkimer to be saying that about you, would you?"

Ambers roared.

"Go away," he said.

One of the reporters asked him if he had been hunting woodchucks lately.

"No," he said, grinning. "The woodchucks are hibernating."

He remembered the word from early last spring when he said he could not find any woodchucks. Somebody told him the woodchucks were in hibernation.

"But I'll get them when they come out," he said.

"You're hell on those woodchucks," a reporter said.

"Yes," he said. "Did you ever go hunting?"

"No," the reporter said.

"Oh, boy," Ambers said. "You don't know what you miss. You go hunting once, you'll never do anything else. I'm going to get a new .16-gauge automatic and a 25-20 rifle."

Al Weill came in the room just in time to overhear this.

"Are you a hunter, too?" he asked the reporter.

"No," Ambers said. "He never hunts. Al never hunts, either."

"What's the use of hunting when you can't hit anything?" Weill said.

Ambers was ready for the ring now, and Whitey came in.

"All right," he said. "Come on."

One of the reporters asked Ambers, as they were leaving the room, if he had brought his saxophone with him.

He made a gesture of disgust.

"No," he said. "I bought three saxophones, but I couldn't learn to play them right, and I gave them away."

"How's your clarinet?" the reporter asked.

Ambers laughed.

"I was playing it every day, and I just got so I was learning to play it pretty good when the lady downstairs came up and asked me, 'Please don't play that thing anymore. My baby can't sleep when you play it.'"

"Just when I was learning it pretty good, too, so I had to quit."

"Come on," Whitey said. "They're waiting for you."[22]

Ambers used welterweight Jack Giacaione and lightweight Irving Eldridge as his sparring partners. Eldridge had good hands that gave Ambers trouble. It prompted Ambers to say that Eldridge might be the boy who would someday take his title just as he took it from Canzoneri.[37] Eldridge finished a good career with a record of sixty-two wins, fifteen losses, and eleven draws. He rated the eighth-ranked lightweight from 1938 to 1940 by *The Ring* magazine. No one ever gave him a title chance.

On November 19, Ambers's training was completed. Odds makers had him a three-to-one underdog against the former welterweight champion McLarnin, who had defeated, and made a large amount of money, conquering lightweight champions. He beat Tony Canzoneri, Barney Ross, Sammy Mandell, Al Singer, and Benny Leonard.[39]

McLarnin outweighed Ambers by eight pounds. They billed it as a light welterweight fight. They fought at Madison Square Garden on November 20, 1936. No one had knocked out Ambers in more than three years of professional fighting. There were no knockdowns. Ambers, on the brink of being knocked down a few times, exhibited his toughness and durability by not hitting the canvas once. He staggered several times. At the end of the bout, Ambers was covered in his own blood.[40] McLarnin won a unanimous decision. Ambers retained his lightweight crown since it was not a lightweight fight. McLarnin had a long and brilliant ring career. This was the last fight for the twenty-eight-year-old former welterweight champion Jimmy McLarnin. Lou later said that McLarnin was the hardest puncher he ever faced.

"It was a mistake to fight," manager Al Weill admitted.[26]

CHAPTER 25

Death, a Carnival, and a
Baer in the Woods

Early in 1937, yet another former heavyweight champion came to Madame Bey's Camp. It was Max Baer. He won the world heavyweight championship on June 14, 1934, when he knocked out Primo Carnera. He lost it in his next fight on June 13, 1935, to James Braddock in New York.

They called Baer the Livermore Larupper or Madcap Maxie. He wore a prominent Star of David embroidered on his boxing trunks during his defeat of Max Schmeling in 1933 and subsequent fights. His mother was Protestant and his father Jewish on his father's side. That made Max one-quarter Jewish. He was born in Omaha, Nebraska, in 1909. At the age of twelve, Max Baer's family moved to Livermore, California, to be cattle ranchers. He credited his powerful shoulders to working as a butcher and carrying heavy carcasses of meat.[1] He became a professional boxer in 1929.

Like Carnera and Ambers, Baer killed a man in the ring. Baer fought Frankie Campbell on August 25, 1930, in San Francisco. Campbell's brother was Brooklyn Dodgers Baseball Hall of Famer Adolph Camilli. Manager Jack Kearns and former heavyweight champions Jim Jeffries and Jack Dempsey were at ringside. Baer's punch struck Campbell with such power, his brain detached from the connective tissue securing it. Between rounds, Campbell told his corner men he felt something snap in the back of his head. He continued to fight. In the fifth round, Baer knocked Campbell out. He never regained consciousness. After he lay on the canvas for almost an hour, medics brought Campbell by ambulance to a nearby hospital where he died of extensive brain hemorrhaging.[2] Campbell's death devastated Baer. Authorities charged him with manslaughter but later acquitted him. The State Boxing Commission banned him for the next year.

Baer quit boxing for several months after Campbell's death. After returning, he lost four of his next six fights because he did not fight as he did before the tragedy. One of the four losses was against Tommy Loughran. After the fight, Loughran told Baer that he was looping and telegraphing his punches. Jack Dempsey helped Baer shorten his punches and assisted him the rest of his career.[3]

Joseph Goebbels, minister of propaganda and public entertainment in Germany, banned Baer's movie *The Prizefighter and the Lady* from playing in his country.

"Is the film barred because Max Baer is a Jew?" someone asked Goebbels.

"Ja," he snapped.

"They didn't ban the picture because I have Jewish blood," Baer said when contacted for comment. "They banned it because I knocked out Max Schmeling."[4, 5]

Max Baer's lifestyle as a playboy and his unencumbered comments were a source of annoyance for boxing commissions.

In February 1937, Max Baer came to Madame Bey's Camp. He was the sixth world heavyweight champion to use Chatham Township to train. He was there to train for a fight with Bob Pastor, a fight that many doubted would occur because Baer needed a license to fight in New York. Along with Max came his heavyweight-boxing brother, Buddy Baer, trainer, Izzy Kline, and his manager, Ancil Hoffman.[6]

After appearing before the New York Commission, they granted Baer a license in late February to fight Pastor in New York. The commission gave a date of March 19 for the bout at Madison Square Garden. New York Commissioner Bill Brown made it clear how he felt.

"I want no mistake about how I feel on Baer," he declared. "I still think Baer as a fighter is an ordinary bum. My opposition to him has not changed. I still consider him a detriment to boxing. But if the Garden wants to be burdened with this kind of a burden, I'm willing to cooperate. I'll vote in favor of giving him a license."[7]

For Baer's manager, Hoffman, the actions of the Garden and commission were too late. He had made plans for Max and his brother, Buddy, to fight in England. To add to the confusion, a press member telephoned Baer at Bey's where he expressed enthusiasm for fighting Pastor.

"Max is going to fight in London April 15 and has another bout scheduled for May 31," Ancil Hoffman said. "We will not return here until June. If during the outdoor season, Pastor wants the bout and the erroneous impression that Max is a bum as a fighter has been corrected, we'll be glad to consider it."[7]

English promoters General Albert Critchley and Sid Hulls came to America to sign Max Baer for fights in England. When the Garden heard this, they told Hoffman they would take legal action if he broke the contract to fight Bob Pastor on March 19. The Garden sent their matchmaker, Sam McQuade, to Bey's to talk to Max Baer. Baer informed McQuade that the decision rested with his manager, Hoffman. He expressed a willingness to fight Pastor, provided his manager agreed.[8] Hoffman had plans for the Baer brothers to sail to England in two days on the ship *Berengaria*.[9] Despite the legal action, they left Madame Bey's and went to England.

Lou Ambers trained at Bey's in March and April 1937.[10] Ambers had won four fights and drew another since losing to Jimmy McLarnin on November 20, 1936. That fight sent McLarnin into retirement. In March, Ambers lost by a decision in a nontitle bout against Puerto Rican Pedro Montañez, who had a record of sixty wins, four losses, and three draws, and had not lost in his last forty-three fights. Two weeks later, Ambers beat Phil Baker. Next, he was going to fight Tony Canzoneri again on May 7. This time the world lightweight title would be at risk. Ambers would stay at Bey's to train for Canzoneri.

"That fellow Lou Ambers can take a punch with the best of them," observed an anonymous veteran fight manager at Bey's Camp. "And anytime you get a fighter to ride a punch like the Herkimer kid, it is going to take a lot of fighting to beat him. Speed and ability to take a punch are two attributes that every champion must possess and do not forget that Lou Ambers has both of these assets."[11]

Canzoneri trained at Dr. Bier's Camp in Pompton Lakes, New Jersey. The younger and faster Lou Ambers was the favorite against the older Tony Canzoneri. The five-time titleholder Canzoneri would be going for an unprecedented sixth. Ambers would have little trouble getting in shape—he had fought six times since the beginning of the year.

On April 24 in Ridgewood Grove, Brooklyn, Canzoneri had a warm-up bout against Joey Zodda. Ambers did not pass up the opportunity to watch his next opponent. He came to watch Canzoneri dance, feint, and jab. Ambers kept especial attention on how he used his powerful right.[12] Ambers would need to root for Canzoneri so as not to hurt their draw for their bout in May. Canzoneri knocked out Zodda in the seventh round.

Al Weill, who made it a point not to make prefight predictions, broke with his tradition. He advised his friends to bet a few bucks on Ambers. He could not see how Ambers could lose against his old rival.[12] He was training well at Bey's, which pleased his manager, Weill, and his trainer, Whitey Bimstein.

Canzoneri moved to his home in Marlboro, New York, to finish training while Ambers remained at Bey's Camp.[13] From Madame Bey's Camp, there were reports Ambers was a much better fighter now than at any time since he won the title from Canzoneri. At the camp, Ambers laughed when someone suggested that Canzoneri would knock him out. He said that he would be the one to apply the crusher if there were any knockouts delivered.[14]

The former world welterweight champion Jack Britton and his past manager, Dumb Dan Morgan—one of the best during his time—visited Ambers at Madame Bey's Camp. Morgan was the man who gave Joe Jacobs his start in boxing. Britton retired in 1930 with a record of 103 wins, twenty-nine losses, and twenty draws. Morgan also was retired. After Morgan retired from managing fighters, Mike Jacobs for Madison Square Garden employed his expertise to help with fight promotions. Jack Britton traveled to Bey's to watch his son, welterweight Bobby Britton, spar with Ambers. An average fighter, the son never obtained the heights of his father.

Ambers and Al Weill planned a tour of Europe after the Canzoneri bout. Weill wanted to visit his sister in his native France. Ambers had no objections.

"Al and I want to go places," Ambers announced before he boxed five rounds, three with Bobby Britton and two with welterweight Jackie Reemes.

"I never saw Ambers look better," Morgan said.

"I'm not having any trouble with the weight," Ambers volunteered without being asked. "I'm down to one hundred thirty-six pounds and will come in under one hundred thirty-five. I've got to be fast for Tony. He's always dangerous."

Ambers, who was again having trouble making weight, tried to dispel the rumor. The rumor was true.

"You'll beat him easy," Morgan assured Ambers.

"He hasn't got it anymore," Weill agreed.[15]

Actor and singer Al Jolson offered $25,000 for a bout between his Henry Armstrong and the winner of the Ambers-Canzoneri title fight.[16] On May 7, 1937, at Madison Square Garden, a crowd of 11,005 fans paid $40,746[17] to watch the twenty-three-year-old Ambers fight the twenty-eight-year-old Canzoneri. Each weighed 135 pounds; Ambers barely made weight. Canzoneri had fought about 150 fights and earned close to a half-million dollars in purses, but he was on the decline. Ambers destroyed Canzoneri in a lopsided, unanimous decision. There were no knockdowns. Ambers was unmarked at the finish. One of Canzoneri's eyes was closed completely. There was a cut on the other, and he bled from a cut on the nose. Newspapers wrote it was a pitiful shadow of Canzoneri. For the man who used to meet them all and beat them all, the fight probably marked the passing of Canzoneri as a major fighter. The crowd gave the five-time champion Canzoneri a tremendous ovation as he left the ring.[17, 18] The judges scored it thirteen to two and fifteen to zero while referee Arthur Donovan had it twelve to two with one even. The Associated Press score sheet gave twelve to Ambers, two to Canzoneri, and one even.

Canzoneri had promised the week before to hang up the gloves if he failed to defeat his former Madame Bey sparring partner. After the bout, he said he intended to keep fighting. Canzoneri refused to admit he was finished as a fighter.

"Ambers was much improved tonight," he said, "but I can lick him. He hit me with a lot of backhand slaps tonight that should not have been counted."[17]

As planned, Ambers and Weill left to tour England, France, Germany, Belgium, and Italy[16] soon after the bout.

In June, trainer Ray Arcel returned to Bey's with former world middleweight champion Teddy Yarosz. He won all seven of his fights since losing the middleweight title. He knocked out Young Terry in Youngstown the last August. He beat Babe Risko, Ken Overlin, and Eddie Maguire in Pittsburgh, Solly Krieger in New York, and upset Lou Brouillard in Boston. Many considered Yarosz a threat to regain his title.

He trained for a bout with Billy the "Pittsburgh Kid" Conn, who would later hold the world light heavyweight championship from 1939 to 1941. Billy Conn would become best known for his classic 1941 fight for the world heavyweight championship with Joe Louis and their rematch in 1946. In 1941, with Conn ahead on points, Louis knocked him out in the thirteenth round. The Brown Bomber said it was one of his toughest fights.[19] Both Yarosz and Conn were from the Pittsburgh area. The Yarosz-Conn bout would be contested in the middleweight division.

Ray Arcel left Madame Bey's and Teddy Yarosz to travel to Chicago. His assistant, Lefty Castron, worked with Yarosz in his absence. Arcel was employed by world heavyweight champion James Braddock as a second. It was for his title fight against Joe Louis at Comiskey Park.[20] On June 22, 1937, one minute into the first round, Braddock dropped Louis with a right uppercut to the chin. Louis got up and proceeded to dominate the rest of the bout. Due to severe bleeding and a badly swollen face, Braddock's manager, Joe Gould, wanted to stop the bout between rounds seven and eight, but Braddock convinced Gould to let him continue. In round eight, Louis threw a left to the body and followed with a hard right to the chin that put Braddock down. The referee counted him out at one minute and ten seconds of the round.[21] Braddock later said, "When he hit me with that left-right combination, I could've stayed down on the canvas for three weeks." It was the first and only time anyone knocked Braddock out. Ray Arcel traveled back to Madame Bey's the next day.

One day before his fight, Yarosz worked out for fifteen rounds, boxing for twelve. He sparred with Walter Woods, who would be fighting on the Yarosz-Conn undercard, and former world middleweight champion Ben Jeby, who had contested his last professional fight on July 15, 1936. After a month's work, Yarosz developed a tan from working outside. Trainer Arcel, manager Foutts, and Yarosz said they would fly out of Newark Airport the next day.[22, 23] Newark was the first major airport in the metropolitan area, opening on October 1, 1928. The airport, built on sixty-eight acres of marshland by the city of Newark, quickly became the world's busiest commercial airport.

The next morning, both fighters appeared at McClelland's office in the Law and Finance Building for the prefight weigh-in and physical. Yarosz went with trainer Ray Arcel and manager Ray Foutts. On June 30, 1937, the twelve-round fight took place at Forbes Field, Pittsburgh, Pennsylvania. On the undercard, Yarosz's sparring partner, Walter

Woods, won over Joe Duca in a fifth-round technical knockout. Yarosz was a two-to-one favorite. He lost a twelve-round split decision to the nineteen-year-old Conn. Referee Al Grayber scored it five to three, Judge George MacBeth scored it three to eight, and Judge Alvin Williams scored it six to four. The crowd pelted the ring with seat cushions and bottles after they announced the decision; they thought Yarosz had won. The intensity of booing drowned out the cheers from the Conn fans. Seat cushion sales and soda sold in bottles was disallowed for future bouts because of the incident.[24]

For the young, tall, handsome Conn, it was his thirty-fourth consecutive win. He had not lost a middleweight bout. Conn had terminated a remarkable comeback by Yarosz since he lost the title to Risko in their second match in September 1935. Conn now became Pittsburgh's favorite son.

"Billy is a good boy," Yarosz said after the fight. "But I am certain I beat him."

The year 1937, again, was bringing many boxers of world renown to Madame Bey's Camp. It was a time of celebration of her business. It was also a year of deep sorrow for Madame Bey. Her husband, Sidky Bey, developed heart problems in early 1937. On a Sunday, July 11, Sidky Bey died of heart failure. His wife, son, daughter-in-law, two granddaughters, and sister living in Turkey survived him. His family held funeral services at the Bey Camp on July 13.[25] The man she had married forty years before, who had brought her to the American shores under the auspices of the Turkish delegation, was gone. The man whom she married at sixteen years old was dead at the age of sixty-two.

No longer would the quiet, soft-spoken Sidky Bey wander around camp as he was inclined to do daily. Journalist Damon Runyon said, "He always struck us that he must be slightly bewildered by the prodigious efficiency of a helpmeet who successfully manages a home for prize fighters and makes the deadliest punchers, and the most ferocious gladiators, toe the mark of her rules."[26]

Madame Bey, now fifty-five years old, was devastated by her husband's death. She would need to take solace in her boys to get through this dark period of her life. The heartbeat of the camp would need her guidance to survive. She would immerse herself into what had been her life's work. The camp continued to thrive with her at the helm.

In July 1937, promoter Mike Jacobs had the idea to put together an unprecedented boxing card with four championship bouts. He would promote it as the Carnival of Champions. Jacobs committed to four title fights to be staged at the Polo Grounds. The four championship bouts would match world lightweight champion Lou Ambers against Pedro Montañez, world welterweight champion Barney Ross against Ceferino Garcia, world bantamweight champion Sixto Escobar against Harry Jeffra, and French middleweight champion Marcel Thil against Fred Apostoli. Before the fight date arrived, controversy arose over the middleweight bout. Thil regarded himself as the world middleweight champion. The New York State Athletic Commission (NYSAC) recognized Freddie Steele as the champion. Under NYSAC compulsion, both boxers had to sign an agreement stipulating that no title would be at stake if they wanted to fight in New York.

Jacobs signed a contract stipulating for him to pay lightweight champion Lou Ambers $65,000 with an opportunity of 20 percent of the gate. It was an all-time high guarantee for a lightweight. In time, Jacobs had every fighter signed to an elaborate scale. Besides Ambers's contract, he signed his challenger, Montañez, for $40,000. He signed Ross for $35,000, Thil $30,000, Escobar $12,500, Garcia $5,000, Apostoli $5,000, and Jeffra $2,500. If his receipts reached the $350,000 mark, Jacobs predicted he stood to realize a sizable profit. Jacobs did not ignore his philanthropy for the event. He committed 10 percent of his profits to the House of Calvary Cancer Hospital.

Mike Jacobs had committed about $200,000 of his own money. He believed that with the Polo Grounds tickets scaled from $3 to $16.50, he might achieve a gate of $500,000. When it was suggested that a financial loss on the event was a possibility, he grinned and shrugged.

"What of it?" he said. "We'll all have a lot of fun, won't we? We'll see some good fights and give a lot of fellows some work."[27]

Promoter Jacobs wanted his fighters to be in the best of shape to stage a good show for the paying patrons. He sent many of his fighters to his friend Madame Bey. He was a frequent visitor when fighters he was promoting were there. Mike Jacobs would have three of his Carnival of Champion fighters train at Bey's Camp. World lightweight champion Lou Ambers, world bantamweight champion Sixto Escobar, and middleweight challenger Fred Apostoli. Whitey Bimstein trained all three. Ambers had a new manager, and his former manager, Al Weill, took the position of matchmaker for Mike Jacobs's Twentieth Century Sporting Club.

Charley Goldman was Ambers's new manager though he was more known as a trainer. Weill and Ambers, thought to be inseparable, remained good friends, and Weill would check in on his former charge during his training at Bey's Camp. In later years, Weill and Goldman would collaborate to campaign many fighters, including undefeated world heavyweight champion Rocky Marciano.

Charley Goldman stood just over five feet tall and weighed a little over one hundred pounds. He wore a signature black derby and horn-rimmed glasses. He had a gruff face that hid his gentle, jovial temperament. That face most often held a big cigar. He was born Israel Goldman in Warsaw, Poland. He grew up in the tough Red Hook segment of Brooklyn and discovered how to fight on the streets. He dropped out of school in the fourth grade and began fighting in unsanctioned fights to earn money. He turned professional at the age of fifteen, fighting mostly as a bantamweight. He fought bantamweight champion Johnny Coulon in a no-decision bout in 1912. Goldman retired in 1914 with a record of thirty-six wins, six losses, eleven draws, and eighty-four no decisions. Goldman claimed he fought about four hundred times. He idolized world bantamweight and featherweight champion Terrible Terry McGovern and was his protégé. He wore the same trademark derby hat in imitation of McGovern.[3, 28, 29]

In Goldman's career, he trained Joey Archibald, Kid Gavilan, Al McCoy, Carlos Ortiz, Marty Servo, Jersey Joe Walcott, Fritzie Zivic, and Rocky Marciano. Goldman's philosophy was to improve upon, but not change, a fighter's style. The *New York Times* quoted Goldman describing the difficulty training young boxers.

"Training a promising kid is like putting a quarter in one pocket and taking a dollar out of the other."

One of the most remarkable facets of the training of Lou Ambers, Sixto Escobar, and Fred Apostoli at Madame Bey's was the friendliness among them in the camp. When the press was told they would share Madame Bey's Camp for the Carnival of Champions, many anticipated that animosity would result. Nothing transpired. Madame Bey structured their training to avoid conflict. Escobar started first at one o'clock, Ambers followed at two o'clock, and Apostoli at three o'clock. Just one happy family, a reporter said.[30]

Ambers and Escobar were veterans of Bey's Camp, while Fred Apostoli was a new addition. Fred Apostoli was born in San Francisco's North Beach district. He worked as a bellhop before boxing. The press called him the Boxing Bell Hop and Handsome Freddy. He was a classmate and friend of baseball legend Joe DiMaggio.

Journalists, photographers, and fans inundated the camp before the Carnival of Champions date. On September 13, Al Buck reported on the fighters for the *New York Post*. He asked Ambers if he thought he had won the night Montañez received a close and disputed decision in their ten-round nontitle bout at Madison Square Garden.

"I don't know," Ambers answered. "I never know who is winning when I'm fighting."

Ambers was asked how he liked his new manager, Charley Goldman.

"Fine," Ambers said as he winked. "Swell."

Goldman said nothing. Heavyweight Tony Galento, Dumb Dan Morgan, Kid McPartland, the former lightweight boxer who retired in 1905 and now was a boxing judge and referee, Al Weill, and manager Joe Jacobs were also at the camp. Weill asked how Ambers looked.

"Better than he's looked for some time, but he gets hit with too many right hands," Joe Jacobs observed. "I counted ten during the three rounds he boxed with Augie Gonzales."

"I'm rolling with 'em, Joe, and I'm not quite right yet," Ambers explained to Joe Jacobs. "Gonzales is a smart young fellow, and I honestly only felt three of his punches."[31]

Dr. Vincent Nardiello, New York State Athletic Commission physician, came to Madame Bey's on September 16. He came to weigh and examine Lou Ambers, Sixto Escobar, and Fred Apostoli. He pronounced them in excellent condition for the Carnival of Champions. Dr. Nardiello was especially impressed with the condition of Apostoli.[32]

Making weight was becoming problematic for Ambers. Many press members were unaware that Ambers was starving to make weight. He was outgrowing the lightweight limit. Whitey Bimstein had all three in such good condition that he had to decrease their training less than a week before the fight date.[33]

A few days later, Whitey commented on his fighters' weights.

"We haven't any weight problems in this camp," Whitey said. "My big job is not to let the boys get down too fine. Escobar weighed one hundred eighteen and three-quarter pounds after today's workout. Ambers is down to one hundred thirty-six and Apostoli is only two pounds over the middleweight limit of one hundred sixty pounds. All could go in and fight tonight."

Ambers deviated from his dancing style of boxing. He fought in close with his sparring partners.

"I'm going to slug with him, and I'll be ready and willing to take a good punch in order to land one," Ambers said.

"I have never seen Lou as rough or as determined as he is for this fight," Harry Lenny said, a veteran New York fight manager. The crowd cheered as Ambers sparred.[34]

After Ambers, Escobar sparred with Jimmy English and Cyril Josephs. Apostoli only did bag punching and shadowboxing. Whitey declared there would be one more day of boxing for all three. After that, they would do light training before the fights.

On September 17, Fred Apostoli sparred with Tony Fisher and Young Terry for five rounds. He hit Fisher hard for two rounds, and then with the veteran Terry it appeared to be a real fight. Apostoli focused on his body punches with both sparing partners. He used short, vicious left hooks to the body with consequence. Ambers had a day of rest while Escobar did limbering exercises. The two were to box the next day while Apostoli would rest.[35]

The next day, September 18, the press asked Escobar about his two previous defeats against Jeffra, his opponent in the Carnival of Champions.

"No, he beat me," Escobar declared in referring to the decisions he lost to Jeffra. "I think I win in Baltimore. He win all right in Hippodrome. This time I do better. He too big to make weight."

Escobar's opponent, Jeffra, was having legal issues in the Supreme Court with a breach of contract for a previous match. Lou Brix, Escobar's manager, was asked about Jeffra's legal problems and if the match was in danger. Brix said that was for Mike Jacobs to worry about.

"I fight," promised Escobar, assuming that Jeffra would be able to fight. "I win, too."[36]

After the journalists' questions, champion Escobar sparred with Jimmy English and Cyril Josephs. He expressed uncertainty, at least for publication, that his fellow Puerto Rican Pedro Montañez would do as well against Lou Ambers.

"It is tough fight," Escobar observed. "Tough for both of them."[37]

The press asked Whitey Bimstein, trainer of all three, about the bouts.

"The winners?" Whitey said. "They're all here, Escobar, Ambers, and Apostoli."[36]

Promoter Mike Jacobs made a shift in the order of the fights for the Carnival of Champions at the Polo Grounds. Marcel Thil of France would open the event against Fred Apostoli. Jacobs said he changed the fight order to enable European newspapers to receive news of the fight some hours earlier than if it had been later. In the second bout, he put the Barney Ross match with Ceferino Garcia. The third bout would be Lou Ambers against Pedro Montañez. The finale would be Sixto Escobar and Harry Jeffra. A preliminary bout would open the program at 7:45 in the evening, and the Thil-Apostoli bout would begin at 8:10.[38]

Three days before the fight date, the three fighters at Madame Bey's undertook their final intense workout. Lou Brix, in a tactical move, or unethical, went to New York to get Harry Jeffra's chief sparring partner, Kitzuma Mirioka, and brought him to Madame Bey's Camp to spar with Escobar. Fred Apostoli did the most arduous sparring. He boxed six rounds with three sparring partners. He fought Solly Farina for two rounds, Buster Hall for one round, and Young Terry for three rounds. Again, he concentrated on hitting to the body. Lou Ambers went three rounds with Carl Guggino and two with Augie Gonzales. Ambers again fought in close with his sparring partners.[39]

On September 23, 1937, Mike Jacobs held his Carnival of Champions at the Polo Grounds. It was an unprecedented event in boxing history. The event started at 7:45 with a four-round preliminary bout of such little importance that Mike Jacobs forgot to list the fighters. Amongst the crowd of 45,000 were governors, United States senators and congressmen, mayors, judges, lawyers, bankers, stockbrokers, industry leaders, society people, stage and screen stars, and figures from many fields of sport. WNBC broadcast the fight over the radio.[38]

It was fifty-five rounds of championship fights. Not one knockdown occurred. Ambers retained his lightweight title by avenging his previous loss to Montañez. Both judges gave Ambers the edge, with the referee scoring it even. Lou Ambers sang in his dressing room, "Put on your old gray bonnet with the blue ribbons on it."

"Save those gloves," Ambers shouted, hardly missing a note in his song and then started to dance. He traveled to Herkimer after the bout with his brothers Joe and Angelo, his friend Father Gustave, and a lucky pair of boxing gloves.[40]

Barney Ross retained his welterweight title with a unanimous decision over Filipino Ceferino Garcia, who claimed Ross head-butted him. Fred Apostoli, in the only fight not to go fifteen rounds, defeated Marcel Thil. The Frenchman was stopped in the tenth round with a severe cut over his right eye. Thil led on the scorecards at the time of the stoppage. This was the thirty-two-year-old Thil's final career bout. Apostoli, along with most of boxing, considered Freddie Steele the world middleweight champion. Only the Boxing Federation of Europe considered it a championship bout. Apostoli could not claim the title.

Sixto Escobar lost his bantamweight title to Harry Jeffra in a one-sided match to the surprise of many. Harry Jeffra, despite winning, complained because he fought around midnight. Escobar also stated his annoyance claiming the delay made him cold.

"Ten o'clock's my bedtime," Jeffra declared.[40]

Of the 45,000 in attendance, 32,600 were paying customers. The gross receipts were $232,644. After the $20,000 stadium rental and other expenses, the net amounted to $198,634.[41] After paying the $190,000 guarantees to the fighters, Mike Jacobs had a little profit, but it set future matches for Jacobs that made the night worth it.

CHAPTER 26

My Max Returns

W hitey's Carnival of Champion fighters who had trained at Bey's had won two and
lost one. Ambers and Apostoli had won while Escobar took the loss. The camp
welcomed the next boxers now that the men of the Carnival of Champions had vacated
the grounds. Some of the best in the heavyweight division would be present at the camp.
They would dominate the camp's last two months of 1937.

A special time for Madame Bey came in the middle of November. The man she had
helped when he had nothing and parlayed her graciousness into fame, fortune, and a world
heavyweight title would be back. Her Max was returning. To many, this was a different
Max Schmeling. By affiliation, he represented the German Nazi regime. To Madame Bey,
he was the same Max that showed up at her door looking for help years ago.

The year before, Schmeling found himself caught in the politics of boxing. On August
8, 1936, Schmeling arrived at Lakehurst, New Jersey, on the *Hindenburg* airship. He came
for the expressed purpose of signing and fighting for the world heavyweight title against
James Braddock. Schmeling and Braddock signed contracts for the bout shortly after
Schmeling's arrival. The fight was tentatively scheduled for September 26. In mid-August,
Braddock's manager, Joe Gould, said that Braddock suffered from a bone enlargement of
the little finger on his left hand and postponed the match.[1]

In December, they signed again for a bout on June 3, 1937. A picture of Schmeling
and Braddock after the signing appeared in newspapers.[2] Ten hours before the rescheduled
fight, Schmeling appeared at the weigh-in. The commission president, General Phelan,
stood and greeted Schmeling with a formal statement. Braddock did not show, the fight
was cancelled, and Braddock was fined one thousand dollars. Schmeling called the fine
ludicrous.[3] Tickets and posters had been printed, and the Madison Square Garden Long
Island Bowl marquee displayed the fight. A newsreel called *Ghosts Stalk in Empty Arena for
"Phantom Fight"* showed the weigh-in and empty arena.[4] Braddock had signed a contract
for a title fight with Joe Louis. That fight took place in Chicago a few weeks later with
Louis winning the title. A clause of that contract, not publicized, stated that Braddock
would receive 10 percent of Louis's earnings for the next ten years.[5] Joe Louis defended

his title twenty-five times in that decade. By not fighting Schmeling, Braddock became a wealthy man, as did Mike Jacobs.

Schmeling awaited a title opportunity. His close links to the Nazi Party and the fact that there was more money to be made from Braddock verses Louis shunted him aside. As Louis stopped Braddock and claimed his crown in June 1937, a furious Schmeling, with the backing of Hitler and the Nazis, planned a showdown with the Welshman Tommy Farr. They labeled it "the real world championship."

Before the Schmeling-Farr bout took place, promoter Mike Jacobs outmaneuvered Schmeling to protect his fighter—Joe Louis. Mike Jacobs did not want an alternate heavyweight champion recognized in Europe. He made a big-money offer to Farr. He guaranteed him a fight with Louis on August 30, 1937. It would be Louis's first title defense. Farr accepted the fight and Mike Jacobs's terms.

Thomas Farr was born on March 12, 1913. He was one of eight children. Farr grew up in a poor part of Wales. His mother died when he was nine. His father, an Irish bare-knuckle fighter, died shortly after. Farr became the main source of income for his family. He began working in the mines where his father had sustained injuries that led to his death. Farr bore blue coal scars on his back, received from crawling around small holes in the mines at the age of twelve. Welsh boxing historian and referee Winford Jones said it was his loathing of the mines rather than any love of boxing that first drove twelve-year-old Farr into boxing.[6] He became the British heavyweight champion and never lost the title in the ring; he relinquished it to fight Joe Louis.

About ten million Britons stayed up in the middle of the night to tune into the radio broadcast of the fight, which some ringside observers thought Farr had won.[7] He became the second man to take Louis the fifteen-round distance, losing the decision. The fight verdict outraged Farr's fans in Wales. Farr admitted the better man won that night.

"My face looked like a dug-up road after he'd finished with it," Farr said. "I've only got to think about Joe Louis, and my nose starts bleeding."[8]

Years later, Farr was quoted as having said, "At the end, I thought I might have got it. If they had made it a draw, I would have been happy."[7]

Schmeling had to forget the boxing politics from the prior year to achieve his goal of regaining the heavyweight title. Max landed in America aboard the ship *Bremen*. It was his seventh arrival in two years and his seventeenth since he first entered America in 1928 as an unknown heavyweight. The press started calling him Commuter Max. As usual, accompanying Max was his trainer, Max Machon. Manager Joe Jacobs met them upon their arrival.[9] The transatlantic commuter Schmeling arrived in America to launch anew his campaign for the heavyweight championship he once held.

Germany was under Nazi control, and Schmeling was a product of Germany. The crowds in America that once adored him now despised what he represented. His large Jewish following dissipated. Pictures of Schmeling and Adolf Hitler were in print for everyone to see. The Nazis used their star athlete as propaganda for what they thought a superior Aryan race. Schmeling's actions were duplicitous. He had met with Nazi officials to free Jews, gays, and other Nazi undesirables from incarceration. They were friends from his fond days during the Weimar Republic. He took the endeavor with personal risk. It was a risk that would prove to have consequences. Schmeling did admit he liked the attention he received from his Nazi association. He gave reason for detractors and supporters to reinforce their views.

Schmeling was to fight Harry "Tarzan" Thomas with a record of thirty-eight wins, nine losses, and two draws. Thomas had played football at Trinity College in Morningside, Iowa. He was a cowboy on a ranch near Intake, Montana.[10] For this fight, Schmeling had Mike Jacobs on his side; he was promoting the fight.

The media reported that Schmeling tried to secure exclusivity to Madame Bey's Camp. That request she would not grant, not even for her Max. Reportedly, Joe Louis had tried to train at Madame Bey's, too, but wanted complete control over the camp. That also met with her rejection.[11] Madame Bey would not put any of her boys out, not even to host the biggest names in boxing. Like all other fighters, they would have to come on her terms or not at all.

Schmeling decided upon Madame Bey's Camp, without the exclusivity, to prepare for his next fight. Manager Joe Jacobs stated that Max had obtained many offers to prepare at places where spectator money to watch him train would be lucrative. Max balked at all offers so that he could train where he was first befriended by Madame Bey.

"I like the camp and am happy to get back," Schmeling said. "It is quiet here, and the air is better."[12]

A few days before Schmeling came to Madame Bey's, Frank Graham interviewed him in a suite at the Essex House Hotel in New York. With Schmeling for the interview was his friend Otto Petrie, famed former bicycle race rider. Petrie was a constant companion to Schmeling while he was in America. Joe Jacobs was also present. Despite the continued Nazi efforts, with a personal request from Joseph Goebbels, Schmeling kept Jacobs as his manager. The Nazis found it a source of embarrassment that Schmeling maintained his Jewish manager over their objections.

Schmeling knew Joe Jacobs's power in boxing and took risks to keep him as his manager. "I received a letter from the Reich Ministry of Sports. They want me to split from Joe Jacobs, my manager since 1928. … I really need Joe Jacobs. I owe all my success in America to him."—Max Schmeling to Adolf Hitler, 1935.

Frank Graham described Schmeling as looking just the same. He was big, broad-shouldered, brown and healthy, eyes clear, flesh firm, and ready to fight.

"Well, what had he been doing?" Graham asked.

"Hunting," Schmeling replied.

"Anything else?"

"I bought a new place in the country, a farm."

"How big?"

Schmeling turned to Otto Petrie and said something in German.

"Six thousand acres," Petrie said.

"Yes," Schmeling said. "I do not know how big an acre is, but I remember now, six thousand acres."

"As big as Central Park," Joe Jacobs said.

"Bigger," Petrie said.

He waved his hand toward a window below where the park stretched north.

"This would be his front lawn," Petrie said.

"Field Marshall von Blucher owned it," Schmeling said. "You have heard of him, eh? He beat Napoleon."

"And after that, Bismarck owned it," Petrie added. "You know Bismarck, the Iron Chancellor?"

"There is cattle on it," Schmeling continued. "And horses and chickens and pigs. It is a real farm."

Graham asked him what his plans were.

"I will go to Madame Bey's at Summit to train in a couple of days," Schmeling said. "I will stay there until the fight on December 13. After the fight, I will go home for Christmas. I will fight Ben Foord in Hamburg on January 30, and a couple of weeks after that I will come back here. I would like to fight here in March again.

"I have been out of the ring for eighteen months. The only way to get back in fighting shape is to fight. That will give me the work in the ring I need and keep me in training. I will be in training, and I will have my mind on fighting. I will train here for a month, fight, go home, rest for a couple of weeks, and then start training again. Then I will fight, rest for a couple of weeks and then come over here and train again and fight in March, I hope. Then, I will not do any more until I fight Louis. But I will be in good shape."

Graham commented that he appeared to be in good shape now.

"I am," Schmeling said. "I weigh about one hundred ninety-six or one hundred ninety-seven. What did I weigh last June?"

"For Braddock?" Graham asked.

"Yes," Schmeling said. "For Braddock."

"A hundred and ninety-six," Petrie said.

"You see?" Schmeling said.

Graham asked if he knew anything about Harry Thomas, the man he would fight in America on December 13.

"No," Schmeling said. "I never heard of him."

"I told Max about him when I went down the bay to meet him," Joe Jacobs said. "I told him he was a big, rough, strong kid. You ought to know. You saw him fight."

Graham asked who did.

"You did," Joe Jacobs said. "You saw the Braddock-Louis fight. He was the fellow who stopped Brescia on his last fight; he beat Max Marek and had him on the floor three times. He has won most of his fights by knockouts, and he can take a punch. He is just the kind of a fighter to give Max a good fight. When I told Max about him, Max said he wanted the fight made for fifteen rounds because it might take him eight or nine rounds to catch up with a young fellow like that who can take a punch. And I mean he can take a punch. It's just a question of how long he can take it from a fellow who can punch as good as Max can."

Graham told him there was a report that he was going to fight Walter Neusel.

"I heard it," Schmeling said. "I was on the boat, and I got a cable from a German paper about it. I answered the cable. I said, 'I am matched with Harry Thomas and Ben Foord. I do not know anything about a Neusel fight.'

"Neusel," Schmeling said, "I beat him bad over there, and nobody would want to see me fight him again. I know what this is about, they want to match him with another fellow, and they are using my name for advertising. They will say they offered the match to me first, but they couldn't get me."

"Neusel couldn't beat Strickland," Joe Jacobs said. "They gave him the decision, but he got licked."

"Yes," Schmeling said. "Even the German papers said that. They said Strickland should have got the decision."

"And after the fight, Daley, Strickland's manager, gave Paul Damski a good going over," Joe Jacobs said.

Damski was Neusel's manager.

"Yes, I hear this, too," Schmeling said.

Joe Jacobs laughed.

"It must have been a big night," Jacobs said.[13]

Protests were immediate, as they were when Schmeling fought Joe Louis the year before. They did not want the perceived Nazi fighting in America. Schmeling last fought on June 19, 1936, when he surprised everyone by beating the undefeated Joe Louis in the twelfth round. The Nazi regime exploited the victory to its fullest.

The Non-Sectarian Anti-Nazi League to Champion Human Rights urged its supporters to boycott any event in which Max Schmeling might participate. They also opposed the proposed James Braddock fight against Schmeling earlier in the year. The Anti-Nazi League's letter, from organization president Samuel Untermyer, read in part:

"On August 30, we informed you that we shall be forced to urge our members and supporters to withhold all support from any event in which Max Schmeling may participate. According to reports in the press, Schmeling has been signed to fight Harry Thomas at Madison Square Garden, December 13. At this time we desire to repeat that we shall have to advise our members to withhold all support from the above event.

"Our reasons for this action have been stated before. Max Schmeling is a citizen of Nazi-Germany and on his return there, he will take with him the money he earns as a result of his participation in prize fights. It is not against Schmeling personally or because he is a German, but because whether he wins or loses the result of the fight will be to take American money to Germany and to that extent destroy the efficacy of the boycott If a way can be found or suggested by which the money paid to Schmeling can be invested and kept invested in this country, we should not be interested in the situation. But we know of no such way ..."

"There doesn't seem to be anything we can do about it," Mike Jacobs said. "I doubt if I will have any comment."

"I think the Anti-Nazi League has been fair in giving Schmeling a clean bill of health personally," Joe Jacobs remarked before leaving to join Max Schmeling at Madame Bey's Camp. "Of course, he is a German citizen and there is nothing he can do about that."[14]

Alberto Lovell of Argentina, the 1932 gold medal Olympic heavyweight champion, completed training at Madame Bey's before Schmeling arrived.[15] He had won all seven of his fights since arriving in America. He was training at Bey's for his New York debut against Eddie Blunt in the Hippodrome on November 12. Blunt was considered by many to be one of the hardest hitters in the heavyweight division. Lovell won by a unanimous decision. He won his next fight and then lost in December. He returned to Argentina and won the South American heavyweight title the following year. He fought until 1951 but never returned to America to fight. He retired after he lost to Archie Moore, who would train at Bey's for many fights, in a first-round knockout after forty-six seconds. The fight was held at the Estadio Luna Park, Buenos Aires, Distrito Federal, Argentina. Moore would win the world light heavyweight title in 1952, a title he held for almost ten years. Lovell's final career record after the loss was seventy-six wins with fifty-five knockouts, eight losses, and three draws.

On November 15, Schmeling returned to Madame Bey's Camp. He lived next door to Madame Bey's in a large wooden house. It was a pleasant, sunlit house on the side of a hill. Madame Bey's son, Rustem, owned the house. Rustem Bey, now thirty-nine years old, had worked as the acting police chief of Chatham Township since 1936 when Rowe, the police chief, died. Schmeling would be in the house where Rustem, his wife, Mildred, age thirty-eight, and two daughters, Muriel and Bette Anne at twelve and eight years, old lived.[16]

The living quarters gave Schmeling privacy and security. There was no animosity toward him among the boxers at Bey's Camp. Some of the public still disapproved of the German, though, and the safety of any boxer in public had always been a concern. No matter how strong and fierce these men were, many would bring armed bodyguards with them, especially those that were champions or famous. Schmeling's fame went beyond boxing. He was political, something beyond his control. He had a bodyguard.

"He took over my son's house next door to mine," Madame Bey said, "had his private chef and also had a bodyguard who carried a gun. That is not uncommon, as most of the champions feel it necessary to have someone around for protection in case enemies or gamblers should try to damage them, and even if they don't want the protection, the promoter of the fight will insist on it. But I think most of them secretly enjoy it because it stresses their importance."[17]

Billy Beauhuld, a Jersey City, New Jersey, native, was at Bey's when Schmeling arrived. Beauhuld, a lightweight division boxer,[18] had not lost a fight in his first thirty-eight professional bouts. Beauhuld had been at Bey's since August. He was to fight Al Roth in the main event at Madison Square Garden on September 9, but Beauhuld injured his right hand while training for the bout and canceled. Paul Junior, an aggressive lightweight from Lewiston, Maine, replaced Beauhuld.[19] The fight resulted in a draw.

Beauhuld's hand healed. He would fight world featherweight champion Henry "Homicide Hank" Armstrong, who was so fast and hard-hitting that some that fought Armstrong thought there were two men in the ring. No title was at stake. The fight would be in the lightweight division. Armstrong was eight-to-five odds he would win by a knockout. He planned his next fight before the Beauhuld bout had begun. Armstrong wanted to fight Pedro Montañez next—the man Ambers had just defeated in the Carnival of Champions.

"Armstrong intends to defend the featherweight title whenever a challenger shows," his manager said, "but while we're waiting for the opposition, he'll do a little fighting as a lightweight. That is if Beauhuld doesn't prove too tough tomorrow night."[20]

Beauhuld completed his training at Bey's with a final workout while Armstrong finished at Stillman's in New York. Before Beauhuld completed training, he had publicity pictures taken with Max Schmeling.[18] A thrill for a twenty-one-year-old boxer, as it was for Schmeling when he first met Jack Dempsey in Germany.

On November 19, 1937, at Madison Square Garden, the Armstrong-Beauhuld bout took place as the main event. Beauhuld hit the canvas in the first round. In the fifth, he went down again; the bell rang at the count of seven. Referee Art Donovan then decided "that the hopelessly beaten Jersey fighter had absorbed enough punishment."[21] Beauhuld experienced his first loss.

On November 25, one of the era's premier journalists Damon Runyon came to file a story on Max Schmeling. His column made mention of the ex-heavyweight champion, but the story evolved into one about Madame Bey and her establishment. Runyon was more impressed by the incredible story of Madame Bey than that of the former world heavyweight champion. The story entitled "Madame Bey Makes Fighters" read, in part:

"We note in sports news of the day that Madame Bey's is again a point of sporting attention … With Max Schmeling and his training we have no concern here. Our concern is with Madame Bey, the lady who runs the place known as Madame Bey's, a famous training camp for prize fighters."[22]

Schmeling was there to train. He would need to block out everything around him and concentrate on his upcoming fight. He trained daily. On December 6, with an admiring crowd of five hundred at Madame Bey's, he sparred with three opponents. The crowd was more interested in the boxer than the political hype about him. Schmeling sparred two rounds each with Jack Tebo; amateur Bill Schloeman, weighing 203 pounds; and wild swinging Steve Colucci, a Phillipsburg, New Jersey, heavyweight weighing 195 pounds. Schmeling showed that he still had that powerful ring hand. With it, he dropped Colucci to his knees.[23]

Though Schmeling was training to fight Harry Thomas, the fight everyone wanted was a rematch with Joe Louis. In September, Mike Jacobs had an agreement in place that the two would fight in June. The main points of the contract Schmeling signed was that the title bout would be staged somewhere in the United States in June, and Schmeling would get 30 percent of the net receipts and a large part of the radio and movie revenue. Louis would get 40 percent.[24]

The next day on December 7, Madame Bey's was abuzz with talk that another champion was to arrive. Retired ex-heavyweight champion Gene Tunney was to visit Madame Bey and watch Max Schmeling go through his workout. Few at the camp gave credence to any of the talks. The press said the thirty-nine-year-old Tunney had not done much for the sport that gave him his fortune and fame besides from his prefight ring appearances.[25]

To the surprise of many, Tunney came. It was the first time he had returned to the camp since before his first fight with Dempsey in Philadelphia eleven years ago. He was exquisite in dress. He wore a dark suit with a handkerchief exposed from the left breast pocket, light dress shirt, and a tie with a clasp. His hair was short and neatly in place.[26] His appearance belied his wealth obtained from the ring and marriage to Carnegie heir Polly Lauder. Tunney no longer donned trunks but sat on boards of corporations. He could associate with literary figures without fear of condemnation in the press, which was not the case when he was boxing.

Accompanying Tunney were two friends. He was with Robert Wilkin, a former Dartmouth football player and college boxer, and Frederick Faust, a writer famous for his Western fiction under the name of Max Brand. Faust was one of the most prolific authors of all time. He wrote more than five hundred novels and almost as many short stories. He penned more than thirty million words.

The reporters who remembered Tunney could not believe this was the same Gene Tunney as he sat in Madame Bey's dining room. The man they had tried unsuccessfully to be acquainted with when he was the champion. This was a softer Tunney.

"I can't believe it's the same man," one reporter said.[25]

Tunney proclaimed that he deplored the attempted boycott of the match because Schmeling was thought to be a Nazi. Tunney and his friends met Schmeling while they were having lunch in the dining room. Schmeling had already eaten in the house he was living in next door. Schmeling had come over after he finished his meal. He had met Tunney before. He had shaken hands with Tunney while he was in the ring waiting to fight Louis and again when all the former heavyweight champions gathered for introductions before the Louis-Farr fight.

They greeted each other and seemed interested in meeting.

"Do you do much running?" Gene asked Max. "I mean, real running, sprinting and so forth?"

"Oh, *ja*," Max said. "Real running, I walk and sprint and trot."

"Do you do any boxing on those days when you do roadwork?" Tunney asked.

"No," Max said, "but I walk around a bit in the morning on the days when I box."

"That's what I used to do," Tunney said.

Schmeling revealed that the first fight he saw in America was Tunney against Tom Heeney, which was Gene's last ring appearance. After they had exchanged a few reminiscences about a club they both had visited in Europe, Max said he was going to get ready and would wait for Gene to finish his luncheon before starting his workout. After he left, the conversation in Madame Bey's crowded dining room changed to an article Tunney had compiled some years ago in which he had selected outstanding fight descriptions and stories from classical literary works. Tunney talked with enthusiasm about an essay written by William Hazlitt. Now the reporters were getting a dose of the Tunney they remembered. Faust suggested that present newspaper fight stories were badly done. That a good snappy two thousand words concentrated on the blow that did the trick, instead of too much incidental writing about the whole bout, was the better idea.

"Like Homer did," Faust said with violent enthusiasm.

"Why, you could write two thousand words just on that one punch with which Louis knocked out Paulino," he said.

"Not in my paper," a reporter said.

Gene Tunney, followed by the dining room guests, walked across the driveway and climbed the hill to watch Schmeling go through his workout. Townspeople, fans, reporters, and photographers packed the gymnasium. They gave Tunney a rousing welcome. He watched the German closely. Schmeling sparred with Bill Schloeman and Steve Colucci two rounds each as he had done the day before. Reporters besieged Tunney after the workout. He did not hesitate in picking Schmeling to knock out Joe Louis again next June.[27]

"Schmeling has one of the best right hands I ever have seen," Tunney said, "and he's a smart and deliberate fighter. He has kept himself in such fine condition and has taken such good care of himself that I think the layoff will affect him less than it would another boxer. His blocking, footwork, and timing are perfect. If and when he meets Joe Louis again, I predict another knockout victory for Max."

Tunney had some final advice.

"But he should not take this fellow Thomas too lightly. I saw him stop Jorge Brescia in Chicago, and the boy can really hit."

A reporter pointed out to Schmeling that the bout with Thomas would be his thirteenth in America and would be fought on the thirteenth day of the month.

"I'm not superstitious," Max replied.[28]

There was plenty of time left for photo opts of Tunney and Schmeling in the indoor ring, with the backdrop of the wall plastered with fight posters of former Bey trainees. Schmeling, having just finished his workout, wore his usual sleeveless shirt and still had his boxing gloves and trunks on for pictures in the gymnasium.

Madame Bey said that having "her two big boys," Tunney and Schmeling, back home at once was the biggest event in her life since the day she saw President William McKinley mortally wounded.[25] It was an odd life's comparison. The gravity of an event leaves an indelible mark on our memory, whether pleasant or horrific.

There was one story the writers never became tired of telling for anyone inclined to listen after Tunney had made such a different impression on them. They would say on one occasion on a chilly autumn day, there were many sportswriters at the camp to watch a champion workout with his sparring partners. They hinted to Madame Bey that it would be gracious of their host if she gave them some whiskey to warm them up.

Prohibition was over, and even Madame Bey kept some spirits around. She set out the whiskey glasses. As the writers were going for their drinks, a car pulled into the driveway. Madame Bey quickly gathered the glasses and put them under the table. She told the reporters, "It is Gene! You understand, boys, I could not have that liquor out when he comes in. That dear Gene, he would be furious if he saw it!" Tunney entered the room where the growling writers were, who had never liked him. Tunney ignored them to give his old friend a warm greeting.

"Brrrrrr, it's a bit raw, Madame!" Tunney declared. "Er—do you think you could—ah—find a little whiskey about the place?" Tunney was the American Distilling Company chairman.[17]

Another heavyweight arrived at Madame Bey's Camp the day after Tunney came. On December 8, Buddy Baer, brother to Max Baer, joined Schmeling. Baer would train for his bout with Eddie Hogan December 17, 1937.[29] Baer would win that fight by a technical knockout in the third round.

On December 9, manager Joe Jacobs took a group composed of promoter Mike Jacobs and three newspapermen to Madame Bey's Camp to see Max Schmeling train. On the way there, a newspaperman asked Joe Jacobs if he had seen Thomas, who was at Dr. Bier's in Pompton Lakes.

"No," Joe said.

"He's a tough guy," the newspaperman said. "How he can hit! When he punches the heavy bag he has a fellow hold the bag, and he hits it so hard it takes the fellow right off his feet."

Joe did not say anything.

"If he hits Schmeling with one of those punches, he'll knock him dead," the newspaperman said.

"Are you going to Germany with Max for Christmas?" Mike Jacobs asked.

"No," Joe Jacobs said. "I'm going over in January."

"If this Thomas hits him on the lug you'd better not go back at all," the newspaperman said.

"If he hits Max on the lug I won't want to go," Joe said.

"I think Thomas is a good short-end bet, myself," the newspaper man said. "He's a big, strong kid—and confident! Say, you never saw such a confident guy. He's the best salesman I ever met. After listening to him talk, I wanted to run right out and make a bet on him. No wonder Max is sore at you."

"Max isn't sore at me," Joe said.

"Maybe not," the newspaperman said. "But Machon is."

Joe did not say anything.

They arrived at Bey's and went to her son's house where Schmeling was staying. There was a white-capped chef in the kitchen and Schmeling, Machon, and Otto Petri were playing a German card game called skat in the dining room.

Schmeling wore a soft shirt with a dark green tie, a green pullover sweater, flannel trousers, woolen socks, and black patent leather slippers.

"Did you have your lunch?" Schmeling said.

"Yeah," Joe said, "Did you?"

"We just finished," Max said.

He called the chef and said something to him in German.

"Ja," the chef said. "Right away."

"Your lunch will be ready right away," Max said.

They put the cards away, and everybody went into the living room.

"The weather is nice out here," somebody said.

"Yes," Max said. "It is nice today. It was windy yesterday."

"I saw Thomas train the other day," the newspaperman who had been ribbing Joe in the car said.

"So?" Max said.

"Yes," the newspaperman said. "He is in good shape."

"How's business?" Schmeling asked.

"The sales looks pretty good," Joe said.

"Have you ever seen Thomas?" a newspaperman asked.

"No," Max said.

"He's wild," the first newspaperman said. "But he can punch. And he is always trying."

"How are his sparring partners?" Max asked.

"Not so good," the newspaperman answered.

Joe and Mike went out.

"Have you seen any motion pictures since you have been out here?" one of the newspapermen asked.

"About thirty-five or forty," Max said. "We didn't go last night. We played skat."

"Who won?" a newspaperman asked.

"I did," Otto said, beaming.

"For a change," Schmeling said.

Joe and Mike came back. Joe set the table in the dining room.

"Your lunch is ready," Joe said. "I ain't going to eat. I ate in Hymies just before we came out."

"I will go lie down," Schmeling said.

He went into his bedroom and shut the door. Machon went over to the training quarters. The visitors sat, and the chef waited on them. While eating, another newspaperman came in. Joe laughed when he saw him.

"You're the fellow said I was fired and couldn't come back to the camp," he said.

"I didn't say that," the newspaperman said, pulling up a chair.

"They put that in the head. I didn't say it in the story. I just said Machon was sore because you put Schmeling on the spot."

"I have been trying to steam up Joe and Machon to take a punch at each other," the first newspaperman said. "It would be a swell story. But they won't do it."

Joe laughed.

After lunch, the visitors returned to the living room. Schmeling came in and put on a hunting coat.

"I am going over now," he said. "There is no hurry. I will take a little time getting dressed."

After a while, the visitors walked over to the training quarters.

The gymnasium was crowded. Every seat was occupied, and many persons were standing, but others kept coming in. There were a few fighters and fight managers there. Heavyweight Buddy Baer and his manager, Ancil Hoffman; Billy McCarney, a promoter and part owner of Schmeling; and Steve Dudas, an Edgewater, New Jersey, heavyweight and future Schmeling foe. Most of the crowd was drawn from the countryside made of men, women, and a few small children.

Max suddenly bounded up the stairs from his dressing room. Behind him came two sparring partners. Max bowed and smiled, and Machon adjusted his head guard and laced on his gloves. The first sparring partner was Bill Schloeman, a heavyweight who recently left the amateur ranks. Schmeling boxed two rounds with him and two with Steve Colucci, who had served as a sparring partner for other heavyweights in the New Jersey camps. He gave them a drubbing, firing his right hand at them and never missing.

"I never saw him look better," Joe said.

After that, Max shadowboxed, punched the heavy bag, engaged in calisthenics, and then skipped the rope. The crowd watched him in silence, impressed by his intensity. At the conclusion, he bowed from the waist, smiled broadly, and, turning quickly, ran down the stairs to his dressing room.

Joe remained with Schmeling. He said he would come back to town later. The others climbed into the car and drove away.

"I'm glad I came," Mike said in the car. "That feller is in great shape."

"It was the most impressive workout I ever saw," one of the newspapermen said. "The guy fascinated everybody there, including me."

"What do you think now about Thomas being a good bet at the price?" another newspaperman asked the one who had been talking about Thomas on the way to Bey's Camp.

"I was only kidding," he said. "Still, Thomas has nothing to lose, as Schmeling has, and if he ever lands one of those right-hand punches—"

Mike Jacobs lighted a cigarette.

"You never can tell," he said. "Anything can happen when two heavyweights get in the ring."[16]

The next day, Schmeling's trainer, Max Machon, expressed concern that Max had peaked too soon.

"Max was just right when Tunney was here Tuesday," Machon admitted. "Next day, he misses openings and sometimes he gets out of position."

"Max ought to cut out boxing," Joe Jacobs insisted, "but he is advertised to box tomorrow, and though I've suggested no more boxing, I'm afraid Max is too stubborn to yield to this suggestion ... I hear Max and Machon are blaming me for picking a dangerous one in Thomas. If anything goes wrong, it looks like little Joe is on the spot, which isn't fair."[30]

Harry Thomas was training at Dr. Biers in Pompton Lakes, New Jersey, where champion Joe Louis trained. Thomas claimed that he knocked Joe Louis flat a couple of years before when Joe was training for a fight on the West Coast. He said that as a result, he was fired from the Louis camp without even receiving the ten dollars due to him.

"I can't remember it," Louis said, "and I usually remember these fellows who knock me down. But I'll pay him the ten if he says I owe it to him."[31]

Ex-heavyweight champion Jack Johnson visited Thomas. After Johnson's visit and seeing Thomas go through two sparring partners, he said, "Thomas will make plenty of trouble for Schmeling."[28]

When Jack Dempsey heard that Gene Tunney had visited Max Schmeling at Madame Bey's, Tunney's old adversary decided to make the trip to Harry Thomas's camp.[32] Dempsey appeared at the training camp of Thomas. He thought Thomas would get better as the fight progressed and Schmeling had made a mistake insisting the fight be fifteen rounds.

"Maybe I made a mistake. I had that fellow four years ago," Dempsey confessed, "but could not look after him because of my other business interests. I'm not picking him to lick Schmeling, but you certainly have to give him a chance. I like his style and I think he's going places."[33]

After Dempsey watched Thomas perform at camp, he did not share Jack Johnson's impression. Dempsey made a statement before he hastened away from the camp.

"It might be a good fight—for a few rounds. I would judge that Thomas is very, very slow to get started."[32]

That was about the most generous thing he would say about Thomas.

The day before the fight, the press said Schmeling had been in the best shape of his life. He had spent twenty days at Madame Bey's and did not rest one day. He completed the most rigorous course of training in which he had ever engaged. Schmeling had gone through no fewer than 116 rounds of boxing. There was not a day when he was not scheduled to box in the afternoon. His conditioning, hitting, and timing were perfect. It was hard to believe he had not fought for eighteen months. He did eight-mile runs on the road in addition to his sparring. In the afternoons and evenings, he took long walks,[34] as did many boxers after a long day's work. It was a means of keeping your head clear. Schmeling had no fewer than eight sparring partners to box with at Bey's Camp.

Some newspapermen asked Schmeling at Bey's while he was training if he had tired of fighting.

"No," Max said. "Why should I? Only when you are down low, you get tired."[35]

A crowd of 16,125 that paid $74,000 came to see Schmeling fight at Madison Square Garden on December 13, 1937.[36] The boycotts and Nazi accusations did not keep boxing fans away, but there was a heavy police presence to keep order. Side streets were patrolled by police on foot and horse, and police cars were parked at the curbs. In front of the stadium, there was a line of picketers carrying signs denouncing Schmeling. Police officers watched the picket line for disturbances. A woman yelled, "Don't send money to the mad dog of Europe! Schmeling is an agent of Hitler!"[37]

Former heavyweight champion James Braddock, current heavyweight champion Joe Louis, middleweight champion Freddie Steele, and some other fighters were introduced. For the first time in a while, the popular Braddock was booed by some of the fans, which journalist Frank Graham attributed to "probably Schmeling rooters still smoldering over the pushing around that Max received from Braddock last summer."[37] Joe Louis also received jeers from the crowd. Upon entering the ring, Schmeling was met with a voluble reception. Before the fight started, Joe Louis went over to Schmeling's corner. He leaned over, placing his right hand on top of Schmeling's left glove, and spoke some private words. They both smiled.[38]

The fight began with Thomas winning three of the first four rounds on the United Press score sheet. Again, Schmeling started a fight at an unhurried, measured pace. Schmeling did connect with an uppercut in the first round that Thomas later said hurt him plenty. In the sixth round, Schmeling landed at least a dozen short, jarring rights that staggered Thomas. Another hard right to Thomas's jaw in the seventh knocked him down for the first time in a five-year, seventy-two professional fight career. Thomas was on one knee as the bell ended the round. In the eighth round, another right to the chin put Thomas on his knees. After getting up, another right sent him to the canvas again. After going down five times in the round, with six seconds left, the crowd pleaded for the fight to be stopped. Referee Donovan obliged and prevented further carnage. Schmeling had sent Thomas to the canvas six times.[36, 39]

"Thomas was a hard boy to hit and gave me some trouble until I hit my stride," Schmeling said. "I needed a fight like that because I wanted to make sure my fists still carried the sting that knocked out Joe Louis in 1936. My timing was off at first, and I'm glad it lasted as long as it did because I needed the work."

In his dressing room, the press asked Thomas why he did not take a nine count each time he hit the canvas.

"Hell," Thomas said. "I didn't even know I was down until I was getting back on my feet and saw Schmeling start for a neutral corner."[36]

Another ranked heavyweight contender arrived at Madame Bey's Camp after Max Schmeling left. Late December witnessed the arrival of the twenty-four-year-old Welshman and former British heavyweight champion Tommy Farr. His last fight was a loss to Louis in what was Louis's first title defense. The Louis fight was Farr's debut bout in America. Before the Louis bout, Farr had gone twenty fights without a loss. One of those fights included the defeat of Max Baer when he was touring England. Farr's next bout was to be against James Braddock on January 21, 1938, at Madison Square Garden. It would be Braddock's first fight since losing the title to Joe Louis.

At the end of 1937, they were training for a different kind of battle at Madame Bey's Camp. The spelling bee of the century, the press called it, between boxers and wrestlers was going to be broadcast over the nation's airways on the night of January 15, 1938, from Madame Bey's Camp. Mike Jacobs, Twentieth Century Sports Club promoter, selected the spelling bee candidates. He stated that the boxers would insist on a one- or two-letter handicap since most "wrasslers" are college men with mighty degrees.[40]

There would be five boxers and five wrestlers. The captain of the boxers was Mushky Jackson,[41] a man with little command of the English language. He could knock out the language with the best of them. Mushky Jackson, born Morris Ladisky, worked as a boxing manager, trainer, second, and publicist. If something needed to be done, Mushky was your man. He was promoter Mike Jacobs's number-one handyman.[42] He had spent much time in Joe Louis's camps. The Brown Bomber liked hanging around with Mushky; everyone liked hanging around with Mushky. He would have people laughing uncontrollably with his unconscious wit, based on his inability to pronounce words of more than one syllable. At Louis's camp, he was an assistant publicist, but the press called him the chief king's jester, spar-boy handler, and official "welcomer."[41, 43]

Earlier in the year, June 1937, Mushky was at Joe Louis's camp while he was training for his title bout with James Braddock in Kenosha, Wisconsin, on the shores of Lake Michigan. Everyone in Kenosha awaited Mushky's announcements for Louis's training schedule.

"Joe Louis will train in dis arena Totsday and Sat'day," Mushky announced on one occasion. "Dat in case a t'reatnin wedder Louis will box in Moost Hall."

Mushky defined a "moost" as a "cow wid branches."[43]

Tentative selections were Tommy Farr, Henry Armstrong, Nathan Mann, and Frankie Blair. Every one of them, Mushky assured the press, possessed at least a swell high school education.

"They'll surprise these wise-guy rasslers, too," Mushky Jackson commented. "As a regular thing they might not be such tough spellers, but they're gonna get two slugs ($2) for every word they get spelled correct on this card and that'll make 'em tough. I know fighters."[41]

Ray Fabiani, mat czar of New York and former concert violinist, regarded the result as a foregone conclusion.

"Why, it's going to be ludicrous, matching these boys of mine against those resin-monkeys," Fabiani said. "Half those boxers couldn't spell beer. I can put a full team of college graduates in there if I want to."

Mushky Jackson asked only one question when offered the job and told to choose his men.

"Sure," he said, "what weights?"[41]

The press exploited the competition in a write-up.

"They are coming together in a spelling bee on WJZ-NBC at 8:30. Tommy Farr, British heavyweight, is to head the boxing team of words with Mike Mazurki in charge of the wrestlers. The bout is to originate at Farr's training camp at Summit, N. J."[44]

Paul Wing would announce the spelling bee. He was an assistant director during the 1935 Academy Awards in the short-lived category Best Assistant Director. He won for the film *The Lives of a Bengal Lancer*, starring Gary Cooper. Wing also worked as a radio announcer.

"I will see to it," Paul Wing said, "that for boxers there will be no seconds allowed; for wrestlers no grunts allowed. Mouthpieces will be prohibited and no backbiting tolerated."[40]

Results from the spelling bee were unknown.

The recognized world middleweight champion arrived at Madame Bey's Camp before Schmeling came to train for his fight with Thomas. The twenty-four-year-old Freddie the

"Tacoma Assassin" Steele arrived before Schmeling came to fight Thomas.[45] He had a record of 120 wins, two losses, and eleven draws. He was to fight Fred Apostoli, who had just beaten Thil in the Carnival of Champions. The Steele-Apostoli bout was scheduled for January 7, 1938. The two were well acquainted, both coming from the West Coast. They had met in one official fight in which Steele stopped Apostoli in the tenth and final round. It was Apostoli's first defeat.

Steele was born in Seattle, Washington. He showed skill in basketball, soccer, and baseball. He chose boxing where opportunities, fame, and fortune existed. At the age of twelve, he started attending a gymnasium in Tacoma, Washington. After several months, the gymnasium's proprietor, Dave Miller, decided to manage Steele. Miller put Steele in his debut professional fight a month before his fifteenth birthday.[46] He went undefeated in his first thirty-nine fights. By the age of twenty, Steele had compiled a record of seventy-two wins, two losses, and eight draws. He avenged both of his decision losses in return matches. He won the world middleweight championship by defeating Eddie Risko on July 11, 1936, in Seattle.

While Steele was at Bey's, he used light heavyweight Walter Woods as a sparring partner. Madame Bey called Freddie Steele "my little prince." She said he trained at her camp for all his eastern fights. She recalled one night that Steele, not yet accustomed to her camp life, asked her for more potatoes at supper. Madame Bey looked at Steele's plate and saw some string beans there. Madame Bey told him to eat the string beans first, and then he would get his potatoes.[17] Steele looked at her surprised. After all, he was the world middleweight champion—the Tacoma Assassin. Here was this middle-aged woman telling him what to do. Madame Bey, not in awe of her new tenant, saw him as one of her boys. She had seen so many champions at her camp with more notoriety and fiercer sounding names. If Steele thought himself special, he was mistaken. After a moment, Steele laughed. Madame Bey and Freddie Steele became good friends after the incident. Again, another fighter understood the camp rules and who was in charge.

Madame Bey's little prince, Freddie Steele, started 1938 with his scheduled fight against the man he had defeated on the West Coast, Fred Apostoli, on January 7. The middleweight title was not at stake. Apostoli weighed over the 160-pound limit. The crowd of 7,970 saw one of the most ferocious and spectacular fights ever at the Garden. Each hit the other continuously. By some counts, it was the greatest middleweight fight seen in a generation, topping the Greb-Walker bout.[47]

In the seventh, a left hook to Steele's groin from Apostoli sent Steele writhing in pain. Referee Arthur Donovan stepped between them, waved Apostoli away, and permitted Steele some seconds rest. No decisions based on fouls were still recognized under the New York State boxing regulations as a direct result of the Schmeling-Sharkey heavyweight championship that Schmeling won on a low blow. Donovan exercised his judgment in calling a brief halt to the fight. The fight was even after eight rounds, but Steele looked worse than Apostoli. By the ninth round, blood streamed from Freddie Steele's left eye, and his right eye was just a slit. In the middle of his face was a ring of red where once a nose had been. Steele absorbed terrible punishment. He was virtually out on his feet when Donovan stopped the fight after fifty-four seconds of the ninth round to save the world middleweight champion from further punishment.[47, 48]

In his dressing room, Steele needed almost an hour to recover from the drubbing. Dr. William A. Walker, the commission doctor, examined Steele and discovered a bruise caused by the low blow in the seventh round. Steele's breastbone was broken and his face a bloody mass.

"I just was beginning to get right. It sent a terrific pain all over my lower body. I know Apostoli didn't do it on purpose, but it won the fight for him. After that I was strictly a catcher," Steele said about the seventh-round low blow.[47]

By giving Steele a rest in the seventh round, Donovan broke the rules. After the fight, referee Donovan defended his actions.

"To hell with the rules. Steele was hurt. All of us saw that. He was helpless and if I had let Apostoli clip him, he might have knocked him out, broken his jaw, or otherwise seriously injure him.

"Those people paid to see a fight, and I was in there to help them see it. If I had let Apostoli knock him out, I would have been panned for the rest of my days."[48]

With the spelling bee over, it was back to hard work for Tommy Farr. Snow piled up from a recent storm at Madame Bey's Camp on January 17, 1938. Uncle Mike Jacobs arrived to check on Tommy Farr. It was Jacobs's Twentieth Century Sporting Club, which was promoting Farr's bout with James Braddock. It seemed Uncle Mike came to Madame Bey's whenever he could. While Tex Rickard was never known to frequent Madame Bey's, but his fighters were there many times, Uncle Mike took every opportunity to come to the camp. Mike Jacobs arrived in a limousine that the driver drove into a snow bank. Jacobs barked orders and assisted with words of suggestion to those engaged in extracting the limousine out of the snow bank. He also directed traffic while the vehicle remained stuck.

After the limousine issue was resolved, Jacobs went inside Madame Bey's farmhouse. She had made a chicken that he consented to carve. Joe Jacobs, the manager of Max Schmeling and Tony Galento, was at Bey's, too. Afterward, they went to watch Farr work out.

Tommy Farr had started his day with a six-mile jog over the snow-covered hills. He skipped rope for ten minutes before punching both the light and heavy bag. He shadowboxed a round and sparred a round with Jack Tebo, a Canadian heavyweight. Tebo was the only sparring partner to remain on his feet for two rounds. Farr knocked down Paul Pross with a left hook to the jaw and knocked Steve Colucci down twice. Jack Tebo and Steve Colucci were the men knocked around by Max Schmeling the month before during his training for Harry Thomas.

"He looks good, doesn't he?" Mike Jacobs asked when Farr knocked down Steve Colucci for the second time with a short right to the jaw.

"Damn good," Joe Jacobs agreed.

"I like the way Tommy uses his left hand," Gunnar Barlund commented, a heavyweight whose next fight was against Buddy Baer.

"Schmeling or Galento would kick the hell out of him," added Bud Gorman, a good heavyweight from ten years earlier and one of Bey's first boys. Madame Bey's became a gathering place for fighters past and present.

"Say, Joe, how about a go at Galento?" Farr inquired, his workout finished.

"Anytime," manager Joe Jacobs replied, "Mike here's a promoter."

"Well, I've nothing to do after Friday night," Farr declared.

"Galento's ready," Joe Jacobs insisted. "Mike can make the match now."

"How about it, Mike?" Farr asked.

"Say, you and Braddock are going to draw a lot of people from New Jersey," Mike Jacobs answered, ignoring both Tommy and Joe's interest in a Galento match.

Mike Jacobs was asked what he thought of Farr's chances against James Braddock.

"He likes to fight and just because he's swapping punches in there with his sparring partners doesn't mean he's going to lead with his chin," Uncle Mike explained.

"I'm the promoter and can't pick a winner, but this fellow's ready for a hard fight. He's in better shape than he was when he finished at Long Branch for the Joe Louis fight."

Joe Jacobs said he wanted to see James Braddock work before committing himself but joined in the general approval voiced for Tommy Farr. After his workout completed, Farr went for a rubdown. After the rubdown, Farr began conversing with Joe Jacobs again.

"Say, Joe, Schmeling has nothing to fear from Ben Foord," Farr predicted of the man he had defeated for the British heavyweight title. "Foord could be a great fighter, but won't train. He's got a big head."

Galento's activities, Jacobs said, might prevent him from traveling to the Schmeling-Foord battle on January 30, 1938, in Hamburg, Germany.

"I'll be ready in September if Max beats Joe Louis," Farr declared.

"Okay," Joe said.

Mike Jacobs, pleased with Farr, now focused on promoting problems he was having outside the heavyweight division.

"I'm holding March 18 open at Madison Square Garden for Armstrong to box Pedro Montañez," Mike Jacobs declared.

He revealed that an effort was being made to satisfy world featherweight champion Henry "Homicide Hank" Armstrong, who was threatening to fight Barney Ross for the world welterweight crown in Chicago unless given a lightweight title chance at the Garden with Lou Ambers.[49] The Ambers-Armstrong battle would assume later significance at Bey's Camp.

The next day, January 18, Chairman John J. Phelan of the New State Athletic Commission came to Madame Bey's Camp. He brought Dr. William H. Walker with him to examine Farr. He found him to be in excellent shape. Dr. Walker thought he should lessen his work and told that to Farr.[50]

Farr heeded the advice and rested the next day. The day after, his workout consisted of sparring four rounds instead of the seven to eight he had been doing every day. Using the same sparring partners, Farr knocked down Colucci. He slowed in his work against Pross and Tebo, concentrating more on defense. He instructed Pross and Tebo to throw right hand punches. Farr focused on fending the leads.[50]

Ted Broadribb, the former manager for Farr, who had parted from him after the Louis fight, came to Madame Bey's Camp. Broadribb said he had no intent to enforce his contract with Farr. He brought three fighters with him and introduced them to American fight manager Charles J. Harvey. The boxers, some trying to enter into American boxing, were Irish heavyweight Dominick Lydon, who claimed to be the second cousin to Gene Tunney; Austrian flyweight Ernst Weiss; and one of Britain's best lightweights, Jimmy Vaughn. Harvey was to manage Weiss and Vaughn. Lydon came to America only to meet Gene Tunney and watch the Farr-Braddock bout. He said he did not come to fight. He predicted Farr would win.[51]

Farr decided to forego sparring the next day, the final day before the bout. He skipped rope for half an hour and did calisthenics, bag punching, and shadowboxing. That same day, James Braddock, training at Dr. Biers in Pompton Lakes, New Jersey, was visited by world heavyweight champion Joe Louis and New York Yankee outfield star Joe DiMaggio. Louis had beaten Farr and Braddock.[52]

"Braddock appears faster than he was in Chicago," Louis commented, referring to their title fight. "I don't want to forecast a result. Braddock punches harder than Farr, but Farr has youth and speed with him."[51]

A capacity crowd of more than 18,000 attended the fight at Madison Square Garden on January 21, 1938. Gross receipts were $80,645.23. The fighters received about $20,000 each. Farr was ten years younger than Braddock. Farr started strong for the first eight rounds of a ten-round fight. He took the fight to Braddock. It was in the last two rounds that Braddock turned the tide. He showed his superior power.[53]

When the men came out for the last round, the Braddock biased crowd roared. Braddock was desperate, as he must have known he was behind. Both men, exhausted, showed their resolve. Braddock hammered away at Farr. It was a savage fight. The Garden emitted a tremendous roar. Braddock had come back. Braddock had beaten off the years that weighed upon him. Now he was beating Farr. The ending bell rang. The two kept fighting; neither heard it as the crowd drowned it out. Journalist Wilbur Wood wrote, "Napoleon cynically remarked that God is on the side which has the heavier artillery. James J. Braddock demonstrated that when he opened up with his big guns in the last two rounds."

"It is too bad Jim didn't start sooner," somebody said after the bout.

"He couldn't," the man sitting beside him countered. "He wouldn't have had enough left to carry him through the tenth round."

Now the fight was over, and the ring was swarming with seconds. Joe Gould, Braddock's manager, shook hands with Farr as the fighters went back to their corners. The seconds sponged off the men, and the crowd stood waiting for the decision. Then the announcement came.

"The winner—Braddock!"

Braddock won a split verdict over Tommy Farr. The scoring was as close as a fight could get. Judge Charley Lynch scored it four to six; Judge George LeCron six to four; referee Johnny McAvoy had it four to four with two even. The scorecard was a draw, but the referee gave it to Braddock on points.

A roar came from the pro-Braddock crowd. Braddock clenched his hands over his head in greeting his fans. Farr was dumbfounded by the decision, thinking he had earned it by his dominant performance before the ninth round. In anger, Farr threw his robe draped about him. Braddock went to shake Farr's hand, but Farr turned away and left down the steps from his corner. In the ring, Braddock's handlers jumped about as the crowd still roared. The crowd had seen a game old fighter come from behind to win.[54]

Newspapers printed that Farr said referee Johnny McAvoy was coaching Braddock during the last round. Farr denied the accusation. Farr said after the fight that he had an injured left hand, but nothing had been stated before the fight. Farr would apologize a few days later to Braddock, but the damage was already done. He met with Mike Jacobs to make amends. Unable to hide his disgust, the meeting did not go well. Summing the sentiment of the journalists toward Farr, Al Buck wrote, "Within the next few days, Tommy Farr would go to Miami with the best wishes of the sportswriters who hope, quite sincerely, that he never returns."[55]

Eleven days after the fight on February 1, Braddock announced his retirement. He knew his thirty-two-year-old body had had enough. The time arrived to leave the game.

He did not need to subject himself to more punishment. He had a $500,000 payday from the Joe Louis fight and a percentage of the champion's future earnings. He was financially secure.

Tommy Farr returned to Madame Bey's Camp and was welcomed. It never mattered to Madame Bey what the newspapers printed; she judged her boys on a different set of criteria—her own. She had come to know the rigors of preparing for a fight and the psychological toll it took. She understood the disappointment after hard preparations and the difficulty in acceptance of losing a close decision. Farr was back for his third consecutive fight against a world champion. It would be against ex-heavyweight champion Max Baer, the man he beat in England. It would be Farr the boxer against Baer the puncher.

Journalist Edward Van Every went to Madame Bey's to report on Farr's preparation. He reported that to his surprise, Farr seemed to be working at a tireless pace and punching harder than ever before. Paul Pross, Charley Massera, and most sparring partners engaged were on the verge of a knockout daily.[56]

When fight day arrived, March 11, 1938, at Madison Square Garden, a crowd of 18,222 paying $63,380 saw the fight. Gone were Baer's clowning antics. He knocked down the rugged Farr in the second and third round. Farr lasted the full fifteen rounds. The decision was unanimous and not close. Scoring was thirteen to two, eleven to three with one even, and nine to five with one even in favor of a more serious Baer.[57]

Farr would fight two more times in America, losing both by a decision. Though all his fights went the distance, he would be winless in America. His last loss in America would be against Red Burman. Three months later, after returning to England, he would defeat Burman in London. Farr never fought in America again. For the year and a half he was in America, the Welshman fought the best the heavyweight division had to offer. Madame Bey's became his home for many of those fights.

Figure 1. Last posed picture of President William McKinley taken at the Pan-American Exposition. From left to right: Madame Bey; Mrs. John Miller Horton; John G. Milburn; Senor Asperoz, the Mexican ambassador; President William McKinley; George B. Courtelyou, the president's secretary; Col. John H. Bingham. (Library of Congress)

Figure 2. Madame Bey during her days in Washington, DC.

Figure 3. Madame Bey beside her sign advertising Bey's Training Camp. (Associated Press)

Figure 4. Madame Bey conversing with promoter Mike
Jacobs in her gymnasium. (Associated Press)

Figure 5. January 10, 1938, Madame Bey with British Empire heavyweight champion Tommy Farr in the Bey gymnasium. Farr was training for a bout with James Braddock. Farr had won acclaim the previous summer by going fifteen rounds against Joe Louis. (Associated Press)

Figure 6. July 27, 1938, Madame Bey, second from the left, visited her competitor's camp in Pompton Lakes, New Jersey, to see Henry Armstrong, world featherweight and welterweight champion, train. Armstrong was training for a bout with Lou Ambers, lightweight champion, who was training at Madame Bey's camp. (Associated Press)

Figure 7. Madame Bey's outdoor boxing ring where exhibitions that rivaled Madison Square Garden boxing cards occurred. (Chatham Township Historical Society)

Figure 8. Signed photographs left to Madame Bey with inscriptions. Clockwise from upper left, world lightweight champion Freddie Welsh, "With Every Good Wish"; world heavyweight champion James Braddock, "Best Wishes Your Friend Jimmy Braddock"; five-time world champion Tony Canzoneri, "a mother to boys from one of her boys"; heavyweight challenger Red Burman, "The real mother of fighters with lots of luck & success." (Chatham Township Historical Society)

Figure 9. Signed photographs left to Madame Bey from world middleweight champion Ken Overlin with the inscription, "You're a very dear person—Thanks a million for everything." (Chatham Township Historical Society)

Figure 10. Signed photograph left to Madame Bey from light heavyweight Johnny Krieger, "To one who is a mother to fighters." (Chatham Township Historical Society)

CHAPTER 27

Tony

Two-Ton Tony Galento; Fat Tony; The Jersey Water Buffalo; The Newark Night Stick; Tarzan Man because of his off-key Tarzan yell; The Fighting Fat Man; The Belting Beer Barrel; The One Man Riot; The Beer Barrel that Walks Like a Man. There were Presidential buttons printed with the slogan "Tony Galento For Pres. Prohibition Party's Choice." He went through no fewer than eight managers. He was one of the most colorful boxers. He had his followers and detractors. If you loved him, you read to follow his exploits in and out of the ring. If you despised him, you read about him to justify your hatred.

Born Dominic Anthony Galento on March 12, 1910, in Orange, New Jersey, he started his boxing career on March 10, 1928, two days before turning eighteen.[1] Boxing knew him mostly by the name of Two-Ton Tony Galento. His boxing nickname was not for his size, as many thought. His manager called him Two-Ton after he drove his ice truck to an arena. He arrived late before the start of one of his fights. When his manager confronted him in the parking lot to inquire where he had been, Tony replied, "I had two tons of ice to deliver on my way here."

The press exploited his atypical boxing frame of five feet eight inches, 240 pounds, and a forty-three-inch waist.[2] He was balding in his twenties and looked older than his years. "'How old are you, anyway?'" Tony said someone would ask. "Then they take a look at this thin hair and begin addin' more years."[3] They called him a fat man and referred to him as a clown or buffoon. He did not discourage it since it meant more publicity. He was a tireless self-promoter. His press conferences were a comedy routine. No matter how the press felt about him, they knew Tony would give them plenty of material for their newspaper columns. Tony knew how publicity influenced fight gates. He gave the writers what they wanted, sometimes unintentionally, and used them to his advantage. Tony was boisterous. Before bouts, he disparaged his opponents and directed ethnic and racial slurs toward them. *Bartlett's Familiar Quotations* lists his enduring quote, "I'll moider da bum." He was a headache for boxing commissions. They were not amused by his actions. They thought it was degrading to their sport.

Tony was a rugged, strong, hard puncher. Despite his antics inside and outside the ring, he was one of the toughest boxers. He could endure great punishment and pain.

"I like fightn'," Tony said. "I want to see that blood flow. Naw, I ain't worried what happens to the other guy. Let him take care of hisself. If he don't wanta get hurt, he sh'unt be in the fight game. Anyway, he hadn't ought to fight Galento."[4]

He had a hard head literally and figuratively. He never lost by a knockout. His losses resulted from technical knockouts from bad cuts. Journalist Lemuel Parton wrote, "Tony fought with his mouth open, as if he were trying to catch flies."[5] His publicist, Carmine Bilotti, said he had five effective punches and used them all. "He used his two fists, two elbows and of course, his head."[6] He was more of a barroom brawler than a skilled boxer. His fouls in the ring included deliberate head-butts, low blows, eye gouging, and elbows. It gave him the reputation of being a dirty fighter, but he possessed a boxer's punch. His was a lethal left hook, a roundhouse punch that could stagger the world's best boxers. Tony called it his beer punch.[7]

Ray Arcel had trained Galento for a brief period and worked across the ring from him in his fights with Max Baer, Lou Nova, and Nathan Mann.

"Nobody really liked him except maybe the guys who hung out in his saloon," Ray Arcel said. "He was a crude guy, to put it mildly, who would resort to all sorts of foul tactics to win a fight."[8]

He was notorious for his street-fighting style that flaunted the rules and often led to fouls. Many boxing insiders despised him. The public watched his every move. He had a connection with the blue-collar crowd. His rise to the top started when he hired Joe Jacobs as his manager. The two became friends.

"Joe Jacobs is a smart manager," Tony said. "He looks at me close, he has always liked me, from the time I nearly lick Risko. He says, 'Tony, you've got the build, the strength, the courage, and a punch. I'll take you, but I ask only one thing. You get in that gym, let me do the rest. If you don't—and we lose—don't let me hear a squawk. I'll do my share; you keep up your end. If that's O.K. by you, it's a deal.' I stuck out my hand, Joe shook. And I ask you, have we been doin' all right since then? I just ask you."[9]

Tony did his training, as he lived, on his terms. He liked to train in his tavern and a local gymnasium. When he was not fighting people, Galento would battle with animals. He fought kangaroos, bears, and an octopus named Oscar. He fought the octopus in Seattle as a promotion for a local business.[10] At the Million-Dollar Pier in Atlantic City, New Jersey, Galento fought a pair of 175-pound kangaroos—Peter the Great and Battering Bukaroo. "I'll fight anyone—anything," Tony proclaimed. He said the last animal he would conquer was the lion.

"Who has that lion ever licked?" Galento demanded in a New York press conference. "What right has that big bum to go popping off that he is king of the jungle?" He declared that he would "punch his mane off."[11]

Gene Tunney joined Tony's antics. In jest, he attempted to match Galento with Gargantua the gorilla. The gorilla was part of Ringling Brothers Circus. Everyone there called him Gargy. Gene Tunney proposed the bout to manager Joe Jacobs.

"It's beneath our dignity," Joe Jacobs said. "Who did this chimpanzee ever lick?"

Tunney, acting as a promoter, assured Jacobs that Tony could not lose.

"Gorillas are overrated," Tunney said. "Gorillas have no stamina, no intelligence, and hardly any ribs. Even your bum, Mr. Jacobs—I mean to say, even your fearless fighter, Tony Galento could whip this unfortunate simian."

"You could throw six Tony Galentos into that cage," Dick Kroener, Gargantua's trainer, said, "and I would still bet on Gargy to tear them to pieces."[12]

He was the last person you would think would come to Madame Bey's Camp with her rules. Galento had trained at Bey's in 1935 for his winning fight against Anthony Ashrut on the undercard of the Baer-Braddock heavyweight title. In 1937, he trained at Bey's for his bout against Arturo Godoy,[13] a bout he lost. Galento was familiar with the camp and Madame Bey. Two people could not be more different. They were opposites in both the way they approached boxing and life. They did not get along, but Madame Bey would not discuss it with the press.

In February 1938, the New York Boxing Commission and promoter Mike Jacobs had it with Tony Galento, his antics, and training style. Galento had a third round knockout of Charley Massera at the Armory in his hometown of Orange, New Jersey, on January 5, 1938. His next fight was to be against Harry Thomas on February 18 at Madison Square Garden. Uncle Mike Jacobs was the promoter.

General John J. Phelan, chairman of the New York State Athletic Commission, and Tony had a dispute over how and where he should train. Phelan said that unless Galento left his Orange tavern for Madame Bey's Camp, he might refuse to allow Galento to fight Thomas. Phelan said that Two-Ton must drink no more beer, smoke no more cigars, and pose for no more pictures while drinking beer and smoking cigars. Phelan ordered Galento to Madame Bey's Camp.

Phelan telephoned Madame Bey's Camp to determine if Galento had complied with the order, but they told him Tony had not arrived. Irate, Phelan called promoter Mike Jacobs at the Twentieth Century Sporting Club, but he was in Florida on business. He demanded from the matchmaking department to know why Galento was not at Madame Bey's Camp, but they had no explanation. Phelan called Galento at his Orange, New Jersey, tavern. Tony answered the call and told Phelan he was not at Madame Bey's because he had never promised to go to Madame Bey's and had no intention of training at Madame Bey's Camp.

"I told Mr. Phelan that Madame Bey had a nice camp, but that I hadn't promised him I would go there and preferred to train here," Galento explained.

Galento said he worked out in the Parkview Gymnasium.

"I got in good enough shape here to knock out Al Ettore, Lorenzo Pack, Leroy Haynes, and Charley Massera, and I'm doing everything else Mr. Phelan asked me to do," a defiant Galento said.

"Why, I even had my picture taken drinking milk.

"I don't drink whiskey, only beer.

"If I train here I can be home and my wife, Mary, cooks the food I like and am used to. Besides, I can watch my tavern. I only weigh two hundred twenty-six pounds right now. I told Mr. Phelan that he can send his deputy over here, and that he'll find me in good shape."[14]

Phelan continued to insist that Galento train for Thomas at Madame Bey's Camp. Galento, adamant, insisted on training at the Parkview Gymnasium.

"Not me," Galento once said about going to Madame Bey's Camp. "That's out where that brunette tells you what to do, hey? Well, nothing doing!"[15]

The commission continued to instruct Galento to stop posing for press photographs while guzzling beer and smoking cigars. Tony retaliated with a subtle poke at the commission by allowing the press to snap photographs of him sipping milk through a straw and licking a heart-shaped lollipop.[16] One picture showed Galento in his hometown of Orange, New Jersey, eating spaghetti and meatballs, an apparent large glass of beer to his right. Tommy Farr flanked him on his left and guitar player Nick Lucas to his right. The picture printed below that one was the one that drew the commission's ire. It showed Tony in his boxing trunks sitting on a boxing corner stool drinking from a bottle of milk with a straw while one of his trainers, John Burke, was trying to wrestle it away from him.[17]

"This fellow belongs in a circus, not in a ring," Commissioner Bill Brown declared. If Tony did not report to a "recognized training camp," the commission threatened to cancel the bout. Promoter Mike Jacobs met with Galento's manager, Joe Jacobs, and ordered Joe Jacobs to get Tony to Madame Bey's place. "Or I'll cancel the match myself," he stated.

"We ain't going to Madame Bey's or any other training camp," one of Tony's trainers Frain said.[16]

The commission also opposed Galento tending bar in his tavern. They thought it was degrading to boxing.

"You can't be a bartender and an athlete at the same time as far as I can see," Brown said. "We owe it to the public to bar Galento if he refuses to condition himself properly and unless something unforeseen occurs before Friday, I feel certain the commission will withdraw sanction of the bout at its regular meeting."[18]

With the risk of losing the money for the bout, Galento relented. He agreed to go to Madame Bey's to train for the fight but argued that he could get in better condition at home.

"What more could I do at a training camp?" he asked.[18]

Then Galento surprised everyone when he stated he was injured.

"I intended to go to Madame Bey's training camp as I promised I would," Galento admitted from this home in Orange, "but when it came time to go I found my hand was still giving me trouble. So, I tried to put off going to the camp as long as possible, as I knew soon as I started to box it would be a giveaway as to my condition, and I wanted to go through with that Thomas fight so much. However, Al Weill, the Garden matchmaker caught up with me this morning, and I had to fess up."[19]

Mike Jacobs, confronted with contradictory accounts regarding Galento, had no choice but to substitute Jimmy Adamick of Detroit, a Jack Kearns-managed heavyweight, against Thomas. Galento, according to the Mike Jacobs, told him via telephone that he had refused to train at Madame Bey's to conceal the fact that he had a fractured left hand.

"What fractured hand?" demanded a surprised Mike Jacobs over the telephone.

Tony explained he had aggravated an injury to a bone in his hand sustained in his recent fight with Charley Massera.

"If I went to Madame Bey's, the commission would find out about it," Tony said.

"Couldn't they have discovered it at your gym, too?" Mike Jacob's said.[20]

Tony did not answer the last question.

Mike Jacobs charged that all this had been another excuse for cancelling Galento's New York appearance so he could fight Thomas in Newark, New Jersey. Dr. J. Hiti examined Tony's hand at the Orange Memorial Hospital and said X-rays revealed a slight healing fracture.[20] That ended the ordeal between Tony and the commission, which had begun the week before when the boxing commission forbade him to pose for any pictures drinking beer or smoking cigars. Tony withdrew from the match with Harry Thomas. Whether Galento's injury was legitimate or an excuse, as Mike Jacobs believed, one thing for sure—he was not coming to Madame Bey's Camp.

That same month, February 1938, another heavyweight came to Bey's Camp. His name was Nathan Mann, and he would be the second challenger to Joe Louis's heavyweight title. They called him Natie. His real name was Natale Menchetti from New Haven, Connecticut. At the age of twenty-two, he had been a professional for three years. Now he was preparing for a fifteen-round championship bout with Joe Louis on February 23. On that date, he expected to win the title. It was a belief that was not shared by those gathered outside the ropes at Madame Bey's Camp. The fight would be the first time the heavyweight title would be contested indoors since 1920 when Jack Dempsey knocked out Bill Brennan at the old Madison Square Garden. For Joe Louis, the fight would be a tune-up for the forthcoming return match between him and his conqueror, Max Schmeling, in June.

Mann would be the first in a long line of heavyweights to train at Madame Bey's to challenge a superior Joe Louis for his title. Others had trained at Bey's to fight Louis, but those were not for the championship. Joe the "Brown Bomber" Louis had become so dominant that his challengers were deemed "the bum of the month" by the press in later years. The press took its liberties with the term bum. They were not. Louis was a rare heavyweight champion; his opponents were overmatched.

Mann settled into his training routine at Madame Bey's Camp. Jimmy "Fat" DeAngello, manager; Ray Arcel, trainer; Billy Brown Jr., assistant manager; Harry Newman, press agent; and Marty Krompier, another team member, completed the group that gathered for Mann at Madame Bey's Camp. The team was convinced that Nathan Mann had a chance to win the world heavyweight championship. Natie was the least excited man in camp. Journalist Al Buck said he lacked the imagination to fear Louis.[21] When he knocked down Bob Pastor in the first round in November at the Garden, he became convinced that he had the punching power to knock out the world champion.[21]

"When Mike Jacobs offered us the Louis fight I hesitated," manager DeAngello explained. "I talked it over with Billy Brown and for the first time we decided to put it up to Mann himself. So, we asked Natie and all he said was, 'Well, you signed didn't you?' It didn't take us long to hustle back to the Hippodrome and sign."[21]

Tony Galento infuriated the commission when having his picture taken while drinking milk. Every day following his workout in Madame Bey's gymnasium, Mann would drink a quart of Bey's fresh milk. Mann refrained from having his picture taken while drinking.

"We're putting weight on him," Ray Arcel explained. "Right now he weighs one hundred ninety-four pounds. He'll scale at least one hundred ninety pounds when he boxes Joe Louis."

"I'm used to the country, and I like it here," Mann said.

"Natie eats two meals a day," Arcel said. "He has breakfast at nine-thirty A. M. and dinner at five-thirty P. M. Occasionally he has a snack between meals."

When he was not working in the gymnasium or running on the road, he played cards with his trainers, press agents, and managers, like many before him. He was a movie fan and went to the theater in Summit, New Jersey, every night. Gary Cooper and Greta Garbo were his favorite actors.[22]

There was enthusiasm at Madame Bey's because Mann had impressed in his training. Despite the optimism at Bey's, the odds were four to one against him. Natie was sure he would knock out Louis, and so was his team at Bey's Camp. That included the famed camp proprietor.[23] Again, Madame Bey gave her support to the one that trained at her camp. When asked by the press for a prediction, she picked her boy to win.

"It's a chance I hadn't dreamed of getting this quick," Mann said. "It's a wonderful break for me, and I won't muff it. Did you know that the governor of Connecticut and about a thousand others are coming down from New Haven to watch me win?"

Mann's confidence was heightened because he had never been knocked out.

"I had to sign an agreement to fight Louis again within sixty days if I win the title," he revealed, "but that doesn't bother me. If I whip him once, I can whip him again."

Someone asked Mann about fighting Schmeling.

"No, I won't necessarily fight Schmeling after that. I'll fight whoever looks like pulling the biggest crowd," Mann replied.

Mann explained that Louis offered an easy target for a body attack and did not like a good right hand on the jaw.

"Schmeling proved that," he added, "and did you notice how he batted his eyes and covered up any time Farr threw a right at him?"

While not everybody shared Mann's optimism, many conceded that he was at the top of the country's young heavyweights at age twenty-two. His manager, Jimmy DeAngello, said he had done everything asked of him. He beat both Bob Pastor and Gunnar Barlund the year before. He beat Pastor more impressively than Louis did. He was at least as good a man as Tommy Farr, who lasted fifteen rounds with Louis, and maybe better.[23]

"Louis is just another fight for me," Mann said.

It was more than just another fight to Natie's Connecticut followers. They would be at ringside in large numbers to see him attempt to win the crown. In a Sunday workout, with promoter Mike Jacobs absent in Florida, his brother, Jake, represented the Twentieth Century Sporting Club on an official visit to Bey's Camp. Mann weighed 184 pounds. In his workouts with Johnny Whiters, a heavyweight from Detroit, Mann had Whiters throwing lefts every round. Mann shortened his left hook and used his right to the head with accuracy. If there was a fault, it was his inability to get away from the left jabs that Johnny Whiters and George Fitch, his sparring partners, kept poking into his face.

"He's in a crouch, and he's moving on his feet the way I told him to," DeAngello explained.

The style of fighting from a crouch would become important when a fighter met Joe Louis. It was noticed that Louis showed restraint when his opposition fought from the crouch. He lost his leverage when punching downward and feared injuring his hands hitting the top of his foe's head. He kept his distance to prevent a head butt from when a man rose from the crouch. It gave Louis trouble but only delayed an inevitable outcome. Louis was too smart a fighter, and he would determine a strategy to overcome the crouch.

"Mann is a better fighter than Tommy Farr," trainer Ray Arcel commented. "His record proves that and Louis couldn't do anything with Tommy. Mann is stronger now than he was, he's heavier, and he's punching better than he did."

"I tell you he's the next champion," Billy Brown insisted. "I'm going to open the Queensboro with him next spring. Why, my son here, Billy Jr., is telling his friends that his daddy's fighter will beat Louis."

"Don't sell Natie short," advised Harry Newman, his press agent.

Mann said little. In quiet, he drank his daily quart of milk and trained hard for Joe Louis.[21]

Mann met Louis for the heavyweight title on February 23, 1938, at Madison Square Garden. A crowd of 19,490 spectators paid $111,698. Louis collected 40 percent and Mann 12.5 percent of the gate.[24] The night started great for the Bey contingent. Natie's sparring partner, Johnny Withers from Detroit, outpointed Henry Cooper, from Brooklyn, in a preliminary heavyweight bout.

The good fortune continued when Mann looked great in the opening round against Louis, who had not fought for six months. By the end of the second round, Louis shattered Mann's dream when he sent Natie to the canvas. He took a count of nine. The bell ending the second round saved him. In the third round, Louis put Mann down three more times; he did not recover from the last blow. Mann, bloodied, took the final count in one corner of the ring. He rested on one knee but so shaken that he did not even appear to hear referee Arthur Donovan's final count of ten. Louis had knocked out the man who had never been knocked out before at one minute, fifty-six seconds of the third round of a scheduled fifteen-round fight. It took Louis less than eight minutes.[24]

"Louis sure can punch," Mann said after the fight. "I must have run into a good left in the second round. I don't remember a thing from then until I heard them counting me out. I didn't even see the punch that did it."[25]

Mann would win his next two bouts. He knocked out Louis LePage in the second round in March. Then he knocked out Hans Havlicek in the third round in April. In May, Mann was to fight Tony Galento; his hand healed. It was another showdown with the New York Commission. Again, Tony ignored the commission and trained in the poolroom gymnasium. The controversy began again.

The commission allowed the bout to transpire on May 13, 1938, at Madison Square Garden. It was Tony's first main event bout at the Garden. Tony outweighed Mann by forty pounds. Tony landed only four punches in the match, each with power. The first was the lethal left hook followed by a straight right and another left hook that sent Mann down for a nine count. Mann continued until he was caught with another left hook that put him on the canvas again. Mann was on one knee near Tony's corner as referee Arthur Donovan counted him out at two minutes, four seconds of the second round.[26]

After the fight, the National Boxing Association named Tony the number-one challenger to Joe Louis in the heavyweight division. With the resounding defeat, the commission gave

Tony permission to train at his preferred Parkview Gymnasium.[27] Now that Tony could choose his training quarters for his next fight against world light heavyweight champion John Henry Lewis, Tony decided he would train at Madame Bey's Camp.

The New York Commission was in an uproar. It was not because of his choice of training camps that made the commission irate but his choice of opponents. The New York Commission, for what the press described as only reasons of its own, did not want Tony to fight John Henry Lewis. They had little influence since the fight was being held at Municipal Stadium, Philadelphia. The New York Commission threatened to suspend Tony if he fought Lewis. It was their only recourse.

"I'll fight Lewis suspension or not," a defiant Galento said as he hit the bag with a big cigar stuck between his teeth, "and after I knock him out try to keep me away from a Joe Louis battle. I can lick both the Lewises no matter how they spell their name.

"It took me two rounds to knock out Fiducia," Galento continued. "I can knock out Pastor in two, and I won't need more than four to knock over Joe Louis," Tony said while still punching the bag.[28]

Unlike most boxers at Madame Bey's Camp, Tony would not be a resident. He had his convertible automobile in the camp and made nightly trips to his Orange, New Jersey, home. He trained at Bey's during the day, tended to his tavern at night, and said hello to his friends and patrons.

After Tony had settled into a routine at Madame Bey's, besides getting orders from the New York Commission, he was getting them from the Pennsylvania Boxing Commission. Jules Aronson, of the Pennsylvania Commission, ordered Galento to Philadelphia. The betting line was three to one, not that Tony would win or lose but that the fight would not happen. The situation was created because a suspension of Galento loomed by the New York Commission if he defied the directive not to fight John Henry Lewis. This made Philadelphians skeptical that the bout would occur.[29]

The same Madame Bey Camp where the New York State Athletic Commission had so much difficulty in getting Galento to go, he now objected to leaving. It took a wire from Jules Aronson of the Pennsylvania Commission to persuade Galento to leave Madame Bey's for the Broadway Arena in Philadelphia.[30] After pressure, Galento agreed and moved to the Philadelphia camp. Going to Philadelphia to train meant Tony would not be able to travel to his home at night. His tavern, because of his fame, was making $1,500 a week. Tony was a celebrity.

Galento completed one more day of training at Madame Bey's before going to Philadelphia. He boxed six rounds, two with John Bill, two with Lou Brown, and two with Larry Johnson. After the workout, he weighed 223 pounds. The hot summer in the East persisted, and the press wrote that his lighter weight resulted from the heat.[29]

Accompanying Tony to Philadelphia was his team. His trainers, that Tony called his First, Second, and Third Brooms were Jimmy Frayne, Jimmy Burke, and Dick O'Connor; Joe Jacobs, manager; Harry Mendel, press agent; and Lou Brown, a sparring partner. Amply proportioned Mary Galento, Tony's wife, was to make the trip but stayed behind to operate the tavern. She had planned to attend the fight via a special train from Newark bound for Philadelphia that would be provided on the morning of the fight. Aside from the train, there were fifty special buses planned to be available to carry Galento followers to Philadelphia.[29]

A Philadelphia brewery offered Galento a piece of their business if he knocked out John Henry Lewis. A department store presented him with a suit. A hotel put him in a suite with a piano in it. Promoter Taylor wanted to sign him to a long-term contract. Tony did not accept the last offer of the contract. He would train indoors at the Olympia Club on South Broad Street. While in Philadelphia, fans mobbed Tony on the streets, wanting a glimpse of the heavyweight.

"They must have been thinking about Tony when they called Philadelphia the City of Brotherly Love," Joe Jacobs said. "Crowds followed him on the street, everybody wanted to buy him beer, and so many people packed into the Olympia Club when he trained that you couldn't breathe."[31]

The heat in Philadelphia remained oppressive. It took a toll on the big man during training.

"Tony has been complaining to me about the air in the Olympia," Joe Jacobs said. "He says he cannot breathe properly, and that he was anxious to train outdoors … working indoors on these scorching days has taken a lot out of him. Prior to coming here, he trained fifteen rounds daily. Here I have had to make a halt at the end of nine rounds, he has become so fatigued."[32]

After four days in Philadelphia, Tony wanted to return to Madame Bey's Camp.

"I told Commissioner Jules Aronson what we were up against," Joe Jacobs said, "and as he knows boxing from actual experience, he agreed that the only thing to do was take Galento back to Madame Bey's."[31]

"Herman Taylor, the promoter, was satisfied because he wants to get a little publicity on Lewis," Jacobs continued. "There's been so much publicity on Galento that a lot of people don't know the name of the fellow he's fighting."[32]

"Tony had to get away," Jacobs explained. "That's all there was to it. I told Taylor that Galento will fight anybody he can get in September—Max Baer, Tommy Farr, or Bob Pastor. The heat in Philadelphia was so oppressive and the opportunity for doing proper roadwork so limited."[31]

Joe Jacobs said they would go back to a "real training camp."[32]

Back at Madame Bey's, Joe Jacobs conveyed he expected Tony to win and win early by a knockout. Tony was happy to be within driving distance of his Orange, New Jersey, tavern again. It gave him the opportunity to train in the outdoor ring at Bey's, too, where the oppressiveness of an indoor ring was absent. Tony thought the fight was as good as won. The moving about did not affect ticket sales. The prefight sale satisfied the promoters, having passed the $50,000 mark.[31]

Lou Ambers joined Tony and his team at Madame Bey's Camp. The Herkimer Hurricane arrived with his dog to begin work for his lightweight title defense against Henry "Homicide Hank" Armstrong. The fight was to be held on August 10 at the Polo Grounds. Ambers came from his Herkimer home with Skid Enright. Al Weill came to Bey's, too. Weill once again was Ambers's manager after resigning his position in the spring as the Madison Square Garden matchmaker. Weill kept Charley Goldman on the team to train Ambers with Whitey Bimstein. Charley Goldman was known as a better trainer than he was a manager. Ambers boasted one of the best corners one could have. He had one of the best managers in Al Weill and two of the best trainers in Whitey and Charley. As well as Whitey being the best cut man you could have.

"I'm feeling fine," Ambers declared before singing a song.

"He's going to win, too," Weill insisted. "They're out of their minds when they offer three to one on Armstrong."[31]

On July 18, Tony drove to Bey's Camp in the afternoon. He entertained over one thousand fans gathered at the training camp. He knocked out sparring partner Joe McDougall. Then he proceeded to belt Phil Serio and Lee Brown. He had done this in a manner that impressed experts among the Bey crowd. It included Nat Rogers, Twentieth Century Sporting Club matchmaker; Charley Lucas, Australian promoter; Lou Ambers, the world lightweight champion; Al Weill, Ambers's manager; Charley Goldman, Amber's trainer; and Sid Wolfe, manager of the New York flyweight champion, Filipino Small Montana.

It was one of Bey's largest crowds in a while and one of the most for a nontitle holder. Ambers was not scheduled to start working until July 20. He would be using Joey Fontana and Sammy La Porte as sparring partners. "Homicide" Hank Armstrong had left Los Angeles and arrived at Stillman's Gymnasium in New York to begin training. He would then transfer to Dr. Biers in Pompton Lakes, New Jersey.

"If this Ambers would have boxed, I wouldn't have bothered," Galento said. "My wife and I would have driven to the seashore. But somebody had to entertain all those people."

After Tony's exhibition, he traveled back to his Orange, New Jersey, home in his open automobile. Galento took to relaxing at the end of a busy day. The citizens started to refer to their local hero as TG before it became fashionable to call star athletes by their initials.

It was more common to refer to a president, such as Franklin Delano Roosevelt, as FDR. Citizens also referred to Tony as the Prince of Orange. If you did not believe him to be invincible, he would get his pictures and show you. He would convince anybody, friend or stranger, who entered the Galento tavern and stayed long enough for the show.

The show that night was a motion picture shown, in color, of the Princeton invitational track meet featuring Glenn Cunningham and Archie San Romani in a mile race. Galento refused to stop playing a card game known as knock rummy with his manager, Joe Jacobs, long enough to watch Cunningham beat Romani. Tony was winning and could not be bothered, at least not until the motion picture of himself and Al Ettore appeared on the screen. Then Tony dropped the cards.

"This one started it," Tony explained to those lining the bar. "It took me eight rounds to knock out Ettore. Then, I knocked out Lorenzo Pack in six rounds. It took me three rounds to knock out Leroy Haynes. You watch the next picture."

The next film showed Galento's fight with Charley Massera. It ended in the second round with Massera on the canvas. Next, Nathan Mann was the victim. It showed Madison Square Garden, where the referee counted Mann out in the second round.

"Do you get it?" Tony asked. "If you don't, you're dumber than I am. I knocked Ettore out in eight and each time out since then I've made it a little shorter. Massera was around a few seconds longer than Mann."

"Now do you get it?" Tony inquired. "If you don't I'll tell you. I'll knock out John Henry Lewis in a round. Then I'll knock out Louis in half a round. Then I'll knock out Joe Jacobs."

The customers cheered in agreement.

"Have a beer," Tony growled as he prepared to resume his card game with Joe Jacobs.[33]

On July 21 at Bey's, Tony was preparing for his workout. The press listened and took notes as Tony reminded everyone that he was going to knock out John Henry Lewis in their July 26 bout in case no one had heard him say it the many times before.

"He must be a better fighter than Joe Louis because he isn't afraid to fight me," Tony proclaimed.

"It may be his income tax," Tony said. "If it isn't, he's afraid. Promoter Muggsey Taylor has a fellow ready to put up half a million dollars for the fight. What's his name, Joe?"

"George La Fontaine," manager Joe Jacobs replied. "Never mind Joe Louis, Tony, you worry about John Henry Lewis and Max Baer."

"Baer. All he does is talk," Tony declared. "Max Baer can lick anybody he thinks he can lick, but he knows he can't beat me.

"And these foreign fighters. You newspaper guys give them too much attention. Why, Tommy Farr is nothing but a curiosity like my trainers," Tony insisted.

Galento's three trainers—Jimmy Frain, Johnny Burke, and Dick O'Connor looked at one another, puzzled, but nobody said anything.

"Come on. It's time for you to go to work," manager Jacobs decided.

Galento started boxing his shadow. Clowning around, he pretended to knock down his absent opponent. He followed that with a kick to his shadow. To make sure the foe stood down, he jumped on the stricken shadow with both feet.

"That's what I'll do to John Henry," Tony boasted while the gallery laughed.

Galento boxed five rounds with three sparring partners, shadowboxed two more rounds, punched the light bag, and then skipped rope for nine minutes without a rest. Tony continued to engage the spectators with his antics. He gave his Tarzan yell and insisted Gargantua the gorilla deserted him.

"If I have to, I'll chase this John Henry," Tony declared when asked his plan of battle. "I'm in perfect shape. I've been on the road every morning, walking, jogging, and running five or six miles."

The press wrote about the wounds over Tony's eyes. They were old cuts that Lewis, the master boxer, figured to rip open with left jabs. Cuts during his fights caused many losses for Tony. Opponents were still unable to score a knockout over him.

"Do you know I haven't had a cut in over a year?" Tony explained. "In none of my last five fights was the scar tissue broken."[34]

The next day was to be Tony's last day of serious training. Whitey Bimstein, the trainer of Lou Ambers, predicted victory for Two-Ton Tony Galento over John Henry Lewis at Philadelphia's Municipal Stadium.

"I know what I am talking about because I seconded Bob Tow last April in Philadelphia," Whitey said. "Lewis won the decision, but he is not fifty percent the fighter he was a year ago.

"Galento is rough and strong," Whitey continued. "He's in good shape. He'll wear Lewis down and then knock him out. I don't see how Tony can miss.

"There are two winners in this camp," Whitey predicted. "A lot of people will be surprised when Lou beats Armstrong and Galento is a cinch to stop Lewis."[35]

The next day, with Tony Galento acting as an announcer, Ambers did three rounds of sparring. He sparred two rounds with Joey Fontana, a lightweight, and one with Sammy LaPorte, a featherweight. Tony predicted victory for the Herkimer Hurricane, who was, Tony declared, a second edition of the late Harry Greb. Ambers weighed 139 pounds the day before,[36] four pounds over the lightweight limit. Ambers continued to have difficulty making weight.

"Lou is in no hurry," manager Al Weill explained. "He's just starting. A week from now you'll see a different fighter."

The experts gathered at the ringside agreed that Ambers's physical appearance looked great. He had plenty of speed, and it was too early to judge his boxing. Before this day, Ambers was at Madame Bey's a few days loafing. The lightweight champion continued to be contented because there was a piano and a radio in the camp. Ambers played, sang, and took long walks in the country.

"Galento keeps me laughing all the time he's in camp," Ambers explained while laughing. "Do I think he'll beat John Henry Lewis? Sure."[36]

Ambers and Galento posed for a publicity photograph downstairs from the gymnasium in one of Madame Bey's all-wooden rubdown rooms. Tony lay on his back, a towel wrapped around his waist, bare-chested. Ambers kneeled over the top of him rolling his belly with a rolling pin.

Tony posed for many pictures taken in fighting positions by newsreel men and press members. He would give a savage growl and would pound his chest to show his ferocity. He bragged that he was the best heavyweight in the world and believed he would beat John Henry Louis quickly. When he stood to be photographed, Tony jokingly asked manager Joe Jacobs if Max Schmeling was in the other corner. Joe managed Max too. Tony then announced he had more money than Max.

"Maybe," Jacobs countered, "but not half as much sense."[37]

Of the eleven sparring partners he had in the last three weeks, Tom Schenk, George Lark, and Joe MacDougall remained. They helped Tony entertain a large delegation from Philadelphia. Whitey Bimstein; Herman Taylor, the Galento-Lewis bout promoter; and Jules Aronson, Pennsylvania Commission chairman, saw Tony knock out his three sparring partners in his final day of boxing. Stepping on the scales for Aronson, Tony weighed 226 pounds. It was eleven pounds less than he weighed for Nathan Mann the April before at Madison Square Garden. Dr. Clune of the Pennsylvania Commission could find nothing wrong with Tony physically. Promoter Taylor, after being chased from one end of the camp to the other by Tony, doubted his mental condition.

"I gotta have two hundred more seats in the front row," Tony insisted after chasing Taylor around the camp. "I gotta have 'em for my customers in my bar in Orange. I tell you I gotta have 'em."

"Be reasonable, Tony," Taylor begged. "The first row is sold out. The advance sale is more than $50,000. Leave me alone."

Taylor informed Galento that he sold the motion picture rights for $5,000. The promoter had not received what he considered a fair price for the radio rights. Indications were that there would be no broadcast.[35]

The day over, Ambers retired at Madame Bey's and Tony went back to Orange in his convertible automobile, as he had done every day while at Bey's Camp. It was Tony's last day before the Lewis fight. This trip home would be different from the others.

When he arrived home, Tony served a few beers. He also had a few; at times he had been his best customer. Soon, he trembled with a chill. Tony thought he had nothing more than a slight cold. He called Dr. Joseph G. Higi, his physician, who immediately diagnosed the illness as influenza pneumonia. Dr. Higi rushed Tony to Orange Memorial Hospital at seven that evening when his temperature failed to drop below 104.4. Attending to Tony were Dr. Higi and Dr. Norman Plummer, who specialized in pneumonia. Dr. Higi ordered an oxygen tent. Tony was fighting the most critical battle of his career. His temperature remained 104.4. His pulse beat at 120, and respiration measured thirty-two. Dr. Higi summoned two New York doctors for consultation. Doctors deemed his condition critical. Defiant, even in crises, Tony demanded that the oxygen tent be removed, and he would be ready for the Lewis bout.[38]

"Take that thing away," Tony insisted with a swing of his giant fists. "I'll be ready Tuesday, and I'll knock Lewis out."

A slight overnight improvement brought his temperature down to 103 degrees. They said he rested comfortably. Considered so ill by his physicians, promoter Herman Taylor, after rushing from Philadelphia to Orange, had no alternative but to cancel the fifteen-round bout. He postponed it indefinitely. Joe Jacobs said that Tony had a strenuous day's training on his last day. He knocked out three sparring partners and then had driven home in the cool night air while wet and overheated.

"Galento is a very sick man and his illness may keep him in the hospital from five days to three weeks," Dr. Higi stated in a bulletin. "He will be unable to return to the ring for two or three months at least."

Although Tony kept insisting he would be fit to fight, Aronson issued the following statement:

"Tony Galento right now is a very sick man and my sympathy first goes to the man. While I feel for Herman Taylor, who through his efforts has put over the finest promotion in his long and successful career, Mr. Taylor agrees with me that at a time like this we do not measure monetary consideration or disappointment when a life is at stake. My sincere wish is for the unfortunate man and his speedy recovery."[38]

Taylor estimated that his loss would amount to between $14,000 and $15,000. He said the advance sale exceeded $60,000 and that he had anticipated a gate of at least $150,000.[38]

Dr. Higi Issued the following bulletin that night:

"The causative organism was typed after culture and animal inoculations and identified as Type 3 pneumococcus. An X-ray of his chest showed the lower lobe to be involved a spot on the lung, confirming the findings of a physical examination. At 4 p. m. his temperature was 104; his pulse 92 and respiration 32. Normally Galento's pulse beat is between 50 and 60, and his respiration between sixteen and twenty."

Joe Jacobs said from Orange that Tony's condition was "very critical."

"His life is at stake and will be for the next thirty-six hours. Dr. Higi says we'll know then—one way or the other," he added, in a broken whisper.[39]

Joe Jacobs appeared visibly moved.

"Please don't ask me any questions," he told a writer. "I don't want to talk to anyone." His voice broke momentarily.

"Tony is very bad," he added. "That's all I can say. The important thing now is for Galento to recover."[39]

When Tony awoke at nine the next morning, he asked for his wife, who had been waiting to see him since early morning.

"Hi, Mary, how do I look?" were Tony's first words.

"A lot better," she answered.

"What's wrong with me?"

"You've got a bad cold."

"Well, what are these docs whispering around about? It must be something pretty bad?

"Hey, Doc, spill it. What's the matter with me?" Tony asked.

"Bronchitis," Dr. Higi answered, "a bad case that has to be treated like pneumonia."

"When am I goin' to get outta here?"

"Monday."

"When'll I be able to fight again?"

"Oh, about two weeks."

"I can't stay in here. I can't disappoint all my friends and Joe Jacobs."

No one but Joe Jacobs and Mrs. Galento were allowed to visit Tony. When Joe came into the room, he told Tony he had pneumonia.

"You'll have to fight like you never fought in the ring."

Tony looked relieved. He smiled slightly. Then he spoke softly. He did not sound like the Galento who used to bellow his words.

"Thanks, Joe. I feel better already now that I know what I'm fighting. I'll lick this bum like I licked all those others I met in the ring."[40]

Tony would later recall, "When I see all them priests hangin' around I says, 'Here boy, you better get up 'fore they count you out.'"[41] In time, he would make a full recovery. He would return to the Tony everyone loved or hated.

CHAPTER 28

Homicide Hank in a Hurricane

With Two-Ton Tony Galento gone from Madame Bey's and recovering in his Orange, New Jersey, home, Lou Ambers was again the main attraction at the camp. He would risk his lightweight title against Henry Armstrong. For the world featherweight title, Armstrong defeated Petey Sarron in October 1937. Then in May 1938, for the world welterweight crown, he defeated Barney Ross in a fifteen round decision at the Long Island Bowl. He had the two titles on either side of the lightweight crown owned by Lou Ambers. If he defeated Ambers for the world lightweight title, he would be the holder of three simultaneous titles. The experts did not think Ambers had a chance. Armstrong was a winner by a knockout in thirty-five of his last thirty-eight fights. The odds stood at three to one in favor of Armstrong and even money that he would knock out Ambers.

Gayle Talbot from the United Press wrote, "The consensus of those who sat through the slow, agonizing destruction of Ross, one of the truly great little fighters of the decade, was that Ambers has a similar fate in store …"

Armstrong was relentless in the ring. He appeared never to tire. He bounded around punching in continuum, giving him the alternate ring names of Hammering Hank and Perpetual Motion Henry. Why could Henry Armstrong travel at such a high speed through so many rounds? Where did he find all that amazing energy? Journalist Grantland Rice questioned Armstrong after he had been bouncing around during a workout and still not taking an extra breath.

"Two or three specialists asked me the same thing," Armstrong said. "At first they couldn't figure it out. Later on, they made a complete examination of my physical makeup and finally decided it was the size of my heart. They told me that weighing around one hundred thirty pounds, I happen to have a heart that should belong in a one hundred ninety pound body. I don't know much about these things, but I suppose it is like having a big motor in a small car."[1]

He was born Henry Melody Jackson on December 12, 1912, in Columbus, Mississippi. Armstrong's family worked as sharecroppers. They moved to St. Louis, Missouri, when Henry was a child, where he learned how to box but had little success when he became an amateur. He moved to California in 1931 with his manager, Harry Armstrong. At that time, he took his manager's last name and called himself Henry Armstrong. He lost three of his first four professional fights. In late 1932, he started to show talent. He lost only one of his next thirty-four fights, all in California.[2]

In 1936, Henry Armstrong formed a relationship with entertainer Al Jolson, a fight fan. He saw Armstrong fight in Los Angeles. Jolson, along with actor George Raft, decided to back Armstrong. Jolson changed his manager to the experienced Eddie Mead.[3] In the 1930s, Jolson occupied the stature of America's most famous and highest paid entertainer. He performed in blackface makeup. The practice would receive condemnation today, but Jolson advocated equality. He introduced African American music to white audiences. As early as 1911, at the age of twenty-five, Jolson was already noted for fighting discrimination.[4] He was the only white man allowed into an all-black nightclub in Harlem.[5]

At the end of July, Sixto Escobar joined Ambers at Madame Bey's Camp.[6] Escobar had regained the world bantamweight championship by defeating Harry Jeffra in February after losing it in the Carnival of Champions. He would train for a series of preparatory matches before risking his title.

On July 27, Madame Bey made an unusual trip. She went to Dr. Biers's Camp in Pompton Lakes, New Jersey, to see Ambers's competition, Henry Armstrong, train. The newspapers, instead of running pictures of Armstrong training, printed a picture of Madame Bey paying her admission fee to the camp like any other customer. For a woman who shunned going to fights and stayed out of the way of her boxers as they trained, this was unusual. The press called it a social visit.[7] Madame Bey did not divulge what her intentions were. Ambers's team back at Bey's Camp had to be interested in what she observed.

On July 30, after Ambers had been training at Madame Bey's for a week, the press questioned Al Weill about his plans for the upcoming bout.

"Lou won't plan any special style for Armstrong," Weill said, "just wait a round or two and suit his style accordingly. Then watch out!"

The press stated that Weill liked Madame Bey's Camp.

"The mental attitude is just as important as physical condition in a fight," Weill explained why he chose Madame Bey's site over cheaper arrangements. "Madame Bey knows Lou, understands the kind of food he likes. He won't have to be giving orders to strange chefs."[8]

Charlie Goldman and Whitey Bimstein, Ambers's trainers, had Ambers using his known speed in workouts and had him using his left jab that would keep Armstrong away.[8] That seemed to be the logical plan, to keep Armstrong away and not get into a slugging match. Whitey had other ideas that would manifest a different plan as the fight approached. To everyone's surprise, Ambers would start slugging with his sparring partners and not show his brilliant boxing ability. Everyone, except Ambers's team, thought the new strategy was a mistake and would benefit Armstrong.

At Bey's Camp, Weill had heard Armstrong and Eddie Meade, his manager, wanted to postpone the bout from August 10 because Meade believed it would help the gate. Meade explained at their training facility in Pompton Lakes, New Jersey, that the Saratoga horseracing season neared its climax around that date, and there were several New York attractions, which may interfere with the gate. Weill was not in favor of a delay.

"The fight has been postponed once and when promoter Mike Jacobs picked August 10 at the Polo Grounds he knew about the Hambletonian at Goshen, Saratoga, and the night ball game at Ebbets Field that night."[9]

The press overwhelmingly favored Armstrong, but Henry did not take Ambers lightly.

"Lou Ambers is a definite problem," Armstrong said on a sultry day at Pompton Lakes. "He's a tough nut to crack, not because he's so tough, but so shifty and fast. I can beat him. I know, but I expect much more trouble out of him than I would out of Mike Belloise or Petey Sarron, or even Barney Ross."

On August 3, one week before the showdown with Armstrong, Ambers was getting into shape. Three prominent boxing figures came to see Ambers train—Bill Brown of the New York State Commission; friend, foe, and five-time champion Tony Canzoneri; and former world heavyweight champion James "Cinderella Man" Braddock.

Braddock would frequent the camp many times to watch top boxers train. On one occasion, he left a signed boxing-pose photograph for Madame Bey.

"T. Madame Beyes Best Wishes Your Friend Jimmy Braddock."

He misspelled her last name.

"This kid is one in a million," Al Weill, said referring to Ambers. "That's why he will lick the Mammy Singer."

Weill called Armstrong that because he was Al Jolson's fighter, who was known for singing the song "My Mammy."

Outside, the sun was beating down. The dining room in Madame Bey's farmhouse looking over the hills felt comfortable. It was filled with New York Boxing Commissioner Bill Brown, James Braddock, Tony Canzoneri, Lou Brix, Sixto Escobar, Al Weill, Whitey Bimstein, and some newspapermen. The newspapermen were drinking beer and eating sandwiches. They expressed opinions about the anticipated Armstrong-Ambers fight. Ambers, having already started some early work, rested in his upstairs room, and nobody, not even Whitey Bimstein, who trained Ambers, seemed to be in a hurry to wake Lou and put him to work.

The storytelling tradition at Madame Bey's continued with Al Weill.

"He's one in a million," Weill said again. "I'll tell you what he done once, and I don't know anybody else that would have done it.

"Remember the first time be fought Canzoneri? Well, everybody in Herkimer came down for that fight. Everybody you could think of. They were sure he was going to win, and they were there yelling for him. But you know what happened. Canzoneri knocked him down in the third round, and he made an up-hill fight after that, but it was too much for him. He wasn't ready for it. Well, he felt bad, and so did I, but I consoled him and sent him home for a couple of weeks.

"And you know what happened? He went home and his mother consoled him, and he felt better, and then he went out around the town to meet his friends, and they ignored him. Even the fellow he thought was the best friend he wouldn't have nothing to do with him. They said he threw the fight to Canzoneri after they bet all their money on him. They said Skid, who was in his corner, sprinkled stuff in the water bottle, even.

"There was only one fellow in the town who stood by him. That was Charlie Clough, the village blacksmith. He told Lou he still had faith in him and not to pay any attention to the other fellows.

"Lou came back to New York, and he came right to my office, and he said, 'When can you get me another fight with Canzoneri?'

"I said, 'Why, Lou, I don't know. You got to go some distance before you can get another fight with Canzoneri. What do you want to fight him again for now?'

"He wouldn't tell me. He just kept saying he wanted another fight with Canzoneri.

"'I'll go through anything to get it,' he said to me. 'I don't care what it is.'

"Well, we started out, and everything happened to him. He got his jaw broke, and then there was that unfortunate thing with that poor Scarpati, who died in the ring with him. But he kept on going and winning, and finally he was in a spot again where I could challenge Canzoneri. Tony didn't want to fight him. He wanted to fight Montañez because he thought he could draw more money with Montañez, and we milled around for a while, and finally the commission said there must be an elimination and they picked Ramey and Montañez and him and said the winner would fight Canzoneri.

"Montañez wouldn't enter the elimination, and Ramey went into the St. Nicholas one night and got licked by Leonard Del Genio, so we got the match. I don't have to tell you what happened. He beat Canzoneri.

"Well, now he is the lightweight champion of the world, and I get a telegram from the boys in Herkimer. They want to give him a big reception. I showed him the wire, and he said, 'Sure, I'll go. I want to go. I want to go up there because I got something to tell those fellows.'

"And then for the first time he told me what they had done to him when he went back after he got licked by Canzoneri, and that is why he was so determined to lick Canzoneri and wouldn't rest until he had done it.

"We went up there, and they gave us a big reception. They had bands and school kids and his teacher, Margaret Tucker, who taught him when he was in school. And they had his mother and all his brothers and sisters in cars, and they paraded through the street, and you never saw such a time. There was an uproar, and they were all shaking hands with him and with me, and the bands were playing.

"That same night they had the dinner. The Mayor couldn't be there because he had to be some place that night, but State Senator Schall was the master of ceremonies. They had Lou's mother up on the dais, and it was a very swell dinner. They all made speeches, and when they called on me, I made a speech. I said, 'I am very glad to be here.' And I told them what a wonderful little fellow Lou is and what a great fighter, and how he beat Canzoneri—there was only about half as many came down for the second fight as there was for the first—and I said, 'And now I am going to ask the champion to say something because I know he has something to say to you.'

"They all cheered, and Lou got up. You know how he is. He never had any chance to learn how to make a speech. That was the first thing he said. He said, 'Mother, and all you gentlemen and ladies, I don't know how to make a speech. But I want to say something: I had my back burned, and I had my foot smashed. I still have a silver plate in my foot. I got my jaw broke, and I felt terrible the time poor Tony Scarpati died. But nothing that ever happened to me hurt me as much as you did when I came home after Canzoneri licked me, and you said I threw the fight.'

"And then he sat down. How many guys you know would have had guts enough to do that? That's why I say he is one in a million, and I say he is right when he says he will lick this Mammy Singer."[10]

Ambers awoke. He prepared and worked with his sparring partners lightweight Slugger White of Georgia and featherweight Victor Corchado of Puerto Rico, whose style resembled that of Armstrong. After watching his colleague work, Canzoneri made a comment.

"It's going to be one of the toughest fights you ever saw, but I'm not picking a winner yet. Ambers is in good trim, and it's not going to be any tea party for Armstrong. Armstrong can hit harder, but Lou will land oftener, and if he fights the fellow right, can nag him to death. Personally, I don't think Lou is working right for the fight. He should move around more, step from side to side, instead of taking all those punches he absorbed this afternoon."[11]

The same day, retired former world lightweight champion and one of the top-ranked lightweights ever, Benny Leonard, went to Pompton Lakes to watch Armstrong train. It was almost five years since his second retirement in 1932. His first retirement lasted seven years, but a comeback was necessitated when he lost his ring earnings in the stock market crash of 1929. Leonard was unwilling to give the fight to Armstrong like many experts.

"Henry is going to meet a smart boxer who knows how to slip punches and then counter, a boxer who is fast, shifty, and smart. Ambers has what it takes to beat Armstrong," he said after watching Armstrong train.[11]

Later, Leonard came to Madame Bey's Camp. After watching Ambers, Leonard shared Canzoneri's concerns about how Ambers decided to approach the fight. He was still fighting inside instead of measuring his opponent from a distance that he had been so adept at doing.

"It would be a good idea to be a bit afraid of Henry," Leonard said. "Be enough afraid to keep away from him."[12]

Whitey thought the best way to beat Armstrong was with both hand and foot speed. He believed Ambers needed to prepare for a fight at close range.

"There are times when you gotta get in close," Whitey said. "And what is the best punch to use in close? A right hand uppercut. And this is where Ambers comes in. Ambers has as good a right uppercut as you'd ever want to see."[13]

The press questioned Whitey, well respected as the best, about the tactics he was using with Ambers.

On August 4 from Madame Bey's Camp, Al Weill predicted trouble for Armstrong. On that day, New York Commissioner Phelan and Dr. Walker visited the camp. They observed Ambers spar with Slugger White and Victor Corchado. Dr. Walker pronounced Ambers in top condition. He scaled at 135.5 pounds, a half a pound over the limit.[14] Unknown by many, Ambers's weight problem took a physical toll. He was starving to make weight. He found himself in a dilemma no fighter wanted. He could move up in weight class, which meant fighting stronger opponents, foes who could withstand a solid punch, which would knock down a person in a lower weight class. If he stayed in the lower weight class, it meant a weakened body from lack of caloric intake and nutrition.

On August 6, the press asked Mike Jacobs, promoter of the Armstrong-Ambers bout, who would win.

"Who's gonna win the Armstrong-Ambers fight next Wednesday night at the Polo Grounds? How in the heck do I know? I'm a promoter, not an expert. It oughta be a swell fight, though. Hey, take a look at that line at the box office window. Looks like I'm giving the people what they want, don't it?"[15]

The press printed the obligatory publicity pictures of a boxer. As often the case at Bey's Camp, Ambers's pictures involved farming. One picture showed him milking a cow. Another one had him holding a hoe while tending to a garden. A third had him doing roadwork while others paced him on bicycles.

Ambers, while still hard at work, had time for entertainment. The Blue Streak Quartet came to the camp to harmonize with Ambers. He played the ukulele while flanked by two members of the quartet on each side. The pictures of the five of them appeared in newspapers, Ambers smiling as he sang, happy as always. One quartet member wrote a parody of the bout that Ambers sang with enthusiasm. They sang it to a tune named "Ti Pi Tin," a top song from 1938. Sometimes boxers will do anything to relieve the tension before an important match.

> This week while the weather was mellow,
> We met that Lou Ambers fellow,
> He liked us, you bet
> The Blue Streak Quartet,
> And we got along rather swell-o.
> 'Twas after a game of ping-pong.
> We asked him how he'll fare with Armstrong.
> He waited awhile
> And then with a smile
> Upon his old uke he strummed this song:
> (Chorus)
> I'll tip his chinny-chin, chinny-chin,
> Tap his tummy-tum, tummy-tum,
> You can bet I'll cut him
> When I uppercut him,
> Slam him all around.
> His head will start to spin, spinny-spin,
> Legs will weigh a ton, tonny-ton,
> And when it's all over
> I will be in clover,
> Still the lightweight champion of the town.[16]

On August 8, two days before the Armstrong-Ambers bout, world heavyweight champion Joe Louis flew in from Detroit and then rushed over to Madame Bey's Camp. He wanted to see Ambers in his final workout. Louis refused to make a prediction after seeing Ambers work.

"That Ambers boy is awful fast," Louis told reporters. "He's quick to see openings. He'll give Armstrong a tough fight. It ought to be nip and tuck."[17]

While at Madame Bey's Camp, Joe Louis took publicity pictures with Charles Atlas, the proclaimed strongest man in the world. One showed Louis, Ambers, and Atlas in the gymnasium during Ambers's workout. Another photograph showed Joe Louis and Charles Atlas standing in front of Madame Bey's farmhouse. Louis was dressed in suit and tie. Atlas was bare-chested, wearing long, light-colored pants. Louis's right hand squeezed Atlas's triceps while his left hand squeezed Atlas's biceps. Atlas also posed with Sixto Escobar. Many believed Atlas had perfect body symmetry. In the 1920s, he occupied the spot as the top male model. He performed many feats of strength. The most known one was towing a seventy-two-ton Pennsylvania railroad car 112 feet along the tracks.

Louis returned to his camp that night in Pompton Lakes, New Jersey, where Armstrong did his training. As in the case when Madame Bey visited Armstrong's camp, Louis said nothing about why he came to watch Ambers.

Louis was to speak with Mike Jacobs to discuss plans for a September title defense. Possibilities were Tommy Farr or Max Baer. Max Baer's mother had died the previous night, and it was believed he would not fight until the indoor season started.[17] A September defense never transpired. Louis would not fight until January.

With Joe Louis's visit, every heavyweight champion from Jack Dempsey to Joe Louis had either trained in Chatham Township or visited. In total, all eight heavyweight champions who reigned from 1919 to 1948 spent time there. Joe Louis would make frequent visits from his Pompton Lakes facility where he trained for the majority of his fights. Louis's promoter, Mike Jacobs, was on good terms with Madame Bey and continued to visit the camp and send fighters there for bouts that he promoted. Jacobs sent Louis there to help promote his other bouts.

On August 10, the day of the fight, Ambers just made the 135-pound limit. It would not matter. The evening at the Polo Grounds started with a light rain. By the time the main event arrived, the skies opened, and a deluge of rain ensued. It was the peril of scheduling an outdoor bout. After promoter Mike Jacobs consulted with a commission representative and the boxers' managers—though Al Weill opposed the delay—they decided to postpone the match.[18]

"It never rains in the Garden," Mike Jacobs stated, where the rescheduled bout would be held.

"No, not Friday," Al Weill, Ambers's manager, dissented. "Ambers is on edge tonight. This is the greatest break Armstrong ever got for Lou was ready to step out and turn on the heat."[19]

Promoters had held fights in the rain before. There was the first Dempsey-Tunney fight in Philadelphia. It rained all night flooding the ring. The fight went until the end. Even worse was a Chicago night when Ace Hudkins fought Mickey Walker. They had just started the bout when the rain came in torrents. It kept pouring, but the fight went to the finish.[20]

The Armstrong-Ambers bout postponement saved Mike Jacobs from a complete financial disaster. The Polo Grounds ticket sales were poor. Of nine thousand tickets sold, only five thousand braved the weather. Mike Jacobs rescheduled the bout for one week later.[18]

The two fighters returned to their respective training camps. Ambers was back at Bey's and worked more in the ring. He punched at sparring partners and did other training activities. At the end of the day, he would retire to his room and play one or more of his many musical instruments. He was a one-man band. Of his many instruments, he would play piano, clarinet, and snare drum. He began to play a new instrument at Bey's Camp. He started playing the trombone. One writer called it the swing band at Madame Bey's bungalow of bop. His manager, Al Weill, had a different view. Weill never in all his life saw anything to equal the trombone as a sharpener of fighters.

"Before he took up the trombone, Lou's right hand was just another right hand," Weill said. "Not bad, not good. But a week on that instrument and his right hand became a killer diller. The snare drum helped him, too. To play one of those darn things, and play it hot, you got to swing your body like a monkey on a limb. Lou would get to swinging a piece and then ask his sparring partners to try and hit him. They couldn't put a glove on him when he was really going to town on 'Flat Foot Floggie.'"[21]

The rescheduled bout looked better for promoter Mike Jacobs. He told everyone it would be different than the Polo Grounds when the two little champions charge into each other at the Garden.

"Already we've sold more ringside and $11.50 seats than we sold for the Polo Grounds," Mike Jacobs said. "The pasteboards are moving today, and I look for a crowd of 19,000 and a gate of around $100,000."[22]

Other estimates placed the gross receipts nearer $70,000 or $80,000. Jacobs had the seat prices arranged so that a sellout would bring in a gate of $130,000. No more than 9,000 tickets sold for a $60,000 gate in the cancelled soggy Polo Grounds match.[23]

The New York State Athletic Commission ruled that only Ambers's lightweight title would be at stake. Neither of Armstrong's two titles would be at risk. The commission had promoter Mike Jacobs and managers Eddie Mead and Al Weill sign an agreement specifying they would only fight for the lightweight championship.[22]

Armstrong remained a favorite at three to one with even money that Armstrong would win by a knockout. The largest single bet reported was Al Jolson laying $1,100 to $1,000 that Armstrong would win by a knockout.[22] The layoff did not appear to have an adverse effect on the fighters. If either had felt affected, it was Ambers; he had to keep the weight off for another week. The press reported him in the best shape of his fighting career before the cancellation. A rumor continued from Madame Bey's that Ambers had trouble making weight. Weill laughed about it. He said Ambers weighed 134 pounds, one under the limit, after his last workout.[22] Weill was covering for his fighter.

The day before the fight, Lou Ambers sang while he played the piano in Madame Bey's cool, shadowy parlor.

Ain't misbehavin'
Up on the shelf
Ain't misbehavin,
'Cause I'm happy by myself ...

Madame Bey smiled at a reporter and nodded toward the cheerful champion Ambers, who now sat singing in an old rocking chair.

"He's happy, that boy," Madame Bey said. "He's full of good food, real milk, sunshine, and lots of sleep. He's got four weeks of training under his belt, and he looks like a million. He's in the pink. And he's confident, too."[24]

On the day of the fight, August 17, 1938, it was hot and muggy. The change in venue, as Uncle Mike Jacobs had predicted, helped ticket sales. There had been a last-minute rush to gain entrance to the fight. They sold the $1.15 cheap seats to the $16.50 ringside ones. The amounts were a Garden high-ticket price for a non-heavyweight title bout. The fight drew a surprising gate. Gross attendance reached 19,216. The paid attendance came to 18,240. Gross receipts reached $102,280.94 with net receipts $90.203.92. Ambers's share of 37.5 percent amounted to $33,860.22. Armstrong's share of 22.5 percent gave him $20,766.13. On the undercard, Slugger White, Ambers's sparring partner, won his lightweight bout.

In attendance, and introduced, were Jack Dempsey, James Braddock, Benny Leonard, Tony Canzoneri, Joe Louis, and Tommy Farr. Barney Ross also attended. One reporter joked that the retired three-division champion Ross came to check if Armstrong, who had taken his welterweight crown, was one man.[25] One person at the fight received no introduction but knew everyone introduced. Madame Bey attended the bout. It was the second time on record that she made an appearance at a fight. The last time was in 1926 for one of her boys, light heavyweight champion Paul Berlenbach. She chose one of the hardest fought and bloodiest of fights.

The United Press noted that blood normally sold for twenty-five dollars a pint. That was the hospital price. At Madison Square Garden, people saw two blood donors. Henry Armstrong and Lou Ambers shed a quart or so in a dogfight for the lightweight championship.[26]

Armstrong dominated the early rounds. Everybody expected Armstrong to fight in close. The surprise was that Ambers, who possessed great footwork, decided to stand

and trade punches with Armstrong just the way he trained at Madame Bey's Camp. In the fifth round, Armstrong knocked Ambers down. The bell saved him. In the next round, Ambers went down again and got up. Armstrong could not keep him on the canvas. Armstrong was repeatedly warned about low blows and penalized. Ambers won later rounds, but Armstrong never took a backward step. Ambers caused a horrific cut on Armstrong's lip in the tenth round.[27] In the twelfth and thirteenth round, Billy Cavanaugh considered stopping the fight. Armstrong was losing too much blood from the cut on his lip.

"Look at the ring, it's full of blood!" Billy Cavanaugh said. "If you spit anymore blood onto the floor, I'm going to stop this fight."[25]

Armstrong would swallow the blood to prevent spillage on the canvas and the referee stopping the bout.

Armstrong came out for the fourteenth round with his left eye closed; his appearance was "grim and deathlike."[28] A right by Armstrong in the fourteenth round sent Ambers staggering backward with the ropes preventing him from going down.[29] In the fifteenth and last round, both boxers exchanged punches at the end. The bell could not be heard because of the roar of the Garden crowd. They continued to fight after the bell until referee Cavanaugh separated them. Armstrong was so disorientated that he went to the wrong corner after the fight ended.[29] The epic battle was over. In 1996, *The Ring* magazine would rank it as the twelfth greatest title fight of all time.

At the finish, most of the press was splattered with blood, and the canvas was full of blood. Only twice during the entire fight did the referee have to separate the fighters. When he did split them, he endangered himself because as the two fighters neared closer, they fought harder.[26] Fights of this nature weigh on the body and influence future fighting ability. It proved too hard for Madame Bey to see one of her boys receive such punishment. She charged out of her seat before the fight had completed.

"You cannot tell me that the boy I saw fighting was the same boy I know as Luigi D'Ambrosio," she declared in contempt using Ambers's birth name. "My Lou Ambers is a gentleman. All my boys are gentlemen. I don't want to know how they act when they fight because they aren't that way when they are with me."[30]

She could watch them train at her camp and listen to their fights on the radio but could not endure a visual display of brutality. She understood what they did for a living. She supported them with all their needs. When confronted by the stark reality of the sport, she could not watch. Training is far different from an athlete in the throes of competition. Prepare all you want; you cannot approach the frenetic pace of the contest. Adrenaline will force you faster. Endorphins will mask body pain. The mind ignores the body's signals that would cause a sane person to stop the continued punishment.

Madison Square Garden was a roaring, wild place where men were throwing their hats away, and women were screaming. A sudden quiet came as a voice boomed through the loudspeakers.

"The winner and new lightweight champion of the world—Henry Armstrong!"[27]

Referee Cavanaugh walked over to the exhausted new champion's corner and lifted his hand. He had to lift it; Armstrong was too spent to raise it himself.[26] Al Weill threw his towel on the canvas and kicked it in disgust.[31] The Garden voiced its disapproval. Jeers came rolling down from the rafters. Ambers stood in a blue robe drenched in sweat, an empty look on his face. Armstrong got the lightweight title. Ambers got the cheers. Then, showing his sportsmanship, he shook Armstrong's hand.[27] Ambers fought the way he had trained with his sparring partners at Madame Bey's under the direction of Whitey Bimstein. Twice he hit Armstrong so hard on the chin that his mouthpiece bounced out of his mouth and across the ring.[27]

If fighters are artists, the black Armstrong and the white Ambers used the same color, blood red, to paint the canvas upon which they fought. The wet blood lingered on the canvas, where the two men fought and bled, while the crowd continued its roaring, demanding a return bout.

It took thirty-seven stitches to close Armstrong's mouth wound. Armstrong threw up a quart and a half of blood, which he had swallowed during the fight, in the doctor's office an hour later.[25]

After, the fighters left the ring and retired to their dressing rooms. Ambers appeared borderline delirious, sitting naked in front of reporters in a straight-backed chair. Welts covered his body, and a large lump adorned the top of his left eye. He sang his favorite song, laughed, and babbled.

"I want a girl, just like the girl that married dear old dad," he chanted in one breath.

"Whoop-a doopy. He can't punch. He ain't the best puncher. Hiya pal," Ambers blurted out.

"I want a gal … Yeah, I coulda gotten up … Just like the gal … Hiya everybody," he sang and talked alternately.

The press tried to take notes of his nonsensical babble. As he sang and jabbered, his tired body still swayed as though he were rolling punches. His head bobbed as though he was ducking a right, and his feet did little miniature double shuffles.[26]

"I beat him," Ambers said as his bravado took over and spoke the line repeatedly.

"Hurt me? Hell, no. Armstrong's not half the puncher they say he is. Look at the way I cut him up.

"Armstrong never hurt me once—even when he knocked me down. I knew what I was doing every second. I'd like to fight him again. He wasn't a hard puncher. He just keeps after you. I want to fight him again, any time and any place. He fights with his head, and that's no fairy tale. Not one of his punches hurt, even when he knocked me down. He's all right that Armstrong."[32]

The mood differed in the other dressing room—somber. Armstrong just sat. His eyes bruised and his raw, tender lips stood out. He licked them as he answered questions with weariness.

"It was the toughest fight of my career. Ambers punches fair, but he don't hurt much. I wasn't in the best of condition. Yes, I'm going to keep the featherweight title. Find me a good one hundred twenty-six pounder and I'll fight him."[32]

When they sloshed iced water on his back, or flashbulbs exploded in his face, he never changed expression.[26]

The referee awarded the seventh, eleventh, and twelfth rounds to Ambers on penalties. Armstrong had a margin on points in each of those rounds. The scorers rendered a split decision with one round deciding the fight. Judge Marty Monroe gave the decision to Ambers, eight rounds to seven. Judge George Lecron gave Armstrong eight rounds with Ambers winning six and called one even. That left the outcome of the fight to referee Bill Cavanaugh, who gave Armstrong seven, Ambers six, and called two even. The press's scorecards were not as close as the official ones. The United Press score sheet gave Armstrong eight, Ambers five, and called two even. Lawton Carver from the International News Service commented that the crowd reaction of booing the decision was unjust. James P. Dawson from the *New York Times* went further, calling the crowd's display "a sad demonstration after a glorious bout." Dawson scored the bout for Armstrong by a ten-to-five margin. In his opinion, Armstrong had the better of all three rounds lost for the foul deductions. Caswell Adams from the *New York Tribune* also had Armstrong winning ten to five. Alan Gould from the Associated Press had Armstrong in front by an even wider margin, favoring the new champion by an eleven-to-four count. In Gould's opinion, Ambers had only outfought the challenger in the thirteenth round. *Scripps-Howard* sportswriter Joe Howard wrote, "Personally, I didn't see how any other decision could have been given. Armstrong hit harder and landed more often. There is no other basis on which a decision can or should be given." Ambers won but one round on points, as Damon Runyon scored it.

Al Weill had a different view than the writers.

"It was murder," Weill shouted. "… They let Armstrong butt and hit low all night. Fight him again? Sure, but go in and take a look at him. Armstrong won't be able to fight again for six months. How did anybody reach a decision like that?"[31]

"There's no doubt in my mind who won," Weill continued loudly. "And all we want is a return match—the sooner the better."

At first, Ambers conveyed more respectfulness than his manager did. He refused to blame Armstrong's rough tactics as a reason for his defeat. Instead, Ambers said that he did not know whether he had won or lost but just hoped it had been a good fight. He added that he wanted the rematch his manager called for but only after he had "a good long rest."

"I started with a badly cut lip that got much worse after the tenth round. It wasn't a matter of heart or breathing or condition, but the blood I had to swallow slowed me down," Armstrong would later recall.[33]

"Henry Armstrong," Damon Runyon wrote, "the brown skinned fighting fury from Los Angeles … completed the total extinction of the Caucasian race from the pugilistic world championship map."[34] Of eight recognized titles, Joe Louis held the heavyweight title, John Henry Lewis held the light heavyweight title, Sixto Escobar of Puerto Rico held the bantamweight title, and Henry Armstrong held the three titles from featherweight to welterweight. There was no recognized flyweight champion, and the white Al Hostak held the middleweight title.

With Armstrong's victory, for the first time a fighter held three titles simultaneously. He paid the price. It took Armstrong three days to recover. Ambers strolled around town the next day.[24]

A month after the fight, the Reverend Edward Lautenschlager, chairman of the Amsterdam's Recreation Commission, visited Madame Bey's Camp. He hoped to see Battlin' Sam Crocetti, but he was in training at a West Side gymnasium in New York for his fight with Matt Perfetti at Lanzi's arena on September 15. Madame Bey gave the Reverend Lautenschlager a message to give Ambers.

"Lou Ambers should have gotten the verdict in that battle with Armstrong—watch him give the colored boy a thorough going over the next time."[35]

CHAPTER 29

Recognition

Time weighed upon Madame Bey, as it had for many of her boys. Now fifty-seven years old, her slim figure that once graced the Seventh Avenue drawing rooms had widened. Her back had a slight hunch. The long black hair, now short, just reached her ears on the side and touched the bottom of her neck in the back but remained black. Her dramatic, expressive eyes and strong-featured face remained, as did her indomitable spirit.

Madame Bey had refused long interview requests and had avoided photographers since she opened her camp in November 1923. She preferred spotlighting her boys. She continued to be content behind the scenes, providing her champion boys with all she could give them to be the best at what they did. Starting in 1937, after her husband died, she began to be more visible in the press. She visited an opposing camp and attended a fight. Late in 1938, a magazine requested an interview for an article. The request came not from a boxing journal, sports periodical, or prominent newspaper column. The request came from the American women's magazine, *Family Circle*. She accepted the invitation, and journalist Stewart Robertson came to the camp to write the article. The interview occurred during the time Galento occupied the camp for John Henry Lewis and Ambers for Henry Armstrong. It gave us an insight into Madame Bey.

She reminisced to Robertson about her days in Constantinople as a young girl and her early days in Washington, DC, as a young woman. There were the days of dancing in the East Room of the White House. She said it had been when there were "handsome men in uniforms and decorations, and the women were beautiful and gracious." She explained her duties as part of the Turkish Diplomatic Corps. She talked about her late husband, Sidky, with whom she was always together, until his death a little over one year before.[1]

"Those were joyful and exciting years we spent in Washington," Madame Bey told Robertson. "And as I was the only woman at the legation who could speak English, I had an exceptionally lively time at all the dinner parties and entertainments, I made friends everywhere, and ex-Queen Liliuokalani of Hawaii (the last Hawaiian queen), who had been deposed and was living at the capital, was so fond of me that she wanted to adopt me as her daughter. She used to give me many of the songs she wrote, and once presented me with a gorgeous amethyst ring mounted in the shape of a crown, which had been given to her by

Queen Victoria of England. You see, I also speak Greek, Italian, French, Armenian, and Spanish, and quite a little German that I picked up from Max Schmeling. It seems strange to you that I should speak of queens and pugilists at the same time? Not to me, my friend. Each of them is a part of my life, and life to me has always been a fascinating adventure.

"But I was to know horror as well. When President William McKinley went to Buffalo to attend the Pan-American Exposition in 1901, the diplomatic corps made the journey also, and many of us were near him when he was shot on that fateful September 6. I was photographed with a group of officials surrounding him in front of the Temple of Music, and was in almost the same position a little later when the assassin Leon Czolgosz approached to shake hands with the President. Czolgosz had a revolver bandaged into the palm of one hand to make it look as if he was injured, and when the President reached out to take his good hand, Czolgosz shot him. There was a terrible scene, and I can remember hearing President McKinley saying, 'Don't let Mrs. McKinley know about this!' while he was being carried away. He died eight days afterward."

After leaving the Turkish Legation, Madame Bey explained they wanted to stay in America. She told him about their entry into the rug business and its failures.

"Well, in the diplomatic service, one is continually being shifted to distant parts of the world, and when the time came for my husband to be transferred, we were so much in love with America that we wanted to stay here always. It is the same thing now with my son Rustem Bey, who is the chief of police for Chatham Township, but he doesn't mind. He was born while I was in Washington, and the American ways are good enough for him, as they are for me," she explained.

"We were not getting any younger, so we decided that we would settle down on a little place in the country, grow our own vegetables, and take things more easily. And I suppose I would be doing that today if Freddie Welsh, the ex-lightweight champion, had not dropped in to tell me his troubles. Freddie, who had been a wizard with his fists, had retired to run a training camp and health farm.

"Never before has there been a training camp run by a woman," Madame Bey continued. "And also remember that I am the only woman around the place. I have my rules about conduct and hours, and because the boys know I have their interest at heart, they obey me without the arguments that there sometimes are in other camps."

Robertson asked Madame Bey if she went to see her boys do their battling, but she shook head. This happened to be a short time before she attended the Armstrong-Ambers bloodbath.

"Not anymore," she told Robertson. "Because it hurts me to watch them getting hurt when all the time I know they are not really bruisers, but artists in a sense, who are doing the thing they know best in order to earn a living. I cannot bear to see them cut up, and then when they win, which my boys do most of the time, I prefer to hear about it over the radio. But the boys always offer me ringside seats, and I guess I am about the only person in the country who regularly turns down $27.50 chances to see world's championship contests.

"I see these boys not only as punishing boxers but also as human beings with a burden of doubt under their youthful pose of being extremely hard and wise. Don't you suppose they worry about being punched deaf or blind, or having to take punishment that will injure them internally? You bet they do! And the worry is multiplied if they are beginning to age and find it harder to get into shape. That is what makes most of them except the rarities like Lou Ambers out there …

"Early in the training period I allow their girlfriends," continued Madame Bey, "sisters, or wives to come out to see them in the afternoons, but during the last week, they are shut off from everything. Sometimes a manager will not allow his boy to see any girls all the time he is here, but that is up to him. And I would like to say that I have never seen the crooked type of manager that one sees in the movies. All the ones I know work their heads off to get their men in condition, and if more fighters listened to their managers, they would be better off. Whenever the boys tell me about their love affairs, all I do is to advise them to marry their own kind. Some of them never give girls a thought, but think only of making good in some business after they retire.

"Somehow the happy ones stay longest in my memory. Paolino Uzcudun, the Basque heavyweight, who never was knocked out until he met Joe Louis, trained here, and nothing ever worried him. To me, he was my rough diamond, and although he may be fighting for his life in Spain now, I am sure he finds time to sing and laugh. Then there is that gorgeous boy Tommy Farr. Tommy is musical and has made English phonograph records, and used to sit at my piano and sing duets. I forgot to tell you that I was a professional singer in my younger days—a mezzo-soprano and good enough to give concerts at Carnegie Hall in New York—so I still can accompany Tommy when he puts on steam. Now, there is a boy who used to be a coal miner in Wales, and yet he has more instinctive politeness than many raised in better surroundings.

"It's funny about politeness. Do you remember Battling Siki, that Senegalese from French Africa who was light-heavyweight champion? Siki lived alone in a little cottage here when he was training, and to our eyes he was a strange, half-wild man from the jungle. Yet he had a complete knowledge of how to conduct himself with other people. He liked to dress loudly, and sometimes he wore a silk hat, but when they brought me the news that he had been murdered in a New York street, I could think of him only as one of the most courteous man I had ever known.

"Then there is Freddie Steele, my little prince. He lost the middleweight championship in August, but that was in Seattle, and he could not train here. Freddie trained at my camp for all his eastern fights …

"You see, they are just like children, and they sometimes have to be made to eat everything on their plates so that they will get a balanced meal.

"And now I do not want to give you the impression that I am always around these boys. Not at all, they see me principally at mealtimes, and I make it a practice to keep out of the way during the sparring, the gymnasium work, the road races, and all the rest of it usually the boys will want to talk to me for a while after supper, but I try to avoid having them feel that a woman is around to cramp their style," Madame Bey said.

"Some of them really need me to talk to, though. Andre Routis, the Frenchman who was featherweight champion, was homesick for someone who could speak his language, and there I was, ready to oblige. But mostly the boys play cards and games or listen to the radio, and they are great for detective stories. If their managers are agreeable, they sometimes drive to Summit for the movies, and they cry at the sad scenes just the same as people who couldn't punch a hole in a paper bag."

Robertson said that Bey did not want to get a reputation for philanthropy, but there were always several discouraged or financially embarrassed youths who were allowed to train with their eyes on a distant future, and nothing was said about the bills, provided they lend a hand with odd jobs now and then. It was one of these boys who, shouldering up to a press photographer who had come out to grab some pictures at the camp, pointed to Madame Bey and advised in a whisper, "Make her look like Greta Garbo, see, or else ..."

Robertson said there was only one boxer on record as spurning the Bey facilities, and that was Two-Ton Tony Galento. Not in the *Family Circle* article, there was an incident where another reporter along with Madame Bey watched Galento train. Madame Bey shrugged her shoulders and said, "Well, it's a little business,"[2] referring to Tony training at her camp. She would say no more. It was a rare for Madame Bey to voice disparagement upon a boxing tenant no matter what they said about her. She was more prone to praise a fighter, even those known for questionable ring tactics and illicit non-boxing activities.

CHAPTER 30

Lewis for Louis

The man Tony Galento was to fight before he became ill, John Henry Lewis, arrived at Madame Bey's Camp on December 27, 1938.[1] John Henry Lewis, age twenty-five, became the next challenger to fight Joe Louis, his good friend, for the world heavyweight crown. For the second time, and the first time in America, two black men would battle for the heavyweight title; the first was on December 19, 1913, in Paris between Jack Johnson and Battling Jim Johnson. John Henry Lewis had held the world light heavyweight title for the past three years. For those three years, Lewis discovered it was hard to make money from the light heavyweight title. Lewis moved up to the heavyweight division where the purses were larger. Many said the fight amounted to his friend Joe Louis giving him an opportunity to make money by giving him this bout.

Born in California, May 1, 1914, John Henry Lewis moved to Arizona when his father took a job as a trainer for the University of Arizona. Lewis turned professional at the age of fourteen as a welterweight. He rose to prominence in 1932 when he defeated James Braddock in San Francisco. In addition to Braddock, he defeated Maxie Rosenbloom, Bob Olin, Red Burman, Al Ettore, Bob Godwin, and Johnny Risko.

John Henry Lewis hired a new manager, Gus Greenlee, in May 1935. He became the light heavyweight champion under his guidance on Halloween night 1935 in St. Louis. Gus Greenlee was an African American businessman, numbers runner, bootlegger, and racketeer. In 1933, he was the owner, officer, and founder of baseball's Negro National League. He owned the Pittsburgh Crawfords that everyone called the Craws. A wealthy man, he spent his money freely. He showed generosity with his baseball players that included Hall of Famers Satchel Paige, Josh Gibson, Judy Johnson, and Cool Papa Bell. He built a stadium that seated about 7,500 at an estimated cost of $100,000. Greenlee financed half of the cost. He named the team after his Crawford Grill. The Crawford Grill was one of black Pittsburgh's favorite nightspots, where Lena Horne, Louis Armstrong, Dizzy Gillespie, Ella Fitzgerald, Stanley Turrentine, Count Basie, Duke Ellington, Cab Calloway, Billy Eckstein, Miles Davis, and Bill "Bojangles" Robinson entertained. The club became a hangout for both black and white entertainers and sportsmen. The football Pittsburgh Steelers owner, Art Rooney, a friend of Greenlee, frequented the Grill. With his money, Greenlee built the Pittsburgh Crawfords into one of the best teams.[2, 3, 4, 5, 6] Greenlee came to Madame Bey's to watch John Henry Lewis.

When John Henry Lewis came to Madame Bey's, he learned that *The Ring* magazine in its annual boxing rankings had made it unanimous in placing him at the top of the light heavyweight division. Joe Louis was ranked as the top heavyweight.[7] Noticeably missing from the list of ranked heavyweights was Max Schmeling.

This fight would be Joe Louis's fifth title defense. His last fight was against the only man that defeated him—Max Schmeling. Max did not train at Bey's for that fight.

"I don't want nobody to call me champ until I beat Schmeling," Louis said.

Joe Louis met Schmeling for the second time on June 22, 1938, at Yankee Stadium before a crowd of about 80,000 paying $1,015,096. Louis received 40 percent of the net gate of $803,113, which amounted to $321,245. Schmeling received 20 percent or $160,622. Bookmakers installed Joe Louis as a three-to-one favorite to avenge his only loss.

In the first round, Louis hit Schmeling with two left hooks and a right to the chin and then a crushing blow to Schmeling's kidney. Schmeling went down. He got up only to be twice more knocked down under Louis's unrelenting blows. At the count of three, Schmeling's trainer, Max Machon, threw in the towel. It sailed through the air while referee Arthur Donovan kept counting. When Machon tried to climb into the ring, the referee ordered him to get out.[8]

"Further counting was useless," the *New York Times* reported. "Donovan could have counted off a century and Max could not have regained his feet."

The Ring magazine hailed the knockout of Madame Bey's Max in two minutes, four seconds of the first round as the outstanding achievement of the year. Schmeling had to be taken to the Polyclinic Hospital in Manhattan, where doctors diagnosed him with two broken vertebrae.

"Mr. Schmeling has suffered fractures of the transverse processes of the third and fourth lumbar vertebra with a hemorrhage of the lumbar muscles," Dr. Brennan, who treated him, said.[9]

Schmeling's team differed from what was printed in the press that doctors had said about his injuries. About a week after the fight, Schmeling remained in the hospital. He was sitting up in his bed at the Polyclinic Hospital. There was a table across the bed and a box of cookies on the table. A nurse brought a pot of tea, cup, and saucer. She poured the tea, and Max sat there drinking and eating the cookies. The cookies were from an uncle of his who had a bakeshop in Irvington, New Jersey, and had sent them to him. Joe Jacobs, Eddie Walker, Frank Graham, and two German newspapermen watched him.

Max's face, so tanned at Speculator, was paler. The corner of his left eye and the eyebrow were discolored. He was depressed and looked listlessly out the window at the falling rain. Joe Jacobs talked about the boxing commission meeting from which he had just returned, but Max paid no attention to what he was saying. A nurse came in and stuck a thermometer in his mouth, and he smiled for the first time, pointed to the thermometer, and shook his head.

An orderly came in with a bundle of mail and handed it to Joe Jacobs.

"More mail," Jacobs said. "You should see all the letters he has got."

Jacobs shuffled the letters. Letters from Seattle … from Cherryville, North Carolina … from Harrisburg, Pennsylvania … from Patterson, New Jersey … from all over the country.

"They're all the same," Jacobs said. "They all say they are sorry he was beaten and wish him good luck."

The nurse came in, took the thermometer out of Schmeling's mouth, wiped it off, and looked at it. She slipped it into her pocket and left.

"Look at all these flowers," one of the German newspapermen said.

There were flowers on two tables, a mantel, and the windowsills.

"All sent by people he does not know," the German newspaperman said. "There were many more. Many more. We sent them to the wards."

"Look at this," Schmeling said.

On a low table beside his bed, there was a portable combination radio set and phonograph.

"Somebody sends me this," he said. "I have great pleasure with it. Show him how it works."

Jacobs pulled a switch, and a phonograph record played. Soft music filled the room.

"Turn it on the air," Schmeling said.

Jacobs pulled another switch, the phonograph record stopped, and the radio played.

"You don't have to change the records, only every eight times."

"This thing here pushes one record in when another has been played," Jacobs said.

"Last night I thought I would time it and see how long the records played," Schmeling said. "I lay back here and listened to them, and before they were through I fell asleep. So, I still do not know how long they play."

He laughed for the first time.

"When I woke up, I turned on the shortwave radio. I listened to Germany and London and Paris."

Max Machon, Schmeling's trainer, came in, and at the sight of him, Schmeling seemed to brighten. They spoke in German for a few minutes. Schmeling had finished his tea and cookies, and Walker and Jacobs pulled the table to the foot of the bed and lowered the bed so that Schmeling was reclining. Someone asked him if he was in pain.

"No," he said. "When I move, it hurts. But that is all. The doctor says I must stay quiet and then it will heal."

He was silent for a moment.

"Always I thought a kidney punch was a foul. All over the world it is not allowed. In every country but New York State, it is not allowed."

"Somebody said maybe he hurt his spine when he fell," Jacobs said. "I was talking to a doctor last night, and the doctor said that was impossible."

"It was a terrible punch," Schmeling said. "The pain was terrible. Nobody can take a punch in the kidney. The pain was so much I did not know anything."

"The doctors said they never saw a man take a blow like that and stand up," Machon said. "But Max is strong, and he was in perfect condition and so he stood up."

There had been so much discussion as to when the punch was struck that someone asked Schmeling, who wanted to be clear on that point.

"Early in the fight," Schmeling said. "When I was on the ropes."

Louis had hit him with many punches about the head before he went to the ropes. How about those punches? Had they dazed him? Someone asked.

Max shook his head.

"No," he said. "They did not bother me. In the first fight, he hit me many times in the head. After the fight, the reporters came to my dressing room and said:

"'Why did you let him hit you in the face so many times with a left in the first three rounds?'

"And I said, 'Because I wanted to be in a position to hit him with my right hand, and those punches did not bother me.'

"It was just like this the other night. In the first fight when Louis hit me in the face in the first round, I heard the people around the ring say, 'There he goes!'

"I heard them. They said, 'There he goes!'

"But this did not bother me. And in this fight it is like this, too. But then he hit me this punch, and I did not know what I was doing."

He rubbed his hand across his forehead.

"I could not think what to do," he said. "I could not move around. It was an accident that punch."

"If it wasn't for that punch it would have been a different fight," Jacobs said.

Someone asked Schmeling whether he wanted another point cleared up. It had looked following the first exchange, when they were close, Schmeling had hit Louis with a short right punch to the chin.

"Yes," Schmeling said. "And I heard the people yell when I hit him."

"But Max's feet were like this," Machon said.

He planted his feet on a line and close together.

"He could not hit hard from that position," he said.

Then he took a stance with his left foot extended and his right foot back, in perfect position for punching.

"If he had been like this, he could have hit him like this."

He smashed his right fist against an imaginary chin.

Schmeling did not say anything. He lay there looking at the rain.

Someone asked if he intended to fight again.

"Why not?" he answered.

Someone said there were several reasons why he should not. He was happily married, he had two estates, an apartment in Berlin, and plenty of money. What else did he want?

"Money isn't everything," he said. "I lost my last fight. I do not want my last fight to be a defeat. I get even."

"It is up to him," Machon said. "He must make the decision. When he is healthy again, he will want to fight. If the time comes when he knows he is not good any more, he will say no, he does not want to fight."

It was his pride, then, someone asked, that made him want to continue. What if he did lose his last fight? He won many fights. He had been the heavyweight champion of the world. Nobody was going to forget him even if Louis did beat him.

Schmeling shrugged.

"Well, anyhow," he said.[10]

For two weeks, Schmeling remained hospitalized. He was bedridden and immobilized as he sailed back to Germany. This time, no welcome home materialized. The Nazi regime had no more use for a German beaten by a black man. They could no longer propagandize him.

"And I believe he would be champion today if Joe Louis hadn't caught him in an unguarded moment ..." Madame Bey said. "As for Max, I am afraid he needs plenty of encouragement in these days, and I don't suppose he will get it in Germany now that he has been beaten."

At Madame Bey's Camp, John Henry Lewis harbored a secret. He was nearly blind in his left eye. If that fact reached the authorities, his boxing career would have been over. No organization would allow him to fight with so much at risk. He had concealed it for four years. Lewis would later admit that the injury, which had led to the blindness, occurred during a 1935 bout with Abe Feldman, a fight he lost. John Henry Lewis would win the world light heavyweight title in his next fight three months later against Bob Olin. He fought over three years with the handicap and never lost the light heavyweight title in the ring.

When John Henry Lewis met Madame Bey, she gave him the most coveted room in the house. He would be sleeping in the bed where Gene Tunney once awaited a fight with Jack Dempsey.[11] Accompanying John Henry Lewis were his manager, trainer, publicity man, and four sparring partners. Lewis's trainer, Larry Amadee, was once the assistant to Jack Blackburn, the trainer for Joe Louis. His manager, Gus Greenlee, had confidence he could defeat Joe Louis, as did his trainer and publicity man, John Clark. The public and press did not share their view. Installed as a seven-to-one underdog, no one gave John Henry much of a chance. The press at Madame Bey's found his confidence nothing short of surprising.[11]

Madame Bey did the cooking for her boys, but sometimes fighters brought their own cooks. This was the case when Lewis came. He brought his cook, Frank Sutton, to camp. Sutton was the cook for the former heavyweight champion Jack Johnson. It became a point of controversy. The point of contention arose not from Madame Bey; it came from Joe Louis's camp. Sutton used to be Joe Louis's cook, and his camp claimed Greenlee stole him. Greenlee, resentful of the charge that he stole Sutton away from Louis, addressed the claim.

"Why, Larry Sutton was always my cook," Gus Greenlee declared. "He cooked for Jack Johnson, and I only loaned him to Joe Louis."[12]

As the fight approached, reporter Chester Washington drove to Bey's Camp to watch Lewis work. Beside him sat Joseph Forcier, the trainer who worked with Gene Tunney when he readied for his fight with Jack Dempsey. They watched John Henry's workout. John Henry Lewis went through six rounds of boxing. He worked with a light heavyweight and a middleweight for speed and skill and two heavyweights for power. He demonstrated to be fast and elusive against his lighter sparring partners, strong and rugged against the heavier foes. Against heavyweight Bob Smith, a slugfest developed with John Henry revealing punching power in his right hand. Forcier expressed his opinion that the boxing history that Gene Tunney made the night he outsmarted Jack Dempsey might be repeated when John Henry Lewis went against Joe Louis.[11]

"Gene was the master boxer," Forcier said. "And so is John. Jack was the hardest hitter, and so is Joe.

"But the master boxer won, and I think John will win," he continued. "And so does John's trainer, Larry Amadee."[11]

Reporter Chester Washington declined to endorse Forcier's assessment. He had seen both Joe Louis and John Henry Lewis train. He concluded Joe Louis to be the most powerful puncher in the ring. He conceded John Henry Lewis may be the best foe yet to face Louis, but Louis's punching ability stood out. Washington said it would be the old story of the master boxer versus the superior puncher, and this time it looked like punch prowess would win out. Washington supported another Joe Louis victory.[11]

Gus Greenlee continued to defend his fighter.

"John Henry has had ninety-nine fights and has lost only five," Greenlee explained. "Jimmy Braddock and Izzy Gastanaga are the only fighters to have him on the floor, and he beat both of them. Braddock won in the Garden, but John won out on the Coast, and my fellow came back to beat Gastanaga in a return bout. Nobody has knocked John Henry out and nobody, not even Joe Louis, figures seven to one over him."[12]

Amadee expressed satisfaction with John Henry's condition, and Lewis exuded confidence. John Henry Lewis, so convinced that neither Louis nor any other boxer deserved seven-to-one odds over him, instructed Greenlee to bet $1,000 on him. That was provided he could persuade Mike Jacobs, the promoter, to loan him the money against the 17.5 percent he would receive as the challenger.[12]

"I sure have waited a long while for this chance," John Henry Lewis said as he mused while sprawled on a table at Madame Bey's having his hands bandaged for the last few rounds of sparring before the fight.

"I know what I'm up against. I don't know, though, just how I'll work in there against him. Naturally, I'm not going to try any slugging. But I'm not going to run either. I think it's possible to beat him with experience, speed, and boxing ability. I think these are in my favor. Of course, if I see a chance to throw a finishing punch, I'll try that."[13]

Jack Johnson, the first African American to hold the world heavyweight championship, came to Madame Bey's to watch Lewis in his final days of training. Johnson held the title from 1908 to 1915. It continued the long parade of heavyweight champions to occupy Madame Bey's Camp. He became the ninth heavyweight champion to appear in Chatham Township. There were fifteen heavyweight titleholders at that point. Seven of the fifteen were before Madame Bey's Camp had opened.

Much had been written about Jack Johnson. Aside from being the first African American heavyweight champion, it befell on him to be the first African American pop culture icon. He was photographed in excess. Newspapers scrutinized him. The masses had been eager to read about him.[14, 15]

Time had passed and Jack Johnson's notoriety with it. At sixty years of age, no longer the object of scrutiny, he was not hounded by the press at Madame Bey's Camp. Gone was the time when there could not be found enough space in newspapers to print all the stories, both true and fabricated, about Jack Johnson. Older, no longer champion, neither the press nor public cared about his sex life, statements, conduct, nor even his opinion on boxing matches. The press relegated his newspaper space to a few quotes about his view on the historic bout of Lewis versus Louis.

"John is a much better boxer. I think he will outpoint Joe," Jack Johnson declared after John Henry Lewis's workout.[11]

At his Pompton Lakes camp, Joe Louis spared six rounds in one of his finishing preparations. One of Joe Louis's sparring partners was the future world heavyweight champion Jersey Joe Walcott,[13] who would train at Madame Bey's in later years. Louis punished him so much that Walcott darted from the ring and refused to fight longer. Louis and Lewis boxed four rounds on the final day of training. They both rested the day before the bout.

On January 25, 1939, the crowd at Madison Square Garden exceeded promoter Mike Jacobs's expectation. It started with empty seats, but they filled during the preliminary fights. At the close, attendance reached 17,350, with the gross gate at $102,015.43. The crowd and gate were a tribute to the lure of Joe Louis. With the night's financial gross, the champion's four times at Madison Square Garden had never failed to attract less than $100,000.[16] For those that thought Joe Louis would not fight hard with his friend, they were mistaken. Undetectable was the friendship between the two when the bell rang. Joe Louis showed no mercy.

Sparring for a brief time in the first few seconds of the opening round, neither threw anything hard. Then Joe Louis threw a right that whistled by John Henry's head, just missing. That punch gave warning to John Henry Lewis. He did not occupy the ring with a friend. He represented to Louis any boxer trying to take away what he had worked so hard to obtain. The world champion would end this as quickly as possible, intent on nothing but a win. Joe Louis wasted no more time sparring. A right hit John Henry on the jaw. He went down. John Henry, shaken, got up at the count of two. His legs were uncertain. He lurched forward and somehow managed to land a good right hand punch to Joe Louis's ribs[17]—it would be the last punch he threw worth mentioning.

Joe Louis rattled rights and lefts into John Henry's head. He forced him to the ropes, worked him on the body, and had him bleeding from the nose and mouth. There came regular flurries from Joe Louis, and John Henry pitched to the ropes, falling half over the lower strand. He hit the canvas for the second time. He rose at the count of three. John Henry tried to stumble away, but Joe Louis pursued. He pumped blows to the head and body, and John Henry fell back on the ropes. With no compassion, Joe Louis landed a hard right on his chin. John Henry plunged over and felt the canvas for the third time in the first round. He got up at the count of five. Referee Arthur Donovan saw enough. He waved Joe Louis away. The fight was over. Joe Louis won by a technical knockout at two minutes, twenty-nine seconds into the fight.[17]

According to figures from the Twentieth Century Sporting Club, Joe Louis received $34,413.70. John Henry Lewis took $15,056. Heavyweight champion Joe Louis earned money at the rate of $230.96 a second at the calculation of a writer.[18] He neglected to figure into his calculation the great many hours of hard work and sacrifice to get to the point where he could display such a brilliant performance. It takes effort to make your performance appear effortless.

"It was tough luck," Mrs. Mattie Foster, mother of John Henry Lewis, said from the house her son built for her.

"It's all over, that's all," dejected, Lewis's younger brother Paul, remarked.[19]

People packed Joe Louis's dressing room immediately after the bout. The champion posed for photographers and shook hands.

"What was the time of the knockout?" someone asked.

"Two minutes, twenty-nine seconds." someone replied.

"Shucks, that ain't as good as I done against that feller Smellin'. I done knocked him out in two minutes four seconds, didn't I?" Joe Louis said.[20]

"I didn't think he hit me at all," he explained to the press later. "It was an easy fight—I just worked up a light sweat, and that was mostly from the lights."[16]

It was becoming apparent that Joe Louis was a superior heavyweight champion.

In John Henry Lewis's dressing room, the vanquished challenger made statements and took questions. John Henry said he was in full possession of his faculties and could have continued the fight. Referee Donovan saw it differently, and the press said he did well in stopping the fight. Another hard right could have injured him severely.

"I felt funny all of a sudden," Lewis explained.[16]

"I don't think referee Arthur Donovan should have stopped the fight," John Henry said.[20]

When asked why he did not stay down for a nine count the three times Louis floored him, he claimed he never felt hurt at any time.

The huge Garden crowd did not question if referee Donovan had done the right thing, and there were cries of "Stop it!" even before he intervened.

"I wasn't hurt at all," John Henry said.

"Did you know you were on the floor?" someone asked.

"No. I didn't."[21]

John Henry Lewis thought he deserved another chance. The public and boxing thought otherwise. It would be John Henry Lewis's last official fight, not because of the drubbing by Joe Louis but the blindness in his left eye. John Henry Lewis had been scheduled for a light heavyweight title defense against Dave Clark on March 31, 1939, in Detroit. On March 17, two physicians examined his vision and determined him essentially blind in his left eye.[22] Doctors discovered Lewis's secret. The postponement of his bout with Dave Clark ensued. Michigan banned him from boxing in their state. For his safety, other boxing jurisdictions followed. Then, Lewis unsuccessfully pursued a London light heavyweight title defense against Len Harvey. His eye trouble led to its cancellation, too.[23] Lewis would retire and never fought again.

Lightweight Tippy Larkin, heavyweight Freddie Fiducia, and light heavyweight Walter Woods[24] were a few of the boxers who came to Madame Bey's Camp early in 1939 after John Henry Lewis had left. Tony Canzoneri and Lou Ambers, who had seen Tippy Larkin train at Bey's Camp, praised him.[25] Tippy Larkin would defeat Billy Beauhuld on January 6 at Madison Square Garden. In a rematch on April 10 at Laurel Garden, Newark, New Jersey, he beat him again. Freddie Fiducia lost to Bob Pastor in a ten-round decision on June 12 at the Meadowbrook Bowl, Newark, New Jersey. Walter Woods lost to Ceferino Garcia on June 15 at Madison Square Garden.

Tony Galento received the fight he had been waiting for. He would fight Joe Louis for the world heavyweight championship. After recovering from his illness, he had won his next six fights over a three-month period. He won every one by a knockout or a technical knockout. He defeated Harry Thomas in three, Otis Thomas in nine, Dick Daniels in three, Jorge Brescia in one, Natie Brown in four, and Abe Feldman in three.

The fight for Louis and Galento was set for June 28 at Yankee Stadium. The commission wanted assurance of Galento's health. In late March, five physicians examined Galento in New York to determine whether he was healthy to fight Joe Louis for the heavyweight title. General John J. Phelan, boxing commission chairman, started to explain the examination report but gave up when he tried to describe the use of a sphygmomanometer to measure Galento's blood pressure.

"I don't know any more about it than you guys do," Phelan said. "Come back Friday when they got the findings translated into English, and I'll let you know whether we're going to approve the match."

"This is worse than waiting for the jury's verdict when you're on trial for murder, which I never was," promoter Mike Jacobs stated.[26]

"What is this?" Tony asked as one of the physicians turned a dial on a machine. "First you put me in the electric chair, then you tune in the radio."[27]

"Those guys give me a better goin' over then I'm gonna give that Louis bum," Galento said.

"They had wires on me arms, poked lights in me eyes, and they even looked into me brain with some phoney-lookin' gadget."

"Well, that proves one thing boys," Joe Jacobs observed, "Galento has a brain."[26]

Galento passed the physical examination and in June 1939 signed to fight Joe Louis for the world heavyweight title under the promotion of Uncle Mike Jacobs. The question became where Tony would decide to train. Would it be the barroom gymnasium or the quiet woods of Madame Bey's Camp? Now that the commission had approved both, Tony decided to go where the restful sound of ocean waves lapped against the sandy shore. He would train in the resort town of Asbury Park, New Jersey. The reaction from General

John J. Phelan and the commission proved unfavorable. Once again, a rift between Tony's team and the commission ensued.

Asbury Park lacked boxing facilities. Merchants that knew having Galento would be a boon to their businesses agreed to contribute the money to build accommodations. Manager Joe Jacobs closed the deal in mid-May. They established a plan for the erection of a grandstand, ring, and ticket booth at Third and Ocean Avenue. It was across from the site where Max Baer had prepared for his title losing battle with James Braddock. The writers made the quick association, stating Galento was following in Baer's losing path; Tony was a ten-to-one underdog.

Tony weighed 262 pounds when he arrived in Asbury Park. All went as planned as the National Boxing Association's number-one contender for the world heavyweight title trained.[28] Merchants expressed satisfaction with crowds Tony drew. He posed for pictures and became the subject of a short newsreel piece in which heavyweight contenders Max Baer and Lou Nova joined him. The newsreel started with Tony in the ring with awkward, arrhythmic, speed bag punching.

"Try to get my good looking face in that picture, will ya!" he commented.

Clumsy rope skipping followed as he joked with the crowd that had gathered. At the end of his session, Tony put on a suit jacket over his workout attire, both hands still taped. To his right stood former heavyweight champion Max Baer wearing a suit and tie with large sunglasses. Flanking Tony on his left stood heavyweight contender Lou Nova, with his left ear bandaged and wearing an unbuttoned suit exposing his suspenders. Tony pounded his chest and yelled. The three laughed, as did the crowd.

"And I thought I was crazy," Baer said, laughing.

Nova stood silently with a smile.

"I wish most of you people had my bank account," Tony responded. "And you'll see how crazy I am."[29]

In response to an announcement by Joe Jacobs proclaiming that he would make a revelation of great importance, a large delegation of newspapermen gathered. They had just arrived from New York and made themselves comfortable in the sunroom that served as press headquarters in Asbury Park.

"I have something to say to you fellows," Joe said.

There existed tenseness in his voice that caused everybody to look at him with interest.

"For a year, everybody has been asking me what happened to Schmeling," he said. "Nothing happened to Schmeling. Give me a match, Harry."

"Nothing happened to Schmeling, hey?" one reporter said to another. "What happened to him shouldn't happen to me."

"Nor to my worst enemy," another reporter said.

Harry Mendel handed Joe Jacobs a match. Jacobs proceeded to tell his story. He accused Joe Louis of using a gimmick—a foreign object, usually metal, placed in the glove. Louis was not the first boxer accused of the practice. When Jack Dempsey destroyed Jess Willard for the heavyweight title, some accused him of using plaster of Paris in his gloves. Many expressed outrage by the accusation posed by Joe Jacobs against Louis. Commissioner Phelan and promoter Mike Jacobs were on their way to Asbury Park when Joe Jacobs made the statement.

"Do you fellows know why Joe Louis knocked out Max Schmeling last June? Do you think Louis is as hard a hitter as his record would leave you to believe? Joe Louis uses a gimmick that's what. He has a special instrument, sort of like the handle of a dumbbell, and he carries it inside his glove. That's what he used on Schmeling and all those other fighters he knocked out so easily. But he won't do it to Galento because I'll ask the commission to watch that Louis every minute from the time he puts his gloves on till the time he's carried out."

Shortly after Joe Jacobs finished, Braddock, who lost the title to Louis, walked in and heard what happened.

"Had you ever seen a gimmick, Jim?" somebody asked.

"Yep! That's right. He does use a gimmick. I was hit with one in Chicago. The same gimmick that Schmeling was hit with, and all it was made up of was four fingers and a thumb."[30]

Mike Jacobs arrived with Phelan. The press immediately asked both about the gimmick allegation. The pair laughed at the question. When both realized that the reporters were serious, they summoned Joe Jacobs. Mike Jacobs, John Phelan, and Joe Jacobs discussed the matter for several minutes. They were far from the curious reporters. Then Joe Jacobs addressed the reporters in a clear, firm voice.

"Gentlemen, I retract the statement about the gimmick."[31]

It could have been just a stunt to attract more gate revenues. Boxing experts said that manager Joe Jacobs's stunt had added anywhere up to a couple of hundred thousand dollars to the gate for the Louis-Galento fight.

The talk about the use of a gimmick reached Louis's camp. Jack Blackburn, Louis's trainer, laughed at Jacobs's statement.

"Only gimmick that Louis boy needs is the five-fingered one he's got hanging on the end of his arm," Blackburn chuckled.

Asbury Park sizzled under the scorching sun, and Tony wilted. It became obvious the heat and damp air affected him.

"You don't look so good," John Phelan told Galento. "I think this sea air has gone to your head where it has the most room to operate!"[32]

After he conferred with promoter Mike Jacobs, John Phelan issued an order to Joe Jacobs that Tony move to Madame Bey's Camp. A police officer kept the reporters beyond hearing distance. Uncle Mike said little. The promoter did his best to distract everybody from Galento's poor workout by serving ice-cream cones. The order was a command with which Galento had become familiar. Tony had not returned to Madame Bey's since his illness. He did not offer resistance as before.[33] The cool wooded camp of Madame Bey's would be a relief from the sweltering heat of Asbury Park. This created a problem with the town of Asbury Park, which had spent money for Tony to train. Asbury Park residents were irate at Phelan for implying that their climate had been unhealthy for Galento. They pointed out that Max Baer trained there to win the heavyweight title from Primo Carnera.[32] They did not add that Baer also prepped there when he lost the title to James Braddock.

"Fellows, this is the last day that Galento will do any training in Asbury Park," Joe Jacobs informed the crowd. "He feels that the sea air robs him of his snap, and tomorrow he will set up headquarters at Madame Bey's Camp in Summit, New Jersey."[31]

An Asbury Park committee requested Joe Jacobs to refund the money they had spent to erect an arena and to issue a statement setting forth the scenic and other virtues of Asbury Park. This Joe Jacobs did. He promised to reimburse at least $1,000 that local merchants had contributed to back the training venture. That satisfied most.

Joe Jacobs explained that Galento had been "lazy and tired" recently.

"Dr. Edward Walker, New York Commission physician, after examining Tony and finding him in good condition decided this feeling might be the result of the sea air and excitement of crowds at the shore," Joe Jacobs continued.[34]

On his last day at Asbury Park, James Braddock and Lou Nova visited Tony. Braddock looked at Tony and insisted he had a chance of beating Joe Louis. Nova did not agree and picked Louis to win. Nova added that he was convinced he could outthink Louis should they meet in the ring. In his five rounds of ring work, Galento looked unimpressive in his last workout in Asbury Park. He offered an easy target for his opponents, and they hit him frequently.

Tony and his caravan of thirty-five-dollar-a-day sparring partners,[35] attendants, sportswriters, photographers, and other members of Tony's entourage completed their trek from Asbury Park to Madame Bey's Camp.[36] Tony had little to show for the first half of his training at the shore resort. His first day at Madame Bey's, he addressed his manager's assertion that Louis had used something in his glove. He had some distance between where he stood and the press.

"Say, if anybody tries to use a gimmick on me," he shouted in a whisper that could be heard far away, "I'll bite him."

"But it don't make any difference to me where I train," Tony insisted. "I'll lick that bum anywhere I train. All I need is roadwork to flatten him. Yeah, and I won't get rough unless he does—and anyway, my head is twice as hard as his.

"Sure, it cost me $1,800 to move from Asbury," he added, "but what's that much dough compared to winning the heavyweight championship. Anyway, they played too much bingo down there."[34]

The difference between Asbury Park and Madame Bey's Camp was apparent. The writers were amazed by the change in Tony's appearance more than the change of venues. He went five rounds with three sparring partners.

"Who gave him the needle?" Joe Jacobs demanded.[36]

Tony had two weeks to train at Bey's before the fight. His time at Asbury Park, for the most part, wasted. While Tony trained at Bey's, the camp attracted the largest, most consistent crowds for a fighter. Tony outdrew titleholders when they were there. He connected with the common boxing fan because of his style. Gatherings numbered over a thousand and on some days over two thousand. Others were training at the camp, but it was clear they were coming to see Tony. He never disappointed. He did his clowning for the audience. It became evident he took the two weeks to put in serious training. He looked better than he ever had in his career. His trademark stomach disappeared. He looked to be in good form.

On June 16, Tony sat in Madame Bey's dining room with Joe Jacobs and a reporter as Madame Bey prepared a meal for them. She placed an immaculate white tablecloth upon the dinner table. She entered the room with the food and proceeded to serve the men. She placed eight lamb chops in front of Tony, two for Joe Jacobs, and two for the reporter. The men began to consume their dinner.

"There is only one course Tony can pursue when he tangles with heavyweight champion Joe Louis on June 28," the reporter said.

A horrified Madame Bey watched as they drew a boxing ring on her tablecloth. The reporter pointed to Tony in one comer and Louis in the other.

"If Galento doesn't plunge across that ring at the first gong—like a wrestler making a flying tackle—and jolt Louis off balance into the ropes or into a corner, something will be wrong with this fight," the reporter said.

"Whatcha mean? I should get rough," Tony inquired.

The reporter explained that Louis never made much of an impression against any opponent who "used his head," fellows like Natie Brown in Detroit, Bob Pastor at Madison Square Garden, and Tommy Farr at Yankee Stadium.

Tony expressed annoyance and got up as if he were ready for a fight.

"Whatcha mean? I should act like a billy goat? Listen, I've always fought clean, and I'll—"

Manager Joe Jacobs removed the smoldering cigar from his lips and belted Tony backward.

"Shut up. Who's fightin' this fight?" Joe Jacobs interjected.

"Why should I butt him?" Tony said. "I want him to punch at me and open up, so I can nail him on the chin. I'll knock him dead if he opens up."

"Shut up!" Joe Jacobs interrupted again. "Who's fightin' this fight? Keep quiet and listen and learn."

"Okay, have it your way," Tony growled, "but I'll still knock out that bum."[37]

On June 17, eleven days before the fight, fellow Orange resident Dr. Higi, who had helped Tony overcome his pneumonia, visited Tony at Bey's Camp. After examining him, Higi pronounced him "in the best shape I've ever seen him before a fight." Higi advised him "not to bear down too hard from now on." State Athletic Commissioner Abe Greene, known as Mr. Boxing in New Jersey, concurred.

"I'm training for this fight, ain't I?" Tony responded from his dressing room. "I'll work just as hard as I want."

Tony went into the ring and sparred, skipped rope, punched bags, and declared that he continued "training hard and was in good shape and those who even hinted he was not were a bunch of (use of an expletive that was not published)."[38]

On a Sunday, June 18, Tony worked before a large crowd of more than fifteen hundred people, which included Commissioner John Phelan. The crowd was so loud that Joe Jacobs requested them to refrain from unnecessary remarks. A voice from the hillside kept urging Tony to knock out his sparring partners, a request he avoided doing.[39]

He sparred with Abe Feldman, from Schenectady, New York, who Tony beat in his last fight in February at the Orange Bowl, Miami, Florida. Tony sparred from a crouch against Feldman, a style he did not use in the past. Joe Jacobs thought it would be effective against Louis. Next, he sparred with Mickey McAvoy, a Brooklyn fighter who had played the role of James Braddock in the picture *Spirit of Youth* in which Joe Louis appeared, and he was the Brown Bomber's chief second the night Louis won the title from James Braddock. Finally, he sparred with Tom Shenck, a promising heavyweight from Passaic, New Jersey, who had held the New Jersey amateur heavyweight championship in 1937 and 1938. Shenck stood six feet two inches and weighed 207 pounds. He had the skin color, physique, and stance of Joe Louis. Tony then punched the heavy bag, little bag, skipped rope, and did calisthenics.[39]

After the workout, Tony embraced Tom Schenk and Phil Johnson for a press photograph. Shenck, along with Phil Johnson,[40] a fighter with fifteen years of experience, had been with Galento since he started training for Louis. Johnson, who did not work out that day, had fought Jack Delaney, Jack Roper, Johnny Whiters, and Red Barry in his career.

Tony was at Madame Bey's for a week. As training progressed, Tony continued to impress. At Bey's, the training came easily. Each day, he would run over seven miles of terrain encircling Madame Bey's Camp. After a rest, he awaited the workout that usually started at three in the afternoon. He would spar and shadowbox, in his clowning style, for the throngs of people.[39]

Everyone knew Galento was hard to knock down. The fights he lost were stopped because of cuts sustained to his face. One week before the fight, Joe Jacobs employed the best cut man in the fight business. Whitey Bimstein agreed to be in Tony's corner for the fight as a second.[41] Manager Joe Jacobs and trainer Jimmy Frain would complete Tony's corner. Joe Jacobs told the press he had a mysterious liquid that he would apply to Tony's face wounds to prevent them from reopening during the fight.[41]

Journalist Grantland Rice heard that Tony was training well. He sent Clarence Budington Kelland to Madame Bey's Camp to scout Tony. Kelland, an American writer known for his prolific output, was an avid boxing fan. He once described himself as "the best second-rate writer in America." He wrote sixty novels and about two hundred short stories. His works resulted in thirty movies, including *Speak Easy* and *Mr. Deeds Goes to Town*. Kelland's lengthy report disparaged Galento and his chances to defeat Louis. After Grantland Rice received Kelland's report, which he printed in his column, he wrote, "This thoroughly overhauling by Mr. Kelland may help disperse any clouds of doubt that up to date may have obscured a few visions."[42]

On June 22, a reporter, Gayle Talbot, visited the camp and wrote that he would have to stay away from Madame Bey's before he picked Galento to win. He also said the nine-to-one odds in favor of Louis were "about right." With Talbot were three past boxing greats. Former heavyweight champion James Braddock, former featherweight champion Johnny Dundee, and Lew Tendler, a Philadelphia lightweight and one of the best southpaw boxers. They were impressed with Tony. Some predicted Tony would defeat Joe Louis in their heavyweight title fight.

"Tony's got a hell of a chance if he fights Louis like he was fighting today," Braddock said. "I mean it. Joe doesn't like that kind of fighting, and he hasn't been looking good lately. I'm convinced Tony isn't going to be scared or nervous when he goes in that ring. I wouldn't be a bit surprised if Galento licked him and we had another heavyweight champion from New Jersey."[43]

On June 23, Tony, in a publicity stunt, invited Joe Louis to an afternoon cocktail party "in honor of Mr. Joe Louis,"[41] at Madame Bey's Camp. Tony would host. Joe Jacobs issued printed invitations to the press and mailed one to Louis at Pompton Lakes. Tony's manager, Joe Jacobs, had arranged for an exhibition of selected rounds from Louis's fight pictures in which the champion looked unimpressive.[44] Mike Jacobs would come from

Pompton Lakes with Louis's answer later that afternoon. At night, Galento was to submit to a radio interview over station WOR.

General John Phelan, commission chairman, was in Pompton Lakes where Louis trained. Promoter Mike Jacobs also came to watch Louis. Then, Mike Jacobs would take the thirty-minute drive to Madame Bey's to watch Tony. He had been reading from the rulebook in Pompton Lakes to Louis in case Tony committed any fouls.

"What is this bunk?" Tony asked. "Me foul Louis? You bet I will—with a left hook on the chin. As far as I am concerned General Phelan can be sure it's going to be a nice, clean fight."

"I think Louis knows he's licked if he doesn't get help," Joe Jacobs charged. "He's trying to intimidate the officials that Galento will not violate the rules. I can't speak for Louis."[45]

R. G. Lynch, a writer for the *Milwaukee Journal*, also came to report on Galento. Lynch and Joe Jacobs were well acquainted. Invariably, Joe would greet Lynch with "H'ya, Lynch. What time is it in Milwaukee?" It was the result from when Lynch came to Speculator, New York, to watch Schmeling train for his fight with Louis, and he neglected to reset his watch.

"Bring over that coffee pot," Joe told Madame Bey. "We'll finish it up. This fellow is from Milwaukee, where they live on coffee."

Lynch said that Joe Jacobs had no use for Mike Jacobs. Joe remembered the late Tex Rickard and could not see Mike as the successor to Tex. He showed anger about Mike's domination of boxing and had not forgiven him for interfering with the title bout Schmeling had scheduled with James Braddock that led to its cancelation. On this occasion in Madam Bey's kitchen, he had a Newark newspaper before him, open to the sports page, which had a national news service story quoting the writer as saying that Galento was the worst bum he had ever seen. Many men in sports would have been angry about such a statement going all over the country but not Joe Jacobs. Good or bad, it was all publicity to him.

"I try to give you fellows the right steer," Joe said, "and you go and make a sap out of yourself like that. How are you going to feel when Tony knocks out that Louis?"

Joe leaned over, poking a finger into Lynch, with a serious expression.

"Sure, Galento is a funny little fat guy," Joe said, "but he is the first guy that hasn't been afraid of Louis since Schmeling, and he can throw that left mitt of his. If he hits Louis with it, I'm going to have the world champion."

Joe smiled wickedly.

"Then we will have some fun!" Joe continued. "We will show Mike Jacobs that he can't run boxing. Sure, our contract calls for a rematch if Tony wins, but just wait and see! Schmeling had a contract for a title fight …"

Lynch said that Joe Jacobs was the smartest fight manager of his time and the best publicity man we ever saw, and his brain worked on a hair-trigger. If the ticket sales for a fight were lagging, he always figured something to generate interest. No idea ever got past him.[46, 47, 48]

A large crowd had gathered around the outdoor ring. Jacobs took the newspapermen into a large room where a sheet had been hung and a movie projector had been placed. The projector was used to show a film containing all of Joe Louis's moments from fighting where he appeared unimpressive. It contained no rounds in which the champion threw a solid punch. It was made to give Tony confidence. Tony stood with one foot on a low improvised ring. James Braddock was in the crowd of reporters.

"You fellows," Joe said, "seem to have forgotten something. I asked you here to give you a reminder. Okay boys, turn out the lights and let 'er go!"

First shown was a round from Louis's bout with Jorge Brescia in which he landed two punches that sent Louis into the ropes.

"There's your superman!" Jacobs yelled. "Look at him stagger! It took him three rounds to put away Brescia. Tony did it in one."

The next clip showed Nathan Mann fighting Louis.

"So he's invincible!" Jacobs said. "Look at Mann paste him!"

The fourth round of the first Schmeling-Louis fight followed. Schmeling knocked Louis down.

"Now watch how this super fighter hits low when the going gets tough," Joe Jacobs said.

The twelfth round of the same fight showed Schmeling jolting Louis with rights. Louis hooked his left, and it landed low.

"Look it! Look it!" Jacobs yelled. "A sharpshooter, eh? … Watch! Now he gets it! Don't miss this!"

Schmeling hit Louis on the chin, and he went down.

"See that?" Jacobs shouted, "Look at the superman now. He doesn't fall, he just folds up. Look at him shake his head at his corner. Now he lays his glove down so he'll have a soft place to put his head and go to sleep. Do you think a fighter that's really knocked out does things like that? No! He falls down and out."

Next, the Braddock-Louis fight showed Braddock's right uppercut that put Louis on the canvas. The room was filled with excited cries of "Go get him, Jimmy!" despite the fact that everyone knew Braddock lost to Louis a few rounds later, which was forgotten.

"Now! Now!" Jacobs cried. "See how Louis runs. He doesn't know where to go. What a fighter—a super fighter!"

The picture ended.

"Frankly," reporter Frank Bell said, "I don't see what Mann does to Louis, but I may have bad eyes."

"That's the first time I ever saw that picture of me knocking Louis down," Braddock said while walking out.

"What did you think when you saw him go down?" someone asked Braddock.

"I thought I had him," Braddock said. "That spoiled the fight for me. I tried to get him after that. Thought I could slug it out with him."[49]

After the film was over, the press climbed the hill to the outdoor ring to watch Tony train, where were assembled 2,100 people. It was a big crowd, and Tony knew they were there for him. Tony sparred two rounds with Abe Feldman and then two with Mickey McAvoy. Tony fought in a manner that inspired the enthusiasm of the large crowd gathered on the hillside, which included some backhand hits. His sparring partners wore excessive padding. Among the crowd was Mayor Odivio Bianchi of Orange, New Jersey, and Lew Tendler, the former lightweight contender who predicted Tony would knock out the world heavyweight champion. After the sparring, Tony skipped around the ring. As he looked over the crowd, he saw the former heavyweight Bud Gorman, who made some disparaging remarks to the press about Galento that day.

"Come on, Bud." Tony called. "Put on the gloves. I'd like to get you up here!"

"At my age?" Gorman replied.

"Aw, come on. I'll carry you."

"You wouldn't have to carry me," Gorman said.

"Got a wire from Louis," Tony puffed. "Dear Tony, I'll trade you my new car for your left hook. Signed Joe … Robert Taylor wrote me to come out to California; they need handsome guys like me for the movies … Look at this profile."

Tony stuck his nose in the air.

"I turned down a half-million to make a picture. I like this better, killing myself up here."[49]

The crowd laughed. Joe Jacobs was all around the ringside saying how funny Tony was. The press moved around to be sure they heard all of Tony's wisecracks.

Promoter Mike Jacobs and his cavalcade of cars arrived too late from Pompton Lakes to see the workout. He was given a beer and shown the edited film. It was the same film they had shown earlier to the press. Uncle Mike Jacobs informed Galento of General Phelan's stand about enforcing all the rules. He then expressed Louis's regrets about not being able to attend the party Tony was throwing in the champion's honor. The Brown Bomber was attending a birthday party at Pompton Lakes for one of his seconds, Mushky Jackson,[45] who had coordinated the spelling bee at Madame Bey's at the end of 1937.

June 25 was the last Sunday before the fight with Louis on June 28. Many reporters swarmed Madame Bey's Camp. One, reporter Jack Miley, arrived early. He described Tony.

"The condemned man ate a healthy breakfast, a lusty lunch, and a terrific dinner. For a person who is supposed to be only seventy-two hours from the gallows, he shows very little concern."

Tony heard that Miley would be at the camp. He went to the kitchen and demanded a handful of raw eggs. Specifically, he wanted elderly and antiquated eggs. The chef regarded him with suspicion and demanded to know what use he intended with the eggs.

"I'm going to hit that Miley right in the puss with them!" Tony roared. "He's been knocking me long enough; just the other day he called me a pig!"

Somebody suggested that Galento should not execute his plan. He thought for a moment.

"Okay, give Miley some eggs, too, and we'll throw 'em at each other!"

Tony abandoned the egg fight when Miley insisted he wanted his eggs thrown at him sunny side up, fried in butter, and with a slice of ham or a couple of bits of crisp bacon tossed in, not forgetting a cup of coffee as an added starter.

"The man seems totally unaffected by the early indications of this dread disease," Miley wrote. "I know all the symptoms. I have seen them in Maxie Baer, King Levinsky, Primo Carnera, Paolino Uzcudun and many others. They have all shown the same characteristics, and the thing is as unmistakable as smallpox.

"In the first place, these poor, frightened fellows get that dreamy, far-away look in their eyes. You ask them a simple question while carrying on a conversation—something like what time is it? Or is this Tuesday or Friday—and they usually answer with an abstracted, 'Yeah. Huh? What? Sure!'

"They break out in a cold, clammy, gooseflesh. You feel their pulse, but can't find it. They can't sleep, and they can't stay awake. They are in a sort of indescribable coma."

Miley recalled the time Max Baer prepared to fight Louis. He put his right shoe on his left foot, meanwhile babbling something about being the new white hope. Then Jack Dempsey, his chief second, cried out.

"Hey, kid, you forgot to put on your socks!"[50]

Tony started his last big workout before the fight. That Sunday, a crowd of 2,634 people attended Madame Bey's to watch Tony. It amounted to one of the largest crowds at Bey's to watch a fighter train. The crowd included Tony's mother, father, and wife, Mary. Before the sparring session started, Tony requested reporter Jack Miley to box with him. Miley declined. Instead, Tony and Miley had a stimulating verbal argument, in which Miley played the straight man. It ended with them shaking hands.

"I'll read about myself tomorrow," was Tony's parting comment to Miley.

Tony did five rounds of sparring. He mixed in his clowning to the delight of the crowd, which resulted in laughter. He restricted his antics to rule infractions such as low left hooks, holding and hitting, elbowing, kneeing, wrestling, backhand punches, and butting. He did not gouge, bite, or kick. Frank and Nancy Galento, Tony's parents, watched their son, but neither would be at ringside to see their boy fight Louis. Frank Galento saw Tony fight years ago, and it made him nervous. Nancy Galento had always been opposed to her son's boxing career.

Abe Feldman left the ring with a bloody nose, causing Abe Greene, the New Jersey Boxing commissioner, to remark that never had he seen Tony in better form. When he finished working with Mickey McAvoy, former boxer Harry Lenny picked the challenger to win.

"Louis can be hit and this fellow will hit him," Lenny predicted. "Galento will knock the champion out."

"He's a whole show in himself," promoter Mike Jacobs declared.

After completing training, Tony became serious when he discussed the fight against Joe Louis. Someone asked Tony what he planned to do in the ring.

"It all depends on Louis," Tony replied.

A newspaperman asked Tony what he wanted the champion to do.

"I hope he comes at me the way he did at Max Schmeling," Tony answered. "If he does, I'll bring the dog out of him in a hurry."

"Suppose he runs away like he did with Tommy Farr," Galento explained. "What kind of a fight will that be? I want to give the fans a run for their money. I don't want to chase him all over the joint to make him say turkey."

Someone asked what if Louis retreats, jabbing …?

"It may take me a little longer," Tony declared. "I'll knock the bum out in five rounds, anyway."

A reporter asked if Galento thought well of Louis's proposal that he be allowed to have his physician in the corner to rule on the seriousness of any cut the champion may suffer.

"I don't need any doctor," Tony said. "Let Louis have the doctors. He'll need 'em."

A reporter asked if Galento planned a rough fight.

"I ain't going to butt him," Tony replied. "If he don't start anything, I'll fight him fair."[51]

Joe Louis concluded his training at Dr. Bier's in Pompton Lakes, New Jersey, where there was a gathering estimated at 5,000 with many others turned away. It was the largest crowd ever to descend upon the camp where the Brown Bomber trained. He had used it for all his battles in the metropolitan area except his first match with Schmeling. The general belief of the crowd was that Louis would put an end to Galento's bid in about a round. Because of the crowd overflow, many customers climbed trees or perched on thin roofs to see what took place. Many of those who did get into the enclosure could see nothing of what happened in the ring. The crowd so dense, Joe Banovic, Louis's sparring partner, had a hard time getting to the ring. After Louis belted him, Banovic wished he had not been able to make it. After four rounds of sparring, Louis ended his workout when trainer Jack Blackburn told him to stop. Police, camp workers, and Dr. and Mrs. Bier, the camp owners, were relieved when the camp workout ended without any accidents to spectators.[52]

Journalist Ed Hughes came to report on Tony at Madame Bey's the day before the fight. When he arrived, many press members were there, and Tony was playing rummy. Tony was annoyed at interview and photograph requests while he played his card game.

"All week long I'm bothered to death, and now at the last minute here they are again," Tony complained. "No matter how well you treat 'em, they always knock you."

Tony directed some sarcastic comments at a young reporter who had wrote about him derisively. After, he continued playing cards.

"Sure," Joe Jacobs said, "Tony's on edge. That's the way a well-trained fighter should be at this stage. I'm glad to see him that way."

After more remarks, Tony left to dress in his boxing gear for photographs. When he returned, a broadcaster had arrived and set up an apparatus to produce a program featuring a hook-up with Joe Louis's camp.

"I want you to put the questions to Joe," the broadcaster told Tony, "we have them all written out for you here."

"I can't go nowhere?" Tony yelled. "I'm staying right here in this camp? Well, I'm figuring on going out to the movies, so I won't be here."

"If that's the case then," the broadcaster said, "I'll simply call up Mike Jacobs and the station and tell them the program is off."

Galento relented and did as asked. Later, the program aired.

Someone asked whether Tony intended to do some light work in the gymnasium. Joe Jacobs shrugged his shoulders.

"It's all according to the mood he's in. Maybe he will be all right again in a few minutes."

Tony posed for a photograph with a fish bowl stuffed with a picture of Joe Louis. The photographer wanted it to appear as though Tony was prognosticating as he gazed into a crystal ball.

"No kidding," Tony continued his complaining, "I've been bothered like this for a week. Sometimes I don't know how I got any work done. It was pictures and stories all the time. But no kidding, I'm not a bad guy. I ain't got nothin' against nobody. Ask any of my friends. I talk tough and bawl guys out, but the next minute I'm around lendin' those same guys $20."

Before Hughes left, Tony went to the gymnasium. He went into the ring with someone acting as a referee. They simulated a referee pushing Tony away from a clinch, and as he pushed, Tony jumped back and punched at a phantom Joe Louis.[53]

Galento's wife, Mary, was asked about the fight.

"Tony can't and won't lose this fight," she said. "He'll knock Mr. Louis out in the third round. That's all. There are no ifs, ands, or buts about it. The third round, a knockout."

Since Tony was long odds to win, the biggest surprise in the last days before the fight was how it had gained popularity. Mike Jacobs's box offices all reported good action, and a long line of customers formed outside the main ticket window at the Hippodrome, satisfying Uncle Mike's hopes.[54]

On the day of the fight, June 28, 1939, the most comprehensive police precautions ever taken in connection with a local fight provided for an extensive presence in the Bronx and Harlem. The fight arrived. Tony had knocked out his last eleven opponents. The odds on him losing had shortened. The question columnist and experts were asking was not if Tony would win but how long would he last. Few saw it going beyond three rounds. Tony remained a long shot. Louis knocked out his last three opponents in the first round. None had gone more than five rounds since he won a decision over Tommy Farr in fifteen rounds almost two years before.

A crowd of 34,852 filed into Yankee Stadium for a fight most thought Tony had no chance to win. Another forty million people of the 130 million American population listened to the fight on the radio. The turnout for Louis and Galento was a publicity triumph for Joe Jacobs. He had Galento fighting for a title when in the beginning the public showed no interest. He had publicized the fight using any means he could—some tactics being unsavory—to get a crowd into the park. The attendees paid $283,302.68. Radio and motion picture rights were $50,000 bringing the total gross to $333,302. Net receipts were $289,232 after state and federal taxes. Louis's share at 40 percent amounted to $114,332. Galento's share at 17.5 percent amounted to $50,020.[55] Herman Taylor, Philadelphia promoter, collected 5 percent for relinquishing his rights to Galento's services. That left a sizeable profit for the promoter, Mike Jacobs.[56]

In the first round, both started carefully. Tony started in a crouch, and Louis looked at him from an upright stance. Tony threw the first punch, a left to the body, which Louis blocked. Another left to Louis's body was brushed down, and Louis was short with a jab. Then, Galento landed his sweeping left hook that caught Louis on the chin and drove him into the ropes. Louis was visibly shaken. Tony pursued and connected with two shorter lefts and a right to the ear while Louis covered. Louis jabbed while Galento came forward slowly in his crouch. Tony landed a left to the head and missed with a right. Then Louis landed his first good punch, a right uppercut. Tony missed with a left, and a right grazed Louis's chin. Louis timed Galento the next time he came toward him and dropped a stinging left on his jaw but took a left to the head in return. At the finish, Joe connected with a couple of punches to the head, but it was unquestionably Tony's round. With the one punch, to the surprise of many, Tony took control of the fight and won the round. Tony had beat Joe Louis in the first round.

Louis was cautious at the start of the second round and started to jab. Louis started finding his rhythm and struck Tony above his left eye, causing blood to stream down. A left and a right staggered Tony into the ropes, and blood flowed from his mouth and nose. Galento landed a right to the jaw, but it carried no sting, and he clinched. Louis hooked his left to the head, and Tony held and pushed. The champion was pouring punches into Galento. Then a left hook to the head dropped Tony. For the first time in his career, he felt the canvas. In one hundred fights, he had never been down. Tony got up at the count of two before Louis could reach a neutral corner. Tony appeared tired and held on at the bell. Tony's blood covered referee Arthur Donovan and Joe. The round ended, and each man walked to his corner. Even Whitey's magic could not fix the damage to the face of Tony.

The bell rang for round three. Louis started jabbing, and Galento just tried to hold on and push. Then it happened. Both landed rights to the body, the champion's punching being a fraction of a second ahead of Tony's, but Galento landed a looping left hook to the head that lifted Louis's feet off the floor, and Louis, off balance, hit the canvas. A sight no one had expected—Tony standing over the mighty Joe Louis. He hurried to his feet without a count. Tony landed two lefts to the heart, sending Joe into the ropes, following with two more lefts and a right uppercut inside, bringing a trickle of blood from Louis's mouth. Just before the bell, a left to the jaw sent Louis into the ropes, and he held for the first time as Tony tried to rough him. It was Galento's round.

Round four started, and Tony abandoned his crouch. Tony started on the offensive, jabbing and roughing inside, but Louis landed a heavy right to the jaw, and the battle underwent a complete change. Louis sent a hard left into Tony's face, and blood cascaded from his mouth. A few more punches, and Tony was smeared with blood. Louis missed a one-two combination but came back with a right that rocked Tony into his own corner. He was groggy, and Louis drove eight or ten punches into the head, lefts and rights, which came so fast they could not be counted. Referee Arthur Donovan stepped in to stop the punishment, and as he did, Louis paused, and Tony staggered off the ropes and after a few steps went down in a heap. Donovan waved Louis away and reached down to pick up the beaten man. It was over.[57]

There had been nothing clownish about Tony that night. He fought a clean, aggressive fight. He never took a step backward.[58] Referee Arthur Donovan decided he had never officiated at a "hotter" fight and said that until Tony went down under a murderous attack in the fourth, he had no intension of stopping the bout.

"Even when he's hurt," the veteran official explained. "Galento always is dangerous until he's knocked cold."[56]

It lasted only four rounds, but the crowd received their money's worth. Tony said he wanted to fight Louis again. He said if his sight had been unhindered, he would have knocked Louis out.

"I wasn't hurt so much," Tony said. "But something got in my eyes …"[59]

That is what Tony said, but the point remained he was a beaten fighter. Louis cut him up. Beneath each eye was a bruise. A long cut extended down from his nose to the corner of his mouth on the right side. His chin displayed a cut. He looked like a man hit in the face with many punches. It took twenty-three stitches to repair him.[60] Louis looked unmarked.[61]

"Tony berated me something terrible before the fight," Louis whispered to an interviewer after the fight. "He got to me, and I hated him for it. I never hated anybody before. I decided to punish him before I knocked him out. I wanted it to go into later rounds, but he kept calling me dirty names during the fight. So I ended it."[62]

Mrs. Galento, one of the first arrivals at Tony's dressing room, appeared before Tony did. A guard at the door stopped her.

"I can't let you in. Commission rules, lady."

The efforts of Mrs. Galento to identify herself were unavailing. When Galento did come along and bustled his way inside, Mrs. Galento lost sight of him.

Tony was under the shower when Bill Brown, one of the boxing commissioners, came in.

"You put up a great bout, Tony," Brown said.

For the first time, appreciative words toward Tony came from the commission.

Tony came out from under the shower and started to spar.

"I got careless," he said. "If I had done this, and then that, I'd have been all right."

Brown watched him.

"Your friend Donovan stopped it at the right time. You put up a great bout, Tony," Brown added.

The commissioner left, and Galento went back to his shower.

Mrs. Galento returned a half hour later when Galento remained sloshing his way through a shower. Again, she tried to gain access.

"Commission rules, lady," the guard said, still firm. "No ladies in the dressing room."

While Mrs. Galento failed to get in to see her husband, several dozen reporters and other men had no trouble.

An announcer shoved a microphone in front of Tony's battered mouth.

"And for the fine fight you waged, Tony, we want you to have this razor, which has your name embossed in gold letters on the box. Thank you."

"Ugh!" Galento said.

"They should have given him the razor before the fight," someone shouted.[63]

The press that had berated Tony before the fight could not praise his effort enough.

Dan Parker, *Mirror*: "Galento acquitted himself with all the honors that can go to a brave man who has done his best and failed."

Jack Miley, *Post*: "I am not going to kid Tony about being fat any more … That extra weight is his heart."

Hype Igoe, *Journal-American*: "Galento was more glamorous in defeat than he had been in any of his victories."

Jimmy Powers, *News*: "It was the best battle of punchers since Dempsey-Firpo … And make no mistake about this—Galento has a better punch than Louis."

James P. Dawson, *Times*: "Galento missed the title only because in his heavy, awkward-footed way, he could not muster the accuracy to uncork another left hook to the Jaw such as the blow that floored Louis."

Wilbur Wood, *Sun*: "Louis put at rest once and for all any suspicion that he cannot take it or that he will fold when the going is rough."

Caswell Adams, *Herald-Tribune*: "What a great fight! All the yells and all the words can't describe it."

Joe Williams, *World-Telegram*: "Galento was the story … He made the fight … He did the unexpected."

Bill Boni, Associated Press: "Galento was the first beer barrel ever to tap a man."

Tony would keep a picture in his wallet for the rest of his life. If you asked him, but you did not have to ask, he would take the tattered picture out, showing him lifting Joe Louis off his feet with the left hook.

"I should have been champion of the world—retired undefeated," he could not stop saying.[64]

CHAPTER 31

The California Golden Boy

On August 16, 1939, Galento returned to Bey's to train for a bout against Lou Nova[1] less than two months after his loss to Joe Louis. The fight was scheduled to be at Municipal Stadium, Philadelphia, on September 7. The highly regarded twenty-four-year-old Lou Nova had been stalking Galento and Louis at their camps while they trained for their championship fight. Before the Louis bout, everyone talked about a Galento-Nova bout.

Born Jay L. Nova in Los Angeles, he later resided in Oakland, California. He stood six feet three inches and weighed just over two hundred pounds. They called him the Californian Golden Boy because of his looks, a sharp departure from Tony. Nova had one loss in his first twenty-seven fights before this one. He gained prominence by defeating Tommy Farr and Max Baer in his last two fights. The Max Baer fight was the first televised heavyweight prizefight on June 1, 1939. WNBT-TV in New York televised the bout. Nova had hired trainer Ray Arcel, now being called the dean of the corner men. His manager was Ray Carlen. Arcel would later say Nova was a gullible young man. A California mystic named Oom the Omnipotent influenced his boxing. Nova believed he had developed a Cosmic Punch for his future 1941 Joe Louis bout.[2]

Lou Nova attended the Louis-Galento championship bout.

"If I ever staggered Louis the way Tony did, he never would get away from me," declared the confident Nova. "If I'd had him on the floor like Tony did, I would have kept him there. The fellow can't take a punch."[3]

On his first day at Madame Bey's, Tony did not spar. He did four miles of roadwork in the morning. That afternoon he did ten rounds of bag punching, rope skipping, shadowboxing, and calisthenics. He brought some of his sparring partners with him that had helped him prepare for the Louis fight. He had Lee Silvers from the Bronx, New York, Abe Feldman, and Mickey McAvoy.[4]

Tony and his manager created more controversy at Bey's Camp. They disparaged Arthur Donovan, one of the most highly regarded referees in boxing.

"I won't fight Lou Nova if Arthur Donovan referees," Tony said after a workout.[5]

Manager Joe Jacobs said he would appear before the Pennsylvania State Athletic Commission in Philadelphia to insist that George Blake of Los Angeles be the referee.

Galento considered Donovan not objective by taking five rounds from Henry Armstrong on low blows against Lou Ambers.[5] They had not argued his refereeing in the just completed Louis-Galento fight. When managers Jacobs and Carlen signed the Galento-Nova contract, they had agreed that either Donovan or Blake would be acceptable. Tony's demand to the Pennsylvania State Athletic Commission drew an immediate response.

"Neither Tony Galento nor Joe Jacobs, his manager," Leon L. Rains, commission chairman, replied, "will name the referee of a bout so long as I am chairman of the State Athletic Commission. That is against all laws and regulations of boxing in this State, and I am here to enforce these laws. I want Galento and Jacobs to understand right now that I will enforce those laws whether they like it or not."[6]

Joe Jacobs stopped his oversight of Tony at Madame Bey's to phone promoter Herman Taylor,[6] who had collaborated with promoter Mike Jacobs for the bout. He told him that he would be leaving for Philadelphia to talk about the matter with the commission. Joe Jacobs, a persuasive talker, tried to sway the commission. Rains's stance remained—the commission names the referee.

"If Joe Jacobs is coming to see me about naming his own referee," the chairman said, "he will be saving himself time and money by staying right where he is with Tony Galento at Summit."[6]

Rains of the Pennsylvania Athletic Commission telegraphed Tony ten days before his fight on September 7. They ordered him to shift his camp from Madame Bey's to a Pennsylvania site within fifteen miles of Philadelphia.[7] Joe Jacobs said Tony would move to Pennsylvania the next week and go to Jim Dougherty's Camp in Leiperville.[6]

Tony continued his afternoon workouts with Abe Feldman, Tom Schenck, and Lee Silvers. They were all using hard rights to prepare Tony for Nova. As soon as the workout ended, manager Joe Jacobs left for Philadelphia. He met Commissioner Rains the next morning to lodge a formal protest against Arthur Donovan as the referee. He still insisted on George Blake.[6]

Nova, training in Atlantic City, expressed confidence he would defeat Tony early. Onlookers said he looked sluggish in training. Nova did not dispute their assessment.

"I'll snap out of it in a couple of days," he said. "Don't forget, in my last workout before the Baer fight, I looked so bad the betting odds went up."[8]

Bookmakers installed Nova as a four-to-one favorite to beat Tony. Nova was taller, younger, faster, and a much better boxer.

"Tubby Tony is made to order for me," Nova stated. "I'll put him away in five rounds. Of course, I want Louis as soon as possible, but it appears now I won't be able to get him until next spring. So, in the meantime, I'll take on someone in February just to keep from too long a layoff."

"If there's no war over in Europe," Nova's manager, Ray Carlen, interrupted, "Schmeling may be brought back to fight us.

"I've already spoken with Mike Jacobs about it, and he agrees Lou should have a fight in February."[8]

On August 29, Carlen reported to Leon L. Rains, commission chairman, that a cold had hindered Nova's training. Carlen requested an eight-day postponement because of the importance of the bout to his fighter. Rains sent Dr. Terry to examine Nova at the Garden Pier, Atlantic City, where he trained. The commission physician decided that Nova, rid of the cold, needed a day or two of rest before he resumed hard work. Upon hearing Dr. Terry's report, Rains informed promoters Taylor and Mike Jacobs. They all agreed that a postponement was essential. They rescheduled the fight for September 15. Neither the commission head nor the promoters wanted a subpar Nova to meet Galento. Upon hearing of the postponement, Carlen phoned Rains that he would leave the camp on the Atlantic City shore and move to Philadelphia. Nova would go to the Broadwood Gymnasium the next day.

"No promoter likes a postponement," Taylor said. "But I'd rather set back the fight than have Nova go into the ring off form. Our patrons are paying to see a real heavyweight fight, and that's what Mike Jacobs and I want them to have."

Tony, still at Madame Bey's, would still go to Jimmy Dougherty's Camp in Leiperville on September 7. Joe Jacobs, also at Madame Bey's, commented on the fight's postponement.

"It will be all the same to Tee Gee, give or take a week."

"Gettn' cold feet, eh," Tony grunted. "'at bum keeps me waitin' a week, does he? All right, but I won't keep 'im waitin' on de fifteenth. He's just living on borrowed time!"[9]

In late August, the New York Boxing Commission revoked Joe Jacobs's license as a manager. The reason believed to be Jacobs's cry against an alleged gimmick in Joe Louis's glove the night Joe knocked out Max Schmeling. The press asked Joe Jacobs if the New York Commission suspended him because of his talk about Louis using a gimmick. On a site away from the camp, Joe Jacobs addressed the suspension.

"No," Joe said. "They caught up with me before. They only just revoked my license. But I don't know why. It couldn't have been for yelling about the gimmick like they said. That was all settled a long time ago. At least, that's what they made me believe. You were there the day I made the beef. Do you remember General Phelan calling me aside, shooing all the newspapermen away, and talking to me? And me saying to you fellows later that I retracted the story, and that I had given it out just for the publicity? Well, the reason I said that was because the General told me if I didn't retract it, he would have to call me before the commission and suspend me.

"So I retracted it and nothing more was said. Then, they knew that if I was suspended Galento wouldn't go through with the fight, so they didn't do anything. But on July 11, they called me before the Commission and questioned me again. Phelan spoke to me, and Brown spoke to me, and Wear spoke to me. They asked me why I made the statement, and I said, 'Why, I explained that to the General … The fight was dying before I made that statement, and all I was trying to do was to stir up some interest in it.'

"So each of them said to me, 'Well, it's all right this time, but don't do it again.'

"And now they revoke my license. What for? For the beef about the gimmick? Don't make me laugh. That ain't the real reason, don't know what it is, but that ain't it. Maybe it's because I took the Galento-Nova fight to Philadelphia. Maybe it's because after the Armstrong-Ambers fight I said I didn't want Arthur Donovan to referee the Galento-Nova fight. Donovan is one of the Commission's referees, and maybe they didn't like me taking a crack at him, figuring I was taking a crack at them. But I didn't even think about the Commission. I just thought Donovan didn't do a good job in the Armstrong fight, and I didn't want him in there in our fight, and I told that to the Commission in Philadelphia.

"You don't think Louis used a gimmick. All right. That's what you think. And I can't prove he did, any more than you could prove he didn't. But as long as I thought that way, I was going to do everything I could to protect Galento. I got the guy up there, and I was looking out for him and doing everything I could to protect him. I didn't accuse the Commission of anything. I didn't say their inspectors were lax. I didn't say anything about them. But all I succeeded in doing was to get myself jammed up.

"But I guess it don't do me any good to holler. I never did anything to General Phelan, but he's always doing things to me. Why, I've gone out of my way to be nice to him. When he came out to our camp, I was always anxious to see that he was comfortable and had everything he wanted, and once I not only introduced him, but because I was afraid some of those Galento rooters from Orange would give him the buzzer, I asked everybody to give him a big hand.

"Well, anyhow, I don't care if I ain't allowed to operate in New York. I can go somewhere else with Galento and do all right, too. This fight in Philadelphia will do $200,000, and Galento will knock him out, and then we'll get Louis next summer, or if Pastor should beat Louis, we'll get Pastor.

"I don't know what they're going to do about a referee for the Nova fight. Any one of the Philadelphia referees would suit me, and I never said anything about a referee in the beginning, but Ray Carlen said he wouldn't fight there unless they put in Donovan or George Blake from California, and the other day I put the rap in on Donovan, so I don't know what they're going to do. I don't know whether they will pay any attention to my rap or not or whether they will bring Blake in, or whether they will have a Philadelphia referee in there, but whoever they take will be all right with me.

"But excuse me. I got to run out to the camp. Don't forget I told you that Galento will knock him out."

After he had gone, some people were sitting and talking.

"There goes the best fight manager in the business," somebody said.

"I don't know about that," somebody else said. "He's good and he did an amazing job with Galento, but look at the job Joe Gould did with Jim Braddock, and how well Louis is managed, and what Jimmy Johnston has done with Pastor. And how about Sam Plan and Jack Hurley and Pop Foster—to name just a few?"

The first fellow shook his head.

"They're all good managers," he said. "But this fellow got Galento into the ring to fight for the heavyweight championship of the world after he had been just an ordinary fighter for ten years. Everybody laughed at Jacobs when he started his campaign for a Louis fight, but he got the guy in there. And you have to give him credit for that."[10]

Abe Greene, New Jersey boxing commissioner, watched Tony Galento work out in early September at Madame Bey's Camp. After Tony sparred with Mickey McAvoy and Tom Schenck, he said the Orange heavyweight should win by a knockout.

"He appears to be punching harder than he did for the Joe Louis fight," Greene said. "He also seems more vicious. I'm sure his punches will hurt Nova, but I'm not so certain the Californian can punch hard enough to hurt Tony."[11]

As promised, Tony left Madame Bey's Camp on September 7. That evening, Tony attended a parade in Philadelphia meant as a publicity stunt. It became an incredible demonstration. It lasted two and a half hours. The Philadelphia police tried to untangle the resultant crippling traffic snarl. An estimated crowd of 200,000 people lined Broad Street and the Italian district streets to watch. The city called it the greatest parade ever staged for an individual in Philadelphia. The crowd almost tore Tony apart in its enthusiasm.[12]

"What would they of done to him if he had beaten Louis?" his wife, Mary, asked.[13]

Philadelphia, apart from Orange, New Jersey, was Tony's domain. He had tremendous support there before his canceled fight with John Henry Lewis. He had been the center of some astonishing demonstrations ever given a prizefighter since he established his training quarters at Dougherty's Camp. Nova remained favored at four to one. Tony occupied the position of the people's choice. The only friend Nova seemed to have in Philadelphia was his manager, Ray Carlen, and his trainer, Ray Arcel.[12]

Jim Dougherty's Camp in Leiperville had an evil-looking bar and an outdoor ring. Tony brought his sparring partners Abe Feldman and Tom Schenck with him. In his workouts, he attracted about three hundred pro-Galento customers. A small showing compared to the large crowds he drew at Bey's Camp. Each paid a sixty-cent admission charge. Tony was not as talkative as usual—he said he was going to act like a little gentleman—but he impressed with his training.

"I'll knock the bum out," he said to anyone that asked.

As it had been in his training in Philadelphia for John Henry Lewis, it was hot. Tony looked sluggish in his workouts compared to the intensity he showed at Madame Bey's Camp.

"I like him to whip any opponent in the heavyweight ranks," Jim Dougherty remarked. "A great fighter don't always look so good in the gym. But he'll punch the (expletive not printed) outta this Louie Novy. He'll knock 'im out if Novy mixes with him."[14]

The fight took place at Municipal Stadium, Philadelphia, on the rescheduled September 15, 1939. It was the nearest to a championship battle the city had seen since the Dempsey-Tunney fight of 1926. For a city that gathered in droves for Tony's parade, the gate at the fight had a disappointing 25,000 with cash receipts of $69,000. About two hundred police officers kept order outside the stadium. One hundred foot officers kept traffic flowing, helped by fifty-five mounted police and twenty-five police cars. Eighty men were stationed inside the stadium.

Taxicabs by the hundreds brought patrons from out of town that arrived by train from New York, Washington, and western cities. Automobiles numbering over six thousand brought people from as far away as Florida and Illinois. The automobiles jammed the streets and parking lots. The Philadelphians, aware of the impending traffic problems, arrived by subway, bus, and trolley car. The Philadelphia Rapid Transit supplied seventy-five special double-decker busses for the hordes of people. The busses awaited outside the stadium for the rush of people after the fight.

For the main bout, Gene Tunney, former heavyweight champion, and his party were in ringside seats. Gene Tunney, when in New York, said, "I think Galento will beat Nova." Governor "Happy" Chandler of Kentucky attended. Others included heavyweight Al Ettore and Bobby Reynolds, a renowned Philadelphia fighter. Among the old boxers were Jack Johnson, who traveled from New York, and Bobby Barret. Also introduced were Philadelphia's own former light heavyweight champion Tommy Loughran and General Phelan, New York State Boxing Commission chairman. Acting Mayor George Connell, City Solicitor Joseph Sharfsin, and Mrs. Edna R. Carroll, State Board of Censors chairman, were also there with their parties. Promoter Mike Jacobs sat ringside, confident that his Californian Golden Boy, Lou Nova, would win the fight. The victor was scheduled to meet the Joe Louis-Bob Pastor winner. For many, that meant if the winner was Lou Nova.[15]

The crowd was greeted with a clear, star-filled night in the open horseshoe-shaped arena. Tony entered the ring wearing a purple robe that was taken off and draped over his shoulder. His thinned hair glistened with excessive wax. His put on his gloves. Joe Jacobs, with the ever-present black cigar sticking out of the corner of his mouth, looked right at Tony. Nova, in his corner, wore a white robe. He had a white T-shirt and a white towel bunched over his neck. Joe Jacobs protested the grease on Nova's hair.[16] Nova had much on his side when the men climbed into the ring—youth, height, and skill. Tony fought a clean fight against Joe Louis in his previous fight; he had no intention of such tactics in this fight.

In the first round, Tony delivered a foul backhand hit to Nova, so flagrant that many could not have missed it. In the same round, Tony did some effective work with his head. His offenses drew a mild objection from the referee. Manager Joe Jacobs, in Galento's corner, discovered early in the bout that Nova stepped inside of Tony's deadly left hooks. When Tony obeyed his manager's instructions to shorten them up, Nova offered an easy target.[17]

In the third round, Tony hit Nova with a looping left hook, the same one that knocked down Joe Louis. Tony's momentum from the punch threw him off balance, and he landed on top of the fallen Nova. Nova arose, dazed. He never fully recovered from that punch. Nova's efforts to box Tony were futile. Every time he started a left jab, his best weapon, Tony hit him hard to the head. The crowd's boos because of Tony's continuing fouls had no effect on referee Blake and none on Tony.[18, 19] A spectator behind the press rows yelled.

"Either stop that Galento or give him a knife and let him finish the job!"[20]

In the eighth round, Tony had Nova down again for no count. During the intermission between the ninth and tenth rounds, it became evident to the referee and everyone else that the butchered young Californian did not have a chance. The referee looked at Nova's wounds and appeared to want to stop the fight, but Nova's manager, Ray Carlen, dissuaded him.

In the fourteenth round, Nova hit the canvas twice for two and eight counts. Nova was shaken. Tony turned to referee Blake begging him to stop the fight. When he refused, Tony continued to pound Nova. Finally, Blake stopped the fight at two minutes, forty-four seconds of the fourteenth round. Nova staggered Tony a couple of times, but he never went down. Tony would have won by a wide margin of points if the fight had gone the limit. It amounted to a surprising exhibition of hard punching and endurance by Tony—and excessive fouls.

He fouled Nova, especially thumbing Nova's right eye, throughout the fight. It was as rough a brawl as ever seen outside an alley. Referee George Blake—Joe Jacobs's choice—was little more than an interested spectator of the brawl. Tony, the best alley fighter in the world, applied all the technics for which he was famous. He rolled his head into Nova's face, used his elbows and his forearms, heeled and clubbed the back of the neck, backhanded and omitted little save kicking, biting, and gouging.[18, 19]

The December 1939 issue of *The Ring* magazine printed, "One of the most disgraceful fights staged since the days of the barroom brawls. Referee George Blake would have retained his reputation as a great referee had he disqualified Galento. Galento was permitted to thumb Nova's right eye until it reached a terrible condition. Finally, Nova went down in the fourteenth round after being fouled for the last time."

The radio broadcast made little mention of the fouls. It was a tough, hard-fought fight. Tony proved his critics wrong who said he could not win a fight that went into the late rounds. The praise showered on Galento in his defeat to Louis turned to anger for his tactics against Nova. Both fighters were gracious in their post-fight interviews in the ring.

"The man that surprised ninety percent of the country, back again, Tony Galento," the announcer broadcast.

"I fought one of the toughest guys in the boxing game today," Tony replied. "I'd rather box him than box many of the older boxers I box. A tough guy and a good fighter. And good tough … plenty of guts. And thank you mom and pa, hello ma and pa, and my baby home. My wife is here. And I appreciate all the Philadelphia fans that came here tonight to see me. I know they're all my friends."

"Ata boy Tony," yelled someone in the crowd.

"Hello Sam," Nova said in the ring. "It was a tough fight. One of the toughest fights I ever had. And I really haven't any excuses. Tony Galento is a great fighter and a good tough man. I would like at this time, if you don't mind, to greet my wife and little girl. And I'm sorry Mark that I lost. And maybe next time, I'll win for ya kid. So long everyone."[16]

"Blake would have been justified in stopping the bout several rounds before he did," Tommy Loughran said, former light heavyweight champion of the world, "and thus would have saved Nova further cruel and unnecessary punishment. But having permitted the slaughter to extend deep into the fourteenth round, it seems too bad that he saw fit to put the stigma of a technical knockout on the record of a promising young fighter. As a matter of fact, it is very unlikely that Tony, weary as he was when the bout was stopped, could have done Lou much more damage during the three minutes and sixteen seconds remaining."[17]

They took Lou Nova to Hahneman Hospital for the treatment of eye injuries after his bruising battle. It took five stitches to repair the top of his badly cut right eye and five stitches to close a laceration under it;[19] he almost lost it. He also suffered left eye contusions. Galento gave Nova his second loss and worst beating he ever received. It took Nova over a year to recover and get back into the ring.

A year later, Nova recalled the fight and aftermath while preparing for a fight with Pat Comiskey, his second fight since the Galento bout.

"I was so sick," he said, "and had so much pain I thought I never would forget it. But I have forgotten it already. I remember, though, the nights when I couldn't sleep and couldn't move and would just lie there on my back and think about all the things I wanted to do and probably never would be able to do because I either was going to die or, if I got well, I wouldn't even be able to walk, let alone, fight again. … I remember that this eye was cut and bleeding and every time we got together Galento had his thumb out like this, trying to stick it in my eye or pry the cut open with it."

Another heavyweight told Nova about a man Comiskey had knocked out.

"He is a nice fellow," the heavyweight said. "A very intelligent fellow, too."

"He is, eh?" Nova said. "Then what the hell is he doing in this business?"[20]

CHAPTER 32

Show Me a Man Who Never Lost

Arturo Godoy, Chilean heavyweight, returned to America on November 13, 1939. He would train at the place where he had made a new friend on a previous trip to America—Madame Bey's Camp. He had much success training for fights there. Godoy was last at Madame Bey's in 1937. In fifty-five bouts during a nine-year campaign, Arturo Godoy had lost only four decisions and had five draws. He suffered setbacks by Nathan Mann and Roscoe Toles in 1937, Tommy Loughran in 1935, and Billy Jones in 1934. Of his forty-six victories, the Chilean slugger registered twenty knockouts. This would be his first appearance in America since he stopped Eddie Mader in five rounds in New York on November 9, 1937, and his first fight since August when he lost on a foul to Eduardo Prime in Argentina.

He came to fight Joe Louis for the world heavyweight title at Madison Square Garden on February 9. Godoy qualified for the Louis match by virtue of his two triumphs over Tony Galento, the fighter who knocked down Louis. Godoy scored his second decision over Galento in a match on the undercard of the Joe Louis-James Braddock title fight at Comiskey Park, Chicago, June 22, 1937. Louis would be defending his championship for the ninth time and had earned $781,701 since winning the title.

Godoy's wife, Ledda, accompanied him, making her first visit to America. Godoy's manager, Al Weill, and many newspapermen greeted Godoy as he disembarked from the American Republics ship liner *Uruguay*.

"I worked almost daily on the ship," Godoy said. "I intend to remain in the city for about three weeks, then I will go to Madame Bey's place at Summit, New Jersey. I will loaf for a week or ten days there before starting hard training. I want to make the greatest fight of my life against Louis."[1]

While Godoy stayed in New York, Madame Bey hosted another friend for a championship fight. Lou Ambers returned. Ambers had again become the world lightweight champion when he defeated the man who had taken it away from him, Henry Armstrong, in a fifteen-round decision at Yankee Stadium on August 17, 1939. He trained for that second encounter in Carmel, New York. Like their previous bout, it was an epic fight. The two traded blows for the entire fight. Referee Arthur Donovan penalized Armstrong five rounds—the second, fifth, seventh, ninth, and eleventh for low blows. Penalties Armstrong could not overcome.

"The title was not won on competition alone but on fighting rules and ethics," wrote James P. Dawson of the *New York Times*. "Four of these rounds Armstrong won on competition alone without a doubt. … On this observer's score sheet, Armstrong was the victim of an injustice."

Ambers came to Madame Bey's to train for a fifteen-round battle in which he would face Henry Armstrong for a third time. This one would be for Armstrong's welterweight title on December 1, 1939, at Madison Square Garden.[2] Henry Armstrong, who was in Hot Springs, Arkansas, would arrive in the metropolitan area to commence training. Ambers had wed his childhood love, Margaret Celio, on October 5 in their hometown of Herkimer at St. Anthony's Catholic Church. Father Gustave Purificato, who taught Ambers how to box at the church, performed the ceremony.

Ambers had won his previous eleven bouts, including the title bout against Armstrong, in a time span of a year. The last time he lost was against Armstrong on August 17, 1938. He did steady work at Bey's when on the scheduled day of the fight he received word of its cancellation. Promoter Mike Jacobs canceled the fifteen-round welterweight title bout because of Armstrong's ill health. Phelan visited Armstrong with three commission physicians who reported his temperature high and recommended a week's rest to recover. After the cancellation, the New York State Athletic Commission revealed it had amended its rules so that never again could a fighter hold the title in more than one weight division at a time.

"To prevent such mix-ups as now confronts us," General John J. Phelan, the commission chairman, announced, "we are going to make it impossible for a fighter to hold the championship in two weight classes at the same time. We are amending our rules so that an individual holding a championship in one class will not be permitted to enter a title bout with the champion of another class unless he relinquishes the championship he holds."[3]

The commission planned for Armstrong to defend his welterweight title on January 24. Given the new rules, he could not fight Ambers because the winner would hold two titles. Armstrong would fight Pedro Montañez. Ambers would risk his lightweight championship against the number-one challenger to be determined. A third bout between Ambers and Armstrong would never occur.

Armstrong would defeat Montañez in the ninth round of a tough fight. Montañez felt the canvas for the first time in his career in the fourth round. Down again at the end of the eighth, his handlers dragged his half-lifeless body to the corner, then sent him back bleeding and battered for the ninth where Armstrong finished the fight.[4] "For savagery and bruising fighting, virtually all of it displayed by Armstrong, this was a fight that had seldom been excelled. No welterweight or man near Armstrong's inches or poundage could have survived the blistering firepower."[5]

Godoy started training at Madame Bey's Camp on November 30 for his heavyweight title bout against Joe Louis. Joining Godoy in early December was lightweight Tippy Larkin and heavyweight Patrick Comiskey, two outstanding native New Jersey boxers. Larkin came from Garfield, New Jersey, to face hard-hitting, undefeated Al "Bummy" Davis at the Garden on December 15 in the ten-round feature. Comiskey, hailing from Patterson, New Jersey, was to oppose Steve Dudas on the Larkin-Davis undercard scheduled for eight rounds.[6] At nineteen years of age, Comiskey was undefeated in twenty-five fights with one draw. He was a prospect that promoter Mike Jacobs held in high regard. Mike Jacobs wanted to use Comiskey against Buddy Baer and suggested pairing him with Billy Conn after this bout.[7]

The three men trained together at Bey's Camp. A publicity photograph showed all in a row aiming at their prey with rifles. It was not an unusual sight at Bey's to witness a boxer hunting after he finished training. For Larkin and Comiskey, their boxing quarry proved not as easy as that on the hunt. At Madison Square Garden on December 15, 1939, before a crowd of 17,000 fans, they both lost. Larkin, outweighed by eight pounds, lost by a knockout in the fifth round to Al "Bummy" Davis. Comiskey lost his first professional fight in an eight-round decision to Steve Dudas. Comiskey finished with a fractured right hand and a badly bruised left hand. A *New York Times* reporter felt Comiskey was "unlucky not to have received the verdict."

X-rays showed that Comiskey's bruised left hand was severely fractured when he hit the veteran Steve Dudas on the head. In addition, he suffered severe contusions and a split knuckle on his right hand. Dr. Frederick Schwartzberg of Paterson announced that the left hand was shattered, and he put it in a cast with the expectation that Comiskey would need to keep it immobilized for two months. The unfortunate incident in the career of the hard-hitting young Comiskey, that experts were predicting would become a topnotch heavyweight, hurt Mike Jacobs's plan to put him against Buddy Baer and Billy Conn.[7]

As the new decade arrived, Godoy continued his training in a snowbound Madame Bey's Camp.[8] Fred Apostoli and light heavyweight Stan the "Socking Syrian" Hasrato from New York joined him.

"I've never seen a fighter more serious about a bout than Arturo Godoy," Stan Hasrato said from Madame Bey's Camp. "I watch him in training for Joe Louis almost every day and from the way he pummels his sparring partners, the Chilean should be a mighty tough man for the champion to beat."[9]

Hasrato, known more as a sparring partner, boxed almost daily with Fred Apostoli, former world middleweight champion. Apostoli had just lost the championship in October when Ceferino Garcia knocked him out. Apostoli had held the title for over two years. After the loss, Apostoli ascended to the next weight class—the light heavyweight division. Apostoli was to meet Melio Bettina on January 5, 1940, at Madison Square Garden. The Socking Syrian would fight on the Apostoli undercard.

Fred Apostoli fought a determined Melio Bettina. The fight demonstrated boxing's brutality as the two light heavyweights pounded each other. Apostoli felt the canvas in each of the first three rounds; Bettina went down in the tenth. Apostoli won by an unpopular decision.[10] The referee scored it six to four with two even, and one judge scored it six to five with one even, both for Apostoli. The other judge made it a six-to-six draw. Hasrato the Socking Syrian fought to an eight-round draw on the undercard.

By late January 1940, Whitey Bimstein trained three fighters in the previous five weeks at Bey's Camp.[11] He had trained light heavyweight Fred Apostoli for his winning fight with Melio Bettina on January 5 at Madison Square Garden. He was training Arturo Godoy for his heavyweight title fight against Joe Louis on February 9. He was also training lightweight champion Lou Ambers, his third charge, who would move up to the welterweight division against the undefeated Al "Bummy" Davis on February 23 at Madison Square Garden. Al Weill managed Godoy and Ambers. Larry White managed Apostoli.

Ambers left Bey's to fight Wally Hally, the man he had sparred with at Madame Bey's in November.[12] They fought in Providence, Rhode Island, on January 29, 1940. Ambers hit Hally easily and had a wide margin in every round,[13] winning the fight. In February, Lou Ambers rejoined the fighters at Madame Bey's Camp. Solly Krieger, the former National Boxing Association world middleweight titleholder, was one of the fighters in the camp. Krieger had not fought in seven months since losing his title to Al Hostak. Krieger weighed almost 190 pounds. He tried to get down to 175 pounds for a comeback among the light heavyweights.[14] Krieger would win his bout against Texas Joe Dundee on February 2 in Ridgewood Grove, Brooklyn, New York.

Whitey Bimstein had both Godoy and Apostoli in excellent condition. If Apostoli could win, he would receive a chance to fight Billy Conn for his light heavyweight crown. If he lost, his career may be over. Godoy had a cold over one weekend, and the press worried that he would be unable to fight Louis on the scheduled date.

"What's all the fuss?" Whitey told concerned reporters. "He had a cold and a slight sore throat, so I gave him some fish oil and put him to bed for a day. He's not a bad looking sick man now, is he?"

While he was speaking, Godoy climbed into the ring for a sparring session with Jimmy Smith. Someone commented that if he got any sicker before he met Louis, Joe would get something, and it would not be Arturo's cold. Godoy, a crouching, bobbing type of fighter, figured to give the Brown Bomber trouble.[15]

In Fred Apostoli's last training session before the bout, he went through five rounds of sparring. The press wrote his final workout looked outstanding. He boxed three rounds against Tiger Smith and two with Stanley Hasrato. At the end of the workout, Apostoli weighed 169 pounds.[16] When he finished sparring, he looked and felt strong. When he woke the next morning, he had a bad cold. The morning after that, the day of the fight, he felt worse and talked as little as possible so no one would hear how hoarse he had become. He had coughing fits. He feared that his manager or the commission doctor would discover it, causing a postponement of a fight that meant so much to him.[17]

Bettina worked his final day at Stillman's Gymnasium in New York City. Jimmy Grippo, his manager, declared Bettina would surprise Apostoli.[16] The odds makers made Apostoli a favorite at five to six.

On his twenty-seventh birthday, February 2, 1940, Apostoli met Bettina at Madison Square Garden. Bettina battered him over the last three rounds. Apostoli took a horrific beating. After the twelfth round ended, his face battered and swollen, his team carried him back to his corner and decided to stop the fight. They took him to Polyclinic Hospital after the bout due to his suffering from nausea and shock. Dr. John Hammond, the Garden physician, ordered Apostoli to bed for a couple of days and revealed he had a heavy chest cold and a fever of 103 degrees when admitted to the hospital. Some thought he had suffered a concussion, but an examination failed to reveal any internal head injury.

The next day, Apostoli looked much better though his left eye was still badly bruised, and a plaster covered his right eyebrow. He lay on his bed at the Polyclinic Hospital and told reporter Jack Mahon in an interview that he would make one more try to regain the ring glory that he once held. His manager insisted the twenty-seven-year-old should retire from the ring.

"I think I might have caught cold from Arturo Godoy with whom I worked at Madame Bey's Summit, New Jersey, camp all week," Apostoli said. "I felt fine all day Friday and in the dressing room before the fight. I was sure it was my night and that I would knock Bettina out."[18]

The press stated that Godoy had something in his style. Godoy, as anyone who had watched him in training at Madame Bey's Camp could see, looked bigger, faster, and a better fighter than he had been. During his boxing at the camp, he had his head down in a bouncing, fast-stepping fashion that made him a hard target. He hit with both hands to the body with such speed it kept an opponent busy on the defense.

The way Galento fought Louis was not lost on the astute Al Weill. He instructed Godoy in the flaws in Louis's style and prepared Godoy to take full advantage. He had Godoy practice fighting from a crouch, the style Galento used that gave Louis trouble. Godoy had used it already, but Weill made it more pronounced. The fact the Godoy was fighting from a crouch reached Louis's camp in Pompton Lakes. The onlookers saw Louis sparring with fighters that were in a crouch. Louis readily admitted the style gave him problems. It forced him to punch downward, robbing some potency from his blows. It made him cautious, fearing hurting his hands on opponents' hard heads.

"Godoy is a heavyweight Henry Armstrong," judged Lou Ambers, the lightweight champion, training at Madame Bey's for his over-the-weight bout with Al Davis on February 23.

"The difference is that Arturo hits to the body instead of the head. In stamina and whirlwind attack, he is a larger edition of Henry. Like Henry, the big fellow is not so easy to hit as he looks, is hard to hurt, and gives an opponent no rest."[19]

"He's fast, much faster than Louis," Ambers said. "Louis is a great fighter and a sharpshooter, but he's not going to find it easy tagging Godoy, the way that guy bounces around, and the way he rolls under a punch and belts away for the body. It won't surprise me if Godoy gives Louis a surprise, and I mean it."[20]

Ambers, like other experts watching Godoy, said he would give Louis trouble. They would not predict a win for the challenger.

Godoy loved music, danced, and had a pronounced weakness for the bass violin.

"That bull fiddle gets on yer nerves," one handler said.

Arturo Godoy, getting the gist of this remark, toweled the source of it into silence. They said Godoy took his fiddling seriously. Godoy confessed he wanted to lead a band when he finished his boxing career.

"A big band, like so many I see in New York," he said with clumsy gestures and interpretation. "All over South America, I will lead them. We need music in South America."

Another joy the Chilean shared with his foe—Louis was a fan of bands and dancing—was ice cream. Boxers at Bey's said he consumed on average two quarts a day but had to reduce his intake to get in shape. He weighed around 202 pounds, almost the same as Louis.[21]

During sparring, James J. Johnson, his sparring partner, unintentionally landed a punch to Godoy's stomach. Immediately, the ring became a roughhouse. Godoy thought the punch was a cheap shot. Johnson's quick and complete annihilation was the only proper response. A journalist said in the earnestness of his action that he all but wrecked the joint.

He continued, if he could hit half as hard as Galento, or with a tenth the accuracy of Louis, he would be an international menace.

Godoy boxed six rounds during one day of his last week of training. He went two rounds each with Bill Poland, James J. Johnson, and Jimmy Smith. He showed plenty of speed. Later in the week, Arturo Godoy engaged in his final sparring for his championship bout. The Chilean weighed 206 pounds when he returned from his roadwork. Major General John J. Phelan, New York State Athletic Commission chairman, and Dr. William Walker attended the last session of Godoy's training at Bey's Camp. Dr. Walker examined Godoy and found him in excellent condition.[22] General Phelan was made aware of Godoy's questionable boxing tactics. He came to tell the Chilean he must desist.

"No heeling, no butting, no kicking, gouging, or disemboweling," the general said, assuming his sternest pose.

Godoy listened to his words with an expressionless nonresponse. His handlers made promises that no such infractions would be used. General Phelan, satisfied, went away. Then the challenger crawled into the ring and demonstrated an exhibition of atrocities. He boxed four rounds with James J. Johnson, the only sparring partner left. Godoy had beaten the others so much they had fled, which was the best indication of how his boxing had gone at Madame Bey's Camp. James J. Johnson, a man with staying power, reported for work, and on him, Godoy vented his last training camp fury. Johnson gave him a good workout.[21] Godoy finished two months of arduous training. He weighed ten pounds heavier than when he campaigned in America two years before but had lost none of his speed. Godoy had boxed one hundred rounds since he began training at Madame Bey's on November 26.[23]

Much of Godoy's training at Madame's Camp was devoted to perfecting his crouching style. The press called it a turtle crouch, owing to how low he squatted. They could not decide whether he looked like Paulino Uzcudun or a first-round Galento against Louis. Then Godoy announced that he would put the gloves away until he entered the ring against the champion.[21]

Arturo Godoy sat in his steaming dressing room after the day's work.

"This is my big chance. It is the chance that comes once into every man's life. It is the million-dollar chance. I hold it like this, and it cannot get away," Godoy said as he leaned forward, resting his hands on a small table. He clenched them violently as if gripping something important that belonged to him. He expressed sincerity and determination.

A reporter asked if he had ever seen Louis fight.

"Oh, yes, many time. I saw his first against Jack Sharkey, then with Ettore, Brescia, Braddock, Farr, and Pastor."

Among these, he thought Louis's best showing was against Braddock. He was asked what he thought of Louis and his chances against him.

"He is a very good fighter," Godoy replied. "I do not say it will be easy for me. Oh, no. But I know I will do my best just as I do against any other fighter."

Someone suggested that Godoy was at his best in a rough fight such as those he won from Tony Galento. Arturo misunderstood the question. He bristled.

"If Louis wants a dirty fight I can take care of that! But he is a clean fighter, and that is how I hope it is. You want rough? I give you rough!"

Godoy handled his English and was talkative and animated. Without much prodding, he sketched his life and his career as a fighter. Arturo Godoy said he was not the least bit annoyed when Tony Galento ran the laces of his glove across his face, butted him a few times, backhanded him, and punched him on the breaks.

"You like fight this way? I like too," Godoy said.

There had been few rougher fights than that staged by Godoy and Galento at the old New York Hippodrome and repeated in the undercard of the Joe Louis-James Braddock fight in Chicago. Galento enjoyed a rough fight, but Godoy took pleasure in one even more. He proved he had more experience than Galento at it, twice gaining decisions over the man who sat Louis on the canvas. Godoy promised he would try to observe the rules when he faced Louis in the fifteen-round world heavyweight championship match at Madison Square Garden.

"But this fight business, she no picnic," Godoy said. "A fighter he try to win best way he know how. Sometimes rules they get in way a little bit—so best sometimes forget about rules. Louey and me we fighting for big championship. Louey, he world champion. I got to win this, and how. I try best way I can. Maybe I get a little rough Friday night. Louey he should no be scared. I no mind if he try little bit rough stuff too. That make good fight, no?"

To the press's surprise, they learned that Godoy was almost entirely Indian. His father was a full-blooded South American Indian of the Auracano tribe. Both his mother and father had the name Godoy. Based on an antiquated Spanish custom, it entitled Arturo to call himself Godoy-y-Godoy. He was born in a little seaport town in Chili and worked as an angler until he entered the army.

"I had no idea of being a boxer until I got in the army," Godoy told a reporter. "One day I put on the gloves for the first time. I didn't care much about it then, but the captain told me I must be a boxer. He said I was made for it. After that, I did no work in the army but box every day. After that, I boxed amateur and won the championship of Chili. A man asked me to be a professional. I said no. I was a fisherman and had my family to think of. But he said he would give me money so I wouldn't have to fish and could fight. That's how I got started."

Godoy's first big victory occurred over the first famous South American heavyweight, Luis Firpo. Godoy had knocked Firpo down nine times in four rounds when the referee stopped the fight. Godoy belittled it. Poor Firpo was washed up, he explained. Godoy then confided that he was a fine swimmer and once held the one-hundred-yard title in his country. He proudly recalled, too, that he saved a woman in the surf in Miami when the waves were "very mad." Godoy fully dressed jumped in and made the rescue. Arturo disclosed that he was an exceptional tango and rhumba performer. He claimed that he had an offer to strut his art at Brooklyn's St. George Hotel.

American football fascinated Godoy. He stated football to be among his favorite games because so many could get hurt at it.

"If I had lived here, I would have played that game and done something," he said. "It is great stuff."

His fondest admirer as a fighter was his mother. She saw several films of Louis's battles. She wrote her son predicting that Louis would not last more than four rounds.

"Nobody will know Louis after you are through with him," Mom added.

Godoy's wife was a Chilean of Italian extraction. She stood in New York while her husband trained. She would not be attending the fight.

"We are expecting a baby soon," Godoy noted, smiling.[24]

With Godoy's hardest work behind him, the press turned their attention the day before the fight to the camp proprietor—Madame Bey.

Prizefighters are "lovely children," Madame Bey declared. She was counting on one of her boys to forget his charming manners and knock out the world heavyweight champion, Joe Louis, in the following night's heavyweight bout.

A reporter asked Madame Bey her opinion of Godoy against Louis.

"In my opinion, he is tougher than any man Louis has ever met," she said. "Of course, he's going to win—maybe even by a knockout."

As always, she predicted a win for one of her boys.

Reporters were still unbelieving of a woman running a successful camp for prizefighters, especially for a woman with the socialite, refined, aristocratic background of Madame Bey. She had developed a camp for some of the toughest men in the world. A reporter queried her about the business.

"It was the necessity of doing something," Madame Bey said of her entrance into the business that is now the "work of my life.

"But now I love my boys; they all seem like members of the family," she said. "I believe you can never make a success of any business unless you like it, and I certainly like mine."

She was asked about watching her boys fight.

"I stay by the radio, keep my ears closed, and practically die with nervousness."[25]

At his camp on the frozen shore of Pompton Lakes, New Jersey, Joe Louis trained for his ninth title defense. Louis's camp knew Godoy butted with his head. When Galento boxed Louis, Tony fought from a crouch in the first and third rounds, both of which he won. When he stood straight in the second and fourth rounds, Louis battered him. Godoy would fight from a crouch.

At his camp, Joe Louis developed a new punch for his fight with Arturo Godoy. It was a left uppercut, and like most of Louis's punches, it did damage. The strategy was designed not to knock Godoy down; the purpose was to straighten him up from his crouch. On his final day of hard training, Louis tried the left uppercut followed by a straight right in his workout several times against Emil Scholz of Boston, and each time the crouching Emil stood up straight.[22]

Tony Galento came to watch the champion work out on the final day. Tony gave Louis some unwanted advice. He figured Louis would win by a knockout if he got a good shot at Godoy.

"Hello, Joe—howya feel?" Galento shouted to Louis during the workout.

"It wouldn't surprise me if Godoy lasted the full fifteen rounds. He's a game guy and takes a punch well, and his awkward style will bother Joe. Louis always has trouble with anyone who bobs and weaves. I know I gave him a lot of trouble and so did Max Schmeling."

"I know that South American man is tough, and I ain't gonna take no chances with him," Louis said. "I aims to knock him out as quick as I can. Maybe in the first round."[26]

The Louis-Godoy world heavyweight championship occurred on February 9, 1940, at Madison Square Garden. The card drew a gate of 15,675 fans paying $88,523.89, a disappointment for a Louis fight. His previous Garden appearances each topped the $100,000 mark.

In Chile, there was fervor over the fight. Most of South America rooted for Godoy, especially Argentina. Chilean crowds gathered around loudspeakers at newspaper offices and cheered for Godoy to beat Louis. Chile's president, Pedro Aguirre Cerda, listened to the radio in his summer palace at Vina Delmar with friends and ministers riveted to the broadcast. Godoy's most ardent fan, his mother, listened in Iquique, a Pacific Coast port city in northern Chile. She had thought her son would be champion if he got past the fifth round.[27]

Arturo Godoy wore purple trunks with the letter G on the left pant leg. Joe Louis had black trunks with offset letters J and L on the left pant leg. Godoy's corner included the two men who had spent so much time with him at Madame Bey's Camp—Al Weill and Whitey Bimstein. Godoy, as taught, had no intension of slugging with Louis. His strategy was designed to stay out of range of Louis's superior punching power or tie him up in a clinch where his hits would have less effect.[28]

Joe Louis faced a style that baffled and frustrated him. He tried to find a spot for his famed punch on a crouching, bobbing Godoy, who came out for the first round so low his gloves brushed the canvas. Just as Al Weill had Godoy practice it at Madame Bey's Camp. Technically, it could have been ruled a knockdown, but the referee did not apply the exact measure of the rule when Godoy's gloves touched the canvas.[28] Godoy dove for Louis's thighs and then crept upward until he could bury his chin into Louis's neck, butting with his head and whaling away. The Garden erupted as the Chilean bulled the champion around the ring, often throwing looping punches with both hands. The press wrote that if they had the potency of a Galento punch, it would have been disastrous for Louis.[29]

The fight reached the fourteenth round when, to the surprise of everyone, Godoy planted not a punch but a kiss on Louis's face. Godoy never deviated from his planned tactics. When the bell rang opening the fifteenth and final round, Godoy was still strong. When the final bell sounded, Godoy grinned with joy. He had lasted fifteen rounds with the Brown Bomber. It was the first time any challenger had gone the distance with Louis since Tommy Farr two and a half years before. Louis was unmarked. Godoy's left eye was closed, his right eye puffy, and there was a cut on his cheek.[30] Whitey rushed into the ring to put his arms around the Chilean who hopped about. Al Weill followed, still barking orders to Godoy.

"Please, please, Arturo, listen, do what I tell you."[28]

It was no use; Godoy could not contain his enthusiasm. He went into his crouch, jumping into the air with joy several times as he awaited the verdict. Then the announcer uttered, "The winner and still world champion …" A thunder of boos swept from the Madison Square Garden rafters. Godoy's manager, Al Weill, waved his left hand in disgust, thinking they had won. It appeared close to many Garden fans. Godoy shrugged, held his arm in the air, and went over to congratulate Louis. He planted several kisses on the champion's left cheek. Louis looked more stunned than from any of the punches he received from Godoy's gloves.[28]

The judges rendered a split decision. Tommy Shorten, one judge, gave Godoy the fight with ten rounds to five. Referee Arthur Donovan gave Louis ten and Godoy five, the same as the Associated Press score sheet. The other judge, George Lecron, gave Louis ten, Godoy four, and called one even. The only rounds in which the three agreed were the third and eighth, both to Godoy, and the fourteenth for Louis. Godoy thought he deserved a draw, but the *New York Times* reported the decision as "eminently fair"—its reporter scoring it ten to five for Louis.[31] Other reporters had similar results. Godoy's punches had little effect on the Brown Bomber. The more punishing blows came from Joe Louis, who retained his title.[29]

In his dressing room, a reporter asked Louis what went wrong.

"What was wrong with me?" Joe said, "Huh, what's wrong with him? He bobs around and keeps butting you in the head. It sure is hard to hit him."

"When Godoy kissed me in the fourteenth round that was a new one on me," Louis said.

In the other dressing room, Al Weill rushed Godoy under a shower. He explained his fighter's effort.

"I think Godoy won the fight—at least he should have got a draw, in my opinion. He was only hurt by one punch early in the fight."

Godoy gave a different version of the kissing episode.

"Louis kissed me with his best punch, and it had no effect, so I just kissed him right back. He is a fine, clean fighter—the cleanest I ever met.

"Boy, he hurt me once in the fifth, but it wasn't a staggering punch. He is a wonderful puncher.

"Sure, I want a return match but not until after one more fight. I'd like to get Tony Galento. You know I beat him twice. I think I'm entitled to another crack at Louis."[30]

The Chilean president, Pedro Aguirre Cerda, cabled Godoy, "Congratulations on your valiant, plucky fight."[27]

Most Chileans regarded it as a moral victory for Godoy. They saw him as a hero in defeat. He proved a worthy opponent for the world's best fighter. South America had its best fight since Louis Firpo had knocked champion Jack Dempsey out of the ring. Fans in Argentina objected to the decision. The Buenos Aires newspaper *El Mundo* printed, "… all radio listeners … gained the impartial feeling that the Chilean fighter gave the same thing and the decision was unjust." *La Nacion* in Buenos Aires printed that Louis got the "smelly benefit of the doubt" but lost prestige in the fight.

The next day, the boxing world was abuzz with the name of Arturo Godoy. Many figured that a return meeting during the outdoor season the following summer was a certainty. The *New York Times* printed, "Louis won sloppily against a bruising, mauling, and rushing fighter that knew no fear or retreat."

Godoy received $13,540.10. Champion Louis took $32,848.81. Louis received 40 percent of the purse against Arturo's 17 percent. Godoy wore dark glasses the next day because of the bruises to his eyes. Louis's face appeared unmarked except for a slightly bruised right ear.[32]

Al Weill softened his fight assessment from his words the day before. He thought that maybe Louis had won.

"But if we'd had a fight under our belts—Godoy's been idle since last August—we'd have took it," Weill said. "We'll lick Louis in the return next summer."

Al Weill and Whitey Bimstein could not dwell on the Godoy fight. They had another fighter at Bey's Camp—Lou Ambers. The top Bey fighters were on a losing streak. Godoy lost in a valiant effort. Apostoli had the cold excuse but remained a fighter with his best years behind him. The lightweight champion Ambers appeared to be destined for the same result. He was to fight the undefeated Al "Bummy" Davis with a record of thirty-five wins, no losses, and two draws. In his last two fights, Davis beat Apostoli in the third round and Tippy Larkin in the fifth round. Ambers could take comfort in Whitey Bimstein's theory.

"Show me an undefeated fighter and I'll show a guy who's never fought anybody," Whitey once stated.

Fight experts were calling for the first knockout of Ambers in this contest. They figured that this was a preliminary fight toward a welterweight championship bout between Henry Armstrong and Davis. Ambers would not have to worry about his weight; the fight was in the welterweight division. Ambers's lightweight title would not be at stake.

Al "Bummy" Davis, born Albert Abraham Davidoff, stood five feet five inches, with short, wavy dark hair. He came from the Brownsville section of Brooklyn, New York, where he was idolized by the Jewish neighborhood. It was where the notorious Murder, Inc. originated. Davis possessed one of the hardest left hooks in the history of the sport. In 2003, *The Ring* magazine listed him as number fifty-four of the top one hundred Greatest Punchers. Al was called Boomy or Vroomy as a child by his family, but his nickname was changed to Bummy by his manager, Johnny Attell, prior to Davis's first professional fight in May 1937. Upon learning of his new nickname, Davis stormed into Attell's office.

"… I don't want to be called Bummy."

"… You want to make money fighting, don't you? People like to come to fights to see guys they think are tough," Attell responded.[33]

His toughness was solidified in 2003 when he became the subject of the book *Bummy Davis vs. Murder, Inc.: The Rise and Fall of the Jewish Mafia and an Ill-Fated Prizefighter*, by Ron Ross. Murder, Inc. was the name the press gave to groups in the 1930s through the 1940s that acted as the enforcement for American organized crime, composed of principally Jewish Americans and Italian Americans from the Brooklyn neighborhoods of Brownsville, East New York, and Ocean Hill.[34] Davis was known for his street fights as well as those in the ring.

Whitey and Weill prepared Ambers, who had won his last twelve bouts. On February 23, 1940, with a gate of $66,749, the two met at Madison Square Garden. Al Davis's left hooks to the stomach and ribs hurt Ambers in the first four rounds. He was wincing and appeared worried, but he weathered the punches. In the fifth round, the fight shifted in favor of Ambers as he showed his great boxing ability. Ambers out-boxed his man with swings to the jaw, and Bummy seemed bewildered and tired. When he clinched, Ambers jerked him away so viciously that Bummy was thrown into the ropes. Bummy's lips were bleeding, and at the end of the seventh, his left eye was swollen. Ambers continued the punishment with his rapid-fire punches through the last three rounds, staggering him at the bell in the ninth.

Referee Billy Cavanaugh scored the fight eight to one, Judge Bill Healy eight to two, and Judge George LeCron seven to two. Lou Ambers, weighing seven and a half pounds less than his opponent, out-boxed and outgunned the bigger Davis, handing him his first loss. After the fight, Davis admitted Lou was "a better man than I am."[35]

Tippy Larkin, the man Ambers and Apostoli had showered with praise, returned to Bey's in March. He had a bout against a fighter gaining recognition fast—Lew Jenkins. Jenkins was a fighter with one of the most powerful right hands for his weight class. He was a small, skinny, lanky-looking man from Texas. His bushy, wild hair befitted his lifestyle. Jenkins was unpredictable, an alcoholic, and known for fights in and out of the ring. He would say, "I was born with a gift—a gift to punch and a gift to drink."[36] Journalists called him the Living Death, the Sweetwater Swatter, and the Texas Tarantula. He wasted his chances in the ring and fought many times under the influence. He could be found in a bar hours before a fight. He did some of his training inebriated and preferred riding his high-speed motorcycles to roadwork. Jenkins sought self-destructive behavior even when training for a big fight.

Jenkins was one of the better and most aggravating fighters to come along in recent years. His boxing career started with great difficulty. Before becoming recognized, he would know privation, defeat, and discouragement. He had worked as a cotton picker and an unskilled fighter. He began his boxing career in carnivals. He fought in small towns, living in boarding houses and tourist cabins. When times were even tougher than usual, he slept in his old, dilapidated car that transported him between towns. He had to fight to live. For his efforts, he received only coffee, cake, rent money, and sometimes there scarcely existed enough of that.[37]

On March 8, 1940, at Madison Square Garden, Jenkins landed a straight right to the chin of Larkin in the first round. The punch staggered Larkin. As he started going down, Jenkins hit him with a left hook. The referee counted Larkin out at two minutes, forty-one seconds of the opening round. Larkin's seconds carried him back to his stool by his corner.[38] Jenkins stood now as a logical choice to fight Ambers for the world lightweight title.

Despite the setback, Larkin would continue his quest. He encountered a non-boxing setback in 1942 when he accidentally shot himself while cleaning his .22-caliber rifle. Larkin said he was "ashamed to admit it, but I didn't know the gun was loaded."[39] The wound only kept him out of the ring for three months. In 1946, Larkin would win the world junior welterweight title and finished his career with 137 wins, fifteen losses, and one draw.

CHAPTER 33

He Could Remedy All but Death

Early in 1940, Joe Jacobs negotiated a Max Baer-Tony Galento bout with promoter Mike Jacobs set for March 4 at Madison Square Garden. The bout winner was to get a title match with Joe Louis. Tony Galento remained the number-one challenger for Joe Louis's heavyweight crown in early January after the fight with Baer had been scheduled. Tony would train at Madame Bey's for the fight.

Tony sat on a bar stool in his tavern and talked about the upcoming fight. His only interest in boxing—the glory it offered.

"I've got a few bucks now," Tony said. "I don't have to worry about money, but I'm gonna murder that Maxie Baer and then meet Joe Louis in June. I want the championship but only for the glory of it."[1]

Joe Jacobs's license to manage Galento remained under suspension with the New York Athletic Commission. Representatives of both charity funds for the fight, promoter Mike Jacobs, friends of Joe Jacobs, and boxing writers tried getting the commission to lift the suspension.

"Three times in the past, we have relented with Joe Jacobs when he was completely in the wrong," Commissioner John J. Phelan replied.

"No license, no Galento," Joe Jacobs said.

"No Jacobs, no Galento, no fight," Tony said.[2]

Unable to stage the fight in New York, it had to be delayed until May at Roosevelt Stadium in Jersey City, New Jersey. Joe Jacobs's license was good in New Jersey.

On April 24, 1940, the little man with the big cigar would no longer cause friction with the New York Boxing Commission. Joe Jacobs, one of boxing's most influential managers, succumbed to a heart attack. Madame Bey and Joe Jacobs had forged a friendship with a professional rapport. He was a fixture at her camp from the early days until his death. Madame Bey pointed Jacobs toward boxers in need of managing help. His skills as a manager had always been clear to her. Jacobs brought some of his best to her camp for some of their biggest fights.

The Jewish American manager was feisty, irrepressible, and sometimes irresponsible, but it was always to get the best deal for his fighter. His quick wit and flashy dress made him one of boxing's characters. He left behind two enduring quotes. He uttered, "We was robbed" after the Schmeling-Sharkey fight. Another of Jacobs's pronouncements had nothing to do with boxing, made while he was attending a World Series game in Chicago on a cold, raw afternoon when he remarked, "I should of stood in bed."

Jacobs even dared to visit Germany when the Jewish persecution was beginning—so audacious was he that he carried through the trip in a grand manner. He alienated his people and raised the ire of those that wanted to destroy them. There had been uproar over a photo of a Schmeling victory in 1935 Germany depicting Jacobs giving the Nazi salute with a cigar in his hand and winking at Schmeling.[3] The Nazis were furious at what they perceived as a Jew mocking the salute. The Jews were mad at one of theirs, giving the salute. On his return to America, Jacobs told outraged friends, "The *Heil* didn't count because the fingers of my other hand were crossed behind my back."

He talked his way out of many tight situations of his own making. He tried to do the same hours before his death when diagnosed with a heart problem. Jacobs's last day started much like a routine day. He spent several hours with Tony Galento in New Jersey in connection with a publicity stunt being arranged for Tony's upcoming battle with Max Baer. Harry Mendel, his friend and promoter of six-day bicycle races, said Joe Jacobs complained of stomach pain. Jacobs did not regard his illness as serious and went about his day as usual. He escorted motion picture photographers to New Jersey to film Galento. He laughed and joked with the movie photographers. Joe Jacobs and Tony posed for pictures behind the bar in Tony's tavern.[4] A newsreel made portrayed the two fighters, Galento and Baer, in conversation, Jacobs's last publicity stunt.

Jacobs left for New York with Harry Mendel. One of the last known pictures of Joe Jacobs appeared in the newspaper the next day with a caption—"Joe Jacobs shown with Tony Galento a few hours before the fight manager died of a heart attack."[5] The picture had been taken in Galento's tavern in Orange, New Jersey, where the little man and the fighter entertained friends. Galento recalled Jacobs had managed him for five years.

Around four o'clock in the afternoon, Joe Jacobs had a conference with promoter Mike Jacobs. They discussed some details of the impending Galento-Baer match. Joe said nothing to the promoter of feeling ill. Shortly after, when he rejoined Mendel, Joe again complained of a pain in his stomach. At Mendel's insistence, they visited the office of Dr. Vincent A. Nardiello. Joe said he thought he had indigestion. He took it as a joke when the doctor advised him a heart condition had developed and that he must consult a specialist at once.[4] Joe Jacobs, trying to talk his way out of a tough spot as he had done in the fight game, laughed. He told the doctor he should go back to medical school.[3] At Dr. Nardiallo's insistence, Joe went with Mendel to the office of Dr. Oswald La Rotunda on Fifth Avenue in New York. He was explaining why he had come and had just taken off his coat when the big cigar dropped from his mouth,[4] and he collapsed into Mendel's arms. Five minutes later at 6:45 in the evening, he was pronounced dead[6] of a heart attack at the age of forty-three.

At Galento's tavern, the news first was told to Jimmy Frain, Tony's trainer. Tony was stunned when notified of his manager's death and cried. Tony could not believe his manager had died shortly after leaving him in Orange, New Jersey. Galento rushed to the New York offices of Dr. Oswald La Rotundo. Tears rolled unashamedly down his face as Harry Mendel, in whose arms Jacobs collapsed, led him to the body. The tough Galento, visibly shaken, was red-eyed and grief-stricken.

"Come on Joey, come back, wake up," Tony sobbed.[7]

After, Galento addressed the press.

"I'm awful sorry. I've lost a good friend. I'm awful sorry," Tony said in an unfamiliar soft tone.[8]

The next day, Tony said he might seek postponement of his scheduled fight with Max Baer.

"I don't know what I am going to do," Tony declared as he sat in the back of his tavern. "Joe was more than a manager to me. I've lost the best pal a guy ever had. How can I think about training, about anything right now?"

"If I find I can't pull myself out of this frame of mind, then I will ask promoter Mike Jacobs to postpone the bout. But I won't decide on anything definitely until after the funeral Sunday."[9]

The midtown Riverside Chapel received the body. Many of New York's fight managers, most top sportswriters, a smattering of city and state political figures, fighters, actors, and gamblers came to pay tribute to the fight game's legendary figure, including Herman Taylor, Abe Greene, Dan Morgan, Billy McCarney, Hymie Caplin, Abe Attell, Benny Valger, and Max Waxman. Among others, there were brothers, Benjamin and Caswell Jacobs; two sisters, Mrs. May Grieb and Miss Rose Jacobs; and Jacob's fiancée, Connie Drake. The honorary pallbearers were Tony Galento, Harry Mendel, Max Baer, James Braddock, General John J. Phelan, and Jimmy Johnston.[10] Some pallbearers had had differences with Joe Jacobs, and among themselves, but they put it aside in honor of one of the greatest fight managers. Rabbi Ginsburg explained that because of the Passover, he was not permitted to deliver a eulogy, "but one cannot help realizing," he said, "that the greatest eulogy that could be given is represented by the men and women here to pay their last respects to the one they loved."[11]

The press said they had lost a man whose antics and accomplishments probably never would be equaled.

"He was the most colorful manager who ever lived; boxing will miss him," promoter Mike Jacobs said.

"He was the most colorful figure, in the fight game, bar none. The whole sport, from Philadelphia to Keokuk will miss him," promoter Herman Taylor said.[12]

From Germany, Schmeling said, "I'm deeply shocked and sorry. It is too bad, for boxing loses a man who has done a lot for it. Joe and I always got along well together."[13]

Burial occurred at the family plot in Long Island. His controversial stances alienated him from his Jewish people and boxing commissions, but there were few managers with his skills.

Tony would proceed without his friend and manager to train for the Max Baer bout. Joe Jacobs's last publicity stunt proceeded without him. It promoted the Galento-Baer bout. The two fighters did not like each other.

"He's the only fighter I ever hated," Baer said of Tony.

When it meant more money toward their gate, they could appear as best of friends. The newsreel started with Tony behind his Orange, New Jersey, bar serving beer. Then he drank his beer as Joe Jacobs stood beside him with a cigar protruding from the left corner of his mouth. Tony wore casual clothes. Jacobs wore a suit and tie. The scene switched to a truck parked on the roadside with Baer talking into the telephone.

"Hello, operator. Operator would you give me Galento's dumb, I mean tavern in Orange, New Jersey."

"Hello, who is this?" Tony queried. "This is Galento's joint."

"Hello Tony," Baer replied, "how are you? Yeah, this is the man you're going to fight. The fella that's a bum. Yes, that's me."

"Why you big bum, what you startin' that stuff. That's my line you big bum. I'm gonna moider you ..."

"Ah, say listen, Tony, I'd like to speak to you, so would you put your interpreter on. Yes, alright, thanks."

"Hello, this is Max Baer. Say, I just wanted to call you up and let you know that I'm gonna knock that fella out of yours when I fight him this coming twenty-eighth day of May. Yeah, you know that muscle-bound fighter that you work for. You do the interpreting for him, don't you? Yeah, well, that's swell. Just convey that message to him."[14]

Tony would train at Madame Bey's for Baer, but first, two other noteworthy fighters would be there—Lou Ambers and Ken Overlin.

August 22, 1939, was the day that world lightweight champion Ambers won against Henry Armstrong. That date was the last time Ambers made the 135-pound lightweight limit for a fight. It was no longer a secret that Ambers had difficulty making weight. He would risk his lightweight title against Lew Jenkins on May 10, 1940, at Madison Square Garden.

Ambers had to work hard to make the weight. He deviated from the training pattern he had followed ever since he moved up among the fight game's best. He weighed 139 pounds getting into the ring at Madame Bey's a few days before the fight. He would have to forego most of Bey's cooking. Two days before the fight, Ambers weighed 137 pounds. Two pounds in two days was the forewarning coming from Madame Bey's Camp. Cheerful, as always, Ambers boxed for the last time two days before fight day. Ambers went through ten rounds of preparation boxing with young Austin McCann, former Golden Gloves Champion. He then did three rounds of shadowboxing, two skipping the rope, and two on the punching bag. He was working hard.

An assembly of experts scrutinized Ambers from the ringside with unease. Championship fights do that to the experts; they examine, hunting for ways the champion would lose. They shook their heads when Ambers took right counters from the youthful McCann and hit the floor, partially from slipping, during the second round. He was hit with many rights, but a left hook from McCann knocked down Ambers. Despite the right hands, Ambers fought well against McCann.

"I never saw Ambers get hit with so many right hands," one observer said.

"And if Jenkins hits him with a right hand, he'll know it," another said.

Later, Ambers explained the sparring session while on the rubbing table.

"Yeah, I did get hit with a lot of right hands. You know, one of these days I'm going to get sore. You are nice to those kids that box with you … They know it's your last day of boxing, and you're careful. So, they get tough and bait you around. I'll get sore someday and belt them around."[15]

At Jenkins's camp, someone asked about his weak left punch. With considerable ire, Jenkins answered his critics.

"Just because I haven't used my left hand around New York doesn't say I haven't got one. I just didn't use it much because I didn't have to. The only time I really used my left was in my second fight around here against Primo Flores. That didn't quite finish the job because I hit him a little high, so I tossed my right and that was that, but the newspapermen seemed to forget that it was really the left that did the damage."

Jenkins's camp believed it had found a flaw in Ambers's impenetrable defense, and they had Jenkins throwing punches with his left hand. Throughout his career, Ambers was dropped to the canvas by two men—once by Tony Canzoneri and twice by Henry Armstrong in their first meeting. Those knockdowns resulted from right-hand punches. Al "Bummy" Davis, touted as one of the hardest-hitting left handers of the decade, had ten rounds to knock out Ambers, and although he hurt him with a couple of hard hits, he lost.

Ambers and Al Weill at Madame Bey's heard the strategy of Jenkins using his left more than his powerful right.

"It would be just perfect for us," Al Weill said, "if Jenkins depends too much on his left hand. That guy is strictly a one punch fighter, with the right hand. If he goes in there forgetting his right, he'll be going in there with nothing at all."[16]

The day before the fight, Ambers being overweight persisted. The scaled signaled to everyone that he had to lose two more pounds. That forced him to work hard. He did not box but did ten rounds of floor work, shadowboxing, skipping rope, bag punching, and calisthenics that could make him weak. Still, Ambers sweated to make the weight. If it weakened him enough, it would give Jenkins the advantage. Al Weill pretended not to regard the matter seriously. Whitey reflected Weill's sentiment of unconcern.

It was not the right hand or Jenkins that was the chief concern of those guiding Ambers through his workouts but the two pounds remaining. They wanted Ambers to be strong and sharp, and they were hoping that such a small thing as losing two pounds would not dull him. Fight day would give them the answer.

Ambers had to be hospitalized before the fight.[17] It resulted from the consequences to his body caused by his attempts to make the 135-pound weight limit. Somehow, he recovered in time as the fight approached.

A crowd of 13,186 contributed to a gross gate of $57,992 on May 10, 1940, at Madison Square Garden. Ambers lacked speed from the strain of making the 135-pound limit. In the opening round, Jenkins unleashed his right hand into the champion's face. For the first time in a year, Ambers went down. He recovered and endured for the rest of the round. In the second, Jenkins connected with another right, and Ambers hit the canvas. On each of these first two knockdowns, Ambers rose at the count of five, too disorientated from the blows to take the full nine seconds.[18]

In the third, Ambers went down twice. He took a six count, then a nine count. They were both from vicious right hands; Jenkins was in no need of his left. Shaken, Ambers took a two-handed beating in his own corner when referee Billy Cavanaugh halted it at one minute, twenty-nine seconds of the third round. Jenkins's ferocious right-hand punches absorbed by Ambers were hard to watch. Ambers, down four times in three rounds, lost the lightweight championship to a three-to-one underdog. Ambers experienced the first technical knockout of his career.

Jenkins, not one for modesty, said, "I should have knocked him out in the first round," which he came close to achieving.[19] The crowd roared its surprise as not even the experts could predict the rugged Ambers could be knocked out. Al Weill said his fighter was through with the lightweight division. He would vacation through the summer and then come back as a welterweight.[18]

In May, Ken Overlin came to Bey's for a chance at the world middleweight title. He would face the Filipino Ceferino Garcia at Madison Square Garden on May 23.

The twenty-nine-year-old Overlin had a record of 108 wins with seventeen knockouts, seventeen losses, and five draws. He had little power but brilliant boxing ability. He had been boxing for ten years with few scars to show for it. *The Ring* magazine featured him on the cover of the May 1937 issue. That same year he lost a world middleweight title bout to champion Freddie Steele in September. Overlin's odds were nine to five against wresting the middleweight title from Garcia, who had never lost a middleweight fight. Garcia won the title in the previous year from Apostoli. As with so many others, Garcia would prepare at Pompton Lakes for an opponent, Overlin, training at Bey's Camp.

Overlin was from Decatur, Illinois. For seven years, Overlin served as a sailor in the navy. He served on the USS *Tennessee* and then the USS *Idaho*. Overlin fought professionally while in the navy and had been fighting ever since he was discharged, which was ten years before arriving at Bey's Camp. He had nearly two hundred fights and was growing old as a fighter before getting his first chance at the championship. He fought often with a few days of training between bouts. Overlin did not travel outside of America until discharged from the navy. He had been across the country, fighting anywhere his manager, Chris Dundee, would place him. He fought many tough middleweights. Going to Europe and Australia, he fought in Paris, Melbourne, and Sydney.

This would be the first time he had been in a training camp. He said nothing to disparage Madame Bey but equated being at a camp to prison. He left Madame Bey a signed photographed inscribed, "Your a very dear person—Thanks a million for everything." At Bey's, he said as well as he could remember he had 173 fights, in dispute with the official record, which was not always accurate. He said he liked to fight, liked moving about the world, and always enjoyed himself between fights. He was known as someone who went to bed just as the sun was coming up and stayed there until it had gone down. If you asked, and you had to ask, he would tell you about his late-night exploits, nightclubbing, and women.

Overlin's manager, Chris Dundee, was born Cristofo Mirena in Philadelphia on February 23, 1908. He adopted the name Dundee from the world featherweight champion, and his idol, Johnny Dundee. In 1930, he had his first world champion, flyweight Hall of Famer Midget Wolgast. He would later guide Ezzard Charles to the world heavyweight title in 1949. He would promote many fights, most notable the first Muhammad Ali-Sonny Liston world heavyweight title bout in 1964. He was the older brother to the more famous Angelo Dundee. His younger brother, Angelo, during his career, trained Muhammad Ali, George Foreman during Foreman's comeback, Sugar Ray Leonard, Carmen Basilio, Willie Pastrano, and James Tillis among others. Chris Dundee would operate the Fifth Street Gymnasium in Miami Beach starting in the 1950s, where his brother, Angelo, came to help him. The gymnasium flourished. It became an attraction for celebrities like Jackie Gleason, Malcolm X, The Beatles, Sean Connery, Frank Sinatra, Sylvester Stallone, and others.

Overlin trained hard for his middleweight title opportunity that had been hard to obtain. He took the usual route at Bey's Camp, as so many had done before him. There were the morning jogs, breakfast, rest, afternoon rope skipping, bag punching, and sparring. In the evening, he ate dinner, had some downtime activity, and then went to sleep. He had gotten into top shape and felt strong. His confidence was apparent, and he would let anyone know that when asked.

The vanquisher of Lou Ambers, Henry "Homicide Hank" Armstrong, came to Madame Bey's to help Overlin with his sparring. Armstrong had fought Garcia in March to a draw. When Garcia heard Armstrong went to Bey's to coach Overlin, he asked the boxing commission to warn Overlin against thumbing and head-butting.[20] Garcia would not have to worry; that was not Overlin's style.

A few days before the fight, Frank Graham from the *New York Sun* came to Bey's to write about Overlin in his column "Setting the Pace." Overlin sat in a dressing room. He was about to go to the training ring, wearing a quarter-sleeved, white shirt and an old pair of blue trunks.

"How does it feel to be fighting for a title after all these years, Ken?" Johnny Attell, a former little-known lightweight, asked him.

"Swell," he said, "but I'm paying for it by doing time up here."

"How long have you been here?" somebody else asked.

"Do you want the answer in weeks, days, or hours?" he asked.

"Weeks."

"Three," he said.

Overlin looked out the window across the hills.

"I hope it don't do me any harm," he said.

Overlin left the dressing room for the outdoor ring. He slipped through the ropes and shadowboxed a few rounds. His first sparring partner, Al Bernard, got into the ring. Bernard and Overlin fought the year before in Houston, and he gave Overlin a good battle. Overlin liked him and hired him to work with him at Bey's Camp.

"You box four rounds today," Chris Dundee said.

"I'll box five," Overlin replied. "I feel good today. I felt lousy yesterday, but I feel good today, and I want to work."

"Four rounds," Dundee said.

"Five," Overlin said.

He winked at those sitting at the ringside.

"You didn't care how many rounds I boxed last year," Overlin added. "You managed me by wire. I'd get a wire saying: 'Go to Chicago and fight' or 'Go to Frisco and fight.' And I'd just go by myself. Now I'm a big shot, you're around telling me how many rounds to box."

Overlin boxed three rounds with Bernard and two with a Cuban welterweight named Joe Legon, who fought somewhat in the manner of Garcia but faster. This was the first time he had boxed with Legon.

"I wish I had had him up here for a week," Overlin said.

Finished with his workout, Overlin went back to his dressing room, stripped, and lay on the rubbing table where Eddie Ross, his trainer, rubbed him down.

"Be careful with that Garcia when you get him in there," Bill Farnsworth, an American sportswriter, editor, and boxing promoter, said. "He's an old man, you know."

"Yeah," Overlin said. "I know. I know all about these old men. I went into Louisville one night to fight Henry Firpo, and he was an old man, too. Ever see him? He's a bald-headed old guy, and he looked at me in the dressing room and laughed, and he said:

"'I'll give you ten good rounds tonight, young fellow.'

"He did, too. Ten of the toughest rounds I ever had. They had put Vaseline on that bald head of his, and I'd throw a punch at him, and he'd duck and my glove would hit that Vaseline and slip off the top of his head. And he'd rough me around and belt me, and he knew all the tricks. I beat him, but I was glad when the fight was over. We got back to the dressing room, and he said to me:

"'When I was good, I could lick a dozen young punks like you in one night.'

"And I said, 'Well, I'm glad you ain't good anymore because you are tough enough now.'

"I know these old men, and they're never easy to lick. But I'll slow this Garcia down after four rounds and then you'll see Overlin begin to go to town."

Overlin's trainer, Ross, wiped Overlin with a towel as he lay on the rubdown table, and somebody asked him how he started to fight.

"I come from Decatur, Illinois," he said, "and things were pretty tough around our house. I worked as a bellhop and at one or two other jobs, but I could never make any dough, and I figured if I got away, there would be one less mouth to feed. So, I joined the navy. They put me on the *Tennessee,* and we were out in Seattle, Washington, and I was taking part in athletics on the ship. I played football and basketball and one time when we were ashore for rifle practice one of the sailors said to me:

"'I can get a fight for you. Want to fight?'

"I said, 'No. I ain't mad at anybody. If I want to fight I'll pick the guy myself.'

"But when this fellow said he could get $25 for me, that was different. I said sure, I'd fight. So, I licked the guy and got $25, and they put me back the next week, and I licked another guy and got $75. They paid me off in silver dollars, and I had them all in one pocket of my pants, and they were so heavy I was listing when I walked out of the joint.

"After that, everywhere my ship put in I got a fight if I could. I was in Norfolk for a long while when I was on the *Idaho.* Those battleships don't get around much and all

I ever saw in the seven years I was in the navy were the two coasts and the Canal. Well, when I was in Norfolk, I fought in the town a good deal, and I used to get twenty-four hours' leave and ride up to Philadelphia on the bus and fight and then take the night bus back and be on board ship again by seven-thirty the next morning.

"One time a fighter named Joe Comiskey came down there to fight. His manager was looking for a soft touch and when the matchmaker told him he had a sailor for him, he thought he had just the fellow he was looking for. But I beat Comiskey, and his manager is screaming. He says, 'He's a fine sailor! He knows more about fighting than Comiskey.'

"You know who your friends are when you're in the navy," he said.

He sat up and began to put on his socks.

"Two sailors came all the way up from Norfolk yesterday to see me train," he said. "All the way from Norfolk just to see me train, and I looked lousy. If they are going to bet, I know who they're going to bet on. I wish they'd seen me today."[21]

By the night's end on May 23, 1940, at Madison Square Garden, Bey's had produced another world champion. Most experts expected Garcia to defeat his foe with his famed right-hand punch. Instead, the defending champion allowed the challenger to dictate the fight. Overlin proceeded to outpoint him. The decision was unanimous. The official scorecards were ten to five, seven to six with two even, and nine to six with one even, all in favor of Overlin. He was the new world middleweight champion.

On May 27, Tony Galento went to New York. He visited Mike Jacobs to provide a $2,500 forfeit fee for the Max Baer fight,[22] the last fight his late manager, Joe Jacobs, arranged. With Joe Jacobs's death, the fight was rescheduled for July 2. Tony, for the first time in five years, would not have Joe Jacobs in his corner. On May 29, Tony would start training at Joe Jacobs's frequently used camp—Madame Bey's Camp.

On June 23, Joe Louis came to Madame Bey's to watch Tony train. Louis had just fought Arturo Godoy for a second time on June 20 and won by an eighth-round technical knockout. Godoy went down once in the seventh round and was saved by the bell. He hit the canvas twice in the eighth round. After the second knockdown in the eighth, the referee stopped the fight. Godoy charged Louis's corner wanting to continue. His manager, Al Weill, grabbed him; he was in no condition to continue. Louis appeared unmarked from the fight. Godoy was unable to stay away from Louis's punishment as he did in the first fight, and his bloodied face showed the result. Godoy said "he could take it," and he did, receiving thirty-four hard right hands from Louis in the seventh and eighth rounds.[23] Godoy had trained for the fight in Carmel, New York.

The fight mob, what the constant posse of sportswriters and people associated with boxing called themselves, was at Bey's Camp. Louis was there to publicize the Galento-Baer bout for Mike Jacobs.[24] Before the workout commenced, Tony posed with Louis and Tony's young son for newsreel footage and photographs. Two-Ton Galento's son, Tony Jr., was dubbed One-Ton Galento by the press.[25]

Tony, with his hands taped, put boxing gloves on his son. He crouched over and struck a boxing pose toward his son. With unadulterated innocence, Tony Jr. stuck the right glove under his left side and slid it off. He extended his bare hand in an offer of peace to his father causing the crowd to laugh. Next, Joe Louis entered the ring and examined Tony's taped left hand; Louis's face was expressionless. After the photographers had their pictures, Louis put Tony's hand down and returned to his seat.[25]

Galento used a new combination mask and headgear when he boxed for protection from possible cuts in training. It was a padded black leather mask built on a wire frame. Only spaces for his eyes and mouth kept his face from being completely obscured. It was the first time he had used it and bespoke further thought about his condition. It protected his eyes and scars from cuts received over the years. The media wrote it made him appear to be a Martian and called it the Man from Mars headgear.[26] He got the idea from Henry Armstrong, who also used a similar headgear in training.

Louis sat quietly through a half-hour workout while Galento sustained a constant banter that turned the workout into his usual show. Spectators numbering no fewer than five hundred came to watch, fewer than the numbers Tony and Joe drew separately at their camps when they were pitted against each other. Each customer paid sixty cents to see the workout, which was less than the camp received in earlier days. They were amused by Tony's antics. He did not quit talking from the time he started to shadowbox until he finished with skipping the rope. He kept the chatter flowing through two sparring partners and then on the light and heavy bags.

The conversation, strictly one-way, consisted of continual plugs for his tavern in Orange, New Jersey, and innumerable references to bums, Max Baer being one of the several cited. Galento interrupted his buffoonery once for seriousness, saying that Louis was the cleanest fighter he had ever fought. That brought applause that had no effect on Louis. Then Galento went back to show how to knee, butt, and backhand, having the crowd laughing again.

His sparring partners were Phil Johnson and Eddie Cameron. Tom Schenck, who had been a Galento sparring partner for two years, watched the workout from a ringside seat with tape and plaster stretched across the front of his face. Galento broke Schenck's nose in a previous workout.

"This guy wants to knock Baer out fast," promoter Mike Jacobs, also present, leaned over and said. "He wants to win this one more than any other and show he can do it alone."

Tony not quite on his own with Joe Jacobs gone had hired two managers to replace Joe Jacobs. They were Muggsy Taylor and Harry Mendel, Joe Jacobs's friend and whose arms he fell into upon his death.

When it was over, Louis said Galento looked strong and that he was punching fast. He said Tony looked in good shape. Louis was asked to pick a winner.

"I'm not picking anyone," Louis said, and then drove with companions to Atlantic City, where he would vacation until Galento and Baer fought.[24]

On June 27, Madame Bey was scheduled to appear on the radio show *Strange As It Seems*. The show featured people and events that were extraordinary. A woman running a camp for prizefighters satisfied that category. She would discuss her camp and Tony Galento. Two newspapers printed, "Mme. Bey, pug-trainer, on *Strange As It Seems,*" and "How Tony Galento keeps his place among the world's topflight heavyweights on a year round training diet of beer and pretzels will be disclosed by Madame Hranoush Bey, famed proprietress of the Summit, New Jersey, pugilistic training camp, when she is a guest on the *Strange As It Seems* program. Thursday, WABC, 7:30 p. m. Galento is now preparing for his July 2 bout with Max Baer at Madame Bey's Camp."[27]

Less than a week before the fight, a group waiting to see Tony train stood in front of the gymnasium, on a knoll by the roadside in front of Madame Bey's Camp. The air was damp and the grounds wet from a recent rain. An automobile came roaring up and stopped suddenly as the brakes were jammed on. Tony arrived. He climbed out of his automobile and shook hands with some newspapermen who had come from New York and waved his hand to the others. He then went through the gymnasium and down the stairs to his dressing room.

The room was filled with trainers, handlers, newspapermen, and others. Tony took off his clothes. He said little as he struggled into his training attire. The little he had to say was about his new tavern and what a celebrity he was in Orange, New Jersey.

"When I go away," he said, "I send the Mayor a card, and the only address I put on it is his name and 'Tony Galento's Home Town,' and he gets it. Everybody knows me."

Tony started putting on his shoes.

"Tell me about this fight, Tony," a newspaperman from Newark, New Jersey, asked.

"What about it?" Tony replied.

"What will you do with him?"

"I'll knock him out."

"Well, give me some of the details. How do you expect to go about it?"

"I'll just walk out and knock him out," Tony said. "I hope the bum don't quit on me. I want to knock him out."

'When did you see him fight last?" somebody asked.

"I saw him the night he quit to Nova," Tony said. "He wanted to quit in the first round."

Tony spat on the floor.

"He was doing like that," Tony said.

"'Look, ref,' he says, 'I'm bleeding. I'm bleeding.' He wanted to quit in the first round, the bum."

"And what did the referee say to him?" Harry Mendel, one of Tony's managers prompted. "Go on. Tell them what the referee said."

"He said, 'Go ahead, quit, if you want to, you big yeller bum. I won't stop it.' That's what he said."

"Yes," Jimmy Frain, Tony's trainer, said. "We were sitting there, and we heard him. He says, 'I won't stop it. Go on an' quit if you want to.'"

Tony was bandaging and taping his hands.

"Did you hear what they said at Baer's camp?" a newspaperman asked.

"No."

"They said they wouldn't do anything if you got rough in the first two rounds and ignored warnings from the referee, but if you got rough in the third round, they will take Baer out of the ring."

Tony laughed.

"I won't get rough with him," he said. "I'll just hit him on the chin and knock his brains out."

He finished bandaging his left hand and smashed it against the wall.

"Look out for your hand," Mendel said.

"Look out for the wall," Muggsy Taylor, his other manager, said. "If you break it, we'll have to pay for it."

Galento bandaged his right hand and then took the strips of tape that Frain had stuck on the wall and put them over the bandage. He banged his fists together.

"Where am I going to work?" he asked.

"On the hill," Mendel said.

It had been raining, but the sky had cleared.

He threw a playful hook at a newspaperman standing near the door. The newspaperman defended himself with his arm, and Tony laughed.

"I'll break your arm," Tony said.

"Tony, what was the date of your fight with Louis?" a newspaperman asked.

"I don't know," Tony said.

"June 18," Mendel said.

"I forget," Tony said. "That's because I didn't beat him. If I beat him, I would remember the date, and I'd have his gloves hanging up over the bar in my joint."

He went out, and they followed him through the gymnasium back door to the outdoor ring on the hill. Storm clouds were gathering again, and as he punched the bag, the newspapermen suggested to Mendel that they move indoors. They went down the hill to the gymnasium as the wind whipped at the canvas walls about the outdoor ring, and big raindrops fell on them as thunder rolled over the hills.

In the gymnasium, Tony shadowboxed for a couple of rounds, and then Frain put the Man From Mars mask headgear on Tony that he wore while boxing.

"I ain't afraid of getting cut or butted with this thing on," Tony said.

He touched the scars on his face.

"I got all these in training," he said. "That's where you get those things. You don't get them in fights. You get them in training."

As Frain was lacing on his gloves, Tony turned to the crowd.

"Does anybody want me to haunt their house?" he asked, his eyes peering through the mask.

"How much do you charge?" a man asked.

"Cheap," Tony said. "A dollar and a half a room."

Tony boxed with Phil Johnson. Tom Schenck, whose nose was still broken from Tony the last Saturday, looked on.

"He's a mean man," Schenck said.

He did not seem to feel bad about his broken nose. He laughed and shook his head.

"You should have seen Tony," Mendel said. "Schenck is lying on the floor, and the blood is all over him, and Tony says, 'You must have a cold in the head, Tom,' and Schenck says, 'No, I ain't Mister Galento. You really hit me.'"

Galento continued his boxing. Billy McCarney, who was called the Old Professor, looked at him from a ringside seat. McCarney was an American boxing promoter who had been a part owner of Max Schmeling. He also managed heavyweights Luther McCarty and Natie Brown among others.

"He is a very remarkable fellow," McCarney said. "Look how quickly he came back from that beating he took from Louis. That was in June, and in September, you saw him against Nova in Philadelphia. Did you ever see a stronger, tougher fellow than he was that night? Nobody else that Louis ever beat came back as quickly as that. I know from the experience I had with my Natie Brown. A couple of months after Louis knocked him out, I threw him in with a fellow he used to lick every day in the gymnasium, and the fellow licked him. I thought it was a mistake, and six weeks later, I threw him in with the same fellow, and he got licked again. I asked him what was the matter with him, and he said, 'That colored man takes a lot out of you, Bill. I don't feel right yet.'

"But here is this fellow coming back so quickly, and you would never think anything ever happened to him."

In the ring, Galento walked up and down during the minute's rest between rounds.

"I got two managers now," he said to the crowd. "I would like to have you meet my managers. Muggsy Taylor and—er—er Harry Mendel. Stand up and take a bow. Two managers, ain't that something?"[28]

A few days before the fight, at the request of the New Jersey State Boxing Commission's Abe Greene, Dr. Louis H. Dodson visited Madame Bey's Camp for a second time in two months. He pronounced Tony "very fit." He concluded his heart, lungs, weight, blood pressure, and eyes were all good. Dr. Dodson would go to Pompton Lakes, where Max Baer trained, and gave him his approval.[29]

Another visitor, Arturo Godoy, his face still showing bruises and cuts from his second encounter with Joe Louis, sat at the ringside and watched Tony's clowning. It had been eight days since the Chilean lost to Joe Louis. Godoy's left cheekbone was puffed and hidden by sticking plaster, and there could be seen a long, brown scar where a dozen stitches had been in his eyebrow. Having fought and beaten Galento twice, Godoy did not go into elations about Tony.

"I don't think he's so strong as when he fought me," Godoy volunteered. "They can't be so strong again after having pneumonia. My brother in Chile had it once and he never was so good again.

"No, Tony don't hit like Louis. He hit me a left hook in our first fight that hurt, but he hits heavy punches, not sharp like Louis."

Godoy proceeded to discredit another theory about Tony that it was useless to work on the Galento midsection.

"I hit him once to the stomach in our first fight, and he didn't like it," Godoy recalled.

Godoy said he could not make a guess on the winner between Galento and Baer because he never had seen Baer in action. Galento jumped on the scales just before his workout.

"Two hunnert forty-eight and wit' my clothes on," Tony said.[30]

Tony's sparring partners were Phil Johnson, Ed Cameron, an inside puncher, and Steve who gave him the most trouble.[31] It was hard to distinguish Tony's boxing from his wrestling practice, both running concurrently. Several times, he heaved his partners around Madam Bey's outdoor ring. Tony boxed five rounds with the three sparring partners and punched the light and heavy bags. After the exercises, Godoy announced that Tony was much improved from the fat clown he twice outpointed three years ago.

Tony confided to the crowd all his business and building plans for the new "Chez Galento" in East Orange, a flashy block in which would be found the Galento liquor store, Galento tavern, Galento stores, and Galento community house for the convenience of all who wished to hear him on his favorite topic—Galento.

Afterward, Tony became enraged as two attorneys tried to interview him. As usual, it was a busy day for Tony, now approaching his best form. The lawyers came to see Tony after his workout had ended while he sat in a bath. They wanted to know the name of Galento's lawyer so they could complete the affairs of the estate of his late manager, Joe Jacobs. Galento saw in their actions an insidious move to take advantage of him. If there was one thing Tony disliked, being taken advantage of by anyone, in or out of the boxing ring.

He was about to explode when Herman Taylor, his comanager with Harry Mendel, counseled calm. With supreme effort, Tony met the men.

"I have nothing to say," Tony told them in a dignified manner. "I am resting from my workout, I wish to be alone. Here is my lawyer's card."[26]

Tony was not pleased that Max Baer was going to receive the same purse cut as he.

"Where does he come off to get as much dough as me?" Tony demanded. "We're fighting in Jersey, and I'm the drawing card, not him, the big quitting bum."

The clowning, the gabbing, and the exhibitionism was the Galento everyone had become accustomed to watching. Tony continued to perform daily through the week. He went home to Orange, New Jersey, every night where he ate his meals and counted the receipts in his tavern. There was no doubt that he had worked hard for the bout. He looked in good shape. He put in eighty-seven rounds of boxing while at Bey's Camp.[24]

The day before the fight with Baer, Tony asked Whitey Bimstein to ride back home with him that evening. Whitey agreed. The two arrived at Tony's tavern in Orange, New Jersey.

"The night before Tony Galento boxed Max Baer," Whitey recalled, "he said he wanted to go to his joint in East Orange from Madame Bey's Camp in Summit, New Jersey, and I rode over with him."

Tony argued with his brother, Russell, who wanted tickets to the fight. A broken beer bottle found Tony's face, attributed to his brother, and cut him. A doctor was needed to repair it with three stitches, and Whitey covered it with a flesh-colored pigment.[32] The event was much publicized before the bout.

Abe J. Greene, New Jersey's boxing commissioner, examined Tony's wound and determined it was "an abrasion." The gash left on Tony's chin would make an easy target for Max Baer, who was said to have learned about it. All he had to do was read about it in the newspapers.

"It is inconsequential and will only spur me to speedier victory," Galento said, according to Greene.[33]

Promoter Mike Jacobs announced the attendance of 22,711 paying $98,004. They fought at Roosevelt Stadium in Jersey City, New Jersey, under the floodlights of the ballpark on July 2, 1940. The same city where Dempsey and Carpentier drew the first million-dollar gate, and it was the nineteenth anniversary of that fight. Gone was the wooden bowl known as Boyle's Thirty Acres on the Jersey City flats where Tex Rickard called the Dempsey-Carpentier fight the Battle of the Century. The press called Mike Jacobs's fight the Battle of the Bums. Mike Jacobs's promotion did not come close to the 90,000 paying $1,626,580 nineteen years before.

Max drew blood in the first round when he hit Tony on the chin where his wound resided. In the second round, Baer slashed Tony's mouth, and Tony broke his left hand when he hit the top of Baer's head. In the seventh, Baer buckled Tony's knees, and a punch into the midsection from Baer at the end of the round caused Tony to grunt. Tony was unsteady as he retreated to his corner.[34]

"Tony's so tired," someone at ringside said, "that he couldn't answer his cash register's bell."

In the corner after the seventh round, blood dripped from the end of Tony's chin profusely.

"It's a bad cut, this way and that way!" A trainer, pointing to Galento's bloody mouth, shouted to the newspapermen.

The cut ran lengthwise under the lower lip.

"I can't breed," Tony mumbled.

Whitey Bimstein had no solution for the wound. He summoned the referee to examine it. Baer had cut Tony's mouth so badly that referee Joe Mangold halted the fight just as the bell sounded to start the eighth round, giving Baer a technical knockout. Many said Baer should have given Tony's brother, who cut Tony with the glass the night before, a cut of the purse. This carried Baer to victory.

Baer rushed over to Tony's corner, put his arm around him, and said something to him. The photographers clamored for photographs, and Baer held his arm around Tony and turned his face toward the camera. Baer was grinning above the battered face of Galento. Finally, they got Baer away from the corner and back to his own. As Baer started to leave the ring, a little person climbed through the ropes to get his autograph. Baer grabbed him and wrestled him to the canvas. The crowd roared. A writer called Galento, Baer, and the little person three cuckoos. Baer got up laughing, went through the ropes, and stood on the ring apron for a moment, waving to the crowd. Then he jumped down and started for his dressing room through the milling crowd.

Despite their congeniality displayed in the prefight promotional film, their disdain for each other during the fight, and afterward, could not be hidden. There were as many verbal abuses thrown during the fight as punches.

In Max Baer's dressing room, Baer let everyone know about a secret—Joe Louis told him how to fight Tony.

"The old champ here," he pointed to the Joe Louis, who had come into the room, "came up to my camp and showed me what to do, boy. He really did a good job, didn't he?"

"He's no good," Max said. "I should of killed him. Talk about bums! Who's the bum now? I'm glad I cut him up. I'd like to do it again."

In Tony's dressing room, one could see the wound in his mouth was cut through, requiring six stitches. Then, before they ever got into the ring, it was learned Caswell Keppel Jacobs, brother of Tony's late manager, Joe Jacobs, had served papers on promoter Mike Jacobs attaching Galento's purse share.

"The fight shouldn't have gone on," Tony's trainer Frain said in the dressing room after the fight. "Tony's chin was cut so bad by that glass that it opened up on him in the fight and the blood got all over. When he got hit on that place it cut all the way inside his mouth and the blood nearly strangled him.

"He was swallowing blood from the fifth round on and couldn't drink any water, couldn't even get any water into his mouth. The blood made him sick. It was all because of that cut from the glass."

Tony demanded a return match.

"I can lick him," Tony said through his puffed lips. "I can lick that bum. He didn't punch so hard. I can lick him."[35]

Despite Tony's optimism, his best days were behind him. Frank Graham from the *New York Sun* wrote:

"Thus ended one of the most bizarre of all heavyweight fights. Thus ended, too, the big time career of Tony Galento, a brawling, almost unbelievable figure who once had the heavyweight champion of the world on the floor for a couple of breathless seconds."[36]

Max Baer would defeat Pat Comiskey in September by a technical knockout in the first round. Comiskey, from New Jersey, thought to be a challenger for Louis's title, proved otherwise by Baer. It would be Max Baer's second to last fight and his last win. He fought one more time—a loss for the second time to Lou Nova—the man Galento had beaten so badly. Galento would lose his next bout against Max's brother, Buddy Baer, and then win his last three fights. Neither Max Baer nor Tony Galento would fight for the title again or return to Madame Bey's Camp.

In mid-August, Al Weill announced that Arturo Godoy, the Chilean heavyweight who had fought Joe Louis twice, had gone into training at Madame Bey's for a possible match with Max Baer.

"I would like to fight Louis again," Weill stated with confidence. "Godoy goes twenty-three rounds with Louis, don't he? That's tops for any fighter. Pastor went only twenty-one heats, didn't he?"[37]

A fight with Max Baer, or a third fight with Joe Louis, never materialized. Godoy would fight two more times in America, both wins by a decision against Gus Dorazio and Tony Musto before 1940 ended. He would leave for South America after those bouts. He would win the South American heavyweight championship. He never received a third chance at the world heavyweight title.

The Baer brothers, Max and Buddy, went in different directions in October 1940. Max, just from his win over Comiskey, began rehearsal for the musical comedy *Hi 'Ya Gentlemen*, to open in New York about December 9. Buddy Baer went to Madame Bey's Camp. He began training for his next proposed fight with Red Burman in Washington, DC, on November 5, 1940.[38] The fight with Red Burman never materialized, and Buddy Baer left the camp.

By October, world middleweight champion Ken Overlin returned to Madame Bey's to defend his crown against Steve Belloise. He fought seven times since using Madame Bey's as a base to win the title. He lost one of those fights, which was not for the title, against Billy Soose. It was a controversial decision as Soose was fighting in his home state of Pennsylvania.

Overlin, the former navy man, worked out before thirty sailors from the Brooklyn Navy Yard at Madame Bey's on October 29, 1940. By October 31,[39] one day before the fight, Overlin had put in three weeks of hard training at Bey's Camp. For the first time in his career, he had trouble making the 160-pound middleweight limit. Though he would not box on the last day,[40] he would have to work and go through the drying-out process to make the weight—a method that uses excessive sweating and deprives the body of water to reduce pounds.

On November 1, 1940, Overlin weighed in at two pounds under the limit. He fought Steve Belloise, whose older brother, Mike, reigned as the world featherweight champion during the mid-1930s. Overlin was winning until Belloise dropped him to the canvas in the sixth round with a right-hand punch on the chin. Overlin was up at the count of two but badly shaken. Belloise kept the pressure against Overlin, but he did not go down again. The bell sounded, and Overlin stumbled into the ropes. He survived the round. Then came one of the most miraculous comebacks the Garden had seen. Overlin mixed repeated jabs followed by lefts to the ribs; he started to control the fight by making his opponent miss while connecting with his punches. There were some furious exchanges in the later rounds. Belloise landed hard punches in the twelfth, fourteenth, and fifteenth that almost put the champion down. The fight at the Garden was a fifteen-round mixed decision with Overlin retaining his championship. The majority of the crowd shouted their disagreement, but the decision was "eminently just" according to journalist Ed Hughes.[41] The referee scored it a draw. The two judges gave the edge to Overlin.

In December, Overlin returned to Bey's to train for a rematch against Steve Belloise. He was not the only headliner there. Buddy Baer had returned after training at Pompton Lakes where Izzy Kline, the trainer of the Baer brothers and Ken Overlin, had sent Buddy to lose fifteen pounds with no match scheduled.[39] Now Buddy had a match scheduled in a week against Harold Blackshear. Despite the match being across the country in Oakland, California, he trained at Bey's with Overlin.

Ken Overlin sat in his dressing room at Madam Bey's, bandaging his hands. First, he put on gauze, then tape. A sparring partner walked in.

"Give me some tape, Ken," he said.

Ken handed him a roll out of a box on the table beside him.

"That ain't enough," the sparring partner said. "Give me another roll."

Ken handed him another roll, and he went out.

"Can you beat it?" Ken asked. "I buy the tape and those guys use it. They use twice as much as I do."

Izzy Kline, the trainer, took a bar of soap off a shelf and held it up.

"Buddy Baer sent this in, Ken," he said. "He borrowed some from you."

"He's as bad as the rest of them," Ken said. "I give him thirty-five cent soap, and he sends me back a nickel bar. I didn't give him only one bar, either. I never saw a guy use as much soap as he does. But come to think of it, washing him is as big a job as washing a battleship."

He started bandaging his hands. Somebody asked him how long he had been bandaging his own hands.

"Ever since I have been fighting professionally," he said, "or since right after my first fight. I came out of the navy prepared to set the world on fire … and I ran out of matches right away. The fellow who bandaged my hands for my first fight didn't do a very good job, and I smashed both hands and couldn't fight again for eight months. So then I started experimenting on the right way to bandage them, and I finally worked it out."

He leaned over and tapped the wooden side of the rubbing table.

"Since then," he said, "I haven't had the slightest trouble with my hands."

"He bandages his opponent's hands sometimes, too," Chris Dundee, his manager, said.

"That's right," Ken said. "No tricks, either. More than once, I've done it for some kid who didn't know how to do it and didn't have anybody with him who did. I hate to see a kid get his hands broken."

He finished the bandaging and pulled on a sleeveless shirt he was going to wear in the workout. Somebody remarked about how good he looked.

"I feel good," he said, "except that I picked up a little cold the other day. It bothered me for a day or so, but I am shaking it off."

Someone said he did not seem concerned about it.

"I'm not," he said. "It's getting better, but I wouldn't care if it got worse. I could have a very bad cold and still lick this guy."

Overlin talked about Steve Belloise, the man he would fight at the Garden and had fought a few weeks before.

"I got careless," he said. "He hadn't hit me, and I didn't think he could. I never saw the punch he hit me with. He led with his right hand and caught me flat footed. The punch didn't hurt me. If it had, I would have stayed down for a nine count. But when I got up, he hit me again and drove me into the ropes, and I was all tangled up and then he hit me some more and those punches hurt. But I wasn't dazed by any of them, and I rolled with some of them and before the round was over, if you remember, I was punching back.

"This time there won't be anything like that. It should be a better fight. He should start faster than he did, and if he doesn't I'll have to go after him. And I won't make the mistake I made the last time. I can count on my fingers the number of times I have been hit with right hands. And that's the first time I ever was hit with one by a fellow who led with it."

Overlin started getting ready for the ring, and Izzy Kline gathered his stuff.

"Belloise is a nice kid," Overlin said, "but he shouldn't be champion."

Overlin put his robe around his shoulders.

"Belloise is only twenty-two years old," he said, smiling. "A kid of twenty-two shouldn't be champion. They shouldn't get to the top when they're twenty-two. They should have to suffer for a while. Get around the country and get licked sometimes. And go broke and be hungry. Why, the kid hasn't even been out of New York yet. How could he know what this business is all about and what would a championship mean to him? What would he do with it if he had it?"

Overlin looking back on his life prompted this. Overlin told how he had come up in the prizefighting game.

"Let's go," Overlin said.

He went through the narrow corridor and climbed the steps to where the indoor ring stood. He shadowboxed a round or two and then boxed two rounds with Jose Basora, a hard-hitting Cuban middleweight and two more with a lanky young boxer named Johnny Williams—six feet tall and weighing only 143 pounds—who drove a truck and fought occasionally. In the fourth round, Ken hit Williams harder than he meant and knocked him down.

"I'm sorry," he said, as Williams got up.

Williams grinned, and they shook hands.

"Come on," Overlin said. "Hit me. You took one. Now I'll take one."

He stuck out his chin, and Williams, laughing, hit him. Ken fell as though he really had been hit, rolled over, and then got up.

"Now we're even," he said.

"You did that very convincingly," somebody said.

"I should be able to," he said. "I've had enough practice. When you're fighting the town clown for $150 in one of those alley clubs, and you've taken nine rounds from him and can't lose the fight, it doesn't do any harm to take one of those. It makes the kid feel good, and the promoter might be nice enough to ask you back."

A customer on a bench along the wall asked him if he thought he would knock Belloise out.

"Holy smoke, no!" he said. "Say, listen, if I ever knocked anybody out I would be the first one to holler 'Fake!'"[42]

Days before the fight, Overlin transferred his training from Madame Bey's to Lou Stillman's Gymnasium in New York. His sparring was done. He did eight rounds of shadowboxing, skipping rope, bag punching, and calisthenics. He wanted to do more, but his trainer, Izzy Kline, would not allow it. When asked, Kline denied reports that Overlin was having breathing problems.[43] Kline denied the accusation so as not to give an incentive to their opponent. Overlin would have to fight his opponent and a bad cold.

On December 13, 1940, Overlin fought Belloise at Madison Square Garden before 16,353 spectators paying admission of $42,338. The challenger, Belloise, was the favorite because of his knockdowns over Overlin in the previous fight. The fight was between a sick veteran and an unseasoned amateur. Overlin, the master at tactics and phycology of a fight, would not allow Belloise to knock him down as in their prior match. Overlin did contract a cold while in training; it failed to improve before the fight, and he had trouble with his breathing from the opening bell. The result was that he was spent after he had gone a couple of rounds. When Overlin was not making Belloise miss, he punished his younger opponent. Belloise vicious rights connected fewer than six times. Using every trick he knew, a sick Overlin held on to retain his title. The judges rendered a split decision. The scoring was nine to four with two even for Belloise, ten to four with one even for Overlin, and nine to four with two even for Overlin. It was not a good fight. It showed what a smart veteran could do against a young challenger even when handicapped by illness. He did what needed to be done to win.[44, 45]

Ken Overlin had outmaneuvered Steve Belloise in a fifteen-round bout. He had returned to the dressing room, and the door slammed shut. Chris Dundee, his manager, and Izzy Kline, his trainer, and promoter Mike Jacobs and a couple of others came with him. Overlin flung his robe and lay down on the rubbing table. Kline draped the robe on a hook, grasped for a dish of sliced oranges, and passed one to the tired fighter. Overlin was lying on his back, and Jacobs went over and extended his hand.

"Thanks, pal. I know now how you felt, and you did a swell job."

"Thanks, Mike," Overlin said. "I did the best I could."

The two other men who had come into the room were standing in a corner.

"He was a sick guy going into the ring," one of them said.

Dundee quickly turned toward him.

"Don't say that," he said. "He wasn't sick."

"Don't give me that," the man said. "I was sitting right in his corner, and I could tell when he came into the ring that he was sick. I could see it in his eyes."

"You shouldn't say that," Dundee said. "It will hurt Belloise, and Belloise is a good kid, and he shouldn't be hurt."

"Nevertheless," the man said, "your guy was a sick guy. I could see it in his eyes when he came into the ring."

Dundee said nothing. He cut the laces of Overlin's gloves and took them. Then he cut the bandages from his hands. Kline took Overlin's shoes and socks off, and Overlin sat up, took the scissors from Dundee, cut the tape from his ankles, and lay on the table.

"Give me another slice of that orange," he said.

Kline handed him a slice, and he lay there as Dundee was bustling around the table.

"I'll want my bath in a minute," Overlin said.

"No," Dundee said. "No bath tonight."

"I haven't had a bath since the day before yesterday," Overlin said.

"I don't care," Dundee said. "With that cold, I'm not going to let you take a bath. Give him an alcohol rub, Izzy."

"He can have a bath," Kline said. "I'll keep him in here till his pores are closed."

"No," Dundee said. "I'm not going to take any chances with him."

Overlin said nothing. He lay there, chewing on the slice of orange. Jacobs was looking at him.

"Too bad about him," one of the men in the corner said.

Mike Jacobs turned around.

"What do you mean?" he said.

"If he only had some guts," the man said, "he would be a good fighter."

Mike Jacobs smiled.

"Yes," he said. "If he only had some guts."

Mike Jacobs shook hands with Overlin again and left through the half-opened dressing room door. You could hear the crowd outside. Newspapermen, managers, and fighters were there that wanted to see the champion to tell him what a skillful fight he had made. A special police officer closed the door, but in a moment, it was opened again, and they came piling in. There was a swirl of people around the table where Overlin lay. Everybody talked at once. The newspapermen asked questions about the fight. Overlin said that Belloise was a good fighter. Dundee said that Overlin was feeling great when he went into the ring and that Belloise was a good fighter.

No matter what Dundee said in the dressing room, Overlin was ill when he entered the ring. The cold he had contracted during his training and that he had been trying to fight through the last week had drained his energy and left him weak. You could see it in his eyes when he came in. He could not have hurt Belloise. When the opening bell rang, Overlin knew he had to outsmart Belloise for fifteen rounds and make the best possible fight he could and give the customers their money's worth. An indisputable fact was that Overlin, and his trainer, Chris Dundee, exemplified sportsmanship, determination, heart, and the obligation of fulfillment for the match. That was why Jacobs thanked him in the dressing room. Belloise was only twenty-two years old and inexperienced. There were times during the fight when it looked as though anyone could climb into the ring and beat Overlin. There were times when it even looked as if Belloise could win, but he could not.[46]

CHAPTER 34

Final Rounds

Instead of his usual Pompton Lakes facility, Joe Louis, at the end of 1940, trained at Greenwood Lake, New York. He was dominating the heavyweight division. Of his twelve title defenses, eight had gone five rounds or less, including three that did not go past the first round. Only Tommy Farr and Arturo Godoy lasted the distance. Farr had trained at Madame Bey's Camp after his Louis fight. Godoy had trained at Bey's for it. The Bey Camp was becoming known for hosting challengers for the Brown Bomber. Madame Bey's had another challenger for the world heavyweight title arrive on December 26. Clarence "Red" Burman left his Queens home to ready for the scheduled January 31, 1941, heavyweight title bout at Madison Square Garden. He came with his longtime trainer, Eddie Ross, leaving his wife and two young boys behind.[1]

The twenty-five-year-old challenger, with seventy-three wins, sixteen losses, and one draw, had been training at a local gymnasium for two weeks but had done no boxing during that time.[1] A product of Baltimore, Maryland, his real name was Clarence Burns, and he had gone by the ring name of Kayo Burns early in his career. He was of Irish descent. He changed his name to Red Burman. The name Red came from his wavy, red hair. He had a hard body punch and fought from a crouch. The style gave Louis trouble in past fights. His team tried to perfect his boxing from a crouch at Bey's Camp.

Max Waxman managed him, and Red was a Jack Dempsey protégé. Dempsey shared the management with Waxman. Waxman had managed Joe Dundee, Vince Dundee, Harry Jeffra, and Kid Williams, among many other fighters. He advised and promoted many bouts during his long career, including Joe Louis exhibition fights during World War II. He would arrange referee tours for Joe Louis, Jack Dempsey, and James Braddock. His handling of Jack Dempsey's business affairs for over twenty-five years left Dempsey a wealthy man.[2]

A few months before, Red Burman was sitting in Dempsey's bar through the afternoons and evenings eating peanuts and potato chips. He wondered when he would get a fight with somebody that would give him a big payday. There were always Dempsey and Max Waxman to provide for him, but he was averse to continue the arrangement. Burman had

345

a wife and two boys, and he wanted to make money. Burman kept himself in shape by working out almost every day, but he could not get a break.

"What's the matter with me?" Burman would say. "The last time I was in the Garden, I beat Tommy Farr, but the only way I can get in there now is on a Chinee ticket."

Every fight night in the Garden, Red would get a complimentary ticket, sit, and watch lesser fighters being paid. He was not earning anything. Burman said the night he saw Johnny Paycheck fight with Joe Louis was the worst. After he saw that, he wanted to turn west when he came out of the Garden, walk to the river, and jump in.

Dempsey had been interested in Burman for a long time. Waxman found him in Baltimore, where he had done much of his fighting. He took him to Stillman's Gymnasium one day and had him fight a heavyweight Dempsey liked. Red destroyed Dempsey's man so thoroughly that Dempsey lost interest in his man. Since Dempsey and Waxman collaborated in many businesses, Waxman declared Dempsey a partner with him and Burman.

Dempsey sent Burman campaigning around the country, fighting for small purses. Red never asked any questions. He fought everybody Dempsey arranged for him. He won most of his fights, lost some, and never complained. Dempsey instilled experience in the young fighter. Red figured it would amount to something in the future.

Burman hung around with Dempsey between fights, helping him at his restaurant on Eighth Avenue. Burman would be Dempsey's chauffeur at times. He kept frequent Dempsey challengers at bay—probably the hardest job he undertook. There was always someone after having a few drinks who wanted to fight with Dempsey because he thought he could knock out the former champion. They had to be saved from Dempsey's still lethal punch. Not that Dempsey, now in his forties, would ever try to hit them. The devastating power remained in those hands.

Burman would box with Dempsey, and Dempsey would help him with his left hook to the body. Burman was learning, for Dempsey had a tremendous hook to either the body or head.

One day when Ken Overlin finished his training for his second fight with Steve Belloise, Burman was in the gymnasium at Madame Bey's Camp. Overlin asked him if he remembered the time they fought. Red was a young middleweight fighting around Norfolk at the time.

"Yeah," Red said.

"So do I," Overlin replied. "You hit me in the belly with a left hook in the first round, and I ran for the rest of the fight."

Red took a friendly swing.

"Hey," Overlin said. "Keep away from me! You're too big for me now. You bum."[3]

When Red Burman went to Bey's to train for the world heavyweight championship against Joe Louis, he was installed as an eight-to-one long shot or worse. There was no reasonable way of figuring that Burman had enough to beat Louis.

"Of course, I'm Irish," Burman said, resting after training at Bey's one day. "So, I suppose that has a lot to do with my being in the fight game. But it was mother calling me Clarence that had a lot to do with her boy becoming a fighter. As a kid, I attended St. Peter's Parish School and Southern High at Baltimore, and when the kids heard my name was Clarence their taunts started many a scrap.

"But after I got through with those guys who picked on Clarence, they called me Red and everything was swell. I did so well in these schoolyard and street battles it was only natural I should take a fling as an amateur boxer. My simon-pure career, however, was abbreviated.

"All I got out of those three scraps was a cheap bathrobe and a shiner. I was working then as an assistant to my dad, an auto mechanic. After he examined both the shiner and the bathrobe, he said, 'if I couldn't cash in on fighting, I ought to quit fighting.' That's how I became a professional.

"Being a Baltimore kid, it was only natural I should find myself under the management of Max Waxman. Max made both of the Dundee brothers, Joe and Vince, and Harry Jeffra into champs, and he is a big shot manager back in my hometown. And as Max is hooked up with Jack Dempsey, it has been my good fortune to have Jack take an interest in me.

"I was only a welter when Waxman took hold of me, but it was Dempsey who made me a heavyweight. Jack had his restaurant, then across the way from Madison Square Garden, and he turned me loose on his choice steaks. Boy, did I ever give those steaks a working over!

"Being a fighter has its inducements—it helps you go places. I stopped Buddy Knox in Chicago, beat Johnny Risko down in Miami, halted Joe Sekyra in Dayton, beat Gus Dorazio in Philadelphia, and Tommy Farr in Madison Square Garden. I've also fought a couple of times a heavy, back in my hometown, where I decisioned Tony Musto and Eddie Blunt, who beat Buddy Baer last week on the Coast."[4]

Early in his training at Bey's Camp, Burman received a warning from a heckler as he walked down the aisle to meet a sparring partner.

"Watch out, Burman, there's Joe Louis!" the heckler hollered.[5]

The startled Burman turned showing fear. No Joe Louis was found. His face turned red![5] Louis's presence was felt at Madame Bey's even when he was not there.

Burman had the confidence, but the fight mob thought of him no more than the next victim of Joe Louis. In late January, in the snowy hills of Madame Bey's, sports columnist Bob Bumbry came to see if Burman had a chance against Louis.

"I bet $200 against $2000 on myself to beat Louis," Red announced. "I have two hands, two feet. I know I have the guts to stay in there with him. So why haven't I a chance?"

Journalist Bumbry had heard that line before from opponents Louis had dismantled. He came to determine if Red was different.

"Louis has never faced a good body puncher," Burman told Bumbry. "I'll upset Louis as sure as I am sitting here.

"I have the incentive. I am a hungry fighter. I have a wife and two kids. I'll win for them."

Bumbry left with the impression that Red's chances against Louis were no better than any previous challenger. The public agreed, increasing Louis's odds to ten to one. In his column, Bumbry concluded:

"If I were Burman, I think I would flee Madame Bey's, where a guy can get ideas like he has …"[6]

Madame Bey's could do that to a man. It could give the confidence to him who appeared to have no chance. There had been many at her camp given no chance, only to proceed to victory to the surprise of the experts. The walls were plastered with posters of those men as reminders. Red would need that confidence the camp bestowed.

Burman would leave behind a signed photograph of himself in a boxing pose for the woman who ran the camp and meant so much to the fighters.

"To Madame Bey, The real mother of fighters with lots of luck & success 'Red' Burman."

Uncle Mike Jacobs and the rest of Joe Louis's team were already looking for a fight after Burman. They signed with Gus Dorazio, with a record of fifty-one wins, nine losses, and one draw. The fight scheduled for February 17 at Convention Hall, Philadelphia, was just two and a half weeks after the scheduled Burman bout. Dorazio joined Burman at Madame Bey's Camp. Louis's next two challengers were now preparing together at one camp. If you listened to Burman, Dorazio was wasting his time. Red believed he would be the champion before February 1.

Burman continued to train the next day.

"Get down," shouted one of Burman's two trainers Heinie Blaustein, working in the ring as if he were the referee. Burman boxed with Johnny Kapovich, a young light heavyweight.

"Don't straighten up. Punch, punch to the body. Keep down."

"Every fighter Louis has met punched to the head," Burman's other trainer, Eddie Rose, pointed out as he watched. "Red is going to hit him in the body. Before the fight is over you're going to see a very sick champion in the ring."

"I'm not a washed up fighter going in there for the loser's end," Red explained. "I've got pride and I have a family to support. If I can win the heavyweight title, the Burmans are set for the rest of their lives."

"Do you know I've never been beaten in the Garden?" Burman continued. "I knocked out Italo Colonello in a round and I outpointed Tommy Farr. I'm going to win my third fight at the Garden next week. Go and bet on it."[7]

Burman had been training for nearly six weeks at Madame Bey's Camp for his chance against the champion, but even before that, he had been getting in shape for nearly two months. Burman had been going through his training energetically, using Bob Smith, Sepia Detroiter, Joe O'Gatty, Ed Wynn, Freddie Fiducia, and Ray Kosky as sparring partners. O'Gatty would defect before the fight; he went over to work as one of Louis's sparring partners.

According to Madame Bey, Burman was the hardest and most earnest worker of all the heavyweights who had ever trained at her noted camp. Madame Bey said that "Red" was drilling harder than Gene Tunney, Harry Wills, Max Schmeling, Paulino Uzcudun, Buddy Baer, and Max Baer.

"None of them, not even Tunney, one of the most conscientious workers I've ever seen," Madame Bey assured, "worked as earnestly as Burman does. They tell me that, even during the three days Burman was away from my camp, he worked two of them in a gymnasium in New York."

"I guess I must have done at least two hundred rounds of boxing during my stay here," Burman said. "You would most likely not believe me if I guessed at how many miles of road work I've done in my training for Louis."[8]

The Saturday before the Friday fight, a capacity crowd gathered around the inside ring at Madame Bey's Camp. Burman boxed six rounds before the largest crowd ever packed into the gymnasium. He sparred two rounds each with Bob Smith, Johnny Kapovitch, and Jim Howell. Jack Dempsey had planned to come to Bey's to watch his protégé work, but scheduling conflicts precluded him from doing so. Dempsey said he felt too nervous and would not be in Red's corner for the fight. He would have a seat in the front. Dempsey said he could not be of any help to second Burman. He added that he picked Red in three rounds. Unlike his boss, Red was not nervous.[9] He had not been in a heavyweight title bout either. Dempsey had fought in many.

A few days before the fight, Doc Morris, Burman's publicist, waited at the Summit Hotel for a group of people coming to see Burman train. They went to Doc Morris's room and had a couple scotches, and then they went downstairs to the dining room for lunch.

"I don't like to hurry you," Doc said, "but he works at three o'clock sharp, and it is nearly half-past one."

"Tell him to wait," one of them said.

"'He'd wait, all right," Doc said, "but his trainers make him work on time, and he hasn't got anything to say about it."

"How far is it from here?"

"Only about ten minutes," Doc said. "I'll go ahead now and tell him you're coming."

Doc Morris left. The others ate their lunch and got back in the car, and in ten minutes, they were at Madame Bey's Camp. Eddie Ross, who trained Burman, met them in the gymnasium.

"He's upstairs," he said. "He hasn't started to get ready yet."

They went upstairs and down a narrow hall lined with bedrooms. One room had been cleared of its furniture except for a table and some chairs. Burman was playing pinochle with Heinie Blaustein, another one of his trainers, and the golf professional from a nearby club. Burman had not shaved for a couple of days, and thick red stubble had grown on his broad face. He wore a flannel shirt, sweater, an old pair of pants, and the shoes he wore for his roadwork. He got up to greet them.

"Do you mind sitting down for a minute?" Burman asked. "I got these guys hooked, and we got one more game to play and I don't want to let them get away."

They sat to watch the game or strolled around the room looking at the markings on the beaverboard walls. Fighters, who had trained at the camp, had scrawled their names or drawn pictures on the walls, and one kid, who probably was homesick while there, had written after his name:

"There is no place like New York."

The card players finished their game. Burman, totaling the score, laughed. It was another big purse for Burman. The golf pro looked glum, and Blaustein was swearing.

"Come on," Burman said while getting up. "I better get dressed."

They went downstairs to the dressing room, where Ross had laid Burman's gear on a rubbing table, cut short strips of tape, and stuck them against the wall for when he would need them to tape the fighter's hands.

One of them asked Burman how much he weighed.

"I weighed one hundred ninety-four when I got up this morning," he said. "I was on the scales just before I went on the road."

"How is the road these mornings?"

"Not so bad. You got to be careful you don't slip, though."

"When it is real bad, I tell him to walk and not run," Ross said.

"How far do you go?"

"About three miles. Some days more. Some days less."

Burman was stripped. He pulled a bathrobe around him.

"Come on," Ross said. "We'll see how much he weighs."

They went down the hall to a room where the scales were located. Burman stepped on and weighed 193.75 pounds.

One of them asked Burman how much he weighed when he fought Tommy Farr in England.

"A hundred and eighty-two," he said.

"I built him up," Ross said. "I only had him six months. I give him a bottle of ale with his dinner every night."

Burman began to put on his training clothes. The door opened and a reporter who had just arrived at the camp came inside.

"Hello. You look good."

"I ought to," Red said. "I been here long enough. I been here so long I am marking the days off on a calendar."

"You fellows should have been out here this morning," Ross said. "We showed the pictures of Louis's fight with McCoy."

"Where? Here?"

"Yes," Ross said. "We got the pictures of most of Louis's fights here. We've been looking at them nearly every day."

"You can honestly say you've seen Louis in your training camp," the reporter who had just arrived said.

"Yes," Red said. "But not behind the trees, eh?"

Burman pulled on his trunks.

"Do you think much about the fight, Red?" a reporter asked.

"Sure, I think about it," Red said. "That's what a training camp is for, ain't it? You come here to get away from good times and things like that and get your mind on the fight; it's my business to think about this fight. If I win it, it will be big business. I can make a million dollars. Why wouldn't I think about it?"

"But you're not worried, like some other fellows who have fought Louis, are you?"

Burman sat on the rubbing table, lacing his shoes. He looked at the reporter.

"That's for them suckers," he said. "I've had plenty of tough fights. I never had anybody picking spots for me and when I was only a kid, I was fighting some of the best middleweights in the country."

"I hope when you're the champion you'll get a new pair of shoes," Ross said.

Burman laughed.

"What's the matter with these shoes?" he asked.

The shoes showed wear and scuff marks. The soles, of thin leather, were nailed on.

"I got them the first time I ever fought on a big show," Red said. "I was in a preliminary on the Baer-Carnera show and the day before the fight I went into a store on Forty-Second

Street to buy a pair of shoes. I thought maybe the fellow would like to know who I was, so I says to him:

"'I'm Red Burman and I am fighting on the Baer-Carnera card, and I want to buy a pair of shoes.'

"So he says, 'I got just the thing for you.'

"He goes in the back, and he comes out with the shoes, and I asked him how much they are and he says, 'Nine dollars.'

"'Nine dollars!' I says. 'Listen, I got five dollars, and I still got to eat until tomorrow.'

"That's true, too. All I got is a five dollar bill, and I pull it out and the lining of my pocket comes with it, and I show it to him, so he will know I ain't stalling and he says, 'Wait a minute. I got a pair you can have for three dollars.'

"He shows me these shoes, and they look all right to me, so I take them. They began to wear out a couple of years ago, and I took them to a shoemaker, and he nailed these soles on and they're still good. I just use them for training now, though. I got good shoes I wear when I am fighting."

"Stop talking and get to work," Ross said.

Burman winked at the others.

"I was just going to tell them about the time you were running a fight club in Baltimore, and you barred me because after I won a sensational fight there. I wanted twelve and a half percent for my next fight."

"Get to work," Ross said. "Tell them later."

They all went upstairs to the gymnasium and watched Burman finish his training for his fight with Joe Louis.[10]

On his last day of training, Burman lessened his work. He did three miles on the road and six rounds in the gymnasium. He wanted to box, but his handlers advised the anxious boxer to refrain; he was too on edge. He broke camp at Bey's the day before the bout and went into New York.[11]

January 31, 1941, the night of the fight, 18,000 fans came to Madison Square Garden to watch the title bout. Burman did not retreat. He charged Louis at every opportunity. They exchanged punches in the opening round. Louis was better, winning the round. Louis had a small cut under his left eye caused by Burman's head. The second and third rounds were also won by Louis.

The fourth rounded ended with a different result as Burman continued his aggressiveness and won the round. Burman, bleeding from a cut over his left eye, still looked fresh as he bulled Louis across the ring in the fifth round. The Garden crowd roared as they sensed Burman may have a chance, and it looked like anything might happen. Red continued to fight with everything he had, but Louis dashed all hope when he knocked Burman down with a right body punch under the heart. Red fell with his head over the lower rope strand near his corner and lay there while referee Fullam completed his count. Louis was the winner in two minutes, forty-nine seconds of the fifth round.[12, 13]

"He's the only fighter besides Galento, who tried to take my title away from me," volunteered Louis after the fight. "He really came after me. I had to hit him the hardest I ever hit a man."

"He fought all he had," Louis said. "That's all you can ask a man to do, ain't it?"[12]

When pressed, the champion admitted Burman never hurt him.

Burman recalled the knockdown.

"The last one—that right under the heart—that was the killer diller, though," he said.[14]

Burman said he might have done better if he had been fighting more often.[12] The journalists did not agree with the challenger's sentiment. To them, he was just Louis's thirteenth victim while champion.

Known for his graciousness, Red would always tell his friends, "Without Joe giving me a chance at the title, the world never would have heard of me. I'm indebted to him, and in my nightly prayers, I never forgot to include his name."[15]

Louis could only rest one week before he went back into training. The other challenger awaited at Bey's for his February 17 bout. Gus Dorazio, whose real name was Justine Vincolota, was born on July 4, 1916, in South Philadelphia. He was thought by many to be a thug, and he looked the part. He was an unorthodox fighter that bobbed and weaved.

Dorazio had been boxing four of his twenty-three years. In the ring at Bey's, he crouched low, weaved, and bobbed. He was another fighter trying to use the crouch to fight Louis. The strategy was not a winning one but allowed one to last longer against the Brown Bomber. As Louis's recent victories proved, he solved the problem of how to attack the crouching style.

Dorazio never had seen Joe Louis fight. He exuded unusual confidence at Bey's for someone about to fight the champion. Bey's Camp extracted what confidence could be found in a fighter. At the camp, he was asked about his chances.

"It's just another fight," he replied. "Those fellows never worried about me before.

"I'll make 'em eat their words. I'm in good shape, and I'm a better fighter than Red Burman. He didn't get killed."[16]

Dorazio spent four weeks at Bey's Camp. He looked in fine physical condition. While there, his daily routine consisted of six miles on the road every morning and boxing six rounds in the gymnasium every afternoon. He ate plenty of Madame Bey's food and slept in a room above the gymnasium. Jimmy Wilson, Dorazio's trainer, worked with him to fight from a crouch. Dorazio had the appearance of a man without a worry. Others were worried. His odds of winning were fifteen to one.

James P. Dawson from the *New York Times* called Dorazio "… one of the most harmless challengers Louis, or any other champion of recent years, for that matter, has ever faced."

"I've been training for three weeks now, and I'll be in top form when I meet Louis," Dorazio told the Associated Press.

"I can't lose. I always fight best against the good boys.

"Why, Burman didn't even train good," Dorazio explained.

"I didn't bother to go to the fight for I knew what would happen. Besides, I've seen pictures of Louis fighting Schmeling, Baer, Galento, Pastor, and McCoy. I can beat all those guys, too."

Jimmy Wilson, Dorazio's trainer, did not instill confidence when he spoke.

"I know Gus will have to get lucky, but I'll bet my life he'll be in there five rounds. He is going to throw punches, for that is his only chance to win. Gus doesn't seem to realize he's fighting for the world heavyweight championship."[16]

His manager, Joe Martino, had more confidence. Martino was convinced Dorazio's style of fighting from a crouch and a newly discovered hard right hand would worry Louis.

"Just as sure as I'm smoking this 'rope' I have the next heavyweight champion of the world," Martino said.[17]

Despite the prognosis Martino built for the twenty-three-year-old Dorazio, the belief persisted among experts that Gus would lose the way other Louis challengers had. It was a question of what round.

On February 17, 1941, a little over two weeks after knocking out Red Burman at Madison Square Garden, Louis entered Convention Hall in Philadelphia to face Dorazio. The joint promotion of Herman Taylor and Mike Jacobs was Philadelphia's largest indoor fight crowd of 16,902 persons paying a gross of $57,552.62. It was the first heavyweight title fight in Philadelphia since the Tunney upset over Dempsey in 1926.

After the first round, Dorazio sat on his stool talking to his trainer, Jimmy Wilson.

"Why this guy isn't so tough," Dorazio told Wilson. "He's a sucker for a hook. I'm going out and stiffen him."

"Better stay down for a few more rounds and see how things go," Wilson counseled.

"But then the bell rang," Wilson explained. "When I saw Gus stand erect I knew it was the end."[18]

Feeling confident, Dorazio abandoned his crouch and tried to land a left hook. As Dorazio rushed in, Louis hit Dorazio with two left hooks. Dorazio, caught off balance, reeled back and for a second stood erect. Louis had an opening, and the Brown Bomber did not miss. He took one short step forward and hit Dorazio with a solid right to the cheek. The punch did not travel more than six inches. Dorazio fell on his face—senseless. Dorazio did not move as the referee counted him out at one minute, thirty seconds of the second round of their scheduled fifteen-round bout.[18, 19]

"They shouldn't have stopped it," Dorazio kept mumbling in his dressing room, so disorientated that he thought referee Irving Kutcher had called a technical knockout instead of a knockout.

"Why did the referee stop it?" he asked.[18]

Louis had solved the problem of how to defeat a fighter that fought him from a crouch. It had been used as a tactic in so many of his previous fights. It prompted him to state after the fight:

"They'll have to get a new gag now. That story about me being a bum against a bobber and weaver won't go anymore."[19]

Dorazio was Louis's fourteenth victim in a title defense, and the press called him Louis's third bum in as many months, two of whom trained at Madame Bey's Camp. He had defeated Al McCoy on December 16, Red Burman on January 31, and Dorazio on February 17. It was the busiest campaign ever accomplished by a champion heavyweight. Louis was never happy with the disparaging label reporter Jack Miley, who originated the phrase, pinned on his opponents.

"Those guys I fought were not bums," Louis told Art Rust Jr. later. "They were hardworking professionals trying to make a dollar, too. I knew the training they went through, and I knew the dreams they had. No different than me. I respected every man I fought."

While Dorazio was training for Louis, light heavyweight Jimmy Webb and heavyweight Melio Bettina[20]—who held the world light heavyweight title in 1939 for five months before losing it to Billy Conn and losing to him a second time two months later—were training at Madame Bey's for bouts at the Garden on February 21. Webb was to meet Tommy Tucker and Bettina to fight Herbie Katz. Both Bettina and Conn had moved up to the heavyweight ranks.

Spike, Webb's Boston bulldog pet, was also at Madame Bey's Camp. Jimmy Webb tried to convince Spike that the light heavyweight championship would not be at stake despite being fifteen rounds when he would box Tommy Tucker. When the match was signed, Billy Conn, the champion, was supposed to relinquish the crown. Since then, promoter Mike Jacobs had decreed otherwise, and the commission had sanctioned an elimination tournament involving Anton Christoforidis, the National Boxing Association title holder, Gus Lesnevich, Tucker, and Webb.

"Spike doesn't understand about boxing commissions," Webb explained. "He's only a Boston bulldog and while he's smart enough, as the breed goes, he can't figure why I should be fighting fifteen rounds if there's no title at stake. I can't figure it out myself."[21]

Bettina and Webb won their bouts.

In late February, the Herkimer Hurricane returned to Madame Bey's Camp. As his manager, Al Weill, said he would do, Ambers had taken time off since the he lost his crown to Jenkins the previous May. Ambers was now a welterweight. He had his first fight after the Jenkins defeat against Norment Quarles on February 14. He won that fight in a ten-round decision. The press said the heavier Ambers looked sluggish in that fight and his workouts since.[22] Ambers said he would challenge Fritzie Zivic for his welterweight title if he beat Lew Jenkins in their rematch at Madison Square Garden. Ambers had outpointed Zivic four years before. The fight with Jenkins would be a lightweight fight, but Ambers had no intension of making the weight, so Jenkins's lightweight title would not be at stake.

Ambers was confident of winning. He used to operate a laundry, and the newspapers showed him in a publicity photograph washing a shirt on a scrub board at Madame Bey's Camp.

"I may be a laundry man," Ambers said, "but I'm not washed up."

Madame Bey smiled when she heard that one-liner.[23]

Ambers had reason to be confident. The twenty-seven-year-old Ambers's confidence stemmed from the fact that no man had ever beaten him twice. During his nine-year career, all four opponents that beat him and fought him again were defeated in return engagements. Steve Halaiko, Tony Canzoneri, Pedro Montañez, and Henry Armstrong were all defeated by Ambers in their second meeting.

Someone asked Ambers at Bey's if he thought he could beat Jenkins.

"Well," Ambers said with a laugh. "I won't say I really know I can beat him, but I think I can. I'll sure give him the best I've got. I'll tell you one thing, this time I'm going to remember not to forget to duck."[24]

When asked after their first meeting why he lost, Ambers said, "He forgot to duck."

Again, a Madame Bey challenger would do his training in Pompton Lakes, New Jersey. Lew Jenkins did his training there. He was the star in town since the heavyweight champion Joe Louis had vacated the camp. He was in Chicago. Louis said he expected an order to report for army duty.

"My draft number is 2611," Louis explained. "This placed me 378th in my local draft board. I returned my questionnaire January 7 and expect to be called any day for a physical examination."

The heavyweight champion also said he thought life as a soldier would not be bad.[25]

While Jenkins trained in Pompton Lakes, his wife, Katie, monitored her husband closely. She made sure he kept away from liquor and that he drank two quarts of goat's milk every day. She even involved herself in his training routine. Jenkins would do roadwork while his wife rode a bicycle beside him.

"I've been training harder for this fight than for any of my others," Jenkins said, "and I don't see why I can't whip Ambers again. I reckon I'll win by a knockout like last time. It may be in the first round, or it may be in the third like it was the other time I beat him."

At camp, it was noticed that Lew Jenkins had the eyebrows above both his eyes bandaged before sparring. It was to protect him against the scar tissue resulting from boxing and non-boxing activities. The tissues were apt to bleed. Ambers was the kind of puncher that cut his opponents' faces, a fact that gave thought that Jenkins would have to knock Ambers out quickly to win the fight.

Jenkins appeared fit at camp. He would go into the ring weighing between 133 and 134 pounds. The scar tissue did not diminish his vicious right punch. He had been working unyieldingly for three weeks, and in that time he had severely injured two sparring partners. He hit Rudy Vastano so hard with his right hand that he broke one of Vastano's ribs. A day later, he repeated the injury on Joe Torres, causing Torres to leave the camp.

"I've learned a lot since the last time I fought Ambers," Jenkins acknowledged as he cooled out after five rounds of sparring. "You can see I've learned how to use my left better, and I reckon you noticed how I was doing on that infighting."

Jenkins had built his reputation on his hard punching with his right hand. The development of his left, noticed by observers, meant trouble for all his future opponents, Ambers included.[26]

Jenkins boasted that in his roadwork he could do four miles in twenty minutes.

"Easy too," Jenkins stated.

They told him that time was remarkable.

"It ain't nothing," Jenkins replied.

This appeared unbelievable to those listening. It was suggested Jenkins offer to meet Gregory Rice, a long-distance runner, in a distance race of three miles. Someone noted that the world record was thirteen minutes, fifty-one seconds.

"Thirteen minutes?" Jenkins asked. "Thirteen minutes for three miles? And that's the world record? Why, hell, I can do it in ten minutes easy. I done it to twelve minutes this morning and wasn't even trying hard. Why, if I couldn't run three miles in better than thirteen minutes, I'd quit."[27]

Being a professional barred Jenkins from running track, which was an amateur sport. His statements went untested.

Mushky Jackson, still the publicity man at Pompton Lakes, got Jenkins to give a statement for the fight. Through Jackson's issuance of Jenkins's statement, it was evident he had not lost his grasp on the English language. Mushky put *Webster's Dictionary* down for the full count again.

"I will give my public plenty of thrills and make their spines quibble."[28]

Two days before the fight, Ambers finished his hard training. He boxed four fast rounds, two against Bill Duffy and two against Pedro Hernandez, as he had done every day during his stay at Madame Bey's Camp. Duffy would fight on the Ambers-Jenkins undercard. Ambers scaled 141.5 pounds after the workout. It was his last major workout before the fight. The next day, Ambers would do only limbering exercises.[29] Ambers had been training hard for his ten-round bout with Jenkins. He would have an advantage of six and a half pounds over his adversary. He was no longer in a position of needing to make weight. They still installed him as a two-to-one underdog to win. Ambers reported that he felt confident of victory.

On February 28, 1941, the day of the fight, Ambers left Madame Bey's to ready for his bout. With four hours left, Jenkins readied, too. He was across the street from the venue at Madison Square Garden. He sat in the corner of a bar having a drink. With two hours left before the opening bell, he remained in the corner of the bar.[30] Without his wife there, the goat's milk nowhere in sight, his pleasure was whiskey. He went to the Garden, trading the bar corner for the ring corner.

The Garden had 15,402 fans that paid $46,443 to see the fight. Ambers's sparring partner Billy Duffy lost his bout prior to the main event. Jenkins started the fight as if he intended to finish it in one round. At the opening bell, as Ambers left his corner, Jenkins swung with a punch that went wild. Twice more he unleashed long rights to the head. Ambers remained out of range and responded with lightning left counterpunches. So inebriated, Jenkins's wild punches did not come close to finding their mark. The round was scored in favor of Ambers.

"I was so high when I got into the ring, I thought I saw two Lou Ambers' in there," Jenkins said.

In the second round, Jenkins threw his devastating right that landed into the jaw of Ambers. Ambers was staggered but kept his feet.

"Ambers did not go down," a ringside witness observed, "but he did a lot of funny things standing up."[30]

Ambers made a comeback, and some of the journalists had him leading at the end of the sixth round. In the seventh round, Jenkins hit Ambers on the chin with a left hook, then a right, which put him on the canvas. He was able to gain his feet, but Jenkins knocked him down again. Referee Donovan stopped the annihilation as Ambers tried to get up. He waved Jenkins away at two minutes, twenty-six seconds of the seventh round.[31, 32]

Jenkins left the ring after putting on his robe and refused to talk to the radio interviewer. As Jenkins left, a ring veteran at ringside shouted to him.

"Champions don't act like that, boy."[33]

Immediately after the fight, Ambers's manager announced that his fighter was retiring.

"Lou Ambers has fought his last fight," Weill said.[34]

"The kid hasn't the same old zip," Weill said, "the snap that he use to have, and I don't want to see him get hurt. He has enough money, and the best thing for him to do is hang it up."[35]

Al Weill told Ambers that his fighting days were over. Ambers argued to continue his career. Weill implored Whitey Bimstein to talk to him. At twenty-seven years of age, Ambers grudgingly agreed. He had earned more money in the ring than any other lightweight. That record would go unsurpassed until 1967 when Carlos Ortiz eclipsed it training for a fight at Madame Bey's Camp. The next day, a press conference was arranged. Ambers, smiling as he always did, had tears streaming down his face.[33]

"Lou will never fight again," Al Weill said.

Ambers went to his home in Herkimer. After a few weeks rest, he called Al Weill on the telephone.

"Al," he said, "I want …"

"Yes," Al said. "I know. You want to fight again. Come down to New York. I got something for you."

Lou hurried to New York. When he arrived, Weill gave him a contract.

"Sign that," he said.

Lou never read anything Al asked him to sign. He always trusted his judgment. He signed a ten-year contract, calling for compensation at the rate of one dollar a year, giving Al complete control of him as a fighter. That was Al's way of telling him it was in his best interest not to fight.[36]

Ambers never again donned the gloves for a professional fight.

In April 1941, Freddie "Red" Cochrane, at age twenty-six, came to Madame Bey's to follow the path of his favorite boxer. It was his onetime neighbor, Mickey Walker. Mickey and Freddie were raised in the Kereigh Head section of Elizabeth, New Jersey. They lived eight houses apart on Bond Street. Cochrane was seven years old when Walker defeated Jack Britton on November 1, 1922, for the welterweight title. He could recite Mickey's record for anyone inclined to listen. When Walker returned home after a fight, he tossed pennies and nickels to kids. Among those scrambling for the coins was Cochrane. With other members of the neighborhood gang, he sat on Walker's front porch, waiting for him to wake in the morning.[37, 38]

Cochrane was scheduled to fight for the world welterweight championship against Fritzie Zivic. Cochrane stood no more than five feet six and a half inches and weighed 142 pounds. He was of Scotch-Irish descent. He had brilliant red hair, blue eyes, a stubby nose, and one of his arms was shorter than the other.[39] Cochrane demonstrated defensive skills; his only facial scar resulted from a head butt.

Mickey Walker was thirty-nine years old and had not been in the professional ring for over five years. It was May, and he was returning to Madame Bey's to meet his admirers in Madame Bey and Red Cochrane. At the camp, Mickey presented Red the boxing gloves he wore when he won the world welterweight championship eighteen years before.[37] It was an inspiring gesture toward his younger fellow welterweight.

World middleweight champion Ken Overlin joined Cochrane at Bey's for his fight against Billy Soose, the man he lost a controversial decision to in a nontitle bout. For this fight, the title would be at stake in a fifteen-round bout at Madison Square Garden. Overlin had fought fifteen times since winning the title less than a year before. During that time, the Soose fight was his only loss.

Soose was an academic who boxed while in college. He had power and knocked out every collegiate boxer he fought. After injuring his right hand, he learned to use his left hand and developed his boxing ability.[40]

On May 4, experts among the crowd of several hundred that came to watch Ken Overlin train at Madame Bey's Camp said he looked in better form than for any of his East Coast matches. Overlin impressed the crowd as he sparred three rounds with Eddie Pierce, a middleweight, hitting him with lefts and rights from every angle. Overlin ended his workout with two rounds against Phil Furr. Manager Chris Dundee said Overlin would don the gloves again the next day.[41]

On May 7, the boxing commission sent for Ken Overlin and Billy Soose and their managers to come in and sign the contracts for their middleweight championship. The three commissioners, General Phelan, Bill Brown, D. Walker Wear, and some of their deputies were there. Also attending were Mike Jacobs, three or four photographers, and a couple of reporters. Overlin came in with his manager, Chris Dundee, and his trainer, Izzy Kline. Overlin wore a white sport shirt open at the throat, a blue and gray checked sport coat, gray flannels, and sport shoes. He even had a faint sunburn. A few minutes later, Soose arrived with his manager, Paul Moss, and his trainer, Ray Arcel. Soose wore a white shirt, pullover sweater, tweed pants, and chamois jacket. The fighters shook hands with each other, and so did the trainers, but the managers ignored each other, and neither fighter had anything to say to the other's manager.

Dr. William Walker did physical examinations of the fighters. The photographers took photographs, and then everybody moved into the main room where the commissioners were waiting. Nat Rogers, the Twentieth Century Sporting Club matchmaker, had the contracts prepared. He also had Sol Strauss, the attorney for the club, ready in case any arguments should unfold. None did, and the fighters signed in the presence of the commissioners, and the photographers took some more pictures. The commissioners shook hands with the fighters and wished them luck, and the meeting was over. Overlin was returning to Madame Bey's for his last day of boxing, and Soose went to Stillman's Gymnasium for the same purpose.

"You look great, Ken," one reporter said to Overlin as the group was dispersing.

He said he looked five years younger than he did the last time the reporter saw him.

"I feel great," he said. "I should. I've been at the camp for twenty-three days."

"There must be something in this fresh air and sunshine, then," the reporter said.

Ken nodded.

"I'm afraid there is," he said.

"Then you haven't minded being in camp this time as much as you did when you were training for the Garcia fight?"

That was the first time Overlin had been in a training camp—Madame Bey's Camp—and he said that he felt as if he was in jail and was marking off the passing days on a big calendar in his room. He would make Garcia pay for making him suffer like that. He did by taking the title from the Filipino. He grinned at the recollection of that.

"Well, it's almost as bad," he said. "I'm glad the fight is only a couple of days away. I don't think I could stand another week out there."

Soose was standing near the door, talking to Moss and Arcel. He was only a few feet from Overlin, but neither looked at the other.

"Tell me about this fight," the reporter said to Overlin.

"He'll scurry him around," Overlin said. "Why shouldn't I beat him? I beat him last summer, and what has he done since then to show that I can't beat him again? He has beaten Mauriello and Vigh—and I could take Mauriello for a week and show him how to beat Soose. Mauriello and Vigh both tried to knock him out in a hurry. That's no way to fight him. But I know how to fight him. I'll not only beat him, but I will make a sucker of him. And I never wanted to make a sucker of a fellow so much in my life."

"Why do you feel that way about him?"

"On account of his manager," he said.

The reporter laughed.

"He's not such a bad fellow," he said.

"The hell he ain't," Overlin said.

"Why?" asked a reporter.

"Why?" Overlin repeated. "Because of what he did to me last summer. Those fellows wouldn't have been in New York yet if I hadn't gone to Scranton to fight Soose. And then they robbed me."

"Was the decision really as bad as that? Or have you been thinking about it so much that it has grown in your mind?"

"Sure it was that bad."

"Did you say so at the time?"

"No, I didn't. I didn't want to squawk about it."

His face relaxed into a smile.

"Anyway," he said, "I don't like these intellects in the prizefight business."

Moss had attended the University of Illinois for two years and finished his formal education at Penn State. Soose was a junior at Penn State when he withdrew to enter professional boxing.

"They don't belong in this business," Overlin said, still smiling. "This is for kids that have to come up the hard way."

Overlin's face became serious again.

"I'll win this fight if it's the last thing I do," he said. "I want this title, and I am going to keep it. I am not going to lose it to a guy like that. When the time comes that I can't keep it, I hope it goes to some poor kid that came up off the streets and had to work hard for everything he got. Soose don't need a title. He's got brains and an education. What is he doing in this business? He can do lots of other things."

The commission was going to have its regular weekly meeting. There were fighters, managers, and matchmakers outside waiting to be heard. The group inside began to drift toward the elevators. Mike Jacobs came over, beaming.

"See?" Uncle Mike Jacobs said. "This is the way things should be done, everything nice and quiet and dignified."[42]

On May 9, 1941, at Madison Square Garden, a crowd of 11,676 paying $35,973 came to see Overlin defend his middleweight title against the five-year younger Soose. Overlin appeared to have the fight in control from the start. Chris Dundee thought that Overlin was so far ahead that he told him to coast the last three rounds.[43] It was a pro-Soose crowd.[44] The Associated Press scored the fight eleven to four in favor of Overlin. Their card did not count. The decision was given to Soose before a stunned Garden crowd. Referee Arthur Donovan gave Soose eight rounds and Overlin seven. Judge Marty Monroe had the same opinion while the other judge, Bill Healy, also chose Soose giving him nine rounds with five for Overlin and one even. It was a unanimous decision.

The *New York Times* printed that although the decision was unanimous "it was a mystifying one, mysteriously arrived at, and so unexpected that it left the onlookers stunned for several minutes."[45] Chris Dundee, Overlin's manager, was so incensed over the verdict he threatened to go before the State Athletic Commission and ask for a reversal.[44] Frank Graham from the *New York Sun* wrote, "The decision … was so bad that the New York State Athletic Commission must do something about it. There have been questionable decisions hereabouts in the last year or so but there was nothing questionable about this one. Overlin won the fight and referee Arthur Donovan and the judges, Marty Monroe and Bill Healy, gave it to Soose."[46]

The decision stood. The following month, Soose appeared on the cover of the June issue of *The Ring* magazine.

Red Cochrane's fight, originally scheduled for May 26, was three times postponed. The postponement did not prevent Zivic from fighting others in nontitle bouts. One of those bouts would be against Al "Bummy" Davis, who would join Cochrane at Bey's in May. The two prepared together for the same opponent, just as Burman and Dorazio did for Louis earlier in the year. Davis had started another occupation. He enlisted in the army in January at the suggestion of his manager, and they attached him to the communications detail of the Sixty-Ninth Antiaircraft Battery. He was on furlough from Camp Hulon, Texas, while at Bey's Camp. Davis would live in the house that Madame Bey's son, Rustem, owned. Rustem had become the full-time chief of police in April when a town ordinance created a permanent police department.[47]

Zivic, notorious for his rough, fouling style of boxing, would say, "You're boxing, you're not playing the piano." Davis had already fought Zivic on November 15, 1940, in his last fight. In that fight, Davis was knocked down in the first round. In round two, Zivic fouled Davis causing him to lose his temper. Davis landed nine intentional low blows, and referee Billy Cavanaugh disqualified him. Davis attempted to resume the fight with Zivic, and when Cavanaugh intervened, Davis kicked the referee in the groin.[48] Davis had not been known as an unsavory fighter before the bout.

"I can't talk about rules now because Davis threw them all out the window," New York Commissioner Bill Brown said. "We won't need Al Davis anymore in New York. You can say for me that Davis will be barred from New York State for life, and I mean it."

Davis was suspended but later reinstated.

In June 1941, General John J. Phelan, who felt personally responsible for Davis, drafted Ray Arcel to be his trainer for the Zivic fight. Johnny Attell, who managed Davis, came to Bey's every day. Mike Jacobs also hired press agent Irving Rudd for the sum of twenty-five dollars a week, for three weeks,[49] to be with Al "Bummy" Davis at Madame Bey's Camp.

Rudd was a short, fast-talking conversationalist. He introduced himself as Rudd, while others called him Unswerving Irving. Rudd made sure you called him a press agent, not a public-relations man, whose ranks he called "posturing phonies."[50] Rudd, one of the most famous boxing publicists, worked throughout his career with Joe Louis, Sugar Ray Robinson, Muhammad Ali, Sugar Ray Leonard, Ray Mancini, and Thomas Hearns.

Lew Jenkins came to Bey's in early June, not to train but to help Davis prepare for Zivic. Jenkins secretly instructed Davis in the dressing room at Madame Bey's gymnasium after he worked out.

"I fought a ten round draw with Zivic, and I know more about him than a lot of those managers, trainers, and advisers," Jenkins told Davis. "Don't pay any attention to what they're telling you. You do it the way I showed you."

Davis nodded in agreement, satisfied that Jenkins had solved his problem.[51]

In late June, journalist Frank Graham came to Madame Bey's to watch one of Davis's final days of training. There was a group with him waiting for Willie the Gypsy, who was Davis's chef, to put their dinner on the table. Davis started talking about the days when he was a kid in Brownsville, selling tomatoes from a pushcart and fighting as an amateur.

"What was the toughest fight you ever had?" someone asked.

"The one I enjoyed or the one I didn't enjoy?"

"Well …"

"The one I didn't enjoy was the Ambers fight. That was a hard fight and he gave me a good licking. He knew too much for me. He outmaneuvered me. Maybe if I was in the army then I could have outmaneuvered him, hey? … The fight I enjoyed was the one with Marteliano. That was a good, tough fight. We just stuck in there with our heads on each other's chest and pounded each other in the belly and then in the last round I switched and hit him on the chin, and I had him on the floor when the last bell rang. That was a swell fight. I really enjoyed that one."

"He really loves to fight," Johnny Attell said.

"How about this Zivic fight, how are you going to fight him?"

"The way Arcel tells me to," Davis said. "He can see better from where he is than I can."

The mention of Zivic's name riled Davis.

"You don't like Zivic, do you?"

"No. Why should I, after what he done to me?"

"They met the other night," Attell said. "Zivic looks at him and he says, 'You look sharp in that uniform Al.' And Al says 'I'm glad you like it. You put me in it.'"

Attell thought that was a good Joke. Davis smiled faintly.

"They told me how he would fight," Davis said. "He done the same thing with all the other fellows he fought, but I guess I was the only one that lost my head when he done it."

"That's the way Zivic always fights," Attell said.

"Nobody ever said I was a foul fighter before," Davis said. "I never hit anybody low. I always hit them in the belly, too, but I never hit them low."

"He never lost a round on a foul before that fight," Attell said.

"How much do you weigh, Al?"

"We're having a little trouble with his weight," Attell said.

"That's the reason we laid him off today. He's got to come in over one hundred forty-seven because this is an over-the-weight match and today he weighed one hundred forty-six."

"You can't fatten him up, eh?"

"No. Well, maybe we could, but that wouldn't be fair to him or those that want to see him win. He's going to be at his best fighting weight."

"Why doesn't Zivic fight him for the title?"

Attell made a wry face.

"Don't make me laugh," he said.

Davis weighed about 170 pounds when he enlisted, but the strenuous life of a soldier caused the weight loss, and he had been training for a couple of weeks and looked sharp. He was awake every morning at six, did roadwork a half hour later, had a light breakfast, skipped lunch, generally boxed six rounds in the afternoon, and had dinner about five o'clock.

"He isn't much of an eater," Attell said. "Stewed fruit, a dry cereal and a couple boiled eggs, toast, and milk in the morning. A steak or chops at night and some more milk. Then, a couple of glasses of milk before he goes to bed. He's a good milk drinker, but no eater."

"How do you like being out in the country, Al?"

"It's swell."

"That's what the army done for him," Attell said. "The only time he was in a training camp before was at Lakewood and after three days he couldn't stand it and ran home. The army got him out in the open air and, see, now he likes it."

"Do you like the army?"

"Yeah," he said. "I do. It was hard at first. It's hard work now but you got a lot to learn and it is interesting."

"I don't have nothing to do with the guns," he said. "My Job is stringing telephone wires. We're down near the Gulf of Mexico and they have us out in the field twelve hours at a time."

There was a story, somebody said, that shortly after he had enlisted he had slugged a sergeant.

"Yeah," he said. "I heard it. I wasn't even in the army. I had enlisted, but they hadn't called me yet. I wasn't in the army and they said I hit somebody."

"Did you have any trouble at all?"

"No. There might have been some guys that would have liked to make trouble for me, but I kept my mouth shut and minded my own business, and I never had any trouble."

"What do you do with all the money you make in the army?"

"He spends it on the other guys," Attell said. "He takes them into town and feeds them. Tell them about that payday when I was down there."

"I would have had to wait in line for three hours for my dough," Davis said. "So I went to see Johnny instead and put the arm on him for my twenty-one bucks."

"What do you miss most being in the army?"

"First," he said. "I miss my family. Next to that, I miss boxing. The general in command of our camp don't think much of boxing, I guess. I offered to box for the boys or put on some boxing shows, but I got turned down. I got a punching bag down there, and now and then I get somebody to box with but not often enough to suit me."[47]

About the time Davis was at Madame Bey's Camp, Foulproof Taylor visited. Foulproof Taylor, who lived in Brooklyn and worked for the Postal Telegraph Company, was an inventor. He had white thatched hair that stood straight up. In the late 1930s, he fashioned a crude baseball safety helmet. His new invention, the Foulproof Taylor Cup, brought him to Madame Bey's Camp. To market his device, he would visit Stillman's Gymnasium or the Pioneer Gymnasium in Manhattan. Wearing his cup, he would stand with his feet apart inviting anyone to punch or kick him in the groin area. The offer was often accepted. Sometimes by a big heavyweight who would throw a mean hook below the belt. Taylor, knocked upside down with his feet above his head, would bounce up unhurt.

Hype Igoe, Hearst newspapers' boxing writer and cartoonist, was at Madame Bey's the same time Taylor was there to demonstrate his cup. Igoe had been covering boxing for the last forty years with exclusive inside stories. Journalist Damon Runyon called Igoe "probably the best informed writer on boxing that ever lived." Taylor asked Igoe to test the Foulproof Taylor Cup. He accepted. Taylor crashed into a baseboard wall. It took several men a number of minutes to extricate him.

Someone placed a makeshift plaque over the hole in the wall that read:

"Hypus Igoe through this wall Knocked Foulproof Taylor—Cup and all!"[49]

On July 2, 1941, a crowd of 8,968 attended the Al "Bummy" Davis-Fritzie Zivic fight at the Polo Grounds. Davis went down in the first round. He took a pounding from Zivic, who appeared to want to punish him. By the tenth round, nearly out on his feet, blood was streaming from Davis's nose, and his lips were swollen. Referee Arthur Donavan stopped the fight. Davis lost by a technical knockout. Davis's share of the purse went to the United States Army Relief Fund.[52]

Since having won the lightweight championship from Lou Ambers, Jenkins had refused to fulfill the obligation that he owed to paying fans. He took no care of himself. He incurred many injuries from careless motorcycle riding. He figured all he had to do to earn his money was to shed his robe in his corner, stall, run, and dodge as long as his weakened legs held him up.[53]

Jenkins was still the lightweight champion; no one doubted his powerful right hand. His fights, for the most part, were watching an out-of-shape fighter trying to land one blow to end the fight. He was in poor shape for his fight with Henry Armstrong on July 17, 1940, at the Polo Grounds, his first fight after wresting the title from Ambers. He inflicted more harm on Armstrong than Henry did on him. He won the first three rounds but went down seven times after that. He folded on the stool in his corner and could not answer the bell for the seventh. Exhausted, he had to be helped from the ring. Jenkins lost the fight, but by agreement, the title was not at stake. He won his next two bouts but was in no better shape for a fight with Fritzie Zivic on December 20, 1940, in which the judges credited him with a draw, although the press wrote the decision rightfully belonged to Zivic. In his next bout, he beat Ambers for the second time fighting through a drunken stupor. Two and a half weeks before his next fight against Bob Montgomery on May 16, 1941, Jenkins rode his motorcycle from Florida to New York in a five-day trek.[54] He put in little effort against Montgomery at the Garden and lost a ten-round decision in a nontitle fight. He still posed a danger with his thunderous right, even being out of shape. Jenkins would put in an effort for his next fight by training at Madame Bey's where outside influences were few.

In the eighteen years that Madame Bey operated her camp, she had staged many spectacular training sessions. July 25 was such a day. She had middleweight Georgie Abrams, world lightweight champion Lew Jenkins, light heavyweight contender Jimmy Webb, and welterweight Freddie "Red" Cochrane all training at her camp. Cochrane had been at Bey's since April waiting for his fight with Zivic.

Jenkins sparred three rounds with Al Dunbar. Webb completed training for a battle with Mose Brown in Pittsburgh by working two rounds with Herbert Marshall. Georgie Abrams did not spar but worked out; he would fight world middleweight champion Billy Soose. It would be Soose's second bout since winning the title from Overlin in May. The title would not be at stake. Jenkins prepared in front of the crowd for a bout with Joey Zodda in Newark on August 4. Cochrane, who was to meet Fritzie Zivic for the welterweight title in Newark, did not work out, as his problem was maintaining his weight, not losing it. He was 142 pounds, five less than the welterweight limit.

Lew Jenkins, known for his lax training effort, decided to satisfy his craving for speed at Bey's Camp. He bought a new automobile to add to his collection of two cars and three motorcycles. He explained his recent defeat to Bob Montgomery by revealing that throughout the fight, he forgot his right hand.

Although Abrams, now a sailor in the navy, was training for a nontitle bout with Billy Soose, he hoped to win so decisively that Mike Jacobs, the promoter, would be forced to alter plans for a Soose-Overlin championship battle rematch in Pittsburgh the following month.

"I'm in a funny situation," Abrams explained after boxing three rounds with Irish Eddie Pierce. "I've beaten Soose twice and can't get a chance at the title. Soose has beaten Overlin twice, and Ken gets a crack at the crown. I can't squawk because Overlin and myself are both managed by Chris Dundee."

What was worrying Dundee and trainer Frankie Doyle was Abrams's weight. He had to weigh over 160 pounds, the middleweight limit.

"I'm in much better shape than I've been in recent years," Abrams continued. "It may be the regular hours I've kept since joining the navy. For a long time, there was something wrong with my vertebra, but the exercises we get at Jacksonville seems to have strengthened my back. Besides, it is hot and naturally a fellow loses weight."

Although Abrams won his two previous fights with Soose by unanimous decisions, he was knocked down once in the second round of the first fight and twice in the first round of the second fight. In the seventh round of the second fight, Soose lay on the canvas when the bell sounded. Both fights were in Pittsburgh.

"I like the service and so do all the other boxers who joined up with Gene Tunney," Abrams, a boatswain's mate, first class, concluded. "In fact, Tommy Tucker is going to make the navy his career. He's always on the flying field fooling around with the mechanics, and he never misses a chance to go up in the big bombers."

For his part, Abrams preferred to be the middleweight champion, and it seemed he might get a chance since Mike Jacobs delayed closing the Soose-Overlin rematch. Whatever happened, Abrams's twenty-day furlough from the navy would end August 1.[55]

The four fighters would all fight over eight days. Bey's fighters would win three and lose one. The first was Jimmy Webb against Mose Brown at Hickey Park in Millvale, Pennsylvania, on July 29. Brown knocked Webb down twice in the opening round. A right hand at fifty-nine seconds in the second round put Webb on the canvas permanently. It was a major upset, as Webb was a six-to-one favorite.

On July 29, 1941, at Ruppert Stadium, Newark, New Jersey, Cochrane's match with Zivic finally occurred, attended by 10,000 spectators. Freddie "Red" Cochrane and Fritzie Zivic were close friends outside of the ring. Cochrane outfought the champion when in close and built a commanding lead. Zivic mounted a late rally in the last five rounds and staggered Cochrane a couple times in the fourteenth round. The fight was decided by referee Joe Mangold, who had the four-to-one underdog Cochrane a winner by scoring seven for Cochrane, four for Zivic, and four even. The result even surprised the new champion's father.

When asked to explain what happened, Zivic said, "I fought three times in a month. That's too much."

Cochrane and friends celebrated the unlikely victory in his dressing room. Earlier in the month, Cochrane had invited Zivic, win or lose, to celebrate at a Hillside, New Jersey, tavern after the fight. Subsequently, the dethroned champion declined his friend's offer.

"I always knew I could beat Zivic if I got the chance," Cochrane said.[56]

"Who'd a thought this was gonna happen?" Cochrane's father said during the post-fight celebrations.

On July 30 at Madison Square Garden, Abrams won a unanimous decision over the middleweight champion Billy Soose. The title was not at stake. The verdict was decisive. Referee Frank Fullam scored nine to one, Judge Bill Healy six to two, and Judge Tom Curley seven to two. After the Abrams bout, Soose fought three more times, winning one, losing one, and drawing one. Soose would never defend his middleweight title. In November, he relinquished his middleweight crown to fight in the light heavyweight division. He fought twice in his new division. He won the first bout and lost the second. Soose retired from boxing in January 1942 and joined the navy.

On August 4, 1941, at the Meadowbrook Bowl, Newark, New Jersey, Jenkins made quick work of Zodda. He scored a third-round knockout. Next, he met Cleo McNeal on September 12 and knocked him out in the third round.

Abe Simon, heavyweight, and Chalky Wright, featherweight, were at Bey's in August 1941. Simon was to fight Buddy Baer. Chalky Wright was to fight Joey Archibald for the world featherweight championship. Chalky Wright had been the movie star Mae West's chauffeur and bodyguard for four months from the end of 1935 to February 1936.[57]

Abe Simon, from Queens, New York, stood six feet four inches and weighed over 250 pounds. He was a man with a powerful presence, a square chin, sturdy legs, and a massive upper body. His frame had an abundance of body hair. They called him the Ape. In spite of his almost frightening appearance, he was a gentleman. The past March, he fought Joe Louis for the heavyweight title in a scheduled twenty-round bout at Olympia Stadium, Detroit, Michigan.

Simon received a chance at the title after winning eight of his previous ten fights. Few gave Simon a chance against Louis. Mike Jacobs had to turn away 3,000 people in a surprising turnout. With 18,990 fans watching, Louis knocked Simon down in the opening round. It was the first time he had felt the canvas in his career. After being knocked down a second time in the third round, Simon grinned while sitting on the canvas until the count of nine, then rose to continue the fight. Simon staggered Louis toward the end of the seventh round. In the thirteenth round, the champion sent Simon to the canvas twice. The referee stopped the fight at one minute, twenty seconds of the round. Louis retained his title. Simon was on the canvas four times before the referee ended the fight. He got some hard punches in during the later rounds, closing Louis's left eye. Simon said after the fight, "The referee should never have stopped it; I may have looked hurt, but I wasn't." Louis said, "He's as tough to wear down as anybody I ever fought." Simon's effort earned him a return match that they scheduled that night.[58, 59]

Abe Simon's fight with Buddy Baer never transpired. Instead, Simon fought Turkey Thomas to a draw at Gilmore Field, Los Angeles, California, in October. For the Chalky Wright-Joey Archibald featherweight championship bout, there was a discrepancy between the boxing commission of New York and Washington, DC, whether it would be for the championship. The New York Commission ruled that it would be for the championship. The District of Columbia Commission, in sanctioning the match, stipulated that no title would be at stake.

Commission Chairman John J. Phelan made New York's position clear during a telephone conversation with Thomas P. Morgan Jr., a Washington board member. He informed Morgan that their commission recognized Archibald as the champion and that Wright, the leading challenger, had posted a $1,000 forfeit binding the title match. The confusion postponed the match until September 11.[60]

By the end of that day on September 11, 1941, Chalky Wright fought Joey Archibald at Griffiths Stadium, Washington, DC. A left hook to the body followed by a right to the jaw knocked Archibald down in the eleventh round. The referee counted him out. Wright won the world featherweight title. Madame Bey had another champion. The gross gate amounted to around $9,000, and the crowd numbered 5,500. With Archibald guaranteed $8,000, the promoters lost money on the venture. Wright received the title but not much in monetary compensation.[61]

CHAPTER 35

On the Ropes

Infrequent is the one unseen punch that puts you down. It is the methodical, cumulative blows from an opponent that wears down the body. You become exhausted and the mind clouded trying to make sense of that which is nonsensical. In this state, a punch that was recoverable earlier would put you down for a final count.

In 1941, Madame Bey's health problems became apparent. Despite health issues, she would continue to operate the camp as best she could. It was her life's work for eighteen years. New boxers came seeking the glory of those that had proceeded, and old ones returned trying to hold on to what they had obtained. Her friends who had built their names in the sport would visit the one that was instrumental in their success.

In the autumn of 1941, the camp was still prospering; Madame Bey was not. Her health was deteriorating. Doctors diagnosed her with a heart ailment and sent her to All Souls Hospital, Morristown, New Jersey. She spent two weeks there before being released. She worked as best she could. The camp endured.

Ken Overlin and Georgie Abrams started training at Bey's Camp that autumn. Overlin was to box Al Hostak at the Garden. Abrams was to get his chance at the world middleweight title in a unification bout with Tony Zale.[1] Lew Jenkins, world lightweight champion, soon joined them. Jenkins trained for a defense of his crown scheduled on December 19 at the Garden against Sammy Angott. The dominant belief was that Jenkins would have to knock out Angott, who was a tireless fighter. Angott had never been knocked out and lost only five fights in the last five years. Three of those losses he later revenged. Only Fritzie Zivic and Sugar Ray Robinson avoided that revenge. They did not fight him again.

The New York Boxing Commission recognized Jenkins as the lightweight champion. The National Boxing Association recognized Angott. The bout would unify the lightweight title. The commission ordered Jenkins to go to Madame Bey's Camp, tiring of his antics and lack of effort in fights. The commission's concern stemmed from Jenkins's last fight with Red Cochrane on October 6, 1941, at the Garden that "showed how many jeering sounds 12,182 fans could make when they were in the mood."[2] The out-of-shape Jenkins lost and put little effort forth. He was called disgraceful by the press.[3] Jenkins said he was still feeling the effects from a motorcycle accident he had three weeks before the fight.[2] Fans were not getting their money's worth, and promoters voiced their displeasure. It could hurt future gates for boxing.

According to the press, Jenkins's $7,000 for the Cochrane fight was held up,[4] whereas it should have been confiscated, and he should have been barred from fighting for a long time, if not for life. Jenkins was ordered to post a $1,500 forfeit as a pledge that he would be in shape for his scheduled meeting with Sammy Angott.[3]

Frank Graham from the *New York Sun* wrote about Jenkins before his title fight against Angott.

"He probably speaks the truth when he says that he cares nothing for money and glory. … he has been taking money by pretending to get ready for a fight and then by pretending to fight and it is high time that something drastic was done about him. Something much more drastic than the penalty just imposed upon him.

"What everybody in the prize-fight business is hoping, of course—and this undoubtedly goes for the members of the Commission—is that he will eliminate himself from the lightweight picture by being knocked out by either Angott or Ray Robinson. It isn't too much for them to wish. Off his showing against Cochrane, he could have been knocked out by two or three of the boys who fought in the preliminaries in that show."[3]

The commission took no chances with the Jenkins-Angott world lightweight championship fight. Lew Jenkins arrived at Madame Bey's as ordered, where again he would be undistracted by outside influences. They could keep track of him there to make sure he fulfilled his obligation to be in shape for the fight and give the fans what they paid for.

Major General John J. Phelan, New York State Athletic Commission chairman, gave his approval to Ken Overlin and Al Hostak to fight. Both former world middleweight championship holders were to fight ten rounds in a light heavyweight encounter at Madison Square Garden. General Phelan went to the Pioneer Gymnasium in New York to watch Hostak box against Harvey Massey, a 165-pound spar mate. Then he went uptown to Stillman's Gymnasium, where he saw Overlin spar against Bunky Wall, the man he had been sparring with at Madame Bey's Camp.[5]

After the workouts, General Phelan expressed satisfaction with the condition of both boxers. Overlin returned immediately to Madame Bey's, where he engaged in his final hard training. Hostak finished training at the Pioneer Gymnasium.[6] Ken Overlin won a unanimous decision over Hostak at Madison Square Garden on November 21. Including the Hostak bout, Overlin fought sixteen times after his last loss, which was to Soose. He never lost another bout. That included a win and draw to future heavyweight champion Ezzard Charles—Charles's first career loss. Overlin never received a title fight again. He retired in 1944 with a record of 135 wins, nineteen losses, and nine draws.

Abrams was still training at Bey's waiting for his title bout with Zale. A doctor examined Zale in November; he was suffering from blisters on his feet and his legs. They were an ugly red color and swollen to twice their natural size. Zale had complained of a slight foot infection, but it appeared to have cleared up. He went to Radio City Music Hall that same day. It was not until he returned to his hotel shortly after ten thirty in the evening that he became alarmed and notified his manager, Art Winch. Dr. Schiff was called, and he in turn summoned Dr. Levin, who sent Zale to the hospital.

Dr. Levin said Zale's stay in the hospital might extend anywhere from two days to two weeks. He marveled at the man's physical condition in spite of the infection. Tony's pulse and temperature were normal. He had no fever. Abrams, who spent the night at Madame Bey's, was the last to be notified. He did not know the fight was cancelled until the morning. Abrams said he planned to call Zale later that day.[7]

Zale recovered. The fight took place the following week on November 28. A crowd of 12,000 filled Madison Square Garden. Abrams put Zale on the canvas in the first round. Zale fought back after the knockdown and became the undisputed world middleweight champion by a unanimous decision.[8]

"Zale is one of the toughest body-punchers I ever fought," Georgie Abrams said after the fight, "and if I hadn't been in the best shape of my life, he might have splattered me all over the ring. After the first round, I came back to my corner and said to myself, 'This is easy. I'm going to win the middleweight title by knockout.' Then in the second round, boom! And you saw what happened. He cut my left eye in the third round, and I never was able to see anything out of it from then on."

Before the Jenkins-Angott fight, commission officials were to scrutinize a workout by Lew Jenkins at Stillman's Gymnasium. Jenkins, directed to be in the gymnasium between two o'clock and two thirty, arrived late. He entered the gymnasium just when General Phelan and officials were departing. The commission was being cautious with Jenkins's condition because he had sustained injuries in another motorcycle accident.[6]

On December 3, the New York Boxing Commission subjected Lew Jenkins to his fourth examination for the Angott fight. Dr. William H. Walker pronounced him in excellent condition. Angott underwent a similar examination with satisfactory results, after which Jenkins, along with Angott, formally signed commission contracts for the championship bout in New York. Angott went to the Pioneer Gymnasium in New York to continue his training.[9, 10] Jenkins returned to Madame Bey's where he was training hard.

In his last workout before the fight, Jenkins only sparred three rounds against Jimmy Pierce. With that workout, Jenkins had done fifty-nine rounds of sparring in the fifteen days he had been preparing for Angott at Madame Bey's Camp. It had been the most comprehensive preparatory endeavor Jenkins had done since winning the lightweight title.[11]

Jenkins prepared well but showed little effort in the fight. Dissatisfied became another Madison Square Garden crowd of 11,343 fans paying $26,816 for a Jenkins's fight. Angott did his best to make a fight of it. He belabored Jenkins with what he had, opening a cut behind Lew's right eye midway through the fight. Angott bruised Jenkins's left cheekbone toward the end. He thumped Jenkins all over the ring at times, but Angott lacked a hard punch. The dull fight caused the crowd to start yelling its displeasure in the fourth round, and they never stopped until it was over. The press printed it may have been the worst championship fight.

All three officials scored the fight thirteen to two in favor of Angott. Jenkins relinquished without a struggle the crown he won from Lou Ambers. The Texan, who rose fast two years before on the strength of a right hand that knocked opponents out, inexplicitly did not use it much. He did not throw more than a dozen hard rights at Angott, and most missed. After it ended, his handlers said, with bewilderment, that they did not know why.[12]

It was an end to a year, 1941, that saw many of the best fighters come to Madame Bey's Camp. Many of her boys were serving in the armed forces as war approached for America. That war became a reality on December 7 with the bombing of Pearl Harbor. Many more of those training at Bey's would join the war effort after that day. The war would change the world and have its impact on boxing. Many continued to come to Bey's to train and fight during furloughs. Madame Bey, who had lived through many wars and the genocide of her people, would continue to fight her own battle. Her strife was an internal struggle. Her heart ailment worsened.

CHAPTER 36

The Crown of Life

Madame Bey had a lifetime that ranged from the exotic Ottoman Empire to the operation of a boxing camp. She dazzled in the diplomatic factions of Washington. She moved in the operatic circles of New York with an extensive concert repertoire and entered the oriental rug and antique business. In a dramatic shift in career, she operated a training camp for pugilists in a rural environment. In every one of these differing fields, she shone. Of all these endeavors, her boxing camp lasted the longest, almost twenty years. It gave her the most pleasure. Her training camp business flourished. Foreign fighters felt at home in her place. Others made it their home.

By the year 1942, the camp had seen the best the sport had to offer during its operation. Many traveled to the remote spot seeking fame, fortune, and a better life. Many succeeded, but more failed. The woman who operated the camp sought none of the fame that her boys did. She contented herself to watch them grow and mature. She concerned herself more with their well-being than their winning of a title or a bout. She came to appreciate her life among her boys more than her years in the whirl of Washington, DC, as a diplomat's wife and socialite.

On January 27, her heart began to betray her again. She was in ill health for six months. She returned to All Souls Hospital in Morristown, New Jersey, for treatment. She lost the bout. She was unable to rally and succumbed to her condition. For the woman who could not be beaten in life, it took a knockout to seize the fight from her. She died on a Friday, January 30, at twelve thirty in the morning.[1] She was sixty years old. The boxing world lost a unique figure, the likes of which would never be seen again.

Her obituary was short but pervasive in newspapers. As in her life, boxing events overshadowed it. The proportion of newspaper space afforded to her compared to that of boxers mimicked the attention she received in life as her boys progressed to fame. She lived contentedly in her role of parent and disciplinarian of rough men. Often her mezzo-soprano voice rolled through the camp as she sang arias from the operas she used to perform for concert audiences. When Madame Bey died, not only a prominent figure in the sporting world passed on but also a person who was resourceful, competent, and talented.

On a Sunday, February 1, her family held the funeral at her boxing camp, where the presence of some of the greatest fighters of the past had always been palpable. A continuous procession of fighters, sportswriters, boxing officials, and neighbors called at her home to pay their last respects to one whom they learned to love and admire. Mostly neighbors and intimate friends attended the funeral services. Her other friends were represented by floral tributes.[2] The Reverend W. O. Kinsolving, pastor of Calvary Episcopal Church, Summit, New Jersey, presided over the ceremonies. Her family had her buried at the Fairmount Cemetery[1] in the Borough of Chatham, New Jersey.[3]

"It's a wonderful life," she once said, "knowing these strong boys, observing their moods and trying, unobtrusively, to mother them."[4]

She championed the idea of a remote training location for boxers. It was an idea that outlasted her. Her camp saw champions from every weight class, and in most cases, multiple champions per class. In the most revered heavyweight division, the town hosted nine heavyweight champions. It would see three more after she had gone. No fewer than forty-three fighters that were inducted into the International Boxing Hall of Fame came to Chatham Township during the time Madame Bey operated her camp. No fewer than fifteen others were inducted as trainers, managers, publicists, and promoters. After her death, no fewer than twenty more inductees would follow.

The number of brilliant boxers who came through the camp over those years was staggering. Nearly every foreign fighter of merit found his way to Madame Bey's door. Champions and top challengers trained there. Past greats came to watch and comment on the talented newcomers. Through the years, Madame Bey had watched her boys grow to manhood and compete in boxing championships. She saw them come to her ragged and saw them rise to fortune and fame. Sometimes they returned to her, beaten and broke, trying to recover a lost glory.

She had her favorites, some boxing legends, others just making a living. She talked often about Gene Tunney, Mickey Walker, Max Schmeling, Lou Ambers, Tommy Farr, Freddie Steele, and Paulino Uzcudun. There were others she tolerated, but she would never express her grievances in the press. Still more that were unknown, she gave a home to, even if they were unable to afford the fee.

She had established a boxing empire that her longtime friend and business partner, Eshan Karadag, would continue. He would not change the formula that Madame Bey had established. The champions kept coming for the next twenty years.

Former world junior welterweight champion Maxie Berger came to train for his fight with Sugar Ray Robinson[5] at the time of her death. Berger would lose to the future multiple titleholder, and one of the best pound-for-pound fighters. Freddie Fiducia was there when

Madame Bey left the camp for a final time.[6] He represented those that came to Bey's to work hard and subsist, though never achieving the heights that so many sought. Fiducia was familiar with the camp; he had been there before. He was a man not renowned in the boxing world but had a twenty-two-year career. He fought in every weight class from flyweight to heavyweight. Freddie Fiducia defeated Johnny Flynn in his bout at Laurel Garden, Newark, New Jersey, ten days after Bey's death. Her boys continued the legacy in her absence.

"Every blow they take," she once said, "I take with them."[7]

She wept with them and over them. She knew all their hopes and fears. She had known several generations of prizefighters and yet had attended only two prizefight cards. She did not like to watch them, especially when it involved any of her boys who had practically grown up at her camp.[8]

Madame Bey appreciated that her boys who were on the verge of success or failure in what at best was a too-short career. She saw that they were not interfered with as their fight neared. She saw them on the way up, as champions, as ex-champions, and then as desperate trudges on the comeback trail. She saw them finally as shaky, old at thirty, has-beens, who came to the camp to watch the latest big names go through their paces.

There was always another prizefighter punching his way to glory, but for Madame Bey, one of the most colorful figures the training camp business had seen, there existed no duplicate.[9] No longer would reporters, promoters, managers, and trainers marvel at the woman running a successful camp for prizefighters, exacting obedience from them by her presence and character. She was without prejudgment and could see beyond their rugged appearances to what existed beneath their exteriors. There was the allure in the championships that Bey's fighters sought. There was another and more important championship, though it carried no name. It went to the person who could conquer defeat and discouragement beyond that of the prizefighting ring. It is earned by those who do not complain about the loss of fame, money, or status to face life anew. It goes to one who can take unselfish pride in those they help and not just in one's own accomplishments. They do not award titles for that.

EPILOGUE

I t was March 1942. Weeks had passed since the death of Madame Bey in the cold of January. Rustem Bey, Madame Bey's son, inherited the boxing establishment. Rustem had a full-time job as Chatham Township's chief of police. Madame Bey's longtime business partner, Ehsan Karadag, operated the camp. Her name lived on in the sports sections of newspapers around the world as top boxers continued to prepare at the camp she had built. The air warmed with the season. The promise of new growth appeared in the hillside camp in New Jersey.

One of the first big-name boxers to come to the camp was the Ape. Heavyweight Abe Simon continued the tradition of using Bey's to attempt to wrest the world heavyweight title away from Joe Louis. He arrived on March 11, just over five weeks after Madame Bey's death. It would be Simon's second title bout against the champion. With Simon were heavyweight Golden Gloves champion, turned professional, Jimmy Carrollo, and lightweight contender Bobby Ruffin.

Ruffin was familiar with Madame Bey's Camp. He was one of the few boxers involved in a physical altercation while training there. Ehsan recalled the incident when both Ruffin and heavyweight contender Gus Dorazio were in training together. While Dorazio was asleep in his room, Ruffin thought it would be fun to light a firecracker under his bed. Dorazio was not amused. Ruffin retreated to his room and locked it. The furious Dorazio found him and broke in the door. The heavyweight proceeded to strangle the lightweight on his bed. Others had to rush in to pry Dorazio's hands off Ruffin.[1]

As he had done many times before, Frank Graham from the *New York Sun* came to report on a fighter. He was there to see Abe Simon prepare for Louis. Graham and others sat around a table after lunch at the Suburban Hotel—renamed from the Summit Hotel— in Summit, New Jersey, listening to promoter and manager Jimmy Johnston tell stories of the old days along Broadway. They could have sat there all afternoon and all evening listening to him, but Abe Simon was waiting for them at Madame Bey's Camp. They were still laughing as they left the dining room.

"I see where you are not going to object to any referee for this fight," one said to Johnston.

"Why should I?" Jimmy demanded. "When you are going to fight Joe Louis you do not have to worry about the referee or the judges or anybody else. The guy never asked for an edge from anybody. He goes in there with nothing but his two fists and lays his title on the line for you, and if you are good enough to take it from him that's all you need."

"And how do you think Simon will do with him?"

"My Abe," Jimmy Johnston said, "will break his nose, close one of his eyes, and give him such a licking that the referee will have to stop the fight in the fourth round."

When they reached Bey's, Freddy Brown, who trained Simon and Bob Pastor and the other Johnston fighters, was waiting at the gymnasium door for them.

"Come right in," he said. "We're all ready."

He led them through the gymnasium, where the paying customers sat against the sidewalls, and down the stairs to the dressing rooms. Simon was sitting on a rubbing table in the same room that Red Burman used when he was there training for Louis.

"Louis's ghost is all over the place," one said.

"Burman trained here and when I came in I saw Gus Dorazio. In one way or another, the guy leaves his mark everywhere he goes."

Simon laughed. He went thirteen rounds with Louis a year before and was on his feet at the finish. He did not fear him.

They stood around the rubbing table or sat on a narrow bench along one side of the room.

"The young man who, by eleven o'clock on Friday night, will be the heavyweight champion of the world," Johnston said, nodding toward Simon.

"That isn't what you told me outside," someone said as he winked at Simon.

"That is what I have been telling everybody," Johnston said.

"Didn't you hear me say that on the radio the other night?" Johnston said as he turned to Simon.

"You said so much I don't remember what you said."

"With a memory like that," Johnston said. "I don't know how you got through high school.

Johnston said a few more words then strolled out of the room.

"Abe," one said, "in your fight with Louis last year, you kept sticking him in the face with your left hand. I don't think you missed with a jab. What is there about his style that made it possible for you to hit him with your left so easily?"

"That night I think I would have hit anybody with my left."

"Why?"

"It was all I had," Abe said. "I couldn't use my right hand at all. I had to hit him with my left or not at all."

"And the knowledge of that sharpened your left?"

'That's what I believe."

"How is your right hand now?"

"It's all right."

"You had no trouble with it this time?"

"None at all."

"What was the matter with it last year?"

"It was broken. I broke it nine days before the fight."

"You fooled me before the fight. I never suspected anything was wrong with it," another one said.

"Neither did Pop," Abe said.

All Johnston's fighters called him Pop.

"I hit a sparring partner three times in a row on the head with it, and I thought at first it was just a sprain, but when the swelling didn't go down I knew it was broken. I almost parboiled it in hot water and epsom salts, but that didn't do any good, and I knew it was broken, but Pop—and even Freddy—didn't know it until after the fight."

Brown stuck his head in the doorway.

"All right," he said. "Let's commence."

Abe climbed into the ring with Joe Baksi.

"This is the fellow that gave Nova hell when he was training for Joe Louis," someone said.

Simon and Baksi boxed two rounds. Baksi hit him repeatedly with straight rights to the head. Simon relied mainly on a left jab and threw his right hand seldom. When he did, he threw it to the body. When Baksi left the ring, Johnny Shkor replaced him and went two rounds. He also had no trouble hitting Simon with right hands, and Abe seldom used his right.

When the workout was over, and they were leaving, someone said:

"I was just talking to Jimmy, and he said that between now and Friday night they would correct that fault in Abe's defense. For his sake, I hope they do. Meanwhile, all I can say is that Abe is in good shape, takes a punch well and is dead game. And I knew all that before I came out here."[2]

A crowd of 18,220 came to see the fight at Madison Square Garden on March 27, 1942. The huge Abe Simon outweighed Louis by over forty-seven pounds. Louis, now a private in the army, fought for no money. He donated his 47.5 percent share of the purse to the charity Army Emergency Relief Fund. Simon reduced his portion of the purse from 20 percent to 15 percent, giving the difference to the fund. In addition, Simon donated another 2.5 percent of his pay for the fight. Being in the army, the Brown Bomber had trained at the army base at Fort Dix, New Jersey.

For Louis, the bout would be the first time he fought without trainer Jack Blackburn, who was hospitalized and would die one month later. Simon went down at the bell in both the second and fifth rounds. Louis sent Simon to the canvas with three punches to the chin in the opening of the sixth round. Referee Eddie Josephs counted ten just as Simon rose and waved Louis away, ending the fight.[3] Simon and Johnston contended he was up at the count of nine, and Simon looked in control of his faculties as he went back to his corner.

"I wasn't hurt," Simon insisted. "I knew what I was doing all the time."[4]

It would be the twenty-six-year-old Simon's last fight. Madame Bey's Max remained the only man to defeat Louis.

It was early spring of 1945. Over three years had passed since the death of Madame Bey. Longtime inhabitants Ehsan Karadag and Tom Finnegan, the man from Northern Ireland whose predictive white pigeon was still making appearances at the camp, operated the business for the last three years. They had been there as handymen for almost twenty-five years under Madame Bey and after her death. Ehsan's relationship extended further to the days when they were business partners as oriental rug merchants. In March 1945, Madame Bey's son, Rustem, sold the world-renowned boxing camp and twelve surrounding acres to Ehsan. He was the sole proprietor of the camp. The large tin sign printed with "Bey's Training Camp" was changed to "Ehsan's Training Camp."

"From now on, the place has a new name, 'Ehsan's Training Camp,'" said Karadag as he was printing his name on the tin marker. "Everything will go on as it did when Madame Bey was here to direct things."

The California Golden Boy, Lou Nova, who had shown promise as a young heavyweight and lost that brutal battle to Tony Galento in 1939, was training at the camp at the time of its sale. He had lost a world heavyweight championship title bout to Joe Louis in 1941. Nova had a room at the Suburban Hotel in the neighboring town of Summit. He would wake and then run the four-mile distance from the hotel to the camp to train. One day, Nova, now thirty, sat with journalist John Beer, Ehsan, and others on the farmhouse porch overlooking the road from where Nova had just jogged from the Suburban Hotel.

"Lou, since that night in 1941, have you thought of anything you missed doing when you had your chance at the heavyweight championship?" John Beer asked.

"That's a good question," Nova said.

"I've thought of it many times, and one word 'wait' is the answer. Every time I think of the word, I get peeved at myself. It goes back to a month before the Louis fight. My handlers drilled me every day with advice of 'wait,' 'wait,' wait.' Keep away from him. Be sure to wait. Well, that was September 1941, and I'm still waiting. My only successful style was to wade in and slug—I've always been able to take a good punch and have two hands to give them. Against Louis, I was foolish enough to take the wrong advice."[5]

Boxers and their handlers continued to come for the next three decades. The old-guard trainers, managers, and promoters returned with old and new charges. They included

Whitey Bimstein, Ray Arcel, Charley Goldman, Doc Kearns, Jimmy Johnston, and Al Weill. New legendary handlers arrived, one being Constantine "Cus" D'Amato, a boxing wizard whose last charge was Mike Tyson.

Tippy Larkin, who had impressed Lou Ambers and Tony Canzoneri, returned. Larkin became the world junior welterweight champion. Freddie "Red" Cochrane also came back, still the welterweight champion. Cochrane carried his welterweight title into World War II where he fought as a member of the navy for three and a half years, causing his absence from the professional ring from 1942 to 1945. On his return, he won his first five fights. After those fights, he trained at Ehsan's for a nontitle bout against Rocky Graziano in 1945.[6] After out-boxing Graziano for eight rounds, he was knocked down in the ninth and then knocked out in the tenth. *The Ring* magazine called it the fight of the year. Cochrane would lose his title the following year to Marty Servo and then retire.

Featherweight Lulu Costantino, undefeated in fifty-six professional fights was there in May 1942 but lost his first fight for the championship to former Bey resident Chalky Wright. Two-time world lightweight champion Bob Montgomery came in 1942. Then Ike Williams trained at Ehsan's to beat Bob Montgomery for the world lightweight title in 1947.[7]

Gus Lesnevich, light heavyweight champion from 1941 to 1948, trained at the camp. He had served in the United States Coast Guard from 1943 to 1945 and named *The Ring* magazine Fighter of the Year in 1947. Lesnevich lost a heavyweight title fight to Ezzard Charles, for which he trained at Ehsan's Camp, in Charles's first defense since he beat Jersey Joe Walcott for Joe Louis's vacated title. It was Lesnevich's last career fight in 1949.

Whitey Bimstein's trainee Billy "Blackjack" Fox, two-time light heavyweight title challenger was there. Some said he had forty-three consecutive knockouts. Fox said that he had thirty-six professional fights, all knockouts, before meeting Gus Lesnevich for the light heavyweight title at Madison Square Garden, February 28, 1947.

"Boxing was my life. I kept track of my fights," Billy Fox said.[8]

Tom Finnegan's white pigeon made an appearance at the camp while Fox trained for his title fight, meaning to Tom that the camp would have a new champion. Despite the fact that the pigeon's lifespan had expired, it kept coming. Once a concept is instilled in one's mind, no logic can dislodge it.

"O' course, it was here," Tom snapped at those unbelievers. "Ain't I been seein' her for years. Don't I know her? … I see her with my own eyes, that's as sure as Fox is goin' to win the title. I know when there's goin' to be a new champion!"[9]

The lore of the pigeon could not overcome the power of Lesnevich. Fox lost.

Ex-world middleweight champion Rocky Graziano trained at Ehsan's in September 1949 with Whitey Bimstein as his trainer. Graziano's wife, Norma, and their daughters,

Audrey, five, and Roxanne, eighteen months, stayed in a cottage at the camp.[10] It was an arrangement that did not occur when Madame Bey operated the camp. Less than a week before his fight with Charlie Fusari, cars were parked along the road, and spectators filled the benches in the gymnasium to watch Rocky spar. Hundreds had occupied the camp every day to watch Rocky.[10] Ehsan Karadag said the crowds that paid to watch the workouts over the Labor Day weekend were the greatest he ever saw at the camp, which exhibited Graziano's allure. During the five weeks Graziano had been training, the camp had the most spectators since it opened in 1923.[11] Tom Finnegan predicted a win for Graziano. Rocky defeated Charlie Fusari at the Polo Grounds on September 14 by a technical knockout. Fusari was ahead by one round on all three scorecards when the fight was stopped.

Archie the "Old Mongoose" Moore came to Ehsan's with Whitey Bimstein and Ray Arcel. When most fighters had long since retired, Archie Moore held the world light heavyweight championship from 1952 to 1962. He was thirty-six years old when he won the title and held it until he reached forty-five. Moore still holds the record of 131 knockouts. He trained at Ehsan's for his 1955 heavyweight title bout against Rocky Marciano in 1955. Moore knocked down Marciano in the second round for a two count but was knocked down four times himself—twice in the sixth, once in the eighth, and then when the referee counted him out in round nine. Moore lost a title bout for the heavyweight championship again in 1956, vacated by Rocky Marciano, to Floyd Patterson.

World featherweight champion Sandy Saddler used Ehsan's as his camp many times. In 1950, Saddler won the world featherweight title from Willie Pep. Johnny Dundee, former world featherweight champion, came to watch Saddler. Dundee, while there, admitted he had never trained at a training camp except once for a fight, against Eugene Criqui.[12] Saddler arrived at Ehsan's to defend his title against Red Top Davis, another user of Ehsan's Camp, at Madison Square Garden on February 25, 1955. With him were Archie Moore and his manager, Jimmy Johnston. Saddler won a unanimous fifteen-round decision.

World middleweight champion Jake "Bronx Bull" LaMotta was in Ehsan's Camp.[13] Jake LaMotta was best known from the movie about his life, *Raging Bull*, in which Robert DeNiro won an Oscar for playing LaMotta. He was also known for his six fights with Sugar Ray Robinson in which he won one and lost five. The one win came after Robinson had won his first forty consecutive professional fights. *The Ring* magazine named LaMotta the fifth greatest middleweight of all time in 2004.

World light heavyweight champion Joey Maxim and his manager, Doc Kearns, were at Ehsan's Camp. In 1951, Maxim had lost a title fight against Ezzard Charles for the heavyweight championship. For his next fight, Maxim was at Ehsan's to train. While at the camp, Doc Kearns would barbecue,[14] as he had done in the past, for attendees. Maxim would retain his light heavyweight title by beating Bob Murphy.

In 1953, Ray Arcel and Charley Goldman, longtime users of Ehsan's Camp, had welterweight champion, Cuban-born, Kid the "Cuban Hawk" Gavilan at the camp. Like his fellow Cuban citizen, Kid Chocolate who used the camp, everyone called Kid Gavilan the *Keed*.[15] The *Keed* would train at Ehsan's for several fights.

Among other fighters to come to Ehsan's were world heavyweight champion Jersey Joe Walcott; Ezzard Charles, world heavyweight champion and *The Ring* magazine's 1949 and 1950 Fighter of the Year; Tommy Bell, who lost a welterweight title bout to Sugar Ray Robinson; Jimmy Carter, three-time world lightweight champion; Beau Jack, two-time world lightweight champion; Willie Pep, two-time world featherweight champion; Ralph Tiger Jones, who defeated Kid Gavilan and Sugar Ray Robinson; Al Weill and Charley Goldman charge Marty Servo—a cousin to world lightweight champion Lou Ambers—who beat Freddie Cochrane for the welterweight crown; Whitey Bimstein's charge, Johnny Saxton, who was a two-time welterweight champion; Tommy Hurricane Jackson, trained at Ehsan's Camp for his world heavyweight title loss to Floyd Patterson; Joey Giardello, world middleweight champion; light heavyweight Lloyd Marshall; Benny Kid Paret, two-time world welterweight champion, who trained at Ehsan's Camp for a title defense against Emile Griffith and died from ring injuries during that fight; light heavyweight contender Jimmy "Cleveland Spider-Man" Bivins, who defeated Archie Moore, Ezzard Charles, Gus Lesnevich, Melio Bettina, Anton Christoforidis, Teddy Yarosz, and Joey Maxim; heavyweight Red Applegate, who went ten rounds with Rocky Marciano; welterweight contender Billy Graham, who had legendary fights with Joey Giardello and defeated Sugar Ray Robinson before Robinson turned professional; middleweight contender Steve Belloise, who fought a losing battle with Ken Overlin for the title; middleweight contender Sam Baroudi, who died from injuries sustained in the ring with Ezzard Charles in 1948; Charley Fusari, who lost a welterweight title bout to Sugar Ray Robinson and Johnny Bratton; Allie Stolz, who fought for the lightweight title; Lee Oma, whose last fight was against Ezzard Charles for the heavyweight title; contenders welterweight Freddie Archer, middleweight Steve Hostak, and welterweight Flashy Sebastian.

World heavyweight champion Floyd Patterson, who had been to the Ehsan's Camp before, arrived in 1959 to train for his title defense against the undefeated Swedish Ingemar "Ingo" Johansson, who had compiled a record of twenty-one wins and no losses. Whitey Bimstein, who knew well the positive effects of Ehsan's on a fighter, was Johansson's trainer. It would be the first of three consecutive title bouts between Patterson and Johansson. Patterson would be the last heavyweight champion to train at the camp. He was there with his discoverer, manager, and mentor, Cus D'Amato.

Patterson had won the title vacated by the retired and undefeated Rocky Marciano, by beating Archie Moore in 1956. Reporter Gilbert Rogin came to Ehsan's to see Patterson before the first Johansson fight.

"When I build a camp," Floyd once said, "you'll have to drive your car, then take a bus, then take a boat across a river, and then walk two miles."[16]

There was not a place remote enough for D'Amato's charge. That made Ehsan's Camp an ideal place for him. He reveled in its seclusion. He collected snakes, for hours, in his spare time.[17] With Patterson was middleweight Ralph 'Tiger' Jones, who was trained by Gil Clancy. Jones was a popular boxer on 1950s television because of his aggressive style of fighting, but he never received a title fight.

When Patterson trained at Ehsan's, he would go to neighboring New Providence on Sundays to attend mass at the Our Lady of Peace Catholic Church.[18] He had converted to Catholicism after meeting his wife.

"I never used to believe in nothing but me," Floyd once said. "What I could see, I believed in—nothing else."[16]

On June 26, 1959, at Yankee Stadium, Patterson and Johansson met for the first time. Johansson sent Patterson to the canvas seven times in the third round. Referee, and former Madame Bey trainee, Ruby Goldstein stopped the fight in the third round. Patterson lost his title before a crowd of 21,961 at Yankee Stadium.

The following year on June 20, 1960, at the Polo Grounds, the rematch was witnessed by 31,892 fans that paid $824,891. Patterson became the first man in history to regain the heavyweight title when he knocked out Johansson in the fifth round. It also marked the return of Humbert J. Fugazy as a fight promoter; he had not promoted a fight for years. When asked in 1959 why he was returning to boxing, Fugazy declared, "Because I think I can make this [the rematch between Johansson and Patterson] the greatest promotion there ever was."[19] *The Ring* magazine called it 1960's Fight of the Year.

In 1961, Whitey Bimstein, sixty-four years old, was in Miami Beach, Florida, training former world heavyweight champion Ingemar Johansson for his third bout with Floyd Patterson for the heavyweight title. Each had a win and loss in their two previous meetings.

"This joint must remind you a lot of Madame Bey's," someone asked, "or maybe Doc Bier's in Pompton."

"I wish it was one of them," Whitey said. "In the old days, a fighter'd be living in the woods like a hermit, running and hiking, and chopping down trees to get in shape for training, which a fighter ought to. And then he'd go someplace like Summit, which was a real training camp and all he'd do is train, just him and the trainer and sparring partners."[20]

Among those that came to watch Johansson spar were two former Bey tenants—Max Schmeling, the ex-heavyweight champion who was a Coca-Cola tycoon in Hamburg, Germany, and Tommy Loughran, unbeaten in his time as the light heavyweight champion. Loughran was a friend of Patterson and his handler, Cus D'Amato.

Patterson trained in Florida as Johansson did, where the bout was held. Patterson was out of his element in Florida. He preferred seclusion. The sparring session was a spectacle more than a training session for a professional boxer. Sam Taub, a journalist and radio broadcaster whose first job was as an assistant to Bat Masterson at the *New York Morning Telegraph*, was the master of ceremonies. At the sparring session were Rocky Marciano, Barney Ross, Tommy Loughran, and Frank Sinatra.

Taub announced each sparring partner and their weight before they entered the ring with Floyd Patterson. Shapely women carried a placard between sessions with the round number. One time after Taub made his weight announcement, someone from the crowd said to one of the women, "How much do you weigh, honey."[21] The solitude and non-glitz of Madame Bey's was a faint memory to those that remembered the way it used to be.

On March 13, 1961, at the Convention Center, Miami Beach, Florida, the two fought. Whitey Bimstein handled Johansson's corner, and Cus D'Amato was in Patterson's corner. Johansson knocked Patterson down twice in the first round; Johansson was then knocked down at the end of the round. Whitey stopped a cut on Johansson after the third round. Patterson knocked Johansson out in the sixth at two minutes, forty-five seconds. *The Ring* magazine called it the fight of the year.[22] Johansson returned to Sweden. He fought two more years and retired with a record of twenty-six wins and two losses—the two losses against Patterson.

The way Patterson and Johansson trained for their third fight in Florida was becoming a standard. Training camps like Ehsan's were becoming part of a past era. A hotel in the Borscht Belt of the Catskill Mountains in New York invited prominent fighters to train. It would serve as entertainment for guests, and the hotel received free publicity from sportswriters. Other hotels followed. They built state-of-the-art gymnasiums. They gave top fighters inducements of free room and board for their entire team. Many would give the fighters all the revenue from admission to their training. It eroded Ehsan's business. He could not compete.

In March 1962, Floyd Patterson agreed to defend his title against Sonny Liston. For the fight, Liston said he would start training at Ehsan's Camp on March 12 or 19.[23] Later, Liston's attorney, Morton Witkin, said, "He'll wait until Patterson formally announces the fight."[24] The fight, originally scheduled for New York, changed to Chicago, which prevented the use of Ehsan's Camp. The New York State Athletic Commission refused to license Liston because of his criminal record and a "pattern of suspicion" he had with people associated with organized crime.[25] On September 25, 1962, Liston won the title by knocking Patterson out in the first round.

By the mid-1960s, Ehsan's still had some top-notch boxers but far from the numbers in the past. Among the camp's best were Jose Torres, world light heavyweight champion; Carlos Ortiz, world lightweight champion; Rubin "Hurricane" Carter, middleweight contender; Isaac Logart, welterweight contender; and Doug Jones, heavyweight and light heavyweight contender.

Doug Jones lost to Harold Johnson for the vacant world light heavyweight championship in 1962. He is best remembered for his March 13, 1963, fight against unbeaten, and highly touted, Olympic gold medalist Muhammad Ali at a sold-out Madison Square Garden. Before the fight, Ali gave his predictive prose, which started with:

"Jones likes to mix,

"So, I'll let it go six."

This prediction would be unfounded. A young Muhammad Ali, The Greatest, discovered the toughness of a seasoned veteran. The officials scored it for Ali, eight to one, five to four, and five to four. The Associated Press poll of fifteen writers at ringside scored seven for Ali, five for Jones, and three even. The United Press International poll of twenty-five writers at ringside scored thirteen for Jones, ten for Ali, and two even. Ali received boos, and Jones received the cheers of a winner, but Ali would obtain greatness. *The Ring* magazine called it the fight of the year.

"I thought I won it no worse than 6–3–1," Doug Jones said.

"I thought I was going to finish him in the fourth, but he's tougher than I thought he was," Muhammad Ali said.

"I'm not knocking his big mouth. He made me a lot of dough," Doug Jones said.[26]

Muhammad Ali exacted his revenge in 1966 when he was the world heavyweight champion in an exhibition match against Doug Jones. He dominated him over six rounds.[27]

By December 1961, Ehsan Karadag was the sole survivor among the old-time proprietors of training camps for only fighters. The hotels took all but a small part of his business. Hundreds of fighters and spar mates had relaxed and played cards in the same living room since the day when Madame Bey had opened the camp thirty-eight years before.

"I can't understand this new attitude of the fighters," Ehsan said. "You'd think they were employed by someone else to get themselves in shape, and they were out to do just enough work to earn a salary—or something.

"They don't do their roadwork or their gymnasium exercises or their sparring with the same all-out determination that was so noticeable when fellows like Charlie Weinert, Joey Maxim, Gus Lesnevich, Kid Gavilan, and even Rocky Graziano trained here. Don't let anybody kid you about Graziano. He was a hard worker."

A reporter asked was 1961 a good year for the Ehsan Camp?

"It was the worst year we ever had," Ehsan replied. "We had only a few boys here. As you can see, the camp is empty right now. But Benny Kid Paret will be back soon to begin training for his welterweight title defense against Emile Griffith in March."

Under present conditions, will Karadag be able to continue running the camp for fighters only, a reporter queried?

"Yes," he said firmly, "I'll run it that way until I die."[28]

Charley Goldman, seventy-five years old, had trained five world titleholders—Rocky Marciano, Al McCoy, Marty Servo, Lou Ambers, and Joey Archibald. In 1963, he came to Ehsan's with a new hope. He was a man with a shaven head and a drooping black mustache—Rubin "Hurricane" Carter. He was training for his nationally televised fight with Farid Salim.

"I'm positive that Carter will be at least my sixth champion and quite likely my seventh and eighth," Charley Goldman said.

"And he can do it, too," Ehsan agreed.[29]

During his training at Ehsan's while on the heavy bag, he would chant a phrase to no one.

"Ain't it a shame the sun won't shine!" Carter repeated after each blow.[30] It meant nothing to anyone but must have meant something to Carter.

"He's the hardest-hitting middleweight since Stanley Ketchel," Goldman explained. "And he hits lot faster and straighter than Ketchel did. Ketchel was a hooker and swinger."[29]

Carter beat Farid Salim in a unanimous ten-round decision. Whether Carter ever would have been a world champion, as Charley Goldman predicted, no one would know. He had one title fight; he lost a fifteen-round decision to middleweight champion Joey Giardello in 1964. Before that bout, Carter had won twenty of his first twenty-four fights, including thirteen by a knockout. Afterward, he won only seven of his last fifteen bouts. His biggest win was a first-round knockout of Emile Griffith, a middleweight and welterweight champion.

"He could have gone a long way," Emile Griffith said. "I should know. He knocked me down and stopped me."

Rubin Carter became more known for his triple murder conviction in 1967 than for his boxing. An extraordinary affiliation between boxer Rubin Hurricane Carter and Fred

Hogan originated at Ehsan's Camp. As a teenage Police Athletic League boxer in Bayonne, New Jersey, Hogan first met Carter at Ehsan's Camp in 1964. Hogan's father worked as a guard at the Hudson County Jail, where Carter's manager, Pat Amato, held the position of a deputy warden.[31]

"My father took me out there a couple of times, that's how I met him," Hogan recalled. "My father knew Rubin's manager."[32]

In June 1966, two black men shot three white men at the Lafayette Bar and Grill in Paterson, New Jersey. An all-white jury convicted Carter and another man, John Artis, mostly on the testimony of two career criminals, Alfred P. Bello and Arthur D. Bradley, who had told the police that they had witnessed the crime. In 1967, Carter was sentenced to a triple life term.

Fred Hogan started working in the public defender's office for its Monmouth County bureau. In his work, he often went to Rahway State Prison to talk to clients. There, he again met Rubin Carter. He started working on his case, and in 1974, Hogan got recantation from Bello and Bradley.[33]

"I knew in my heart that there was no way that Rubin did that," Hogan said. "And the more Rubin told me about the trial, the more I knew it stunk."

Rubin Carter would be retried with the same outcome as the first trial—a conviction in 1976. With the recantations, dozens of celebrities joined Rubin Carter's cause, but Fred Hogan made it possible. The incident aroused widespread controversy and heated public debate among celebrities and the public. Muhammad Ali, the world heavyweight champion, supported Carter and Bob Dylan's 1975 song "Hurricane" depicted the incident. Books and a movie on his life were created.

Carter talked about the one man who did not forget him when imprisoned.

"That one man is Fred Hogan," he said. "If it wasn't for Fred Hogan, I'd be dead now."[34]

In November 1985, Federal District Judge H. Lee Sarokin released Carter. He cited the convictions "were predicated on an appeal to racism rather than reason, and concealment rather than disclosure." Authorities decided against a third trial, and the original indictment against Carter was dismissed on February 26, 1988.[35]

"I wouldn't give up," Carter said in an interview in 2011. "No matter that they sentenced me to three life terms in prison. I wouldn't give up. Just because a jury of twelve misinformed people … found me guilty did not make me guilty. And because I was not guilty, I refused to act like a guilty person."

In the mid-1960s, a Citroen automobile driven by a well-built man in his midthirties arrived at Ehsan's Camp. He explained to those gathered about the automobile's unique suspension, which compensated for various terrains.[30, 36] He was not a boxer but knew more about the history of the sport than anyone did. If there was any place a boxing historian wanted to be, this was the place. His name was Jimmy Jacobs, and he was a six-time singles and doubles world champion in four-wall handball.

Though his sport of choice was four-wall handball, he excelled in many others, including three-wall handball, baseball, basketball, and football. He was credited with running one hundred yards in less than ten seconds, winning a skeet shooting championship, and shooting rounds of golf in the low seventies.[37, 38] In 1966, *Sports Illustrated* wrote, "Jacobs is generally hailed as the finest player of all time. Indeed, there are those who say Jacobs is the best athlete, regardless of sport, in the country."[39]

In his Citroen automobile, he had films of old fights, which was the reason for him coming to the camp. Inside the farmhouse, they placed a projector, showed the films, and discussed them. Jacobs had been collecting boxing films since he was seventeen and was in the process of accumulating the largest collection ever with fellow collector Bill Clayton. In 1984, Jacobs and Clayton signed to manage Mike Tyson, who was being trained by Jacobs's friend Cus D'Amato. Over a year after Tyson won the world heavyweight championship, Jacobs died at the age of fifty-eight. In 1998, Clayton sold their film collection to ESPN for a reported $100 million.[40]

In 1966 and 1967, the last world champion came to use Ehsan's as a base for his training. Like Freddie Welsh, who had brought boxing to the small idyllic community of Chatham Township, he held the world lightweight championship. His name was Carlos Ortiz, born in Ponce, Puerto Rico, on September 9, 1936. He came to mainland America in 1947. Ortiz had eyes that lit his face, even white teeth, tightly curling brown hair, and thick eyebrows dominating his tiny features. His face remained unmarked after eighteen years of fighting as an amateur and professional.[41]

Ortiz held the world junior lightweight championship from 1959 to 1962, followed by two reigns as the world lightweight champion, from 1962 to 1965 and from 1965 to 1968. Most champions were training elsewhere. Some were in hotels in the Catskill Mountains. Muhammad Ali, world heavyweight champion, preferred to do his work in a midtown gymnasium, where the "people can come to see me."

"The Garden wanted to put me up there somewhere, too," Ortiz said, "but there's too many people there. I don't like to be bothered when I'm training."[42]

Ortiz was to defend his world lightweight title against Gabriel "Flash" Elorde from the Philippines at Madison Square Garden. It would be the first lightweight title bout at the Garden in almost thirteen years—since Paddy DeMarco, the Brooklyn Billy Goat, dethroned Jimmy Carter on March 5, 1954.

The now-white, clapboard farmhouse that had housed a great many champions was weather beaten. Inside, Carlos Ortiz played cards, which had been a tradition through the years. Ehsan was seventy-seven years old. He used to have many fighters training, but now he was lucky to have three—Ortiz and two sparring partners. Ortiz also spent a few weeks at Ehsan's earlier that year prior to his title bouts with Sugar Ramos and Johnny Bizzarro. Other than that, Ehsan's Camp had been quiet.

"I love this place," Ortiz said. "I don't want to train at those resorts. Too many people …"[42]

Ortiz dominated the fight against Elorde at the Garden on November 28, 1966. He scored a knockout at two minutes, one second in round fourteen of fifteen. All scorecards showed Ortiz ahead before the knockout. Referee Jimmy Devlin eleven to two, Judge Joe Armstrong thirteen to zero, and Judge Artie Aidala twelve to one. The unofficial Associated Press scorecard was twelve to one, and the unofficial United Press International scorecard was eleven to zero with two even.

Arriving back at Ehsan's in 1967, Ortiz came to prepare for another lightweight title defense. He would defend against the tall Panamanian, Ismael Laguna, a future lightweight champion.

"When I was a kid," Carlos Ortiz said, "I promised myself I would make this title worth more money than it ever was worth before."[41]

With this fight, Ortiz would be able to fulfill his promise to himself. He was to fight for a guarantee of $83,000. When added to his lifetime earnings, it would top by $500 the record for a lightweight, still held by Madame Bey's Lou Ambers thirty years before.

When asked what he would do with his purse, Ortiz said he would buy Ehsan's Camp, and appeared serious.

"… I got to like it. I enjoy walking around here and the little town down the road, New Providence, is a nice place."[41]

On August 16, Ortiz won a unanimous fifteen-round decision over Laguna at Shea Stadium, New York, retaining his world lightweight title.

Ortiz would lose his title in his next fight against Carlos Teo Cruz in a fifteen-round split decision. He did not train at Ehsan's for it. It took place on June 28, 1968, in Estadio Quisqueya, Santo Domingo, Dominican Republic. Ortiz won his next ten fights. In 1972, he was scheduled to fight Roberto Duran, who was the lightweight champion, but Duran withdrew ten days before the fight. Ortiz fought Ken Buchanan instead.

"I had trained for a completely different fighter and was very frustrated. I felt I had nothing to gain and everything to lose," Ortiz said.

On September 20, 1972, thirty-five-year-old Ortiz fought Buchanan at Madison Square Garden. Ortiz did not get up from his stool after the sixth round. He lost by a technical knockout. For the first time in his career, he did not finish a fight.

"I knew this was going to be my last fight," Ortiz said.[43]

In 1969, Willie Ratner, the journalist who coaxed Madame Bey into assuming Freddie Welsh's business forty-six years before, came to visit the camp. Where the sign that used to hang for a passerby to read "Training To-Day" was a new sign—"For Sale."[44]

During its existence, the camp was the best known in the world. Time, economics, suburban sprawl, and a changed world of boxing took their toll. Its past popularity was undeniable. The once sparsely populated farmland was now surrounded by suburban homes and a large apartment complex down the street.

Ehsan would not operate the camp until he died as he had stated. There were no boxers coming to the camp. Three years later, in October 1972, Ehsan died at the age of eighty-two. A revival of the camp was attempted by the man who had purchased the property in the early 1970s. It failed. The farmhouse was razed, and the gymnasium was remodeled into a ranch-style house to blend with the surroundings.[45] The extraordinary events that occurred at the camp live on in the memories and written words of those fighters and sportswriters of the past. The times dictated its success with the brilliant simplicity of its owners. Its time had passed. Change demands embracing, the past—remembrance.

NOTABLES DURING MADAME BEY ERA

Georgie Abrams (1918–1984)

won 48 (KO 9) + lost 10 (KO 3) + drawn 3 = 61

Georgie Abrams was a Roanoke, Virginia, born boxer who fought in the middleweight division. He lost his only title bout. He wore a Star of David on the left pant leg of his boxing trunks. He left Madame Bey a photograph inscribed, "To Madame Bey very grand person indeed—with best wishes Always Georgie Abrams." Abrams retired from the ring in 1948. Afterward, he tried several different professions, including being a salesperson, entrepreneur, and a barkeeper, but none led to success. He was married several times as well. Life after boxing did not afford him the same stability as the ring had. His opponent late in life was Alzheimer's disease, and he died after suffering a stroke in Las Vegas.[1]

Lou Ambers (1913–1995)

won 91 (KO 28) + lost 8 (KO 2) + drawn 7 = 106

Lou Ambers was a Herkimer, New York, born boxer who held the world lightweight championship (1936–1938, 1939–1940). After his retirement from boxing, Ambers operated a restaurant and worked in public relations. He joined the Coast Guard during World War II.[2] He was inducted into the International Boxing Hall of Fame in 1992.

Fred Apostoli (1913–1973)

won 61 (KO 31) + lost 10 (KO 4) + drawn 1 = 72

Fred Apostoli was a San Francisco, California, born boxer who held the world middleweight championship (1938–1939). Apostoli served in the United States Navy during World War II as a gunner aboard the light cruiser USS *Columbia* in the Pacific theater. Wounded in the Battle of Midway, he received a Bronze Star. He rehabilitated at Letterman Army Hospital in the Presidio Base in San Francisco.[3] He retired from the ring in 1948. He was inducted into the International Boxing Hall of Fame in 2003.

Ray Arcel (1899–1994)

Ray Arcel was a Terre Haute, Indiana, born trainer. Arcel's first champion was flyweight Frankie Genaro. Arcel trained over two thousand boxers and twenty-two champions. From 1925 to 1934, Arcel worked in partnership with trainer Whitey Bimstein. He managed and trained his early idol, Benny Leonard, in a comeback attempt. Arcel trained fourteen opponents that fought Joe Louis, which gave Arcel the name of the Meat Wagon. "It was about the fifth or sixth fight I had against Louis," Arcel said, "and when I took my fighter to the middle of the ring for instructions, Joe looks at me and says: 'You here again?' I burst out laughing."[4] He finally beat a diminished Louis with Ezzard Charles. Arcel left boxing but returned in the early 1970s, training Peppermint Frazier, Roberto Duran, and Larry Holmes for his title defense versus Gerry Cooney in 1982. He then retired. He was inducted into the International Boxing Hall of Fame in 1991.

Henry Armstrong (1909–1988)
won 151 (KO 101) + lost 21 (KO 2) + drawn 9 = 181
Henry Armstrong was a Columbus, Mississippi, born boxer who held the world featherweight championship (1937–1938), the world welterweight championship (1938–1940), and the world lightweight championship (1938–1939). After retiring from boxing in 1946, Armstrong opened a Harlem nightclub, the Melody Room. After overcoming alcoholism, he became an ordained Baptist minister. After his death, it was discovered his heart was one-third larger than normal.[5] He was inducted into the International Boxing Hall of Fame in 1990. He was ranked second on *The Ring* magazine's 2002 list of The 80 Best Fighters of the Last 80 Years. In boxing historian Bert Sugar's 2006 book *Boxing's Greatest Fighters*, he ranked Armstrong as the second greatest fighter of all time.

Buddy Baer (1915–1986)
won 53 (KO 49) + lost 7 (KO 2) + drawn 0 = 60
Newspaper Decisions won 2 : lost : drawn
Buddy Baer was a Denver, Colorado, born heavyweight boxer who challenged for the heavyweight title. After retiring from boxing, Buddy followed his brother Max into a career as a bit-part player in films and television from the 1940s through the 1960s. Among his television credits were appearances on the shows *Sheena: Queen of the Jungle, Have Gun— Will Travel, Gunsmoke, Adventures of Superman, Peter Gunn,* and *Rawhide.*

Max Baer (1909–1959)
won 66 (KO 51) + lost 13 (KO 3) + drawn 0 = 79
Newspaper Decisions won 1 : lost : drawn
Max Baer was an Omaha, Nebraska, born boxer who held the world heavyweight championship (1934–1935). During World War II, Baer served as a physical conditioning instructor for the United States Air Force. Later, he starred in a popular nightclub act

with former light heavyweight champion Maxie Rosenbloom. He worked as a referee in boxing and wrestling matches and played roles in movies. He died from a heart attack. Joe Louis and Jack Dempsey were among his pallbearers. The *New York Times* carried his obituary on the front page. Granting his wife's request, Max was buried by her faith, Roman Catholic, in St. Mary's Cemetery in Sacramento. His son, Max Baer Jr., portrayed the character Jethro on *The Beverly Hillbillies* television show. He was inducted into the International Boxing Hall of Fame in 1995.

Billy Beauhuld (1916–1996)
won 55 (KO 8) + lost 15 (KO 8) + drawn 9 = 79
Newspaper Decisions won : lost 1 : drawn
Billy Beauhuld was a Saint Louis, Missouri, born boxer who fought in the lightweight division. He did not lose in his first thirty-eight fights. He retired from boxing in 1946. He was inducted into the New Jersey Boxing Hall Of Fame.

Paul Berlenbach (1901–1985)
won 40 (KO 34) + lost 8 (KO 3) + drawn 3 + no contest 2 = 53
Newspaper Decisions won 1 : lost : drawn
Paul Berlenbach was a New York, New York, born boxer who held the world light heavyweight championship (1925–1926). After retiring in 1933, he owned and operated Paul Berlenbach's Ringside Restaurant in Sound Beach, New York, in the 1950s. He was named number ninety-three on *The Ring* magazine's list of one hundred greatest punchers of all time. He was inducted into the International Boxing Hall of Fame in 2001.

Melio Bettina (1916–1996)
won 83 (KO 36) + lost 14 (KO 3) + drawn 3 = 100
Melio Bettina was a Bridgeport, Connecticut, born boxer who held the world light heavyweight championship as recognized by the New York State Athletic Commission (1939). Bettina would lose the title in his first defense when he lost a unanimous decision to Billy Conn. Bettina won the 1934 Intercity Golden Gloves at light heavyweight by a decision over Tony Zale. He retired from boxing in 1948.

Carmine Bilotti (1913–1988)
Carmine Bilotti was a Brooklyn, New York, born trainer, journalist, and boxing publicist. He started as a copy boy at the *Morning Ledger of Newark* and spent much of his career publicizing boxing and bicycle races. Fighter representatives for the press were rare in his time, but Bilotti started when manager Joe Jacobs hired him as Tony Galento's

pressperson. Promoters used him to publicize many major championship bouts. He did publicity for the Meadowlands Racetrack in New Jersey when it opened in 1976.[6] In 1984, he moved to Cocoa Beach, Florida. He was inducted into the New Jersey Boxing Hall of Fame.

Whitey Bimstein (1897–1969)
Whitey Bimstein was a New York, New York, born trainer. Boxing as a bantamweight under the name Johnny White, he had seventy bouts before becoming a trainer. At nineteen, he joined the navy and served as a boxing instructor in World War I. From 1925 to 1934, Bimstein collaborated with Ray Arcel to train boxers and later, after World War II, teamed with Freddie Brown. In a fifty-year career, Bimstein handled Gene Tunney, Harry Greb, Lou Ambers, Benny Leonard, Louis "Kid" Kaplan, Jackie "Kid" Berg, Lou Salica, Fred Apostoli, Sixto Escobar, Billy Graham, Carlos Ortiz, Bobo Olson, Joey Archer, Rocky Graziano, and Ingemar Johansson among many others. Bimstein was in the corner of James Braddock on June 13, 1935, when the "Cinderella Man" upset Max Baer to win the world heavyweight championship. Bimstein is widely regarded as one of boxing's outstanding trainers, and his expertise as a cut man was unmatched. In the last years of his life, Bimstein suffered from diabetes. He was inducted into the International Boxing Hall of Fame in 2006.

James Braddock (1905–1974)
won 46 (KO 26) + lost 24 (KO 2) + drawn 4 + no contest 2 = 76
Newspaper Decisions won 5 : lost 2 : drawn 3
James Braddock was a North Bergen, New Jersey, born boxer who held the world heavyweight championship (1935–1937). He invested the money won in boxing well and ran several successful businesses after leaving the ring. He enlisted in the United States Army in 1942 and became a first lieutenant. After the army, he worked as a marine equipment surplus supplier and helped construct the Verrazano Bridge in the early 1960s.[7] He was inducted into the International Boxing Hall of Fame in 2001. His fight for the title and Depression era struggles were depicted in the movie *Cinderella Man*, with Russell Crowe playing the role of Braddock.

Jorge Brescia (1915–1989)
won 16 (KO 6) + lost 12 (KO 5) + drawn 0 = 28
Jorge Brescia was an Argentina-born boxer who fought in the heavyweight division. He retired from boxing in 1940.

Jack Britton (1885–1962)

won 103 (KO 30) + lost 29 (KO 1) + drawn 20 + no contest 5 = 157

Newspaper Decisions won 135 : lost 28 : drawn 24

Jack Britton was a Clinton, New York, born boxer who held the world welterweight championship (1915–1917, 1919–1922). He lost his money earned in boxing from investments in Florida real estate. He continued a friendship with his former manager Dumb Dan Morgan. He also became a boxing instructor in New York City.[8] He was inducted into the International Boxing Hall of Fame in the inaugural class of 1990.

Al Buck (1903–1967)

Al Buck was a journalist whose column appeared in the *New York Post* starting in 1935. He was at virtually every important boxing match and championship fight.[9] He was elected president of the Boxing Writers Association three times and was considered an authority on boxing. The Al Buck Award has been given annually since 1967 by the Boxing Writers Association of America to the outstanding boxing manager.

Red Burman (1915–1996)

won 78 (KO 33) + lost 22 (KO 6) + drawn 2 = 102

Red Burman was a Baltimore, Maryland, born boxer who challenged for the world heavyweight championship. He retired from boxing in 1942. Red Burman died of Paget's disease in Baltimore.[10]

Mushy Callahan (1904–1986)

won 48 (KO 21) + lost 15 (KO 3) + drawn 3 = 66

Newspaper Decisions won : lost 1 : drawn

Mushy Callahan was a New York, New York, born boxer who held the world junior welterweight championship (1926–1930). He retired from boxing in 1932. From 1932 to 1960, he worked as a boxing referee in over four hundred matches. During that time, he also worked as a judge in over a hundred fights.[11] In addition, he worked in the entertainment industry as an actor, technical assistant, and stunt man in several movies and television series, including the training of Elvis Presley for his role in *Kid Galahad*.[12]

Victor Campolo (1903–?)

won 21 (KO 17) + lost 8 (KO 3) + drawn 1 = 30

Victor Campolo was a Reggio Calabria, Calabria, Italy, born boxer who challenged for the world dreadnaught championship. His brother Valentin, who was at Madame Bey's with him, fought three losing efforts for the South American heavyweight championship.

Victor was on the cover of the October 1931 *The Ring* magazine. He retired from boxing in 1934 after a second bout with Primo Carnera, which he lost.

Tony Canzoneri (1908–1959)
won 137 (KO 44) + lost 24 (KO 1) + drawn 10 = 171
Newspaper Decisions won 4 : lost : drawn
Tony Canzoneri was a Slidell, Louisiana, born boxer who held the world featherweight championship (1928), the world lightweight championship (1930–1933, 1935–1936) and the junior welterweight championship (1931–1932, 1933). In 1999, the Associated Press ranked Canzoneri as the fourth best featherweight, the third best lightweight, and the third best junior welterweight of the twentieth century. Bert Sugar, in his book *Boxing's Greatest Fighters*, ranked Canzoneri as the twelfth greatest fighter of all time. He fought eighteen world champions and six Hall of Famers in a fifteen-year career. He was inducted into the International Boxing Hall of Fame in 1990.

Primo Carnera (1906–1967)
won 88 (KO 71) + lost 14 (KO 5) + drawn 0 = 102
Newspaper Decisions won 1 : lost : drawn
Primo Carnera was a Sequals, Friuli-Venezia Giulia, Italy, born boxer who held the world heavyweight championship (1933–1934). Always mired in speculation for fixed fights, he had little money after his boxing career. He returned to America and embarked on a professional wrestling career in 1946 to support his family. He became the first person to hold a heavyweight boxing and "heavyweight wrestling championship title." The wrestling gave him some of his fortune back.[13] He also had many roles in movies. He died of psoriasis brought on by alcoholism.

Georges Carpentier (1894–1975)
won 88 (KO 57) + lost 15 (KO 10) + drawn 6 = 109
Newspaper Decisions won : lost 1 : drawn
Georges Carpentier was a Lens, Pas-de-Calais, France, born boxer who held the world light heavyweight championship (1920–1922). Following his retirement from boxing, Carpentier spent a number of years in vaudeville. He authored the boxing novel *Brothers of the Brown Owl*. He appeared in some motion pictures, starring in both silent films and talkies. He made three films in Hollywood, one for director J. Stuart Blackton in England and two in his native France. He became proprietor of an upmarket bar, Chez Georges Carpentier, in a chic Paris neighborhood, and then other locations. He was inducted into the International Boxing Hall of Fame in 1991.

Kid Chocolate (1910–1988)

won 135 (KO 51) + lost 10 (KO 2) + drawn 6 = 151

Newspaper Decisions won 1 : lost : drawn

Kid Chocolate was a Cuban-born boxer who held the world junior lightweight championship (1931–1933). He spent his ring earnings on the New York nightlife and good times. Chocolate retired to his native Cuba, where he operated a gymnasium and lived a quieter life than the partying days of his career. From 1959, Chocolate's fame in Cuba was overlooked by Fidel Castro and his revolutionary forces. In the late 1970s, Chocolate's achievements were finally recognized by the Cuban government, who gave him a small pension. He was the inspiration for the character Chocolate Drop in Clifford Odets's play *Golden Boy*. He was inducted into the International Boxing Hall of Fame in 1991.

Freddie Cochrane (1915–1993)

won 72 (KO 25) + lost 36 (KO 5) + drawn 8 = 116

Newspaper Decisions won 1 : lost : drawn

Freddie Cochrane was an Elizabeth, New Jersey, born boxer who held the world welterweight championship (1941–1946). During World War II, Cochrane fought exhibitions and served overseas in an entertainment unit. He enlisted in the navy but was exempt from combat because he was born with one arm shorter than the other. Although he technically held the title for more than four years, he did not successfully defend it once, due to World War II. In 1945, he fought a losing effort to Rocky Graziano in *The Ring* magazine's 1945 Fight of the Year. After boxing, he operated a tavern and worked as a liquor salesperson. He died at the Lyons Veterans Administration Hospital in New Jersey.[14]

Jack Delaney (1910–1988)

won 73 (KO 43) + lost 11 (KO 3) + drawn 2 + no contest 2 = 88

Newspaper Decisions won 2 : lost : drawn

Jack Delaney was a Saint-Francois-du-Lac, Quebec, Canada, born boxer who held the world light heavyweight championship (1927). He vacated his title, never defending it, to fight in the heavyweight division. Delaney retired from boxing and moved to Bridgeport. After boxing, he refereed and operated businesses and a tavern in New York. He died of cancer.[8] He was inducted into the International Boxing Hall of Fame in 1996.

Al Davis (1920–1945)

won 65 (KO 46) + lost 10 (KO 3) + drawn 4 = 79

Al Davis was a Brooklyn, New York, born boxer who fought in the welterweight division. Davis made close to a quarter-million dollars from boxing. He used it to buy racehorses and a bar and grill. He squandered his fortune by the middle of 1945. Bummy was shot in a bar he used to own, called Dudy's, and died. Davis's funeral had a large turnout with many from his Brownsville, Brooklyn, neighborhood.[15]

James P. Dawson (1895–1953)
James P. Dawson was a journalist who began a forty-five-year career with the *New York Times* as a copy boy in 1908. Eight years later, he became the newspaper's boxing editor and covered boxing and baseball until his death. The annual award presented to the top rookie in the Yankees' training camp is named in his honor.

Jack Dempsey (1895-1983)
won 54 (KO 44) + lost 6 (KO 1) + drawn 9 = 69
Newspaper Decisions won 4 : lost : drawn 2
Jack Dempsey was a Manassa, Colorado, born boxer who held the world heavyweight championship (1919–1926). Jack Dempsey was the most successful athlete of the golden age of sports. He divorced his actor wife, Estelle Taylor, in 1930. He toured the United States and Canada in 1931, boxing in over one hundred exhibitions. He drew crowds and made money. Dempsey managed, promoted, and advised younger boxers. He acted as a referee in many boxing and wrestling matches. During World War II, Dempsey enlisted in the Coast Guard at age forty-seven after first being rejected by the army because of his age. Dempsey opened his famous restaurant, Jack Dempsey's, in 1935. He had financial success after retiring from boxing, unlike others in the sport. Dempsey became part of the 1990 inaugural class of inductees into the International Boxing Hall of Fame.

Gus Dorazio (1916-1986)
won 73 (KO 21) + lost 23 (KO 8) + drawn 1 + no contest 1 = 98
Gus Dorazio was a Philadelphia, Pennsylvania, born boxer who challenged for the heavyweight championship and held the Philadelphia city heavyweight title. He retired from boxing in 1946. In 1946 he was convicted for draft dodging, and in 1949, he was arraigned on a charge of murder by fist. Dorazio claimed that the man and two others had ganged up on him, and he resented taunts that he was punch drunk.[16] The jury found him guilty, and he was sentenced to a twenty-year term.[17] Dorazio spent nearly three and a half years in the notorious Eastern State penitentiary.

Carl Duane (1902-1984)

won 43 (KO 13) + lost 16 (KO 1) + drawn 6 + no contest 2 = 67

Newspaper Decisions won : lost : drawn 1

Carl Duane was a New York, New York, born boxer who held the world junior featherweight championship (1923–1926). He retired from boxing in 1929.

Chris Dundee (1908-1998)

Chris Dundee was a Philadelphia, Pennsylvania, born manager. He managed Ken Overlin at Madame Bey's Camp to the middleweight title in 1941 and Hall of Famer Ezzard Charles to the world heavyweight title in 1949. In the early 1930s, Dundee also started promoting matches and became one of the leading promoters. For nearly thirty years, he owned and operated the world-famous Fifth Street Gymnasium in Miami. This is where his brother, Angelo Dundee, trained Muhammad Ali. He was inducted into the International Boxing Hall of Fame in 1994.

Johnny Dundee (1893-1965)

won 83 (KO 17) + lost 32 (KO 2) + drawn 20 + no contest 14 = 149

Newspaper Decisions won 117 : lost 42 : drawn 25

Johnny Dundee was a Sciacca, Sicilia, Italy, born boxer who held the world junior lightweight championship (1921–1923, 1923–1924), and the world featherweight championship (1923). He had 330 bouts in his career, being knocked out just twice. Only two fighters in history had more fights. He was inducted into the International Boxing Hall of Fame in 1991.

Vince Dundee (1907-1949)

won 118 (KO 29) + lost 19 (KO 1) + drawn 14 + no contest 1 = 152

Newspaper Decisions won 4 : lost 2 : drawn

Vince Dundee was a Palermo, Sicilia, Italy, born boxer who held the world middleweight championship (1933–1934). His family immigrated to Baltimore. He retired from boxing in 1937. He was stricken with multiple sclerosis in 1942 and died at a Glendale, California, sanitarium from its complications.

Sixto Escobar (1913–1979)

won 39 (KO 17) + lost 23 (KO 0) + drawn 4 = 66

Sixto Escobar was a Barceloneta, Puerto Rico, born boxer who held the world bantamweight championship (1934–1935, 1935–1937, 1938–1939). In early December 1935, he returned to San Juan where he was greeted at the dock by many. After regaining his title, Escobar defended it once and then vacated it because he was having trouble making weight. Escobar retired from boxing in 1940 and joined the United States Army in 1941. A durable fighter, he was never stopped or knocked out during his career. He worked for a liquor company in New York temporally and then returned to Puerto Rico where he sold liquor. His alcoholism and diabetes contributed to his death. After his death, the town of Barceloneta, Puerto Rico, honored his memory with a statue. Escobar became the first world boxing champion in history to have a statue in his honor.[18] He was inducted into the International Boxing Hall of Fame in 2002.

Tommy Farr (1913–1986)
won 84 (KO 24) + lost 34 (KO 6) + drawn 17 + no contest 2 = 137
Tommy Farr was a Blaenclydach, Wales, born boxer who challenged for the heavyweight championship. Tommy Farr first retired in 1940. He lost his money from boxing and attempted a comeback at the age of thirty-six to make a living. Farr later ran a pub in Brighton, Sussex, and died on St. David's Day of liver cancer at his home. Farr was inducted into the Welsh Sports Hall of Fame in 1997.

Abe Feldman (1912–1980)
won 35 (KO 15) + lost 14 (KO 2) + drawn 5 = 54
Abe Feldman was a Salt Lake City, Utah, born boxer who fought in the light heavyweight and heavyweight divisions. He was the second ranked light heavyweight in 1935 and fought many good fighters. Feldman never fought in a title bout. He retired from boxing in 1939. He served in the United States Army, but they discharged him in 1941 for medical reasons. Feldman's 1933 bout with James Braddock was featured in the movie *Cinderella Man*.

Freddie Fiducia (1913–1966)
won 61 (KO 15) + lost 21 (KO 2) + drawn 3 = 85
Freddie Fiducia was a New Jersey boxer who fought in 225 bouts, amateur and professional, in a twenty-two-year career that started at the age of fifteen. He fought in all weight divisions from flyweight to heavyweight. After leaving boxing in 1950, Fiducia was a dispatcher for the Continental Can Company of Paterson, New Jersey. He died in St. Michael's Hospital, Newark, after a heart attack.[19] He was inducted into the New Jersey Boxing Hall of Fame.

Jackie Fields (1908–1987)
won 72 (KO 31) + lost 9 (KO 1) + drawn 2 + no contest 1 = 84
Newspaper Decisions won 2 : lost : drawn
Jackie Fields was a Chicago-born boxer who held the world welterweight championship (1929–1930, 1932–1933). He retired from boxing in 1933. Fields earned an estimated $500,000 during his fighting career, which he invested in real estate. The Great Depression left him without money. He worked as an assistant unit manager for the Twentieth Century

Fox film studio, and as a film editor for MGM. In the late 1950s, he bought a large share of stock in the Tropicana Hotel in Las Vegas and was a public relations director for the hotel.[20] He is an International Jewish Sports Hall of Fame inductee and inducted into the International Boxing Hall of Fame in 1994.

F. Scott Fitzgerald (1896–1940)
F. Scott Fitzgerald was born in St. Paul, Minnesota. He became one of America's great writers. He finished four novels: *This Side of Paradise*, *The Beautiful and Damned*, *The Great Gatsby*, and *Tender Is the Night*. A fifth, unfinished novel, *The Love of the Last Tycoon*, was published after his death. *The Great Gatsby* has a prominent place in this book, as Gatsby was much like Fitzgerald's friend Freddie Welsh. Fitzgerald was notorious for his alcohol consumption. He died of a heart attack.

Humbert Fugazy (1885–1964)
Humbert Fugazy was born in Greenwich Village, New York. He was a boxing promoter who competed with Tex Rickard for bouts. In his career, he had been a boxer, prizefight promoter, grand-opera impresario, banker, and travel agency executive. He promoted about one hundred fifty bouts. Fugazy contributed heavy to various charities. In 1927, he pledged $100,000 toward building shelters for homeless youths. His death was attributed to an intestinal obstruction.[21]

Tony Galento (1910–1979)
won 80 (KO 57) + lost 26 (KO 6) + drawn 5 + no contest 1 = 112
Tony Galento was an Orange, New Jersey, born boxer who challenged for the heavyweight championship. Galento retired from boxing in 1943. He went into professional wrestling and acted in film roles. He was thought of as a folk hero by many. He separated from his wife in 1948. He was a diabetic and had circulatory problems. In June 1977, he had surgery to remove his left leg at midcalf and was fitted with an artificial limb. A week before his death, at St. Barnabas Hospital in Livingston, New Jersey, his right leg was amputated.[22] Galento was honored by having a plaza named after him in his hometown of Orange, New Jersey.

Frankie Genaro (1901–1966)
won 79 (KO 19) + lost 21 (KO 4) + drawn 8 + no contest 1 = 109
Newspaper Decisions won 19 : lost 3 : drawn
Frankie Genaro was a New York, New York, born boxer who held the world flyweight championship (1928–1929, 1929–1931). He won the flyweight gold medal at the 1920 Olympics in Antwerp. During his career, Genaro fought ten world champions and three Hall of Famers. He was inducted into the International Boxing Hall of Fame in 1998.

Billy Gibson (1876–1947)

Billy Gibson was a boxing manager of Hall of Fame champions Benny Leonard and Gene Tunney. After Leonard left his manager in 1914, Gibson guided him to the lightweight championship in 1917. Tunney captured the heavyweight title after leaving manager Doc Bagley and hiring Gibson. Gibson retired from boxing after Tunney vacated the world heavyweight title in 1928. During his career, Gibson served as matchmaker and manager at Madison Square Garden for two years. Gibson also managed heavyweight Paulino Uzcudun and featherweight Louis "Kid" Kaplan. In 1925, the NFL president, Joseph Carr, offered Gibson a New York franchise. Gibson, who lost money on the New York Brickley Giants in 1921, refused the offer. He referred Carr to his friend Tim Mara, who established the New York Giants that year.[23] He was inducted into the International Boxing Hall of Fame in 2009.

George Godfrey (1897–1947)

won 96 (KO 78) + lost 21 (KO 6) + drawn 2 + no contest 4 = 123

George Godfrey was a Mobile, Alabama, born boxer who held the world colored heavyweight championship (1926–1928, 1931–1933). Although he never challenged for the world title, likely because of his skin color, he did capture the Mexican and IBU heavyweight titles. He was inducted into the International Boxing Hall of Fame in 2007.

Arturo Godoy (1912–1986)

won 89 (KO 50) + lost 21 (KO 2) + drawn 12 + no contest 2 = 124

Arturo Godoy was an Iquique, Chile, born boxer who challenged for the heavyweight championship. His life was used as the base for the novel *Muriendo por la dulce patria mía*, 1998, by Roberto Castillo Sandoval. He died of cancer in Chile.

Charley Goldman (1888–1968)

Charley Goldman was a Warsaw, Poland, born trainer. In his career, he trained Lou Ambers, Joey Archibald, Kid Gavilan, Al McCoy, Carlos Ortiz, Marty Servo, Jersey Joe Walcott, Fritzie Zivic, and Rocky Marciano. Goldman often worked with Al Weill's boxers but handled others. In the late 1940s and 1950s, Goldman trained undefeated world heavyweight champion Rocky Marciano. He died of a heart attack in 1968. He was inducted into the International Boxing Hall of Fame in 1992.

Ruby Goldstein (1907–1984)

Ruby Goldstein, like so many of the great Jewish boxers of his era, was born on the Lower East Side of Manhattan, New York. He was nicknamed the Jewel of the Ghetto. Goldstein won his first twenty-three fights before Ace Hudkins knocked him out. He started to referee while in the army during World War II. He served as the referee when Joe Louis fought exhibitions at military installations. After his discharge, Ruby Goldstein was one of boxing's best referees, and he refereed thirty-nine title fights. He was inducted into the International Boxing Hall of Fame in 1994.

Bud Gorman (1897–?)
won 35 (KO 14) + lost 14 (KO 7) + drawn 4 + no contest 1 = 54
Newspaper Decisions won 14 : lost 4 : drawn 7
Bud Gorman was a Chicago, Illinois, born boxer who fought in the heavyweight division. He retired from boxing in 1931.

Frank Graham (1893–1965)
Frank Graham was a Harlem, New York, born journalist and biographer. He wrote biographies of politician Al Smith and athletes Lou Gehrig and John McGraw, and histories of the New York Yankees, New York Giants, and Brooklyn Dodgers. He was a man who seldom brought pencil and paper, writing everything from memory. Graham's writing style was notable for his use of lengthy conversations. He was a prolific writer whose books included *Lou Gehrig, A Quiet Hero, The New York Yankees: An Informal History, McGraw of the Giants: An Informal Biography, The Brooklyn Dodgers: An Informal History, Al Smith, American: An Informal Biography, Baseball Wit and Wisdom: Folklore of a National Pastime, The New York Giants: An Informal History of a Great Baseball Club*, and *Third Man in the Ring*—the story of boxing referee Ruby Goldstein as told by Goldstein to Graham, two men who often were at Madame Bey's Camp. Graham developed cancer in 1960. Graham fell at his home in New Rochelle, New York, fracturing his skull.[24] He died several days later at Nathan B. Etten Hospital in the Bronx. Graham was inducted into the writer's wing of the National Baseball Hall of Fame and Museum in 1972. The Boxing Writers Association of America with its highest honor, the A. J. Liebling Award, honored him in 1997.

Abe Greene (1899–1988)
Abe Greene was called Mr. Boxing in New Jersey. Greene is often credited with revitalizing boxing there and positioning it as an attractive venue for major bouts. He worked as a newspaperman, employed at the *Paterson Evening News* for fifty-six years as a reporter and editor.[25] During his many years in boxing, Greene was one of the sports most respected officials and was noted for defending the well-being and rights of boxers. He died of heart failure.[26] He was inducted into the International Boxing Hall of Fame in 2009.

Gus Greenlee (1893–1952)
Gus Greenlee was born in Marion, North Carolina. He was a Negro League baseball owner and an African American businessman. He also served in the black 367th regiment during

World War I. He made money as a bootlegger, numbers runner, racketeer, and the owner of the Crawford Grill nightclub and the Pittsburgh Crawfords baseball team. In 1932, he opened Greenlee Field, the first black-owned and -built baseball park in America. The 1935 team fielded five Baseball Hall of Fame players. He died from a stroke.

Babe Herman (1902–1966)
won 94 (KO 23) + lost 48 (KO 9) + drawn 19 + no contest 1 = 162
Newspaper Decisions won 4 : lost 4 : drawn 2
Babe Herman was a Sacramento, California, born boxer who fought in the featherweight division. He lost in his title fight. He retired from boxing in 1932.

Ace Hudkins (1905–1973)
won 64 (KO 25) + lost 16 (KO 1) + drawn 12 + no contest 1 = 93
Newspaper Decisions won 4 : lost 4 : drawn 1
Ace Hudkins was a Valparaiso, Nebraska, born boxer who fought in the middleweight division. He lost in his two title fights. He fought from lightweight to light heavyweight, won several California state titles, and was Southern California's biggest boxing draw in the 1920s. After boxing, he created the Hudkins Brothers Movie Ranch with his brother, where cowboy stars boarded their horses. Hudkins became friends with Fred Kennedy, Gene Autry, and John Wayne. He did stunt work in movies for Republic Studio. Among Hudkins's horses was Hi Yo Silver for *The Lone Ranger*, which became the Lone Ranger's trademark yell, and Roy Rogers's horse Trigger.[27] Hudkins died in Los Angeles.

Herbert Hype Igoe (1877–1945)
Herbert Hype Igoe was a nationally known journalist and cartoonist for the Hearst newspapers for forty years. He was a native of Santa Cruz, California. He started as a copyboy for the *San Francisco Examiner* and became one of the most respected sportswriters of his era. He covered every heavyweight championship bout from James Corbett to Joe Louis. He was famous for his inside stories and illustrations. With the exception of Gene Tunney, he correctly predicted the rise of every heavyweight champion. He died from a heart ailment in Flushing Hospital, New York.[28]

Joe Jacobs (1898–1939)
Joe Jacobs was a New York, New York, born manager whose charges were Max Schmeling, Ted Moore, Andre Routis, Tony Galento, Mike McTigue, and Frankie Genaro. The colorful, controversial, energetic, and well-connected manager could arrange bouts for his clientele by keeping them publicized. He died of heart failure.

Mike Jacobs (1880–1953)

Mike Jacobs was a New York, New York, born boxing promoter. Like Tex Rickard in the 1920s, Mike Jacobs ruled boxing in the 1930s and 1940s. In 1935, Jacobs signed the young heavyweight Joe Louis. Jacobs controlled the championships of every weight division in boxing.[29] Jacobs suffered a cerebral hemorrhage in 1946. Jacobs struggled with health until he died seven years after his cerebral hemorrhage. He is a member of the International Jewish Sports Hall and was inducted into the International Boxing Hall of Fame in 1990.

Joe Jeanette (1879–1958)

won 83 (KO 70) + lost 10 (KO 2) + drawn 9 + no contest 2 = 104

Newspaper Decisions won 35 : lost 16 : drawn 11

Joe Jeanette was a North Bergen, New Jersey, born boxer who held the world colored heavyweight championship (1909). Because of his skill and skin color, he was avoided for a world title. After his career, he became a referee and a trainer, and he owned a boxing gymnasium in Union City, New Jersey, where he trained hundreds of boxers, including heavyweight champion James Braddock who was born in the same town. Later, he operated a limousine and taxi company named Adelaide, after his wife.[30] He was inducted into the International Boxing Hall of Fame in 1997.

Ben Jeby (1909–1984)

won 54 (KO 22) + lost 14 (KO 2) + drawn 4 + no contest 1 = 73

Ben Jeby was a New York, New York, born boxer who held the world middleweight championship (1932–1933). He retired from boxing in 1936.

Lew Jenkins (1916–1981)

won 73 (KO 51) + lost 41 (KO 12) + drawn 5 = 119

Lew Jenkins was a Milburn, Texas, born boxer who held the world lightweight championship (1940–1941). Jenkins joined the Coast Guard late in 1942. The British decorated him the for his D-Day heroism. After the war, he reenlisted in the army and fought in the Korean War, receiving the Silver Star. He tried a boxing comeback with little success. Lew Jenkins then became a greens keeper at the Antioch golf course in California. An alcoholic as a young adult, he never touched hard liquor again after boxing. "Tell them I'm a sober family man," Jenkins said. "They'll never believe that." He was laid to rest in Arlington National Cemetery.[31, 32, 33] *The Ring* magazine listed him as one of the hardest one hundred punchers. He was inducted into the International Boxing Hall of Fame in 1999.

Jack Johnson (1878–1946)

won 55 (KO 35) + lost 11 (KO 6) + drawn 8 + no contest 3 = 77

Newspaper Decisions won 15 : lost : drawn 3

Jack Johnson was a Galveston, Texas, born boxer who held the world heavyweight championship (1908–1915). He became the first African American to hold the heavyweight title when he defeated Jess Willard. He retired in 1931. He died in a car accident in Raleigh, North Carolina. He was inducted into the International Boxing Hall of Fame in 1990.

James Johnston (1880–1953)

Jimmy Johnston was born in Liverpool, England. He came to the United States at the age of twelve. He was a bantamweight fighter, matchmaker, manager, and promoter. He worked with light heavyweight Mike McTigue, welterweight Pete Latzo, middleweight Harry Greb, welterweight Ted "Kid" Lewis, and featherweight Johnny Dundee, all of whom won world championships. Johnston's brother, Charlie, managed Archie Moore. He was inducted into the International Boxing Hall of Fame in 1999.

Phil Kaplan (1902–1983)

won 66 (KO 34) + lost 14 (KO 1) + drawn 4 + no contest 1 = 85

Newspaper Decisions won 10 : lost 4 : drawn 3

Phil Kaplan was a Newark, New Jersey, born boxer who fought in the middleweight division. A ranked middleweight contender in the mid-1920s, Phil Kaplan never received a title bout. Kaplan was only stopped one time, and that was because of a hand injury; he was never knocked down in his career. He retired from boxing in 1931. He frequented Jack Dempsey's Restaurant, with his manager, Champ Segal, and friends, or at the Aqueduct Race Track watching the thoroughbred race.[34] He was inducted into the New Jersey Boxing Hall of Fame.

Jack Kearns (1882–1963)

Jack "Doc" Kearns grew up in the state of Washington. When he was fourteen, he joined the Alaska-Yukon gold rush. In 1900, he started boxing and claimed to have fought over sixty professional bouts. Kearns is best known as the manager of world heavyweight champion Jack Dempsey and champion Mickey Walker, but he managed over eighty boxers in sixty-five years.[35] He was inducted into the International Boxing Hall of Fame in 1990.

Frankie Klick (1907–1982)

won 85 (KO 24) + lost 26 (KO 4) + drawn 13 + no contest 1 = 125

Frankie Klick was a San Francisco, California, born boxer who held the world junior lightweight championship (1933–1935). He retired in 1939 but attempted a comeback in 1943 before retiring again. His nearly twenty-year career took a physical and metal toll.

He became an alcoholic, panhandler, and had a diminished mental capacity. Writer Pedro Fernandez remembers his father explained to him that Frankie had traded in his senses to entertain fight fans. "Boxing ain't easy," were the words of Fernandez's father, repeatedly.[36]

Johnny Kilbane (1889–1957)
won 49 (KO 24) + lost 5 (KO 3) + drawn 7 + no contest 1 = 62
Newspaper Decisions won 61 : lost 11 : drawn 8
Johnny Kilbane was a Cleveland, Ohio, born boxer who held the world featherweight championship (1912–1923). In the *New York Times* on May 16, 1912, his name was used as a verb, "… Ty Cobb chased after a heckler during a game with the New York Yankees and 'Johnny Kilbaned' him right where he stood …" After boxing, he worked as a referee and operated a gymnasium. In 1928, he campaigned for the office of sheriff of Cuyahoga County, Ohio. He was elected to the Ohio State Senate in 1941. He worked as the Cleveland Municipal Court clerk. He died of cancer.[37] He was inducted into the International Boxing Hall of Fame in 1995.

Solly Krieger (1909–1964)
won 82 (KO 54) + lost 25 (KO 3) + drawn 6 = 113
Solly Krieger was a Brooklyn, New York, born boxer who held the world middleweight championship (1938–1939). He retired from boxing in 1941. He was inducted into the International Jewish Sports Hall of Fame.

Tippy Larkin (1917–1991)
won 137 (KO 60) + lost 15 (KO 10) + drawn 1 + no contest 1 = 154
Tippy Larkin was a Garfield, New Jersey, born boxer who held the world junior welterweight championship (1946–1959). Tippy Larkin was featured on the cover of *The Ring* magazine for July 1944. Larkin never lost a fight that went the distance from 1935 through 1952. He boxed at Madison Square Garden in nineteen main events. He died of kidney failure in New Jersey.[38]

Benny Leonard (1896–1947)
won 89 (KO 70) + lost 6 (KO 5) + drawn 1 + no contest 4 = 100
Newspaper Decisions won 96 : lost 16 : drawn 7
Benny Leonard was a New York, New York, born boxer who held the world lightweight championship (1917–1925). He lost his reported million dollars from the ring in the stock market crash of 1929. In 1931, he started boxing again without losing until his last bout to future champion Jimmy McLarnin. He became a referee and on April 18, 1947, while refereeing a boxing match, Leonard suffered a heart attack and died a few minutes later.[39] He was inducted into the International Boxing Hall of Fame in 1990.

King Levinsky (1910–1991)

won 74 (KO 40) + lost 35 (KO 5) + drawn 7 = 116

Newspaper Decisions won 0 : lost 2 : drawn 0

King Levinsky was a New York, New York, born boxer who fought as a heavyweight. He was featured on the cover of the May 1934 *The Ring* magazine. His 1932 exhibition bout with Jack Dempsey convinced Dempsey to abandon a comeback. A 1932 *Time* magazine article stated: "… would not rate better than tenth among U. S. heavyweights. … as a fighter's ability to earn money at his trade, Kingfish Levinsky might rank as best fighter in the U. S."[40, 41] He left Madame a photograph inscribed "To Madame Bey 'Best training camp I've ever trained in.' With Best Wishes From King Levinsky." He retired from boxing in 1939. Reportedly, after boxing, he exhibited punch drunkenness and sold watches and ties for subsistence.

John Henry Lewis (1914–1974)

won 97 (KO 57) + lost 10 (KO 1) + drawn 4 = 111

John Henry Lewis was a Los Angeles, California, born boxer who held the world light heavyweight championship (1935–1938). Lewis, at age twenty-five, announced his retirement from boxing because of blindness in one eye. He worked after boxing as a liquor salesperson. He suffered from emphysema and Parkinson's disease later in life. He was inducted into the International Boxing Hall of Fame in 1994.

Tommy Loughran (1902–1982)

won 90 (KO 14) + lost 25 (KO 3) + drawn 10 + no contest 2 = 127

Newspaper Decisions won 32 : lost 7 : drawn 3

Tommy Loughran was a Philadelphia, Pennsylvania, born boxer who held the world light heavyweight championship (1927–1929). He was a referee and refereed Floyd Patterson's heavyweight title defense against Pete Rademacher, the first and only time a fighter has challenged for the heavyweight crown in his professional debut. Until the 1960s, Loughran was a successful broker on Wall Street in sugar commodities. He was inducted into the International Boxing Hall of Fame in 1991.

Joe Louis (1914–1981)

won 66 (KO 52) + lost 3 (KO 2) + drawn 0 = 69

Joe Louis was a LaFayette, Alabama, born boxer who held the world heavyweight championship (1937–1949). On March 1, 1949, the longtime champion retired from boxing, holding the title for nearly twelve years—still a record reign. He made more title defenses, twenty-five, than any other champion in any weight class. After boxing, he divorced, had multiple lawsuits from women, was indebted with millions of dollars from unpaid taxes and lenders, and had several business ventures fail. His problems forced him back into the ring. During the 1960s, Louis had health issues, including dementia pugilistica, high blood pressure, and various addictions to narcotics. He worked as a greeter at Caesars Palace in Las Vegas, Nevada. He died of a cardiac arrest.[42] He was inducted into the International Boxing Hall of Fame in 1990.

Joe Lynch (1898–1965)
won 50 (KO 37) + lost 12 (KO 0) + drawn 8 + no contest 2 = 72
Newspaper Decisions won 49 : lost 24 : drawn 11
Joe Lynch was a New York, New York, born boxer who held the world bantamweight championship (1920–1921, 1922–1924). After boxing, Lynch bought a small farm and gymnasium in New York, New York, where he also served as postmaster for many years. Later, Lynch was appointed a judge by the New York State Athletic Commission.[43] In 1965, he drowned in what was ruled an accident in Sheepshead Bay, Brooklyn, but some suspected it was a homicide.[44] He was inducted into the International Boxing Hall of Fame in 2005.

Eddie Mader (1912–?)
won 57 (KO 27) + lost 43 (KO 31) + drawn 8 + no contest 3 = 111
Eddie Mader was a New York, New York, born boxer who fought in the heavyweight division. After retiring from boxing in 1948, he became a boxing promoter in Sarasota, Florida, where he worked for Ringling Bros. and Barnum & Bailey Circus.[45]

Nathan Mann (1915–1999)
won 74 (KO 45) + lost 12 (KO 5) + drawn 4 = 90
Nathan Mann was a New Haven, Connecticut, born boxer who challenged for the heavyweight championship and held the New England heavyweight title. He retired from boxing in 1948.

Eddie Martin (1903–1968)
won 81 (KO 29) + lost 12 (KO 3) + drawn 4 + no contest 1 = 98
Newspaper Decisions won 1 : lost 2 : drawn
Eddie Martin was a Brooklyn, New York, born boxer who held the world bantamweight championship (1924–1925). In his first two years of boxing, he had fifty-one bouts. In three years, he won the world bantamweight championship. He retired from boxing in 1932.

Jimmy McLarnin (1907–2004)

won 55 (KO 21) + lost 11 (KO 1) + drawn 3 = 69

Jimmy McLarnin was a Hillsborough, Northern Ireland, United Kingdom, born boxer who held the world welterweight championship (1933–1934, 1934–1935). Unlike many boxers, McLarnin invested his money wisely and retired a wealthy man. He opened an electrical goods store and did some acting, golfing, and lecturing.[46] He appeared in the movies *Big City, The Crowd Roars,* and *Joe Palooka, Champ.* He was inducted into the International Boxing Hall of Fame in 1991.

Bat Masterson (1853–1921)

Bat Masterson was born in Henriville, Montérégie, Quebec, Canada. He was famous as a gunfighter turned lawman, US marshal, army scout, and gambler. He is credited with killing twenty-eight men and counted Theodore Roosevelt as a friend.[47] In 1877, he joined his brothers in Dodge City, Kansas. He is credited with driving lawlessness out of Dodge City. He served as a sheriff's deputy alongside Wyatt Earp. He traveled the West, gambling and promoting prizefights. He began writing a weekly sports column for *George's Weekly*, a Denver newspaper, and opened the Olympic Athletic Club to promote the sport of boxing. After moving to New York, he wrote newspaper columns for the *New York Morning Telegraph*. He became friends with world lightweight champion Freddie Welsh. He collapsed at his desk from a heart attack after writing what became his final column.[48]

Mike McTigue (1892–1966)

won 77 (KO 52) + lost 26 (KO 9) + drawn 8 + no contest 4 = 115

Newspaper Decisions won 32 : lost 19 : drawn 6

Mike McTigue was a County Clare, Ireland, born boxer who held the world light heavyweight championship (1923–1925). McTigue operated a successful bar on Long Island until the late 1940s. For the last ten years of his life, he was impoverished, had health problems, and was admitted to hospitals around New York.[49] McTigue was honored in his native parish when the porch of the church was named after him.

Jack Miley (1899–1945)

Jack Miley was a native of Milwaukee, Wisconsin. A New York journalist best known for coining the phrase "Bum of the Month Club," referring to Joe Louis's opponents. He would visit the Florida West Coast cities to report on the baseball training season. He served with the First Marine Division in World War I. He joined the navy during World War II where he sustained injuries in New Guinea. He was placed on medical leave, and less than a month before his discharge, he died of a heart attack at his home in New York City.[50]

Tod Morgan (1902–1953)

won 133 (KO 29) + lost 42 (KO 4) + drawn 33 + no contest 2 = 210

Newspaper Decisions won 6 : lost 2 : drawn

Tod Morgan was a Dungeness, Washington, born boxer who held the junior lightweight championship (1925–1927, 1927–1929). He also held the Hawaii welterweight title, California lightweight title, and Australian lightweight title. From 1936 to 1942, he fought exclusively in Australia. In 1942, he retired from boxing. Morgan served in the Australian army, fighting in Africa. He later returned to America and worked as a referee and a bellhop in hotels.[51]

Dan Morgan (1873–1955)

Dan Morgan was born in New York, New York. He boxed as an amateur before turning professional in 1894. He retired from the ring and became a boxing manager. He managed hundreds of boxers and three champions. Morgan is best known for managing welterweight champion Jack Britton. After Morgan retired from managing fighters in 1925, he worked as a promoter for Mike Jacobs.[52] He was inducted into the International Boxing Hall of Fame in 2000.

Walter Neusel (1907–1964)

won 68 (KO 36) + lost 13 (KO 6) + drawn 9 = 90

Walter Neusel was a Bochum, Nordrhein-Westfalen, Germany, born boxer who fought in the heavyweight division. He held the German heavyweight title (1938–1940, 1942–1946). He retired from boxing in 1950.

Kid Norfolk (1893–1953)

won 83 (KO 47) + lost 23 (KO 7) + drawn 6 = 112

Newspaper Decisions won 28 : lost 4 : drawn

Kid Norfolk was a Norfolk, Virginia, born boxer. He never contended for a world title but was considered one of the best light heavyweights of his era. He had to settle for the world colored light heavyweight championship. He had five wins with no losses against world champions. He defeated both Harry Greb and Billy Miske twice. He was inducted into the International Boxing Hall of Fame in 2007.

Jack O'Brien (1878–1942)

won 92 (KO 56) + lost 8 (KO 5) + drawn 14 + no contest 4 = 118

Newspaper Decisions won 56 : lost 9 : drawn 11

Jack O'Brien was a Philadelphia, Pennsylvania, born boxer who held the world light heavyweight championship (1905). He is known for his heavyweight battles against the best of his era. He was inducted into the International Boxing Hall of Fame in 1994.

Bob Olin (1908–1956)

won 55 (KO 25) + lost 27 (KO 4) + drawn 4 = 86

Bob Olin was a New York, New York, born boxer who held the world light heavyweight championship (1934–1935). In 1928, Olin won the New York City Golden Gloves for the 175-pound class. After boxing, he became a restaurateur in New York from 1946 until his death. He died from a heart attack.[53]

Ken Overlin (1910–1969)

won 135 (KO 23) + lost 19 (KO 2) + drawn 9 + no contest 2 = 165

Ken Overlin was a Decatur, Illinois, born boxer who held the world middleweight championship (1940–1941). He rejoined the navy during World War II, where he served for thirty months, including twenty-one months overseas. He attempted a comeback in the light heavyweight division in 1944[54] and then retired from boxing in 1945. He died in Reno, Nevada, where he lived the last twelve years of his life.[55] He was inducted into the International Boxing Hall of Fame in 2015.

Billy Petrolle (1905–1983)

won 89 (KO 66) + lost 21 (KO 3) + drawn 10 + drawn 1 = 121

Newspaper Decisions won 34 : lost 5 : drawn 5

Billy Petrolle was a Berwick, Pennsylvania, born boxer who never won a championship but fought ten current or past world champions and was victorious over five of them. In each of his bouts, he entered the ring with a red and green Navajo blanket as a good luck charm. He made about $200,000 in boxing. After retiring, he owned an iron foundry in Duluth, Minnesota. He then owned a religious goods and gift shop in Duluth and was the chairman of the board of directors of the Pioneer National Bank. He appeared on the cover of *The Ring* magazine in May 1927, March 1931, and May 1932. Petrolle died in Vero Beach, Florida.[56] He was inducted into the International Boxing Hall of Fame in 2000.

Willie Ratner (1895–1980)

Willie Ratner was a Newark, New Jersey, born journalist. He joined the *Newark Evening News* as a copy boy in 1912 and remained with the paper until it closed on August 31, 1972. He worked longer at one paper than any other sports journalist. He was known for his knowledge of boxing and bicycle racing but covered every major sport.[57] He was instrumental in getting Madame Bey into boxing. He was one of the first to practice participant journalism. He was also popular with stars of the entertainment field. He suffered a stroke and died six years later in Beth Israel Hospital.[58] He was inducted into the New Jersey Boxing Hall of Fame.

Grantland Rice (1880–1954)

Grantland Rice was a Murfreesboro, Tennessee, born journalist and an author known for his prose style of writing. He was the first nationally famous sportswriter. In the 1920s, he made in excess of $100,000 a year. He worked the first World Series broadcast in 1922. His sports stories were printed in over two hundred newspapers.[59] He was responsible for the quote "—not that you won or lost—But how you played the Game," from the poem "Alumnus Football." Rice died of a stroke.

Maxie Rosenbloom (1904–1976)

won 207 (KO 19) + lost 39 (KO 2) + drawn 26 + drawn 2 = 274

Newspaper Decisions won 16 : lost 4 : drawn 4

Maxie Rosenbloom was a Leonard's Bridge, Connecticut, born boxer who held the world light heavyweight championship (1932–1934). After and during his boxing career, he acted on radio, television, and films, usually playing comedy roles as a big, clumsy, punch-drunk lovable character.[60] He appeared in the *Fred Allen Radio Show* and in television's first ninety-minute drama, *Requiem for a Heavyweight*.[61] He owned a nightclub, Slapsy Maxie's, which was featured in the 2013 film *Gangster Squad*. The club, which operated from 1943 to 1947, was located in Los Angeles.[62] He was inducted into the International Boxing Hall of Fame in 1993.

Al Roth (1913–1982)

won 47 (KO 12) + lost 30 (KO 2) + drawn 13 = 90

Al Roth was a New York, New York, born boxer who contended for the lightweight title. He lived the later part of his life in Oakland, California, with his wife, Mildred.

Andre Routis (1900–1969)

won 55 (KO 12) + lost 24 (KO 2) + drawn 7 = 86

Newspaper Decisions won : lost 1 : drawn

Andre Routis was a Bordeaux, Gironde, France, born boxer who held the world featherweight championship (1928–1929). He was frugal and used his boxing money to live well. He returned to his native France after retiring from boxing. On his sixty-ninth birthday, Routis died from a heart attack.[63]

Irving Rudd (1917–2000)

Irving Rudd was born in the Brownsville section of Brooklyn, New York. He was one of boxing's great press agents. Rudd worked with world champions Joe Louis, Sugar Ray Robinson, Muhammad Ali, Sugar Ray Leonard, Ray Mancini, Thomas Hearns; promoters Mike Jacobs, Don King, and Bob Arum. Irving was also employed as a press agent for

Yonkers Raceway in New York and for the Brooklyn Dodgers, where he became one of Jackie Robinson's friends. He wore a tie clasp that was a 1953 Dodgers money clip and a 1955 Dodgers World Series ring. He had a sign on his desk with the words "Ulcer Dept." He wrote the books *The Sporting Life: The Duke and Jackie, Pee Wee, Razor Phil, Ali,* and *Mushky Jackson and Me.*[64, 65] He was inducted into the International Boxing Hall of Fame in 1999.

Damon Runyon (1880–1946)
Damon Runyon was a Manhattan, Kansas, born journalist and author. He was a prolific sportswriter for newspapers. He wrote many books and short stories, which were turned into movies and plays. He wrote *Little Miss Marker, The Lemon Drop Kid, Lady for a Day,* and *Guys and Dolls.* He was an infamous gambler, which was a common subject of Runyon's writings. He used to paraphrase from a famous line in *Ecclesiastes:* "The race is not always to the swift, nor the battle to the strong, but that's how the smart money bets." Runyon died in New York City from throat cancer. His body was cremated, and his ashes were illegally scattered from a DC-3 airplane over Broadway in Manhattan by Captain Eddie Rickenbacker.[66] He was inducted into the International Boxing Hall of Fame in 2002.

Lou Salica (1912–2002)
won 62 (KO 13) + lost 17 (KO 1) + drawn 12 = 91
Lou Salica was a Brooklyn, New York, born boxer who held the world bantamweight championship (1935, 1940–1942). Salica's winning title bout against George Pace on September 24, 1940, was called "the final bout of the Golden Age of Bantamweight Boxing" by *The Ring* magazine. After leaving the ring, he would take his two sons and daughter to Madame Bey's Camp. His daughter, Janet Parente, recalled, "I was maybe four or five years old, and I remember riding to the country with my father. We'd go to Madam Bey's Training Camp. I'm sure he wanted to take another shot at the title, but I think he knew it wasn't going to happen." He became an owner of a Brooklyn bar, Lou's Fish Market at the Fulton Market, and had a home in Florida.[67] At forty-six, Salica spent eighteen months in jail for a $150,000 kickback conspiracy. "The way I remember Lou is a guy who was well-liked and with a constant smile," wrote journalist Bill Gallo.[68] He died in the Crown Nursing Home in Brooklyn.

Max Schmeling (1905–2005)
won 56 (KO 40) + lost 10 (KO 5) + drawn 4 = 70
Max Schmeling was a Klein Luckow, Mecklenburg-Vorpommern, Germany, born boxer who held the world heavyweight championship (1930–1932). He was drafted into the

German army during World War II because of his friction with high-level Nazis. He served as a paratrooper, saw action, and erroneously reported dead. After the war, with little money, he embarked upon a comeback in boxing, winning three of his five bouts before a second retirement in 1948. On his first trip back to America, his first stop was to visit the grave of Joe Jacobs, who meant so much to him. During the 1950s, Schmeling worked for the Coca-Cola Company's offices in Germany. Subsequently, he owned a bottling plant and held an executive's position within the company.[69] In 1992, he was inducted into the International Boxing Hall of Fame. He lived his remaining years as a wealthy man and avid boxing fan.

Jack Sharkey (1902–1994)
won 37 (KO 13) + lost 13 (KO 4) + drawn 3 = 53
Newspaper Decisions won 1 : lost 1 : drawn
Jack Sharkey was a Binghamton, New York, born boxer. He was more associated with the city of Boston, which was where he was raised. He held the world heavyweight championship (1932–1933). It is unclear when Jack Sharkey was in Chatham Township, but longtime resident Edward Furneld who knew him remembered him being there.[70] In retirement, Sharkey owned a bar in Boston. He worked as a referee and toured with baseball great Ted Williams in fly-fishing promotions. He supplemented his income with various personal appearances. In 1994, he died just months after he was inducted into the International Boxing Hall of Fame.

Battling Siki (1897–1925)
won 60 (KO 32) + lost 24 (KO 4) + drawn 4 = 88
Newspaper Decisions won 1 : lost 2 : drawn
Battling Siki was a Saint Louis, Senegal, born boxer who held the world light heavyweight championship (1922–1923). He said in a 1922 autobiography, "I want to go on fighting, make money, and save it. Then someday when I am beaten, as all fighters are, I plan to settle down in the country in France with my wife and be a farmer. I like to see things growing."[71] He was never afforded that chance—gunned down in New York City in 1925. In the 1990s, his body was exhumed from Flushing Cemetery in Queens and brought back to Senegal to be placed in a Muslim tomb.[72]

Eric Seelig (1910–1984)
won 41 (KO 8) + lost 14 (KO 3) + drawn 7 + drawn 1 = 63
Eric Seelig was a Bydgoszcz, Poland, born boxer who fought in the middleweight division. Seelig married Greta in the United States. Like Seelig, she was an athlete persecuted under

Hitler's rule. She was prevented from competing in the 1936 Berlin Olympics, where she was to run in the hurdles competition. She, too, had fled Germany. They first lived in New York and then moved to Atlantic City. They ran a chicken farm for a while, and then Seelig opened a boxing gymnasium.[73] Seelig is a member of the New Jersey Boxing Hall of Fame and the International Jewish Sports Hall of Fame. In June 2006, he received the Rocky Marciano AAIB Champions Award.[74] His German titles that the Nazis revoked have never been restored.[75]

Freddie Steele (1912–1984)
won 123 (KO 58) + lost 5 (KO 3) + drawn 11 + drawn 1 = 140
Freddie Steele was a Seattle, Washington, born boxer who held the world middleweight championship (1936–1938). When his boxing career ended, he ran a cigar store in Tacoma. In 1941, former junior welterweight champion Mushy Callahan, who worked for Warner Brothers Studio, got him started in films. Steele first started as a double for Errol Flynn in *Gentleman Jim*. He was also in *Pin-Up Girl*, *Duffy's Tavern*, and *The Story of G.I. Joe*. Ten years later, he returned to Washington state where he operated Freddie Steele's Restaurant in Westport, Washington, for twenty years. He had a stroke in 1980 and died in a nursing home in Aberdeen, Washington, four years later.[76] He was inducted into the International Boxing Hall of Fame in 1999.

Young Stribling (1904–1933)
won 223 (KO 129) + lost 13 (KO 1) + drawn 14 + drawn 2 = 252
Newspaper Decisions won 33 : lost 3 : drawn 3
Young Stribling was a Bainbridge, Georgia, born boxer who fought for the heavyweight championship. Stribling's last fight was a win over Maxie Rosenbloom in 1933. In October of that year, Stribling was struck by a car while riding his motorcycle on his way to the hospital to visit his wife and newly born baby.[77] Stribling's foot was badly mangled, but he said, "I guess this means more roadwork." Physicians were astonished at his ability to hang on to life with a temperature of 107.5 degrees and pulse of 175. He was given a last privilege to see his wife and baby at the same hospital before he died two days later.[78] He was inducted into the International Boxing Hall of Fame in 1996.

Herman Taylor (1887–1980)
From the 1920s until 1975, Taylor dominated the promotions of fights in Philadelphia and Southern New Jersey. Jack Dempsey, Sugar Ray Robinson, Billy Conn, Willie Pep, and about a dozen other world champions attended his eightieth birthday party in 1968.[79] He was inducted into the International Boxing Hall of Fame in 1998.

Lew Tendler (1898–1970)

won 59 (KO 38) + lost 11 (KO 1) + drawn 2 + drawn 2 = 74

Newspaper Decisions won 86 : lost 5 : drawn 6

Lew Tendler was a Philadelphia, Pennsylvania, born boxer who contended for the lightweight and welterweight championships. He never obtained a championship but earned nearly $1 million from his fights. After boxing, he operated a restaurant in Philadelphia from 1932 to 1970, which was a meeting place for famous athletes and politicians. At the time of his death, he lived in Ventnor, New Jersey.[80] He is a member of the International Jewish Sports Hall of Fame and was inducted into the International Boxing Hall of Fame in 1999.

Sid Terris (1904–1974)

won 93 (KO 12) + lost 13 (KO 5) + drawn 4 = 110

Newspaper Decisions won 6 : lost : drawn 1

Sid Terris was a New York, New York, born boxer who fought as a lightweight. He officially retired from the ring in 1933. He lived his later years with his family, friends, and opponents in Miami, Florida.[81]

Young Terry (1911–1977)

won 78 (KO 31) + lost 31 (KO 11) + drawn 7 = 116

Newspaper Decisions won 9 : lost 1 : drawn 2

Young Terry was a Trenton, New Jersey, born boxer who fought as a middleweight. He lost in two middleweight title fights. He was on the cover of the January 1932 *The Ring* magazine. He retired from boxing in 1941.

Jack Thompson (1913–?)

won 20 (KO 31) + lost 15 (KO 11) + drawn 5 + no contest 5 = 45

Newspaper Decisions won 2 : lost 10 : drawn 0

Jack Thompson was a Denver, Colorado, born boxer who fought as a heavyweight. He fought the best African American boxers of his era, including Jack Johnson, Harry Wills, Joe Jeanette, Sam Langford, Kid Norfolk, and George Godfrey. He retired from boxing in 1926.

Gene Tunney (1897–1978)

won 65 (KO 48) + lost 1 (KO 0) + drawn 1 + drawn 1 = 68

Newspaper Decisions won 14 : lost : drawn 3

Gene Tunney was a Greenwich Village, New York, born boxer who held the world heavyweight championship (1926–1928). He won the American light heavyweight championship in 1922 and regained it in 1923. In 1928, he was *The Ring* magazine's first fighter of the year. After boxing, he was successful at business and real estate, making millions of dollars. He served as chairman or director of several companies. He owned a two-hundred-acre estate in Stamford, Connecticut, where he died a wealthy man. He was one of the inaugural inductees into the International World Boxing Hall of Fame in 1990. In 2001, Tunney was an inductee into the United States Marine Corps Sports Hall of Fame. In March 2011, Tunney's family donated to the Smithsonian National Museum of American History many objects from his career, including the boxing gloves he had worn during the infamous Long Count Fight against Jack Dempsey.[82]

Pancho Villa (1901–1925)
won 78 (KO 22) + lost 4 (KO 0) + drawn 4 + drawn 2 = 88
Newspaper Decisions won 12 : lost 4 : drawn
Pancho Villa was an Iloilo City, Iloilo, Philippines, born boxer who held the world flyweight championship (1923–1925). At twenty-three years old, he was the youngest reigning champion to die until 1982. Villa's remains were returned to Manila, and in August 1925, Villa was buried at the Manila North Cemetery. In the Associated Press's Fighters of the Century list, he is listed as the number-one flyweight. He was inducted into the International Boxing Hall of Fame in 1994.

Mickey Walker (1901–1981)
won 94 (KO 60) + lost 19 (KO 6) + drawn 4 + drawn 2 = 119
Newspaper Decisions won 37 : lost 6 : drawn 2
Mickey Walker was an Elizabeth, New Jersey, born boxer who held the world welterweight championship (1922–1926) and the world middleweight championship (1926–1929). He retired from boxing in 1935. Walker made millions of dollars during his boxing career but could not hold on to any of it. He spent his fortune on his lifestyle. He had an unsuccessful acting career followed by working as a traveling salesman. He gave up liquor and continued to play golf. Walker opened a restaurant, and it became a popular dining place in New York City. He became a painting artist, many of his works exhibited at New York and London art galleries. He was married several times, including twice to the same woman. Later in life, he had Parkinson's syndrome, arteriosclerosis, and anemia. He spent the last part of his life in a nursing home in New Jersey.[83] In 1990, he became part of the inaugural class of inductees into the International Boxing Hall of Fame.

Max Waxman (?–?)
Max Waxman was from Baltimore. He started as a boxing manager at the age of nineteen. He managed Joe Dundee, Vince Dundee, Harry Jeffra, Red Burman, and Kid Williams,

among many other fighters. He promoted most of Joe Louis's exhibition fights during World War II. He arranged referee tours for Joe Louis, Jack Dempsey, and James Braddock. He handled Jack Dempsey's business affairs for over twenty-five years.[84]

Al Weill (1883–1969)
Al Weill was born in Gebweiler, Alsace-Lorraine, France. He is regarded as one of the most astute boxing managers in history. Weill came to New York at thirteen. As a manager, his fighters included four world champions—lightweight Lou Ambers, featherweight Joey Archibald, welterweight Marty Servo, and undefeated heavyweight Rocky Marciano. He served as a matchmaker at Madison Square Garden for Mike Jacobs. Weill promoted bouts at many clubs along the East Coast that featured star boxers Kid Chocolate, Barney Ross, Tony Canzoneri, and Max Baer. He left boxing shortly after Marciano left the ring and retired to Florida where he lived the rest of his life.[85] He was inducted into the International Boxing Hall of Fame in 2003.

Freddie Welsh (1886–1927)
won 74 (KO 34) + lost 5 (KO 1) + drawn 7 + drawn 1 = 87
Newspaper Decisions won 47 : lost 24 : drawn 10
Freddie Welsh was a Pontypridd, Wales, born boxer who held the world lightweight championship (1914–1917). He brought boxing to Chatham Township, New Jersey. Welsh fought Benny Leonard, Johnny Dundee, Battling Nelson, Rocky Kansas, Willie Ritchie, Ad Wolgast three times, Packey McFarland twice, Charley White, and Johnny Kilbane, many of whom are considered legends. Welsh managed Jimmy Goodrich in 1925, who won the New York state lightweight title left vacant by Benny Leonard. Many think he was the inspiration for F. Scott Fitzgerald's Gatsby character in *The Great Gatsby*; others would dispute it. He is in the Welsh Sports Hall of Fame and was inducted into the International Boxing Hall of Fame in 1997.

Harry Wills (1889–1958)
won 68 (KO 54) + lost 9 (KO 5) + drawn 3 + drawn 6 = 86
Newspaper Decisions won 19 : lost 1 : drawn 3
Harry Wills was a New Orleans, Louisiana, born boxer. Like Godfrey and Jeannette, he never received a chance to fight for the heavyweight championship because of his skin color. Wills retired from boxing in 1932 at the age of forty-three. He invested his ring earnings in real estate and became a successful businessman. He died from diabetes. He left an estate valued at over $100,000, including a nineteen-family apartment building in upper Harlem.[86] He was inducted into the International Boxing Hall of Fame in 1992.

Charley White (1891–1959)

won 87 (KO 57) + lost 16 (KO 4) + drawn 5 + drawn 2 = 110

Newspaper Decisions won 35 : lost 18 : drawn 10

Charley White was a Liverpool, England, born boxer who fought in the lightweight division. He retired from boxing in 1930.

Johnny Wilson (1893–1985)

won 48 (KO 29) + lost 21 (KO 3) + drawn 2 + drawn 1 = 72

Newspaper Decisions won 14 : lost 8 : drawn 6

Johnny Wilson was a New York, New York, born boxer who held the world middleweight championship (1920–1923). He was Madame Bey's first boxer and helped her financially and physically to build her camp. He retired after fifteen years in the ring. He was not reckless with his ring earnings like many other boxers. He owned several nightclubs in New York and Boston.[87] He lived in a large house on Riverside Drive in New York City.[88] In 1970, Wilson had a short role in the movie *Zabriskie Point* when he was seventy-seven years old.

Chalky Wright (1912–1957)

won 162 (KO 83) + lost 45 (KO 7) + drawn 19 + drawn 3 = 229

Chalky Wright was a Willcox, Arizona, born boxer who held the world featherweight championship (1941–1942). After his retirement, Wright worked as the trainer for lightweight contender Tommy Campbell. In October 1954, Wright opened a bar in Los Angeles called the Knockout Lounge. He claimed that all the bartenders were ex-boxers. By the mid-1950s, Wright lost the money he had earned as a boxer.[89] In 1957, Wright's mother found his body in the bathtub. Rumors of homicide and suicide ensued because Wright had been subpoenaed to testify in a libel suit by Mae West against *Confidential* magazine. Police determined that Wright had a heart attack while in the bathtub, causing him to slip and fall. His death was ruled accidental. Baptist minister Henry Armstrong, a fellow former Bey boxer whom Wright had once fought, delivered the eulogy at his funeral. Other champions attending were Archie Moore, Jimmy Carter, and Young Jack Thompson.[90] He was inducted into the International Boxing Hall of Fame in 1997.

Paulino Uzcudun (1899–1985)

won 51 (KO 35) + lost 17 (KO 1) + drawn 3 = 71

Paulino Uzcudun was a Regil, País Vasco, Spain, born boxer who contended for the heavyweight championship. He retired from boxing in 1935.

Teddy Yarosz (1910–1974)

won 106 (KO 17) + lost 18 (KO 1) + drawn 3 = 127

Newspaper Decisions won 1 : lost : drawn

Teddy Yarosz was a Pittsburgh, Pennsylvania, born boxer who held the middleweight championship (1934–1935). After boxing, he owned and operated a bar called Teddy's Inn and later worked in the steel industry.[91] Yarosz died after a battle with cancer. He was inducted into the International Boxing Hall of Fame in 2006.

ENDNOTES

Prelude

1 How far did the USA achieve prosperity in the 1920s? [Online] December 2015. http://www.johndclare.net/America4.htm.

2 **Bureau, US Census.** No. HS-33. Selected Per Capita Income and Product Items in Current and Real. *Statistical Abstract of the United States.* 2003, p. 62.

3 Boxing in the 1920s. [Online] Wikipedia, April 29, 2015. https://en.wikipedia.org/wiki/Boxing_in_the_1920s.

Chapter 1

1 **Daley, Arthur.** Gem in a Shabby Setting. *New York Times.* June 18, 1959.

2 **Hatem, George J.** *It's in the Genes, a Family History and Autobiography.*

3 **Churchill, Ruth Pierson.** *Memories Entwined with Roses.* s.l.: self-published, 1984.

4 **Cunningham, John T.** *Chatham Township (NJ) (Images of America).* Charleston, SC: Acadia Publishing, 2001.

5 Greenhouse Industry Circa 1880–1999. *Chatham Township Historical Marker.* 2014.

6 **Stoll, Mabel Latham & Marion.** Miss Belcher, Teacher Excerpts from an Oral History with Margaret Belcher Interviewed by Mabel Latham & Marion Stoll on November 6, 1978. *Historical Society of Chatham Township Newsletter.* September 2014.

7 Fashion. *Thoroughbred Heritage Portraits.* [Online] 2005. http://www.tbheritage.com/Portraits/Fashion.html.

8 **Anderson, James Douglass.** *Making the American thoroughbred : Especially in Tennessee, 1800–1845.* Norwood: Plimpton Press, 1916.

9 Fashion. [Online] Wikipedia, February 1, 2016. https://en.wikipedia.org/wiki/Fashion_(horse)#cite_note-1.

10 Engineers Prove That Boxer, 'Hitman' Hatton, Packs A Mighty Punch. *ScienceDaily.* June 26, 2007.

11 **Adams, Cecil.** The True Force of a Boxer's Punch. *Connect Savannah.* [Online] July 20, 2010. http://m.connectsavannah.com/savannah/the-true-force-of-a-boxers-punch/Content?oid=2133328.

12 Fatal Bouts in the Roped Ring Over the Last Two Centuries. *Unknown.* 1900.

13 **Svinth, Joseph R.** *Death Under the Spotlight: The Manuel Velazquez Collection, 2011.* s.l.: EJMAS, 2011.

14 **Robertson, Stewart.** She Puts'em in the Pink. *The Family Circle.* October 7, 1938.

15 **Times, Special Cable to The New York.** ARMENIANS ARE SENT TO PERISH IN DESERT. *New York Times.* August 18, 1915.

16 **Pap.** Max Meets Mickey. *Red Bank Register.* August 31, 1932, p. 16.

17 **Pantalone, Don.** [interv.] Gene Pantalone. December 11, 2014.

18 *Madame Bey's—Training Camp for Championship Prizefighters.* **Hageman, Robert A.** 2004, Summit Historical Society Newsletter.

19 **Press, Associated.** Native of Turkey Mothers Ranking Fighters. *Spartanburg Herald Journal.* August 5, 1978, p. 22.

20 **Shapiro, Michael.** The Boxing Champs Came to Train at Madame Bey's. *Courier-News at Library of the Chathams Received.* August 6, 1978.

21 —. Focus. *Courier-News.* August 5, 1978.

22 **Graham, Dillon.** Former Turkish Society Woman Proves Mother to Ranking Boxers. *Daily Sentinel, Rome, NY.* January 15, 1938, p. 7.

23 **Shapiro, Michael.** Focus, *Courier News.* August 2, 1978.

24 **Knott, Caroline.** *Boxer Training Camps in Chatham Township.* Chatham Township : Caroline Knott, 2013.

25 **Rudd, Irving.** Before Fight Camp Became a Suite Science. *New York Times.* March 1, 1987.

26 Champ Not Yet Down to Limit of 175 Pounds. *Auburn Citizen.* July 14, 1926.

27 **Anderson, Dave.** Ortiz Prefers Simple and Secluded Training. *New York Times.* November 27, 1966.

Chapter 2

1 About Women Charming Mme. Sidky. *Baltimore Sunday Herald.* August 3, 1901, p. 2.

2 Girls College in Turkey. *New York Times.* March 12, 1899.

3 **Robertson, Stewart.** She Puts'em in the Pink. *The Family Circle.* October 7, 1938.

4 Sidky Bey, Modern Turk. *The Tourist* magazine.

5 **Knott, Caroline.** *Boxer Training Camps in Chatham Township.* Chatham Township: Caroline Knott, 2013.

6 **Island, Ellis.** Ship Manifest—Fulda July 7, 1897. New York: s.n., 1897.

Chapter 3

1 Historical Events in 1897. [Online] On This Day, 2016. http://www.onthisday.com/events/date/1897.

2 **Sidky Bey, Mrs. Heranoush Alexan (Agiaganian).** *Turkish Diplomatic Life in Washington Under the Old Rigime, by the Wife of a Diplomat.* New York: Cochrane Publishing, 1910.

3 **Proctor, John Clagett.** Dupont Circle Memorial. *Washington Evening Star.* July 25, 1937, p. 46.

4   Connave.com. [Online] 2011. http://connave.com/dcirc.php.

5   Smokes and Waits. *Washington Bee.* March 8, 1902.

6   **Hubbard, Samuel.** The Social Season. *Courtland Evening Standard.* January 15, 1901, p. 4.

7   President McKinley, and the Diplomatic Corps of 1901 Grouped in the East Room of the White House. *New York Herald.* May 12, 1901, p. 15.

Chapter 4

1   **Robertson, Stewart.** She Puts'em in the Pink. *The Family Circle.* October 7, 1938.

2   **Leech, Margaret.** In the Days of McKinley. New York: Random House. ISBN 978-1-4000-6752-7, 1959, p. 576.

3   **Morgan, H. Wayne.** William McKinley and His America (revised ed.). Kent, Ohio : The Kent State University Press. ISBN 978-0-87338-765-1., 2003, pp. 392-394.

4   Unknown. *Unknown, taken from a newspaper clipping.* September 1901.

5   Ministers and Foreign Legation Here. *Buffalo Courier.* September 5, 1901, p. 9.

6   Guns that Fired President's Salute Break Windows of Car of the M'Kinley Train. *Buffalo Courier.* September 5, 1901, p. 9.

7   The President is Buffalo's Honored Guest. *Buffalo Evening News.* September 5, 1901.

8   Arrival of the Diplomats. *Buffalo Evening News.* September 5, 1901.

9   **Leech, Magaret.** In the Days of McKinley. New York: Harper and Brothers. OCLC 456809, 1959, p. 584.

10 Arrival at the Exposition. *Buffalo Evening News.* September 6, 1901.

11 From the Society Pages. *Buffalo Evening News.* September 6, 1901.

12 Review of the Troops. *Buffalo Evening News.* September 5, 1901.

13 President Sees Many Exhibits. *Buffalo Evening News.* September 5, 1901.

14 Proudist Day in Buffalo's History. *Buffalo Courier.* September 6, 1901, p. 8.

15 Luncheon at N.Y. State Building. *Buffalo Courier.* September 6, 1901, p. 8.

16 Luncheon in Honor of the President. *Buffalo Evening News.* September 5, 1901.

17 Doing The Pan. [Online] 2014. http://panam1901.org/womens/womensdesign.htm.

18 Even at This Late Date Its Purposes. *New York Tribune.* August 8, 1901.

19 Government Building Inspected. *Buffalo Courier.* September 6, 1901, p. 8.

20 Great Day's End is Flashed in Fire. *Buffalo Courier.* September 6, 1901, p. 8.

21 **Leech, Margaret.** In the Days of McKinley. New York : Harper and Brothers. OCLC 456809, 1959, pp. 299-300.

22 Doing The Pan. [Online] http://panam1901.org/music/musicdesign.htm.

23 **Kingseed, Wyatt.** President William McKinley: Assassinated by an Anarchist. *HistoryNet.* [Online] HistoryNet, October 1, 2001. http://www.historynet.com/president-william-mckinley-assassinated-by-an-anarchist.htm.

24 William McKinley: Death of the President. [Online] Miller Center, 2016. http://millercenter.org/president/biography/mckinley-death-of-the-president.

25 **Leech, Magaret.** In the Days of Mckinley. New York: Harper and Brothers. OCLC 456809, 1959, pp. 594-595.

26 *Buffalo Express.* September 7, 1901.

27 .32 Caliber Short Barreled Johnson Revolver - McKinley Death. *AwesomeStories.com.* [Online] October 7, 2013. https://www.awesomestories.com/asset/view/.32-Caliber-Short-Barreled-Johnson-Revolver-McKinley-Death.

28 Pan-American Sketch. Buffalo: s.n., 1901.

29 He Saved McKinley's Life. *Cleveland Gazette.* September 14, 1901.

30 **McElroy, Richard L.** William McKinley and Our America: A Pictorial History. Canton, Ohio: Stark County Historical Society. ISBN 978-0-9634712-1-5, 1996, p. 15.

31 **Miller, Scott.** The President and the Assassin. New York: Random House. ISBN 978-1-4000-6752-7, 2011, pp. 301-303.

32 A Facsimile of Czolgosz's Confession. Source: Karpeles Manuscript Museum, Buffalo, N.Y. Buffalo: s.n., September 6, 1901.

33 **Bos, Carole.** President McKinley—Assassination—TOO LATE . *Awesome Stories.* [Online] June 1, 2005. https://www.awesomestories.com/asset/view/TOO-LATE-President-McKinley-Assassination.

34 **Gado, Mark.** The Assassination of President William McKinley. *EyeWitness to History.* [Online] 2010. www.eyewitnesstohistory.com .

35 **Guenther, Jack.** Madame Bey's Death Saddens Slug Alley. *Pittsburgh Press.* 1942.

36 Work of an Anarchist. *Rome Daily Sentinel.* September 7, 1901, p. 1.

37 **Parker, James.** *Parker's own remembrance of the event as told to a reporter from the Buffalo Times.* [interv.] Buffalo Times. September 1901.

Chapter 5

1 President's Condition. *Gloversville Daily Leader.* September 6, 1901, p. 1.

2 Last Honors For Dead Commander. *New York Times.* September 15, 1901.

3 Service For the Dead in the Capitol Rotunda, Special to the New York Times. *New York Times.* September 18, 1901.

4 **Moberly, C. F.** How the Ceremonies Impressed a Briton. *New York Times.* September 18, 1901, p. 6.

5 **MacDonald, Carlos F.** "The Trial, Execution, Autopsy and Mental Status of Leon F. Czolgosz." New York: the *Journal of Mental Pathology,* 1902.

6 Events in the Social World, Special to The New York Times. *Washington.* November 17, 1901, p. 6.

7 Smokes and Waits. *Washington Bee.* March 8, 1902.

8 **Bureau, Herald.** Homage of Nations Paid to President. *New York Herald.* January 2, 1902, p. 12.

9 A Happy New Year. *Evening Star.* January 1, 1902, p. 1.

10 **Sidky Bey, Mrs. Heranoush Alexan (Agiaganian).** *Turkish Diplomatic Life in Washington Under the Old Rigime, by the Wife of a Diplomat.* New York : Cochrane Publishing, 1910.

11 Diplomatic Changes. *Evening Star.* March 29, 1902, p. 23.

12 An Evening of Music at the White House. *Washington Times.* April 15, 1902, p. 7.

13 **Times, A Special to The New York.** Society in Washington. *New York Times.* May 7, 1902.

14 Washington Gossip. *National Tribune.* November 20, 1902, p. 7.

15 Turkish Minister Gets His Recall. *San Francisco Call.* August 12, 1908, p. 5.

16 **Halford, A. J.** *Official Congressional Directory.* Bowie, MD: Washington Government Printing Office, 1908.

17 Would Welcome Jews. *New York Times.* September 4, 1908.

18 Roosevelt Hails Freedom in Turkey. *New York Times.* September 7, 1908.

19 Ottomans Celebrate. *New York Daily Tribune.* September 7, 1908, p. 2.

20 The Ottoman Union Celebrates. *New York Times.* December 6, 1908.

21 May Oust Turkish Consul. *Sun.* March 9, 1909, p. 1.

22 Mundji Not Coming Back. *Evening Post: New York.* March 20, 1909.

23 **Middleton, Lamar.** Turkish Bey's Wife has Training Camp. *Evening News—Tonawanda.* November 17, 1927, p. 9.

24 **Government, U. S.** *1910 U.S. Census.* Washington, DC: US government, 1910.

25 **Marion E. Porter and Emma L. Teich, Compiled by.** *The Cumulative Book Index, Fifteenth Annual Cumulation, .* s.l.: H. W. Wilson Company, 1913.

26 **Churchill, Ruth Pierson.** *Memories Entwined with Roses.* s.l.: self-published, 1984.

27 Day of Horror Described. *New York Times.* April 28, 1909.

Chapter 6

1 Mme. Sidky to Sing at a Concert. *New York Times.* May 13, 1908.

2 Mme. Sidky Sings for Brooklyn. *New York Times.* May 16, 1908.

3 **Guenther, Jack.** Hardboiled "Lammers' Lane" Mourns Madame Bey's Death. *Buffalo Courier-Express.* January 31, 1942, p. 17.

4 The Metropolitan, Music Notes. *New York Daily Tribune.* January 16, 1910, p. 2.

5 **Guenther, Jack.** Madame Bey's Death Saddens Slug Alley. *Pittsburgh Press.* 1942.

6 Sale of Oriental Art Works. *New York Times.* April 28, 1909.

7 Auction Sales—Advertisement. *Evening Post: New York.* April 26, 1909.

8 Auction Sales—Advertisement. *Sun.* April 27, 1909, p. 7.

9 Sidky Bey Sale Brings $52,567. *New-York Daily Tribune.* May 2, 1909, p. 7.

10 Turkish Art Sold. *New York Herald.* April 30, 1909.

11 Sidky Bey Displays His Rugs. *Boston Evening Transcript.* May 4, 1910, p. 8.

12 **Coffman, Taylor.** Curtis Studio A Story of San Francisco. 2013.

13 Auction Sales—Advertisement. *Montreal Gazette.* April 15, 1911, p. 11.

14 Auction Sales—Advertisement. *San Francisco Sun.* November 16, 1911, p. 17.

15 *Directory of Directors in the City New York, Fourteenth Edition.* New York: Brown Brothers & Company, 1915.

16 **Anderson, Dave.** Ortiz Prefers Simple and Secluded Training. *New York Times.* November 27, 1966.

17 **Robertson, Stewart.** She Puts'em in the Pink—*The Family Circle.* October 7, 1938.

18 **Middleton, Lamar.** Turkish Bey's Wife has Training Camp. *Evening News—Tonawanda.* November 17, 1927, p. 9.

19 **Press, United.** MEET MME. BEY. *Brooklyn Daily Eagle.* December 10, 1937, p. 15.

Chapter 7

1 **Stern, Bill.** *Freddie Welsh Documentary (Boxing Legend) film. Torpedo for BBC Wales, Presented by Trevor Fishlock.* 2006.

2 **Heller, Peter.** *In This Corner …!* New York: Da Capo Press, Inc., 1973.

3 A Rest and Training Resort on Long Hill. *Chatham Press.* May 12, 1917.

4 Freddie Welsh, Boxer, Buys $60,000 Estate for Home and Training Farm. *New York Herald.* March 26, 1917.

5 **Greenspan, Bud.** The Long Last Night in the Ring for Benny Leonard. *New York Times.* April 10, 1983.

6 Freddie Welsh, Farmer. *New York Times.* August 12, 1917.

7 Welsh Says a Champion Should Defend Title Once a Year. *Brooklyn Daily Eagle.* May 13, 1917, p. 2.

8 Freddie Welsh Tries Hand at Building Men. *Milwaukee Sentinel.* August 20, 1917.

9 Registration on Tuesday. *Chatham Press.* June 2, 1917, p. 8.

10 Christie's Lot 233 / Sale 8299. *Christie's Auction.* [Online] November 30, 1999. http://www.christies.com.

11 **Gallimore, Andrew.** *Occupation: Prizefighter: Freddie Welsh's Quest for the World Championship.* Lancashire, United Kingdom : Revival Books Ltd ISBN 10: 185411395X, 2006.

12 **Pilgrim, John.** Watching the Parade. *Binghamton Press.* February 3, 1925.

Chapter 8

1 **Karadag, Ehsan.** *1,307,130* United States, 1919.

2 Freddie Welsh in Uniform. *Tucumcari News.* circa 1918.

3 Freddie Welsh is in the Army. *Le Meschachacebe.* January 25, 1919.

4 Freddie Welsh Coming Home. *Chatham Press.* February 21, 1920, p. 8.

5 French Boxing Champ and His Bride. *Sun and New York Herald.* March 18, 1920, p. 10.

6 Carpentier Feted at I.S.C. Luncheon. *New York Times.* September 15, 1920.

7 Carpentier is Here to Fight. *Evening Telegram—New York.* September 1920.

8 Carpentier to Train in Chatham. *Chatham Press.* September 18, 1920, p. 4.

9 Press Photo. Summit, New Jersey: s.n., 1920.

10 **Carpentier, Georges.** What Georges and "Bat" had to Say To-day. *Syracuse Journal.* 1920.

11 Carpentier Knocks Levinsky Out in the Fourth Round. *New York Times.* October 1920.

12 Chronology of Dempsey-Carpentier Bout. *Troy Times.* July 2, 1921, p. 9.

13 JACOBS, MICHAEL STRAUSS. [Online] Jewish Virtual Library, 2013. https://www. jewishvirtuallibrary.org/jsource/judaica/ejud_0002_0011_0_09907.html.

14 **Daniel, Daniel M.** *The Mike Jacobs Story.* s.l. : Ring Book Shop, 1950.

15 **Lawrence, Jack.** Richard, Bom During Raid on James Boys, Lived Exciting Life. *Syracuse Journal.* January 8, 1929.

16 —. Stoic, Imperturbable Face of Tex Richard Impressed Writer. *Syracuse Journal.* January 15, 1929.

17 —. Richards Were Poor When Tex Was a Kid Back in Kansas City. *Syracuse Journal.* January 9, 1929.

18 —. Richard Was Forced to Earn Living for Ma at the Age of 11. *Syracuse Journal.* January 11, 1929.

19 —. Richard Had Record of Being Fine Shot as Cowboy in Texas. *Syracuse Journal.* January 12, 1929.

20 —. Tex Always Saw to It That His Mother Was in a Cozy Home. *Syracuse Journal.* January 10, 1929.

21 —. Lifelong Friends Made By Tex Rickard in Stay at Circle City. *Syracuse Journal.* January 17, 1929.

22 —. Luck Deserted Rickard in Dawson City Where He Lost Everything. *Syracuse Journal.* January 18, 1929.

23 —. Gans-Nelson Scrap at Goldfield Was Rickard's First Promotion Venture. *Syracuse Journal.* January 21, 1929.

24 —. Rickard Not Sure of Bout Until Nelson Had Entered Goldfield Ring. *Syracuse Journal.* January 22, 1929.

25 —. Mixed Heavy Bout Was Tex Rickard's Greatest Undertaking. *Syracuse Journal.* January 24, 1929.

26 —. Reformers Gave Tex Much Trouble Before Jeffries-Johnson Bout. *Syracuse Journal.* January 25, 1929.

27 —. Rickard Does Lot of Worrying Before Bout Staged at Reno in '10. *Syracuse Journal.* January 26, 1929.

28 —. Dempsey as Hobo. Saw Jeffries, Johnson Bout at Reno, Nevada, in 1910. *Syracuse Journal.* January 28, 1929.

29 **Roberts, James B. and Skutt, Alexander B.** *The Boxing Register: International Boxing Hall of Fame Official Record Book (4th ed.).* Ithica: Ithaca: McBooks Press. ISBN 978-1-59013-121-3, 2006.

30 International Boxing Hall of Fame Biography: Mike Jacobs. *IBHOF.* [Online] Decembe 2015. http://www.ibhof.com/pages/about/inductees/nonparticipant/jacobsmike.html.

31 **Press, Associated.** Mike Jacobs Parlayed Two Tickets Into a Big Industry. *Chicago Sunday Tribune.* January 25, 1953, p. 3.

32 **Skutt, James B. Roberts and Alexander G.** *The Boxing Register.* Ithica: McBooks Press, Inc., 2006.

33 Jacobs, Michael Strauss. *Jewish Virtual Library.* [Online] December 2015. https://www. jewishvirtuallibrary.org/jsource/judaica/ejud_0002_0011_0_09907.html.

34 **Fraley, Oscar.** Saga of Mike Jacobs Comes to End Tonight. *Spokane Daily Chronicle.* May 20, 1949, p. 13.

35 Mike Jacobs is the Big Boss of the Boxing Business Today. *Life.* June 20, 1938, p. 36.

36 **Bak, Richard.** *Joe Louis: The Great Black Hope.* New York: Perseus Publishing. ISBN 978-0-306-80879-1, 1996.

37 *Ottawa Journal .* June 21, 1946, p. 21.

38 **Myler, Patrick.** *Ring of Hate: Joe Louis Vs. Max Schmeling.* New York: Arcade Publishing, 2005.

39 **Margolick, David.** The Beach of Jowly Men. *New York Times.* October 9, 2005.

40 Jews in America: Joe Louis and the Jews. *Jewish Virtual Library.* [Online] December 2015. https://www.jewishvirtuallibrary.org/jsource/US-Israel/louis.html.

41 **Kenefick, Bob.** On the Sport Firing Line. *Unknown.* 1921.

42 Dempsey's Weakness Affection for Kids. *Niagara Falls Gazette.* June 1, 1921, p. 12.

43 **Fernald, Gus.** [interv.] Historical Society of Chatham Township.

44 **Stern, Bill.** *Freddie Welsh Documentary (Boxing Legend) film. Torpedo for BBC Wales, Presented by Trevor Fishlock.* 2006.

45 **Farrell, Henry L.** Kearns Says Dempsey is Only "Playing Around" in Jersey. *Norwalk Hour.* April 29, 1921, p. 19 cite starting from "I'm just resting …"

46 Champion Engages Two More Trainers. *New York Times.* May 5, 1921, p. cite starting from "Dempsey did not wait …"

47 *Capital Times from Madison, Wisconsin.* April 22, 1921, p. 10.

48 Arena is Largest Ever Constructed. *New York Times.* June 26, 1921.

49 **Gustkey, Earl.** This Champion Was a Real Bum. *New York Times.* June 25, 1995.

50 *New York Times.* June 23, 1921, p. 1.

51 **Roberts, Randy.** *Jack Dempsey: The Manassa Mauler.* New York : Grove Press, 1979.

52 New York Governor Forced Fight to JC. *Hudson Dispatch.* July 2, 1971.

Chapter 9

1 **Underwood, George B.** Decision Likely in Jersey Soon. *Evening Telegram—New York.* January 30, 1923, p. 10.

2 Sheriff's Sale. *Chatham Press.* February 11, 1922, p. 7.

3 **Ratner, Willie.** Ehsan's Training Camp on the Ropes. *Newark Evening News.* April 23, 1969.

4 **Shapiro, Michael.** Focus. *Courier-News.* August 5, 1978.

5 **Ratner, Willie.** Punching the Bag. *Newark Evening News.* January 1942.

6 Wilson Starts Training. *Geneva Daily Times.* July 31, 1923, p. 5.

7 **Heller, Peter.** *In This Corner …!* New York : Da Capo Press, Inc., 1973.

8 Duane Made Even Choice Against Kid Wolfe. *Brooklyn Standard.* August 26, 1923, p. 19.

9 Champion is Angry as Partner Lands. *New York Times.* August 25, 1923.

10 Wilson at Weight, Ready to Step Into Ring. *Brooklyn Standard.* August 28, 1923, p. 11.

11 *Pittsburgh Post.* September 1, 1923.

Chapter 10

1 **Robertson, Stewart.** She Puts'em in the Pink. *The Family Circle.* October 7, 1938.

2 **Press, United.** MEET MME. BEY. *Brooklyn Daily Eagle.* December 10, 1937, p. 15.

3 Bantamweight to Box at Rink Thursday Night. *Sun And Globe.* October 17, 1923, p. 31.

4   Jerome to Box Duane in Garden To-morrow Night. *New York Evening Post.* November 22, 1923, p. 10.

5   **Dayton, Alfred.** Siki Pays Visit to Tex Rickard. *Sun and Globe.* November 16, 1923, p. 23.

6   In The Roped Arena. *New York Evening Post.* October 3, 1923.

7   Inspect Fighters. *Evening Leader.* October 3, 1923, p. 8.

8   **Hall, Sam P.** Sheriff Rescues Referee Roche From Angry Crowd When Welsh Gets Verdict. *Buffalo Courier.* September 5, 1916.

9   Welsh and White Bout Proved To Be Some Fizzle. *Journal News Of All Sports.* September 1916, p. cite starting from "I had to fight two men …"

10 Inspect Fighters. *Evening Leader.* October 3, 1923, p. 8.

11 **Gerbasi, Thomas M.** *Ring Ramblings: Tales of a Cyber Journalist.* San Jose: Writer's Club Press, 2000.

12 **Siki, Battling.** *Battling Siki's Autobiography, as told to Milton Bronner.* Bellingham, WA: Bellingham American, 1922.

13 **Runyon, Damon.** War Blamed for Downfall of Negro Star. *Milwaukee Sentinel.* April 26, 1932, p. 12.

14 **Lardner, John.** *The World of John Lardner.* s.l.: Simon and Schuster, 1961.

15 **Boddy, Kaisa.** *Boxing a Cultural History.* s.l.: Reaktion Books Ltd. ISBN 978 1 86189 369 7, 2008.

16 **Island, Ellis.** Ship Manifest. New York: s.n., 1923.

17 Battling Siki is Here in Chastened Mood. *New York Times.* September 2, 1923, p. 18.

18 Senegalese Light Heavy, An Amusing Character, to Train Faithfully for Bout Here. *Brooklyn Standard Union.* October 24, 1923, p. 14.

19 Karpe's Comment. *Buffalo Evening News.* November 20, 1923, p. 32.

20 Battling Siki Will Not Leave Montreal. *Afro American.* October 19, 1923, p. 13.

21 **Underwood, George B.** Big 'Uns Box in Garden Tonight. *Evening Telegram.* November 2, 1923, p. 12.

22 *Tacoma News Tribune.* May 1923.

23 **Middleton, Lamar.** Turkish Bey's Wife has Training Camp. *Evening News—Tonawanda.* November 17, 1927, p. 9.

24 **Shapiro, Michael.** Focus. *Courier-News.* August 5, 1978.

25 **Ratner, Willie.** Ehsan's Training Camp on the Ropes. *Newark Evening News.* April 23, 1969.

26 **Robertson, Stewart.** She Puts'em in the Pink. *The Family Circle.* October 7, 1938.

27 **Guenther, Jack.** Madame Bey's Death Saddens Slug Alley. *Pittsburgh Press.* 1942.

Chapter 11

1   **Press, Associated.** Native of Turkey Mothers Ranking Fighters. *Spartanburg Herald Journal.* August 5, 1978, p. 22.

2   **Coad, John.** Out of the Past: Madame Bey's Training Camp. *Milburn and Short Hills Item, Suburban Section.* September 28, 1950, p. 3.

3   **Robertson, Stewart.** She Puts'em in the Pink. *The Family Circle.* October 7, 1938.

4   **Heller, Peter.** *In This Corner …!* New York : Da Capo Press, Inc., 1973.

5   **Press, United.** MEET MME. BEY. *Brooklyn Daily Eagle.* December 10, 1937, p. 15.

6   **Pantalone, Don.** [interv.] Gene Pantalone. December 11, 2014.

7   **Beer, John.** New Jersey in the Lead as Fight-Training Center. *Newark Sunday Call.* February 3, 1946, p. 3.

Chapter 12

1   Joins New Spiegel Company. *Player.* October 11, 1912, p. 11.

2   **Sorg, Jeff.** Pro-Boxers Jogged Chatham Streets in the 1920's. *Chatham Township Independent.* October 8, 1980.

3   Criqui and Kilbane Receive Their Money. *New York Times.* June 5, 1923, p. 19.

4   Siki Fails to Impress Committee N. Y. Writers; is Wide Open on Defense. *Buffalo Courier.* November 16, 1923, p. 14.

5   **Dayton, Alfred.** Siki Pays Visit to Tex Rickard. *Sun and Globe.* November 16, 1923, p. 23.

6   **Underwood, George B.** Siki, as Seen by a Telegram Expert. *Evening Telegram.* November 17, 1923, p. 8.

7   **Casanova, Louis De.** Curiosity of Boxing Fans Regarding Battling Siki's Ability May End Tonight. *Brooklyn Daily Eagle.* November 20, 1923, p. 2A.

8   **Runyon, Damon.** War Blamed for Downfall of Negro Star. *Milwaukee Sentinel.* April 26, 1932, p. 12.

9   **Webster, John.** Pigeon Augurs Title Success for Billy Fox. *Philadelphia Inquirer.* February 26, 1947, p. 30.

10 Dempsey to Train at Summit, N. J. *Sun And Globe.* December 15, 1923.

11 Jack Dempsey vs. Tommy Gibbons. [Online] BoxRec, October 24, 2014. http://boxrec.com/media/index.php/Jack_Dempsey_vs._Tommy_Gibbons.

12 Jack Dempsey vs. Luis Angel Firpo. [Online] Boxrec, October 17, 2014. http://boxrec.com/media/index.php/Jack_Dempsey_vs._Luis_Angel_Firpo.

13 U. S. Navy Athletes Join Training Camp. *New York Times.* December 19, 1923.

14 Sailors to Engage in Finale Workouts. *New York Times.* December 14, 1923.

15 Vincenti Plans Rest. *New York Times.* December 17, 1923, p. 10.

16 First Northern Fight for Stribling. *Philadelphia Inquirer.* December 31, 1923, p. 10.

17 **Keats, Fred.** New Year's Ring Card Is Big. *Sun And Globe.* December 31, 1923, p. 11.

18 Young Stribling Wheels 'the folks'. *Brooklyn Daily Eagle.* December 29, 1923, p. 11.

19 **Duffy, Edward P.** Stribling is Fit for Rosenberg. *Sun And Globe.* December 31, 1923, p. 11.

20 *Augusta Chronicle.* January 1824.

21 Greb-Wilson Set for January 18. *Sun And Globe.* December 15, 1923.

22 Wilson Leaves the Siki Camp for Bout Tonight. *Brooklyn Daily Eagle.* December 18, 1923, p. 2A.

Chapter 13

1   **Walker, Mickey.** *Mickey Walker: The Toy Bulldog and His Times.* New York: Random House, 1961.

2   **Casey, Mike.** Automatic For the People: Mickey Walker. *cyberboxingzone.com.* [Online] 2007. http://www.cyberboxingzone.com/boxing/casey/MC_Walker.htm.

3   **Andre, Nat Flesicher and Sam.** *An Illustrated History of Boxing.* s.l.: Kensington Publishing Corporation ISBN 0806522011, 2002.

4   **Myler, Patrick.** *A Century of Boxing Greats.* Suffolk: St. Edmundsdurry Press, 1997.

5   **Roberts, James B. and Skutt, Alexander B.** *The Boxing Register: International Boxing Hall of Fame Official Record Book (4th ed.).* Ithica: Ithaca: McBooks Press. ISBN 978-1-59013-121-3, 2006.

6   Keeping in Shape for Benny. *Brooklyn Standard Union.* August 27, 1924, p. 12.

7   **Robertson, Stewart.** She Puts'em in the Pink. *The Family Circle.* October 7, 1938.

8   Marlow and Chick Kansas To Clash at 27th Armory. *Brooklyn Standard Union.* May 26, 1924, p. 13.

9   The Editor's Chair. *Saratogian.* July 5, 1924, p. 9.

10 Bernstein Primed for Zivic Battle. *Yonkers Statesman.* July 21, 1924, p. 10.

11 Payment Made on Mortgage, Adjourn Sale on Welsh Farm. *Chatham Press.* September 20, 1924, p. 1.

12 Tendler Still Under Suspension. *Troy Times.* July 30, 1924, p. 6.

13 Walker Re-Signed For Leonard Bout. *New York Times.* August 5, 1924.

14 Mickey Walker Picks Bernstein to Beat Chilean. *Long Island Daily Press.* August 9, 1924, p. 6.

15 Walker to Start Work Next Tuesday. *Brooklyn Standard Union.* August 27, 1924, p. 12.

16 McTigue Off for Camp. *New York Times.* December 30, 1924.

17 Kramer Will Train at Camp in Jersey. *New York Times.* December 22, 1924.

18 *New York Times.* January 1925.

19 **Dayton, Alfred.** Villa to Risk Title. *Sun And Globe.* February 4, 1924.

20 Burke Starts Training. *New York Times.* April 23, 1924.

21 Tate to Help Train Firpo. *New York Times.* November 7, 1924.

22 Gibbons to Meet Norfolk in Garden. *New York Times.* November 6, 1924.

23 **Malvern, Jack.** The London Times. *Old Sport, it Turns Out Gatsby was a prizefighting Welshman.* January 13, 2007.

24 **Brockway, Anthony.** Babyon Wales. [Online] January 16, 2007. http://babylonwales.blogspot.com/2007/01/was-freddie-welsh-great-gatsby.html.

25 **Gallimore, Andrew.** *Occupation: Prizefighter: Freddie Welsh's Quest for the World Championship.* Lancashire, United Kingdom : Revival Books Ltd ISBN 10: 185411395X, 2006.

26 **Press, Associated.** Scribe Willie Ratner; Plimpton of His Time. *Sunday Register.* April 6, 1980, p. A4.

Chapter 14

1 **Lawrence, Jack.** M'Tigue Claims Siki Will Win Over Paul. *Buffalo Evening News.* March 12, 1925, p. 31.

2 **Wood, Wilbur.** McTigue Likes Siki's Chance. *Sun.* March 12, 1925, p. 30.

3 Berlenbach Stops Siki in the Tenth. *New York Times.* March 14, 1925, p. 9.

4 Mike M'Tigue Yells Hello. *Time-Union.* May 20, 1925.

5 **Cogan, Gene.** Champion Tells Gene Cogan That His Hand, Injured Two Years Ago, Is Strong Again. *Saratogian.* May 20, 1925, p. 11.

6 —. Mike McTigue Expects to Win From Paul Berlenbach. *Saratogian.* May 20, 1925, p. 11.

7 Mike McTigue Loses Crown to Paul Berlenbach. *Saratogian.* June 1, 1925, p. 11.

8 Telling the World. *Sun.* June 26, 1925, p. 26.

9 **Fraley, Oscar.** Days of Wine and Bloody Noses. *Sports Illustrated.* January 20, 1964.

10 Walker Receives Royal Reception. *New York Times.* May 26, 1925.

11 Humbert Fugazy, Boxing Promoter. *New York Times.* April 8, 1964.

12 **Stradley, Don.** Greb, Walker and the tale of the Silver Slipper. [Online] ESPN, July 2, 2008. http://espn.go.com/espn/print?id=3465571.

13 **Walker, Mickey.** *Mickey Walker: The Toy Bulldog and His Times.* New York: Random House, 1961.

14 Fitzsimmons Must Post $100,000 Here. *New York Times.* August 17, 1925, p. 13.

15 **Dawson, James P.** Walker Outpoints Shade; Keeps Title. *New York Times.* September 22, 1925, p. 19.

16 Former Champ Takes Up Foxes. *Borders Cities Star.* July 18, 1925, p. 3.

17 **Press, Associated.** Sports Briefs. *Niagara Falls Gazette.* November 24, 1925, p. 23.

18 **Roberts, James B. and Skutt, Alexander B.** *The Boxing Register: International Boxing Hall of Fame Official Record Book (4th ed.).* Ithica: Ithaca: McBooks Press. ISBN 978-1-59013-121-3, 2006.

19 **Casey, Mike.** Whirlwind: Pancho Villa Was Dempsey In Miniature. [Online] Cyberboxingzone, 2007. http://www.cyberboxingzone.com/boxing/casey/MC_Villa.htm.

20 Battling Siki Shot Dead in the Streets. *New York Times.* December 16, 1925, p. 3.

21 **Robertson, Stewart.** She Puts 'em in the Pink. *The Family Circle.* October 7, 1938.

Chapter 15

1 **Wood, Wilbur.** Glick Scores Over Finnegan. *New York Sun.* November 24, 1925.

2 **Rice, Grantland.** The Spotlight. *Evening Ledger, Corning, N. Y.* January 3, 1925, p. 8.

3 New Ring Flash, Born Deaf Mute, Arouses Fans. *Auburn Citizen.* March 6, 1924.

4 Great Ring Career Predicted for Sensational Berlenbach. *Saratogian.* March 4, 1924, p. 9.

5 **Press, Associated.** Dan Hickey, Former Manager of Berlenbach, Dies in New York. *Independent, St. Petersburg, Florida.* October 19, 1932, p. 7.

6   Sparring Partners are an Asset of the Fight Game. *Pittsburgh Press*. January 8, 1911.

7   Berlenbach Goes to Camp Monday to Train for Bout. *Daily Star, Queens Borough*. February 25, 1926, p. 10.

8   The Light Heavyweight Champion in Action and Repose. *Brooklyn Daily Eagle*. June 27, 1926, p. C3.

9   Press Photo. Chatham Township: s.n., 1926.

10 Berlenbach Ends Hard Work Today. *New York Times*. July 13, 1926.

11 **Kofoed, Jack.** Berly-Delaney Bout for Title Next Week is Ring Event of the Year. *New York Evening Post*. July 1926.

12 Berlenbach, Shorty Press Photo. Chatham Township: s.n., 1926.

13 Berlenbach Shows Form in Workout. *New York Times*. December 4, 1925.

14 Amateurs Usher in Boxing at Garden. *New York Times*. December 8, 1925.

15 Madison Square Garden III. [Online] Munsey & Suppes, 2015. http://hockey.ballparks.com/NHL/NewYorkRangers/3rdoldindex.htm.

16 **Schumach, Murray.** Next and Last Attraction at Old Madison Square Garden to Be Wreckers' Ball. *New York Times*. February 14, 1968.

17 **Troast, Raulf.** History of Garden Goes Back 25 Yeas. *Brooklyn New York Daily Eagle*. 1950.

18 **Press, Associated.** Jack Delaney's Victory Acclaimed in Fistiana as 'Berly' Loses Crown. *Amsterdam Evening Record*. July 17, 1926, p. 6.

19 **Wood, Wilbur.** Some Unexpected Knockouts. *New York Sun*. February 24, 1926, p. 41.

20 Berlenbach Off for Summit to Train for Bout. *Daily Star, Queens Borough*. March 2, 1926, p. 10.

21 Freddie Welsh is Sued. *New York Evening Post*. February 27, 1926, p. 2.

22 Paul's Jaw Pounded Hard and Often; Vaccarelli Wins From Silvers; Suggs Victor. *Brooklyn Standard Union*. March 20, 1926, p. 10.

23 Madame Bey's Training Camp for Berlenbach. *Long Island Daily Express*. June 29, 1926, p. 8.

24 **Press, Associated.** Berlenbach Gives Stribling Beating in 15 Round Fight. *Evening Leader, Corning, N. Y.* June 11, 1926, p. 18.

25 **Wood, Wilbur.** Berlenbach Will Train at Summit for Delaney Tilt. *Brooklyn Daily Eagle*. June 27, 1926, p. C3.

26 Berlenbach to Start Work Friday for Delaney Bout. June 1926, p. 10.

27 M'Graw and Balduc Both Confident. *Unknown Newspaper*. June 1926, p. 10.

28 Berlenbach Draws 2,000 to Exhibition. *New York Times*. July 5, 1926.

29 Johnny and Frenchman to Battle Ten Rounds; Vogel Meets Goodrich. *Brooklyn Standard Union*. August 17, 1926, p. 8.

30 **Robertson, Stewart.** She Puts'em in the Pink. *The Family Circle*. October 7, 1938.

31 Surprising and Decisive Victory for the Challenger. *Schenectady Gazette*. July 17, 1926, p. 13.

32 **Walsh, Davis J.** Delaney Fools 'Em; Experts Predicted K.O. *Daily Star, Queens Borough*. July 11, 1926, p. 10.

33 Boxers' Post-Battle Statements; Paul Asks A Return Engagement. *Daily Stars, Queens Borough*. July 17, 1926, p. 10.

34 Risko and M'Tigue at Garden. *New York Times.* July 1, 1926.

35 Fugazy Lining Large Card Up for Big Benefit Show. *Yonkers Statesman.* July 28, 1926.

36 What Boxers Say. *Brooklyn Standard Union.* August 20, 1926, p. 6.

37 **Graham, Dillon.** Former Turkish Society Woman Proves Mother to Ranking Boxers. *Daily Sentinel, Rome, NY.* January 15, 1938, p. 7.

38 **Cross, Harry.** Punch 'Em Paul Introduces Frenchman to Queer Street. *Buffalo Evening News.* August 21, 1926, p. 9.

39 **Dayton, Alfred.** Jacobs to Sue Mike M'Tigue. *Sun And Globe.* November 17, 1923, p. 13.

40 **Parker, Dan.** Why Yussel the Muscle Died Broke. *Milwaukee Sentinel.* February 2, 1941, p. 28.

41 **Jacobs, Joe.** Explains Bulow Fight. *Syracuse Journal Sports.* June 6, 1929.

42 Delaney Fells Fit After Lohman Bout. *New York Times.* March 10, 1926.

43 **Wood, Wilbur.** Morgan in Town. *New York Sun.* November 9, 1926, p. 40.

44 Morgan Shows Class in Training Session. *New York Evening Post.* May 1926.

45 Harmon Confident of Halting Latzo. *New York Times.* June 29, 1926.

46 Latzo Will Risk Title at Newark. *New York Times.* June 20, 1926.

47 Persson and Risko in Clash Thursday. *New York Times.* August 22, 1926.

48 Ruby Goldstein. [Online] Project Gutenburg Self-Publishing Press, 2016. http://self.gutenberg.org/articles/ruby_goldstein.

Chapter 16

1 **Press, Associated.** Rickard's Bout Plan Still Undecided. *New York Times.* July 20, 1926.

2 **Jr., Frank Graham.** Double Image of a Champion. *Sports Illustrated.* December 4, 1961.

3 GENE TUNNEY, CHAMPION OF THE A. E. F. *Watertown Daily Times.* July 27, 1926, p. 10.

4 Gene Tunney. [Online] Wikipedia, March 10, 2016. https://en.wikipedia.org/wiki/Gene_Tunney.

5 Gene Tunney. [Online] Boxrec, December 18, 2015. http://boxrec.com/media/index.php/Gene_Tunney.

6 Masters of the Sweet Science—Gene Tunney. [Online] Boxing News 24, May 20, 2013. http://www.boxingnews24.com/2013/05/masters-of-the-sweet-science/.

7 Gene Tunney. [Online] World Public Library, 2016. http://www.worldlibrary.org/articles/gene_tunney.

8 **Casey, Mike.** Gene Tunney: The King Of Cool. [Online] Cyberboxingzone, 2007. http://www.cyberboxingzone.com/boxing/casey/MC_GTunney.htm.

9 **Dewey, Donald.** *Ray Arcel A Boxing Biography.* Jefferson: McFarland & Company, 2012.

10 **Anderson, Dave.** Ortiz Prefers Simple and Secluded Training. *New York Times.* November 27, 1966.

11 **Robertson, Stewart.** She Puts'em in the Pink. *The Family Circle.* October 7, 1938.

12 **Runyon, Damon.** Madame Bey Makes Fighters. *Rochester Democrat and Chronicle.* November 25, 1937, p. 9D.

13 Chronology of Dempsey-Carpentier Bout. *Troy Times*. July 2, 1921, p. 9.

14 **Dempsey, Jack.** Why Negoes Rule Boxing. *Ebony.* February 1950.

15 *Reading Times.* July 22, 1926, p. 13.

16 **Press, Associated.** Dempsey Denies Contract. *New York Times.* July 24, 1926.

17 **Ratner, Willie.** Ehsan's Training Camp on the Ropes. *Newark Evening News.* April 23, 1969.

18 **Press, Associated.** Dempsey to Fight Tunney in Chicago. *New York Times.* July 22, 1926.

19 Dempsey Title Bout Suddenly Shifted to Philadelphia. *New York Times.* August 19, 1926.

20 **Press, Associated.** Tunney Keeps Busy with Usual Training. *New York Times.* August 21, 1926.

21 **Vidmer, Richards.** Tunney Welcomed by Philadelphia. *New York Times.* September 2, 1926.

22 **Press, Associated.** Tunney to Train at Stroudsburg. *New York Times.* August 25, 1926.

23 **Davis, Elmer.** Victory is Popular One. *New York Times.* September 24, 1926.

24 **Boyer, Deborah.** The Dempsey-Tunney Fight of 1926. [Online] PhillyHistory.org, January 1, 2009. http://www.phillyhistory.org/blog/index.php/2009/01/the-dempsey-tunney-fight-of-1926/.

25 **Dawson, James P.** City will Welcome Tunney Home Today; Mayor to Hail Him. *New York Times.* September 25, 1926.

26 **Press, Associated.** Carnera-Loughran Title Bout Tomorrow is Finacial "Flop". *Troy Times.* February 27, 1934, p. 11.

27 **Dawson, James P.** Tunney Always Master. *New York Times.* September 24, 1926.

28 —. Tunney Title Bout Set About Sept. 10. *New York Times.* June 20, 1927.

29 —. Fight Fast and Furious. *New York Times.* September 23, 1927.

30 **Hughes, Ed.** Both Fighter Seek 3D Match After Dispute. *Brooklyn Daily Eagle.* September 23, 1927, pp. 1,3.

31 **Press, Associated.** September 23, 1927.

32 **Dawson, James P.** Tunney Scores Knockout Over Heeney in Eleventh; Only 50,000 See the Battle. *New York Times.* July 27, 1928.

33 **Hughes, Ed.** Gene Stops Tom in 11th Despite a Year's Layoff. *Brooklyn Daily Eagle.* July 27, 1928, p. 1.

34 Through With Ring, Tunney Announces. *New York Times.* August 1, 1928.

Chapter 17

1 Freddie Welsh Gets a Respite. *Chatham Press.* April 1927.

2 Freddie Welsh Dies Jobless and Alone. *New York Times.* July 29, 1927.

3 Freddie Welsh, Idol of Boxing, Dies in Solitude. *Brooklyn Daily Eagle.* July 29, 1927, p. 2A.

4 Health Farm Destroyed by Fire in New Jersey. *Lewiston Daily Sun.* October 12, 1927, p. 13.

5 Fire Destroys Health Farm. *Chatham Press.* October 15, 1927, p. 1.

6 Freddie Welsh Losses Summit Health Farm. *Milwaukee Journal.* May 3, 1927, p. 24.

7 **Sorg, Jeff.** Pro-Boxers Jogged Chatham Streets in the 1920's. *Chatham Township Independent.* October 8, 1980.

8 Boxing. *Yonkers Statesman.* January 14, 1927, p. 13.

9   **Press, Associated.** Irishman Hammers Berlenbach to Win by Technical KAYO. *Philadelphia Inquirer.* January 29, 1927, p. 13.

10 **McGonigle, William J.** Sportagraph. *Daily Sentinel, Rome, N.Y.* January 29, 1927, p. 8.

11 **Holmes, Thomas.** Paulino Fought Men Only After Interest in Bull-Fighting Waned. *Brooklyn Daily Eagle.* November 23, 1927, p. 2A.

12 **Morris, William.** Both Seem Sure of Slugging Way to Quick Victory. *New York Evening Post.* April 3, 1927.

13 **Press, Associated.** July 13, 1927.

14 Delaney Bout Sale to Start Tomorrow. *Yonkers Statesman.* August 1, 1927.

15 Uzcudum [sic] May Get Sharkey Contest if He Wins Bout. *Yonkers Statesman.* August 5, 1927.

16 Victory by Kayo is Paulino's Aim; Heeney Confident. *Yonkers Statesman.* September 7, 1927.

17 Basque Woodchopper Has a Knockout Win Over English Heavy. *Brooklyn Standard Union.* October 20, 1927, p. 14.

18 Report on Paulino Expected Today. *New York Times.* October 21, 1927.

19 **Holmes, Thomas.** Paulino Fought Men Only After Interest in Bull-Fighting Waned. *Brooklyn Daily Eagle.* November 23, 1927, pp. 2A cite starting from "Upon reaching his destination, Sidky Bey greeted him …"

20 Johnny Finishes Strong; Gross Defeats Seifert; Okun in Win Over May. *Brooklyn Standard Union.* November 26, 1927, p. 10.

21 **Morris, William.** Around the Ring. *New York Evening Post.* May 17, 1927.

22 **Berger, Phil.** Ray Arcel, Trainer Who Handled Many Boxing Stars, ss Dead at 94. *New York Times.* March 8, 1994.

23 Untitled Article. *Daily Star, Queens Borough.* June 7, 1927, p. 10.

24 **Morris, William.** Both, Hard Punchers, Expect To Score Win by Knockouts Lindbergh Will See Fights. *New York Evening Post.* June 14, 1927, p. 19.

25 Maloney Remains Favorite; Many Backing Him to K. O. Hub Heavyweight Rival. *Brooklyn Standard Union.* May 18, 1927, p. 11.

26 Sharkey Engages in 10-Round Drill. *New York Times.* May 17, 1927.

27 Terris and Martinez Get Ready for Their Scrap at Queensboro. *Daily Star, Queens Borough.* September 22, 1927, p. 12.

28 Terris Starts Work for Bout with Martinez. *Yonkers Statesman.* September 14, 1927.

29 Chief Bey of the Township Has Had Interesting Life. *Chatham Press* . April 26, 1946, p. 1.

Chapter 18

1   **Anderson, Dave.** Ortiz Prefers Simple and Secluded Training. *New York Times.* November 27, 1966.

2   **Government, US.** 1930 US Census. Washington, DC: US government, 1930.

3   Notes of the Ring. *Brooklyn Standard Union.* February 2, 1928, p. 13.

4   Last Rickard List Put Tunney at Top. *New York Times.* January 8, 1929.

5   **Rickard, Tex.** *The Ring.* 1929.

6   **Middleton, Lamar.** Turkish Bey's Wife has Training Camp. *Evening News—Tonawanda*. November 17, 1927, p. 9.

7   **Margolick, David.** *Beyond Glory*. New York : Vintage Books, Division of Random House ISBN-10: 0375726195, 2006.

8   **Schmeling, Max translation by von der Lippe, George.** *Max Schmeling: An Autobiography*. Chicago, IL: Bonus Books, 1998.

Chapter 19

1   **Schmeling, Max.** Max Schmeling's Own Story. *Elmira Star-Gazette*. February 9, 1929, p. 8.

2   **Lloyd, Melarie.** A Tribute to Max Schmeling. *sweetfightingman.com*. [Online] 2008. http://www.sweetfightingman.com/article_maxschmeling.htm.

3   **Schmeling, Max.** Max Schmeling's Own Story. *Elmira Star-Gazette*. February 13, 1929, p. 14.

4   —. Max Schmeling's Own Story. *Elmira Star-Gazette*. February 14, 1929, p. 22 cite starting from "My greatest thrill …"

5   —. Max Schmeling's Own Story. *Elmira Star-Gazette*. February 16, 1929, p. 9.

6   Jack Dempsey. [Online] PBS Online, September 22, 2004. http://www.pbs.org/wgbh/amex/fight/peopleevents/p_dempsey.html.

7   **Ratner, Willie.** Punching the Bag. *Newark Evening News*. January 1942.

8   Max Schmeling. [Online] PBS Online, February 9, 2005. http://www.pbs.org/wgbh/amex/fight/peopleevents/p_schmeling.html.

9   **Schmeling, Max translation by von der Lippe, George.** *Max Schmeling: An Autobiography*. Chicago, IL: Bonus Books, 1998.

10 **Schmeling, Max.** Max Schmeling's Own Story. *Elmira Star-Gazette*. February 19, 1929, p. 24.

11 **Graham, Frank.** Setting the Pace / Eight Years Ago in Schmeling's Life. *New York Sun*. June 16, 1936, p. 28.

12 **Jacobs, Joe.** 10 Rounds With One Arm-Wins. *Sunday Times, Perth, WA*. March 9, 1941, p. 13.

13 **O'Neil, Frank.** Max Schmeling's Life Story. *Syracuse Journal*. February 14, 1929, p. 11.

14 **Kahn, James M.** Tunney is Impressed by Max. *New York Sun*. December 8, 1937, p. 41 cite starting from "Tunney and his friends met Schmeling …"

15 **Robertson, Stewart.** She Puts'em in the Pink. *The Family Circle*. October 7, 1938.

16 K. O. for Montagna. *Chatham Press*. April 5, 1930, p. 6.

17 **McGowen, Roscoe.** Speaking of Sports. *Standard Union*. September 25, 1928, p. 18.

18 **Morris, William.** Frenchman Gave Champion Battle in Previous Bout. *New York Evening Post*. September 28, 1928.

19 **Gould, Alan J.** Canzoneri Beaten by Andre Routis in Title Battle. *Montreal Gazette*. September 29, 1928, p. 21.

20 **Jacobs, Joe.** Explains Bulow Fight. *Syracuse Journal Sports*. June 6, 1929.

21 **Graham, Frank.** Setting the Pace / Schmeling Returns to Madame Bey's. *New York Sun*. December 1, 1937, p. 38.

22 **Parker, Dan.** Why Yussel the Muscle Died Broke. *Milwaukee Sentinel.* February 2, 1941, p. 28.

23 **Press, United.** Famous Fight Promoter is Near Death. *Pittsburgh Press.* January 5, 1929, p. 1.

24 **Dawson, James P.** Schmeling Victor in Bout at Garden. *New York Times.* January 5, 1929.

25 *Vernon Daily Record.* January 7, 1929, p. 2.

26 **Kenefick, Bob.** On the Sport Firing Line. *Syracuse Journal.* January 8, 1929.

27 Sports World Mourns Loss of Rickard. *Syracuse Journal.* January 1929.

28 Where Tex Rickard Was Laid to Rest. *Syracuse Journal.* January 10, 1929.

29 **L.N.S.** Tunney Sends Sympathy. *Syracuse Journal.* January 8, 1929.

30 **Dempsey, Jack.** 'Tex and I', as Told by Ring's Greatest Idol. *Syracuse Journal.* January 10, 1929.

31 —. 'Tex and I', as Told by Ring's Greatest Idol. *Syracuse Journal.* January 25, 1929.

32 **Press, Associated.** Many Relatives Share in Bulky Rickard Fortune. *Buffalo Courier Express.* January 12, 1929, p. 14.

33 **Walsh, Davis J.** Game in Chaotic State. *Syracuse Journal.* January 7, 1929.

34 **Jacobs, Joe.** Schmeling and Paulino Have Old Feud. *Syracuse Journal.* June 8, 1929, p. 11.

35 Schmeling Stops Corri. *New York Times.* January 22, 1929.

36 **Schmeling, Max.** Max Schmeling's Own Story. *Elmira Star-Gazette.* February 20, 1929, p. 8.

37 **Farrell, Jack.** Fans Barred at Workouts of Ringstar. *Rochester Democrat And Chronicle.* January 30, 1929, p. 18.

38 **Press, Associated.** Schmeling in Bad Tangle Over Manager. *Geneva Daily Times.* March 27, 1929, p. 5.

39 **Morris, William.** Contract Tangle Further Involves German Ring Star. *New York Evening Post.* March 26, 1929.

40 **Dawson, James P.** Schmeling is Hero in Boxing Circles. *New York Times.* February 3, 1929.

41 Crowd at Pier as Schmeling Sails. *New York Times.* February 17, 1929.

42 **Press, Associated.** Schmeling Sails Almost Unnoticed. *New York Times.* May 1, 1929.

43 —. German Hopeful Hands Basque Worst Beating of His Career. June 28, 1929.

44 Schmeling Phones Mother at Home. *New York Times.* June 28, 1929.

45 **Press, Associated.** March 28, 1929.

46 Tommy Loughran vs. Mickey Walker. [Online] BoxRec, December 6, 2013. http://boxrec.com/media/index.php?title=Fight:22300.

47 It's Back to the Simple Life for Mikey Walker. *Brooklyn Daily Eagle.* July 27, 1929, p. 6.

Chapter 20

1 Jack Sharkey. [Online] Wikipedia, January 21, 2016. "He was unknown," Madame Bey said.

2 **Hughes, Ed.** Outward Appearance Gives No Indication of Nervous Tension. *Brooklyn Daily Eagle.* June 11, 1930, p. 22.

3 World Listens as Contenderrs Bid for Crown. *Yonkers Stattesman.* June 12, 1930, p. 15.

4 Max Schmeling vs. Jack Sharkey (1ˢᵗ meeting). [Online] BoxRec, February 4, 2011. http://boxrec.com/media/index.php?title=Fight:21765.

5   **McGinley, A. B.** Says Sharkey's Low Blow in the 4th was Foul Beyond Debate. *Brooklyn Daily Eagle.* June 13, 1930, p. 24.

6   *Schmeling-Sharkey Film.* 1930.

7   **Holmes, Thomas.** Max Calm Afterward and Thinks He Would Have Won in Any Event. *Brooklyn Daily Eagle.* June 13, 1930, p. 24.

8   **Jacobs, Joe.** 10 Rounds With One Arm-Wins. *Sunday Times, Perth, WA.* March 9, 1941, p. 13.

9   **Press, Associated.** Schmeling New Heavyweight Champion by Sharkey's Foul. *Troy Times.* June 13, 1930, p. 17.

10 Title Eludes Gob—Falls in Teuton's Lap. *Standard Union.* June 13, 1930, p. 8.

11 Muldoon Says Blow Was Fair. *Standard Union.* June 13, 1930.

12 **Farrell, Jack.** Insist Chicago Charity Benefit By Big Ring Go. *Buffalo Courier-Express.* January 29, 1931, p. 15.

13 **Barker, Herbert W.** Schmeling-Stribling Agreement Likely to Precipitate Boxing War. *Daily Sentinel, Rome, N. Y.* January 14, 1931, p. 8.

14 **Morris, William.** German Arrives in Good Condition Despite Layoff. *New York Sun.* January 28, 1931.

15 **Wood, Wilbur.** Schmeling Weighs 193 Pounds. *New York Sun.* January 28, 1931, p. 81.

16 **Press, Associated.** Max Schmeling Faces Law suit in New Jersey. *Daily Illini.* February 6, 1931, p. 8.

17 Dundee Harvey Preparing for Garden Battle. *Long Island Daily Express.* February 7, 1931, p. 9.

18 **Dawson, JmesP.** Schmeling Action Likely Tomorrow. *New York Times.* January 5, 1931.

19 **Dunkley, Charles.** Strib Works Off Excess Pep With Airplane Flight. *Daily Sentinel, Rome, N. Y.* July 1, 1931, p. 10.

20 **Gould, Alan J.** Given Technical Knockout After Furious Battle. *Eugene Register-Guard.* July 4, 1931, p. 6.

21 **Press, Associated.** July 3, 1931.

22 Tony to Train at Summit for Tilt with Berg. *Long Island Daily Express.* August 28, 1931, p. 21.

23 Tony Canzoneri 7-5 Choice to Win Over Berg. *Long Island Daily Press.* September 1, 1931, p. 11.

24 Cany Trains for Berg Bout. *Standard Union.* August 31, 1931, p. 10.

25 Fink to Train Canzoneri for Bout With Berg. *Long Island Daily Press.* August 31, 1931, p. 11.

26 Canzy Strives for Simultaneous Ownership of Five Titles. *Standard Union.* September 3, 1931, p. 9.

27 **Stewart, Dixon.** Canzoneri is Longing for Fith Title. *Urbana Daily Courier.* September 3, 1931.

28 **Neil, Edward J.** Drops Jack for Counts of Nine Twice. *Rochester Democrat And Chronicle.* September 11, 1931, p. 27.

29 *New York Herald-Tribune.* November 20, 1931.

30 **Cox, Monte.** Kid Chocolate, The Cuban Bon Bon. *Cox's Corner Profiles.* [Online] 2007. http://coxscorner.tripod.com/chocolate.html.

31 Chocolate, Bass Wind Up Training. … *And Chronicle.* July 4, 1931.

32 **Press, United.** July 15, 1931.

33 **Neil, Edward J.** Acclaim For Walker as He Battles Sharkey to a Draw. *Troy Times.* October 23, 1931, p. 17.

34 **Press, Associated.** Sharkey Will Meet Walker on July 22nd. *Morning Herald.* Juily 2, 1931, p. 5.

35 The Fight By Rounds. *Troy Times.* July 23, 1931, p. 17.

36 **Wood, Wilbur.** Johnston Lauded by Walker. *New York Sun.* October 23, 1931, p. 45.

37 *New York Times.* November 21, 1931.

38 Victorio Campolo. [Online] BoxRec, October 15, 2007. http://boxrec.com/media/index.php/Victorio_Campolo.

39 *Seattle Daily Times.* September 21, 1929.

40 **Casale, Frank.** Gaucho Impresses in Drill; Hammers 2 Sparring Mates. *Standard Union.* November 24, 1931, p. 9.

Chapter 21

1   Mrs. Mickey Walker Gives Birth to a Son. *Syracuse Journal.* March 19, 1932, p. 10.

2   **Press, Associated.** Max Schmeling Gets Top Rating. *Saratogian.* March 26, 1932.

3   *Salt Lake Tribune.* March 12, 1932.

4   **Morris, William.** Around the Ring. *New York Evening Post.* April 21, 1932, p. 19.

5   —. Around the Ring. *New York Evening Post.* April 4, 1932, p. 15.

6   Walker Beats King Levinsky. *Schenectady Gazette.* April 30, 1932.

7   **Dunkley, Charles.** Walker Beats King Levinsky. *Morning Herald.* June 30, 1932.

8   **Jack Kearns, Oscar Fraley.** *The Million Dollar Gate.* s.l.: Macmillan, 1966.

9   **Press, Associated.** Boils Force Mickey to Postpone Risko Bout. *Buffalo Courier-Express.* May 11, 1932, p. 15.

10 Walker Returns to Garden Ring to Box Paulino. *Long Island Daily Press.* May 23, 1932, p. 11.

11 **Press, Associated.** Illegal Blow Helps Walker Lick Uzcudun. *Binghamton Press.* May 27, 1932, p. 23.

12 **Neil, Edward J.** Max Schmeling Wages Courageous Battle to Keep Sharkey Well on Defensive Onlt to Lose Decision. *Niagara Falls Gazette.* June 22, 1832, p. 16.

13 Max Schmeling vs. Jack Sharkey (2nd meeting). [Online] BoxRec, December 21, 2008. http://boxrec.com/media/index.php?title=Fight:21767.

14 **Press, Associated.** Risko Hands Out 12-Round Defeat to Mickey Walker. *Niagara Falls* . June 25, 1932, p. 14.

15 —. Walker Kocks Out Ruggirello in First Round. *Schenectady Gazette.* July 26, 1932.

16 **Press, United.** Walker Winner by a Knockout. *Daily Argus.* July 26, 1932.

17 **Press, Associated.** Purses are Paid. *Schenectady Gazette.* July 27, 1932, p. 14.

18 **P. Dawson, James.** Schmeling to Box Walker on Sept. 19. *New York Times.* August 16, 1932.

19 **Press, Associated.** Walker's Chance to Equal Record of Fitzsimmons. *Troy Times.* August 30, 1932, p. 11.

20 **Morris, William.** Around the Ring. September 8, 1932, p. 20.

21 **Pap.** Max Meets Mickey. *Red Bank Register.* August 31, 1932, p. 16.

22 Schmeling Departs by Train for Camp. *New York Times.* August 30, 1932.

23 Sharkey's Trainer Picks Mickey Walker. *Syracuse Journal.* August 29, 1932, p. 12.

24 Walker Believes His Style Ideally Suited to Whip Max. *Long Island Sunday Press.* September 4, 1932, p. 13.

25 **Walker, Mickey.** *Mickey Walker: The Toy Bulldog and His Times.* New York: Random House, 1961.

26 **Dawson, James P.** Schmeling Battle Put Off to Sept. 23. *New York Times.* September 12, 1932.

27 ——. Jacobs Loses Plea For New Bout Date. *New York Times.* September 13, 1932.

28 Heavy Advance Sale for Max, Mickey Scrap. *Long Island Daily Press.* September 21, 1932, p. 17.

29 **Wood, Wilbur.** Walker Back to Normalcy. *New York Sun.* September 16, 1932, p. 39.

30 **Lamb, Al.** Delay Irks Walker, Eager to Box Max. *Binghamton Press.* September 21, 1932, p. 18.

31 **Kofoed, Jack.** Rumson Bulldog Sure of Triumph Over German. *New York Evening Post.* September 24, 1933, p. 10.

32 Mickey Walker Will Scale 172, His Heaviest Yet. *Daily Starr.* September 24, 1932, p. 10.

33 Walker Boxes Three Rounds. *New York Times.* August 25, 1932.

34 **Kofoed, Jack.** Principals Ready For 'Heavy' Fight at Bowl Monday. *New York Evening Post.* September 24, 1932, p. 10.

35 ——. Thrills in Sports. *New York Evening Post.* September 24, 1932, p. 10.

36 **Dawson, James P.** Schmeling Ready for Walker Bout. *New York Times.* September 26, 1932.

37 **Ferguson, Frank C.** Schmeling Takes His Own Sweet Time, Making Walker Work Continuously; Eighth Round Finish is a Slaughter. *Daily Star, Long Island City.* September 27, 1932, p. 10.

38 **Press, Associated.** Bout Stopped in Eighth When Kearns Refuses to Let Irishman Continue. *Schenectady Gazette.* September 27, 1932.

39 **Smith, Red.** Sports of The Times; Doc and His Toy Bulldog. *New York Times.* April 16, 1981.

40 Walker and Oster to Fight Tonight. *New York Times.* July 30, 1930.

Chapter 22

1 **Wood, Wilbur.** Jeby Has Old-Fashioned Idea. *New York Sun.* 1933.

2 **Vila, Joe.** Setting the Pace. *New York Sun.* March 20, 1933, p. 23.

3 **Wood, Wilbur.** Pordea Coming Up Third Time. *New York Sun.* March 27, 1933, p. 23.

4 **Gellis, Ike.** Around the Ring. *New York Evening Post.* 1933, p. 44.

5 **Wood, Wilbur.** Canzoneri Flattens Keed. *New York Sun.* November 25, 1933, p. 29.

6 **Every, Edward Van.** Ambers Wears Crown Without Putting on Aors. *New York Sun.* November 17, 1936, p. 37.

7 **Dawson, James P.** *New York Times.* November 25, 1933.

8 **Wood, Wiobur.** Canzoneri Shades Locatelli. *New York Sun.* December 16, 1933, p. 82.

9 **Gellis, Ike.** Popular Italian Proves Showman Against Locatelli. *New York Evening Post.* December 16, 1933, p. 15.

10 Youngster Get Chance in Ring. *Long Island Daily Press.* January 23, 1934, p. 13.

11 **Neil, Edward J.** Tony Canzoneri Wins Over Cleto Locatelli in Twelve Round Battle in New York. *Morning Herald.* February 3, 1934, p. 10.

12 Canzoneri-Klick Clash Wednesday. *New York Times.* June 24, 1934.

13 **Press, Associated.** Referee Halts Match in Ninth. *Poughkeepsie Eagle-News.* June 29, 1934, p. 16.

Chapter 23

1 **Vopelius, Otto.** Chatham Township Fire Department History. [Online] Chatham Township Fire Department, 2016. http://www.ctfd.org/history.

2 Pugilists' Training Camp is Destroyed by Fire. *Chatham Press.* November 16, 1934, p. 1.

3 Fire Destroys Gym, Autographed Photos. *Rochester Democrat And Chronicle.* November 13, 1934, p. 17.

4 Grieves At Less of Fight Photos. *Union-Sun And Journal.* November 13, 1934, p. 7.

5 **Westbrook, Bill.** Bill Westbrook Says. *Milburn-Short—Hills Item.* May 3, 1935, p. 6.

6 Galento is Not Tops but He Hits Hardest. *New York Post.* May 8, 1935, p. 19.

7 **Hecklemann, Charles.** Shirtless Salica Trains Hard for Title Battle. *Brooklyn Daily Eagle.* August 22, 1935, p. 19.

8 **Eyman, Scott.** Life After The Last Bell What Happens After A Two-time World Champ Hangs Up His Gloves? Lou Salica Just Rolled With The Punches. *Sun Sentinel.* March 9, 1986.

9 **Grayson, Harry.** Looking 'Em Over with Harry Grayson. *Saratogian.* October 2, 1934, p. 10.

10 **Press, Associated.** Salica Defeats Escobar for the Bantam Crown. *Saratogian.* August 27, 1935, p. 11.

11 Johnston Sure 'Canzy' - Roth Title Go Will Draw $40,000. *New York Post.* September 27, 1935, p. 17.

12 **Buck, Al.** Only Doc Robb Wizardry Missing From Roth's Drill for Canzoner. *New York Post.* October 2, 1935.

13 **Hecklemann, Charles.** Al Roth Champion Pinochle Player. *Brooklyn Daily Eagle.* September 18, 1935, p. 19.

14 —. Al Roth Ends Hard Training for Title Bout. *Brooklyn Daily Eagle.* October 2, 1935, p. 23.

15 **Schaap, Jeremy.** *Cinderella Man: James J. Braddock, Max Baer, and the Greatest Upset in Boxing History* . New York: Houghton Miffin Company. ISBN 0-618-55117-4, 2005.

16 **Gallico, Paul.** *Farewell to Sport.* Nebraska : University of Nebraska Press. ISBN 978-0-8032-=6761-9, 2008.

17 **Robertson, Stewart.** She Puts'em in the Pink. *The Family Circle.* October 7, 1938.

18 Carnera Faces Homicide Charges. *Daily Star.* February 14, 1933, p. 1.

19 **Neil, Edward J.** Intra Cranial Hemorrhage is Fatal to Boxer. *Citizen Advertiser.* February 14, 1933.

20 Governor Asks Investigation of Fatal Bout. *Buffalo Courier-Expresss.* February 15, 1933, p. 12.

21 **Kelly, Billy.** Before and After. *Buffalo Courier-Express.* February 15, 1933, p. 12.

22 Muldoon Regrets O. K. Of Bout, Blames Second. *Buffalo Courier-Express.* February 15, 1933, p. 12.

23 Primo Carnera vs. Ernie Schaaf. [Online] BoxRec, March 5, 2013. http://boxrec.com/media/index.php?title=Fight:91601.

24 **Neil, Edward J.** Rumors of Title Struggle Between Jack Sharkey and Schmeling in June Die Out. *Morning Herald.* March 29, 1933, p. 4.

25 Max Baer vs. Max Schmeling. [Online] BoxRec, January 5, 2014. http://boxrec.com/media/index.php?title=Fight:21769.

26 **McLemore, Henry.** Schmeling Beaten By Baer in Tenth; Slaughter Halted . *Camden Courier-Post.* June 9, 1933.

27 **Press, Associated.** Title is Next Objective for Winning Baer. *Buffalo Courier-Express.* June 9, 1933, p. 16.

28 Primo Carnera. [Online] Boxing Biographies, January 2016. http://boxingbiographies.co.uk/html/primo_carnera-bb.HTM.

29 **Tunney, Gene.** Sock Won Big Scrap for Baer. *Evening Independent.* June 15, 1934, p. 4A.

30 *New York Times.* March 16, 1935.

31 **Hecklemann, Charles.** Neusel and Carnera Hold Fistic Spotlight. *Brooklyn Daily Eagle.* October 8, 1935, p. 17.

32 **Buck, Al.** Salica Sure Madame Bey's is His Lucky Training Spot. *New York Post.* November 7, 1935, p. 23.

33 **Press, Associated.** November 2, 1935.

34 **Brietz, Eddie.** Champ Wins First Twelve Rounds, Drawing Ovation From 14,210 Fight Fan. *Buffalo Courier-Express.* October 5, 1935, p. 18.

35 The Nazi Party: The Nazi Olympics. [Online] Jewish Virtual Library, 2016. https://www.jewishvirtuallibrary.org/jsource/Holocaust/olympics.html.

36 **Buck, Al.** Hitler's Phiz on Bag Adds Zip to Exile Seelig's Task. *New York Post.* November 6, 1935, p. 19.

37 Madame Bey Picks Seelig For Middleweight Crown. *New York Sun.* November 9, 1935, p. 38.

38 Oh the Pity. *New York Post.* November 11, 1935, p. 23.

39 Joe Louis Planning Tour of European Cities Next Spring. *New York Sun.* November 19, 1935, p. 33.

40 Entire Salica Clan to See Lou Defend Title Against Escobar at Garden Friday Night. *Brooklyn Daily Eagle.* November 13, 1935.

41 **Hecklemann, Charles.** Chapped Lips Fail to Halt Bantam King. *Brooklyn Daily Eagle.* November 8, 1935, p. 23.

42 Herkimer Hurricane has Bout with Jalice in Syracuse Sunday. *New York Post.* December 19, 1935, p. 1.

Chapter 24

1 **Gould, Alan.** Carnera-Gastanaga Match Shadowed As Purses Are Held Up. *Evening Leader.* March 7, 1936, p. 8.

2 So! That Carnera Thinks He Can Fight, Eh! *New York Post.* March 4, 1936, p. 18.

3 Louis? Looka' Haynes! Preem's on Spot Again. *New York Post.* May 11, 1936, p. 15.

4   **Penn, Franklin.** 12,000 See Primo K.O. in Philly Battle. *Pittsburg Courier.* March 21, 1936, p. 5.

5   Jackie Davis Coming to Front. *Syracuse Journal.* September 24, 1934, p. 16.

6   **Press, Associated.** Rare Courage Is Carrying Yarosz Up the Comeback Trail. *Utica Daily Press.* May 18, 1937, p. 13.

7   Sports Stew—Served Hot. *Pittsburgh Press.* May 19, 1936, p. 29.

8   Carnera Attends Cub Scout Meeting. *Milburn and Short Hills Item.* April 10, 1936, p. 2.

9   **Press, Associated.** Attack of Paralysis in Left Leg Forces Primo to Leave Ring; Bout Close with Haynes Disappointing. *Niagara Falls Gazette.* May 28, 1936, p. 21.

10 **Sher, Jack.** The Strange Case of Carnera. *The SPORT Collection.* February 1948.

11 Brescia Punch is His Chance. *New York Sun.* October 6, 1936, p. 34.

12 **Robertson, Stewart.** She Puts'em in the Pink. *The Family Circle.* October 7, 1938.

13 Sports' Sidelights. *Summit Herald.* July 17, 1947, p. 12.

14 Joe Louis vs. Max Schmeling (1st meeting). [Online] BoxRec, November 21, 2014. http://boxrec.com/media/index.php?title=Fight:19807.

15 **Heller, Peter.** *In This Corner …!* New York : Da Capo Press, Inc., 1973.

16 **Runyon, Damon.** Both Barrels. *Philadelphia Inquirer.* October 9, 1936, p. 34.

17 **Buck, Al.** Brescia Bout to Fill Hipp, But No Bets Can Be Found. *New York Post.* October 8, 1936, p. 27.

18 **Press, Associated.** Bomber Wins by Knockout in Third Round. *Evening News Sports.* October 10, 1936.

19 **Graham, Frank.** Setting the Pace / Morning: At the Office. *New York Sun.* November 6, 1936, p. 38 cite stating from "Columnist Frank Graham rode … ".

20 **Heckelmann, Charles.** Escobar Confident of Retaining Crown. *Brooklyn Daily Eagle.* November 11, 1936, p. 19.

21 13 Jinx Holds No Fears for Sixto Escobar. *New York Sun.* November 12, 1936.

22 **Graham, Frank.** Setting the Pace / The Lightweight Champion at Summit. *New York Sun.* November 18, 1936, p. 37 cite starting from "Come on in …."

23 **Press, United.** Ambers Finally Earns Respect of the Experts. *Milwaukee Journal.* February 26, 1940, p. 8.

24 —. He Rates 3-2 on Chance of Another Kayo. *Binghamton Press.* February 27, 1941, p. 29.

25 **Fruman, Andrew.** Until the Real Thing Comes Along: The Night Henry Armstrong Made History Against Lou Ambers Parts 1-3. *The Cruelest Sport.* [Online] August 30, 2012. http://thecruelestsport.com/2012/08/30/until-the-real-thing-comes-along-the-night-henry-armstrong-made-history-against-lou-ambers-part-one/.

26 **McElligot, Pat.** Lou Ambers—The Herkimer Hurricane. [Online] Boxing Insider, 2016. http://www.boxinginsider.com/history/lou-ambers-the-herkimer-hurricane/.

27 **Minnoch, Jack.** Dressing Room Chatter. *Evening Record.* March 18, 1941, p. 12.

28 Al Weill. [Online] IBHOF, 2016. http://www.ibhof.com/pages/about/inductees/nonparticipant/weill.html.

29 **Liebling, A. J.** The Sweet Science. *The Sweet Science.* New York : Farrar, Straus and Giroux. Kindle Edition, 2014, pp. 31-33.

30 **Nelson, Rex.** Ray Rodgers: The cut man. [Online] Sothern Fried, January 31, 2012. http://www.rexnelsonsouthernfried.com/?p=3416.

31 **Talbot, Gayle.** Tony Works Himself Into Best Condition of Career for Bout. *Geneva Daily News.* June 23, 1939, p. 12.

32 Whitey Bimstein. [Online] BoxRec, January 23, 2015. http://boxrec.com/media/index.php/Whitey_Bimstein.

33 **Press, Associated.** Veteran Rated One of Leading Ring Trainers. *Knickerbocker News.* January 31, 1940, pp. 8-B cite starting from "What's all the fuss? …."

34 Whitey Bimstein. [Online] IBHOF, 2016. http://www.ibhof.com/pages/about/inductees/nonparticipant/bimstein.html.

35 **Casey, Mike.** The Recollections of Whitey Bimstein. [Online] Boxing.com, February 1, 2013. http://www.boxing.com/the_recollections_of_whitey_bimstein.html.

36 **Press, Associated.** Scarpati Is Dead After Knockout by Lou Ambers. *Daily Illini.* March 21, 1936, p. 7.

37 **Every, Edward Van.** Ambers Wears Crown Without Putting on Aors. *New York Sun.* November 17, 1936, p. 37.

38 hocalate and Baker Finish Training Today. *New York Sun.* December 5, 1936, p. 49.

39 **Buck, Al.** Lou's Foe Feasts on Lightweights. *New York Post.* November 19, 1936, p. 31.

40 **Press, Associated.** Vancouver Irishman Takes Another Step on Comeback Trail by Gaining Decision. *Morning Herald.* November 21, 1936, p. 4.

Chapter 25

1 **Robertson, Stewart.** Muscles by Mail. *Family Circle.* January 20, 1939.

2 **Shand, Bob.** *Oakland Tribune.* September 26-31, 1940.

3 **Roberts, James B. and Skutt, Alexander B.** *The Boxing Register: International Boxing Hall of Fame Official Record Book (4th ed.).* Ithica: Ithaca: McBooks Press. ISBN 978-1-59013-121-3, 2006.

4 Germany Bans Film Of Baer. *Los Angeles Times.* March 30, 1934, p. 12.

5 Biography of Boxer Max Baer Sr. [Online] MaxBaerBoxer.com, 2006-2009. http://www.maxbaerboxer.com/Max_Baer_Biography.html.

6 Serious Baer Starts Drills. *New York Post.* February 22, 1937, p. 14.

7 **Dawsom, James P.** Baer Receives License as Brown Concurs, but Fight Hits New Snag. *New York Times.* February 27, 1937, p. 37.

8 **Allan, Herbert.** Hoffman Warned. *New York Post.* March 1, 1937, p. 29.

9 Baer Refuses Pastor Match. *New York Post.* February 1937, p. 21.

10 Ambers to Fight Monday. *New York Times.* March 31, 1937.

11 Ambers Proved He Can Take a Punch, Says Vet. *Herald Statesman.* April 13, 1937, p. 10.

12 Canzoneri Looks Ahead to Ambers. *Long Island Daily Press.* April 24, 1937, p. 10.

13 Tony Canzoneri Begins Routine. *Poughkeepsie Eagle-News.* April 21, 1937, p. 11.

14 Money Odds on Ambers to Win. *Long Island Daily Press.* April 27, 1937, p. 12.

15 **Buck, Al.** Cheers for Canzoneri Come From Montanez. *New York Post.* May 4, 1937, p. 23.

16 **Brietz, Eddie.** Sports Roundup. *Evening Ledger.* May 4, 1937, p. 6.

17 —. Ambers Laces Canzoneri for Easy Triumph. *Buffalo Courier-Express.* May 8, 1937, p. 26.

18 **Super, Henry.** Canzoneri Bows to Ambers; Doesn't Want to Quit Ring. *Pittsburgh Press.* May 8, 1937, p. 10.

19 Billy Conn vs. Joe Louis. Part 1. [Online] muhammad-ali-boxing.org.uk, 2016. http://www.muhammad-ali-boxing.org.uk/billy-conn-vs.-joe-louis.htm.

20 Yarosz to be in Best Possible Condition for Fight with Conn. *Daily Times, Beaver and Rochester.* June 23, 1937, p. 9.

21 **McLemoe, Henry.** Bomber Knocks Out Jimmy Braddock in Eighth Round. *Daily Times.* June 23, 1937, p. 8.

22 *Daily Republican.* June 29, 1937, p. 3.

23 Yarosz to Break Camp Today, Will Travel By Plane. *Daily Times.* June 20, 1937.

24 **Anderson, Bill.** Sports Slants. *Daily Times.* August 11, 1937, p. 7.

25 Former Consul of Turkey Dies. *Chatham Press.* July 16, 1937, p. 1.

26 **Runyon, Damon.** Madame Bey Makes Fighters. *Rochester Democrat and Chronicle.* November 25, 1937, p. 9D.

27 **Robinson, Pat.** Ambers Will Draw Down $65,000. *Syracuse Journal.* September 17, 1937, p. 11.

28 ISRAEL "CHARLEY" GOLDMAN. [Online] International Jewish Sports Hall of Fame, 2016. http://www.jewishsports.net/BioPages/IsraelGoldman.htm.

29 **Casey, Mike.** Charley and the Talent Factory. [Online] Boxing.com, November 8, 2012. http://www.boxing.com/charley_and_the_talent_factory.html.

30 All is Harmony When Battlers Camp as Three. *Daily Eagle Sports.* September 16, 1937, p. 24.

31 **Buck, Al.** Montanez Not Scaring Light-Hearted Ambers. *New York Post.* September 13, 1937, p. 20.

32 **Press, Associated.** Apostoli is Found in Fine Condition. *New York Times.* September 7, 1937.

33 —. Garcia Impressive in Sparring Session." *New York Times.* September 19, 1937.

34 —. Carnival of Champs Finds Boxers Geared. *Brooklyn Daily Eagle.* September 19, 1937, p. 2D.

35 —. Montanez Impresses in 4-Round Workout; Apostoli Batters Two Sparring Partners. *New York Times.* September 18, 1937.

36 **Buck, Al.** Weight Angle No Headache, But Escobar Dislikes Alibis. *New York Post.* September 18, 1937.

37 Puerto Ricans Pick Fighters. *New York Post.* September 14, 1937, p. 19.

38 **Dawson, James P.** Four Title Fights to Attract 55,000. *New York Times.* September 23, 1937.

39 **Press, Associated.** Skillful Sparring by Thil Marks Training Sessions for Title Bouts. *New Yorrk Times.* September 20, 1937.

40 **Wade, Eddie.** Ambers Sings Victory Tune. *New York Post.* September 24, 1937, p. 26.

41 **Press, United.** Ambers Beats Montanez to Retain Crown. *Herald Statesman, Yonkers, N. Y.* September 24, 1937, p. 18.

Chapter 26

1   **Press, Associated.** Braddock Bout With Schmeling Postponed; Champ's Hand Injured. *Southeast Missourian.* August 18, 1936, p. 1.

2   **Brietz, Eddie.** Braddock, Schmeling Sign to Meet in Championship Bout on June 3rd. *Daily Illini.* December 13, 1936, p. 1.

3   **Schmeling, Max translation by von der Lippe, George.** *Max Schmeling: An Autobiography.* Chicago, IL: Bonus Books, 1998.

4   *Ghosts Stalk in Empty Arena for 'Phantom Fight.'.* Universal Newsreel, 1937.

5   **Bak, Richard.** *Joe Louis: The Great Black Hope.* New York : Perseus Publishing. ISBN 978-0-306-80879-1, 1996.

6   **Prior, Neil.** Tommy Farr: Boxer Who Fought His Way Out of the Pits. *News BBC Wales.* [Online] March 12, 2013. http://www.bbc.com/news/uk-wales-21697971.

7   **Press, Associated.** Former Boxer Farr is Dead at Age 71. *Gadsden Times.* March 2, 1986, p. C5.

8   —. Tommy Farr, Fighter, Dies; Went 15 Rounds With Louis. *New York Times.* March 3, 1986.

9   Commuter Max. *Brooklyn Daily Eagle.* December 14, 1937.

10 Harry Thomas (of Minnesota). [Online] Bpoxrec, January 28, 2015. http://boxrec.com/media/index.php/Harry_Thomas_(of_Minnesota).

11 Madame Bey's Return. *New York Times.* March 23, 1973.

12 **Westbrook, Bill.** Schmeling at Summit Camp. *Milburn And Short Hills Item.* December 10, 1937, p. 16.

13 **Graham, Frank.** Setting the Pace / That Man Is Here Again. *New York Sun.* November 12, 1937, p. cite starting from "Frank Graham described Schmeling …"

14 **Buck, Al.** Pilot Claims Interferance by Foe, Cites Ignored Cases. *New York Post.* November 16, 1937, p. 22.

15 Bantams Top Fight Cards. *New York Post.* November 10, 1937, p. 33.

16 **Graham, Frank.** Setting the Pace / Journey to a Fight Camp. *New York Sun.* December 10, 1937, pp. 35 cite starting from "On December 9, manager Joe Jacobs …"

17 **Robertson, Stewart.** She Puts'em in the Pink. *The Family Circle.* October 7, 1938.

18 Farmer Comes to Big Town To Settle Old Ring Score. *New York Post.* November 16, 1937.

19 Junior Subs for Beauhuld Tonight. *Kingston Daily Freeman.* September 9, 1937, p. 17.

20 **Buck, Al.** Armstrong's Future Rests With Beauhuld. *New York Post.* November 18, 1937, p. 28.

21 *New York Times.* November 20, 1937.

22 **Runyon, Damon.** Madame Bey Makes Fighters. *Rochester Democrat and Chronicle.* November 25, 1937, p. 9D.

23 Schmeling Floors Sparring Partner. *New York Times.* December 6, 1937.

24 **Press, United.** Schmeling and Louis Next June. *Kingston Daily Freeman.* September 4, 1937, p. 9.

25 **Talbot, Gayle.** Tunney Picks Schmeling to Whip Joe Louis Again in Next Battle. *Leader Republican.* December 8, 1937, p. 4.

26 ACME Press Photo. s.l.: ACME Photo, 1937.

27   **Kahn, James M.** Tunney is Impressed by Max. *New York Sun.* December 8, 1937, p. 41 cite starting from "Tunney and his friends met Schmeling …"

28   **Effrat, Louis.** Two Former Heavyweight Champions Meet. *New York Times.* December 8, 1937.

29   Thomas Givees Mob That Funny Feeling. *Daily Eagle Sports.* December 9, 1937, p. 14.

30   **Every, Edward Van.** Schmeling Camp is Jittery. *New York Sun.* December 10, 1937, p. 35.

31   **Press, Associated.** Champ to Study German's Style in Garden Bout. *Daily Sentinel, Rome, N.Y.* December 18, 1937, p. 18.

32   Jack and Gene Continue Feud, Beating Drums. *Brooklyn Daily Eagle.* December 10, 1937, p. 15.

33   **Dayton, Alfred.** Longer Route Favors Thomas. *New York Sun.* December 10, 1937, p. 35.

34   Schmeling Finishes Stiffest Training Grind of Career. *New York Sun.* December 11, 1937.

35   **Graham, Frank.** Setting the Pace / The Horse of the Year. *New York Sun.* December 11, 1937.

36   **Avery, Lesley.** Referee Donovan Stops Contest When German Batters Thomas to Canvas Six Times to Win Easily. *Niagara Falls Gazette.* December 14, 1937, p. 20.

37   **Graham, Frank.** Setting the Pace / Schmeling Fights at the Garden. *New York Sun.* December 14, 1937, p. 39.

38   Press Photo. New York: s.n., 1937.

39   **Wood, Wilbur.** Thomas Outclassed by Uhlan. *New York Sun.* December 14, 1937, p. 39.

40   Radio Dial Log. *Brooklyn Daily Eagle, N. Y.* January 3, 1938, p. 16.

41   **Press, Associated.** Match Grapplers with Ring Stars. *Daily Sentinel, Rome, N. Y.* December 31, 1937, p. 16.

42   Boxing is in a Repression. *Lockport Union-Sun And Journal.* January 8, 1939, p. 7.

43   **Brietz, Eddie.** The Sports Round-Up. *Geneva Daily Times.* June 15, 1937, p. 10.

44   **Press, Associated.** Best Programs on Radio; Leading Station Features. *Saratogian.* January 11, 1938, p. 11.

45   Lightweights Top Bill. *New York Post.* October 23, 1937, p. 17.

46   **Cuoco, Dan.** The Career of Freddie Steerle Revisited. *International Boxing Research Organization.* [Online] March 2, 2008. http://www.ibroresearch.com/?p=508.

47   Freddie Steele vs. Fred Apostoli (2nd meeting). [Online] BoxRec, February 26, 2015. http://boxrec.com/media/index.php?title=Fight:157857.

48   **Wood, Jimmy.** Sportopics. *Brooklyn Daily Eagle, N. Y.* January 9, 1938, p. 2D.

49   **Buck, Al.** Braddock Foe Shows Better Than at Time He Met Louis. *New York Post.* January 17, 1938, p. 18 cite starting from "He arrived in a limousine …"

50   **Dawson, James P.** Boxing Officials Find Farr in Shape. *New York Times.* January 18, 1938.

51   Foreign Boxers and a Manager on Their Arrival. *New York Times.* January 20, 1938.

52   Braddock Impresses in Sparring Session. *New York Times.* January 19, 1938.

53   **Woodd, Wilbur.** Last Two Rounds Decid It. *New York Sun.* January 22, 1938, p. 33.

54   **Graham, Frank.** Setting the Pace / Braddock Comes From Behind Again. *New York Sun.* January 22, 1938, p. 33 cite stating from "When the men came out …"

55   **Buck, Al.** Voices Belief That He Has Louis Battle Good as Won. *New York Post.* January 25, 1938.

56   **Every, Edward Van.** Farr in Fine Shape for Max Baer Tilt. *New York Sun.* March 1938.

57   **Press, Associated.** March 12, 1938.

Chapter 27

1   **Galento, Tony.** First Pro Bout Convinces Tony Fightin' is Easy. *Philadelphia Inquirer.* September 1, 1939.

2   **Press, Associated.** Galento, at 240 Pounds and 42-Inch Girth, Pronounced Fir for Battle with Max Baer. *New York Times.* June 26, 1940.

3   **Galento, Tony.** Tony Touchy About Age, Insists He's Only 29 Now. *Philadelphia Inquirerer.* September 4, 1939, p. 22.

4   —. Somethin' Gets in Eyes as Fortune Faces Tony. *Philadelphia Iquirer.* September 14, 1939, p. 30.

5   **Parton, Lemuel F.** Who's News This Week. *Cecil County Star.* July 28, 1938, p. 2.

6   *Cincinnati Enquirer.* July 26, 1979, p. 30.

7   Sport: Beer Punch. *Time.* May 23, 1938.

8   **Hopwood, Jon C.** Tony Galento Mini Biography. *IMDb.* 2016.

9   **Galento, Tony as told to Cy Peterman.** Tony Quits Jack Dempsey, Signs With Joe Jacobs. *Philadelphia Inquirer.* September 9, 1939, p. 20.

10 **Press, Associated.** Galento To Fight Another Octopus; Last One Died. *Free Lance-Star.* March 11, 1946, p. 8.

11 **Wilk, Tom.** Two Ton Tony. *Atlantic City Weekly.* March 2, 2011.

12 **Lardner, John.** From the Press Box. *Long Island Star-Journal.* April 15, 1938, p. 11.

13 Pastor Seeks Nestell Bout. *New York Post.* April 21, 1937, p. 21.

14 **Buck, Al.** General Firm in Demanding that Tony go to Mme. Bey's. *New York Post.* February 7, 1938, pp. 19 cite starting from "General John J. Phelan, chairman …"

15 **Robertson, Stewart.** She Puts'em in the Pink. *The Family Circle.* October 7, 1938.

16 **Avery, Leslie.** Group May Halt Beer Drinker's Thomas Battle. *Idaho Evening Times.* February 9, 1938, p. 6.

17 Really Home, Sweet Home to Tony. *New York Post.* February 8, 1938, p. 16.

18 **Press, United.** Galento Must Leave His Bar. *Knickerbocker News.* February 9, 1938, pp. 8-B.

19 **Every, Edward Van.** Krieger Keen to Whip Rossi Tonight. *New York Sun.* February 9, 1938, p. 86.

20 **Mahon, Jack.** Tony Pleads Arm Injury as Varied Reports Surround New Plans for Feb. 18th Bout. *Buffalo Courier-Express.* February 10, 1938, p. 15.

21 **Buck, Al.** Predict He'll Defeat Louis When They Meet in Garden Title Bout. *New York Post.* February 15, 1938, p. 19 cite starting from "He's in a crouch …"

22 Mann Hits Bottle—It's Milk. *New York Post.* February 14, 1938, p. 19 cite starting from "We're putting weight on him …"

23 **Talbot, Gayle.** Camp Attaches Also Figure Natie Might Upset Boxing Dope. *Geneva Daily Times.* February 11, 1938, p. 10 cite starting from "It's a chance I hadn't dreamed …"

24 **Gould, Alan.** Bomber Has the Challenger on Floor Four Times; Rival Shakes Joe in First. *Buffalo Courier-Express.* February 24, 1938, p. 17.

25 *New Haven Register.* February 24, 1938.

26 **Press, Associated.** New Haven Boxer is Floored Twice in Garden Battle. *Montreal Gazette.* May 14, 1938, p. 18.

27 —. Galento Forsakes Old Poolroom. *New York Sun.* July 2, 1938, p. 28.

28 **Buck, Al.** Pastor Lets No Grass Grow Under His Feet—Burman is His Next Foe. *New York Post.* July 1, 1938, p. 16.

29 —. Philly Mayor to Head List of Welcomers for Galento. *New York Post.* July 11, 1938, p. 14.

30 —. Galento-Baer Bout Sought for Newark. *New York Post.* July 7, 1938.

31 —. Philly Admirers Force Tony to Give Up Training There and Return to Mme. Bey's. *New York Post.* July 15, 1938, p. 15.

32 **Press, Associated.** Galento Changes Over to Madame Bey's Camp. *New York Sun.* July 15, 1938, p. 14.

33 **Buck, Al.** Galento Lets Film Back Up He Can Win in One Round. *New York Post.* July 18, 1938, p. cite starting from "After Tony's exhibition …"

34 —. Tony's Weight is Indication He's on Edge for Lewis. *New York Post.* July 21, 1938, p. 21 cite starting from "He must be a better fighter than Joe Louis …"

35 —. Ambers' Trainer Predicts Easy Victory for Galento—Claims Lewis has … *New York Post.* July 22, 1938, p. 15.

36 Hurricane Starts Moving. *New York Post.* July 21, 1938, p. 21.

37 **Westbrook, Bill.** Bill Westbrook. *Milburn—Short Hills Item.* July 22, 1938, p. 10.

38 Sick Galento Wants Lewis. *New York Post.* July 23, 1938, p. 16.

39 **Mahon, Jack.** Galento Losing in Battle for Life in Orange. *Biuffalo Courier-Express.* July 24, 1938, p. 6L.

40 Galento's Temperature 104; Tony Told It's Pneumonia. *Democrat Chronicle.* July 24, 1938, pp. Section C cite starting from "Hi, Mary, how do I look? …"

41 **Galento, Tony.** Tony Won 'Oxygen' Scrap, Earned Bout With Louis. *Philadelphia Inquirer.* September 13, 1939, p. 29.

Chapter 28

1 **Rice, Grantland.** The Sportlight. *Binghamton Press.* August 9, 1939, p. 16.

2 The Official Site of Henry Armstrong. [Online] Henryrmstrong.net, 2012. http://www. henryarmstrong.net/BIOGRAPHY.html.

3 **Bonk, Thomas.** FIGHT OF HIS LIFE : A Boxing Immortal, Henry Armstrong, at 75, Is Enduring Tough Times Again. *Los Angeles Times.* August 14, 1988.

4 **Cryer, A B.** Al Jolson Explained. [Online] Evrything Explained, 2009. http://everything. explained.today/Al_Jolson/#Ref-7.

5 **Ciolino, Joseph.** Al Jolson Wasn't Racist! *Black Star News.* May 22, 2007.

6 Canarsie Boxing, Lull Ends. *New York Post.* July 26, 1938, p. 15.

7 Mme. Bey Goes to Pompton to See Armstrong. *New York Post.* July 28, 1938, p. 23.

8 Ambers Plans No Special Style for Mr. Armstrong. *Afro American.* July 30, 1938, p. 23.

9   **Webber, Harry B.** Henry Will Forsake Feather Crown if He Defeats Ambers. *Afro-American*. July 30, 1938, p. 23.

10 **Graham, Frank.** Setting the Pace / One in a Million. *New York Sun*. August 4, 1938, p. 15 cite starting from "This kid is one in a million …"

11 **Press, Associated.** Canzoneri Sees Ambers in Shape For Bout; Armstrong Uses Special Headgear in Drill. *New York Times*. August 4, 1938.

12 **Middleton, Drew.** Armstrong Keeps Role of Favorite as Fans Turn Out. *Unknown*. August 1938.

13 **Williams, Joe.** Ambers Must Outspeed Armstrong … Both With Hands and Fists. *Pittsburgh Press*. July 30, 1938, p. 14.

14 **Press, Associated.** Dr. Walker Finds Ring Foes in Shape. *New York Times*. August 5, 1938.

15 **Bradley, Hugh.** Hugh Bradley Says. *New York Post*. August 6, 1938, p. 12.

16 Lou Ambbers Singing and Swinging Club's in Session. *New York Post*. August 6, 1938, p. 12.

17 **Brietz, Eddie.** Armstrong Will Put His Welt Title at Stake in Ambers Bout, Despite Talk. *Buffalo Courier-Express*. August 9, 1938, p. 15.

18 **Dawson, Jame P.** Polo Grounds Bout Postponed by Rain. *New York Times*. August 11, 1938.

19 **Buck, Al.** Uncle Michael Would Make His Old Rivall Full Partner. *New York Post*. August 11, 1938, p. 17.

20 **Bradley, Hugh.** Rained-Out Fight Recalls Epic Bouts Held in Downpours. *New York Post*. August 11, 1938, p. 17.

21 **McLemore, Henry.** Today's Sport Parade. *Time Record, Troy, N. Y.* August 17, 1938, p. 14.

22 **Press, Associated.** Challenger Still Heavy Choice to Lift Lou's Title. *Time Record, Troy, N. Y.* August 17, 1938, p. 14.

23 **Ferguson, Harry.** Ambers Rated as Underdog in Garden Battle. *Herald Statesman*. August 17, 1938, p. 8.

24 **Robertson, Stewart.** She Puts'em in the Pink. *The Family Circle*. October 7, 1938.

25 **Fruman, Andrew.** Until the Real Thing Comes Along: The Night Henry Armstrong Made History Against Lou Ambers Parts 1–3. *The Cruelest Sport*. [Online] August 30, 2012. http://thecruelestsport.com/2012/08/30/until-the-real-thing-comes-along-the-night-henry-armstrong-made-history-against-lou-ambers-part-one/.

26 **McLemore, Henry.** 18,000 Fans See Bloody Bout as Little Giants Pound Away. *Herald Statesman*. August 18, 1938, p. 15.

27 **Ferguson, Harry.** Lightweight Champion Beaten by Shade in Thrilling Battle Despite Sensational Comeback. *Herald Statesman*. August 18, 1938, p. 15.

28 **Press, Asociated.** August 18, 1938.

29 Armstrong Outpoints Ambers nn Fast Battle For Lightweight Title, Madison Square Garden. *Ballston Spa Daily Journal*. August 18, 1938, p. 6.

30 **Guenther, Jack.** Hardboiled "Lammers' Lane" Mourns Madame Bey's Death. *Buffalo Courier-Express*. January 31, 1942, p. 17.

31 **Buck, Al.** Henry Wears Three Crpwns. *New York Post*. August 18, 1938, p. 18.

32 So They Say. *New York Post*. August 18, 1938, p. 18.

33 **Rice, Grantland.** Armstrong Aided By Big Ticker. *Desert News.* August 8, 1939, p. 11.

34 **Runyon, Damon.** One Judge Voted for Ambers. *Syracuse Sports Journal.* August 18, 1938, p. 25.

35 **Minoch, Jack.** Dressing Room Chatter. *Evening Recorder.* September 10, 1938, p. 9.

Chapter 29

1 **Robertson, Stewart.** She Puts'em in the Pink. This chapter is mostly from the article written by Stewart Robertson for *The Family Circle* magazine. *The Family Circle.* October 7, 1938.

2 **INS.** Galento No Longer Calls Louis a Bum. *Reading Eagle.* June 21, 1939, p. 14.

Chapter 30

1 Last Twelve Months Most Profitable for Matchmaker. *New York Post.* December 24, 1938, p. 15.

2 **Phister, Bonnie.** Jazz History for Sale in Hill District. *Pittsburgh Tribune-Review.* June 16, 2007, pp. B1, B6.

3 **Harper, Colter.** *The Crossroads of the World: A Social and Cultural History of Jazz in Pittsburgh's Hill District, 1920–1970.* Pittsburgh: University of Pittsburgh, 2011.

4 **Riley, James A.** *The Biographical Encyclopedia of the Negro Baseball Leagues.* New York : Carroll & Graf ISBN 0-7867-0959-6, 1994.

5 *A Historical Look at the Pittsburgh Crawfords and the Impact of Black Baseball on American Society.* **Gilmore, Richard L.** 1996, the Sloping Halls Review.

6 William Augustus "Gus" Greenlee. [Online] Find A Grave, 2016. http://www.findagrave.com/cgi-bin/fg.cgi?page=gr&GRid=5806.

7 **Buck, Al.** John Henry Is Placed in Class by Himself As Ruler of Light -Heavyweight Division. *New York Post.* December 27, 1938.

8 **Press, Associated.** Schmeling Victim of Quickest Kayo. *Evening Independent.* June 23, 1938, p. 8.

9 —. Max Schmeling is in Hospital. *Prescott Evening Courier.* June 23, 1938, p. 5.

10 **Graham, Frank.** Setting the Pace / The Scene Is a Hospital Room. *New York Sun.* June 29, 1938, p. 27 cite starting from "He was sitting up in his bed …"

11 **Washington, Chester L.** A Tale of Two Champions. *Pittsburgh Courier.* January 21, 1939, p. 16.

12 **Buck, Al.** Bomber's Foe Wants to Add More Pounds for Title. *New York Post.* January 17, 1939, p. 13.

13 **Press, Associated.** Had Long Waited Chance to Fight for Ring Laurel. *Daily Sentinel, Rome, N. Y.* January 28, 1939, p. 7.

14 **Burns, Ken.** *Unforgivable Blackness: The Rise and Fall of Jack Johnson.* 2005.

15 **Early, Dr. Gerald.** Rebel of the Progressive Era. *PBS.* January 2005.

16 **Feder, Sid.** 17,350 Payees Bring Gate to $102,015 Total. *Buffalo Courier-Express.* January 26, 1939, p. 14.

17 **Hughes, Ed.** Not a Chance. *Brooklyn Eagle Sports.* January 26, 1939, p. 14.

18 **Feder, Sid.** Brown Bomber Wants One More Shot at Bicycle Bob; Lewis Asks Return Bout. *Buffalo Courier-Express.* January 27, 1939, p. 16.

19 **Press, Associated.** Just Tough Luck. *Brooklyn Eagle Sports.* January 26, 1939, p. 14.

20 **Conrad, Harold.** Chilling of John Henry Points to Bleak Future For Pastor, Galento. *Brooklyn Eagle Sports.* January 26, 1939, p. 14.

21 **Press, Associated.** Max Schmeling and Trainer on Way to America. *Buffalo Courier-Express.* January 27, 1939, p. 16.

22 —. John Henry Lewis Title Fight Off; Physicians Claim One Eye Blinded. *Prescott Evening Courier.* March 18, 1939, p. 5.

23 **Press, United.** John Henry Lewis Will Return Home. *Milwaukee Journal.* May 8, 1939, p. 6.

24 Spoldi to Return to Italy After Fight at Velodrome; Expects Bout With Henry. *New York Post.* June 9, 1939, p. 16.

25 **Every, Edward Van.** Larkin a Fistic Star Without a Fight. *New York Sun.* January 5, 1939, p. 25.

26 **Press, United.** Need Two Days for Data Study. *Schenectady Gazette.* March 22, 1939, p. 16.

27 **Feder, Sid.** Galento Gets Draw in Verbal battle With N. Y. Doctors. *Philadelphia Inquirer.* March 22, 1939, p. 23.

28 Tony, Pastor Rate One, Two. *New York Post.* June 23, 1939, p. 17.

29 *Newsreel.* 1939.

30 **Graham, Frank.** Setting the Pace / It Seems Nothing Happened to Schmeling. *New York Sun.* June 15, 1939, p. cite starting from "In response to a call sent out …"

31 **Nichols, Joseph C.** Phelan Calls Halt to Louis Criticism. *New York Times.* June 15, 1939.

32 **Miley, Jack.** Yussel Jacobs Makes Mistake Choosing Words. *New York Post.* June 15, 1939, p. 23.

33 Tony is Back to First Love. *New York Post.* June 15, 1939, p. 24.

34 **Press, Associated.** Galento Pilot Drops Charges. *Knickerbocker News.* June 15, 1939, pp. B-17.

35 'Two-Ton' Turns Over New Leaf as He Confronts Chance of Life Time. *Pittsburgh Courier.* June 17, 1939, p. 16.

36 **Press, United.** Galento Shows Battling Form. *Schenectady Gazette.* June 16, 1939, p. 31.

37 **Cuddy, Jack.** Tony Sounds Off Again. *Pittsburgh Press. Sports Section.* June 18, 1939, p. 4 cite starting from "She placed an immaculate white tablecloth …"

38 **Press, Associated.** Galento Battles Three Spar Mates. *New York Times.* June 18, 1939.

39 **Dixon, Randy.** Tony Has Power n Left, Tags Spar Mates. *Pittsburgh Courier.* June 24, 1939, p. 17.

40 Press Photo. Chatham Township, New Jersey: s.n., 1939.

41 **Dawson, James P.** Louis Nears Close of Training Grind. *New York Times.* June 22, 1939.

42 **Rice, Grantland.** The Spotlight. *Reading Eagle.* June 21, 1939, p. 14.

43 **Talbot, Gayle.** Talbot, Braddock Impressed With Galento's Form. *Oswego-Palladium Times.* June 23, 1939, p. 14.

44 **Miley, Jack.** Ploy is Afoot to Make Tony Next Champion. *New York Post.* June 23, 1939, p. 17.

45 **Buck, Al.** Bomber Need Have No Fear of Foul Blow, Galento Says. *New York Post.* June 23, 1939, p. 17.

46 **Lynch, R. G.** New York Regards Bout a Joke; New Jersey Takes it Dead Serious. *Milwaukee Journal.* June 27, 1939, pp. 8 cite starting from "H'ya, Lynch. What time is it in Milwaukee? …"

47 —. Unknown. *Milwaukee Journal.* June UNKNOWN, 1939, pp. cite starting from "H'ya, Lynch. What time is it in Milwaukee? …"

48 —. Maybe I'm Wrong. *Milwaukee Journal.* April 26, 1940, pp. 8 cite starting from "H'ya, Lynch. What time is it in Milwaukee? …"

49 —. Tony Galento in Training Is Like a Child Who Happily Shows Off Before Grownups. *Milwaukee Journal.* June 23, 1939, p. 6 cite starting from "A large crowd had gathered …" Many newspapers printed this story, which did not agree on the exact words Joe Jacobs spoke.

50 **Miley, Jack.** Terrible Tony Shows No Sign of Louis Fever. *New York Post.* June 26, 1939, p. 13 cite starting from "The condemned man ate a healthy breakfast …"

51 **Buck, Al.** Serious Tony Explains His Battle Plan. *New York Post.* June 26, 1939, p. 13 cite starting from "I'll read about myself tomorrow …"

52 **Wood, Wilbur.** Louis Only 50 P. C. in Close. *New York Sun.* June 26, 1939, p. 23.

53 **Hughes, Ed.** Hour of Reckoning. *Brooklyn Daily Eagle.* June 27, 1939, p. 14 cite starting from "All week long I'm bothered to death …"

54 **Feder, Sid.** Experts Seek Way to Give Challenger a Chance. *Daily Illini.* June 27, 1939, p. 1.

55 **Hughes, Ed.** Tony's Lefts Befuddle Bomber Before Joe Turns on the Heat. *Brooklyn Daily Eagle.* June 29, 1939, p. 20.

56 **Feder, Sid.** Galento-Nova Fight Here in September! *Philadelphia Inquirer.* June 30, 1939, p. 23.

57 **Wood, Wilbur.** Fierce Fight Thrills 35,000. *New York Sun.* June 29, 1939, p. 24 cite starting from "In the first round …" Many newspapers reported on this fight.

58 **Graham, Frank.** Setting the Pace / Suddenly Galento Began to Fall. *New York Sun.* June 29, 1939, p. 24.

59 **Peterman, Cy.** Tony Lost the Fight But Helped the Game. *Philadelphia Inquirer.* June 30, 1939, p. 23.

60 23 Stitches Used to Patch Up Cuts in Galento's Face. *New York Sun.* June 29, 1939, p. 24.

61 **Wood, Wilbur.** Fierce Fight Thrills 35,000. *New York Sun.* June 29, 1939, p. 24.

62 Joe Louis vs. Tony Galento. [Online] BoxRec, April 3, 2015. http://boxrec.com/media/index.php/Joe_Louis_vs._Tony_Galento.

63 **Kahn, James M.** Galento Eager For a Return Match. *New York Sun.* June 29, 1939, p. 24 cite starting from "I can't let you in …"

64 **Shapiro, Michael.** Focus. *Courier-News.* August 5, 1978.

Chapter 31

1 **Press, United.** Tony Galento Begins Training for Nova. *Knickerbocker News.* August 17, 1939, pp. 12-B.

2 **Ferguson, Harry.** "Cosmic Punch" is Problem. *Citizen Advisor.* June 23, 1941, p. 10.

3 **Talbot, Gayle.** Referee Stops Bout in 2:29 of Fourth, 40,000 are Trilled. *Kingston Daily Freeman.* June 29, 1939, p. 18.

4 Galento to Postpone Boxing Practice. *Philadelphia Inquirer.* August 18, 1939, p. 21.

5 **Nichols, Joseph C.** Mead Hits Conduct of Boxing in State. *New York Times.* August 24, 1939.

6 **Webster, John.** Commission, Not Galento, To Pick Referee, Says Rains. *Philadelphia Inquirer.* August 25, 1939, p. 27.

7 **Press, United.** Orders Site Change. *Schenectady Gazette.* August 25, 1939, p. 27.

8 **Feder, Sid.** Nova Planning Campaign To Capture Louis' Title. *Lockport Union Sun and Journal.* August 28, 1939, p. 27.

9 **Webster, John.** Stadium Fight Re-Scheduled For Sept. 15. *Philadelphia Inquirer.* August 30, 1939, p. 23.

10 **Graham, Frank.** Setting the Pace / Joe Jacobs in His Own Defense. *New York Sun.* September 1, 1939, pp. 21 cite starting from "No, Joe said …"

11 **Press, Associated.** Galento is Impressive. *New York Times.* September 3, 1939.

12 **Kahn, James M.** Galento Idol in Quaker City. *New York Sun.* September 9, 1939, p. 30.

13 **Graham, Frank.** Setting the Pace / Baer Was at Both Ends of the Road. *New York Sun.* July 5, 1940, p. 14.

14 **Webster, John.** Tony Galento Meek in Drill At Leiperville. *Philadelphia Inquirer.* September 9, 1939, p. 20.

15 Galento Fans Go Wild After Victory. *Philadelphia Inquirer.* September 16, 1939, p. 21 cite starting from "The fight took place at Municipal Stadium …"

16 *Galento-Nova Bout.* 1939.

17 **Lewis, Perry.** Fight Repercussions Blake Criticized Carlen Out of Order Fair or Foul Easy for Galento. *Philadelphia Inquirer.* September 18, 1939, p. 20.

18 **Talbot, Gayle.** Tough Tony Galento Bursts Lou Nova's Bubble With Technical Knockout in Fourteenth Round. *Leader-Republican.* September 16, 1939, p. 11.

19 **Cuddy, Jack.** Two Ton Tony Massacred 'Golden Boy' Lou; Bout Was Stopped in 14th Round. *Tonawanda - Evening News.* September 16, 1939, p. 8.

20 **Graham, Frank.** Setting the Pace. *New York Sun.* December 6, 1940, p. 37.

Chapter 32

1 **Dawson, James P.** Godoy Confident of Beating Louis. *New York Times.* November 14, 1939.

2 Ambers Boxes Ten Rounds. *New York Times.* November 22, 1939.

3 **Feder, Sid.** Much-Discussed Clash Called Off, Commission Against Double Champion. *Buffalo Courier-Express.* December 2, 1939, p. 23.

4 **Hughes, Ed.** Referee to the Rescue. *Brooklyn Daily Eagle.* January 25, 1940, p. 14.

5 *New York Times.* January 25, 1940.

6 **Dawson, James P.** Elimination Bout Sought by Garden. *New York Times.* December 7, 1939.

7 **Mahon, Jack.** Broken Left Hand to Keep Comiskey Idle. *Buffalo Courier-Express.* December 17, 1939, p. 10.

8 Warming Up. *Plattsburgh Daily Press.* January 23 or 28, 1940, p. 5.

9 **Worner, Ted.** Sporting Propositions. *Herald Statesman.* January 30, 1940, p. 11.

10 **Conrad, Harold.** Melio Entitled to No Worse Than a Draw. *Brooklyn Daily Eagle.* January 6, 1940, p. 11.

11 **Press, Associated.** Veteran Rated One of Leading Ring Trainers. *Knickerbocker News.* January 31, 1940, pp. 8-B cite starting from "What's all the fuss? …"

12 Sparring Drills Put Off. *New York Times.* November 23, 1939.

13 *New York Times.* January 30, 1940.

14 **Worner, Ted.** Sporting Propositions. *Herald Statesman.* January 30, 1940, p. 11.

15 **Press, Associated.** Veteran Rated One of Leading Ring Trainers. *Knickerbocker News.* January 31, 1940, pp. 8-B.

16 **Dawson, James P.** Apostoli and Bettina End Drills for Battle in Garden Tomorrow. *New York Times.* February 1, 1940.

17 Why Apostoli Wants to Box Again. *New York Sun.* February 6, 1940, p. 24.

18 **Mahon, Jack.** Pictures Fail to Show Signs of Concussion. *Buffalo Courier-Express.* February 4, 1940, p. 9 cite starting from "They took him to Polyclinic Hospital …"

19 **Van Every, Edward.** Ambers Sees Task for Louis. *New York Sun.* February 5, 1940, p. 21.

20 **Clark, Stan.** Daily Dozen. *Observer-Dispatch.* February 7, 1940, p. 6.

21 **Peterman, Cy.** Peter Pan Godoy Favors Hot Music, Rough Boxing. *Philadelphia Inquirer.* February 1940, p. cite starting from "That bull fiddle …"

22 **Press, Associated.** New Punch Added To Louis's Attack. *New York Times.* February 7, 1940.

23 Godoy Engages in Final Drill Today. *New York Sun.* February 6, 1940, p. 24.

24 **Hughes, Ed.** Once in a Lifetime. *Brooklyn Eagle Sports.* February 7, 1940, p. 16 cite starting from "This is my big chance …"

25 **Cochran, Jane.** Madame Bey Picks Godoy Over Louis. *Reading Eagle.* February 8, 1940, p. 26 cite starting from "Prizefighters are …"

26 **Conrad, Harold.** Louis Hopes to Muddle Through. *Brooklyn Daily Eagle.* February 7, 1940, p. 16.

27 **Press, United.** Chileans Cheer, Sing as Arturo Goes Route in N.Y. *Times Record.* February 10, 1940, p. 13.

28 *Louis-Godoy Bout.* 1940.

29 **Press, Associated.** Louis Unable to Floor Challenger Through 15 Rounds. *Daily Sentinel.* February 10, 1940, p. 7.

30 **Pugliese, Anthony J.** Godoy Harder to Hit than Pastor, Joe Says. *Times Record.* February 10, 1940, p. 13 cite starting from "What was wrong with me? …"

31 *New York Times.* February 10, 1940.

32 Paycheck Pans Bomber for 'Stupid' Bout. *Brooklyn Daily Eagle.* February 11, 1940.

33 Davis, Al "Bummy." [Online] Jewishsports.org, 2016. http://www.jewsinsports.org/profile.asp?sport=boxing&ID=78.

34 **Sifakis, Carl.** *The Mafia Encyclopedia.* New York: Facts on File, 2005.

35 **Hughes, Ed.** Bummy 'Gets His'. *Brooklyn Daily Eagle.* February 24, 1940, pp. 10 cite starting from "On February 23, 1940 …"

36 **Schoen, Derek.** 'Hardest Hitter, Drinker,' Jenkins Conquers Alcohol. *Reading Eagle.* September 25, 1966, p. 73.

37 **Graham, Frank.** Setting the Pace / It Rests Mainly With Jenkins. *New York Sun*. May 15, 1941, p. 27.

38 The New York Times. March 9, 1940.

39 **Press, Associated.** Boxer Shot Cleaning Gun. *New York Times*. July 25, 1942.

Chapter 33

1 **Hackett, Jim.** Two-Ton Tony Says Glory is Only Interest. *Buffalo Courier-Express*. January 19, 1940, p. 19.

2 **Press, United.** Tony Won't Fight Without Jacobs. *Times Record*. January 11, 1940, p. 26.

3 **Wood, Wilbur.** Joe Jacobs was a Game Guy. *New York Sun*. April 25, 1940.

4 **Van Every, Edward.** Jacobs a Picturesque Figure. *New York Sun*. April 25, 1940.

5 Just Before Death Struck. *New York Sun*. April 25, 1940.

6 **Press, Associated.** Galento's Colorful Pilot Dies in Physician's Office; Led Schmeling to Title. *Buffalo Courier-Express*. April 25, 1940, p. 17.

7 —. Heart Attack Closes Career of No. 1 Pilot. *Knickerbocker*. April 25, 1940, p. 14B.

8 —. Two-Ton Tony Is Saddened By Death of Ring Manager. *Buffalo Courier-Express*. April 25, 1940, p. 17.

9 **Brumbry, Bob.** Tony, Broken in Spirit By Sudden Death of Manager, Undecided as to His Plans. *Buffalo Courier-Express*. April 26, 1940, p. 21.

10 **Press, Associated.** Notables at Jacobs' Funeral. *Buffalo Courier-Express*. April 29, 1940, p. 15.

11 Ring World Honors Joe Jacobs. *New York Sun*. April 29, 1940, p. 23.

12 Maker of Seven World Champions, Manager of Tony Galento, Yussel the Muscle Dies of Heart Attack. *Niagara Falls Gazette*. April 25, 1940, p. 30.

13 Joe Jacobs, Fight Manager for Schmeling, Galento. *Brooklyn Eagle*. April 25, 1940, p. 15.

14 *Baer-Galento Fight Promotion*. 1940.

15 **Kahn, James M.** Two Pounds Harass Ambers. *New York Sun*. May 1940, p. cite starting from "He deviated from …"

16 **Conrad, Harold.** Right-Hand Crazy? Not Two-Gun Lew. *Brooklyn Daily Eagle*. May 9, 1940, p. 18 cite starting from "Just because I haven't used …"

17 **McElligot, Pat.** Lou Ambers—The Herkimer Hurricane. [Online] Boxing Insider, 2016. http://www.boxinginsider.com/history/lou-ambers-the-herkimer-hurricane/.

18 **Feder, Sid.** Texas Lew Jenkins Stops Lou Ambers in 3rd Round of Title Bout at Garden. *Morning Herald*. May 11, 1940, p. 13.

19 **Conrad, Harold.** Jenkins Ogles Welter Crown. *Brooklyn Daily Eagle*. May 11, 1940, p. 11.

20 Scooparade: Down the Line in Three Dots. *Brooklyn Eagle Sports*. May 23, 1940.

21 **Graham, Frank.** Setting the Pace / Overlin 'Does Time' at Summit. *New York Sun*. May 21, 1940, p. 28 cite starting from "How does it feel to be fighting …"

22 Galento Posts Forfeit. *New York Times*. May 28, 1940.

23 **Press, Associated.** Gets Revenge on Challenger. *Spokesman Review*. June 21, 1940, p. 17.

24 **Kahn, James M.** Joe Louis Provides Contrast. *New York Sun*. June 24, 1940, p. 26 cite starting from "Louis sat quietly through …"

25 *Galento and Louis at Bey's*. 1940.

26 **Peterman, Cy.** Galento, Inc., 238 1-2, Streams Through 5 Rounds. *Philadelphia Inquirer*. June 29, 1940, p. 17 cite starting from "It was hard to distinguish Tony's boxing …"

27 Four Stars To Guest On Music Hall Holiday Show. *Lima News*. June 27, 1939, p. 23.

28 **Graham, Frank.** Setting the Pace / A Car Came Roaring Up the Hill. *New York Sun*. June 27, 1940, p. 25 cite starting from "Less than a week before the fight …"

29 **Press, Associated.** Galento, at 240 Pounds and 42-Inch Girth, Pronounced Fir for Battle with Max Baer. *New York Times*. June 26, 1940.

30 **Talbot, Gayle.** Galento Doesn't Hit Like Louis, Says Arturo Godoy. *Geneva Daily*. June 29, 1940, p. 3 cite starting from "Another visitor, Arturo Godoy …"

31 Physician Says Baer is Ready for Action. *The New York Times*. June 28, 1940.

32 **Smith, Red.** Tony Had Strange Ideas of Training. *Buffalo Courier-Express*. March 5, 1961, p. 36.

33 **Jr., Frank Graham.** Two Flew Out of the Cuckoo Clock. *Sports Illustrated*. June 28, 1965.

34 **Hughes, Ed.** Ed Hughes' Column. *Brooklyn Daily Eagle*. July 3, 1940, p. 13.

35 **Howard, Robert.** Fight Shouldn't Have Gone On-Frain. *New York Sun*. July 3, 1940, p. 16.

36 **Graham, Frank.** Setting the Pace / Galento Couldn't Come Up for the Eighth. *New York Sun*. July 3, 1940, p. 16 cite starting from "It's a bad cut …"

37 **Brumby, Bob.** Cotton's Chip Shots Aimed at Germany. *News Of Sports*. August 16, 1940, p. 30.

38 **Press, United.** Start Training. *Niagara Falls Gazette*. October 18, 1940, p. 25.

39 **Conrad, Harold.** Savold First Real Heavyweight Foe for Conn. *Brooklyn Eagle*. October 22, 1940, p. 14.

40 Overlin has Problem to Make 160 Pounds. *New York Times*. October 31, 1940.

41 **Hughes, Ed.** Ed Hughes' Column. *Brooklyn Daily Eagle*. November 2, 1940, p. 12.

42 **Graham, Frank.** Setting the Pace / The Middleweight Champion at Summit. *New York Sun*. December 10, 1940, p. 31 cite starting from "Give me some tape …"

43 **Dawson, James P.** Virginian Spikes Reports He is Not in Trim for Defense of Middleweight Title at Garden—Rival Works 9 Frames. *New York Times*. December 12, 1940.

44 **Every, Edward Van.** Champ Wins Under Handicap. *New York Sun*. December 1940.

45 **Hughes, Ed.** How Overlin Held the Title. *Brookly Daily Eagle*. December 14, 1940, p. 12.

46 **Graham, Frank.** Setting the Pace / The Winner … And Still Champion. *New York Sun*. December 1940, cite starting from "Ken Overlin had outmaneuvered …"

Chapter 34

1 Burman Off for Camp. *Buffalo Courier-Express*. December 27, 1940, p. 14.

2 Max Waxman. [Online] BoxRec, July 22, 2008. http://boxrec.com/media/index.php/Max_Waxman.

3   **Graham, Frank.** Setting the Pace / Now Burman Is Training at Summit. *New York Sun.* January 24, 1941, p. 24 cite starting from "A few months before …"

4   **Van Everey, Edward.** Clarence to Burman Meant Fighting. *New York Sun.* January 24, 1941, pp. 24 cite starting from "Of course, I'm Irish …"

5   **Washington, Chester L.** Sez Ches. *Pittsburgh Courier.* January 25, 1941, p. 16.

6   **Brumby, Bob.** Burman Bets He'll Beat Louis. *PM Sports.* January 21, 1941, p. 24.

7   **Buck, Al.** Burman's Serious Attitude Shown by Long Training. *New York Post.* January 22, 1941, p. 19 cite starting from "Uncle Mike Jacobs and the rest …"

8   **Every, Edward Van.** Red Believes in Long Siege. *New York Sun.* January 23, 1941, p. 24 cite starting from "According to Madame Bey …"

9   **Buck, Al.** Dempsey Not to Second Burman. *New York Post Sports.* January 27, 1941, p. 14.

10   **Graham, Frank.** Setting the Pace / Red Burman Trains at Madame Bey's. *New York Sun.* January 29, 1941, p. 25 cite starting from "I don't like to hurry you …"

11   Louis Ends Drills for Burman Fight. *New York Times.* January 30, 1941.

12   Champion is Extended by Beaten Foe. *Syracuse Herald-Journal.* February 1, 1941, p. 11.

13   **Conrad, Harold.** Louis Superb in Knockout of Burman. *Brooklyn Daily Eagle.* February 1, 1941, p. 11.

14   **Feder, Sid.** Champ Uncorks Terrific Right to Heart Near End of Fifth to Retain Title. *Morning Herald.* February 1, 1941, p. 13.

15   **Steadman, John.** 'Red' Burman gave Joe Louis a battle in 1941 fight for title Baltimore native dies at 80 after long illness. *Baltimore Sun.* January 25, 1996.

16   **Buck, Al.** Forthcoming Louis Title Bout Fails to Frighten Dorazio. *New York Post.* February 10, 1941, p. 15.

17   **Press, Associated.** Fight Scheduled for Monday Night at Philadelphia. *Times Record.* February 14, 1941, p. 27.

18   **Meier, Ted.** Gus Stands Erect, "Biff," One Punch and Down He Goes. *Times Record.* February 18, 1941, p. 19.

19   **Conrad, Harold.** Louis Again 'the Killer'. *Brooklyn Daily Eagle.* February 18, 1941, p. 13.

20   **Buck, Al.** Boxing Notes. *New York Post.* February 10, 1941, p. 15.

21   —. 15-Round Bout With No Title At Stake Is Puzzle to Webb. *New York Post.* February 19, 1941, p. 20.

22   **Press, United.** He Rates 3-2 on Chance of Another Kayo. *Binghamton Press.* February 27, 1941, p. 29.

23   **Cuddy, Jack.** Ambers Winds Up Training; Ready to Face Jenkins. *Niagara Falls Gazette.* February 26, 1941, p. 18.

24   **Howard, Robert.** Ambers Feels Fit for Jenkins Bout. *New York Sun.* February 24, 1941, p. 25.

25   **Press, Associated.** Joe Louis Expects Army Call Any Day. *New York Sun.* February 26, 1941, p. 31.

26   **Howard, Robert.** Jenkins Confident of Kayo. *New York Sun.* February 26, 1941, pp. 31 cite starting from "Jenkins's wife, Katie …"

27   Lew Jenkins Says He Can Run 3 Miles in 10 Minutes-Easy. *New York Sun.* February 26, 1941, p. 31 cite starting at "Jenkins boasted that in his roadwork …"

28 **Wood, Wilbur.** Has-beens' Ofen Dangerous . *New York Sun.* February 26, 1941, p. 31.

29 Ambers Ends Drill With Boxing Today. *New York Sun.* February 26, 1941, p. 31.

30 **Neubert, Robert W.** Sweetwater's Bombed Bomber. *Sports Illustrated.* October 21, 1968.

31 **Press, United.** *United Press.* March 1, 1941.

32 **Hughes, Ed.** The End of Mr. Ambers. *Brooklyn Daily Eagle.* March 1, 1941, p. 12.

33 **Press, Associated.** Lou Ambers Ends Boxing Career. *Ludington Daily News.* March 1, 1941, p. 6.

34 **Boxrec.** Post Fight Comment. [Online] BoxRec, June 2, 2009. http://boxrec.com/media/index. php?title=Fight:16105.

35 **Conrad, Harold.** Jenkins, Pop Time Gang Up on Ambers. *Brooklyn Daily Eagle.* March 1, 1941, p. 12.

36 **Graham, Frank.** Setting the Pace / New Guy in the Coast Guard. *New York Sun.* February 20, 1942, p. 34.

37 **Press, Associated.** Gets Champions Gloves. *New York Times.* May 4, 1941.

38 —. Acclaim RedHead As Boxing Champ. *Prescott Evening Courier.* August 5, 1941, p. 5.

39 Freddie (Red) Cochrane, Boxer, 77. *New York Times.* January 19, 1993.

40 **Donelson, Tom.** *Boxing Insider.* November 1, 2004.

41 Overlin in Fine Shape. *New York Times.* May 5, 1941.

42 **Graham, Frank.** Setting the Pace / The Champion and Challenger Meet. *New York Sun.* May 7, 1941, p. 35 cite starting from "Dr. William Walker did physical examinations …"

43 **Conrad, Harold.** Soose Pries Away Crown From Ever-Holding Overlin. *Brooklyn Daily Eagle.* May 10, 1941, p. 9.

44 **Press, Associated.** Crowd Boos Decision as Unpopular; Holding May Have Cost Overlin Verdict. *Buffalo Courier-Express.* May 10, 1941, p. 19.

45 *New York Times.* May 10, 1941.

46 **Graham, Frank.** Setting the Pace / It Was a Very Bad Decision. *New York Sun.* May 10, 1941, p. 28.

47 —. Setting the Pace / In the House of Rustem Bey. *New York Sun.* June 26, 1941, p. 29 cite starting from "There was a group with him …"

48 **Conrad, Harold.** Davis Fouls Out on Boxing Career. *Brooklyn Daily Eagle.* November 16, 1940, p. 11.

49 **Rudd, Irving.** Before Fight Camp Became a Suite Science. *New York Times.* March 1, 1987.

50 **Sandomir, Richard.** Irving Rudd, 82, Press Agent In Baseball, Racing, Boxing. *New York Times.* June 4, 2000.

51 **Buck, Al.** Lew Jenkins Preps Al Davis for Zivic. *New York Post Sports.* June 30, 1941, p. 14.

52 **Conrad, Harold.** Zivic Makes Boast Good-And in Spades. *Brooklyn Daily Eagle.* July 3, 1941, p. 13.

53 **Graham, Frank.** Setting the Pace / Three Innocent Victims Went Down. *New York Sun.* October 8, 1941, p. 34.

54 Jenkins Defies Injury. *Syracuse Herald-Journal.* April 25, 1941, p. 38.

55 **Buck, Al.** Abrams Aims at Title. *New York Post.* July 25, 1941, p. 8 cite starting from "She had middleweight Georgie Abrams …"

56 **Mahon, Jack.** Army May Call New Welter King. *Brooklyn Daily Eagle.* July 30, 1941, p. 11.

57 **Press, Associated.** Mae West: 'My, My … Story is Ridiculous …' *Daily Press, Utica.* August 23, 1957, p. 6.

58 **Parrott, Harold.** Lion-Hearted Simon Meets Louis in Return Bout May 16. *Brooklyn Daily Eagle.* March 22, 1941, p. 13.

59 **Press, Associated.** Joe Louis Stops Abe Simon in Thirteenth Round. March 22, 1941.

60 **Buck, Al.** New York Rules Title at Stake in Archibald-Wright Bout. *New York Post Sports.* August 2, 1941, pp. 11 cite starting from "For the Chalky Wright-Joey Archibald …"

61 Wright Worthy Champion. *New York Post.* September 12, 1941.

Chapter 35

1   Boxing Notes. *New York Post Sports.* November 15, 1941, p. 11.

2   **Press, Associated.** Red Cochrane Easy Victor Over Jenkins. *Daily Argus.* October 7, 1941, p. 10.

3   **Graham, Frank.** Setting the Pace / Three Innocent Victims Went Down. *New York Sun.* October 8, 1941, p. 34.

4   **Press, Associated.** State Ring Board Holds Up Jenkins* Purse; Gilsenberg Carlen, Arcel Suspended. *Buffalo Courier-Express.* October 8, 1941, p. 19.

5   Zivic and Davis Gain Top Form for Battle. *New York Times.* June 27, 1941.

6   **Dawson, James P.** Phelan Watches Hostak, Overlin. *New York Times.* November 19, 1941.

7   **Buck, Al.** Zale Suffers Skin Infection Abrams Bout Off to Nov. 28. *New York Post.* November 1941.

8   **Press, United.** Hoosier Rallys to Win at Garden. November 29, 1941.

9   **Dawson, James P.** Boxing Officials to Test Jenkins. *New York Times.* December 2, 1941.

10 —. Robinson-McCoy Fight Arranged; Winner to Get Chance at Title. *New York Times.* December 3, 1941.

11 —. Jenkins and Rival Visit Board Today. *New York Times.* December 16, 1941.

12 **Press, Associated.** Sammy Angott Defeats Lew Jenkins for Boxing Title. *Kingston.* December 20, 1941, p. 11.

Chapter 36

1   Two Ring Figures Claimed by Death. *New York Sun.* January 30, 1942, p. 35.

2   The Passing of Madame Bey. *Chatham Press.* February 6, 1942, p. 2.

3   Heart Attack Fatal to Mme. Bey, Who Kept Boxing Training Camp. *Newark News.* January 30, 1942.

4   **Press, Associated.** Death Takes Madame Bey. *Morning Herald.* January 31, 142, p. 12.

5   Tami Wants Cooper Bout. *New York Post.* January 29, 1942, p. 15.

6   **Press, Associated.** Fiducia, Flynn in Newark Scrap. *Times Record.* January 27, 1942.

7 **Cochran, Jane.** Madame Bey Picks Godoy Over Louis. *Reading Eagle.* February 8, 1940, p. 26 cite starting from "Prizefighters are …"

8 **Runyon, Damon.** The Brighter Side. *Syracuse Journal.* November 23, 1937, p. 11.

9 **Robertson, Stewart.** She Puts'em in the Pink. *The Family Circle.* October 7, 1938.

Epilogue

1 **Heinz, W. C.** Bey's Famous Training Camp Continues Without Amazing Madame. *Ottawa Citizen.* January 9, 1946, p. 3.

2 **Graham, Frank.** Setting the Pace / A Visit to Abe Simon's Camp. *New York Sun.* March 25, 1942, p. 30 cite starting from "Graham and others sat around a table …"

3 *Simon-Louis Fight.* 1942.

4 **Conrad, Harold.** Simon Out of Way, Louis Looks Forward to Conn Go. *Brooklyn Daily Eagle.* March 28, 1942, p. 9.

5 **Beer, John.** John Beer's Corner. *Sunday Call.* April 1, 1945, pp. 2 cite starting from "As he arrived, he noticed …"

6 **Cuddy, Jack.** Welter Champ Wins Fandom Good Will for Graziano Go. *News of Tonawandas.* June 28, 1945, p. 8.

7 **Webster, John.** Williams Assured Trenton Support. *Philadelphia Inquirer.* July 9, 1947, p. 31.

8 **Gary, E. J.** Where are They Now. *The Ring.* April 1981, pp. 66-68.

9 **Webster, John.** Pigeon Augurs Title Success for Billy Fox. *Philadelphia Inquirer.* February 26, 1947, p. 30.

10 **Cuddy, Jack.** They Flock to See The Rock Even in Camp As He Drills for Comeback Go With Fuscari. *Jamestown Post-Journal.* September 7, 1949, p. 19.

11 **Press, United.** Graziano Trains Hard for Clash Against Fusari. *Brooklyn Eagle.* September 7, 1949, p. 26.

12 **Press, Associated.** Sports Roundup. *Courtland Standard.* August 23, 1950.

13 **Hatem, George J.** *It's in the Genes, a Family History and Autobiography.*

14 **Holmes, Tommu.** Outdoor Barbecue in Summit, N.J. *Brooklyn Eagle Sports.* August 15, 1951, p. 16.

15 **Flood, Warren H.** Floodlight. *Knickerbocker News.* January 30, 1953, pp. B-7.

16 **Rogin, Gilbert.** The Invisible Champion. *Sports Illustrated.* January 16, 1961.

17 **N.E.A.** Snakes For Spar Mates. *Kingston Daily Freeman.* June 22, 1959, p. 16.

18 **Press, Associated.** Floyd Attends Church, Then Spars 5 Rounds. *Pittsburgh Post-Gazette.* June 1, 1959, p. 23.

19 Humbert Fugazy, Boxing Promoter. *New York Times.* April 8, 1964.

20 **Smith, Red.** Tony Had Strange Ideas of Training. *Buffalo Courier-Express.* March 5, 1961, p. 36.

21 —. Blonde Distractful at Patterson Camp. *Buffalo Courier-Express.* March 10, 1961, p. 16.

22 Floyd Patterson vs. Ingemar Johansson (3rd meeting). [Online] Boxrec, September 15, 2015. http://boxrec.com/media/index.php?title=Fight:20859.

23 **Press, Associated.** Listori, Floyd Sign. *Binghamton Press.* March 16, 1962, p. 20.

24 —. Title Bout Nearly Set. *Schenectady Press.* March 6, 1962, p. 25.

25 **Hand, Jack.** Interest Mounts in Chicago Bout. *Daily Press, Utica.* September 25, 1962, p. 18.

26 Cassius Clay vs. Doug Jones. [Online] BoxRec, February 25, 2016. http://boxrec.com/media/index.php?title=Fight:22876.

27 **Press, United.** Cassius Humiliates Jones in Exhibition. *Bulletin.* October 28, 1966, p. 8.

28 **Cuddy, Jack.** Boxers 'Employees' Nowadays. *Desert News Salt Lake City.* December 26, 1961, p. 12.

29 —. Today's Sportrait. *Leader-Times.* August 27, 1963, p. 15.

30 **Pantalone, Don.** [interv.] Gene Pantalone. December 11, 2014.

31 **McCormick, Jim.** If It Wasn't For Fred Hogan I'd Be Dead: Rubin Carter. *Daily Register.* March 26, 1976, p. 1.

32 **Anderson, Dave.** The Public Defender. *New York Times.* March 21, 1976.

33 *United States Court of Appeals Docket No. 85-5735.*

34 **Anderson, Dave.** The Public Defender. *New York Times.* March 21, 1976.

35 **Chawkins, Steve.** Rubin 'Hurricane' Carter dies at 76; boxer wrongly imprisoned 19 years. *Los Angeles Times.* April 20, 2014.

36 **Pantalone, Gary.** December 11, 2015.

37 It Was Action Day In Brooklyn. *Sports Illustrated.* September 6, 1966.

38 **Heller, Peter.** *Bad Intentions: The Mike Tyson Story.* ISBN 978-0-306-80669-8: Da Capro Press, 1995.

39 **Boyle, Robert H.** Really the Greatest. *Sports Illustrated.* March 7, 1966.

40 Bill Clayton. *Independent.* October 8, 2003.

41 **Smith, Red.** Carlos Comes High: 83 Gs. *Binghamton Press.* August 11, 1967.

42 **Anderson, Dave.** Ortiz Prefers Simple and Secluded Training. *New York Times.* November 27, 1966.

43 **Hissner, Ken.** Carlos Ortiz the Hall of Fame Junior Welterweight and Lightweight Champion! *Doghouse Boxing.* April 28, 2009.

44 **Ratner, Willie.** Ehsan's Training Camp on the Ropes. *Newark Evening News.* April 23, 1969.

45 **Norton, Mark.** Letter to the Summit Historical Society. Summit: s.n., 2008.

Notables during Madame Bey Era

1   A Look Back: Georgie Abrams. [Online] Jewish Boxing, March 31, 2013. http://jewishboxing.blogspot.com/2013/03/a-look-back-georgie-abrams.html.

2   **Graham, Frank.** Setting the Pace / New Guy in the Coast Guard. *New York Sun.* February 20, 1942, p. 34.

3   Fred Apostoli. [Online] World Public Library, 2016. http://www.worldlibrary.org/articles/fred_apostoli.

4   **Berger, Phil.** Ray Arcel, Trainer Who Handled Many Boxing Stars, Is Dead at 94. *New York Times.* March 8, 1994.

5   Henry Armstrong Biography. [Online] Biography.com, 2016. http://www.biography.com/people/henry-armstrong-9188829#later-years-and-legacy.

6   A cigar-chomping sports publicist for … *Orlando Sentinel*. May 24, 1988.

7   *James J. Braddock.Dictionary of American Biography, Supplement 9: 1971-1975*. s.l.: Charles Scribner's Sons, 1994.

8   **Roberts, James B. and Skutt, Alexander B.** *The Boxing Register: International Boxing Hall of Fame Official Record Book (4th ed.)*. Ithica: McBooks Press. ISBN 978-1-59013-121-3, 2006.

9   **Press, Associated.** Al Buck. *Montreal Gazette*. June 26, 1967, p. 41.

10 **Steadman, John.** 'Red' Burman gave Joe Louis a battle in 1941 fight for title Baltimore native dies at 80 after long illness. *Baltimore Sun*. January 25, 1996.

11 Mushy Callahan. [Online] BoxRec, 2016. http://boxrec.com/boxer/041498.

12 Mushy Callahan (1904–1986). [Online] IMDb, 2016. http://www.imdb.com/name/nm0130237/.

13 **Sher, Jack.** The Strange Case of Carnera. *Sport*. February 1948.

14 Freddie (Red) Cochrane, Boxer, 77. *New York Times*. January 19, 1993.

15 Davis, Al "Bummy". [Online] Jewishsports.org, 2016. http://www.jewsinsports.org/profile.asp?sport=boxing&ID=78.

16 **Press, Associated.** Gus Dorazio, Ex-Boxer, Held in Fatal Fight. *Gettysburg Times*. January 8, 1949, p. 2.

17 Dorazio Convicted, Faces Long Sentence. *Reading Eagle*. May 20, 1949, p. 30.

18 **Barahona, Marvin Fonseca.** *Puerto Rico: Cuna de Campeones*. Puerto Rico : ISBN 978-1-60643-254-9, 2007.

19 *New York Times*. May 11, 1966.

20 Olympian Fields Dies at 79. *Palm Beach Post*. 1987.

21 Humbert Fugazy, Boxing Promoter. *New York Times*. April 8, 1964.

22 **Rogers, Thomas.** Tony Galento, Brawling Heavyweight, Dies. *New York Times*. July 23, 1979.

23 **Association), Coffin Corner (Professional Football Researchers.** Mr. Mara. *Pro Football Hall of Fame*. 1984.

24 Frank Graham Rites Friday. *Telegraph*. March 10, 1965.

25 Abe Greene, 89, Dies; Jersey Boxing Official. *New York Times*. September 23, 1988.

26 Abe J. Greene. [Online] IBHOF, 2016. http://www.ibhof.com/pages/about/inductees/nonparticipant/greene.html.

27 **Fleming, E.J.** Ace Hudkins. [Online] IMDb, 2016. http://www.imdb.com/name/nm0399731/bio.

28 **Press, Associated.** Hype Igoe, Famous Boxing Writer, Dies. *Lewiston Daily Sun*. February 12, 1945, p. 8.

29 Michael "Mike" Jacobs. [Online] International Jewish Hall of Fame, 2016. http://www.jewishsports.net/BioPages/Michael-Jacobs.htm.

30 **Rosero, Jessica.** Boxing Sensation Joe Jeanette. *Union City Reporter*. February 19, 2006.

31 **Red Smith.** Sgt. Lew Jenkins. *New York Times*. November 4, 1981.

32 Lew Jenkins. [Online] Arlington National Cemetery, November 25, 2005. http://www.arlingtoncemetery.net/ljenkins.htm.

33 **Schoen, Derek.** 'Hardest Hitter, Drinker,' Jenkins Conquers Alcohol. *Reading Eagle*. September 25, 1966, p. 73.

34 'K.O. Phil' Kaplan. [Online] New Jersey Boxing Hall of Fame, 2016. http://www.njboxinghof.org/k-o-phil-kaplan/.

35 **II, Jack Kearns.** Jack "Doc" Kearns. *The Boxing Biographies Newsletter.* January 6, 2011.

36 **Fernandez, Pedro.** Pacquiao Fans Never Met Frankie Klick. [Online] Ring Talk, 2016. http://ringtalk.com/pacquiao-fans-never-met-frankie-klick.

37 **Press, Associated.** May 31, 1957.

38 Tippy Larkin, Boxer, 74. *New York Times.* December 13, 1991.

39 Sport: Benny the Brain. *Time.* April 28, 1947.

40 Sport: Dempsey v. Fish. *Time.* February 1932, 1932.

41 Sport: Levinsky v. Walker. *Time.* May 9, 1932.

42 Joe Louis. [Online] BoxRec, November 21, 2014. http://boxrec.com/media/index.php?title=Human:9027.

43 Joe Lynch. [Online] Cyber Boxing Zone, 2016. http://www.cyberboxingzone.com/boxing/lynch-j.htm.

44 Joe Lynch. [Online] BoxRec, September 17, 2014. http://boxrec.com/media/index.php/Joe_Lynch_(Boxer).

45 Eddie Mader. [Online] BoxRec, January 27, 2014. http://boxrec.com/media/index.php/Eddie_Mader.

46 **Lewis, Mike.** Jimmy McLarnin. *Guardian.* November 11, 2004.

47 Gunman of Old Wild West Days Dies at His Desk. *Washington Herald.* October 26, 1921, p. 1.

48 Bat Masterson, US. Marshal. [Online] GENi, 2016. http://www.geni.com/people/Bat-Masterson-US-Marshal/6000000014101666627.

49 News. [Online] 2016. http://www.mikemctigue.com/page2.htm.

50 Lt. Jack Miley Dies Suddenly. *Milwaukee Sentinel.* June 18, 1945, p. 8.

51 *Portland Oregonian.* December 24, 1942.

52 Dan Morgan. [Online] IBHOF, 2016. http://www.ibhof.com/pages/about/inductees/nonparticipant/morgan.html.

53 **Press, Associated.** Boxer Bob Olin Is Dead at 48. *Sarasota Journal.* December 17, 1956, p. 11.

54 —. Ken Overlin Plans to Try Comeback. *Reading Eagle.* August 1, 1944, p. 14.

55 —. Ken Overlin Dead at 59. *Pittsburgh Post-Gazette.* July 26, 1969, p. 10.

56 Billy Petrolle. [Online] BoxRec, November 20, 2015. http://boxrec.com/media/index.php?title=Human:10128.

57 **Shannon, Bill.** Willie Ratner. [Online] New-York Historical Society, 2016. http://sports.nyhistory.org/willie-ratner/.

58 **Press, Associated.** Willie Ratner. *Daytona Beach Morning Journal.* April 4, 1980.

59 **Inabinett, Mark.** *Grantland Rice and His Heroes: The Sportswriter as Mythmaker in the 1920s.* Knoxville : The University of Tennessee Press, 1994.

60 **International, United Press.** Former Light-Heavy Champ Maxie Rosenbloom Is Dead. *Ellensburg Daily Record.* March 8, 1976.

61 **Crosby, John.** 90-Minute Drama Packs a Punch. *Toledo Blade.* October 16, 1956.

62 **Foster, Charles.** *Once Upon a Time in Paradise: Canadians in the Golden Age of Hollywood.* s.l. : Dundurn ISBN 978-1550024647, 2003.

63 **Press, Associated.** Andre Routis. *Montreal Gazette.* July 18, 1969, p. 17.

64 **Sandomir, Richard.** Irving Rudd, 82, Press Agent In Baseball, Racing, Boxing. *New York Times.* June 4, 2000.

65 Irving Rudd. [Online] IBHOF, 2016. http://www.ibhof.com/pages/about/inductees/nonparticipant/rudd.html.

66 **Lewis, W. David.** *Eddie Rickenbacker: An American Hero in the Twentieth Century.* Baltimore : Johns Hopkins University Press ISBN-10: 0801889723, 2008.

67 **Lorenzo, Stephen.** Daily News Golden Gloves Hall of Fame: Lou Salica. *Daily News.* April 16, 2014.

68 **Gallo, Bill.** Ringing in Some Super Memories. *Daily News.* February 3, 2002.

69 Max Schmeling. [Online] PBS, February 9, 2005. http://www.pbs.org/wgbh/amex/fight/peopleevents/p_schmeling.html.

70 **Furneld, Edward.** Letter From Edward Furneld to the Chatham Township Historical Society. Chatham Township: s.n., 1985.

71 **Siki, Battling.** *Battling Siki's Autobiography, as told to Milton Bronner.* Bellingham, WA : Bellingham American, 1922.

72 **Anderson, Dave.** Sports of The Times; Battling Siki Finally on His Way Back Home. *New York Times.* March 28, 1993.

73 **Shelly, Jared.** Champ Gains a Bit of Recognition. *Jewish Exponent.* July 6, 2006.

74 Eric Seelig. [Online] New Jersey Boxing Hall of Fame, 2016. http://www.njboxinghof.org/eric-seelig/.

75 Eric Seelig. [Online] International Jewish Sports Hall of Fame, 2016. http://www.jewishsports.net/BioPages/EricSeelig.htm.

76 Biography. [Online] Boxing Biographies, 2016. http://boxingbiographies.co.uk/assets/applets/Freddie_Steele-bb.pdf.

77 "Young" Stribling Dead. *Tuscaloosa News.* October 4, 1933, p. 8.

78 Young Stribling. [Online] BoxRec, September 8, 2015. http://boxrec.com/media/index.php?title=Human:12052.

79 Herman Taylor. [Online] IBHOF, 2016. http://www.ibhof.com/pages/about/inductees/nonparticipant/taylor.html.

80 **Press, Associated.** Lew Tendler, Veteran Ring Star, Is Dead. *Prescott Courier.* November 6, 1970, p. 7.

81 **Blady, Ken.** *The Jewish Boxers' Hall of Fame.* New York : Shapolsky Publishers ISBN 0-933503-87-3, 1988.

82 **Dahlberg, Tim.** Famous Long Count Fight Still Resonates. *USA Today.* March 19, 2011.

83 Mickey Walker. *The Boxing Biographies Newsletter.* March 2, 2012.

84 Max Waxman. [Online] BoxRec, July 22, 2008. http://boxrec.com/media/index.php/Max_Waxman.

85 Al Weill. [Online] IBHOF, 2016. http://www.ibhof.com/pages/about/inductees/nonparticipant/weill.html.

86 Former Heavyweight Boxer Harry Wills Leaves $100,000 Estate. *Jet.* January 15, 1959.

87 Johnny Wilson. [Online] BoxRec, June 30, 2011. http://boxrec.com/media/index.php?title=Human:11328.

88 **Marcus, Norman.** Johnny Wilson: Middleweight Champ 1920-1923. [Online] Boxing.com, May 2, 2012. http://www.boxing.com/johnny_wilson_middleweight_champion_1920_1923.html.

89 New York Beat. *Jet.* October 14, 1954.

90 Chalky Not a Suicide Say Police. *Afro American.* August 27, 1957, p. 14.

91 Teddy Yarosz. [Online] IBHOF, 2016. http://www.ibhof.com/pages/about/inductees/oldtimer/yarosz.html.

INDEX

Gene Pantalone is a boxing enthusiast who had the opportunity to visit Madame Bey's camp in its waning years when boxers still trained there. Today, he lives near the original boxing camp site and is familiar with the camp's storied existence. Madame Bey's: Home to Boxing Legends is his first book.